ADOLESCENCE

ADOLESCENCE

Marguerite Malm
Professor of Education
Indiana State Teachers College

Olis G. Jamison
Chairman of the Department of Education
Indiana State Teachers College

FIRST EDITION

New York   Toronto   London
McGRAW-HILL BOOK COMPANY, INC.
1952

ADOLESCENCE

THE MAPLE PRESS COMPANY, YORK, PA.

PREFACE

This is the proposition upon which our book is based: Since adults make and govern the homes, the schools, and the communities where adolescents spend their time, and since adults influence the adolescent's behavior in countless ways, it is their duty to see that the adolescent years are good ones and that the adolescent be given all the assistance needed to develop into a fine maturity. The objectives of our book, therefore, are three: to help adults get along better with the adolescent, to help them understand what the adolescent needs to live wholesomely and happily, and to show them how these needs may be met.

Specifically the authors have attempted to do the following:

1. To give a picture of the adolescent today so that the adult may understand him, see life, as it were, through his eyes, and sympathize with his problems, needs, and interests.

2. To acquaint the reader with the adolescent's social setting—both as to the patterns and demands of the adolescent's own age group and as to adult influences which bear on him.

3. To clarify the concept of what a good life for the adolescent *as an adolescent* is and also to make clear what kind of adulthood we hope to help him reach.

4. To supply definite and workable suggestions as to how the adult may live most harmoniously with the adolescent and do the most to help him.

In preparing this book, the authors have carefully reviewed all pertinent materials and while much of worth could not be included, they believe that their selections from the research and comment will all prove valuable to the reader. Information has been gathered, too, from adolescents currently enrolled in high school, both through interviews and through written responses to questions. Finally, the authors have, of course, called upon their own extensive experience with adolescents and with teachers of adolescents.

Mention should be made of the fact that no chapter has been included in mental development. Too often such a chapter in an adolescent psychology is largely repetition of general and educational psychology material on the nature of intelligence, intelligence tests, constancy of IQ, and the like. We have chosen to avoid such repetition and have included any useful material on the adolescent's intelligence in the chapter on the world of the adolescent and the chapter on the school.

v

We sincerely hope that all of this book will be truly helpful to the reader and that through it he will find his insights enlarged, his sympathies broadened, and his knowledge of what to do and how to do it made concrete and definite.

In conclusion we extend our sincere thanks to the many writers and publishers who have so willingly allowed us to quote from their work. We wish to express our appreciation also to the junior and senior high school teachers who have helped us get material directly from adolescents: Francis Adams, Marguerite Haddon, Margaret Riddle, Donna Stuebe, Frances Williams, and those many Vincennes, Indiana, high school teachers who so generously assisted us.

MARGUERITE MALM
OLIS G. JAMISON

TERRE HAUTE, IND.
February, 1952

CONTENTS

Part I

THE ADOLESCENT AND HIS WORLD

Chapter 1. WHO IS THE ADOLESCENT?

Who is the adolescent? He is fifteen-year-old Dick, who, as tall as his father, thinks he ought to be allowed to drive the car alone. He is seventeen-year-old Jim, who shaves every day but still has to tell his parents where he is going when he leaves the house at night. He is eighteen-year-old Tom, who has been going steady for over a year with the same girl and wants to marry her but knows he couldn't support a wife.

She is thirteen-year-old Peggy, who longs to wear lipstick but whose mother won't allow it. She is fourteen-year-old Nancy Jo, who loves bubble gum and who is going to her first formal dance next week. She is sixteen-year-old Helen, who is only a junior in high school but who goes with a college boy of twenty-one and looks to all she meets like a college girl herself.

He is—she is—any boy or girl who is on the path from childhood to adulthood.

In the life of every person there occurs a time when the body begins the process which will change it from a childish structure to that of an adult. At first the change is hardly noticeable, but soon it becomes pronounced enough in body form and in body feelings to take the person definitely out of the realm of childhood.

When the young person begins to *feel* these changes himself, even though he doesn't identify them, feel that he is becoming radically different from the child that he was, feel that he is becoming more like the adults around him, sense emotions in himself that he hadn't known before, then the beginning of the psychological growing-up process has started. That psychological process may continue beyond the time when his body has finished its growth. It will continue until he has become adult in his interests and behavior.

This period of psychological growing up we call *adolescence.* Though its beginnings are roughly the same as the beginnings of the growth toward sexual and physical maturity, they are not coincidental. Though its ending will be related to the end of physical growth, it may come later.

The length of the period of adolescence differs from person to person, but it is customarily thought of as encompassing the teen years, and that age span will do as well as any for our definition of adolescence by age period.

As far as numbers are concerned, according to the 1950 preliminary census reports there are 15,234,000 young people in our country between the ages of thirteen and nineteen. This is 10 per cent of the total population. Of these 8,680,000 are urban; 3,352,000 are rural nonfarm; 3,202,000 are rural farm.

During the time of adolescence the individual moves from the dependence and restrictions of childhood to adult independence and freedom from parental restriction. In our society this is a lengthy process because adults have chosen to make it such. They keep the growing youth in school until he is sixteen (in most states) and urge him to stay there even longer. By law and by public opinion they prevent his marrying until he is close to the end of, or out of, his teens. They refuse him adult work or wages comparable with those of adults. His parents, in their concern for his welfare, and out of habit also, keep him under their jurisdiction until he is in the later part of his teens or in the early twenties. In our society, too, adolescence is often a difficult period for youth because adults are loath to give him the independence he craves and needs and he must himself struggle with them for his emancipation.

The reminiscences of a twenty-year-old girl will give us some insight into what it feels like to be an adolescent:

I guess whenever anyone looks back over the past events of his life, he sighs wistfully, and says, "If only I had it to do over! How much easier it might have been!"

Such a period of confused, chaotic, and emotional behavior was that of my adolescence. This I know very well—my parents always said that I had a very, very severe case of growing up.

I'm twenty now, and as I look back over the past seven or eight years, I know they are years that I shall never forget. Going along at an even keel was impossible to this adolescent—my life was a continuous roller-coaster ride—I was either riding ecstatically on a pink cloud, or plunged to the most depressing depths of black despair.

Life first became noticeably difficult for my parents when I entered the seventh grade. Having attended an elementary school consisting of six grades, I entered junior high school and was plunged headlong into the seventh grade and into various emotional difficulties. I was changing both mentally and physically, and of course the change in schools altered my outside environment to a great degree.

Several things bothered me. I had matured early and this set me apart from the other girls in my class. I also had to wear glasses, and I had the idea that my legs were too short.

These grievances were small and slight, but it is very often this type that bothers the adolescent. He magnifies them and soon they develop into a state of mind or social attitude. I know this is the way it was with me. I was on the defensive, because I felt inferior in looks and in my ability to get along with others.

In looks I really wasn't worse than average but no one could have made me believe this at the time. Like most teen-age girls, I was an inveterate movie-goer, and seeing such beautiful, graceful and poised creatures on the screen only made me feel homelier and more awkward than ever. Lana Turner was my ideal. I felt that no one in the world could be quite so beautiful. For masculine perfection, I alternated for several years between Tyrone Power and Errol Flynn, but fell madly for Cornel Wilde when he first came into prominence. I disliked going to the movies except by myself, for only in that way could I lose myself completely and become oblivious to the drabness of everyday life. Most of my allowance went for shows.

My relations with others were extremely hard for me. Coming from a small elementary school, I was thrown in with one particular group of girls who had come from a larger one—they were a clique, and while outwardly friendly, they took no real interest in anyone outside their particular group. I was very self-centered and this made it difficult for me to make friends, because I was really interested in no one but myself. I think that if it were possible to teach a child only one thing, it should be this, that he develop a sincere and affectionate interest in other people.

When I entered the eighth grade, things were easier. I still had the old inferiority complex, but I did manage to fit into the group. Boy-girl activities began. Dancing class opened at the Y.M.C.A. More social contacts occurred. First loves blossomed. We began to have parties—dances—hayrides.

I developed my first crush. He, in turn, was unresponsive, being smitten with a very close friend of mine. The situation taxed my emotional powers and divided my loyalties. It made life extremely difficult for me.

With the eighth grade came one of my first fond ambitions—to be a violinist. (I ignored the fact that I had gotten a very late start.) I had the determination and desire, but lacked the talent and stick-to-itiveness. I practiced devotedly (when I practiced, which was about once a week).

Eighth grade came and went, and ninth grade appeared. Class work became a little harder, but then that had always been the least of my worries. I was always at the top of my class with ease. In fact, I was a good example of the stereotyped picture of The Student: serious, shy, frightened and completely introverted.

I developed a very close friendship with another girl. Although we were entirely different personalties, we had several things in common:

1. We both had difficulty in adjusting to other people. We used each other to "lean on."

2. We were both introverted and were going through that extremely romantic stage—I don't mean romantic in the sense of love interest, but more in an aesthetic sense—a love for culture and refinement and gentility.

We felt that we were above the "common herd." This was an attitude that seriously hampered our attempts at enjoying other friendships and social events.

We went overboard for each other. It was a Damon and Pythias sort of relationship, and yet I can see now how unwise it was. It is a good thing to have a close friend with whom to share the problems of adolescence, but even a good thing can be carried too far, because our development was hindered by dependence on each other.

Finally, the ninth grade was over, and the tenth came with even more problems and opportunities to "sink or swim." For again we changed schools, progressing to high school itself, which presents itself to every entering adolescent as the ultimate in excitement and adventure.

For the senior high school adolescent there is no such thing as being an individual; the crowd rules—and the person who stands firmly by his individuality is regarded as either a "brain" or a recluse or as probably just "queer."

What I yearned for so painfully was to "be accepted"—to be popular, gay and flirtatious, and yet not stoop to the silly inaneness of the group. I felt that boys were very difficult—I was interested, but sometimes their foolishness and loudness annoyed me so that I could hardly stand them. What I dreamed of was someone cultured, poised, and debonair—perhaps with a little bit of artistic temperament.

This probably accounted for my first Big Crush. It started in the ninth grade. More than anything else it was in the category of the movie-star adoration that I had experienced in the past. It was hero-worship and infatuation with a capital "I." The fact that I knew nothing—absolutely nothing—about the fellow had no effect on me—he was tall, he was dark, he was handsome. I knew his name and his background, which I managed to find out from various sources, but there my information stopped.

One night he brought me home from an informal school dance. (One of those affairs that everyone attends stag.) I was soaring high in the clouds—at the same time, I was dumbfounded that he had even looked at me. I was elated and ingratiating. Every time he looked at me, I practically gasped. Naturally he never came back, and my heart was broken. My life had ended—I made this very clear to my family. It was all over—I would never love again.

Of course my poor family suffered with me in this, my first crisis, but they finally had too much of my sighs and moans, and soon I had an unreceptive audience. (Eventually I got over it, but it took several months.) Of course the inferiority complex asserted itself with redoubled vigor, and my hopes of ever being poised or attractive immediately fled. I was destined to be a misfit. I regressed practically to my seventh grade sensitivity and once more my family groaned and gently tried to stir me out of my shell. I can see now how the mother of a teen-ager has to have an infinite amount of patience—I don't think I would have survived this period without the patient understanding of my mother.

Then came the second Big Crush. He was, of course, even more charming than the first. (He *was* accessible.) Our love affair progressed awkwardly for two or three months. He was a senior in high school; I was still in the ninth grade. (I always did fall for older men.) However, when it came to weighing bashfulness and timidity, the scales balanced pretty evenly for both of us.

The slightest change of attitude on the part of either of us would give rise to feelings of insecurity, and then we would both be nonchalant for awhile. It was extremely agonizing.

The difference between our classes (he was in the twelfth, I was in the ninth) made our compatibility a little difficult.

However, I believe that compatability counts very little in adolescence. This might be because the Crowd is the Supreme-Guide-of-All. Everyone goes to the same places, and does the same things. Consequently, mutual interests are not as necessary—because the All-Powerful Group does the deciding.

I think this is one of the things that teen-agers should take into consideration when they plan to get married at a very early age. It is very possible that they fall in love with the crowd, with the activities and the life they lead. All these things will inevitably change with marriage. You can find very few groups that after graduation continue to keep in contact through the years. Intimate friendships of high school may last, but seldom do its group activities. Marriage and differential occupational interests are usually the cause.

At any rate, my second love died as my first had, if not quite as abruptly. Once more my life was over. I would never love again. Anyone who sees a movie portrayal of a teen-ager laughs and finds it quite ridiculous, but I believe that an adolescent can suffer just as much over an infatuation as an adult can over a real love. The teen-ager's feelings are just as deep but his sense of habit and routine and the "life must go on" attitude are not so thoroughly ingrained.

My complex returned, but this time it was a little bit fainter. I still went to social activities and tried to put up a big pretense of having a good time. About this time a song came out that I felt expressed perfectly the state of my emotions. It went "I'm laughing on the outside, crying on the inside, 'cause I'm still in love with you." I pictured myself bravely fighting the adversities of Fate, and struggling to hide my broken heart. Perhaps if I hadn't concentrated so hard on making people *believe* I was having a good time, I could actually have had one.

During my sophomore year I met someone else who was destined to go down in my adolescence as Big Crush Number Three. (I'll call him Joe.) He was entirely different from the other two. He wasn't suave, or exceptionally good looking. I guess his charm was his bashfulness, naturalness, and lack of pretense. Anyway I found him very attractive and we got along easily. Pretty soon we were dating regularly. The inferiority complex began to disappear, and I had no trouble getting along with others. What amazed me more than anything else was that I had no trouble attracting the boys. I began to feel just a trifle pleased with myself. I learned that the old adage "Pride goes before a fall" is very very true indeed. When Joe got very sentimental one night and asked me to "go steady," I refused. "Let's not tie ourselves down," I suggested grandly. (The fact that we had been dating only each other for several months was overlooked.) I found him very attractive but my wandering eyes had hit upon a certain senior, and I was pondering the possibilities. My decision was something that I was to regret almost immediately. For when Joe heard my words, he decided to beat me at my own game. I must admit that he won. Because when he started giving me the indifferent routine, I decided that the handsome senior wasn't worth it, and I longed to have him back. This led to the third completely miserable and agonizing period in my life.

We were playing a game—when he was penitent and anxious to make up, I was cold, unrelenting and sarcastic, and when I decided to be sweet and forgiving he turned on the nonchalance with full force. Several agonizing months followed. By now I had no trouble getting dates, but my stubborn one-track mind held me to one thought—the only reason I dated others was to make *him* notice my popularity and want to come back.

After about four months the game grew tiresome, and in one of my dates, I met someone even more wonderful. I tumbled head over heels (as usual). In less than a month, I had completely forgotten the agonies of my lost love for I was now completely engrossed in a new one.

This was always my main trouble—the lamentable fact that I would concentrate on only one thing at a time. My complete devotion to One Cause—whatever or whoever it happened to be—contributed a great deal to such intense suffering, I think.

Anyway, Big Crush Number Four arrived, and it was undoubtedly more stable than any of my other loves. (Proof of this can be seen in the fact that it lasted for three years.) The romance between us started when I was still a sophomore and lasted until I was a freshman in college. It was saner and quieter than the others. I felt for the first time that I was in love in a sort of serene way. I guess that I wasn't really in love—the fact that it didn't last seems to bear that out. But I do know that it was on a more unselfish level than any of the others had been.

I believe now that it was the fact that we both needed someone—someone with sincerity and a serious attitude toward life. At first it worked out all right, but soon differences of opinion and ideals and basic ways of living became apparent. I guess you could call it the first flaw in our compatibility—we were "geared" differently. In my opinion, each person is geared to the way he grew up—the general speed of his life—if it was a lazy easy life with the opportunity for avoiding obstacles, he will want to live the rest of his life that way. That was the trouble between my steady and me. He had grown up in a kind of lazy indifference to the demands of life, and had a disgust at having to meet them. I was not very tolerant of this attitude—I wanted to be more active, to get something accomplished, although the whole idea *was* rather vague in my mind.

He was an idealist—he *wanted* to do something worth while, but when he started out and saw what a big job it was, he soon lost his enthusiasm. He wanted luxury—not necessarily material luxury—but kind of a luxurious laziness of the mind.

I found that I couldn't believe in him, and had no respect for this attitude of his. Every person has to believe in someone, and I could see that I had to wait to find someone who was "geared" the way I was. Thus ended romance Number Four. I suppose that an easier way to say all this would be, simply, that he was lazy and I nagged him. But at any rate, I came to the conclusion (after three years) that it just wouldn't work.

However, this romance of mine had lasted through three years—very important ones in my life—my high school days. In three years I changed a great deal.

As a sophomore, I was shy, frightened and studious with just beginnings of good social behavior. I hadn't quite grown out of my idolizing stage. Every teen-ager believes at one time or another that his life is completely colorless and drab. He yearns for glamour and sophistication. I remember when I did— I was a quiet little sophomore sitting in the school library, watching the beautiful senior girls walk by. One in particular fascinated me—she was always perfectly groomed, and wore very expensive clothes. She went to all of the school dances and occasionally wore an orchid in her hair. I remember her particularly in one outfit—she wore a beautiful fuzzy pink angora sweater with pink angora socks to match, and then, of course, the orchid in her hair. I was entranced. Someday, I thought, I'll have a pink angora sweater with socks to match, and even the orchid. And believe it or not, I did!

And when I was a senior, I sat in the library in my angora sweater (with socks to match) and the orchid and sympathetically enjoyed the wistful stares of several little sophomores.

By the time I had reached my senior year, the inferiority complex was definitely submerged. I participated in many activities and was far from being unpopular. It was then I realized that I had managed to struggle through all the big problems of adjustment. Perhaps I didn't do the best job in the world, but I guess that every teen-ager handles his problems in a rather awkward emotional manner.

Here we see the adolescent—not a child, not an adult. We shall picture him more fully in the chapters that follow.

Chapter 2. WHY STUDY THE ADOLESCENT?

Why should the teacher, the parent, or any other adult who works with young people study the adolescent?

The answer seems clear enough when we look at those adults who are ill-advised, awkward, bungling, or even cruel and vicious in their treatment of young people. When we see parents who dominate their children and refuse to let them grow up, parents who are cold and unfeeling toward their sons and daughters, parents who are harsh and demanding, when we see teachers who have no understanding of what makes life interesting and worth while to the teen-agers with whom they work, teachers who have no sympathy with the adolescent who is having difficulty in his adjustment, teachers who are envious of the happiness of youngsters getting along well, teachers who inflict their own feelings and discontent on those in their charge, when we see townspeople who have no interest in providing good recreational facilities for boys and girls, who are untroubled by the vice spots in the community, who let poorly chosen police and court officials handle the juvenile-delinquency cases—when we see people like these, we feel rather sure that some of them would become more considerate, more sympathetic, and more effective in their dealings with the boys and girls in their homes and in their classes and would become more concerned with providing good schools and good community life for youth if only they could study the adolescent and learn more about his needs, his problems, his interests, his likes and his dislikes.

Yes, these types of adults should study adolescent psychology, we might all agree, because they might thereby become less inept, less thoughtless, less negligent, and less inconsiderate in their dealings with the many boys and girls whom they influence.

But what about the more accomplished teachers, the more successful parents, the more intelligently concerned townspeople?

"We're getting along all right," the parents of fifteen-year-old Patty say, "and neither one of us has ever read a book on adolescent psychology." And it would seem that they *are* doing a good job in rearing their daughter, doing it, too, without excessive friction or worry. It is true that they meet many problems in connection with Patty's growing up, but on the whole they handle them with good common sense, and they are probably justified in assuming that Patty will continue into adulthood the happy, well-balanced person she is now.

"And I'm getting along all right," Patty's English teacher, Miss Bryson, says, "even though I've never studied adolescent psychology." The onlooker might agree with her as he sees how much her students enjoy her classes and how well they do their work. Miss Bryson seldom has any trouble with discipline, and her personality, which is marked by good humor, kindness, and a genuine liking for people, helps make the classroom atmosphere a wholesome and pleasant one.

Should we agree with Patty's parents and her English teacher? May we assume that the sympathetic, kindly, intelligent adults who work effectively with teen-agers can depend on their common sense and intuition to do the right thing on most occasions—that any extended study of the adolescent through courses or books is unnecessary for them?

Not at all. For even the most accomplished teachers and the most skillful parents need to see the whole of the adolescent problem—and this "whole" is bigger than most people realize. It involves understanding not only the boys and girls of our acquaintance but understanding also in what respects they are like all adolescents and in what respects they diverge from the pattern. It involves knowing the problems that beset the adolescent even though he may not tell us about them and knowing also when we should try to help him and when we should leave him alone. It involves knowing what happy, well-adjusted adulthood for the adolescent really means and knowing what we can do for him in his growing-up years in order that he actually may become the best that he has the possibility to be. More than that, if we really understand adolescent psychology, we shall be able to recognize maladjustments in the boy or girl and then be able to give the often delicate and subtle assistance which will enable him to develop as he should. We shall comprehend the whole story of delinquency—its causes, its manifestations, and its remedies. We shall see wherein the community fails the adolescent, know what some towns and cities are doing to remedy their defects, and have a clear idea of what good community life for young people includes.

Helping the adolescent requires vision beyond that which our daily experience with him is likely to bring. It requires greater breadth of understanding than that which comes from dealing with two or three teen-agers or even a hundred, a knowledge of methods other than those each of us is individually able to devise, and that magnitude of insight and objective which comes only when many people contribute their best thinking to our learning.

It might be different if we were just onlookers of adolescence. But we are more than that. All of society influences the adolescent, and some

have assumed the responsibility of *guiding* him. In effect these latter say
to youth: "Put your life in our hands. Do what we tell you. Confide in
us. Ask our advice. Follow our dictates. Trust in us. Then when you are
eighteen or nineteen, or a little older, you will be the kind of adult who
can live happily and well." Often, if not always, we make this great
promise without half realizing how complex and even hazardous at times
is the development of the child into the adult.

The adolescent is the child who is going through the process of becoming an adult. It is important that we realize how all-embracing, how
difficult at times, how fraught with possibilities for maldevelopment is
this process of growing up.

As adults we affect the progress of this growth in many ways, sometimes indirectly, sometimes very deliberately, sometimes in minor details,
and sometimes in life-shaking degree.

Now our answer to Patty's parents and her teacher is this: When a
growth process is as vital and complex as is that of adolescence, it cannot
be fully comprehended without serious study. When a group of people
affect a growth process as much as adults do that of the adolescent, it
behooves those people to reach a thorough understanding of the process
and of their own role in it.

We shall elaborate on these two points.

THE ADOLESCENT GROWTH PROCESS IS VITAL AND COMPLEX

Adolescence Prepares for Adult Responsibilities

The adolescent period is the time when the child grows into the adult
and becomes ready for adult responsibilities.

Imagine yourself visiting a large high school and attending a senior
class meeting. As you look over the crowd of boys and girls there, you
realize that you could say this to most of them: "Before very long you'll
be looking for work, finding jobs, and beginning to earn your own living.
Before very long many of you will be choosing a husband or wife. Before very long many of you will be parents."

These are big responsibilities. Yet whatever the high school does for
the adolescent or does not do, however the parents help him or fail him,
when adulthood arrives the youth seemingly has achieved a readiness to
take on these major tasks. We can say for the average adolescent that
when grown up he *does* get a job and manage to earn a living, he *does*
vote, he *does* choose a mate and maintain a home, and when his children
are born, he *does* manage their upbringing.

We cannot and should not be confident, however, that he does these things well. Rather to the contrary, we know that many young adults fall into the wrong first job and that of these a goodly number never do find the work in which they can be well content. Many twenty-one-year-olds are ill-informed about public affairs, are easily swayed by propaganda and emotional appeals, and have little sense of responsibility toward their community duties or their duties as voters. Many marital choices are hasty or in other ways unwise, and divorce or lifelong unhappiness in marriage often results. Many children are given the poorest kind of parental care, often not from ill will but from sheer ignorance.

We must not take these failures complacently. While many of the people who dislike their jobs, who are poor citizens, and who make failures of their marriages and of their child rearing do seem to get by, yet the cost in individual happiness and in social welfare is almost beyond comprehension. And if we are the ones who have taken on the task of helping the adolescent, *we* must take some of the blame for this failure.

By the very fact that adolescence is the time between childhood and adulthood, it is the time when the child becomes the kind of adult he will be. During that time he will give much thought to the kind of work he may do as an adult and be eager for help both in choosing his vocation and in preparing himself for it. He will become interested in dating and going steady and will begin to consider the possibilities of marriage. He will take on a more adult interest in the front page of the paper, will be strongly aware of adult attitudes toward matters of public concern, will take pride in the fact that he is moving closer and closer to the age of twenty-one and full citizenship. During that time the girl will begin to view homemaking from the woman's rather than the child's point of view. This is a period, then, when the adolescent can become a good adult—or a bad one. Much depends on the help we give him.

Let us consider the importance of the adolescent period as far as each of these adult responsibilities is concerned.

✓**Vocational Preparation and Choice.** Having a job that is suitable and satisfying is one of the requisites for happiness. When we consider that a goodly share of our waking hours every week is spent at work, we realize that we insure a large amount of our life's success if we can enjoy work and feel fulfilled in it.

This means more than just finding the right job. It means being able to find pleasure in work rather than considering it a necessary evil, being able to accomplish something that we can be proud of, being able to get along with our associates. These are long-term developments in a person. One does not take them on automatically with his twenty-first birthday.

That is one reason why the adolescent years are so important. They can be used to shape the personality of the boy or girl so that he can be, in the fullest sense, vocationally successful. This means that the adolescent must have experiences such as these:

1. Discovering that work can be pleasurable.
2. Learning to make the most of work opportunities through proper aggressiveness, alertness, willingness to apply oneself, and pride in achievement.
3. Developing the qualities of perseverance, reliability, and responsibility.
4. Comprehending the importance of work in one's life.
5. Comprehending the place of the worker in the nation's life.
6. Growing in the ability to get along with others in work relationships.
7. Coming to understand one's own abilities and work fitnesses.
8. Coming to understand one's temperamental needs as far as the kind of work is concerned.
9. Knowing the kinds of work that are available to someone of one's own capabilities and interests.

All of these achievements take time, and many of them will not even occur at all if the years of adolescence are not used for their development. This is one reason why we stress the fact that the adult must understand all of the potentialities of the adolescent and how they may be brought to fruition.

✓**Citizenship.** Being a citizen, of course, means much more than voting. The good citizen and the poor citizen may both vote, and they may both vote alike. But the good one will have qualities of character and interests that the poor one will lack: neighborliness, honesty, cooperativeness, respect for the law, respect for the rights of others, interest in good government and willingness to contribute his own effort to the needs of his community and his country.

These qualities are not the product of the adolescent period, to be sure. Character, generosity toward others, a social rather than a wholly egoistic center of one's interests—these have their beginnings early in life. But it is in adolescence that they can take on significance in terms of the adult world. Adult problems and adult behavior have, naturally, more meaning to the person about to become an adult than to the child. The adolescent also explores adult behavior more fully than does the child—both in his activities and in his speculative thinking. He observes the adult, he questions his motives, he weighs his values, he imitates some of his behavior, and he develops habits that will be of use to him in the world he is to enter.

It is highly possible that the adolescent could in these years develop a code of social responsibility, get practice in making right choices, and see implications in human relationships such as to give him values in regard to citizenship which would function firmly in his adulthood. Even the child whose character and adjustment have not developed wholesomely in childhood has, so to speak, a last chance in adolescence. Anyone who has worked with delinquent boys and girls will know that some of them have changed from wrongdoing to right-doing, from self-centeredness to cooperative ways, from antagonism toward others to a liking for others, given the right influences and the right environment.

✓ **Marital Choice and Marital Happiness.** Adolescence is the time when interest in the other sex develops. For that reason it is a time when interest in sex itself and in relationships with the other sex is higher than it has ever been before. It is a time of romance, a time when thoughts of marriage take on reality, a time for viewing relationships in the home with newly critical eyes. If a youth is given the right opportunities, it is during adolescence that he can comprehend not only the facts about sex but also its relationships within his life. It is then that he can experience the many typical adolescent infatuations, get them out of his system, one might say, and grow into the ability to make a choice on a strong and permanent base.

As our common sense tells us and as such investigations as Terman's show, marital happiness depends greatly on the good personal adjustment of the two people involved in the marriage. The selfish, the insecure, the touchy, the easily discouraged, the overdependent, the irritable, the fearful, the dominating, the cruel, the self-centered—in other words, the maladjusted—are not good marital risks.

The period of adolescence cannot remake a personality. But when you consider that in these five or six growing years the desire to be liked and accepted by others and the desire to be "grown-up" are strong, you must realize that there is great opportunity for that growth to be guided along lines that will lead to a sweeter natured, more lovable, and more cooperative personality.

✓ **Parenthood.** Good parenthood means two things: that the parents be wholesome, happy, kindly people themselves and that they have that knowledge of the needs of children and skill in meeting those needs which will enable them to give their children the right kind of care. The first requires that same good personality development we have just discussed in connection with marriage.

As far as the second, the special knowledge and skills of parenthood, is concerned, this is perhaps best acquired when the motivation is the highest—at the actual time of need. Adult education is the answer. But until some sort of systematic adult education really functions, adolescence seems to be the only time when such teaching can be made to reach all prospective mothers and fathers.

Adolescence Is the Time of Momentous Psychological Changes

We see that the time of adolescence is important to adulthood because it readies the boy or girl for adult responsibilities. But it is important also because it is at this time that three momentous psychological changes must occur if the child is actually to become a mature adult:

1. He must become independent of his home; that is, his psychological weaning must be accomplished.

✓ 2. He must make a heterosexual adjustment; that is, he must reach the point where he is able to choose, love wholeheartedly, and live happily with someone of the opposite sex.

3. He must adopt adult viewpoints, values, morals, standards, and ideals; he must learn to direct his own activity and make his own decisions—and do so as an adult should.

We have called these changes momentous. The fact that they are such will be brought home to anyone who visits the sixth or seventh grade and who then goes on to look at a group of near-adults—say, sophomores in college. So different have these mature young people become in their last seven or eight years of growth that it is actually difficult for some of them to recall just what life was like to them at eleven or twelve.

These changes *must* be accomplished by the end of adolescence for the greatest adult well-being. We might well say to the young thirteen- or fourteen-year-old: You have only these five or six years. Use them to full effect; for in them you *must succeed* at your three tasks.

Independence of the Home. The prepubescent child of nine or ten has a child's relationship to his home. The decisions he makes are concerned with minor issues and in areas delegated to him by his parents. Thus he usually decides with whom he will play and what he will play, what he will wear each day, though the clothes were originally picked out for him by his mother, how he will spend his rather small allowance, what he will read, what radio program he will listen to, and what movies he will attend, although even his parents' suggestions may sway his judgment. But otherwise he is expected to be docile (and in the main he is) in regard to the innumerable decisions by which his parents regulate the greater part of his living—when he should go to bed and when rise, how often he should bathe, what he should eat, what type of clothing he should wear, whether or not he should go to church and Sunday school, how much he can be away from home, how much allowance he is given, and what recreational objects, such as a bicycle or roller skates, are bought for him.

His parents treat him as a child, protecting him, governing his behavior.

and often expecting from him blind obedience and blind respect. He, in turn, looks upon his parents from the distance of childhood. To him they are wise and strong, the proper source of protection, help, and direction.

The young adult of twenty-one, ideally, has an entirely different relationship with his parents and his home. His mother and father make none of his decisions for him, and when he asks their advice, he feels free to accept it or reject it as his judgment dictates. He decides how he will spend his money, which in most cases he has earned himself. He decides what he will wear, how he will spend his leisure time, when he will go to bed, when he will rise, what he will eat, with whom he will associate, how much time he will spend in his home, when he will come in at night. His attitude toward his parents, ideally, is one of affection and friendship rather than one of dependence.

This change in home relationship should occur between childhood and adulthood, that is, during the period of adolescence. It is, obviously, revolutionary, and it is often difficult. The child must grow up to assume complete responsibility for his own actions, he must learn to handle money and time, he must learn to feel secure without his parents' protection. What is more, he himself must be the one to initiate the separation from his parents' dictation, guidance, and protection. *He* must be the aggressor in his battle for independence. Often he has much opposition, for his parents continue to feel protective toward him and continue to want the satisfactions that come from dominating a relationship. They cling to the child as he grows up, and friction results. But he must persevere in his growth toward freedom and responsibility.

Heterosexual Adjustment. The magnitude of the heterosexual adjustment can best be shown by a comparison again—this time between the child and the adolescent. The child has the body that he has had all of his life, though it has gradually become larger and he has gradually become more competent to handle it. The adolescent has a body which rather suddenly has taken on characteristics which mark it as being different from what it was and as being adult—the breasts develop in the girl, the hips widen, hair grows under the arms and in the pubic region, menstruation occurs; in the boy, the Adam's apple develops and the voice deepens, hair grows on the face, under the arms, and in the pubic region, the genitals develop, breast knots may appear, nocturnal emissions occur.

The child is not disturbed by strong and often upsetting feelings when he is in the presence of those of the other sex. The adolescent becomes aware of new tensions and excitements of a sexual nature which are sometimes difficult to understand, if comprehended at all, and troublesome to cope with. The child is not concerned with the special problem of being accepted by the other sex. The adolescent is much concerned with this and, what is more, *must* make himself acceptable. The child may know about the structure and mechanics of sex, but he is not personally too much involved in this knowledge. The adolescent must adjust his new feelings and his new personal interests to his knowledge of sex and make some kind of workable whole of the two.

By the end of adolescence the youth should be well adjusted heterosexually. This means that he should have adequate knowledge of sex and its place in life, should be able to get along naturally and easily with associates of either sex, should have companions of both sexes, should have had the experience of dating with several, and should be ready to settle down to going steady and to thoughts of marriage.

Attaining the Behavior Directives of Adulthood. Many types of ideas, ideals, standards, beliefs, viewpoints, and values which are commonly found in adulthood are either not present in the child or, if there, are but vaguely formed. This is true of ideals of marriage, concepts of what sexual morality consists of, standards for adult friendship, concepts of religion, attitudes toward work, attitudes toward laws, adult recreational interests, attitudes toward spending and saving money, ideas as to the purpose of life, ideas as to women's working and women's place in the home, mature ideas of the social worth of the various vocations, viewpoints on social problems, self-imposed standards of personal grooming, and others.

The child doubtless has precepts which govern him in some of these areas. But with every behavior directive in the list given above, the actual adult formulation is first considered and first put into an adult-worthy form during adolescence.

As we have said earlier, the importance of childhood as it affects personality formation cannot be overemphasized. The adult personality has innumerable childhood learnings in it. Nevertheless, the precise mind stuff that directs adults is largely of adolescent and adult making. In all probability we cannot say that the adolescent completes the formulation of these directives. But certainly in many cases he is forced to devise some kind of viewpoint on many of them, and often it is this viewpoint with slight modifications which becomes the final one.

There are, then, three great psychological changes that the adolescent must accomplish before reaching adulthood: He must become emancipated from his home; he must become heterosexually adjusted; and he must formulate adult directives of behavior. The fact that he must do this and also prepare for the adult responsibilities of vocation, citizenship, marriage, and parenthood, would be enough to make the teen years of tremendous importance to adult adjustment and happiness. But in still a third way this time of life is vital. For the adolescent period is in a sense the last chance to ensure all-round wholesome personal adjustment.

Adolescence Is a "Last Chance" for Achieving Good Personal Adjustment

Good adjustment is absolutely essential for happy and effective adulthood. Such good adjustment, ideally, is developed from infancy on. But if good adjustment is not present in childhood, adolescence is the next best time for achieving it. It is not accurate to say that it is the last chance, actually, but it is certainly true that major improvements in adjustment after adolescence are difficult to achieve for many reasons: the maladjustments are well set, the opportunities for manipulating the environment so as to help bring about readjustment are few, and the accessibility of help has greatly decreased.

Among normal adults there is a great deal of maladjustment of all kinds. An inferiority complex, inability to win affection, socially displeasing personality characteristics, parent fixations, lack of courage, lack of enterprise, temper, needless fears, emotional coldness, proneness to grow irritated on slight provocation, touchiness, jealousy, hatreds, lack of aesthetic feeling, reliance on rationalization, giving up too readily, the use of alcohol to excess, troublemaking, boasting, lying, sulking, inability to adjust oneself to changed circumstances, suspiciousness, worry, repressed hostility, and repressed guilt feelings are all examples of maladjustments that occur rather frequently. Each will contribute something to the unhappiness of the person who harbors it.

If a person is well adjusted in childhood, he is likely to get along all right in adolescence and be a well-adjusted adult. If he is maladjusted in childhood and continues to be maladjusted in adolescence, the struggle for good adjustment in adulthood will be at best difficult and never completely successful.

Since there are so many children who are maladjusted, adolescence takes on great importance because it is a last chance for *adults to help youth* and it is an especially good last chance, too, since the adolescent is highly flexible and is strongly motivated to make the most of himself. The very fact that adolescence is a time when so many new adjustments are being made, when social relations take on great importance (and much adjustment centers around social interaction), when there is much idealism and hopefulness about the future, makes it a most opportune time for accomplishing major changes in outlook on life, attitudes toward self, emotional control, and the like.

Every high school teacher has seen some boys and girls become more self-confident, others rid themselves of disagreeable personality traits, others learn to look upon the world with more courage, develop greater perseverance, stop boasting, become less unpleasantly aggressive, become less dogmatic, or make similar improvements in personality adjustment. Every high school teacher surely must know that changes in adjustment much more complex than these can occur.

This then is another reason why the period of adolescence has such importance. The selfish child can grow into a less selfish adult, the timid child can become more at ease socially, the child who runs away from difficult situations can develop more strength of character—these changes and many, many others are possible if adolescence is used wisely—often more wisely than the adolescent knows how to use it and sometimes more wisely, unfortunately, than many adults know how to suggest.

One phase of personal adjustment which deserves special word is social adjustment. Briefly, the socially well-adjusted person is one who can get along with others easily in work, play, and family situations and who has both a sense of social responsibility and the willingness and the ability to assume that responsibility.

Now since the adolescent is almost pathetically eager to be accepted and to get along smoothly with others and since he is also eager for adult responsibilities and the feelings of adulthood, his is perhaps the most receptive age for becoming mature in social relationships and for becoming mature in social responsibilities. If we fail him in his desire to become well socialized, we are doing him a great wrong—and we are also doing wrong to his adult associates and adult society.

In summary we see that good development in adolescence is of major importance to a happy adulthood. Not only is adolescence the preparatory period for vocational choice, citizenship, marital choice, and parenthood, but it is also the period when three major psychological adjustments must be made, that of independence from the home, heterosexual adjustment, and the adoption of adult directives. Still more, it is a time when good personal adjustment even though not achieved in childhood may still be attained.

Our Civilization Makes Adolescence Complex and Even Hazardous

Many years ago the anthropologist Margaret Mead (1925) spent nine months in the South Sea island of Samoa, where she could study adolescence in a much simpler culture than ours. She went there to try to find the answer to this question: Are the disturbances which vex our adolescents due to the nature of adolescence itself or to our civilization?

She discovered that the adolescent girl of Samoa did not find the period of adolescence either complex or troublesome. She gives five reasons to explain this:[1]

1. Growing up is easy in Samoa because society there is so casual. No one plays for very high stakes, no one pays very heavy prices, no one suffers for his convictions or fights to the death for special ends, no one is hurried.

2. Choices are simple. Nor is there any pressure to make important choices.

3. There is a lack of personal relationships and lack of specialized affection. No one cares for any one person greatly; no one sets high hopes on any one relationship.

4. No secrecy surrounds the matters of sex, birth, and death. These are a normal part of living, and the child has many and varied experiences with them upon which to base emotional attitudes.

5. Children learn to work at a very early age at tasks which have significance in the structure of the whole society.

Our civilization, in contrast to that of Samoa, is very complicated in its structure and makes for complexity in choice and decision. Indeed for many adolescents, it presents hazards which the boy or girl cannot withstand. We shall look at the many ways in which this is so.

1. Life may be difficult for the youth because he is kept a child when he is physically nearly an adult. As a result, the adolescent has an ambiguous position in society: he looks like an adult; he is most often treated like a child. Even when he does not appear an adult to adults, he himself may feel like one. He is approaching adult height. His body has adult contours and adult sexual characteristics. Yet in spite of this, the attitudes of parents and teachers toward him are very similar to their attitudes when he was in the first decade of life. As Dollard says:[2]

"It is possible that under ideal circumstances the new behavior patterns might be learned without producing a measurable amount of frustration. In certain primitive environments the reaching of adult status is recognized as soon as it is attained. The post-pubescent is tested to determine whether or not he is worthy of entering into the society of adults and, if he satisfactorily fulfills the requirements, he is accepted by his superiors as one of them. In American society, however, these newly acquired abilities are prevented from functioning. Although the individual is physiologically an adult, he is sociologically a child. This period is one of 'detachment of the young person from family control and marked dependence upon his age-group before achieving the degree of individual

[1] Margaret Mead, *From the South Seas* (New York: William Morrow & Company, Inc., 1939), pp. 198–199, 203–204, 215–216, 226–231.

[2] John Dollard, Leonard Doob, Neal E. Miller, O. H. Mowrer, and Robert R. Sears, *Frustration and Aggression* (New Haven: Yale University Press, 1939), p. 94.

independence in the making of decisions characteristic of adult status.' He is expected to conform to the adult restrictions and mores, and yet he is allowed very few of the advantages and privileges which should accrue at maturity. His sphere of activity is circumscribed, his efforts to assert himself are suppressed, his possessions are definitely limited, his economic independence is not tolerated, his status as an adult is unrecognized, and many of the restrictions of his childhood remain in force. . . . "

2. Life may be difficult for the adolescent because he often finds himself in conflict with his parents. There is, of course, some conflict between parents and children from babyhood on in any home, but adolescence may magnify the discord greatly. The parents of the teen-ager have, for the past twelve years at least, been accustomed to making many of his decisions for him, to protecting him, and to having their judgment about his affairs and about many other matters respected and deferred to. Both the long-established habit and the sense of worth and importance the parents derive from it combine to make them cling to their prerogatives. Add to this the fact that parents have their own ideas of what is proper in youthful behavior, these ideas probably stemming from their own youth and often at variance with the ideas of their children, and we see how parental behavior may gall and cause rebellion in the boy or girl who is coming to look and feel like an adult, is branching out in his interests, and is seeing the importance of parents and home become smaller as his world outside the home becomes more vital to him. The adolescent struggle for independence in the home sometimes results in conflict so severe that the home is thereby made miserable for all within it.

3. Life may be difficult for the adolescent because he is confronted with such variations and disagreements in ideals, standards, values, and social customs, and also with such hypocrisy on the part of adults, that the establishment of his own code of living and the making of moral choices may become very difficult—or, as it may be, he is left without any strong imprint on his character of the more difficult and abstract ideals and values.

Thus honesty is preached as a desirable type of behavior; yet political dishonesty is condoned or even made light of, and cheating is practiced in school by some of the "best" children.

Parents and teachers advocate law enforcement. Yet some of the most respected people "get by" when they can with excessive speed on the highway and with minor income-tax evasions—as adolescents are well aware.

It is assumed that sexual abstinence before marriage and monogamy represent the most desirable behavior. Yet the adolescent reads of glamorous adults who violate these principles and seem to suffer not at all for so doing. Often, for that matter, the movies associate romance and personality charm with very free sex behavior.

We live in a country where democracy is the key-word and we preach democracy for other countries as if we truly had it ourselves. At the same time we recognize the presence in our country of innumerable class and race and financial discriminations.

Lynd suggests that these dualisms, among others, exist in American thinking:[3]

Everyone should try to be successful.

BUT: The kind of person you are is more important than how successful you are.

Hard work and thrift are signs of character and the ways to get ahead.

BUT: No shrewd person tries to get ahead nowadays by just working hard, and nobody gets rich nowadays by pinching nickels. It is important to know the right people. If you want to make money, you have to look and act like money. Anyway, you only live once.

Honesty is the best policy.

BUT: Business is business, and a businessman would be a fool if he didn't cover his hand.

America is a land of opportunity and people get pretty much what's coming to them in this country.

BUT: Of course, not everybody can be boss, and factories can't give jobs if there aren't jobs to give.

Women are the finest of God's creatures.

BUT: Women aren't very practical and are usually inferior to men in reasoning power and general ability.

Patriotism and public service are fine things.

BUT: Of course, a man has to look out for himself.

The American judicial system insures justice to every man, rich or poor.

BUT: A man is a fool not to hire the best lawyer he can afford.

Poverty is deplorable and should be abolished.

BUT: There has never been enough to go around, and the Bible tells us that the poor you always have with you."

As Bergen Evans says:[4]

" . . . modern society sometimes looks as if it were deliberately designed by some fiendish experimenter in order to drive us insane. We are brought up to expect rewards for certain kinds of behavior and then thrown into a world in which none of the signals work. We are taught as children to be kind, self-sacrificing, and helpful, never to be greedy

[3] Robert Lynd, *Knowledge for What?* (Princeton, N. J.: Princeton University Press, 1939), pp. 60, 61, 62.

[4] Bergen Evans, *The Natural History of Nonsense* (New York: Alfred A. Knopf, Inc., 1946), p. 188.

or aggressive. Then we must live in a ruthlessly competitive economy. We are taught to be honest, in preparation for a world in which honesty is often penalized and dishonesty in a thousand forms is often rewarded. Our ambition is stimulated and we are assured of success if we will only 'apply ourselves,' when actually, by the very nature of things, nine out of ten must be disappointed, and chance carries as much weight as merit."

4. Life may be difficult for the adolescent because he has many choices to make. They may not seem important to us but they are important to him. What is more, some of them are actually so crucial that the wrong decision may be disastrous.

He must ask himself: What should I take in school? Latin, Spanish, French, or no foreign language at all? Bookkeeping or chemistry? Speech? Woodworking? Typing? Algebra?

What should I do tonight? Listen to the radio? What program? Go to a movie? Which one? Read a magazine? What story?

Should I go to church or not? To Sunday school?
Should I smoke?
Should I take a drink?
How much should I neck and pet?
Should I go steady?
What kind of work should I choose?

5. Life may be hazardous for the adolescent because his recreation is often carried on far from the supervision of any adults who have personal interest in his welfare. He may go some distance by car, by streetcar, or by bus to a movie, skating rink, party, restaurant, or tavern. In one small town where the recreational opportunities for the youth are very wholesome, the young people nevertheless spend their Saturday nights—provided that they can get the family car and have sufficient money—across the state border in cheap night clubs where no one cares what they see or what they do.

6. Life may be hazardous for the adolescent because he has access to adult vices. No one would question the statement that the use of alcohol can become a degrading habit. No one, similarly, would condone the use of marijuana or of other drugs. No one who respects himself or other would accept as justifiable behavior resort to prostitutes. No one feel that the reading of salacious literature is good for a person. Or that gambling is anything but harmful. Yet all of these adult vices are easily available to some adolescent; and because they are pleasurable, provide thrill and suggest that one is experiencing adulthood, they are tried out by more young people than we realize.

In one large Middle Western city, a recklessly and wildly driven car was spotted by the police one evening. When the car was finally stopped, its occupants were found to be two sixteen-year-old girls, a seventeen-year-old boy, and the eighteen-year-old boy who was driving. All were very drunk. Later when asked how they got the liquor, one of the boys said "Nothing to it. We were having a party at our house. My folks were out. I just called the liquor store and had them deliver it."

7. One of the major urges and experiences of men, that of sex, is subject to much misinformation, little regulation, and great commercial stimulation. As was stated earlier, with the Samoan child there is no "secrecy, ignorance, guilty knowledge, or faulty speculation" regarding sex. With the present-day adolescent, almost the opposite is true. Often he gets his information piecemeal and from unreliable sources, and often it is a half truth or a distorted truth that he receives.

When sex knowledge is received surreptitiously, and even sometimes when it is acquired scientifically pure from parents or others, it is not apt to be set in a framework of idealism. Sex with many a youth means only thrill, excitement, and pleasure. The very fact that it is kept such a secret part of life helps account for the fact that all of its import is not comprehended.

When ignorance of the facts about sex and lack of understanding of the interrelations of sex with the other phases of living are coupled with an emphasis upon the importance of sex attractiveness and also with actual sex stimulation by movies, advertisements, and some magazines, we have ignorance combined with such stimulation to action as to result in misadventure in some cases and in guilt feelings, fears, and unwholesome conditionings in others.

8. Finally, life may be difficult for the adolescent because we live in a world where there are many forces too big for individual handling. We hear about the inevitability of war, we read of corruption in government, we may work in organizations where the individual has but a pin point of importance. In all of these cases both the worth and the power of the individual seem very slight. The adult is confused and frustrated, and we may well suppose that the adolescent, too, finds these situations disturbing.

From all this we see that becoming an adult in our world is not the simple matter that it is for the Samoans. Ready for adulthood in body build, in sex development, in interests, in feelings of independence, the youth must conform to the adult's view of the correct in-between status, a status which may often be repressive and irksome and against which he may rebel, or which may lead to his putting his adult body and desires to unfortunate uses.

Civilization offers confused and confusing standards and ideals to the youth; it presents sophisticated adult influences which he cannot escape—influences often harmful to the adult and doubly so to the adolescent; it gives the adolescent great freedom in his recreation and then sometimes puts dangerously unwholesome recreational opportunities before him; it provides as many stumbling blocks to healthy sex adjustment as could possibly be needed to cause all kinds of sexually maladjusted personalities in adulthood. It is too big and unwieldly to allow him to feel that his part in it has any worth or any effect.

No wonder that we say that our civilization makes life complex and even hazardous for the adolescent.

The Physical Changes of Adolescence May Make Life Difficult

The period of adolescence is marked by hormone changes and consequent development of the primary and secondary sex characteristics. As a result of these changes, the adolescent must make adjustments which would be difficult for any of us. We shall mention some of them and suggest how they may add problems to the adolescent's life.

The growth of the genitals, seminal emissions, menstruation: Supposing some change in appearance or in physical behavior as major as these happened to you right now. Might you not be puzzled, or embarrassed, or even disgusted and rebellious? Might you not wonder whether or not you were developing normally?

The growth of the breasts and the rounding of the hips in the girl: Picture the girl of nine, flat-breasted and straight-hipped, and then picture her five years later with rounded breasts, curved hips, a definitely womanly figure. Can you realize how striking a change just this alone is to the girl? With many, of course, the change is welcome, and the adjustment to it is easy. With other girls, however, embarrassment, conflict, and feelings of awkwardness and conspicuousness may occur.

The sudden growth of the long bones and lack of muscular adjustment: So many adolescents are awkward in their movements that we generally picture the typical teen-ager as awkward, gangling, and self-conscious. Perhaps it is hard for the adult reader to recall how painful it is to feel clumsy, inharmonious of gait, all hands or all feet, but if he has recently known any occasion of embarrassment, he can multiply this one feeling of uneasiness by many and somewhat understand the recurring discomfitures that many adolescents experience.

The change in voice: Many adolescent boys experience no difficulty in connection with the changing voice; but some, of course, find this but an added inconvenience attendant upon the process of growing up.

Bad·complexion: A bad complexion is not the rule with the adolescent, of course, but many are afflicted with pimples and blackheads, enough so that when one sees a young girl whose age is difficult to determine and notices that her face is broken out, one's reaction is: "Oh, an adolescent."

In a society such as ours—where the adolescent leads a very public life and not one limited to his family, relatives, and close friends, where he is so often under the surveillance of adults, where social success among his peers means so much, where an attractive appearance helps so greatly in heterosexual adjustment—body changes which disrupt coordination, lead to feelings of self-consciousness, and make one wonder about his normalcy may be highly disturbing.

ADULTS HAVE A GREAT RESPONSIBILITY TOWARD THE ADOLESCENT

The adolescent is not a free agent. However much he might wish to live his life unhampered by adult supervision, he is unable to do so. And even if we wished to set him free from adult influences, that would be impossible. In some cases adults have purposefully taken upon themselves the direction of the adolescent; in others their effect on him is unplanned, as the following five points show:

1. The adolescent usually lives upon his parents' bounty. As a result, he must generally adjust his living to theirs. He lives in the house they have chosen, taking the room or bedroom space they wish to give him. He follows their home routines as to time for meals and eats the food they buy and prepare. He may or may not use the family car as they decide.

2. For the same reason he is influenced by them, guided by them, or actually follows their dictates. The younger adolescent wears the clothes that his parents pick out or that he knows they will approve of; he has the spending money they give him; he often must ask permission when he goes to a movie, goes swimming, or goes out with his friends; he does the family chores that are assigned to him; he hears his parents and others in the family discuss friends, acquaintances, statesmen, political parties, religions, and the like, and his opinions are affected. He sees or is a party to amiable or quarrelsome exchanges in the home and inevitably learns attitudes and techniques there in regard to human relationships. He sees examples of loyalty, distrust, hatred, love, kindness, cruelty in home situations and cannot help reacting to these situations in a way that will have some effect on his own personality.

The older adolescent is usually less affected by home circumstances, but he, too, receives their imprint. Except for rare family situations, he, too, is dictated to at times, has strong suggestions made to him at others, is given advice, is scolded when he does wrong. He, too, is influenced by his family's opinions and actions.

3. The adolescent must spend six or seven hours in school each weekday. During that time, he does for the most part what adults *tell* him to do. He is seldom free from their observation, their plans, and their decisions. The school rules are generally adult-made rules—he must not be absent; he must not be tardy; he must not whisper; he must not loiter in the halls; he must not smoke on the premises; he must recite when he is called on. He must hand in this paper, study that lesson, take that test. He is watched over all of the time, reproached when he does what the adults do not like, given grades, awards, or demerits in accordance with their ideas of what is good and what is bad.

4. Adults have circumscribed the adolescent's working by law: he cannot get a full-time job until he is sixteen in most states, and until he is even older than that in others.

5. The adolescent's leisure-time interests are often prepared for him by adults. This is true of the movies he sees, the magazines he reads, the radio broadcasts he listens to, the dance halls he frequents, the skating rink, the swimming pool, and the libraries he patronizes. In other cases adults help plan his recreational activities and help direct the way they are carried out, as, for example, with the many organizations for youth: the Boy Scouts, Girl Scouts, Y activities, boys' clubs, girls' clubs, 4-H clubs, and the like.

Moreover, since adult recreation is so much in evidence, the adolescent is inevitably influenced by it. He sees adults play cards, and he learns card games too. He sees adults going to baseball games, dancing, frequenting night clubs and taverns, and naturally he, too, becomes interested in trying some or all of these.

As we have tried to show in the above, the adult inevitably influences the adolescent and in many cases directs his behavior or takes on the responsibilities of giving him guidance.

The adolescent of today is tomorrow's adult. The kind of life he lives today will help determine what kind of citizen he will be, what kind of spouse, what kind of parent, what kind of worker, how he spends his recreational time, how he meets his problems, how he treats his friends, how he maintains his health, how honest he is, how tolerant, how dependable, how courageous, and much else.

The kind of life he leads today will help determine what he is tomorrow. And we adults presume to say to the adolescent: Put yourself in our hands, and we will help you be happy now and help you become a worthwhile adult. Follow our directions, take our suggestions, watch us. Then when you are twenty-one, you will be ready to choose a mate and build a happy marriage, you will be ready to vote and participate in government, you will be able to handle your frustrations wisely and meet your needs for companionship and the like successfully, you will be able to make choices prudently, you will be able to use your leisure time advantageously.

This is a serious commitment. When we make mistakes in our dealings with him, when we advise him foolishly, influence him harmfully, direct him ineptly, those mistakes are indeed visited not only upon the adolescent himself but also upon the world of tomorrow of which he will be one of the citizens, upon the family of tomorrow, upon industry of tomorrow, upon friendships of tomorrow. When we are careless, when we are neglectful of his interests, when we forsake him or mistreat him, he, and society through him, bear the imprint of our failure.

It is true that there is much neglect today of the adult responsibility toward the adolescent and the adolescent still seems well able to grow into a normal adult, able to carry on the business of living with fair success. But this is no indication that we are exaggerating the enormity of adult responsibility. Probably there isn't a person who reads this book who can't look back upon his twelve-to-twenty years and see much that might have been done for him to make his living better then and better now. We are not referring here to having greater luxury, more pampering, or the like. Rather, we are talking about opportunities for making friends which might have been better, opportunities for learning more about getting along with people, opportunities for recreation which might have been more varied, opportunities for developing hobbies, opportunities for becoming better adjusted, and so on, which would have made our adolescence happier and our own adulthood more successful.

If the reader can think of such instances, he will be the better convinced that even though adolescents are seemingly getting along "all right," the adults who influence them and work with them could help them get along much better than just "all right" if they would be fully aware of their responsibilities and do something about them.

The Adolescent Has a Right to Effective Help from Adults

A teacher remarks about a senior student: "Bob is about the most solitary boy I've ever known. He is always alone, never goes around with any other students."

Another teacher comments: "Bill never gets anything but A's in my class. He's the one person I don't have to worry about."

A mother says about her sixteen-year-old daughter, Ruth, who is very quarrelsome and unpleasant in the home: "It's just the way adolescents behave, I guess. There's nothing to do about it."

Another mother thinks: "Ann doesn't seem to be popular at all. I wish I knew what to do about it."

A father says: "John's getting so that he doesn't want to mind me any more. But I won't have any behavior like that from a sixteen-year-old boy. I'll make him come to time."

A principal says: "Miss Haynes can't seem to get along with her students. She has more disciplinary difficulties than all of the other teachers put together."

And Miss Haynes says: "Half of the boys and girls in my class are more interested in each other than they are in the work they're supposed to do. It's disgusting."

Another school principal remarks: "I wonder why it is that we have so much trouble with Max. And I wonder what we should do with him."

A businessman, Mr. White, comments: "Here's an article on juvenile delinquency and what they're doing about it in River City. Seems as if they've almost gotten rid of it there. Wonder if that can really be done."

Look over these remarks. They were actually made by some parents, teachers, and school principals and by a businessman.

Consider Bob's teachers. What should they know? What are their responsibilities? Have they ever thought out the kind of person Bob might become at his best if conditions were right for him? Do they realize that it isn't good for him to be without friends? Have they thought how they might help him?

What about Ruth? Is it good for her to be so quarrelsome and unpleasant at home? Is this kind of behavior typical of adolescence? Should we ignore it? Should we try to change it? Are the parents helping to make Ruth this way?

How about Bill? All that the teacher knows about him is that he gets A's in her class, that he is quiet, courteous, attentive, and fairly well liked by the other students of English IV. Should she know more than this? Perhaps he worries a great deal, lets his parents make most of his decisions for him, doesn't date. Should she know of this? Should she know what his aspirations are, how he spends his leisure time, how happy he is at home and at school?

Ann is not popular. Her mother would like to help her develop a more attractive personality. Can she? Could someone else help her more effectively?

Miss Haynes looks at the adolescents in her class and is annoyed by the strong interest the boys and girls have in each other. Should she be? Or is she showing a considerable lack of understanding? Are the adolescents out of line, or is she?

John and his father aren't getting along well any more. Who is to blame: John? His father? Both of them?

What is the matter with Max? What will help him? Punishment? Greater leniency? Or what?

What is being done with the adolescents who have been brought before the court? Are we, like Mr. White, informed only to the extent that we chance to read some magazine article on the subject?

All of these people are talking about some of the teen-agers in our country. They are talking about the boys and girls who in 10, 20, or 30 years will themselves be parents, teachers, community leaders, neighbors, lawmakers, or lawbreakers.

And the people who are talking about them, the parents and the teachers and the others who help make the conditions under which youth grows up, are the ones who will be able to say:

We helped these people to become honorable, thoughtful, decent, kindly, well-adjusted adults.

or

We failed to do as much as we should have, and as a result there are some who are unsocial, some who are unhappy, some who are fearful, some who are immoral, and some who are criminal.

It is our contention that the adolescent has a right to the best possible help from adults. This means that all of us who work with youth—teachers, parents, and other workers—must undertake these two major responsibilities: We must understand the adolescent, and we must try to promote his happiness and well being.

WE MUST UNDERSTAND THE ADOLESCENT

We must know what the adolescent's world is like and be able to see it from his point of view. We must know what his interests, desires, needs, problems, hopes, and fears are like.

Some evidence of the importance of this understanding is shown by the fact that there have been many extensive studies of adolescence carried on by schools and by individuals in recent years. The University of Chicago's study of adolescent character and personality and of the impact of social classes on adolescents, the California Adolescent Growth Study, the Harvard Growth Study, the Brush Foundation Study, the less recent American Youth Commission's study of young people in Maryland, and the Progressive Education Association's Study of Adolescents, as well as such less extensive studies as the Washington survey of senior problems, Fleege's study of the Catholic adolescent boy, and Dimock's two-year study of 200 boys, and innumerable smaller investigations, all attest to the importance of understanding youth.

We shall describe each of these studies mentioned since they make fine contributions to our knowledge of the adolescent.

The California Adolescent Growth Study: This study, under the direction of Dr. Harold E. Jones, was started in 1932. Two hundred and fifteen cases were selected from the fifth and sixth grades of the elementary school, and these young people (and additional cases) were measured in various ways every six months for seven years. The sample, drawn from six schools, covered a wide range of socioeconomic status. These examinations and records were made:[5]

Physical examinations.
Anthropometric measurements.
Body photographs.
Optometric records.
Roentgenograms (X-ray records of hands and knees).
Metabolic measurements.
Basal measures of pulse, blood pressure, respiration rate, and temperature.
Measurements of physiological changes under stimulation, such as by motion pictures, association words, and interview questions.
Reaction to exercise.
Urine analysis.
Physical ability tests.
Motor skill tests.
Intelligence tests.
Learning tests.
Achievement tests.
Teacher's ratings in senior high school upon interest in school work, school achievement, and college aptitude.
Tests of interest and attitudes.
Activity records.
Associates' ratings by "guess who" test.
Miscellaneous personality measures such as annoyance inventory, adjustment inventory, Rorschach test, observational records, interviews.

The University of Chicago's study of adolescent character and personality: The Committee on Human Development of the University of Chicago conducted an investigation in regard to character development of all youths in "Prairie City" who were sixteen years old in 1942. An

[5] Harold E. Jones, "California Adolescent Growth Study," *Journal of Educational Research,* 31:561–567 (1938).

actual Middle Western community with population between 5,000 and 10,000 was used. All of the boys and girls who became sixteen in 1942, 144 in all, were studied in an effort to find answers to these questions:

"1. To what extent is character development influenced by the value systems or the social groups to which the individual belongs, or to which he relates himself positively or negatively?

"2. How is character development influenced by the quality of emotional relations with parents? with adults? and with age mates?

"3. To what extent is the individual's character influenced by his values, interests, and goals?

"4. To what degree is character development influenced by the individual's ability to intellectualize problems of conduct?

"5. To what extent is character development influenced by other personality factors of an individual, namely, his drives, his physical make-up, his intelligence, his dispositions toward other people, and his self-adjustment?"[6]

The results of this study are set forth in the book *Adolescent Character and Personality* by Robert J. Havighurst and Hilda Taba.

The University of Chicago's study concerning the impact of social classes on adolescents (also under the auspices of the Committee on Human Development): One hundred seventy-five adolescents were the subjects of this investigation, "all of the boys and girls who either were or belonged in high school, irrespective of age, by virtue of their membership in a class that finished the eighth grade between 1938 and 1941—one high school 'generation.'" The town is the same as in the study above though in this case called Elmtown.

"This study was focused on the study of the social behavior of high-school-aged adolescents . . . to determine whether the observed behavior of the adolescents was related to the position their families occupied in the community's social structure."[7]

The results of this investigation are set forth in *Elmtown's Youth* by A. B. Hollingshead.

The American Youth Commission's study of young people in Maryland: This was a study begun in 1935 of 13,528 youth in Maryland between the ages of sixteen and twenty-four. "The whole body of data, gathered over a period of seven months with a field staff of thirty-five interviewers, can well be divided into two kinds—facts that reveal condi-

[6] Reprinted by permission from *Adolescent Character and Personality* by R. J. Havighurst and H. Taba, published by John Wiley & Sons, Inc., 1949, pp. 11–12.
[7] Reprinted by permission from *Elmtown's Youth* by A. B. Hollingshead, published by John Wiley & Sons, Inc., 1949, p. 12.

tions and expressed opinions that indicate attitudes."[8] The report of the investigation covers the following topics: National implications of the Maryland data, youth and the home, youth and the school, youth at work, youth at play, youth and the church, attitudes.

The survey data are presented in the book *Youth Tell Their Story* by Howard M. Bell.[8]

The Progressive Education Association's Study of Adolescents: This study was begun in 1934 and concluded in 1939, the staff including educators, psychologists, psychiatrists, physicians, anthropologists, sociologists, and psychiatric social workers under the chairmanship of Caroline B. Zachry. Its objective was to improve the understanding of adolescents as an aid to education. The findings of the study have been presented in more than 10 books. Among them are *Emotion and Conduct in Adolescence*, by Caroline B. Zachry and Margaret Lighty,[9] and *The Adolescent Personality*, by Peter Blos.[10]

The Harvard Growth Studies: The Center for Research in Child Health and Development at Harvard University was initiated in 1932. Emphasis has been on studying one group of children over a period of years (longitudinal studies—that is, continual or repeated studies of the same children). Seven years after the beginning of the study, 296 children had been registered, and of these 224 (111 boys and 113 girls) were still undergoing examination at regular intervals. For each child there are psychometric tests, psychological observations at play, health examinations, dental examinations, combined orthopedic (skeletal build and body mechanics) and anthropometric (weight, total length, sitting length, trunk length, sitting height, head length, and so on) examinations, roentgenograms (X-ray photographs), photographs, and blood samples.[11]

Brush Foundation Study: This is a study of the growth and development of a large number of Cleveland children, begun in 1931 and ended in 1942. Examinations included psychometric tests, anthropometric determinations, and roentgenograms. In 1935 and 1936 particularly, children aged ten, eleven, and twelve years were enrolled in the program to be studied into adolescence. This study was supported principally by funds from the General Education Board of the Rockefeller Foundation.

The Washington Study: Under the direction of L. J. Elias, State Col-

---

[8] Howard M. Bell, *Youth Tell Their Story*, Washington: American Council on Education, 1938, p. 3.

[9] New York: Appleton-Century-Crofts, 1940.

[10] New York: Appleton-Century-Crofts, 1940.

[11] Harold C. Stuart, "The Center, the Group under Observation, Sources of Information, and Studies in Progress," *Monographs of the Society for Research in Child Development*, No. 1 (1939).

lege of Washington at Pullman, a survey was made of 4,500 seniors from 154 of Washington's approximately 300 high schools to determine their opinions concerning their schools, their families, their friends, and their futures. A 12-page printed inventory was used, and the results are tabulated in *High School Youth Look at Their Problems*.[12]

Fleege's study of the adolescent boy: Urban H. Fleege studied the problems of 2,000 Catholic adolescent boys between the ages of twelve and twenty, using what he called a "problemmaire" and securing their views on some 200 vital questions. Students from 20 Catholic high schools in 12 different states were sampled, Dr. Fleege presenting his objectives personally to the boys (selected at random) in every case. His findings are presented in *Self-revelation of the Adolescent Boy*.[13]

Dimock's study: Hedley S. Dimock systematically studied 200 boys, twelve to fourteen years of age at the beginning of the study, for two years. The boys lived in the cities of Milwaukee and Kenosha, Wisconsin. An effort was made to get answers to such questions as when boys undergo pubescence, whether or not awkwardness is typical of the adolescent, whether or not moral and religious ideas and attitudes develop more rapidly in adolescence than earlier, what the most common and popular play interests are, how the adolescent spends his time, what factors make for mutual friendships, and so on. The results of his study are presented in *Rediscovering the Adolescent*.[14]

All of these studies and the many others which might be mentioned show how important it is felt to be that we do know what the adolescent is like. There are several reasons why we need this understanding. Let us consider them from the point of view of a high school teacher. It is his objective to work pleasantly, sympathetically, and helpfully with the young people in his classes. Surely one requisite for this is that he know what they are like.

He should know, for example, how adolescents differ in their physical development. He should know that one fifteen-year-old boy may be sexually mature, that another may not yet have achieved such maturity, and that a third may have reached sexual maturity some time previously. He should understand the psychological difficulties a late maturer may have if all of his associates are early maturers. He should understand how a boy may feel if he alone among his comrades has reached puberty.

[12] L. J. Elias, *High School Youth Look at Their Problems* (Pullman, Wash.: College Bookstore, State College of Washington, 1949).

[13] Urban H. Fleege, *Self-revelation of the Adolescent Boy* (Milwaukee: The Bruce Publishing Company, 1945).

[14] Hedley S. Dimock, *Rediscovering the Adolescent* (New York: Association Press, 1937).

He should know what the social life of the adolescent is like, as, for example, what makes for popularity in the seventh grade as compared with what makes for popularity in the tenth grade or the twelfth.

He should be able to distinguish between an adolescent who is experiencing what might be called normal adjustment disturbances and the adolescent who has serious personality maladjustments.

He should know what the ideals of adolescents are like, what their hopes for the future are, and what they consider their most serious problems to be.

He should know this and a great deal more if he is to work with the adolescent without friction and in an intelligently helpful way.

WE MUST TRY TO PROMOTE THE ADOLESCENT'S WELL-BEING

Only too often it is the aim of the adult to have teen-agers behave in such a manner as to make adults happy. Many adults feel that the adolescent is properly a miniature adult in his ways. This is unfair and often even harmful. The boy or girl must be helped to live well as an adolescent and to live, too, so that he will be a happy and socially valuable adult.

If we are to help the adolescent, we must understand:

1. What he is like.
2. What good living for him as a teen-ager is.
3. What will help him become the best adult he is capable of being.
4. Which forces in our culture are helpful to him and which are harmful.
5. What our own strengths and weaknesses are as leaders.

It is the purpose of the authors of this book to help the reader attain that knowledge which will make his association with the adolescent pleasant and rewarding both to the adolescent and to him. For that reason we shall confine our discussion to the following matters:

The world of the adolescent: what life is like as seen through the eyes of the teen-ager.

The physical development of the adolescent: how he grows and how his growth changes affect him psychologically.

Social adjustment: the importance of the peer society, problems of the adolescent in the area of social development, and how good social growth may be promoted.

Heterosexual adjustment: what the adolescent is like in his heterosexual interests, in his heterosexual problems, in his sex knowledge and his need for sex education. How he can be helped to make a good adjustment in this area.

Emotional adjustment: the nature of emotion, what the adolescent is like emotionally, and how he may be helped to become emotionally mature.

Standards, ideals, morals, and religion: how these internal directives of behavior are formed, what they should be ideally, how we can help the adolescent develop suitable ones.

Personal adjustment: what good adjustment means and how the adolescent may attain it.

Vocational adjustment: the importance of good vocational adjustment, the present status of the adolescent, and how he can be helped.

Delinquency: the nature of delinquency, its causes, and what teachers, communities, and schools can do to prevent it.

The home: how the home influences the adolescent, problems in home relationships, the ideal home.

The community: what the adolescent needs from the community, how the community fails him, the way to improvement.

The school: what a real *school for the adolescent* should be like.

To the Teacher and the Student

Following each chapter except the first are a number of suggestions for making your learning more meaningful, more interesting, and more extensive. There are questions involving your own adolescence which might well be used in small discussion groups or for written work. There are other questions suited to whole-class discussion, though also useful in panel or small-group discussions. The periodical readings are timely, interesting, and, in almost every case, ones not used in the text. The books listed are those which student and teacher will find worth reading in their entirety. The movies are especially selected for their suitability and worth.

Reminiscences

1. Were the years from twelve to twenty as good for you in every way as they might have been? If not, what could parents, school, or community have done for you that would have made life better for you then or would have made you into a better adult today?

2. Your own adolescence may not be very long past. Nevertheless, can you see any ways in which the world has become more complex or more difficult for today's adolescent than it was for you?

3. What preparation did your adolescence give you for choosing a vocation and for marriage?

4. Which of your childhood dependencies and restrictions were the last to go?

Observation

If you can interview some high school seniors, find out the following:
1. Have they had any help on vocational choice?
2. In what ways are they still treated like children by parents or teachers?
3. In what ways are they treated like adults?

4. Are they looking forward to being full-fledged adults? Why or why not?

5. What are their principles of honesty, of obligation to fellow man, of loyalty, and the like? (Do these seem sufficiently mature to you?)

6. What do they feel about the importance of religion in life?

7. Of what prevalent adult standards do they disapprove?

8. Do they feel that they have been helped sufficiently by the school?

9. If they had sons or daughters growing up in the community, how would they want the community to be organized to be the best for these boys and girls?

General Discussion

1. Give thought to the description of Samoan life. What aspects of it would be desirable in our culture? Could we attain them?

2. Consider the various measurements in the California study. Of what value would each of these be to teachers or parents (as made on many adolescents)?

3. How is the Chicago study of adolescent character and personality helpful to teachers and parents? ·

4. The Chicago study of the impact of social classes on the adolescent?

5. The Maryland study?

6. The Harvard growth study?

· 7. What standards for living would you put high on the list of necessities for the adults of tomorrow?

8. What ideals?

9. Why does attaining emancipation from the home prove so difficult for some adolescents?

10. Why is it important that parents know what adolescents are like in general?

Panel Discussion

1. What are the hazards for adolescents in the city in which you live?

2. Is life in general better for the country adolescent or for the city?

3. Wherein do we adults say to the adolescent: "Do as we say and not as we do"?

4. What would the adult be like ideally if we could break the old mold and make an entirely new pattern?

5. Evans says: " . . . modern society sometimes looks as if it were deliberately designed by some fiendish experimenter in order to drive us insane." Elaborate on this with concrete examples from your own experiences and observations.

Research

1. Listen to the radio or look at television for a period, and tell what you think of the caliber of program for adolescents.

2. Visit a newsstand, and page through some of the seemingly more lurid periodicals available to youth. What do you think of them?

3. Interview as many adults as possible on the topic "Was life more wholesome for adolescents when you were a teen-ager than it is now?"

Further Reading

For this and all subsequent chapters, we recommend the full reading of the periodical articles to which reference is made in the body of the chapter.

For this chapter, page through or read the books mentioned in connection with the discussion of studies of adolescents. In addition:

BOND, JESSE, "Can the High School Help Youth Meet Its Basic Needs?" *School Review*, 58:389 (1950).

BOSSING, NELSON L., "Readjustments in the School Program for the Adolescent," *School Review*, 49:428–435 (1941).

CLINE, E. C., "Social Implications of Modern Adolescent Problems," *School Review*, 49:511–514 (1941).

GROVES, E. R., and G. H. GROVES, "The Social Background of Wartime Adolescents," *Annals of the American Academy of Political and Social Science*, 236:26–32 (1944).

HANKINS, DOROTHY, "The Psychology and Direct Treatment of Adolescents," *Mental Hygiene*, 27:238–247 (1943).

JUDD, CHARLES H., "Real Youth Problems," *School and Society*, 55:29–33 (1942).

REUTER, E. B., "The Sociology of Adolescence" (abstract), *American Journal of Sociology*, 43:414–427 (1937).

ZACHRY, CAROLINE B., "Customary Strains and Stresses of Adolescence," *Annals of the American Academy of Political and Social Science*, 236:136–144 (1944).

Chapter 3. THE WORLD OF THE ADOLESCENT

They sit behind you in the movie theater, four adolescent girls, and you hear, "Isn't he cute?" "Isn't he a dream?" They pass you in a dilapidated 1930 car, seven adolescent boys, three of them with their legs hanging over the side, all looking relaxed, happy, and without a care in the world. When you go into the neighborhood drugstore in the late afternoon, you find the booths filled with fifteen-, sixteen-, and seventeen-year-olds and the place noisy with their laughter and talk. You walk behind two high school juniors, a boy and a girl, who are sauntering slowly down the street, holding hands and saying very little to each other. You watch a girl of about fourteen across the aisle on the train as she painstakingly powders her nose, applies lipstick, takes a little bottle of perfume from her purse and touches some to her ear lobes, puts the perfume back and withdraws next—an all-day sucker, which she carefully unwraps and puts in her mouth.

What are adolescents like?

If we are to get along well with the adolescent, be sympathetic toward his ideas, interests, and needs, and truly help him, we must understand him. This is not too easily done, for we tend to see other people in our own image and when we do this to the adolescent, we very readily arrive at a false picture of him. We assume that he wants what we want, that he is interested in what interests us, that his angers and irritations, fears and excitements occur to the same extent and for the same reason that ours do, that he hopes for what we hope for, that he dreams as we dream, and that he sees the world from the same perspective as we do.

When we do this, we are led astray, for looking upon the adolescent through the eyes of adulthood, we fail to discern him as he really is. As a result, we may be unsympathetic and critical when he is following most wholesomely the dictates of his nature; we may attempt to force him away from interests that are strong and worthy and into those whose only merit is that they are dictated by adulthood; we ignore some of his more fundamental needs; we fail to show appreciation when it is deserved; we look upon him as being "cute" or "amusing" or "annoying" just because he is different from us, ignoring the complexities of his nature.

Anyone who works with the adolescent must try to comprehend the world of the adolescent. What is the adolescent like? What are his problems? What are his interests? What does he look forward to? What are his religious beliefs? How does he spend his time? What is he seeking?

WHAT IS THE ADOLESCENT LIKE AS A PERSON?

The Younger Adolescent

Here are four different descriptions, one from Meek,[1] the other three from junior high school teachers.

He is a boy (or girl) of many, but often short-lived interests. Talkative, noisy, and daring, he has little insight into his own behavior or into the behavior of others. His great concern is to build relationships with boys and girls—he is seeking peer status and has a high respect for peer standards. He wants to be identified with the herd, the crowd of boys and girls. His acceptance by others is based on his own merits and is little influenced by family status. He has many friends, but his friendships are often rather temporary. He rarely dates and his social activities are of an informal kind. He needs reasonable rules to give his life stability, but adults will find him divided in his willingness to accept adult authority.

He is usually loud and boisterous, usually full of excitement and physical activity. He likes to associate with members of his own sex. He likes to attend Western or mystery pictures. He listens to radio thrillers and serials. He swims in the summer if there is a place available. He likes to take part in all kinds of sports. He often aids in chores at home that require physical activity. He rides his bicycle everywhere. He likes to be in club activities. He reads many comic books. He gets odd jobs to earn spending money. He participates in band and orchestra and other school activities. He is usually up rather early in the morning and in bed early at night.

In one sentence, the younger adolescent is unstable in his emotions, gullible, not too clean, sociable, and self-conscious.

The seventh-graders are more immature, more eager to please, more enthusiastic. Their attention span seems shorter, but their interest is more easily captured. The eighth-graders are less homogeneous, there is greater disparity in size and in sophistication. Many of the girls are very different

[1] Adapted from L. H. Meek, *The Personal-Social Development of Boys and Girls* (Committee on Workshops, Progressive Education Association, 1938), p. 121.

from what they were in the seventh grade. They wear lipstick, and their clothes are not little-girl clothes any more; they have much more poise than the boys do.

A more detailed account comes from Cameron. In writing of the early-adolescent personality, he gives the results of observations at a clubhouse for junior high school students:[2]

"Let us imagine ourselves as present with sixty or seventy children in the two main downstairs rooms during a typical noon-hour. . . . At first the noise of shouts and laughter nearly deafens us. As we move closer to the radio, dance music can be heard. A crowd is bent over it, beating time, swaying rhythmically, and picking out the words of a new tune. Fifteen or more couples are dancing, two or three boys and about thirty girls. A few of the dancers are getting fiendish delight out of bumping into a particular couple, scooting after them with fast, romping dance steps from one room to another. It is rather obvious that some of the smaller girls are still in the process of learning to dance—their movements are so conspicuously stiff and awkward.

"Suddenly a door bangs; there is a loud crash of feet, followed by a scream. Mary has provoked Arthur again, and the chase is on. Down the hall first one and then the other runs and slides, and then back through the rooms to the distress of those dancing—for the majority of the group are too intent upon their own good times to stop and watch this familiar episode. Finally he catches her and forces her into a corner, both arms pinned behind her back in a double hammer-lock, and then slaps her face and head until Mary is about ready to cry. At which point she is released, only to start molesting Arthur afresh so that she may get more and more of this delicious punishment at the hands of her hero. If we are observant, we shall see that in one way or another Mary actually succeeds in keeping Arthur's attentions directed toward her; and, most important of all, before the school bell rings Arthur has asked Mary to dance, and they glide away across the floor together.

"It is significant to note that Mary has grown up in a relatively wealthy home, whereas Arthur's parents live in very modest circumstances. Both happen to be slightly above average in intelligence; although, in these clubhouse social activities there was practically nothing on the surface which distinguished the bright from the dull, or the rich from the poor. Not until later adolescence was the stage set for such distinctions to assume importance, and then, it was often through strong parental pressure.

[2] W. Jaffray Cameron, "A Study of Early Adolescent Personality," *Progressive Education*, 15:553–563 (1938).

TABLE 1. SEX DIFFERENCES IN THE EARLY-ADOLESCENT PERSONALITY*

Girls	Boys
They are motivated by the desire to conform	A major motivation is the desire to know how to control their anger, hostility, and aggression
	They have poor relations with their teachers
They manipulate children of their own age and younger in ways to get the affection and approval they lack	If accepted by their friendship clique, they are accepted because of their tendency to spontaneous self-expression
	They have found that friendly ties with others leave them freer for self-exploration
They picture their world as unfriendly and threatening. This is a source of their feelings of anxiety	A source of guilt or of feelings of anxiety is their concern over their lack of control of anger, hostility, and aggressions. They are aware that their impulsiveness is not adult-approved, and they feel either guilty or anxious as a result
They accept their impulse life inwardly but do not allow it outward expression	
They use fantasy, fantasy escape, and day dreaming as an outlet for their anxiety feelings	They have sensual self-comfort outlets other than fantasy for their inner feelings of anxiety. A means of compensation or adjustment for them is the adoption of activities which afford sensual gratification, such as excessive eating, body-contact sports, certain hand-skill hobbies, swimming, excessive verbalism, raising animals
	Their overt behavior is a reactive, covering-up "front" for their anxiety feelings. Their "tough-guy" behavior is a defense
Their outer control is often overrigid as a reaction to their feelings of anxiety	They are in an active process of developing impulse control
They find the accomplishment of set tasks satisfying	They tend to direct their emotional energies inward in self-love or in self-preoccupation
	They conform to outer demands only enough to be left free enough to satisfy their impulses

* Rearranged from Esther Milner, "Effect of Sex Role and Social Status on the Early Adolescent Personality," *Genetic Psychology Monographs*, 40:231–325 (1949).

"But let us mingle further with the noon-hour crowd. In marked contrast to such blatant and sophisticated activities as we have already noted, other children are very differently occupied. Perhaps a dozen smaller boys who still regard girls in a very matter-of-fact manner, are most fascinated with the equipment available for playing basketball, throwing horseshoes, or with turning flips on the horizontal bar out in the back yard. Rarely do they venture into the flirtatious atmosphere of the crowded clubhouse rooms. Still another group of boys does come inside, but remains strangely silent and reserved. We may notice several of these tucked away in the corners of the rooms, their noses buried in ten-cent books of mystery, sports, and adventure. Occasionally, one of them may look up to watch the dancers, peeking momentarily out from his shell of shyness. Or another, if he can be reasonably certain of getting away with it, may stick his foot out to trip a couple dancing by."

The young adolescent girl differs, of course, from the young adolescent boy, and Milner's extensive and intensive case-study materials on 15 boys and 15 girls between the ages of ten and fourteen indicate what some of these differences may be. These are summarized in Table 1.

The Older Adolescent

For the older adolescent we have three descriptions, the first again from Meek,[3] the other two from senior high school teachers.

The older adolescent has fewer interests than the younger, but they are deeper and more lasting. His friendships, too, are fewer, but they, too, have greater depth and permanence. He seeks identification with a small select group, and family socioeconomic status is an important factor in determining his associates. He dates and, in many cases, goes steady. He enjoys formal social activities such as dances and also individually satisfying activities in line with talent development, proposed vocation, academic interest, or hobby. His behavior has considerable dignity and control and reflects adult cultural patterns. He is developing good insight into human relations and is seeking relations with adults on an equality basis.

The older adolescent leans toward activities that don't require much strenuous physical exercise and ones that are unorganized. Very often he wants that activity to include both sexes. He listens to music and romantic programs on the radio. He likes informal parties with both sexes present. He likes to ride around in an automobile with his friends. He attends romantic movies and musicals, with a date. He talks endlessly over the telephone. He likes picnics and outings. He may read comic books but begins to lean toward romantic literature. He attends dances with a date or stag. He has a spare-time job. If he doesn't participate in sports, he is apt to be a spectator.

[3] *Loc. cit.*

TABLE 2. PERSONALITY TYPES*

Type	General description	Social adjustment	Moral values
Self-directive...	Conscientious Orderly Persistent Ambitious Self-critical Strong-willed Self-sufficient	Does not seek companionship May be socially backward Accepts leadership though he does not always enjoy it	Somewhat uncertain, though behavior proper and reputation good Severe conscience
Adaptive......	Sociable Friendly Vivacious Usually good-looking Usually great physical vitality Lack of aggressiveness Conforms naturally to expectations of those he associates with	Good "social intelligence" Enjoys leadership but does not strive hard for it	Moral criteria not strict Permissive conscience
Submissive.....	Waits for others to take the lead Lives by authority Passively accepts surroundings	Frequently a nonentity Ignored rather than actively approved or disapproved Little or no desire to be a leader	Lives by authority
Defiant........	Openly hostile to society Maladjusted Irresponsible Needs help of psychiatrist	Aggressive, selfish Self-centered Quarrelsome Bitter Unkind Unfriendly	Bad
Unadjusted (not a definite type but potentially one of other four)	Discontented Insecure Frustrated Not openly hostile Actively but unsuccessfully seeking to establish a satisfactory relationship with his environment		

* Information taken from Robert J. Havighurst and Hilda Taba, *Adolescent Character and Personality* (New York: John Wiley & Sons, Inc., 1949), pp. 124–175.

He is radical, secretive, snobbish, cocky, giggly, with a know-it-all attitude. He lacks moderation, he passes rapidly from one interest to another, he has a blind loyalty to his friends, he dramatizes himself, he is idealistic and rebellious.

Further insight into the adolescent personality comes from Havighurst and Davis, who describe five personality types in their book *Adolescent Personality and Character*. They warn the reader, and we emphasize this, that these types should not be used as the five pigeonholes into which all personalities can be fitted. Many adolescents will not be like any one of these. But if the adult will have in mind these five personality descriptions, he can orient himself through them and then branch off to more individual characterizations. We have summarized their data in Table 2.

WHAT DOES THE ADOLESCENT WANT FROM LIFE?

What does the adolescent want from life right now, and how do his wants differ from those of adults? Figures 1 and 2 summarize the wants of the younger adolescent and those of the older.

How Does the Adolescent Differ from the Adult in His Wants?

The adult who wishes to understand the adolescent should try to think through the difference between his own wants and those of the teen-ager. Thus an average adult might say to himself: As far as the younger adolescent is concerned, he is very unlike me. He most unashamedly wants the lazy pleasures of life—much comfort, little work, not too much cleanliness, plenty of food at and between meals, something active and fun to be doing, and a pal to be doing it with. He takes adult life seriously chiefly when adults force a serious consideration upon him. Life is not necessarily all fun for him, nor is he irresponsible. But if he had his way, he would concentrate on the simple pleasures and excitements and comforts in life.

As for the older adolescent, he is more like me, the adult might continue, although he differs in that his satisfactions are not so well established, he is more unsure of himself, he is newer at the game and therefore he feels his wants more intensely.

The Home. I have my own. He hasn't. I have the right to say who will come into my home. He most often must abide by the choices of someone else. I have an important share in all decisions made. He is often not consulted. I can help determine whether or not there will be quarreling and

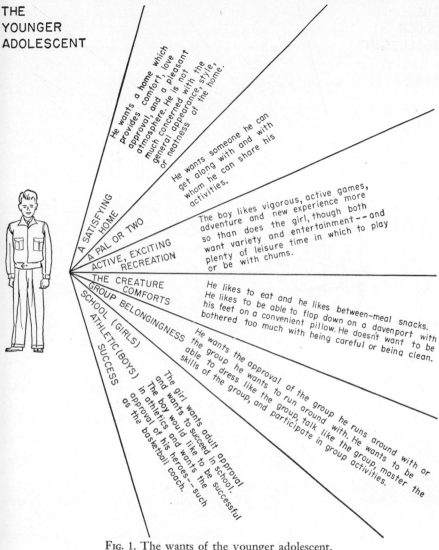

THE
YOUNGER
ADOLESCENT

He wants a home which provides comfort, love approval, and a pleasant atmosphere. He is not much concerned with the general appearance, style, or neatness of the home.

He wants someone he can get along with and with whom he can share his activities.

A SATISFYING HOME

A PAL OR TWO

ACTIVE, EXCITING RECREATION

The boy likes vigorous, active games, adventure and new experience more so than does the girl, though both want variety and entertainment—and plenty of leisure time in which to play or be with chums.

THE CREATURE COMFORTS

GROUP BELONGINGNESS

SCHOOL (GIRLS)

ATHLETIC (BOYS) SUCCESS

He likes to eat and he likes between-meal snacks. He likes to be able to flop down on a davenport with his feet on a convenient pillow. He doesn't want to be bothered too much with being careful or being clean.

He wants the approval of the group he runs around with or the group he wants to run around with. He wants to be able to dress like the group, talk like the group, master the skills of the group, and participate in group activities.

The girl wants adult approval and wants to succeed in school. The boy would like to be successful in athletics and wants the approval of his heroes—such as the basketball coach.

Fig. 1. The wants of the younger adolescent.

bickering in my home. He is often the helpless onlooker when parents quarrel. I am treated as an adult in my home. He is often forced to fight for such treatment and even then doesn't achieve it.

Work, Money, and Possessions. I have a job which is highly important to me. He has a part-time job which may be interesting but which in most cases has little to do with his life plans. The way I succeed in my job is

**THE
OLDER
ADOLESCENT**

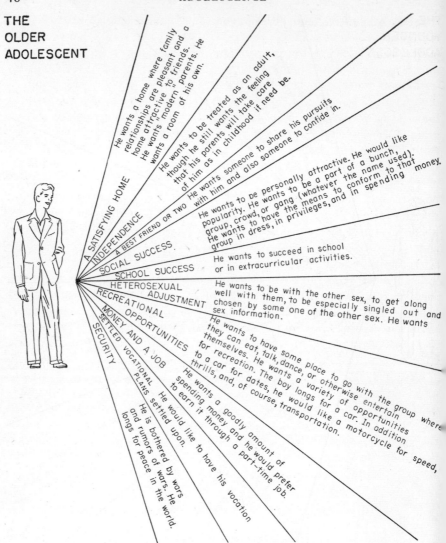

He wants a home where family relationships are pleasant and a home attractive to friends. He wants a "modern" parents. He wants a room of his own.

He wants to be treated as an adult, though he still wants the feeling that his parents will take care of him as in childhood if need be.

He wants someone to share his pursuits with him and also someone to confide in.

He wants to be personally attractive. He would like popularity. He wants to be a part of a bunch, group, crowd, or gang (whatever the name used). He wants to have the means to conform to that group in dress, in privileges, and in spending money.

A SATISFYING HOME

INDEPENDENCE

A BEST FRIEND OR TWO

SOCIAL SUCCESS

SCHOOL SUCCESS   He wants to succeed in school or in extracurricular activities.

HETEROSEXUAL ADJUSTMENT   He wants to be with the other sex, to get along well with them, to be especially singled out and chosen by some one of the other sex. He wants sex information.

RECREATIONAL OPPORTUNITIES   He wants to have some place to go with the group where they can eat, talk, dance, or otherwise entertain themselves. He wants a variety of opportunities for recreation. The boy longs for a car. In addition to a car for dates, he would like a motorcycle for speed, thrills, and, of course, transportation.

MONEY AND A JOB   He wants a goodly amount of spending money and he would prefer to earn it through a part-time job.

SETTLED VOCATIONAL PLANS   He would like to have his vocation settled upon.

SECURITY   He is bothered by wars and rumors of wars. He longs for peace in the world.

Fig. 2. The wants of the older adolescent.

one of my major concerns. He is more interested in the money he collects I must spend my money for all of the necessities of life and save for the future. He is not so concerned about saving except for special purchases in the near future. I am fairly well satisfied as far as possessions are concerned. He has intense longings for possessions which in some cases are out of his reach—a car always, but otherwise it may be an expensive watch an expensive camera, more clothes than he can afford, and the like.

Social Acceptance and Participation. As far as personal attractiveness is concerned, I have done the best I can with myself; now I accept myself pretty much as I am, following established routines of grooming. He is unsure and still experimenting. I have a circle of friends which remains stable and wherein I have fairly well established myself. His group is somewhat more fluid, and his position in it is often far less secure than mine. I am not so eager to be on the go with my friends, nor do I have as much energy and time for this as he does. Close association with a "best friend" is not vital to me, and if I have a close friend, I am not likely to share with him all of my confidences; I have many interests which I do not consider the concern of a friend or of interest to him. He needs a "best friend," and he is apt to confide in that friend to the extent of leaving nothing untold. Popularity doesn't mean a great deal to me. I want to be liked; I want to have friends; but I don't long for overwhelming acceptance. Popularity has importance for him, for it "shows" more in high school than in adult living.

Sex Relationships. I know the truths about sex, and I have integrated them into my general understanding of life. Either I have married, or I can take the possibility of not being associated closely with someone of the opposite sex calmly and without perturbation. He is likely to be puzzled and disturbed about sex. He is just beginning his search for a life partner.

Adventure and Entertainment. My time for entertainment is rather limited, and what I seek is likely to be quiet, nonexciting, and sedentary, such as bridge playing, radio listening, movie going, and reading. He likes the same things I do, but he has more zest for and longing for the daring, the exciting, the thrilling, the adventurous, and the dangerous. He has the wanderlust and wants to find out "what's around the corner." The average adult has found out and is satisfied with his own back yard.

HOW DOES THE ADOLESCENT SPEND HIS TIME?

On weekdays, the younger adolescent rises at seven or seven-thirty and goes to bed between nine and ten. He spends as much time as possible outside playing whatever athletic game is seasonal or else more informal games. He may also read, listen to the radio, practice his music, deliver papers. He spends little time in study at home. On Friday evening he may go to some club meeting.

On Saturdays he sleeps later, does chores, plays, listens to the radio, reads, or goes to a movie.

On Sundays he may go to Sunday school, read the funnies, play, visit with relatives, go to a movie.

As for the typical sixteen-to-eighteen-year-old, he uses his out-of-school time in this way, according to several recent studies.[4]

Athletics: Fifty-nine per cent of the boys and 31 per cent of the girls participate in some athletics.

Work: Most girls do some housework, and a number earn money outside the home through baby sitting, jobs in drugstores, and the like. A majority of the boys have part-time jobs.

Home study: Most high school seniors say that they spend an hour, more or less, each evening studying.

Loafing with friends: Most of the older adolescents spend six or seven hours a week on an average loafing with friends. When boys are together, they talk about sports, girls, school, social activities, sex, and movies, time spent according to the order given.

Listening to the radio: More than 90 per cent of one group investigated say that they listen to the radio seven or eight hours a week. They listen chiefly to popular music, comedy and variety shows, detective, crime, and mystery programs, and drama. Television attention will probably be greater than this.

Movies: In one study, 67 per cent of the boys and 72 per cent of the girls say that they go to one movie or more every week and spend, on an average, four hours per week there. The first three choices for the boys are comedy, mystery, and Westerns. The first three for the girls are comedy, love, and mystery.

Reading: Most older adolescents spend a half hour or more reading. In the daily paper they read the comics, the sports section, the headlines, and any news or features that have a sensational or human-interest appeal. They read the popular magazines—*Life, Saturday Evening Post, Ladies' Home Journal, McCall's, Time,* and the like. About one-half of them read both newspapers and magazines. Only about one-fourth read books as well.

[4] Data from, Hedley S. Dimock, *Rediscovering the Adolescent* (New York: Association Press, 1937), pp. 15–26; L. J. Elias, *High School Youth Look at Their Problems* (Pullman, Wash.: College Bookstore, State College of Washington, 1949), p. 8; E. B. Olds, "How Do Young People Use Their Leisure Time?" *Recreation,* 42:458–463 (1949); Nettie Pauline McGill and Ellen Nathalie Matthews, *The Youth of New York City* (New York: The Macmillan Company, 1940), p. 222; Urban H. Fleege, *Self-Revelation of the Adolescent Boy* (Milwaukee: The Bruce Publishing Company, 1945), pp. 231–234; W. R. Clark, "Radio Listening Habits of Children," *Journal of Social Psychology,* 12:135 (1940); F. L. Meine, "Radio and the Press among Young People," in P. F. Lazarsfeld and F. N. Stanton, *Radio Research* (New York: Duell, Sloan & Pearce, Inc., 1941), p. 194; P. A. Witty, S. Garfield, and W. G. Brink, "Interests of High-school Students in Motion Pictures and the Radio," *Journal of Educational Psychology,* 32:180 (1941); Harold H. Punke, "Dating Practices of High School Youth," *NEA Bulletin of Secondary School Principals,* 28:47–54 (1944).

Table 3. Most Popular Leisure-time Activities as Ranked by Adolescent Girls, According to Age*

Activity	Age of girls reporting					
	14 years	15 years	16 years	17 years	18 years	19 years
Talking	1	1	1	1	1	
Attending movies	2	2	2	2	2	
Participating in sports	3	6	5	7	10	
Attending school affairs	4	3	3	3	3	
Listening to phonograph	5	..	8—			
Attending church affairs	6	10	7	..	8	
Doing homework	7	5	9	5	5	
Attending parties	8	4	4	6	6	
Going for walks	9					
Dancing	10	8	6	10	7	
Riding	..	9	10			
Walking	..	7	..	9	8	
Playing games	..	..	..	4	4	

* Frances G. Bibb, "Study of the 1042 Sophomores, Juniors, and Seniors of a Midwest High School" (unpublished master's thesis, Indiana State Teachers College, 1949).

Table 4. Most Popular Leisure-time Activities as Ranked by Adolescent Boys, According to Age*

Activity	Age of boys reporting						
	14 years	15 years	16 years	17 years	18 years	19 years	20 years
Participating in sports	1	1	1	1	1	1	1
Attending movies	2	2	3	2	..	2	
Attending school affairs	4	5	..	8	2		
Attending sports	3	3	4	4	..	2	
Attending parties	5	10	10	7	5		
Talking	6	3	2	3	1	1	1
Playing games	7	7	5				
Doing homework	8	9	9	6			
Walking	9	..	7				
Fixing things	10	4	6				
Attending church affairs	..	8	..	9			
Riding	..	6	8	10	3		

* Frances G. Bibb, "Study of the 1042 Sophomores, Juniors, and Seniors of a Midwest High School" (unpublished master's thesis, Indiana State Teachers College, 1949).

Dating: According to one investigation of high school seniors, all but 22 per cent of the boys and 14 per cent of the girls date, with dates running from 1 per month to more than 10 per month. One or two dates a week seem typical.

Further information on leisure time activities is given in Tables 3 and 4.

Most older adolescents spend from two to five evenings a week out of the home. This is particularly true of Friday and Saturday evenings, when they may attend some athletic event, go to a mixed party, go to a movie, or just hang around with the crowd.

WHAT ARE THE PROBLEMS OF THE ADOLESCENT?

What are the problems of the adolescent? What are the serious decisions he must make? What requires long thought on his part? What are present obstacles to him? For an answer to these questions, we have asked many high school students to write about their problems. These are a few of the answers we have received:

"I am only fifteen years old and one of my problems is finding a way to earn my own money. I am not of age yet to work in a store and all the baby-sitting jobs are taken. After all I don't want my mother and father to give me all my money." (*Sophomore girl.*)

"These are my problems: my mother's heart trouble; my sister's dates (by this I mean her boy friend); my father's driving—he figures that he owns the road and figures that everyone should get out of the way for him. My parents recently were on the verge of divorce and I had to decide which parent to go with. Thank goodness, there was a reconciliation." (*Junior boy.*)

"I worry about the mess of the world today and wonder if we will ever grow up and be able to live a happy life in a peaceful world. I worry about how my character is forming and the opinions others have of me. I, as well as other girls, worry about small love affairs on the side and often wonder if it doesn't affect my studies at some times. I have decided to take certain subjects in high school which I do not want to take but which are of value to me. I recently found out that I was adopted when I was three months old. With the shock of this, one of my biggest problems is that I turn out in a manner that will please my foster parents that have done so much for me. I don't want to hurt them in any way." (*Junior girl.*)

"It is almost time for our Junior-Senior Prom. A fellow asked me to be his date. I wanted to go but it took a lot of thought as to what to do. Around school he is quite a clown and none of the teachers like him. All of the kids seem to like him and especially the kids I run around with. We are double-dating with one of my best friends and I know he will be swell and we'll have a wonderful time. After about two days' thought and a talk with my mother, I decided to go. I wanted to go all along but there's always a little doubt right at first. I hope I didn't do the wrong thing." (*Junior girl.*)

"Mostly I think I worry about little things such as dances, parties, clothes, friends, and how to save money. These things don't seem too important to older people but to us they create quite a problem." (*Senior girl.*)

"What do I worry about? That covers a large territory, because I worry about anything anywhere and anytime. For example, will I get my geometry right? Will Jane and I get married after graduation? Will we have war all of the time? Just any little thing worries me. I sometimes wonder if I am going crazy." (*Sophomore boy.*)

"I made a decision on whether I would stay working over to the Hinky Dink or quit and stay healthier. This is a problem because I like extra spending money just like anyone else." (*Freshman boy.*)

"I feel like I have many problems. I am self-conscious about every little thing—hair, how I look all of the time, just any little thing." (*Freshman girl.*)

"I worry about my grades. I usually make all A's in all of my subjects but it requires a lot of hard work and plenty of worry. A decision I have made just recently was a very hard one to make. I wanted very much to go to a party with a group of friends and I had a test to study for. The test won out. I thought I had better get a good education while I could and go to parties later." (*Sophomore girl.*)

"I worry about college and my life afterwards, what to prepare for, what I am suited for, where I can do the best work. I worry about what is natural for a boy my age. I worry about *me*. When am I being myself and when am I 'putting on'? I worry about religion and God. I worry about the seemingly degraded and mercenary people of our world. I question 'why' almost to a fault. I want to know why people say the things they do, what right they have to say them. I am self-conscious; I often fear walking to a juke box and playing it—feel that everyone is staring at me. I tend to feel inferior and lack confidence in myself. I take general criticisms and apply them to myself. I am sometimes indecisive and I procrastinate." (*Senior boy.*)

"I was faced with the decision 'college or not'? I was recently faced with the problem 'to drink or not to drink.' And another problem is that of smoking. These may not seem serious to you, but to us they are." (*Senior girl.*)

"I worry about later life and about marriage and all the problems of

TABLE 5. PROBLEMS OF TEEN-AGERS*

Per Cent

1. My school
   Wish I knew how to study more effectively...................... 54
   Wish I was more calm when I recite in class..................... 56
   Have difficulty in keeping mind on studies....................... 53
   Would like to know more definitely how I am doing in schoolwork 40
   Worry about tests... 43
   Would like to obtain practical work experience................... 49
   Difficulty in expressing myself in words......................... 41
   Do not know how to use library................................ 21
   Doubt the value of what I study................................ 21
2. After high school
   Don't know how much actual ability I have...................... 59
   Would like more information about my real interests.............. 42
   Worried about choosing a vocation.............................. 50†
   Don't know if I have ability for college work.................... 42
   Don't know what people do in college........................... 36
   Don't know whether I should go to college....................... 33
   Don't know requirements for college............................ 33
   Don't know how to select a college............................. 38
   Don't know what jobs are open to high school graduates.......... 40
   Don't know what training different vocations require.............. 29
   Don't know what fields are overcrowded......................... 27
   Want to know about the possibilities of being drafted (boys)...... 57
   Don't know how to go about finding a job....................... 35
   Don't know where to get help in finding a job................... 24
   Don't know for what kind of job to apply....................... 27
   Don't know how to act during interview......................... 19
   Don't know how to write good letters of application.............. 18
3. About myself
   Worry about "little things".................................... 35
   Can't help daydreaming.. 35
   Must always be "on the go".................................... 29
   Nervous.. 27
   Have guilt feelings about things I have done.................... 26
   Ill at ease at social affairs.................................... 25
   Want someone to discuss personal problems with................. 24
4. Getting along with others
   Want people to like me more................................... 54
   Want to make new friends...................................... 50
   Wish I was more popular....................................... 42
   Aren't enough places for wholesome recreation................... 50‡
   33§

*H. H. Remmers and Benjamin Shimberg, *Examiner Manual for the SRA Youth Inventory* (Chicago: Science Research Associates, Inc., 1949).
† Ninth-graders.
‡ Rural.
§ City.

TABLE 5. PROBLEMS OF TEEN-AGERS.*— (*Continued*)

Per Cent

5. My home and family

Barrier between me and family.................................. 10
Can't discuss personal things with parents....................... 20
Afraid to tell parents when I've done something wrong............ 19
Parents too strict about letting me go out at night............... 18
Parents too strict about letting me use family car............... 16
Allowance too small.. 12
Parents interfere with the way I spend money.................... 11
Parents pry into private affairs................................ 9

6. Boy meets girl

Boys:

Seldom have dates.. 48
Don't have a girl friend...................................... 41
Bashful about asking girls for dates.......................... 34
Don't know how to ask for a date............................. 26
Don't know how to keep girls interested in me................ 25
Wonder whether there is anything wrong with going places stag.... 23

Girls:

Seldom have dates.. 39
Don't have a boy friend...................................... 30
Feel I'm not popular with boys............................... 23
Don't know how to keep boys interested in me................. 33
Would like to know how to refuse a date politely.............. 36
Wonder whether it is all right to accept blind dates.......... 29
Don't know how to break up an affair without causing bad feelings 22
Wonder whether I should kiss date the first time I go out with him 20

Both: *Boys Girls*

How far should high school students go in love relations......... 24 26
My parents avoid discussing sex with me....................... 22 18
Should I go steady... 19 25
I wonder if high school students should pet and make love....... 18 18
I think about sex a good deal of the time..................... 17 8
I need more correct information about sex..................... 16 14
Must I neck to be popular.................................... 14 14
I don't understand how children are born..................... 5 3

7. Health

Concerned about losing or gaining weight....................... 52
Want to learn how to select foods that will do me most good........ 25
Want to improve figure (girls) or improve posture and body build (boys) 50
Concerned about skin... 33
Teeth need attention... 16
Frequent headaches... 12
Frequent colds... 12

8. Things in general

Worried about next war....................................... 31
Mixed up about world affairs................................. 14
How can I help make the world a better place................. 30

TABLE 5. PROBLEMS OF TEEN-AGERS.*—(*Continued*)

	Per Cent
How can I help get rid of intolerance	15
What can I do about race prejudice	25
Is there any way of eliminating slums	24
Confused by religious beliefs	10
Bothered by thoughts of heaven and hell	12
Not living up to my religion	22
Wonder about the afterlife	22
Concerned about what life is all about	18
Concerned about right and wrong	19
Difficulty in deciding what is important in life	12
Need to develop a satisfactory philosophy	8

marriage. I worry especially about finding a good job now that I am almost out of school—and other less important matters." (*Senior boy.*)

"What are the problems in my life? They are appearance and what people think of me. They seem little to adults but big to me." (*Senior girl.*)

"These may not seem serious to adults, but to us they are," these boys and girls so often say. They are right on both counts. Adults too often think that the worries, troubles, and problems of the adolescent are trivial and of no importance. Such an attitude shows little understanding. The problems of the adolescent to him and for him are just as important as those we face in adulthood. It is true that the results are not apt to be so serious and life shattering as are some of those of adulthood. But they have the same range from the trivial to the vital that adult problems do and sometimes require as much thought and anguished consideration.

In four recent studies of the problems of adolescents,[5] the problems which occurred among the first five in importance were those of school life, those concerning preparing for a vocation and getting a job, home and family problems, financial problems, problems concerning personality development and personal adjustment, problems in regard to social (and particularly boy-girl) relationships, war problems, and problems regarding future plans.

A more detailed picture is presented in Table 5 from Remmers and Shimberg's study of 15,000 teen-agers throughout the country.

[5] Lucile H. Williams, "Problems of California High School Seniors," *California Journal of Secondary Education*, 24:74 (1949); Olive Yoder Lewis, "Problems of the Adolescent," *California Journal of Secondary Education*, 24:219–221 (1949); Hugh S. Bonar, "High-school Pupils List Their Anxieties," *School Review*, 50:512–51 (1942); Charlotte Pope, "Personal Problems of High School Pupils," *School and Society*, 57:443–448 (1943).

WHAT IS THE FINANCIAL SITUATION OF THE ADOLESCENT?

The younger adolescent depends mainly on his parents for money. He is likely to have an allowance, he gets money as gifts at birthdays and at other times, now and then he finds odd jobs by which he earns a little. If he lives in the country, he may be working on a 4-H project which will bring in some income.

Having an opportunity to earn his own spending money is probably not so important to the younger adolescent as it is to the older. He does not mind so much asking his parents for money when he needs it. Nevertheless, an allowance is an asset to him in more ways than one. Having some money of his own to spend gives him a sense of worth, gives him equality with others who have an allowance, and helps him learn to make decisions about money.

The older adolescent would like to earn his own money and in a great many cases does have a part-time job which makes him financially independent of his parents to some extent.

Table 6, which presents data from several investigations, gives us a picture of the adolescent and his work and money relationships.

TABLE 6. THE ADOLESCENT AND HIS FINANCES*

How many work at part-time jobs?	Of 879 freshmen studied, 16% reported working at part-time jobs
	Of 5,500 seniors studied, 51% of the boys and 39% of the girls reported working
How much do they work per week?	Of all of the students working in one large high school, the greatest percentage of girls (55%) worked from 10 to 19 hours per week. The greatest percentage of boys (44%) worked from 20 to 29 hours per week
What do they do?	Freshmen boys reported doing selling, stock work, messenger work, selling papers, setting up pins, light factory work, restaurant work, driving trucks
	Boys in a general vocational school reported working as bowling-pin setters, grocery clerks, paper-route carriers, helpers in machine shops,

* Sources of data: Salvatore G. DiMichael and Marion C. Meyersieck, "Ninth Year Pupils Engaged in Part-time Employment," *Occupations*, 23:405–410 (1945); L. J. Haas, *High School Youth Look at Their Problems* (Pullman, Wash.: College Bookstore, State College of Washington, 1949), p. 11; Mary Reynolds Fisher, "Part-time Employment of High School Students," *Occupations*, 23:161–163 (1944); K. G. Horvath, "Earnings and Expenditures of 130 Boys in a General Vocational School," *NEA Bulletin of Secondary School Principals*, 29:59–72 (1945); Percival M. Symonds, "Economic Problems and Interests of Adolescents," *School Review*, 48:97–107 (1940).

TABLE 6. THE ADOLESCENT AND HIS FINANCES.*—(*Continued*)

	automobile mechanic's helpers, janitor's assist ants, movie ushers, gasoline-station attendants truck driver's helpers, newsboys, and the like They also reported such minor employment a running errands, cleaning snow off walks, doin household chores, washing cars, and taking car of children
	Freshmen girls reported clerking, soda-fountai work, taking care of children, doing light fac tory work, acting as waitresses, and doin housework
How much do they earn?	Of 5,500 seniors studied, 21% earned between $ and $9 per month, 24% earned between $10 an $29, 19% earned between $30 and $69, and 6 earned $70 or more
How do they spend their money?	The most common expenditures of 130 boys in general vocational school (as far as entertai ment, luxuries, and recreation are concerne were for moving pictures, drinks and cand comic books and magazines, transportatio other than school, gifts and treats, cigarett and tobacco, athletic activities, and games chance, in the order mentioned. Only 29 these boys reported spending money on date In other groups, one would expect, a larg number would report expenditures for dates
What are their attitudes to- ward economic problems?	Adolescents are vitally concerned with the pe sonal aspects of money problems—getting job, the unemployment situation, saving mone and opening a bank account—but little co cerned with weighing the values of gamblir betting, speculating, charge accounts, buying installment, or investing in stocks and bonds.

WHAT ARE THE RESPONSIBILITIES OF THE ADOLESCENT?

The responsibilities of the adolescent are not to be compared with t adult's in seriousness or in reasons for taking them on, for the adolescen responsibilities are in many cases forced upon him by parents or teache and he may undertake them without any sense of their meaning or i portance. Nor do responsibilities equal to the most serious of adults' ha on his shoulders. Still from the viewpoint of the adolescent himself, p ticularly the older adolescent, his duties and obligations may at tim seem just as burdensome as those of the older person.

At home and at school the younger adolescent's and the older adole cent's responsibilities are similar—doing household tasks, caring f brothers and sisters, taking care of room, clothes, and personal grooming at home; getting to classes on time, meeting assignments, and assuming extracurricular responsibilities at school. Elsewhere the older adolescent's are heavier: getting a job, being responsible for that job, spending his money, being responsible for a car, choosing a vocation, and making many important personal choices such as whether or not to date, where to go on a date, how to behave on a date, and so on.

Many of the average adolescent's responsibilities either weigh rather lightly upon him or else weigh heavily because they irk him. For the most part they do not, as do the adult's in many cases, utilize his full abilities, draw upon his character strength, or really test his worth.

WHAT IS THE ADOLESCENT'S SOCIAL WORLD LIKE?

Younger adolescents have three small social worlds which, as far as the superficial social relationships are concerned, are of about equal importance to them. One is the home, one is the school, and one is the world of friendship.

If there are brothers and sisters, then the home may provide a considerable amount of companionship in sharing work, in talking, in listening to the radio, in going to movies, and so on. In many homes, too, the family is together not only for meals but also in recreation. The young teen-agers are likely to go to movies with their parents, visit relatives with them, go riding on Sundays with them, and so on.

When a thirteen-year-old girl was asked: "How many friends do you have?" she answered: "All of my class." When a thirteen-year-old boy was asked: "How many people of your own age do you like?" he replied: "Almost everyone at school." Quite obviously with them the school is their second social "home," as the job world is apt to be the second social "home" of the grown man.

The younger adolescent generally has a best friend or two of the same sex and also a more extended group of friends of the same sex with whom he runs around. This is a small closed world of intimate companionship, where thoughts and speculations and worries are shared, but where the greatest sharing is in doing something together.

The older adolescents may be said to have four social worlds in many cases: the world of the home, that of the school, that of friends, and that of the job. In addition there are of course other scattered contacts.

In the home the older adolescent is likely to have graduated to a friendly relationship with his parents, more casual and more on a basis of equality than it was in earlier years. At the same time, he depends little if at all upon his parents for companionship, although they do, of course, give him a passive sort of companionship in that the warmth of their presence in the home is socially comforting.

The school is the scene of much casual but significant social activity with older boys and girls. Whereas the younger adolescents go with their friends to school, the older youth go to school to find their friends. Whereas the younger adolescents like to use their spare time at school for play, the older ones like to use theirs for a more adult type of social behavior—talking. The older adolescent is probably more aware of the personalities, clothes, and status of others in the classroom than is the younger. And to the older adolescent more than to the younger, school is a place where social groupings and distinctions are important.

Friendships are with both boys and girls, but friendship with a member of the opposite sex is likely to be the strongest. The older adolescent is usually a member of a mixed or same-sex crowd of his own age and interests. He dates frequently and is often going steady. Some girls are seriously considering marriage.

The world of the job while often very important socially to the adult is probably fourth in importance to the adolescent *socially*. The hours he spends at work are fewer, and his importance to the others in the work situation is often slight.

WHAT DOES THE ADOLESCENT LOOK FORWARD TO?

The younger adolescent looks forward to immediate concrete pleasures or those not too far distant, as, for example, a new watch, a new dress, a new radio, driving the car, a spot on the team, dates with older high school students (girl), going to a certain movie, a party, vacations. The older adolescent, like all of us, also looks forward to close-at-hand pleasures, as, for example, a new formal, a car, having a latchkey, being senior, the junior prom. But the older adolescent is also looking ahead to the more remote future. He is thinking about college or else about getting a job. When he is asked about his future, he shows that he has given enough thought to it to be able to picture it rather clearly. Contrary to the expectations of many adults, the adolescent is down-to-earth, realistic, and conservative in the hopes he has for himself. Witness the statements written in recent months by adolescents:

"Ten years from now I would like to be married to a guy that has a good job and that can give me happiness. I hope to have three children, a set of twins and one other. I would like to live in the southern part of the United States in a prosperous city that has a lot of nice people living there. I would like to send my children to a good school and to college if they want to go. I hope I will never be sorry that I pick the man I do for a husband. By this I mean, I hope I never want a divorce." (*Senior girl.*)

"I have two desires for the future. The first is to be married and have at least two children. I would like to be living on the outskirts of town. The second is to be a beauty operator and owner of my own shop." (*Senior girl.*)

"In ten years I hope to be married, have a home and a son and a daughter. I want to go to college and become a certified public accountant. I want to work for two years before I marry, because I don't want to get married on nothing. These are the plans I have, but in six years you never know what will happen." (*Senior boy.*)

TABLE 7. PERCENTAGES OF BOYS' AND GIRLS' VOCATIONAL ASPIRATIONS*

Item of test	Group	Grade						
		6	7	8	9	10	11	12
'I want to be a very great person and do great things that people will talk about."	Boys	10	11	13	13	15	13	20
	Girls	4	7	8	10	14	11	10
'I want to be one of the leaders in whatever town I live in."	Boys	1	3	4	8	10	14	8
	Girls	1	4	0	3	1	1	4
'I want to be a happy ordinary person with a good job."	Boys	75	80	79	77	72	72	72
	Girls	87	85	89	83	81	89	85
'I would rather not grow up."	Boys	14	6	4	3	3	3	1
	Girls	7	4	3	1	0	1	1

* H. E. Jones, *Development in Adolescence* (New York: Appleton-Century-Crofts, Inc., 1943), p. 137.

"If in ten years from now I am happily married and have a healthy family of children and my parents are still healthy and happy and my sister happily married, I shall be satisfied. I haven't yet decided what field of work I am going in to, but I only hope that I make my life a happy and successful one and I also hope that I bring happiness into the lives of others." (*Senior boy.*)

"Ten years from now I would like to be living in Indianapolis with my husband, who I hope is the one I have in mind right now. I would like to have behind me three or four years of nurse's training which I can always use either in my home life or in the professional world. I would like to spend most of my life with my three or four children and my husband, doing things together with happiness." (*Senior girl.*)

"I want to marry, primarily. My father has always laid importance on a woman's accepting her duty of raising a family and I've laughed and decided I'd be a career girl. Now that I am older I want to have a home where I can do a good job—that job of being a mother. I want to work preceding marriage in order to feel I have something I could fall back on if anything happened to my husband. I also think I can learn best the value of money by earning and spending my own. After marriage I hope to be happy in bringing up my children to choose their type of lives and carry on this endless chain of individual freedom and happiness." (*Senior girl.*)

Jones gives us information about the vocational aspirations of boys and girls in Table 7.

WHAT IS TRUE OF THE ADOLESCENT'S ACHIEVEMENTS?

First let us consider what some of the achievements of the adolescent are: getting an A on a test, getting on the team, a date with a much-admired boy, making a good cake, making an attractive dress, learning to swim, learning to dance, winning over one's father or mother to some proposal, learning to drive the car.

Adolescent achievements are of two general types: those demanded of him by an adult in authority over him and those which his own heart desires. The adults say: "Study these lessons; write these papers; take these tests; give these talks." As a result, these achievements, which sometimes take much effort, may mean very little to the boy or girl who must attain them, though on the other hand, many who dread the task do get a glow of real satisfaction from its accomplishment. Sometimes too, these achievements are not at all in line with the boy or girl's ability or interests. In fact, he may know before he starts that he cannot accomplish the task set for him; yet he must make the attempt because someone else tells him to.

In contrast to these are the achievements which are of the adolescent's own desire and planning. These may be of the utmost importance to the adolescent and yet seem trivial to the onlooking adult.

Social achievements: Making a new friend, getting in a desired crowd, getting the lead in the play, attaining athletic prominence, becoming a good dancer.

Personal improvements: Getting new clothes to impress the crowd, fixing one's hair some strikingly attractive new way, keeping rein on one's temper, getting a higher grade in a test than previously.

Creative achievements: Making a dress, repairing the car, writing a poem, cooking a satisfactory dinner, giving a good talk in English.

In general the adolescent's achievements differ from those of the adult in that they are often on a short-term basis, they are often made under the supervision of adults, and they are not connected with his lifework

For a few, achievements are attended by much acclaim, as in athletics, dramatics, leadership positions. Others, however, are doomed to little recognition for what they accomplish.

The adolescent doubtless takes joy in any achievement, but it is achievement of his own planning and design or that of a group of which he is a part that does him the most good, for then he sees purpose in his effort, he works with undivided will, and he has practice in setting a task and completing it.

It is these achievements which help give the adolescent a place among his peers. They may be crude and lack polish in the eyes of the adult, but they should be judged in terms of adolescent ability and value and not disparaged because they do not meet the standards of adulthood. The adolescent wants his achievements to be recognized, and he takes his failures to heart—of this, too, the adult should be aware.

WHAT IS THE ADOLESCENT'S RELIGIOUS STATUS?

Speaking very generally, we can say that about half of the adolescents belong to a church and probably far less than that attend services regularly. Those who do not belong to a church and those who do not attend services may reflect parental attitudes, for if the home has been one without strong religious allegiances, the adolescent will tend to follow a similar pattern. However, there are other reasons, of course, for the failure of the adolescent to participate in church activities. Some are

TABLE 8. ADOLESCENTS AND RELIGION*

Church membership........	In a study of 5,500 seniors it is reported that 49% of the boys and 57% of the girls are church members
Church attendance.........	In a study of 840 Missouri sophomores, juniors, and seniors, 43% of the boys and 58% of the girls report engaging in religious activities every week
	In a study of 81 seniors in a small Middle Western town, 71% report attending church regularly, 12% irregularly
	In a study of 3,676 Los Angeles seniors, 36% report attending church regularly, 52% attending irregularly

* Sources: L. J. Elias, *High School Youth Look at Their Problems* (Pullman, Wash.: State College of Washington, 1949); E. B. Olds, "How Do Young People Use Their Leisure Time?" *Recreation*, 42:458–463 (1949); Erma Pixley and Emma Beekman, The Faith of Youth," *Religious Education*, 44:336–342 (1949); Emma Beekman, What High School Seniors Think of Religion," *Religious Education*, 42:333–337 (1947); Raymond G. Kuhlen and Martha Arnold, "Age Differences in Religious Beliefs and Problems during Adolescence," *Journal of Genetic Psychology*, 65:291–299 (1944).

TABLE 8. ADOLESCENTS AND RELIGION.*—(Continued)

Reasons for attending....... The Los Angeles seniors gave these reasons for attending, in the order mentioned: desire to honor God, parental influence, requirement of religion, Bible, or duty, opportunity for fellowship

Reasons for not attending.... They gave these reasons for not attending, in the order mentioned: work, other social interests, feeling that regularity is not essential to belief, dissatisfaction with church, lack of parental interest, change of residence, and lack of transportation

Prayer................... In the study of 81 seniors, all but one reported praying at times

Problems................. In a study of 547 twelve-year-olds, fifteen-year-olds, and eighteen-year-olds, the most common problem mentioned (and with about equal frequency in all groups) was that of "sin." Other major problem in all groups, in the order mentioned, were: failing to go to church, getting help on religious problems wanting to know the meaning of religion, wanting communion with God, "heaven and hell," and conflicts of science and religion. Two problems which increased somewhat with age were: wondering what becomes of people when they die and disliking church service

Beliefs remaining stable...... Certain beliefs remained fairly stable from the twelfth year to the eighteenth. They are: "I know there is God." "There is a heaven." "The main reason for going to church is to worship God." "Prayers are source of help in time of trouble." In all cases these beliefs were held by 70% or more of the students

Beliefs losing ground....... Other beliefs lost ground. They are: "God is someone who watches you to see that you behave yourself and who punishes you if you are not good." "Only good people go to heaven." "Hell is a place where you are punished for your sins on earth." "People who go to church are better than people who do not go to church." "Young people should belong to the same church as their parents." "Good people say prayer regularly." "Prayers are to make up for something that you have done that is wrong." "Every word in the Bible is true." "It is sinful to doubt the Bible" Showing some loss, though not much were these two "Only our soul lives after death." "Prayers are answered"

Beliefs gaining ground...... "It is not necessary to attend church to be a Christian." "Catholics, Jews, and Protestants are equally good" dissatisfied with what the church offers. Others are too lazy or too much occupied with other plans to get to church.

Most adolescents pray, some from habit, others purely because of the urgency of a need that has arisen.

Most adolescents believe in God, believe in Heaven and Hell as distinct places for reward and punishment, and believe that prayers are answered. In general their religious beliefs are conservative although in the later years of adolescence there seems to exist much tolerance for beliefs not their own.

More specifically, we present Table 8, which summarizes information about adolescents and religion.

WHAT ARE THE SECURITIES OF THE ADOLESCENT?

What gives the adolescent a sense of secure well-being? With the adult, it is a friend, husband, or wife whose loyalty, faith, and love are unquestioned; a job that is adequate to financial needs and whose continuance is not questioned; a savings account and insurance; and, perhaps most important, an inner sense of adequacy. What are the securities of the adolescent? Table 9 summarizes them.

TABLE 9. THE SECURITIES OF THE ADOLESCENT

	Younger adolescent	Older adolescent
Personal....	An inner sense of security Healthy, normal body Skill in sports	An inner sense of security Healthy, normal body Physical attractiveness
Family.....	Sheltered home life Loving parents	Happy home life Congenial parents
School......	Equality with peers in appearance, spending money, clothing Acceptance by a group A best friend	Equality with peers in appearance, family social status, spending money, clothing Acceptance by a group A best friend Attractiveness to the opposite sex Access to a car
School......	Ability to keep up with class Acceptance by the teacher (particularly with girls) A sense that everyone will be treated fairly	Ability to keep up with class The feeling that he has a real friend in some teacher or that all of the teachers are his friends An integral part in some extracurricular activity A sense that everyone will be treated fairly Athletic success (boys)

Like the adult, the adolescent needs an inner sense of security. Like the adult's security, the adolescent's depends partially upon being able to feel that people in authority will be fair in their treatment of him. But further they differ. While the typical adult's security has considerable basis in the love of one person, husband or wife, the typical adolescent's security is found to a considerable extent in the family affection he receives. While the adult must earn part of his security by working at a job, the adolescent must earn part of his by winning the acceptance of his peer society.

HOW READY IS THE ADOLESCENT FOR ADULT LIFE?

The younger adolescent has some rudimentary readinesses, but in the main he is not ready: he lacks experience; his judgment is unreliable; he is not used to assuming responsibility for his behavior; he lacks steadiness in viewpoints, allegiances, and intentions; he has little if any philosophy of life; he is easily hurt and easily influenced; he has few ideas of his responsibilities as a citizen; he doesn't have sufficient vocational tools to support himself.

The older adolescent has grown up fast in the past few years that have elapsed since he entered upon his adolescence. He has acquired a good deal of common sense and a considerable amount of experience in adult ways.

According to Strang,[6] we see in many adolescents such manifestations of maturity as the ability to see other person's points of view, objectivity, ability to meet disappointment head on, and the ability to form opinions based on sound reasoning. Our own judgment would bear this out. Anyone who listens to older adolescents discuss personal codes, religion, family affairs, and so on, must appreciate their good sense and maturity.

They *are* grown up in many respects and as ready for adult life as many adults. But along with this there are aspects of childishness still clinging to them. For example, they are still unstable and easily swayed by their emotions. This story is illustrative: A large high school was having a home-coming celebration, part of which was the home-coming parade. A girls' club in the school had been lent a large, handsome convertible, which the president of the club (a girl of seventeen who could drive a car but was not particularly skillful at it) was going to drive at a snail's pace through the marked-off city streets, definitely not a hazardous undertaking.

[6] Ruth Strang, "Manifestations of Maturity in Adolescents," *Mental Hygiene* 33:563–569 (1949).

The elaborate decorations to be applied to the car took longer than the girls had expected. Consequently they were late in getting to the place where the parade was assembling. Their position was eighth in line, and the girls were at a loss as to how to get to that place since the street where the lines were assembled was now impassable. Finally they decided that if they could go up a crowded street for half a block, turn into the alley, go through the alley, and then turn back half a block, they would be at about where they wished and could edge into their proper place.

The parade was about to start. The young driver of the car started up the street, found the pace of the other cars too slow for her, put her hand on the horn to keep it sounding while she went pell-mell up the left side of the street, turned crazily into the alley, drove at top speed through it, burst out into the street on the other side, depending on the ever-sounding horn to clear her way, and went careening down to the parade. It was sheer luck that she didn't crash into another car or run down one of the many children who had to skitter out of her way as she approached. Though a bright girl, the excitement of the occasion completely swept away her good judgment.

And even though adolescents are adult in many of their interests, social skills, and moral viewpoints, they do lack the experience which will bring them the moral stability and social insight which will be typical of them when they are older.

Reminiscences

1. In what ways were you a "typical" teen-ager in your adolescence?

2. Did you fit into one of the Havighurst and Davis types? Which one? Did you diverge from it in any major ways?

3. Consider the ways the adolescent spends his time. Did your time expenditures as an adolescent agree with these?

4. Consider Bibb's listing of the most popular leisure-time activities. Which were the most popular with you during your adolescence? Which the least? Are you still the same in these respects?

5. What were your major problems during adolescence?

6. Did you work during your teens? In what ways was the experience good for you?

7. What were your responsibilities as an adolescent? How heavy do they look to you in retrospect?

8. Have you changed greatly since your high school days in your aspirations? What has brought the change?

9. What were the achievements that meant the most to you during your adolescence?

10. How do your religious beliefs compare with those given in the text as

remaining stable and as losing ground? Have you changed greatly in the last few years?

General Discussion

1. Do you agree with Milner's descriptions of young girls and young boys? Elaborate on her statements with concrete examples.

2. Have you known anyone who is the self-directive, the adaptive, the submissive, the defiant, or the unadjusted type? Describe him.

3. Of what use to the parent or teacher is a knowledge of what the younger adolescent and the older adolescent want from life?

4. In the light of the discussion as to how the adolescent spends his time, do you believe he should be given homework?

5. Assuming that adolescents spend their leisure time as Tables 3 and 4 show, with the most time for those rating high and the least for those rating low, do you think this a suitable use of their time?

6. Study the problems of Table 5. Which ones should the school try to give help on? Are there any that the school must stand aloof from?

7. Consider the adolescent's responsibilities. Should they be made heavier by home, school, and community?

8. Should the school try to do anything about the adolescent's aspirations?

9. Are the facts about the adolescent's religious beliefs reassuring or disheartening?

10. Is the adolescent radical in his religious beliefs? Atheistic? Agnostic?

Panel Discussion

A panel of parents and/or of teachers on "What is the adolescent like?"

Further Reading

Adolescence, 43d Yearbook, National Society for the Study of Education (Chicago: University of Chicago Press, 1944).

DIMOCK, HEDLEY S., *Rediscovering the Adolescent* (New York: Association Press, 1937).

EDMAN, MARION, "Attendance of School Pupils and Adults at Moving Pictures," *School Review*, 48:753–763 (1940).

FENDRICK, PAUL, "Newspaper Reading Interests of High School and College Students," *Journal of Educational Research*, 34:522–530 (1941).

FLEEGE, URBAN H., *Self-revelation of the Adolescent Boy* (Milwaukee: The Bruc Publishing Company, 1945).

HICKS, J. A., "Study of the Characteristics of 250 Junior High School Children," *Child Development*, 9:219–242 (1938).

HILDRETH, GERTRUDE, "Social Interests of Young Adolescents," *Child Developmen* 16:119–121 (1945).

HOLTORF, EVELYN E., "What Pupils Do after School," *Nation's Schools*, 30:14–1 (1942).

JONES, H. E., *Development in Adolescence* (New York: Appleton-Century-Croft: Inc., 1943).

LIMBERT, PAUL M., "New Light on the Needs of Adolescents," *Religious Education,* 45:287–291 (1950).

PARHAM, LILLIAN C., "Out-of-school Environments and Activities of Junior High School Pupils," *Social Education,* 6:27–30 (1942).

TEAD, ORDWAY, "Young People in the World Today," *Religious Education,* 45:48–55 (1950).

WITTY, PAUL, and ANNE COOMER, "Activities and Preferences of a Secondary-school Group," *Journal of Educational Psychology,* 34:75–76 (1943).

Part II

THE ADOLESCENT AND HIS ADJUSTMENT

Chapter 4. GROWING UP PHYSICALLY

The adolescent is a boy or girl who is changing before our very eyes from a child into an adult. We see the boy getting closer and closer to his final adult height, his hands and feet approaching man size, the down on his face changing to darker and heavier hair, his skin losing its baby-like delicacy, and his face assuming the contours of maturity. We see the girl changing into a woman, her hips rounding, her breasts maturing, and her features taking on the firmness of adulthood.

And for all of these outer signs of physical growing up, we know that there are many physiological changes which we cannot see but which make life very different—and sometimes temporarily difficult!—for the boy and the girl who are experiencing them.

WHAT ARE THE CHANGES THAT TAKE PLACE?

The changes which we associate with the growing-up process may be grouped into four divisions:

1. The growth spurt. Some time between 8½ and 11½ girls begin growing more rapidly than before. The same thing happens with boys at some time between 10 and 14½. This spurt of growth continues for about two years and then the rate declines until, four years or so later, it stops altogether.

2. The primary sex changes. These are the changes that take place in the organs housing the germ cells, the ovaries and the testes. Associated with these primary changes are changes in the accessory organs. In the girl these are the Fallopian tubes, uterus, and vagina. In the boy these are the efferent ducts, epididymis, vas deferens, ejaculatory duct, seminal vesicles, prostate gland, and Cowper's glands.

3. The growth of the ability to be sexually excited, to feel sexual desire.

4. The secondary sex changes. These are all of the other changes that make the body characteristically masculine or feminine—the deepening of the voice, the growth of hair on the face, in the pubic region, and under the arms, the widening of the pelvis and growth of the breasts in the girl, the broadening of the shoulders of the boy.

WHEN DO THESE CHANGES TAKE PLACE?

We have little information on when the primary sex changes begin (some, of course, cannot be observed), but for menstruation, ejaculations, and the secondary changes, average times of occurrence can be given:

73

In the girl:

Hips begin to widen as early as the age of eight to ten.

Breasts begin to develop between ten and fourteen.

Pubic hair appears after the breasts start to develop but before the first menstruation.

The first menstruation occurs on an average at 13.

Hair under the arms appears after this.

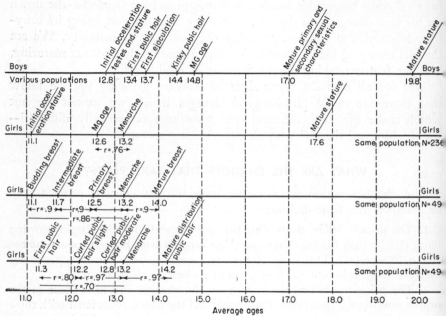

FIG. 3. Schematic picture of the typical sequence and interrelation of events in the process of sexual maturation of boys and girls. (Based on an analysis of data of Kinsey, Reynolds, Schonfeld, and Shuttleworth.) (From F. K. Shuttleworth, *The Adolescent Period: A Graphic Atlas,* Monographs of the Society for Research in Child Development, Inc., Vol. XIV, No. 1, 1949. Child Development Publications, 1951.)

In the boy:[1]

The voice changes on an average at 13.4.

Pubic hair appears on an average at 13.6.

Ejaculations first occur on an average at 13.8.

These facts are shown graphically in Fig. 3.

[1] Glenn V. Ramsey, "The Sexual Development of Boys," *American Journal of Psychology,* 56:217–233 (1943).

WHAT CAUSES THESE CHANGES TO TAKE PLACE?

These changes are initiated by a hormone secreted by the anterior lobe of the pituitary, the gonadotropic (*tropic* meaning *tending to change*). This hormone, as the name suggests, causes the gonads (that is, the sex glands, or ovaries and testes) to develop. The gonads then produce their own hormones, and it is these hormones which bring about the other sex changes.

Wolf writes:[2]

"If we assume that the essential primary function of man is to be a repository and, as it were, a culture medium for the sex cells, we should expect the growth hormone to function undisturbed during the growing age until the body has assumed sufficient size and quality to afford proper conditions for the comfort and safety of the sex cells. This is indeed the case, for only at the age of puberty do the antagonistic sex-stimulating hormones of the pituitary assert themselves and arouse the sex cells from their hibernation. The gonadotropic secretions stimulate the sex activities, at the same time checking bodily growth by antagonizing the growth hormone. By this time most of the growth increment has taken place and henceforth the body tissues require a growth stimulus sufficient to increase only slightly in size here and there, that is, to provide for the replacement of worn-out cells.

"The sex-stimulating hormones of the pituitary and sex glands now assume the upper hand, since the medium for their healthy and undisturbed functioning has been sufficiently prepared. Thus, at puberty, ova in the female and spermatozoa in the male begin to ripen, indicating that reproduction may soon begin."

THE GROWTH SPURT

As is suggested by Wolf above, the body begins to get its final growing over with, so to speak, before the sexual changes are accomplished.

This is the second and last spurt of growth the body experiences. The first period of rapid growth occurs in the first twelve months of life—nine months before birth and three after. Following this first growth spurt there is a long period of eight to ten years or more during which time the rate of growth gradually decreases.

The second growth spurt begins with girls at some time between 8.5 and 11.5. Then *on an average* by the age of 12.5 the height of rapidity

[2] William Wolf, *Endocrinology in Modern Practice* (Philadelphia: W. B. Saunders Company, 1940), p. 36.

of growth has been reached, and the rate declines from then on until growth is over at some time between 15 and 18. The most rapid growth in stature occurs about a year and a half before the first menstrual period.

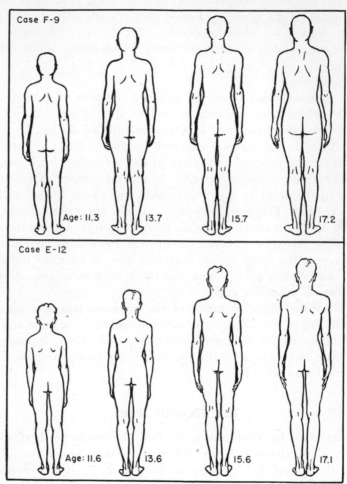

FIG. 4. Contrasting the growth of an early-maturing boy (*above*) and a late-maturing boy (*below*). (Based on data of Bayley and Tuddenham.) (From F. K. Shuttleworth, *The Adolescent Period: A Graphic Atlas*, 1951.)

With boys the pattern is similar, though the spurt does not take place so soon. It begins at some time between 10.0 and 14.5, reaches its maximum rate *on an average* at 14, after which the rate declines more and more until growth is over at some time between 17 and 20. Figure 4 contrasts the growth of an early-maturing boy with that of a late-maturing boy.

A recent report[3] on the somatic development of boys gives us the following information on the growth spurt in boys: In a study of 81 boys, 9 began their growth spurt between the ages of 10.5 and 11.5; 35 began theirs between 11.75 and 12.5; 22 began theirs between 12.75 and 13.5; 13 began theirs between 13.75 and 14.5; 2 began theirs between 14.75 and 15.0.

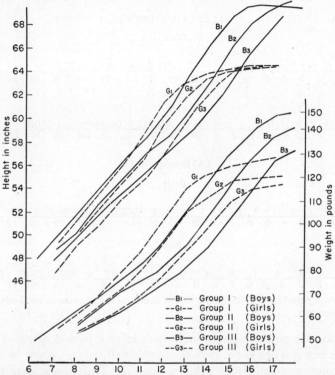

FIG. 5. Growth trends in average height and weight of boys and girls of early- (B₁ and G₁), middle- (B₂ and G₂), and late- (B₃ and G₃) maturing groups. Note that the early-maturing groups are consistently taller and heavier. (Based on data of Richey.) (From F. K. Shuttleworth, *The Adolescent Period: A Graphic Atlas*, 1951.)

The duration of the growth spurt varied from 1.95 years to 4.05 years, with the median 2.85 years. During this puberal growth period one boy gained only 4.76 inches in height while another gained 11.77 inches, the mean gain being 8.35 inches.

Growth trends in the height and weight of boys and girls are shown in Fig. 5. In general boys are taller than girls at 10, but girls are taller

[3] Herbert Rowell Stolz and Lois Meek Stolz, *Somatic Development of Adolescent Boys* (New York: The Macmillan Company, 1951).

than boys at 11, 12, and 13, when boys again become superior in height. On the average, the greatest gain in weight for girls is between 11 and 13 while the greatest gain in weight for boys is between 14 and 15.

As we have indicated earlier and as Fig. 6 shows, the boys and girls who are maturing at the early or late extremes of the range are definitely out of line with many of their classmates. As Bayley says:[4] "A striking difference between early maturing children and late maturing children is

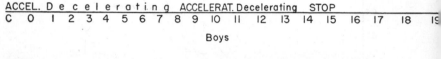

EARLY MATURERS

Girls

ACCEL. D e c e l e r a t i. n g ACCELERAT. Decelerating STOP
C O I 2 3 4 5 6 7 8 9 IO II I2 I3 I4 I5 I6 I7 I8 I9

Boys

ACCEL. D e c e l e r a t i n g ACCELER. Decelerating STOP
C O. I 2 3 4 5 6 7 8 9 IO II I2 I3 I4 I5 I6 I7 I8 I9

LATE MATURERS

Girls

ACCEL. D e c e l e r a t i n g ACCELER. Decelerating STOP
C O I 2 3 4 5 6 7 8 9 IO II I2 I3 I4 I5 I6 I7 I8 I9

Boys

ACCEL. D e c e l e r a t i n g ACCELERAT. Decelerating
C O I 2 3 4 5 6 7 8 9 IO II I2 I3 I4 I5 I6 I7 I8 I9

Fig. 6. Showing the time of acceleration and deceleration of growth for early maturers and late maturers.

that the former go through a much more intense period of rapid growth while the latter, when their growth spurts finally occur, grow less rapidly but continue growing over a longer period. This means that the early maturing child suddenly becomes relatively very large, but after a few years is again back to normal in size; while the late maturer lags behind remaining small when his peers have far outdistanced him, and only gradually, after several years, does he regain his physical status. In general these differences between the early and late maturers are true of both sexes, but in certain respects there are sex differences in these trends. The growth and sex hormones which are active during this adolescent period of physiological maturing, being different for the sexes, affect growth somewhat differently. . . .

"The slow-maturing girls, on the other hand, are the ones who are

[4] Nancy Bayley, "The Long and the Short of It," *Educational Leadership*, 2:331–33 (1945).

growing up along with the boys of their own age. Although they are, before about 13 or 14 years, smaller than other girls their same age, their growth, though slow, is continuous over a longer period of time. For the same degree of skeletal maturity the later maturers are larger than the early maturers. They have a moderate spurt of growth around 13 to 15 years, after which age they are usually the taller girls, and become the tall adult women. (This, of course, is on the average—there are always wide variations due to inheritance, health, and nutrition.) . . .

"The boys present a different picture. The early maturers are growing rapidly at about the same time as the main group of girls is growing fast. The late-maturers, on the other hand, lag far behind. They are still little boys at 13, 14, and often even at 15 years. They simply cannot keep pace with the other children in their age group."

DISPROPORTION IN GROWTH

The parts of the body do not grow at the same rate. This is well illustrated in Fig. 7, where we see dramatic differences in the growth rate of the brain, body as a whole, and genitals. The disproportion is probably most disconcertingly evident to the adolescent in the difference in growth rate in arms, legs, and trunk and the difference in upper part of the face as compared with the lower.

At the time of the growth spurt, arms and legs lengthen rapidly. With the early maturing, the legs are long in proportion to the trunk at around ten for girls and twelve for boys. But with the late maturing they are long at around the age of thirteen for girls and fifteen for boys. This can be shown by diagrams indicating the change in proportion of sitting height to standing height, which may be represented thus:

$$\frac{\text{Sitting height}}{\text{Standing height}}$$

When this ratio is smaller, it means that trunk length compared with leg length is smaller. When this ratio is larger, it means that trunk length is, comparatively, catching up with leg length. Figure 8 shows the change.

This disproportion in growth rate is much more evident in some boys and girls than in others, of course. Some, like young colts, look "leggy"; others go so smoothly from childhood into adulthood that no age finds them other than well proportioned.

With some boys and girls the face also gives evidence of different rates of growth, the upper part (forehead and nose) reaching its mature size before the jaw does. One young man of twenty with well-balanced features says he recalls that his profile at fifteen seemed to be all nose.

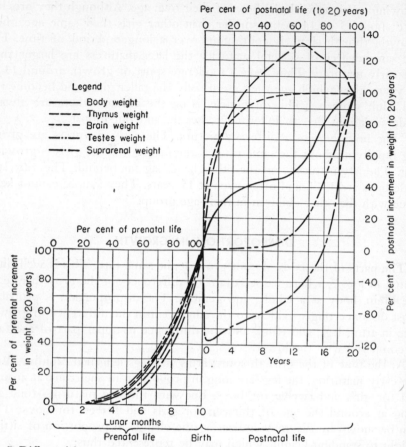

Fig. 7. Differential growth in weight of the human body and of various organs during the fetal period and postnatal life; fetal and postnatal time periods expressed as 100 per cent and fetal and postnatal increments expressed as 100 per cent. Brain weight at age 6 has attained 90 per cent of maturity while testes weight does not attain 90 per cent of maturity until age 19. (Based on data of Harris *et al.*) (From F. K. Shuttleworth, *The Adolescent Period: A Graphic Atlas*, 1951.)

"When I'd try on clothes and see myself in a three-way mirror, I'd always get a shock upon seeing my profile, for my chin just slid off into my collar and my nose looked like an eagle's."

OTHER DETAILS OF GROWTH

It need not be said that along with growth of height and weight in the individual's approach to final adult form and size, there are other changes in size and structure. The shoulders of the boys widen as do the hips of the girls. Figure 9 illustrates this.

Many adolescents go through a fat period. Stolz and Stolz[5] found this to be true of about one-half the boys they studied. This cycle of increase and then decrease in fat centers near the onset of the growth spurt.

With girls such a fat period leads to concerns about dieting. With boys there is concern because their bodies have a feminine look, for the fat accumulates around the nipples, and over the abdomen, hips, and thighs.

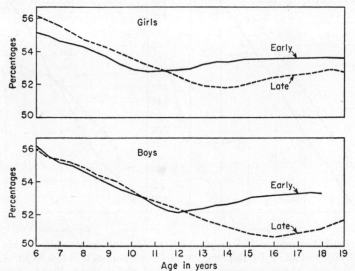

FIG. 8. Age changes in the proportion of sitting height to standing height. (After Shuttleworth.) (From Nancy Bayley and Read Tuddenham, "Adolescent Changes in Body Build," Chap. III in 43d Yearbook, National Society for the Study of Education, Part I, *Adolescence*, p. 42. Used by permission of the Society.)

This may well lead to great distress in some who feel that they are thus developing wrongly.

Muscles achieve much of their ultimate growth by sixteen. As Jones says,[6] the period of most rapid growth for manual strength is between twelve and thirteen for girls and between fifteen and sixteen for boys. At eleven, he says, boys are twice as strong as at six, and by sixteen their manual strength has doubled again.

The heart doubles in size, the lungs make their greatest increase at the

[5] Stolz and Stolz, *op. cit.*, p. 357.

[6] Harold E. Jones, "The Development of Physical Abilities," Chap. VI in Nelson B. Henry (ed.), 43d Yearbook, National Society for the Study of Education, Part I, *Adolescence* (Chicago: University of Chicago Press, 1944), p. 101.

time of the growth spurt, the stomach and intestines get longer and the walls thicken, the liver increases in weight. Though not a matter of change in size, it might also be mentioned here that the second molars erupt between twelve and fifteen, the wisdom teeth between fifteen and twenty-five.

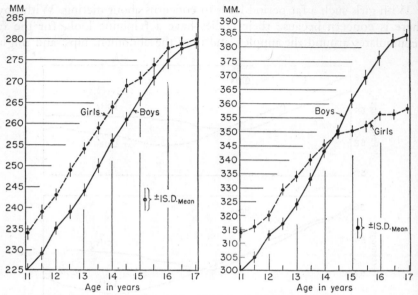

FIG. 9. (*Left*) Growth in hip width. (*Right*) Growth in shoulder width. (From Nancy Bayley and Read Tuddenham, "Adolescent Changes in Body Build," Chap. III in 43d Yearbook, National Society for the Study of Education, Part I, *Adolescence*, p. 42. Used by permission of the Society.)

PUBERTY

As we have said, the sudden spurt of growth that heralds the approach of physical maturity begins before we see evidence of sexual maturity. In other words, it occurs before puberty.

The word *puberty* is subject to various interpretations. We shall define it as it is most commonly used: *Puberty* refers to the attainment of sexual maturity, that is, the attainment of the ability to conceive a child. When a boy or girl has reached puberty, his or her body has reached the point where it can procreate.

Pubescence refers to the process of becoming sexually mature. The *prepubescent* child has not begun the process. The *pubescent* child is undergoing the change. The *postpubescent* boy or girl is sexually mature

WHEN BOYS AND GIRLS MATURE

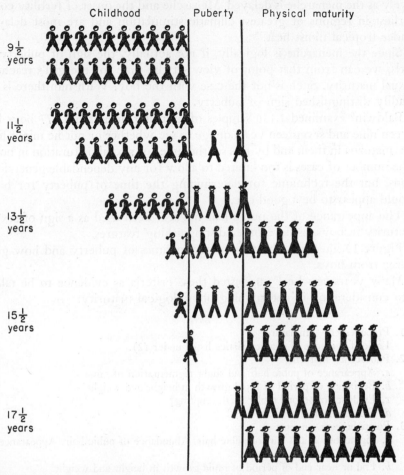

FIG. 10. The occurrence of puberty in boys and girls, showing the wide range in times. (Pictograph from A. V. Keliher, *Life and Growth*, (New York: Appleton-Century-Crofts, 1938, p. 159. By permission of Appleton-Century-Crofts and Pictograph Corporation.)

Since the first menstrual period of the girl (or the *menarche*) indicates that her uterus has for the first time been in readiness to receive the fertilized egg, the menarche is often used as the sign that the girl has reached sexual maturity, or puberty. Actually, however, this may not be a proper sign of sexual maturity, for there is considerable evidence to the effect that the girl is sterile for some time after the occurrence of her first menstruation. This sterile period may possibly be for as long as from three to six years. As Mills and Ogle say:[7] "This sterile period shortens progressively as the menarche is delayed. Menarche and the onset of fertility come earliest in regions of greatest climatic stimulation and are most delayed under tropical moist heat."

Since the menarche is logically, if not actually, the sign of puberty in girls, we can from that point of view set the time for the girl's reaching sexual maturity. Such is not the case with the boy. With him there is no readily distinguished sign of puberty.

Baldwin[8] examined 1,136 samples of morning urine from 177 boys between nine and seventeen years of age to see whether or not he might find spermatozoa in them and by this set the time for sexual maturation in boys. The number of cases is too limited to allow for any dependable generalizations, but the technique for determining the time of puberty for boys would appear to be a good one.

The appearance of the pubic hair has also been used as a sign of sexual maturity in boys, as have other distinguishing features.

Figure 10 illustrates the wide range in times of puberty and how girls differ from boys.

Many years ago Leal[9] suggested these criteria as evidence to be taken into consideration in determining physiological maturity:

Boys

1. Prepubescent—immature
   Lack of evidence of characteristics listed under (2).
2. Pubescent—maturing
   a. Appearance of pubic hair and slight pigmentation of same
   b. Beginning of period of rapid growth in height and weight*
   c. Evidence of second molar teeth erupting†
   d. Enlargement of genitals
3. Postpubescent—mature
   a. Pigmentation and curl of pubic hair. Abundance of pubic hair. Appearance of beard
   b. End or near end of period of rapid growth in height and weight*
   c. Second molar teeth erupted
   d. Full development of larynx—change of voice
   e. Seminal emissions

* Difficult if not impossible to determine.

† Physicians who worked with Miss Leal in her study said that the eruption of the second molars in boys when appearing without other signs was not sufficient evidence of stage 2.

[7] C. A. Mills and Cordelia Ogle, "Physiologic Sterility of Adolescence," *Human Biology*, 8:607–615 (1936).

[8] William Walter Greulich, "Some Genital Changes Associated with Puberty," Chap. IV in *A Handbook of Methods for the Study of Adolescent Children* (Society for Research in Child Development, 1938), Vol. III, No. 2, p. 65.

[9] Mary A. Leal, *Physiological Maturity in Relation to Certain Characteristics of Boys and Girls* (Philadelphia: University of Pennsylvania Press, 1929), pp. 33–34.

Girls

1. Prepubescent—immature
   Lack of evidence of characteristics listed under (2)
2. Pubescent—maturing
   a. Appearance of pubic hair and slight pigmentation of same. Also axillary hair
   b. Beginning of period of rapid growth in height and weight*
   c. Evidence of second molar teeth erupting
   d. Enlargement and change of appearance of breasts
   e. Enlargement of pelvis breadth
3. Postpubescent—matured
   a. Pigmentation and curl of pubic hair. Abundance of hair. Hair under arms
   b. End or near end of period of rapid growth in height and weight*
   c. Second molar teeth erupted
   d. Full development of larynx
   e. Menstruation

*Difficult if not impossible to determine.

The most dependable way of determining physical maturity, however, seems to be to take X rays of the long bones of the hand and knee. Skeletal age has been used for some time to give a measure of bodily maturation, for it seems to be closely related to the development of the reproductive system. Any part of the skeleton might be used, but some parts present more easily identifiable criteria than others.

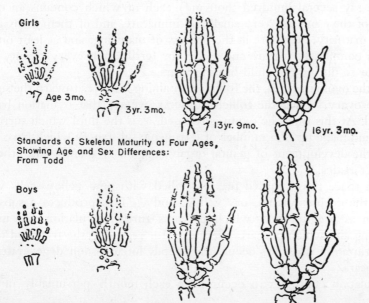

Girls

Age 3 mo.   3 yr. 3 mo.   13 yr. 9 mo.   16 yr. 3 mo.

Standards of Skeletal Maturity at Four Ages,
Showing Age and Sex Differences:
From Todd

Boys

Fig. 11. Age and sex differences in ossification of the hand and wrist. (From F. K. Shuttleworth, *The Adolescent Period: A Graphic Atlas*, 1951.)

The ends of the long bones are called epiphyses. These are cartilaginous early in life but shortly develop a bony cap at the end. "Maturity determinators in the skeleton are successive change in outline of shaft ends and in contour of epiphysical ossification centers which mark the progress in skeletal maturation to its final adult form."[10] Figure 11 illustrates this progressive ossification of the hand and wrist.

THE REPRODUCTIVE SYSTEM

Puberty means that the reproductive system has matured enough to make it possible to conceive a child. It seems necessary to give a brief explanation of the nature of the female and the male reproductive systems before we enter into a discussion of the changes of puberty. Figures 12 and 13 show the human reproductive systems diagrammatically.

The Female

The reproductive cells of the female, the egg cells, or ova, are stored in the ovaries, a pair of flattened, oval, grayish-pink bodies about 1½ inches long which lie on either side of the uterus in a slight depression of the pelvic wall. These contain a great number of tiny follicles or sacs (some say several hundred thousand) each of which contains an ovum. Most of these ova are very small and immature, and of them many never reach maturity. Some are in the process of maturing, and at least one becomes completely mature and ready for fertilization every twenty-eight days or so during the child-bearing years.

As the ovum matures, the follicle containing it moves toward the surface of the ovary. When the follicle ruptures, we say that ovulation has occurred. At this time the ovum is released, as is the fluid which surrounds it, a fluid made up of a number of estrogenic substances which have to do with the development of genital organs, mammary glands, and other sex characteristics.

The space thus emptied becomes filled with new yellow cells which form the corpus luteum, or "yellow body." This produces a substance known as *progesterone*, which prevents further ovulation and uterine bleeding and which prepares the uterus for receiving the fertilized ovum. If fertilization does not occur, the corpus luteum soon degenerates and disappears.

Ovulation continues to occur once each month—presumably midway

[10] T. Wingate Todd, *Atlas of Skeletal Maturation* (St. Louis: The C. V. Mosby Company, Medical Publishers, 1937), p. 40.

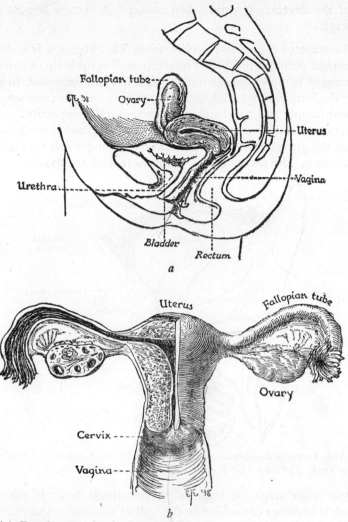

FIG. 12. (*a*) Female reproductive system. (*b*) Internal female reproductive organs. (From Harold Diehl, *Textbook of Healthful Living*, New York: McGraw-Hill Book Company, Inc., 1950, pp. 396-397.)

between the menstrual periods—until the end of the child-bearing period of a woman's life at some time between forty-five and fifty.

The ovum released in ovulation is caught by the funnel-shaped opening of one of the 4-inch-long Fallopian tubes (also called the *oviducts* or *uterine tubes*), and it passes through the tube and via an extremely small opening into the cavity of the uterus.

The uterus, a pear-shaped, hollow organ less than 3 inches long, is the home of the developing child when conception occurs. It goes through three stages:[11]

1. The stage of repair and proliferation. This begins a few days after the menstrual period is finished. The uterus wall is made up of three layers, the innermost being a mucosa lining called the *endometrium*. In preparation for the fertilized egg, this lining becomes thicker, becomes filled with blood and lymph, and its glands grow in size and complexity.

2. Premenstrual, or secretory, stage. The processes mentioned above continue, the glands growing larger and much longer and becoming filled with secretion. The uterus is now ready to receive the ovum.

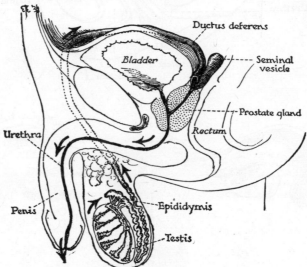

Fig. 13. Male reproductive organs. (From Harold Diehl, *Textbook of Healthful Living*, New York: McGraw-Hill Book Company, Inc., 1950, p. 395.)

3. Destructive stage, or stage of the menstrual flow. If the ovum is fertilized, it becomes embedded in the wall of the uterus and the endometrium continues to develop, finally becoming the placenta (the vascular structure by which the fetus is nourished in the uterus).

If the ovum is not fertilized, it degenerates and is absorbed in the Fallopian tubes or the uterus. In this case, the preparatory material in the uterus is not needed. The extra layers of tissue are now shed, thus opening the tiny blood vessels. This sloughed-off part of the endometrium, along with the interstitial blood, is expelled periodically through the contraction of the uterus. This is called the menstrual flow.

[11] Charles Herbert Best and Norman Burke Taylor, *The Physiological Basis of Medical Practice* (Baltimore: The Williams & Wilkins Company, 1950), pp. 878–87.

The organ of copulation through which sperm are received from the male is the vagina, a tube 3 or 4 inches long reaching from the vulva to he uterus. Before intercourse has ever taken place, the outer opening of this is normally covered in part by the hymen, a fold of mucous membrane. However, even without intercourse, this hymen is sometimes ruptured.

The external part of the female reproductive organs is called the vulva. It consists of:

Mons pubis: The rounded eminence, covered with hair by the time of puberty.
Labia majora: The outside two longitudinal folds of skin.
Labia minora: Two smaller folds between the labia majora.
Clitoris: Two small erectile cavernous bodies.
Vestibule: Cleft between labia minora.
Vestibular glands: Two small rounded bodies which lie on either side of he vagina and open into the vestibule between the hymen and labia minora. They secrete a lubricating substance.

The Male

The male germ cells, the sperm, or spermatozoa, are found in two void bodies, the testes, which hang in the scrotum, a pouch of thin skin with no fat which provides a cooler place for the sperm than would a cavity inside the body. In addition to housing the sperm, the testes produce hormones, the androgens, concerned with the development of the accessory sex organs, secondary sex characteristics, sebaceous glands, subcutaneous fat, and muscles. The course of the sperm from the testes to the vagina of the female is as follows:

Efferent ductules, or ducts: Fifteen to twenty ducts which carry the seminal fluid from the testes to the
Epididymis: A long, flat body which lies on the testis and which is really a extremely long, much folded tube. The convoluted masses of efferent ductules form the head of the epididymis. The body and tail are made up of a much convoluted duct at least 20 feet long. Here the spermatozoa are stored, and here they mature. The epididymis empties into the
Vas deferens, or seminal duct: A tube about 45 centimeters long which lies within the spermatic cord. This is joined by the
Duct of the seminal vesicles. The seminal vesicles are two pouches which produce a secretion to be added to the seminal fluid. Their duct, together with the seminal duct, forms the
Ejaculatory duct, which enters the
Prostate: A gland about the size of a chestnut which contributes its secretion to the semen. This secretion is believed to serve the purpose of making

the sperm, which have been kept quiescent in the epididymis, active. The prostate is poorly developed until the time of puberty. In the prostate the ejaculatory duct empties into the prostate portion of the

Urethra: A tube 17.5 to 20 centimeters long which serves to transport both semen and urine. The ejaculatory duct is closed when the urethra carries urine. Similarly, when the tube carries semen, a valve closes the outlet of the bladder. The urethra is contained for the most part in the

Penis: The male organ of copulation as well as of elimination. This is a cylinder made up largely of erectile tissue, a meshwork of spaces which fill with blood and thus cause the erection of the penis. During intercourse, there occurs an ejaculation during which the semen is delivered into the urethra, which then expels it. In the ejaculation there may be 120,500,000 spermatozoa or more.

SOME PUBESCENT CHANGES IN THE BOY

Growth of the Genitals

Like the rest of the body, the testes and penis also have a period of rapid growth during adolescence. According to Stolz and Stolz,[12] the testes begin their accelerated growth from .25 year to 1.75 year before the growth spurt in height and finish it a year or so after. Somewhat later (coincidentally with the onset of the growth spurt) the penis begins growth spurt which ends before the growth spurt in height is over.

Nocturnal Emissions

Many pubescent boys have ejaculations of semen during their sleep. These nocturnal emissions are perfectly normal and are caused by stimulation received in dreams or by some physical condition such as a full bladder, the pressure of bed clothing, and so on. According to Ramsey,[13] in study of 291 boys between the ages of 10 and 20, nocturnal emissions were experienced by 75 per cent of the boys by the age of 18.

Breast Knots

Breast knots (slight enlargements of the breast) often develop in boys during pubescence, disappearing in a short time. Of Ramsey's[14] group of 291 boys, about a third reported such enlargement of the breast as appearing at the age of twelve, thirteen, or fourteen. They caused little or no difficulty. Of those who had them, 47 per cent remembered them

[12] Stolz and Stolz, op. cit., pp. 337, 342.
[13] Ramsey, loc. cit.
[14] Ramsey, Ibid.

lasting less than two weeks, 47 per cent as lasting between two and twelve weeks, and 6 per cent as lasting between three and twenty-four months. Breast knots are a normal occurrence, though the fact that they may occur in only one of the breasts in some boys, that they may be painful, and that they may exude a secretion may cause alarm in the boy who doesn't know just what is happening to him.

Body Hair

Hair appears in the pubic region, on the face, under the arms, and on other parts of the body. At about the age of fourteen pubic hair begins

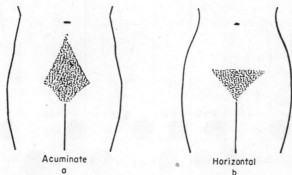

Acuminate
a

Horizontal
b

FIG. 14. Typical pubic-hair distribution of man (*a*) and woman (*b*). (From C. W. Dupertuis, W. B. Atkinson, and H. Elftman, "Sex Differences in Pubic Hair Distribution," *Human Biology*, 17:138 (1945).)

to appear at the base of the penis and then later extends upward. In most boys it takes shape *a*, in the girl shape *b*, as Fig. 14 shows. However, according to one study[15] the horizontal, or feminine, type is found in only nine-tenths of women and in 17 per cent of adult males, while the acuminate, or masculine, type is found in half of the men and 10 per cent of the women. Two other types of hair distribution are also found, but much less frequently.

Axillary (armpit) hair appears somewhat later.

The hair on the body of the child is a downy type called *vellus*. Much of this is replaced in maturity by a longer, heavier, darker hair, called *terminal* hair. This terminal hair is found on many parts of the body. It appears on the face of the boy at the time of puberty, first on the upper lip, later on the chin and sides of the face, and then over the whole beard area. Terminal hair also develops on the limbs and trunk.

[15] C. W. Dupertuis, William B. Atkinson, and Herbert Elftman, "Sex Differences in Pubic Hair Distribution," *Human Biology*, 17:137–142 (1945).

Voice Change

The voice deepens during pubescence. Ramsey[16] found that the median age for voice change was 13.4 years. The male voice is about an octave below that of the female. The change of voice usually occurs after some

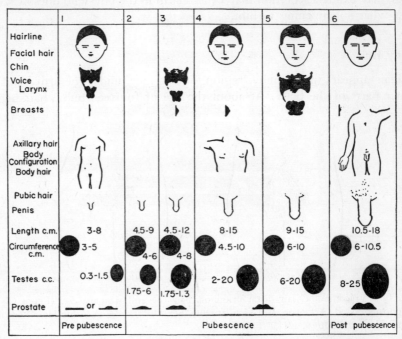

	1	2	3	4	5	6
Hairline						
Facial hair						
Chin						
Voice Larynx						
Breasts						
Axillary hair Body Configuration Body hair						
Pubic hair Penis						
Length c.m.	3-8	4.5-9	4.5-12	8-15	9-15	10.5-18
Circumference c.m.	3-5	4-6	4-8	4.5-10	6-10	6-10.5
Testes c.c.	0.3-1.5	1.75-6	1.75-1.3	2-20	6-20	8-25
Prostate	___ or ___					
	Pre pubescence	Pubescence				Post pubescence

FIG. 15. Schematic diagram illustrating the typical sequence and correlation of male primary and secondary sex characters for each of six stages of development. (From Schonfeld.) (From F. K. Shuttleworth, *The Adolescent Period: A Graphic Atlas* 1951.)

pubic hair is present. As Greulich says, except in extreme cases there is no necessary relationship between depth of voice and masculinity—that is, we cannot assume that the person whose voice is deep is more masculine than the person whose voice is higher.

A summarization of the sex changes in boys is presented in Fig. 15.

SOME PUBESCENT CHANGES IN GIRLS

Sex Organs

The ovaries, Fallopian tubes, and uterus develop during pubescence. Scammon's graph indicates that the ovaries begin a spurt of rapid growth between the ages of about thirteen and eighteen which continues for some time.

[16] Ramsey, *loc. cit.*

According to Ljubetzki,[17] the uterus weighs on an average 5.3 grams
at eleven to twelve years and 43.0 grams at sixteen. This is based on only
a small number of cases but does show what is probably a fact, that the
uterus grows rapidly at this time.

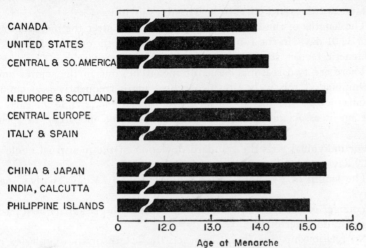

FIG. 16. Average age at first menstruation in the Americas, Europe, and Asia, data
presented separately for northern, central, and tropical or semi-tropical areas. Note
that the menarche is consistently early in central temperate areas and delayed in
colder northern and warmer southern areas. Menstruation is earlier in the United
States than in any other area. (From F. K. Shuttleworth, *The Adolescent Period:
A Graphic Atlas*, 1951.)

Menstruation

The menarche (or first menstruation) occurs at about the age of thirteen. Mills and Chenoweth,[18] in a study of 2,644 University of Cincinnati
girls, give the mean menarcheal age at 13.1607. Simmons[19] gives 12.58 as the
mean found for the girls studied at the Brush Foundation. Further data
are given in Fig. 16.

Reymert and Jost give us the following data regarding menstruation
from the Mooseheart Laboratory for Child Research:[20]

[17] Greulich, *op. cit.*, p. 51.
[18] C. A. Mills and L. B. Chenoweth, "Is the Human Growth Tide Turning?"
Human Biology, 10:547–554 (December, 1938).
[19] Katherine Simmons, "The Brush Foundation Study of Child Growth and Development, II. Physical Growth and Development," *Monographs of the Society for
Research in Child Development*, 9 (No. 1) (1944).
[20] Martin L. Reymert and Hudson Jost, "Further Data Concerning the Normal
Variability of the Menstrual Cycle during Adolescence and Factors Associated with
the Age of Menarche," *Child Development*, 18:169–179 (1947).

1. Length of the menstrual cycle (time from beginning of one menstrua flow to the beginning of the next) varied from 10 days to 150. The mod was 27 days, and the mean was 29.8 days.

2. There is a definite seasonal variation in the cycle. There are shorte cycles in the winter and longer in the summer. The cycle varies from ar average of 28.2 days in February to 31.4 days in July.

3. The lengths of the cycle during the first year after the menarche have mean of 32.01 days. In the fourth and fifth years the mean is 29.03 days.

4. Genetic factors seem to influence the age of menarche.

5. There are two seasonal peaks of menarche, one in the winter and on in the summer. A relatively late menarcheal age is frequently associated with the occurrence of the menarche in winter or summer, while an early menarcheal age is associated with the occurrence of the menarche in spring o fall.

6. For individual girls the standard deviation of the menstrual cycle varie from 2.9 days to 12.9 days.

7. The length of the flow varied from 1 day to 14 days, with a mean o 4.85 days.

8. Younger girls have a more irregular cycle with greater tendency towar missing than do older girls.

9. No relationship was found between the length or the regularity of th menstrual cycle and the age of the menarche.

10. Some girls are relatively regular in their periods, and others are mos irregular. Not one is absolutely regular.

Breast Development

The breasts begin to develop at some time between ten and fourteen One of the earliest signs of pubescence in the girl is the appearance o the breast buds. According to one investigator,[21] the mean age for this i 10.7. This early developmental stage, the bud stage, is illustrated in Fig 17b. As Greulich says, the breasts of some adult women never attain th final stage of development but remain in the third stage throughout life

Body Hair

Hair grows in the pubic region and under the arms. The pubic hai in the girl appears some time after the breasts have started to develop bu often before the menarche and appears first on the labia majora (the oute lips of the vulva). According to Dupertuis et al., it finally takes on the so called "horizontal" distribution in nine-tenths of the women. Hair unde the arm appears at some time after the pubic hair has appeared and als

[21] Earle L. Reynolds, "Sexual Maturation and the Growth of Fat, Muscle and Bon in Girls," *Child Development*, 17:121–144 (September, 1946).

after the menarche. In some girls there may be a slight growth of hair on the upper lip and on the sides of the face. This is no indication of masculinity.

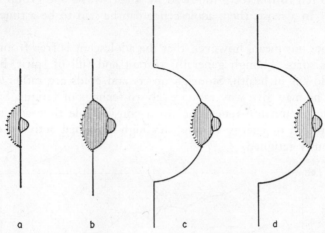

a   b   c   d

FIG. 17. Stages of breast development. (After Stratz.) (W. W. Greulich *et al.*, *A Handbook of Methods for the Study of Adolescent Children*, Society for Research in Child Development, 1938, Vol. III, No. 2, p. 41.)

THE SKIN IN ADOLESCENCE

There are three kinds of glands in the skin:

The merocrine sweat glands, found all over the body.
The apocrine sweat glands, found under the arms, in the mammary, genital, and anal regions, and on the groin.
The sebaceous glands, found wherever there are hair follicles.

The sweat glands under the arms, both merocrine and apocrine, become increasingly active during pubescence, even before the growth of the axillary hair. The apocrine glands appear to be particularly active just before and during the menstrual cycle. The secretion of these glands is somewhat fatty in nature and has, as we all probably know, a pronounced odor.

The sebaceous glands, which secrete a fatty substance called *sebum*, keep the skin pliable and a little moist. They too become much more active during adolescence, as is rather easily evident to anyone who studies the skin of children and compares it with the skin of the pubescent boy or girl. A clogging of these glands or infection of them produces the blackheads and pimples to which so many adolescents fall victim.

HEALTH AND VIGOR IN ADOLESCENCE

According to Frank, the lowest death rate for all ages occurs in the age group ten to fourteen, followed by a rise in the age group fifteen to nineteen.[22] In a sense, then, adolescence can be said to be a time of good health.

This does not mean, however, that the adolescent is free from ailments of various sorts. Though generally vibrant and full of spirit, he has his ups and downs in health. Stomach upsets and colds are rather common. Then too he may give way rather easily to feelings of fatigue. Sometimes we see him abundantly energetic for a considerable time and then suddenly, depleted of energy through his high-tensioned activity, quiescent and obviously fatigued.

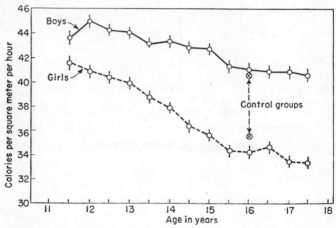

Fig. 18. Age changes in basal metabolism based on repeated observations on 50 boys and 50 girls. (From F. K. Shuttleworth, *The Adolescent Period: A Graphic Atlas*, 1951.)

Girls, particularly, often seem to have less energy in adolescence than previously. Lund explains this in terms of both physical conditions and social motives:[23]

"Well known differences in metabolism [as shown in Fig. 18] and in glandular balance are perhaps of chief importance. Thus, the superior muscular development of the male is correlated with higher protein and general metabolism (17 per cent higher in the male than the female at the age of 17) and with somewhat higher adrenal output. In turn, the relatively

[22] Lawrence K. Frank, "Adolescence and Public Health," *American Journal of Public Health*, 31:1143–1150 (1941).

[23] Frederick H. Lund, "Adolescent Motivation: Sex Differences," *Pedagogical Seminary and Journal of Genetic Psychology*, 64:99–103 (1944).

lower metabolic rate of the female is coupled with larger fatty deposits and with important changes in body proportions. Variations such as these tend to reduce physical activity in teen-age girls and create a dislike for all exercises, unless, indeed, they serve some social purpose, as is true of dancing. In passing, it may be noted that a good illustration of this is found in the failure to interest women in the physical fitness campaign conducted in Philadelphia and other large centers. The classes for women (as compared with those for men) are poorly attended, and those who do attend are interested chiefly in reducing—that is, in physical fitness only as it related to physical appearance. . . .

"Data collected in two junior and two senior high schools, having a total population of 8,200, showed that the incidence of pupils asking to be excused from gymnasium classes on the basis of alleged physical disabilities increased markedly during the adolescent period, an increase which was confined almost entirely to the girls. The increase in the case of the latter—400 per cent between the 7th and 12th grade—is attributed, not to any change in susceptibility to disease, but to changes in interests and motives. These interests and motives, which are given strong social direction in the girls, are often out of accord with the demands of the gymnasium floor. The resultant disinclination is reinforced by vast internal changes, by an increase in fatty deposits, and by important shifts in body metabolism and body proportions."

Specific health defects of adolescents in Philadelphia are shown in Table 10.

TABLE 10. PHYSICAL-DEFECT INDICES FOR THE ELEMENTARY SCHOOLS AND JUNIOR AND SENIOR HIGH SCHOOLS, 1942*

Defect	Per cent elementary schools	Per cent junior high	Per cent senior high
Dental decay	33.0	57.6	61.6
Malnutrition	21.0	9.4	17.9
Defective vision	19.0	7.1	11.7
Diseased tonsils	12.4	3.9	2.5
Nasal obstruction	7.5	1.9	2.6
Flat feet	5.1	5.1	5.3
Hearing defects	2.5	0.8	1.0
Stoop shoulders	2.4	2.6	3.4
Heart disease	1.0	1.0	1.2

* Frederick H. Lund, Earl R. Yeomans, and Ellwood A. Geiges, "Health Indices in Relation to Age, Sex, Race, and Socio-economic Status," *Journal of Social Psychology*, 4:111–117 (1946).

As for the causes of death among adolescents, we have data as presented in Figs. 19 and 20.

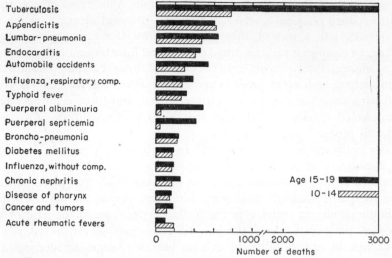

Fig. 19. The more important specific causes of death among females age 10 to 14 and age 15 to 19 in 1932 for the United States as a whole. (From F. K. Shuttleworth, *The Adolescent Period: A Graphic Atlas*, 1951.)

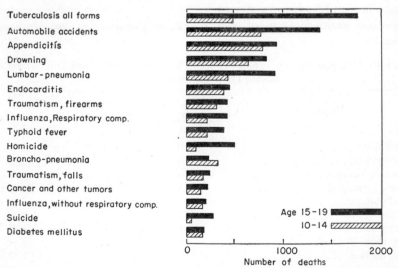

Fig. 20. The more important specific causes of death among males age 10 to 14 and age 15 to 19 in 1932 for the United States as a whole. (From F. K. Shuttleworth, *The Adolescent Period: A Graphic Atlas*, 1951.)

HOW TIME OF MATURING AFFECTS THE YOUTH

The fact that some boys and girls mature at an earlier age than do others has psychological significance which parents and teachers of adolescents should understand. Bayley summarizes the effects of early and late maturing in this way: [24]

"Practically, in status and social acceptance within their age-grade groups, these differences in size and build of children who are physically extremely accelerated or retarded may be very important. The greatest hazards to good social adjustments may be expected among the two groups who are most extreme—the early-maturing girls, and the late maturing boys.

"The accelerated girls, though eventually their size and builds will not be unusual, are conspicuously out of the ordinary at an age when they are usually most sensitive and easily disturbed at being different from their associates.

"On the other extreme are the late maturing boys. In addition to being left far behind in their growth they have the further disadvantage of being slender-built, poor-muscled, and weak. (There is, among boys, a fairly close relation between increases in strength and physical maturing.) These little boys cannot compete in athletics requiring strength and size. They must seek their social satisfactions elsewhere—often among younger children who are below them intellectually. Or they may, with their own age group, make use of compensating characteristics of intellectual or social interests and abilities.

"Being different from the group with whom one is thrown is always a possible hazard in social and emotional adjustments, but especially so during the adolescent years of growing into adulthood, when there seems to be a hypersensitivity to any deviations from the accepted norm. The physical differences which are thrust on some children by the mere difference in their velocities of maturing are among those hazards. The adult who is aware of these hazards and recognizes them when they occur, may through his understanding guidance help such children to understand themselves and to develop adequate compensations in other ways. Often, when the deviations are only temporary the knowledge of their temporary nature may help a youth to accept them with less emotional disturbance. For more permanent deviations, an honest evaluation of one's self in relation to others is an important start in the formation of a sound basis for building emotional attitudes which make for happy social adjustments."

One nineteen-year-old girl writes: "When I was fourteen I was one of

[24] Bayley, *loc. cit.*

the tallest, thinnest girls in my class, I remember many times threatening (in a half-hearted way) to cut my legs off, so I'd be short like the other kids. This was the period when I found myself beginning to be much interested in boys, but they didn't seem to respond and I immediately blamed this on my height. It seemed that most of the boys were at least two inches shorter than I. I cried many times over my height and slouched and did everything possible to make myself shorter."

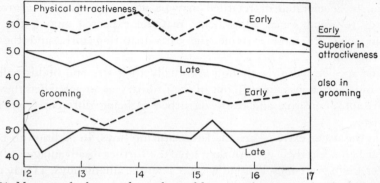

Fig. 21. Mean standard scores for early- and late-maturing groups, in physical appearance. (From M. C. Jones and N. Bayley, "Physical Maturing among Boys as Related to Behavior," *The Journal of Educational Psychology*, 41:134 (1950).)

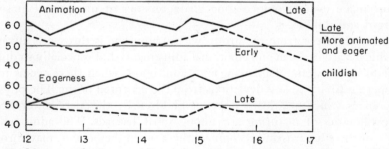

Fig. 22. Mean standard scores for early- and late-maturing groups, in expressive traits. (From M. C. Jones and N. Bayley, "Physical Maturing among Boys as Related to Behavior," *The Journal of Educational Psychology*, 41:136 (1950).)

A thirteen-year-old girl, writing a theme on self-consciousness, says "This may seem funny to you but it is really what I am self-conscious about. I just simply feel terrible when somebody mentions how big I am. Last year I really felt it the most. You see all of the kids in my class were so small that I simply towered over them. They would kid me about it too, but I have learned to take it without any hard feelings."

Jones and Bayley studied sixteen early-maturing boys and sixteen late

maturing boys (judging their maturity by skeletal age) and found:[25]
"Those who are physically accelerated are usually accepted and treated
by adults and other children as more mature. They appear to have relatively little need to strive for status. From their ranks come the outstanding student body leaders in senior high school. In contrast, the physically
retarded boys exhibit many forms of relatively immature behavior: this

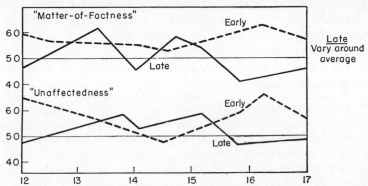

FIG. 23. Mean standard scores of early- and late-maturing groups, in attention-seeking
behavior. (From M. C. Jones and N. Bayley, "Physical Maturing among Boys as
Related to Behavior," *The Journal of Educational Psychology*, 41:137 (1950).)

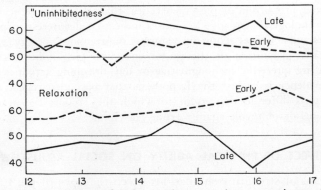

FIG. 24. Mean standard scores of early- and late-maturing groups, in emotional pattern-
ing. (From M. C. Jones and N. Bayley, "Physical Maturing among Boys as Related to
Behavior," *The Journal of Educational Psychology*, 41:138 (1950).)

may be in part because others tend to treat them as the little boys they
appear to be. Furthermore, a fair proportion of these boys give evidence
of needing to counteract their physical disadvantage in some way—usually
by greater activity and striving for attention, although in some cases by
withdrawal."

These facts are illustrated in Figs. 21, 22, 23, and 24.

[25] Mary Cover Jones and Nancy Bayley, "Physical Maturing among Boys as Related
to Behavior," *The Journal of Educational Psychology*, 41:129–148 (1950).

THE EFFECT OF PUBERTY ON THE ATTITUDES AND INTERESTS OF GIRLS

In the same classes in junior or senior high school there will be girls who have not yet reached puberty and girls who have for some time been sexually mature. Will these girls differ from each other very much in their outlook and interests?

Stone and Barker studied 1,000 girls in two larger junior high schools of Berkeley, California, comparing the attitudes and interests of the premenarcheal girls with those of the postmenarcheal girls. They found that the premenarcheal and postmenarcheal girls of the same chronological ages and social status responded differently to the items of an attitude-interest questionnaire:[26]

"1. Post menarcheal girls favor the chronologically 'mature' response more frequently than premenarcheal girls; *i.e.*, greater proportions of similar age-groups of post menarcheal than of premenarcheal girls give responses that are favored by increasing proportions of girls who are chronologically older.

"2. A greater proportion of post menarcheal than of premenarcheal girls of similar chronological ages favor responses indicating heterosexual interests.

"3. A greater proportion of post menarcheal than premenarcheal girls of the same chronological ages give responses indicating interest in adornment or in display of person.

"4. A greater proportion of post menarcheal than of premenarcheal girls of the same chronological ages give responses indicating disinterest in participation in games and activities requiring vigorous or strenuous activity.

"5. A greater proportion of the post menarcheal girls indicate that they engage in or are interested in imaginative or day dreaming activities.

"6. The evidence is against the hypothesis that post menarcheal and premenarcheal girls differ in the extent to which they report the presence of family frictions or of revolt against family discipline."

THE EFFECT OF PHYSICAL ABILITY ON SOCIAL ADJUSTMENT

On the basis of strength examinations given the boys of the California study at the age of seventeen years six months, Jones selected the 10 strongest boys and the 10 weakest. Since strength is apt to be accompanied by a good physique, physical fitness, and early maturing and since these all have prestige value with the adolescent, it is not surprising that Jones found the 10 strongest boys to rank high in social prestige, in social stimulus value, and in personal adjustment. Conversely, the 10 weakest boys showing as they did a pronounced tendency toward an asthenic physique

[26] Calvin P. Stone and Roger G. Barker, "The Attitudes and Interests of Pre menarcheal and Post Menarcheal Girls," *Pedagogical Seminary and Journal of Genetic Psychology*, 54:27–62 (1939).

late maturing, and poor health, ranked low in social status and in personal adjustment.[27]

Van Dalen administered strength tests to 348 boys and to 348 girls in the seventh, eighth, and ninth grades and then compared those of high strength with those of low. He found that those of high strength exceeded those of low in total number of play activities engaged in and in total duration of time devoted to play activities.[28] Here again we see that physical ability leads to greater social activity and, one would probably be safe in concluding, better social and personal adjustment.

It is probably true in general that those of good physique have a real advantage in the social world of childhood and adolescence and pile up more and more successful social experiences to give them a pleasing personality and assurance of success in dealing with people. We should be glad that these boys and girls are thus successful, but we should also keep in mind the fact that many others are handicapped in their social experience by the accident of inheritance, and we should try to compensate for their initial slow start on the road to social success with much opportunity for social participation where physical superiority is not the key to achievement.

It is of course understood that we are talking here about the typical adolescent of good physique and the typical adolescent of poor physique. There are many exceptions to these conclusions we have given.

NORMAL—BUT POSSIBLY DISTURBING

A great many of the physical changes which are a most normal part of growing up are nonetheless troublesome in the case of some adolescents. We shall consider each of these.

Sex Differences in Development

As we know, the development of girls is ahead of that of boys even at birth, and by the time of puberty girls are as much as two years ahead of boys, as the data for pubescent changes and skeletal growth show. Nevertheless, at any age the average boy is still taller than the average girl except for one brief period, roughly from eleven to thirteen. For this very reason, that it is unusual, the time when the height roles are reversed may well be disconcerting to some. One girl, for example, whose growth spurt

[27] Harold E. Jones, "Physical Ability as a Factor in Social Adjustment in Adolescence," *Journal of Educational Research*, 40:287–301 (1946).

[28] D. B. Van Dalen, "A Differential Analysis of the Play of Adolescent Boys," *Journal of Educational Research*, 41:204–213, (1947); and "A Differential Analysis of the Play of Junior High School Girls," *ibid.* 43:22–31 (1949).

came early felt that she *towered* above the other girls and boys in her room at school and developed a disturbing sense of ungainly bigness which she carried with her for some time after the rest of the girls caught up with her and the boys grew taller.

A young man of twenty-one recalls that at fourteen he was the "little shrimp" of the class. The girl who greatly attracted him and who returned his liking was at least 4 inches taller than he, and for this reason he was always embarrassed in her company. One time she invited him to go with her to a party. Wanting very much to go, he accepted, but at the last minute he pretended to be sick and stayed home because he couldn't endure the prospect of, as he puts it, their "Mutt and Jeff" appearance.

A thirteen-year-old girl says: "I am always wondering what I look like when I dance with someone shorter than I. And, oh, that feeling. Sometimes it gets pretty bad. It seems as though every eye in the room is upon me. Of course that is just my imagination, but I would also like to pass through the floor. I guess it is just my tallness that makes me feel that way. Yes, I'm pretty sure it is."

Anyone who teaches in the junior high school knows that the difference in development between boys and girls makes for many problems. Interests are different; what will appeal to the boys will often not be appealing to the girls, and vice versa. More troublesome to the boys and girls themselves is the fact that the girls are ready for romantic association with boys for which the boys of their age group are actually too young. If the junior high school is not located near a senior high school, the girls have, in their opinion and in reality to a considerable extent, no suitable companions at school among the boys and a considerable unrest may develop among them. If the senior high school and the junior are together, the girls will find companions among the older boys.

"All Arms and Legs"

Many adolescents grow gradually enough so that they don't seem to experience an "all arms and legs" period of growth. In contrast, there are some whose long bones have grown so fast in proportion to the trunk growth that they not only don't seem to know what to do with arms and legs as they sit or stand but are also awkward in their movements. These are the ones whose arms hang as if they were not a part of the corporate body, who twist their legs around the chair where they sit or stretch them out in graceless positions, who walk with a gangling lope, who knock into things, who break anything breakable they handle. However funny they may seem to the adult, this overawareness of part of the body may bring on a self-consciousness which is very painful to them, and the awkwardness may call attention to them in ways that are minimizing and unpleasant to experience.

Big Nose—Small Chin

Similarly, a few adolescents develop unevenly enough so far as their facial growth is concerned as to make them fear that they are going to be all nose and no chin. Facial appearance means a great deal to all of us, and doubtless there are few normal people who wouldn't like to be handsome or beautiful. To the adolescent who is at the socially most crucial time of his life such displeasing facial disproportion as the big nose-weak chin combination may be very upsetting. Eventually, of course, the jaw catches up with forehead and nose, but many do not know that this will happen—and even if they do, that fact does not change the actual appearance at a time when it counts so much.

Change of Voice

Boys and girls both experience a deepening of the voice, but that of the boy is, of course, much more radical than that of the girl. We often think that every adolescent boy goes through a period of time when he is much embarrassed by lack of control of his voice. Actually the majority of boys find the change-of-voice process gradual enough to be largely unnoticeable. In several casual investigations of college classes three out of every five young men say that they remember little of interest about their change of voice. The others remember occasions when the momentary change from the high voice of childhood to sudden gruffness or when the unexpected shooting of the new low voice into the upper registers has either embarrassed them or been cause for mirth on their own part as well as that of companions. Not a few of these recall that they enjoyed the freakishness that their voices developed during this period. Probably only in music classes is the boy's change of voice rather widely disturbing.

Excessive Perspiration

Adolescents do perspire more than they did as children or than they will when they are well into adulthood. Emotional situations so often occurring in adolescence may augment perspiration even more. As with so many other normal physical occurrences, most make an easy adjustment to this one. A few, particularly those whose hands and armpits perspire excessively, find it a source of embarrassment and a cause for worry about social acceptibility.

Menstruation

Even in this day there are still girls who are not prepared for the menarche and who may be shocked by its occurrence. Other girls harbor foolish or hurtful misconceptions about the menstrual period—that menstruation is a "sickness," that they should never bathe while menstruating, that it is harmful for a boy to be near them at such a time, that they must not prepare food during the period for fear of polluting it.

Even when the nature of menstruation is well understood, it may still be disturbing on occasion—painful, inconvenient, a cause of embarrassment, or a cause of worry. It might be mentioned also that many girls are depressed or irritable just before the menstrual period because of the level of hormones in the body at that time. They don't feel at their best, and their relationships with others are likely to be easily disturbed.

Some girls suffer from headache, backache, nausea, faintness, or severe cramps at the beginning of the menstrual period. With a few the pain for some four or five hours (or more) is as great as the girl will ever have to bear in a lifetime from any cause. One teacher remarked about a girl who left her class to go home to bed for this reason: "That sort of thing doesn't happen any more. I know the girl is just faking." She herself had never experienced any menstrual discomfort and had no sympathy for those who, in her words, "claimed" they did. Such a teacher is mistaken, of course, as as many as 1 out of every 10 girls can testify. Every teacher should also understand that a girl may suffer almost unbearably for several hours and then have the cramps cease so that she can be up and around again surprisingly soon, looking in the best of health. It is sometimes hard for a teacher to realize that a girl may be out of his class at ten in the morning because she is unable to do anything but lie writhing with pain in her bed and yet be at the basketball game that night at eight looking as if she hadn't known a moment's discomfort in her life.

In a few cases, a girl will have a nosebleed just before her menstrual period. Sometimes too, at this time, the mammary glands become enlarged and sore to the touch.

It is important that parents and teachers feel that a normal, comfortable menstrual period is to be expected, for if they don't, they can infect the girls with unwholesome expectations of pain. But at the same time they must remember that the beginning of the period for some girls will not be comfortable no matter what care is taken to ensure good health.

Almost every girl has at some time or other experienced the inconvenience or disappointment of being unable to participate in some social activity because her menstrual period has just started. Swimming or any other active sport, dancing, a school entertainment, or a school trip may have to be given up on occasion because participating would be too great a source of discomfort.

The menstrual period can be a cause of embarrassment, particularly with the younger girls who are afraid that they will have stains on their dresses or that the napkins worn will bulge and show. But even the older girls have their difficulties. A senior girl stood weeping in the women's rest room of a college student union building where the senior dance was being held. When the chaperone who discovered her there asked her what was the matter, she explained that although she had been at the dance for only half an hour, she thought she'd have to go home. She had started to menstruate, and she had no belt or napkin to wear.

The fact that the menstrual period is likely to be so very irregular with the just-beginning girl may also be a source of worry to the girl who thinks that to be normal her period must occur every twenty-eight days.

Nocturnal Emissions

It is very common for boys to have so-called "wet dreams," that is, to have ejaculations in their sleep. If a boy is prepared for this occurrence, he will not be frightened or embarrassed by it. Boys should understand too, however, that nocturnal emissions are not inevitable and that if they fail to have them, they are not by that sign lacking in masculinity.

Erotic Stimulation

In addition to the presence of girls who attract them, there are a number of other stimuli which will arouse erotic feelings in the boy. According to Ramsey, they are:[29]

Age 11 to 14 Years	Age 15 to 18 Years
Sex conversation	Female nudity
Female nudity	Daydreaming
Obscene pictures	Obscene pictures
Motion pictures	Motion pictures
Daydreaming	Sex conversation
Burlesque or stage shows	Burlesque or stage shows
Nude art	Dancing
Motion when riding	Nude art
Literature	Motion when riding
Own body	Own body
Male nudity	Literature
Dancing	Male nudity
Music	Music

[29] Ramsey, *loc. cit.*

These are natural and not unwelcome feelings, but a boy may be embarrassed or ill at ease in public when such stimulation brings the centering of feeling in the external sex organs, with often resultant erection. Girls, of course, also receive erotic stimulation, but because their feeling is more diffused, they are not so likely to find it so much a reason for self-consciousness.

Skin Disturbances

About half of any college class will respond affirmatively to the question: "Did you have any trouble with your skin during adolescence?" In some cases pimples and blackheads result from a diet too rich in sweets and fatty foods or from lack of cleanliness. But in other cases, one can only say, "It's adolescence," and trust to time to cure the difficulty. Such trust is in almost every case rewarded by the time a boy or girl is nineteen or twenty.

The complexion troubles of the type we must call normal may result from a clogging or infection of the sebaceous glands, which are producing more oil than can be freely eliminated, or may be due fundamentally to endocrine imbalance of not too great seriousness.

No one can deny that disfigurement of the complexion is a hard cross for the adolescent to bear, and while many refuse to let it interfere with their social life or their self-confidence, a few do develop ideas of inferiority and become shy and withdrawn because they feel themselves too ill-looking to be acceptable. The teacher should, with great tact and subtlety, attempt to build up their confidence. He should, of course, in no way suggest that the boy or girl *is* handicapped or to be pitied but should be motivated by the feeling that a bad complexion is trivial compared with all the personality assets possessed or to be developed.

A FREQUENT QUESTION: AM I NORMAL?

There are many adolescents who find reason to be seriously concerned about their normality, those who develop very early in some cases but those who develop very late in more. The boy who stays small and immature much longer than the others, the boy whose external genitalia are very immature, whose pattern of pubic-hair distribution is not like that of most of the boys, the girl who doesn't menstruate until she is seventeen or eighteen—all of these can understandably ask themselves "Am I normal?" Such may also be the question with the boy whose body contours are somewhat feminine. Boyishness of contour is seldom so distressing to the girl as is femininity of build to the boy.

Zachry writes:[30]

"If physical development in all of the persons of an age followed a like pattern and took place at the same time, individual adjustment to this change might be a simpler task. For an important consideration with most boys and girls is that such changes in physique as they are making be as nearly as possible 'right' changes—that is, that they be of the sort that the adolescents believe are to be expected of them at their age. In the general uncertainty attendant upon bodily change it is reassuring to believe that this is a universal necessity, that in one's own case it is proceeding properly. But as the adolescent looks about him he sees that he is different from others, since the growth process varies for each individual. And in his uncertainty it often seems to him that all the others are more alike than he is like them. Is there something wrong with him?"

A PERVADING FEELING: AM I ACCEPTABLE?

Social acceptance is of great importance to every normal human being from infancy to old age. To be happy we must be received by some people as friends, companions, and desirable coworkers. It is doubtful if anyone could endure being disdained and rejected by all.

Physical appearance will aid our acceptance or will interfere with it, as we all know, and almost everyone will give some effort to making his appearance pleasing, if only to the extent of slicking down his hair. A great many people go to great lengths to enhance their appearance, one of the chief reasons, if not the chief one, being the desire to be well thought of by others and pleasing to them.

The adolescent is more concerned with his acceptance by others than are those of any other age group. What would naturally bother any of us in our appearance—a bad complexion, protruding ears, gaps in the teeth, and the like—bothers him to a greater extent. Much that we don't like in our appearance but have become accustomed to is cause for concern with him.

A high school freshman writes:

"As you probably know, I'm a very large girl. I know it's my fault, but still I can't help but feel sorry for myself. I'm very self conscious of this being-big business.

"I always feel, when I walk down the hall at school, that everyone is looking at me, and they are saying, 'Look at that big slob.' People probably don't even notice me, but I think they are all staring at me.

"The way I feel at these times can be described in only one way. I wish that the floor would open up and swallow me.

[30] Caroline B. Zachry, *Emotion and Conduct in Adolescence* (New York: Appleton-Century-Crofts, Inc., 1940), p. 49.

"I'm self conscious only at school. What I mean is I'm not self conscious in front of older people. They seem to understand your predicament better than young people."

A high school senior says:

"The main thing that bothers me is my small eyes. It seems as though everybody notices them. I do not see why they should cause such a fuss over them. That is how they are and nothing can be done about it.

"People found out that when I laugh my eyes go completely shut. Every once in a while, I will catch the kids who know about it watching me or rather my eyes. It sometimes is rather embarrassing.

"When I had my picture for the Annual taken, the photographer noticed my eyes right then. For he said I had him puzzled, because I had a pretty smile and such terribly squinty eyes.

"I have no idea about how to get over my self-consciousness. I guess I will have to try to ignore the people who do make fun of my eyes. I was meant to have eyes like these, and no doubt I always will have."

Frazier and Lisonbee asked 580 high school sophomores to rate themselves as to weight, height, and time of development and then to indicate their degree of concern (never think about it; think about it now and then; worry about it a little; worry a good deal; worry a lot). The latter three were considered indications of concern. Table 11 gives the results.

TABLE 11. PER CENTS OF 580 TENTH-GRADE BOYS AND GIRLS GIVING CERTAIN DESCRIPTIONS OF THEIR PHYSIQUES AND PER CENTS EXPRESSING CONCERN ABOUT THE CHARACTERISTICS DESCRIBED*

	Boys		Girls	
Description	Per cent so describing themselves	Per cent expressing concern	Per cent so describing themselves	Per cent expressing concern
Thin...................	21	22	16	48
Heavy.................	13	3	30	55
Short...................	26	39	27	22
Tall...................	28	4	22	49
Development early..........	19	6	24	15
Development late..........	17	40	13	36

* Alexander Frazier and Lorenzo K. Lisonbee, "Adolescent Concerns with Physique," *School Review*, 58:397–405 (1950).

These same students were also asked to describe themselves as to other aspects of their appearance. Table 12 gives these data. We see here, what actual observation would also tell us, that many boys and girls are afflicted with irregularities of appearance which could well make them wish to be better favored of face and which may be very troublesome to their spirits.

TABLE 12. ITEMS OF SELF-DESCRIPTION CHECKED BY 10 PER CENT OR MORE OF 580 TENTH-GRADE BOYS AND GIRLS, WITH AMOUNT OF EXPRESSED CONCERN

Boys			Girls		
Item of description	Per cent checking	Per cent of concern	Item of description	Per cent checking	Per cent of concern
Blackheads or pimples....	57	51	Blackheads or pimples....	57	82
Lack of beard..........	34	2	Heavy eyebrows........	24	11
Heavy eyebrows........	27	1	Freckles..............	23	24
Scars, birthmarks, moles...	20	13	Oily skin.............	22	52
Irregular teeth..........	17	39	Scars, birthmarks, moles..	22	30
Heavy lips..............	14	5	Glasses................	21	31
Protruding chin..........	13	6	High forehead.........	19	8
Ears stick out...........	13	6	Too round face.........	19	21
Oily skin...............	12	27	Too homely............	18	42
Freckles................	12	..	Dry skin..............	16	43
Heavy beard............	11	13	Irregular teeth..........	16	42
Glasses.................	11	23	Thin lips..............	15	13
Dark skin..............	10	4	Low forehead..........	13	3
Receding chin..........	10	4	Too long nose..........	11	23
Gaps in teeth...........	10	26	Too big nose...........	11	44
Too long nose...........	10	8	Receding chin..........	10	13
Too thin face..........	10	15	Odd-shaped nose.......	10	23
Too large ears..........	10	8			

Table 13[31] shows the physical manifestations which disturbed boys and girls as reported for the California study by Stolz and Stolz.

Stolz and Stolz go on to say: "The foregoing 31 per cent of boys and 1 per cent of girls who suffered known anxieties concerning physical factors represent a minimum accounting, since others undoubtedly had, at one time or another, some degree of disturbance in this area which did not come to the physician's attention."

In another discussion Stolz writes:[32]

"One of the vicissitudes of growth which is apt to be passed over as

[31] Herbert R. Stolz and Lois Meek Stolz, "Adolescent Problems Related to Somatic Variations," Chap. V in Nelson B. Henry (ed.), 43d Yearbook, National Society for the Study of Education (Chicago: University of Chicago, 1944), Part I, *Adolescence*, 86. Quoted by the permission of the Society.

[32] Herbert R. Stolz, "Helping Youngsters Adjust to Their Physical Growth," *Educational Leadership*, 2:340–342 (1945).

unimportant and even humorous by adults, but which may cause acute suffering to a sensitive boy, is the period of increased fatness which occurs just prior to and during the early stages of adolescence. The common assumption that fat boys are happy boys is far from true. Indeed, it may be said with certainty that the sufferings a boy may endure while he is passing through this fat period are frequently reflected in his attitude towards life for many years and in many ways.

TABLE 13. PHYSICAL MANIFESTATIONS FOUND DISTURBING BY 93 BOYS AND 83 GIRLS

Boys		Girls	
Item of description	Number	Item of description	Number
Lack of size—particularly height	7	Tallness	7
Fatness	7	Fatness	7
Poor physique	4	Facial features	5
Lack of muscular strength	4	General physical appearance	5
Unusual facial features	4	Tallness and heaviness	3
Unusual development in the nipple area	4	Smallness and heaviness	3
		Eyeglasses and strabismus	2
Acne	3	Thinness and small breasts	2
Skin blemishes, scars	2	Late development	2
Bowed legs	2	Acne	1
Obvious acoliosis	2	Hair	1
Lack of shoulder breadth	1	Tallness and thinness	1
Unusually small genitalia	1	Big legs	1
Unusually large genitalia	1	One short arm	1
		Scar on face	1
		Brace on back	1

"To be fat during the early years of the second decade is peculiarly handicapping to boys because of the great value they place upon participation in active games, and even boys are usually sensitive to the jibes and nicknames which an excess of subcutaneous tissue seems to invite. Here again, knowledge of the frequency with which this period of fatness occurs among boys and an understanding of the transiency of this phase of development is distinctly comforting. Actually about 25 per cent of all boys show this tendency in some degree and for varying durations. It is true that a few of them will continue to be fat after high school graduation, but by that time the great majority will have lost their plumpness and will fall very easily within the normal group so far as appearance is concerned. One or more series of photographs showing how boys may be quite fat for a period of two or three years and yet emerge with not only passable but really splendid physiques are more useful in reassuring the self-conscious youngster than any amount of conversation."

In connection with appearance and social acceptability we may mention here the matter of posture. Many girls who feel themselves too tall for their group slump or stoop in a conscious or unconscious attempt to look smaller. Other girls and boys, of course, have poor posture because they fall into bad habits of standing or sitting and/or because their muscles are weak.

Nagging about poor posture will seldom change it and will inevitably cause friction or feelings of inferiority. Boys and girls should be helped to see that good posture makes a strong contribution to good looks. They should know that any normal person in adolescence can develop good posture through exercise and determination.

How Can Adults Help?

In helping the adolescent adjust to his physical changes, the first and the simplest thing for parents and teachers to do is to inform him of what to expect in his physical growth and development, the reasons involved, and the wide range of development that occurs among normal boys and girls. In other words, he should be given the facts contained in this chapter.

Second, all those who work with young people should be aware of the difficulties that may arise during pubescence and should take care not to add to them in any way. Adults must be able to meet adolescent embarrassment with poise, awkwardness with tactful unconcern, irritability with patience and tolerance, diffidence with generous liking and evidence of confidence. At the same time, adults must be cautioned not to expect difficulty where none exists. Oversolicitude, saccharine sympathy, or the casual assumption that the adolescent is having troubles or will have them—all are wrong and must be avoided.

Finally, the adult who works with the adolescent must make opportunity for him to have the physical activity he needs to develop well and the social experience that he needs for self-confidence and social ease.

Reminiscences

1. When did the growth spurt take place with you? Were you in line, developmentally, with the majority of your classmates? If not, did your rate of growth make for any psychological difficulties?

2. Did you go through an awkward age? Was your treatment by adults at that time what it should have been?

3. Do you remember any worries about the changes in your facial proportions?

4. Were there any ways in which you were highly dissatisfied with yourself physically during your adolescence?

General Discussion

1. Why are the primary sex changes called *primary?*
2. Why are the secondary sex changes called *secondary?*
3. Boys are likely to be taller than girls, in general, for all of the years excepting which ones? Does the fact that girls are taller at one stage make for any psychological difficulties?
4. If you had a son, would you choose to have him an early maturer rather than a late? Why?
5. If you had a daughter, would you want her to be an early maturer or late? Why?
6. How does disproportion in growth make for psychological difficulties? Should the teacher try to ease these difficulties? If so, how can it be done?
7. Why is it logical to say that the menarche is the sign of puberty in girls?
8. If a boy is worried about nocturnal emissions, what would you tell him?
9. What questions might young girls have about menstruation which the Reymert and Jost data might answer?
10. Does the idea that girls have less energy than boys during adolescence have any basis in fact?
11. What personality differences can you expect in early-maturing boys as compared with late, judging by Jones and Bayley's data?
12. If you have premenarcheal and postmenarcheal girls in the same classrooms, what differences can you expect in their attitudes and interests? Should you make any adjustments to these differences? If so, how?
13. Consider the "normal, but possibly disturbing" changes one at a time. What can the teacher do, if anything, to ease the disturbance?
14. In regard to that prevalent feeling, "Am I acceptable?" what should the teacher do?

Movie

How to Be Well Groomed, Coronet Films, 10 min., b. & w. or color, 1948

Further Reading

BAYLEY, N., "Tables for Predicting Adult Height from Skeletal Age and Presen Height," *Journal of Pediatrics,* 28:49–64 (1946).

FINESINGER, JACOB E., "The Physiological and Psychological Factors in Adolescen Behavior," *Psychiatry,* 7:45–57, (1944).

JENSEN, KAI, "Physical Growth and Physiological Aspects of Development," *Review of Educational Research,* 20:390–403 (1950).

JONES, MARY COVER, and NANCY BAYLEY, "Physical Maturing among Boys as Relate to Behavior," *Journal of Educational Psychology,* 41:129–148 (1950).

STUART, H. C., "Normal Growth and Development during Adolescence," *New England Journal of Medicine,* 234:666–672, 693–700, 732–738 (1946).

WETZEL, N. C., "Physical Fitness in Terms of Physique, Development, and Bas: Metabolism with a Guide to Individual Progress from Infancy to Maturity, *Journal of the American Medical Association,* 116:1187–1195 (1941).

Chapter 5. SOCIAL ADJUSTMENT

One of the best selling of recent books is one on how to win friends. The fact that it has sold so widely gives testimony to the hunger in people to make friends and to get along with associates smoothly and without friction. We do not need such evidence, however, to be convinced of the importance of being able to adjust easily to people—to be likable, poised, self-confident, and effective in social relationships—for we need only to think of how necessary such abilities are to good living to be impressed with the value of good social adjustment. No one can live happily without some friends, and, conversely, one has the assurance of a considerable amount of pleasure in living if he can attract friends and have comfortable associations with them. No family can be a happy family if there is much conflict and dissension within it. Similarly in neighborhood relations, work relations, and business relations, it is important that a person have the ability to be, in the best sense, a social being. Then, too, we cannot help being aware of the importance of good person-to-person relationships because each one of us has opportunities every day to experience failures and successes in our personal associations and to suffer or feel happy accordingly.

Equally important but not so immediately felt, and for that reason not so often a source of concern to the individual, is the need for social responsibility. A sense of duty to fellow man, the willingness to contribute effort and thought to group welfare—the more of this that we have in individuals, the better will be the society that nourishes them.

Good social adjustment is important at any age—in childhood, adolescence, or adulthood. Perhaps adolescence has especial significance, however, for it is then that the person most ardently longs for and seeks after social success and it is then that much occurs to make the person what he will be socially in the long years of adulthood.

THE PEER CULTURE

By the *peer culture* we mean the life and ways of the same-age society within which the individual finds himself situated.

The Importance of Peer Culture

Meek writes:[1] "For most children during the secondary school years the greatest influence on their behavior is the opinion of the group of children with whom they associate." She further says: "We have long realized that boys and girls during this period care more about what their friends or gang or clique think than what either their parents or teachers think."

Why is this so?

1. The adolescent is leaving his childhood dependence on the home and as he breaks away from its security, he must find replacement security in his other social relationships. The "crowd" often becomes his real home base. It is here that his most lively emotional ties exist. It is here that the most interesting discussions take place, that he is apt to have the most fun, and that he does in a sense most truly belong.

In contrast to the adult, the adolescent's greatest personal possession is his friends. The adult has an engrossing and time-consuming job and is apt to have such other roots in the ground as a bank account, a car, a home—in many cases—and a family, as well as the feeling of being stable and settled through his own effort and his own choosing. The adolescent's stabilities (outside of his confidence in himself) are his home, from which he is gradually divorcing himself, his school, against which he often feels rebellious, and his world of friendship, where relationships are likely to be the most gratifying to him.

2. The adolescent often resents the disparity between the way adults treat him and his sense of adulthood, but in his own social groups he is on a level with the others. What he does is generally in accord with what his associates think he *should* do. In expressing his opinions he isn't handicapped by being "too young" or by a feeling that perhaps his judgment is worth little in the face of the adult's experience.

3. The adolescent is still child enough to want to play and have fun, and he still follows the childish pattern of wanting to play with a number of companions. It is true that because the physical changes of the girls make them less interested in vigorous activity, they fall into more sedentary patterns of play, with the boys following their lead. But it is still "play," and it is this continuing interest which helps to make the peer culture so important.

4. The adolescent now gets much pleasure out of the very presence of the other sex. Consequently a social situation where the activities allow

[1] Lois Hayden Meek, *The Personal-social Development of Boys and Girls with Implications for Secondary Education* (New York: Progressive Education Association, Chairman, Committee on Workshops, 1940), p. 43.

for an interplay of personalities, for awareness of individuality, and for the delicate rise of pleasing emotion is very satisfactory.

5. Acceptance by associates is always important to us, whatever our age. But the sex attraction that draws boys and girls together in adolescence makes acceptance even the more important, for without it the youth is denied the success that his being particularly demands at the time, that of being recognizably attractive in his sex role and of receiving an emotional response from someone of the other sex. His own age group is the place where he can seek this acceptance and response. Thus it is inevitably the scene of important strivings, failures, and successes.

How Does the Importance of the Peer Culture Express Itself?

We have said that the peer culture is very important to the adolescent. In many ways this is a matter of intangibles, but we also see external evidence of how the adolescent feels toward his own age group:

1. In the following of fads. In the *Ladies' Home Journal* "Profile of Youth" series, we read about Iowa teen-agers:[2]

"One crowd of girls trades single shoes at school in the morning as a friendship gesture; a gang of fellows wear peaked white railroad engineers' hats for everything from gym class to dance dates; one basketball team sports athletic socks with bright red tops. Both fellows and girls wear ribbed white number socks, with class numerals stamped on turned-down cuffs."

This is typical of teen-agers. They want to be different as a group, set apart from children and adults, but they also want to be one with the group. They like the feeling of belonging and of being marked as belonging, and the following of fads in hair styles and dress is at least in part due to this desire.

2. In acceptance of group ideals, standards, principles. Any parent of an adolescent has doubtless heard, "But, Mother, all of the others do it," as if no argument could be more convincing. And it is true that to most adolescents, the way of the group is the proper way, the way which must be followed.

3. In the secrecy shown. Often the feeling "It's ours. It's ours alone. You wouldn't understand what we do, what we think, and what we say" prevails with the adolescent in regard to his own age group. This sense that the peer group is special and not subject to discussion and criticism is another mark of its importance to the teen-ager.

[2] "Iowa Teen-agers Step Out," *Ladies' Home Journal*, August, 1949, p. 43. Reprinted by special permission from the *Ladies' Home Journal*. Copyright, 1949. The Curtis Publishing Company.

4. In the urge to be with age mates. This is the prime evidence that the peer culture is highly important to the adolescent—that if he is typical he is sure to seek the companionship of his own age mates and will want to be with them often and for long periods of time.

WHAT IS THE ADULT'S RESPONSIBILITY IN THE ADOLESCENT'S SOCIAL DEVELOPMENT?

Typically the adult's relationships with the youth's social life and social adjustment may be categorized thus: With some of the adolescent's social activity and development, particularly that which takes place in the small unorganized groups, the adult takes no hand in the management and does little if anything to influence its direction. With other activity he provides the opportunity for adolescents to get together and may or may not offer some guidance, as at home, at school parties, committee meetings, and the like. In still other cases he provides strong direction and supervision, as at the boys' club or Y, for example.

This, however, does no more than suggest what his responsibilities are as far as adolescent social development is concerned. A full list includes the following:

1. The adult should know what the typical social activities of the youth in his community are—movie going, party giving, hanging around at the drugstore, playing at the youth center, or the like. He should know enough about these activities to be able to judge their values and harms.

2. The adult must understand the importance of this social life to the adolescent. He should know how much time is so spent, how the adolescent regards it, what his successes and failures mean to him, how it influences his behavior, what he will become as a result of the right kind of activities, what harm the wrong kind can do him.

3. He must know what wholesome social development for the adolescent consists in. A standard is imperative if he is to make any judgment as to how the boy or girl is getting along or to decide what ought to be done for him.

4. The adult must help the adolescent find enough desirable social activities. In one town of 60,000 people, almost every adolescent voices this complaint: "There's nothing for us to do here except go to movies." Adults generally agree with them—there *is* nothing to do. But no one does anything about it. It is true that the adolescent will grow up in any kind of environment and that he will find recreation even though none is provided. But his growth will be stunted. We should be intelligent enough to understand this even though evidence that the adolescent's social life is not good may not be so easily seen as to shock us.

Long tested 78 adolescents for their social maturity by studying their interpretations of typical episodes in family living. She found that more than half of those with average intelligence rankings were below average in social maturity. Those who ranked very high were found in all classifications of home, age, and intelligence levels except the lowest. Two years later she retested them. She found that although some maintained their earlier positions, others had shifted position greatly, for better or worse.[3]

Here we have evidence of the fact that high social maturity might be achieved with all adolescents and also of the fact that the experiences of even two years can bring about great changes in social adjustment.

The adolescent becomes what he has practice in becoming. If he has few opportunities to converse in groups outside the family, if he has little chance to take part in group projects, if he receives little encouragement to be generous with people who are not friends or relatives, he will not become skillful in these respects. It is a part of our responsibility to give the adolescent a chance to be the best that he *can* be.

5. The adult must be aware of those adolescents who are having difficulty in their social adjustment and try to help them. There are techniques for discovering the socially maladjusted adolescent but most adults are satisfied to let a passable adjustment suffice. We must realize that the socially inadept adolescent is an unhappy person and if he continues as he is, he will be an unhappy adult. We owe him help.

THE SOCIAL LIFE OF THE ADOLESCENT: THE HOME

The first socializing influence on the child is the home. There he learns to respond to the touch, the voice, the facial expression, and the act of others. He develops attitudes of generosity or of selfishness, he learns ways of expressing his hostilities toward people or he learns to repress them, he develops likes and dislikes as to particular characteristics in people and particular kinds of behavior, he learns ways of conducting himself with family, with friends, with guests, and with strangers. His family experiences may make him shy and withdrawing, or they may make him aggressively social. They may make him trusting toward people or suspicious. They may develop in him a taste for solitude or a taste for always being with others.

Because there are as many kinds of homes as there *are* homes, adolescents differ widely in regard to the social advantages and disadvantages they have received and as to the kind of social life they are now experiencing at home. Just a few of these variations may be mentioned, and then only the extremes will be suggested.

[3] Alma Long, "Social Development among Adolescents," *Journal of Home Economics*, 41:201–202 (1949).

The number of people in the home: The adolescent who is an only child and whose home relationships involve only two people (his parents) has a very different social experience from the adolescent who is one of several children. Then, too, some adolescents are used to a family social life which includes many family friends and acquaintances, while in contrast there are others whose families are greatly limited in their contacts with outsiders.

The relationships in the home: Some adolescents are used to a kindly, friendly, pleasant relationship among the members of their family. Others see much quarreling and lack of consideration for others. Some adolescents have dominating parents; others are overpampered. Some adolescents have parents who try to select their children's friends for them; others are allowed complete freedom of choice.

The social polish in the home: Some adolescents are used to good manners and know the right thing to do in almost any situation. Others have been brought up in surroundings where the behavior is crude and even vulgar.

Free time from home responsibilities: Some adolescents have much time to spend with their friends. Others are kept so tied to family chores or to outside work that they have little leisure for recreational association with those of their own age.

Availability of the home for entertaining friends: Some adolescents have homes which they may use for entertaining and parents who are glad to have the home a meeting place for the crowd. Others have homes they are ashamed of or homes where they are not allowed to have their friends congregate.

Indirectly, too, the home affects the adolescent's social life. Thus John Sanders, a boy studied in the California Adolescent Growth Study, was not invited to enter any of the social clubs of the high school he attended:

"As far as avenues of approach to these cliques were concerned, John was evidently in many of the 'wrong' ones. Chiefly these 'wrong' alleys had to do with money, family status, the neighborhood he lived in and the junior high school attended. With superior personal qualifications however, an individual, especially a boy, could thread his way to success in spite of these social handicaps. John's classmate Karl, from his neighborhood and from the same elementary and junior high school, became one of the accepted leaders of the student body. But John as we know did not have the necessary personal qualifications to overcome other handicaps."[4]

[4] Harold E. Jones, *Development in Adolescence* (New York: Appleton-Century-Crofts, Inc., 1943), p. 23.

One high school senior writes bitterly: "To be a popular person around this town, you have to be a son or daughter of a *rich* man. In school, you have to be a teacher's pet, and to be appointed on a committee you have to have lots of pull. Most popular people think of others as some form of low animal life and not equal to themselves. To be recognized as a member of the teen-age canteen, you practically have to wear a tuxedo and drive a car. In my opinion, *some* people aren't worth knowing."

In an Illinois town, as we read in *Elmtown's Youth*,[5] a Class IV girl summarized the effect of the class system in the high school on the lower ranking boys and girls, in so far as it pertains to extracurricular activities, when she said:

" 'Frankly, for a lot of us there is nothing here but just going to classes, listening to the teacher, reciting, studying, and going home again. We are pushed out of things. There is a group of girls here who think they are higher than us. They look down on us. I won't mention any names, but they are a group of girls from the higher families. They have a club that is supposed to be outside of school, but it's really in the school. They just go from one club to the other and hog all of the offices. They're in all the activities. They talk about what they're doing, what they're going to do, and they won't pay any attention to us. They snub us and they won't talk to us. Some of them will speak to us sometimes, but most of the time they just ignore us. I'd like to be in the school activities and the school plays, go to the dances, and things like that, but they make us feel like we're not wanted. I went to some of the activities when I first started high school. Last year, I was in the Home Makers' and the Cheer Club, but they ignored me. Now I'm not in anything. If we go to the high school dances, nobody will dance with us. They dance among themselves and have a good time and we're nobody. If we go to the football games, is the same way. Those Cheer Club girls are supposed to sit together at a game and root, but they don't. They break up into little groups and you're not in one of the groups, you're left out of things.' As she said this, she turned her palms upward, shrugged her shoulders and said, 'Well, why go? We're made to feel out of place and that's the way it is.' "

FRIENDS AND CHUMS

Every adult will understand the adolescent's need for a best friend—someone to go around with, someone to confide in, someone to give him support in his ventures. The normally adjusted adolescent will have a best

[5] Reprinted by permission from *Elmtown's Youth* by August B. Hollingshead, published by John Wiley & Sons, Inc., 1949, p. 203.

friend—sometimes more than one, as when an adolescent replies to the question, "Who is your best friend?" with "I have two best friends. We three do everything together." The adolescent without a best friend, a pal, a chum, is not only out of line in social adjustment but is also missing an association which adds greatly to his sense of well-being and social security in addition to giving him a valuable experience in a close social relationship with someone outside his own family.

As Meek says:[6]

"Gradually, there emerges the need for a friend of similar age with whom we can identify ourselves, who seems in some way almost a projection of ourselves; someone who accepts us as we are, who loves us in spite of our faults; someone with whom we can drop all pretenses, with whom we can 'think out loud.' This human longing for a friend or friends is deep-rooted and makes life joyous and bearable. The lack of a close friend leaves one dependent upon one's self and few of us have enough inner resources to meet life alone."

How are friendships formed? According to Dimock,[7] a boy is likely to become the friend of another boy who lives in his neighborhood, has the same economic and cultural background, attends the same school and is about the same chronological age. But, as he says, a score of boys may meet these conditions and yet just two become mutual best friends. He concludes that the crucial determinants of friendship are in the realm of the more complex aspects of personality and conduct.

Are the attitudes of girls toward their best friends different from the attitude of boys? Sister M. Lucina used an attitude test containing 3 items on the order of "My best friend is always true to me" and "I am sometimes jealous of my best friend" to investigate this question, testing 600 adolescents in all. She concluded that there is a difference between boys and girls in attitudes toward best friends:[8]

"The statistically reliable sex differences found are as follows: (1) Boys trust their pals to back them up more than girls do their chums. (2) Boys more than girls envy the success achieved by their best friends in school and in sports. (3) Boys more than girls think that their friends give in to themselves too much. (4) Boys get tired of their pals more than girls do of their chums. (5) Boys more than girls think that their friends take up too much of their time. (6) Boys more often than girls are jealous of their best friends. (7) Girls are more proud than are boys to be seen

[6] Meek, *op. cit.*, p. 16.

[7] H. S. Dimock, *Rediscovering the Adolescent* (New York: Association Press, 1937), pp. 108–109.

[8] Sister M. Lucina, "Sex Differences in Adolescent Attitudes toward Best Friends," *School Review*, 48:512–516 (1940).

with their chums. (8) Girls more than boys like their chums too well to give them up. (9) Girls tend to feel lost without their chums more than boys do. (10) Girls more than boys have the attitude that their chums cheer and comfort them."

A friend can be and often is an important influence in the social growth of the adolescent. An illustration occurs in the life of John Sanders, the boy mentioned earlier in this chapter:[9]

"Throughout the tenth and low eleventh grades, John's social contacts were limited chiefly to a few boys who, like himself, were not conversant with or particularly successful in the folkways favored by the group as a whole. . . .

"During this darkest period, however, John had the saving support of a friend. In a number of classes he had come in close contact with Ralph Souza, an earlier acquaintance of junior high school days. Ralph was in some respects a more extroverted edition of John himself—with similar interests—but with a quite decidedly positive and outgoing way of expressing these interests. In Ralph, John found a vicarious means of realizing his own inhibited social aims and intellectual enthusiasms.

.   .   .   .

"John and Ralph came to the office today. John, arriving somewhat earlier, was brusque and uncommunicative. When Ralph entered, he became more ready to talk. His manner was tentative, and his voice light and lacking in confidence. Ralph supplied most of the conversation.

.   .   .   .

"The John-Ralph combination paid us a visit after school. John as usual was a rather uneasy second to Ralph's ready flow of speech—occasionally he offered suggestions in a tentative manner, and then apologetically withdrew them. Seemed quite dependent on Ralph's opinions and decisions.

"If continued, this attitude of discipleship could hardly have been very helpful to John. But under the stimulus of Ralph's fluent expressiveness, and with the support of Ralph's genuine liking and confidence in him, John gradually came to play a more equal role.

"At the same time, John was achieving a closer and more mature relationship with several teachers and staff members. A boy of intellectual interests, with a great need for social approval, might be expected to turn frequently to adults for some renewal of faith in his own status. Except in the case of a few less appreciative and more easily exasperated teachers, John's rapport with adults was more satisfactory than with his own class-

[9] Jones, *op. cit.*, pp. 57–59.

mates. It is not surprising that in the latter years of school he was rated as 'frequently seeking adult company.'

"These personal relationships appear to have been of genuine importance to John. With Ralph, and with a few adult acquaintances, he became able to express himself almost with Ralph's own facility."

Unfortunately there are many adolescents who do not have the friends they need. What Dimock writes of adolescent boys is of course equally true of girls:[10]

"Many of them we would find in virtual social isolation, impoverished in personality in the midst of an abundance of potential friends. Their deep and eager longing for the comradeship of understanding friends denied, they feel the dejection and loneliness of those who are in the social group but not of it. Others, how many we cannot accurately tell, feel the sting of being ridiculed, unwanted, and unliked by those for whose opinion and approval and friendship they care the most. With shriveled ego and punctured sense of self-esteem they seek by devious ways to convince themselves that they possess a worth and a social status that their world of associates, cruelly and unremittingly, daily denies."

GROUP RELATIONSHIPS

Adolescents vary greatly in their group memberships. Some few are solitary or associate chiefly with younger or older people. Thus, Victor a boy of seventeen, of better than average intelligence, of pleasing appearance and good manners, doesn't associate with any crowds, nor does he have a close companion of his own age. When he is with others, it is likely to be with his twenty-one-year-old brother and his group.

Another boy, Tom, also seventeen, has a steady girl friend and spends most of his leisure time with her. He is seldom with groups of his own age. A girl of sixteen, Florise, dates more than do most girls of her age and she seems to depend entirely on these boys for companionship, having no group affiliations.

The majority of adolescents, however, have some group with which they associate, either a group of their own sex or a mixed group. Customarily the younger adolescent associates with a group of friends of his own sex, while many older adolescents are members of a mixed crowd. For example, one such group is a self-styled "gang" composed of seven girls and eight boys. Their ages are from fifteen to eighteen. Five of the girls go with five boys in the gang, but others date outside the group. They usually gather at the drugstore in the morning and proceed from

[10] Dimock, *op. cit.*, p. 125.

there to school. At noon they meet at a place called the Soda Shop, where ice cream, soft drinks, and lunches are sold and which is particularly the hangout for high school students. They meet there after school again for something to eat, staying only a half hour or so.

This gang go to the movies together, often go to a neighboring city for entertainment on Saturday nights, and spend much time at one another's houses where they listen to records, play cards, and do a great deal of talking.

In answer to the question "If you are a member of a 'crowd' or 'clique,' tell what it is like," the following are typical:

"The 'crowd' I am a member of consists of both boys and girls, eight of us, ages of 15 to 18. We take in movies together, go for short trips, go to different ones of our homes. All go to church, though not always together. I am glad to be a member, because all are swell persons—we have fun together. When we do things together, everyone is in on it and no one is more outstanding than the others." (*Ninth grade.*)

"I am a member of a crowd of five boys including me. Their ages range from 15 to 18 and once every week a member of our crowd gets his father's car to ride around in. We go to the show on Friday and Sunday nights and ride around on Saturday night. We never get into trouble and our gang is known as the 'Woman Haters'; that is, we don't mess around girls." (*Ninth grade.*)

"We have a very small crowd of six people. There are three boys and three girls. I am very proud to go with them because they are well groomed and very mannerly. They are ordinary people, none with a real lot of money or too conceited. We talk over our problems with one another and date together. We also take turns going over to one another's house for get-togethers or parties. The girls each go with a fellow of the crowd and therefore there is no arguing over boys or girls. We all like each other very much and none of us has ever lowered ourselves to do anything that is wrong." (*Ninth grade.*)

"There are five boys in our 'crowd.' We live on the same street. We hunt and fish, play games and go to the shows together. We also belong to a scout troop. After you go with a crowd for a certain length of time you feel that when one goes some place, the others should go too." (*Ninth grade.*)

"I belong to a 'crowd,' the main part of which consists of four girls—so you see we are quite limited. Our crowd of four girls has no immediate crowd of boys because we four girls go with four boys, all of whom are high school graduates, and we do not run around together except when we double date. The four girls in our crowd are all seniors in school. We always have fun with our crowd—we do things at each other's house, attend school and social activities together, and in general just have fun. Our crowd is not a type of crowd where we exclude everyone else in school. We only call ourselves a crowd when we have parties and go places together all the time. We aren't entirely shut off from the rest of the world. That type of a clique is a bad thing for a high school student." (*Twelfth grade.*)

"The ages range from 17 to 18 for the girls and 18 to 21 for the boys. There are five girls and six boys. We skate and go to shows and dances. We hang around at the Donut Shop. I'm glad I belong because the kids are swell and people look up to them. They are popular and they like everyone. They hold no grudges and enter no fights. They go out to have a good time and always achieve their goal because you couldn't help but have a good time with them." (*Twelfth grade.*)

"I am a member of a crowd and I like it very much. I often wonder how the people that are not can really enjoy themselves. We have boys and girls both and there are about two dozen of us or more. We do just a bit of everything. In the summer we have hayrides, swimming parties, and often we go to a large park to spend the day. We belong to several organizations; therefore, we have several dances. In the winter, we usually go to someone's house to dance and now everyone loves to play Canasta. Several of us belong to a 'Young Peoples Society' at church and we sing in the choir. There is just ever so much for a teen-ager to do. The ages of the girls are 17 to 18, but some of the boys are 21 and are in the university. Most of us prefer going with a fellow out of school, as they don't act so silly as high school boys, at least some of them. We all just have lots of fun." (*Twelfth grade.*)

"I am a member of a clique of ten girls. We all have very much in common in our interests and our home lives are very similar. Our parents all have good jobs and most of us have very nice clothes, entertain, and are usually in the best clubs in school and are very active in outside school activities. We are all seniors in high school at the present and all ten of us will be going to college in the fall. The ten of us have a very good time together and usually double-date together because there is a group of senior boys our same age who usually do things with us. Most of u date boys in that gang; however, I don't. We plan picnics together about two times a week in the summer and go swimming practically every day Our same group of girls has been running around together since junior high days because our friendships were started there when we wer placed in classes according to our scholastic ability. I enjoy being a member of this group because they all are nice, wholesome friends that would never be ashamed to be with anytime." (*Twelfth grade.*)

"I am a member of a so-called 'clique.' We are all boys, eight in numbe and we are between the ages of 17 and 18. When we are together, we usually don't plan anything specific to do, for we get along well and usually can come to a quick conclusion on what to do. In my memory there has never been a time that we've been together that we haven't enjoyed ourselves. I am glad to be a member of the 'clique' because we enjoy each other's company very much. We always have good times when just sitting and talking amongst ourselves. When we are together we seem to be more free than we would be otherwise. We have been running around together since we were in the eighth grade. We seem to have the same interests and can have a good time with just two of us together, for we don't always have to be all together. We have become so close that we seem to tell each other everything and to know each other completely. To us our 'clique' is very important." (*Twelfth grade.*)

"In our gang there are about five or six boys at the present time. We are all 16 or 17 and have somewhat the same interests. Mostly we will go riding, sometimes to other towns, or play cards or something. Three of us like to go hunting and fishing and we frequently go together. I believe that the main reason for forming these 'crowds' is to have someone to do things with. As it is, we are assured of having at least two or three other fellows to fall back upon. I don't believe that a crowd of boys is as tight as one of girls. We are drawn together mainly because of likenesses and not from any desire to exclude anyone. Some crowds are merely snobbish." (*Eleventh grade.*)

"I am a member of a crowd. We are a crowd of eight boys all 17 years old and seniors. We date girls in a small circle, seldom varying from it. Three of us go steady. I am very happy to be in this gang. Not in a bragging way I say we are a powerful gang. We control many school clubs. I am proud to be a member of 'The Dirty Eight.' I think gangs are swell. The eight of us do everything together because we have the same interests. We don't make these friends our only buddies—I can have fun with other fellows too. For these reasons I am glad to be a member of the 'gang.' " (*Twelfth grade.*)

"There are five boys in our 'crowd'; all are between 17 and 18 years old. Usually we all have dates on Sundays and go to the show together—on Saturdays and some free days we usually try to go camping or fishing or have sports according to the season. I think the best reason I like the crowd is because everyone seems to understand the other fellow. We don't stick together all the time like some 'crowds.' If we want to do something with someone else we do it. The one thing I like is when you don't like what the other fellow is doing you just tell him and no one gets mad, and that one fellow never gets his way all the time and no one is the leader." (*Twelfth grade.*)

The activities in which mixed crowds of teen-agers engage are summarized in Table 14.

TABLE 14. MOST POPULAR LEISURE ACTIVITIES OF HETEROSEXUAL GROUPS AS RANKED BY ADOLESCENT BOYS AND GIRLS, ACCORDING TO AGE*

Activity	Age of boys and girls reporting						
	14 years	15 years	16 years	17 years	18 years	19 years	20 years
Playing games........	1	3	2	4	3	3	3
Dancing.............	2	1	1	1	1	1	1
Listening to phonograph.............	3	2	3	2	2	2	2
Participating in sports	4	6	4	10			
Attending movies.....	5	4	6	5	5		
Talking.............	6	5	5	3			
Attending school affairs	7	10	10	9			
Attending parties......	8	9	9	7			
Attending sports......	9	8	7	6			
Riding.............	10	7	8	8	4		

* Frances G. Bibb, "Study of the 1042 Sophomores, Juniors, and Seniors of a Midwest High School" (unpublished master's thesis, Indiana State Teachers College, 1949).

Hollingshead, writing about Elmtown, says:[11]

"Persistent study revealed the vast majority of a particular boy's or girl's waking hours are spent in the company of a few pals. When he leaves home in the morning he generally walks or rides to school with them. In and around the high school he can be seen talking, laughing, walking, playing with them. Through the day he is with them whenever some formal demand on his time, such as classes or the job, frees him for informal activities. Before school opens in the morning little groups of friends can be seen talking together, laughing over some joke or prank, planning future activities, or reliving past ones through talk and shared memories. Later the same little band of boys or girls can be seen going to class together. At noon they may be seen going to or from lunch, and usually together; if they pack their lunch they may be grouped in a corner of the Commons Room or in the Central School gymnasium.

"After school two or three out of a group of five or six may go uptown to the pool hall, if boys, or to the drug store or bowling alley if girls. The same two or three boys or girls may be seen early in the evening on their way to a show or a friend's home. This persistent relationship

[11] Reprinted by permission from *Elmtown's Youth* by A. B. Hollingshead, published by John Wiley & Sons, Inc., 1949, pp. 204–207.

between a few boys or a few girls which carries over from one activity to another throughout the day, and day after day, is the most obvious thing about the behavior patterns of the high school pupils.

"These small, informal groups, which we shall call *cliques*, consume most of the interest, time, and activities of the adolescent. We shall call the more or less permanent ties the members of a clique have with one another a *clique relation* to differentiate it from other kinds of social relationships. The clique relationship exists only through the social relations the members of a clique maintain with each other. A clique relationship lasts as long as a person is a member of the clique, whereas social relationships in the clique are ephemeral, multiform, and almost infinite in number.

"A clique comes into existence when two or more persons are related one to another in an intimate fellowship that involves 'going places and doing things' together, a mutual exchange of ideas, and the acceptance of each personality by the others. Perhaps the most characteristic thing about the clique is the way its members plan to be together, to do things together, go places together. Within the clique, personal relations with one another involve the clique mates in emotional and sentimental situations of great moment to the participants. Confidences are exchanged between some or all members; often those very personal, wholly private, experiences that occur in the family which involve only one member may be exchanged with a best friend in the group. Relations with the opposite sex, with adults, and with young people outside the clique are discussed and decisions reached on the action to be taken by the clique, or by a particular member involved in a situation.

"Membership is voluntary and informal; members are admitted gradually to a pre-existing clique and dropped by mutual consent of its participants. Although there are no explicit rules for membership, the clique has a more or less common set of values which determines who will be admitted, what it does, how it will censure some member who does not abide by its values.

"As the clique comes to be accepted by other cliques as a definite unit in the adolescent society it develops an awareness of self, a 'we feeling,' sentiment and traditions which impel its members to act and think alike. Its members frequently identify their interests with the group in contrast to the interests of the family, other cliques, the school, and society. Generally clique interest comes before those of the individual member or any outside group or interest. This attitude often results in conflicts between the clique and the family, between the clique and the school, or between the clique and the neighborhood. If this conflict element becomes the *raison d'être* of the group, the clique develops into the gang.

"The impact of clique control on the adolescent produces a sense of personal importance in his relations with other members, as well as with persons outside the clique, for the clique has a powerful emotional influence on him which he tends to carry over into outside social relations, using it to bolster his own conception of himself. Each member has a group status derived from his ability to achieve something or to contribute something to the well-being of the clique. This group-derived status is often valued very highly by the boy or girl. Thus, the clique is a powerful influence in the life of the person from its formation in the pre-adolescent years until it is dissolved by the development of the dating pattern.

"Outsiders, especially parents and teachers, often fail to realize the meaning which the clique has for its members; consequently there is a tendency for them to deprecate it. This may produce more resistance and withdrawal into the sanctuary of the clique on the part of the adolescent, for, in a conflict situation that involves him as a member of the group, the youngster tends to look to the clique for support. The adolescent, bolstered by his sense of belonging to a group that backs him in his efforts to emancipate himself from adult and institutional controls, feels a sense of power, of belonging, of security, and consequently makes decisions in collaboration with his clique mates he would never make alone, as long as his decisions meet with clique approval. Each member of the clique, reinforced by the presence of his 'pals' and their agreement that some line of action is desirable or undesirable, that something must be done or undone, produces a cohesive social situation in which the clique acts as a unit. Controls operating in the clique tend to produce uniformity of thought and action on the question at issue. Individuals who do not go along with the decision of the majority are coerced into acquiescence or ostracized, since deviation is tolerated only with narrow limits. Adherence to the group code is guarded carefully by the clique's members for cliques develop reputations and have favorable or unfavorable statu attached to them by other cliques, parents, teachers, preachers, and adult on the basis of their membership and activities."

Advantages and Disadvantages of the Crowd

Membership in a well-knit mixed group of friends can have man advantages for the adolescent. These lie not only in the pleasures of com radeship and in the securities that a friendly and acceptant group ca give but also in the social skills and adjustments that develop.

At home one need not win acceptance and affection; he has it whethe or not he merits it. Nor is it difficult there to take rebuff or criticisn But the social world outside of the home is different. There one mu earn acceptance, be pleasing if he is to be liked. And there he must be able to take in his stride coldness, disregard, or even dislike from some.

The mixed crowd, if it is wholesome, can be an excellent practice group for developing social adulthood, for it provides a miniature society where the adolescent must learn to make adjustments to others and where, at the same time, he has the security of being accepted to membership in the group.

If the situation is ideal, he will grow in the direction of being socially pleasing, of being altruistic in a larger circle than that of his own family, and of being able to take slights, coldness, or censure without hurt.

On the other side of the picture are some possible disadvantages. Coyle[12] mentions the fact that groups may harden into exclusive loyalties and develop hostilities to those outside. Smucker studied college cliques. Some of his conclusions in regard to them are applicable here. He found that since members tended to pattern their behavior according to the values of the clique their standards were sometimes narrow. Since cliques encouraged considerable uniformity, individuality and generosities that extended beyond the group were often inhibited. Then, too, as he says, unwanted or left-out individuals may be badly hurt by being rejected.[13]

According to Scheidlinger,[14] the group is a source of strength to the adolescent in his striving for independence from parental authority. If the group make-up and activity are satisfying to the adolescent, he feels secure and his attitude toward adults is likely to be friendly. Yet if the adult leader becomes overidentified with parental authority, then the group may turn against him, too. When the group is on the defensive against the adult, the adult may be able to break through these defenses if he can make himself psychologically indispensable to the group, as, for example, by becoming an agreeable part of the adolescent's group life.

Adolescent Cruelty

Adolescents can be very cruel to their age mates:[15]

"Mary Alice J——————— was a big, good-looking girl. When she smiled

[12] G. L. Coyle, "Contributons of Group Experience to the Development of Older Children," *Proceedings of the National Conference of Social Work*, 1941, pp. 387–395.
[13] Orden Smucker, "The Campus Clique as an Agency of Socialization," *Journal of Educational Sociology*, 21:163–168 (1947).
[14] Saul Scheidlinger, "Understanding the Adolescent in a Group Setting," *Journal f Educational Sociology*, 23:57–64 (1949).
[15] "Teen-age Cruelty," *Ladies' Home Journal*, November, 1949, p. 66. Reprinted y special permission from the *Ladies' Home Journal*. Copyright, 1949. The Curtis Publishing Company.

—and that was often—she made you feel good. Most people liked her, but she was shy and she never thought of herself as 'popular' and no one else did either. To be popular in the high school she went to, meant being at 'the' hangout a lot, going with a boy who was well known, and being 'in' with 'the gang.' Mary Alice usually dated on Friday nights, but not with one of the 'smoothies.' Thus, when she was elected queen of the junior prom through a freak, no one was more surprised than she was. Her pleasure, however, didn't last long. The 'popular' girls ganged up on her and, after a series of whispered conferences in the halls, punctuated with snickers and sneers, they persuaded 'the gang' to boycott the prom and have a party of their own instead. Although there were only 40-odd of them, and there were some 250 students in the class, they were the 'big shots,' the kids to be envied, and their absence ruined the mood of the prom. They sent in word that they weren't coming to any party by 'the cheap kids,' and some even went so far as to say their parents had forbidden them to attend. Another girl might have fought back, but, as her brother said, 'Mary Alice didn't know what hit her.' She told her best friend she 'couldn't take it any longer' and left home. She got a job as a waitress in Chicago and her whole life was changed."

Jones writes:[16]

"The harshness and blunt cruelty sometimes found in the adolescent culture are illustrated in such observations as the following [concerning John at age fourteen]:

"Allen and Clayton were playing catch with one of John's gym shoes. While John rushed from one to the other, they would toss it back and forth and skillfully keep it out of his reach. John finally started to walk away without it; Tom, watering the lawn, tried to sprinkle him with the hose. Tom (to protesting staff member): 'Oh, we're in his scout troop we understand him.'

"Pete and Tony succeeded in getting a library book away from John and threatened to hide it. They paused in shocked surprise, when John showed signs of beginning to cry. They were obviously both ashamed of him and a little sorry for him when they found he couldn't 'take it.' Pete approached him rather awkwardly and patted him on the shoulder.

"*Clubhouse living room.* John chose a chair but was told to get out of it because 'it belongs to someone out of the room.' There seemed to be a coordinated effort to make him uncomfortable, to which he responded in a rather petulant manner.

"*Clubhouse porch.* John came in with his lunch. Asked if someone would play backgammon with him.

"Douglas: I can play but I wouldn't play with you.

[16] Jones, *op. cit.*, pp. 54–55.

"Marilyn (to John): He's beat better people than you. John dropped the backgammon board, and Douglas and Marilyn laughed at him. He was disconcerted, but still remained on the porch and later played a game with Bill. Bill trotted away abruptly as soon as the school bell rang.

"John: I'm always the one that's left to pick things up.

"*Evening party at the Clubhouse.* Most of those present are playing a game which involves penalties. John is reading magazines in a corner. Louise is given the penalty: 'Go up to the best looking boy in the room and vamp him.' When she balked one girl said, 'Oh, you just go up and say "I love you," and then give him a kick.' Louise looked relieved at the apparent simplicity of this assignment, but still hesitated.

"Dorothy: Say it to sissy-babe John. He doesn't know the difference anyway.

"John responded with a sarcastic 'Thank you,' without looking up from his reading.

"*In the Clubhouse yard.* John rides up on his battered bicycle.

"Joe: Hello Johnny.

"John: Hi.

"Joe: Aw, don't be so darned stuck up, or I'll knock you off that bike."

THE SOCIALLY SUCCESSFUL ADOLESCENT

What makes an adolescent acceptable to his peers? This question has been the subject of much study. One of the most thoroughgoing investigations took place in the California Adolescent Growth Study. Table 15 shows the qualities that make adolescents well liked at the seventh-, ninth-, and twelfth-grade levels.

According to Dimock, the five kinds of behavior that seem to make a boy popular are: cooperates and helps willingly, is courteous and considerate of others, assumes leadership in groups, is truthful and "aboveboard" in conduct, and controls temper in annoying situations.

The five kinds of behavior that work against a boy's being liked are: shows off, bluffs, boasts, seeks limelight; bullies, is quarrelsome, arouses antagonism in others; thinks he is "picked on," misunderstood; harbors grudges, is resentful; and uses excuses, alibis, escape mechanisms.

Dimock goes on to say:[17]

"There are some indications (suggested by observation rather than research) that if the individual had more status, security, and sense of belonging in a vital social group, he might be less quarrelsome, boastful, shy, resentful, etc., and more cooperative, unselfish, and considerate of others. It is expecting a great deal from a person who is suffering from

[17] Dimock, *op. cit.,* pp. 137, 140.

TABLE 15. QUALITIES WHICH MAKE BOYS AND GIRLS POPULAR AT THE DIFFERENT GRADE LEVELS*

Seventh Grade

Boys	Girls
Expertness in organized games	Friendliness
Readiness to take daring chances	Prettiness
Ingenuity in leading or directing games	Tidiness
Aggressiveness, boisterousness, unkempt-ness	Popularity
	Sedateness in school
Restlessness, talkativeness, attention getting	Submissiveness and nonaggressiveness
(Gentle, pleasant, lovable boys accepted but not emulated)	(Tomboyish girls acceptable but not admired or well liked)

Ninth Grade

Physical skills	Buoyancy
Strength	Amiability
Bravery	Aggressive good sportsmanship
Aggressiveness	Popularity
The above share importance with:	Friendliness
Social ease and poise	Enthusiasm
Personableness	Happy nature
Likableness	Daring
	Humor in relation to jokes

Twelfth Grade

Skill in athletics or interest and leadership in group activities or ability in art or leadership in a forum group	Prettiness
	Good grooming
	Good taste in dress
Good looks and careful grooming	Attractiveness to boys combined with poise, polish, and even tact
Being tall and looking grown up and mature	Ability in activities so as to be able to do something with boys when not dancing
Easy social manners	Acceptance by a select group rather than popularity with a large group
Ease and poise with girls	
Good dancer	Popularity with a desirable boy
Brains if accompanied by social maturity; otherwise not	Interest in play for the fun of it, not for success

* Lois Hayden Meek, *The Personal-social Development of Boys and Girls with Implications for Secondary Education* (New York: Progressive Education Association, Chairman, Committee on Workshops, 1940), pp. 46–50.

a sense of insecurity, whose own ego is in a precarious position, to lose himself in the interest of others! He must almost inevitably become more aware of his own ego and tighten his defenses for its protection. A poised personality is usually one with a sense of status and security."

Kuhlen and Lee[18] investigated the traits that make for social acceptance

[18] R. G. Kuhlen and B. J. Lee, "Personality Characteristics and Social Acceptability in Adolescence," *Journal of Educational Psychology*, 34:335 (1943).

and found that friendliness, enthusiasm, and popularity ranked high with boys and girls, sixth grade or twelfth grade. Disliked by all were these traits: enjoys fight, seeks attention, bosses others, and restless.

Anastasi and Miller[19] studied the preferences of 100 high school students in a suburban community in the vicinity of New York City, 50 being pre-college students and the other 50 being noncollege students. They found that for both groups there was agreement in preferring the following characteristics in classmates:

Has many friends
Friendly
Well mannered
Cooperative with a group
Enjoys hearing or telling jokes
Enthusiastic
Loyal to friends

However, the two groups differed in some of the characteristics they gave preference to:

Precollege	Noncollege
Serious-minded	Good listener
Talkative	Athletic
Talented in arts and crafts	Enjoys practical jokes
Enjoys working on his own hobbies	Peppy
Enthusiastic	Neat in appearance
	Grown-up
	Hail fellow well met

There are four major conclusions we can come to on the basis of all of these data:

First, in general the qualities that adolescents appreciate are the same qualities one appreciates at any age—friendliness, enthusiasm good manners, a sense of humor, cooperativeness, and the like. We can assume that the likable adolescent will in most cases be a likable adult.

Second, there are nonetheless changes from one age to another as to what the adolescent considers the most desirable characteristics in age-mates. To return to the data from Meek, you will see that the boy who is likely to be very popular in the seventh grade would not be so popular in the ninth grade if he retained all of those same traits—he might even fall to the level of toleration. Similarly a girl popular in the seventh grade would have to become more aggressive and daring to retain this height of popu-

---

[19] Anne Anastasi and Shirley Miller, "Adolescent Prestige Factors in Relation to Scholastic and Socio-economic Variables," *Journal of Social Psychology*, 29:43–50 (1949).

larity in the ninth grade. It follows, therefore, that some boys and girls in their progress through junior and senior high school will move out of popularity into mediocrity or from mediocrity into popularity. For the first group, this loss of position would be difficult to adjust to.

Third, we see again how the girls precede the boys in their adjustment. The popular girl in the seventh grade is far more akin to the popular ninth-grade boy than to the seventh-grade boy.

Fourth, as we would expect, for we see it happening with adults also, traits that are appreciated may differ from group to group. We saw, for example, that serious-mindedness was more valued in a group of students going on to college than in a group not going to college. With some students extreme daring to the extent of lawbreaking is regarded as admirable, while with others it is looked upon with abhorrence. Similar examples might easily be found.

It is important to remember that a trait which makes a boy or girl attractive to his or her fellows might make that person very unattractive to the teacher. Actually the seventh-grade boy who is popular may be the very one who makes life difficult for the teacher. It is, of course, the relationship here which makes for the strong difference in viewpoint. The teacher who is trying to control a group may find that traits which would be highly pleasing among equals can be very disconcerting in the classroom.

OF WHAT IMPORTANCE TO THE TEACHER IS THE ADOLESCENT'S SOCIAL ACCEPTANCE?

Being accepted by one's associates is a necessity for happiness at any age, and if we believe that the adolescent will be the best off and will make the best adult when he gets along well in adolescence, then it is imperative that we help those adolescents who are not finding a place for themselves in a wholesome social group of their own age.

Meek writes:[20] "One must somehow belong to and be accepted by a group, have at least one close friend of the same sex and be accepted by the other sex and have someone who chooses him above all others. There is probably no other area of development which consumes so much of the energy and time and interest of adolescent boys and girls as the establishment of these intricate relations with their peers. In consequence, there probably is no problem so important for teachers in the secondary schools to face as the problem of providing not only adequate social experiences for each student but also opportunities for each individual to become more acceptable to his classmates."

[20] Meek, *op. cit.*, p. 16.

Dimock says:[21]

"The three sets of findings that have been reviewed unite in yielding three major conclusions. First, they testify that relatively few boys in ordinary group situations are unanimously popular or acceptable. The friendship preferences of all the members of a group do not converge on a single boy, but are distributed among a few at least. The second conclusion follows in part from the first. A substantial number, probably a majority, of the boys enjoy a moderate degree of acceptability or popularity among their associates. The final conclusion is that a minority, but a highly significant group of perhaps 15 to 25 per cent of the boys, possesses an acceptability status that we have arbitrarily judged to be below the minimum needs for wholesome and satisfying personality."

A further very important point, according to Vickery,[22] is that it is likely to be the adolescent who is well adjusted in his relationships with his peers who can also become most wholeheartedly interested in social problems which go beyond the personal. She studied 12 informal club groups of girls from fourteen to eighteen. By various devices she was able to locate in the group the well-socialized girls as well as those less well adjusted socially. Each girl was asked to indicate her interest in problems of larger concern. She found enough difference between the well-socialized girls and the less well adjusted to conclude that the girls who are making a satisfactory home adjustment and who are learning to give and take with their age mates are also the girls who tend to relate themselves to the welfare of the larger social group.

UNDERSTANDING THE INDIVIDUAL'S SOCIAL STATUS AND SPECIAL NEEDS

Observation

Inevitably everyone who has any contact with adolescents learns something about them through observation, but that observation may vary from the casual, insensitive kind which brings forth such obvious remarks as "Noisy bunch, aren't they?" to the intelligent, perceptive, sympathetic mind which results in understandings like this: "Nancy is not well accepted by the boys and girls in my room—probably because she is very self-centered and 'won't play' unless everything is done her way; yet she has much to make her pleasing to others. She is a nice-looking girl and she is always clean and attractive. She has good manners; if she only had gener-

---

[21] Dimock, op. cit., p. 125.

[22] Florence E. Vickery, "Adolescent Interest in Social Problems," Journal of Educational Research, 40:309–315 (1946).

ous intentions back of them she'd be very likable. Of course, she *wants* to be liked. I could be sure of this even though I saw no signs. However, I see evidence of it, too. Nancy has more spending money than most of the girls and she is very free with her money. A few days ago she bought four girls, not her particular friends, each a bar of candy. Yesterday, I notice, she invited Joan and Cassie to a movie. Is she trying to buy their friendship? She wants to be liked but she needs help in going about it the right way."

If one is to come to know the individual adolescent very well through observation, that observation must be based on an understanding of all adolescents and often is best if directed toward certain ends.

Newman[23] describes the making of several scales in connection with the California Adolescent Growth Study, these to be used to rate the adolescent as he functions in a social situation. After several forms were devised and used experimentally, the final revision, Scale D, was made and used during the last three years of the study. The points upon which boys and girls were rated were:

Attractiveness of appearance	as shown by initiation of social contacts
Attention to grooming	
Amount of overt activity	Seeking of adult company
Interest in opposite sex as shown by attempts to attract attention	Compliance with authority
	Social self-confidence
Interest in opposite sex as shown by seeking of physical contacts	Attention seeking
	Affection
Interest in opposite sex as shown by hanging around them	Social stimulus value
	Popularity
Interest in opposite sex as shown by conversational reference	Self-assertion
	Sensitivity; dependence on approval
Interest in social contacts in general as shown by attention to others	Leadership
	Group (vs. self-) interest
Interest in social contacts in general	

The "Guess Who" Technique

The "guess who" technique was originated by Hartshorne and May and used in their study of the nature of character. It is nowadays sometime used by teachers and others to discover an individual's reputation with members of his group. Those in the group are given a list of descriptive sentences and asked to name the person or persons described. The direc tions given may be of this nature:

"Below we give statements or questions describing people in this class After each is a space for writing the name of the person described. Wri

[23] Frances Burke Newman, *The Adolescent in Social Groups* (Stanford Universit Calif.: Stanford University Press, 1946), pp. 86–89.

that name in. If the statement fits more than one person, write the names of all described. If it fits you, write in your own name."

Thus, Symonds and Jackson have devised an Identification Sheet, using this technique, which measures social adjustment. Sample items from this will illustrate the method:[24]

Positive Items	Negative Items
Who is very quiet, calm, and possesses exceptionally good self-control?	Who is always grimacing or twitching his face, neck or some part of the body?
Who is wide-awake in class, pays good attention, always knows the place, and takes an active part in the class activities?	Who is always bullying or teasing someone younger and smaller than himself?
Who is always friendly and helpful especially toward those younger or smaller than himself?	Who is always pushing or shoving or tripping up other people?

Moreno's Sociometric Technique

J. L. Moreno has invented a special technique for arriving at the structure of social relations within a group, these relationships then being diagramed in a sociogram.

First the members of a group are asked to make some kind of choice involving others in the group. Thus a high school class may be told: "It seems advisable to divide the class into committees to work out this presentation of *The Merchant of Venice*. In order to get committees whose members work well together, I am going to ask each one of you to put down the names of the people you would like to work with and also the names of those you would *not* want to work with. Make a first, second, and third choice. Consider those who are absent today as well as those who are here."

Or: "We are going to take a trip to Vincennes to see places of interest next Monday. We are taking six cars, and we would like to arrange people so that congenial ones are together. Put down your three choices (first, second, and third) for the ones you prefer to be with and also the names of the three you would least like to be with."

Two examples of the sociogram are given in Figs. 25 and 26.

Jennings emphasizes the fact that the original agreement (the committees in the first case; the trip to Vincennes in the second) should be carried out and gives these principles for doing this:[25]

[24] Percival M. Symonds and Claude E. Jackson, *Measurement of the Personality Adjustments of High School Pupils* (New York: Bureau of Publications, Teachers College, Columbia University, 1935), p. 40.
[25] Helen Hall Jennings, *Sociometry in Group Relations* (Washington: American Council on Education, 1948), p. 45.

"1. In order to carry out as many expressed wishes as possible, it is generally best to start with the children who have not been chosen at all or only seldom. It is usually better to give an unchosen pupil his own first choice.

"2. Give any pupil in a pair relation the highest reciprocated choice from *his* point of view: his first choice if this is returned, his second if this is returned and his first is not, or his third if this is the only reciprocated choice on his list.

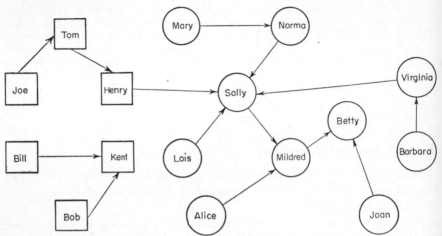

Fig. 25. Sociogram of a tenth-grade class in sociology. First choices only are given. Question asked: "We are going to form into several committees to study . . . What person in the class would you most like to have on your committee?"

"3. If a child has received choices only from people other than the ones he chose, then give him his first choice.

"4. If there have been any rejections, make sure that no such unchosen child is put with those boys and girls who have asked not to be with him.

"5. Check the final arrangements to make sure that every child has been placed with at least one of his indicated choices."

A sociogram will reveal a youth's position in the classroom regarding committee work, trips, parties, and so on, depending on what questions are asked. It will not, of course, tell why the students react as they do toward those they choose and those they reject.

It cannot be emphasized too strongly that the sociogram data should be kept confidential. A teacher might hurt a boy or girl immeasurably by revealing his position on a sociogram.

Cook[26] describes a study which shows how a sociographic study may

[26]Lloyd Allen Cook, "An Experimental Sociographic Study of a Stratified 10th Grade Class," *American Sociological Review*, 10:250–261 (1945).

be used to advantage in understanding and furthering the social adjustment of students. A tenth-grade social studies class of 44 pupils was given
a blank asking for reactions to extracurricular activities and having midway
on the blank two sociometric directions: "Give the names of your best
friends in school." "Give the names of the boys and girls about your own
age whom you don't like so well, don't care to associate with."

From these data a sociogram was made and studied with a view to
finding the isolates, the pairs, the cliques, the leaders, and so on. Throughout the next two years efforts were made to bring about better social

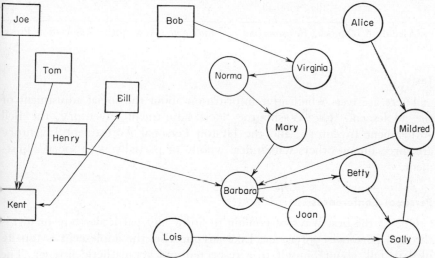

FIG. 26. Sociogram of a tenth-grade class in sociology. First choices only are given.
Question asked: "For our excursion to Vincennes we are going to divide the class
into carloads of five to a car. What person would you most like to have in the same
car as you?"

adjustments within the class. Sociograms at six months intervals were used
to discover what changes in group relationships were occurring.

The Friendship Record

Dimock used a "friendship record" to learn more about the adolescent's
social status. Each student is asked to name the 10 boys he knows best,
ranking them in the order of his liking. Then the boy is asked to star the
names of the four he would choose for some special enterprise, such as
cabin mates at camp, and so on.

FRIENDSHIP RECORD*

Name of boys known best	Activities engaged in with that boy	How often per week	Hours spent in each activity
1. James Barrett	Go to and come from school together	5	2½
	Play at recess	2	2
	Play football	2	4
	Visit home, listening to radio	1	2
4. Bill Thompson	Play together at recess	5	2
	Go to Scout meeting	1	2½
	Play football	2	4

* Hedley S. Dimock, *Rediscovering the Adolescent* (New York: Association Press, 1937), p. 95.

Tests

There are tests which give information about the social adjustment of the adolescent. The Washburne Social-adjustment Inventory, the Bell Adjustment Inventory, and the Heston Personal Adjustment Inventory are three among others which deal wholly or partially with social adjustment.

Personal Conferences

One of the best ways of coming to know any particular boy or girl is through personal conference. Like anyone else, the adolescent is usually glad to talk about himself to a respected and sympathetic listener. The authors have found again and again that a personal conference with a student, requested for the purpose of obtaining information, is always met with a frank readiness to talk about personal problems, interests hopes for improvement, and the like.

Such a conference must not be motivated by idle curiosity. It is when the friendly, noncritical teacher asks a teen-ager about his leisure-time interests, his hobbies, his friends, and so on, in the spirit of friendship that the teacher really comes to understand the boy or girl.

WHAT KIND OF LIFE SHOULD THE ADOLESCENT BE LIVING, SOCIALLY

There are two questions that concern us as far as the adolescent's social experiences are concerned. One: Is he living a good life now socially? The other: Is he developing into the most desirable kind of social being Emphasis can usually be placed upon the first since, if his life at present is all that it should be, the chances are good that his personality will form along desirable lines. However, the adult can be most helpful if he clarifies not only his ideas of what is good now but also his concepts of what it is good to become.

What Is the Good Life Now for the Adolescent?

1. The adolescent should be enjoying wholesome companionship in many different kinds of activity:

a. In play:
  (1) In participative sports.
  (2) In onlooker sports.
  (3) In social gatherings such as parties.
b. In work:
  (1) In classroom activities.
  (2) In all-school concerns.
  (3) In out-of-school projects.

2. The adolescent should have a best friend or two.

3. The adolescent should belong to a wholesome group, preferably though not necessarily of both boys and girls.

4. The adolescent should have opportunities for social service—opportunities which are appealing enough to him so that he takes on responsibility from personal choice and with a real sense of wanting to help others.

What Should the Adolescent Be or Become Socially?

The adolescent is developing into an adult, and the kind of life he lives in his teens will inevitably play a strong part in molding him into the kind of adult he will be, socially and otherwise. Since he is in the process of *becoming*, it is important that his leaders know what he should become. The ideal might be indicated in this way:

Person-to-person Relationships

Knowledge and skills	Easy good manners, good conversationalist, tactful, many interests in common with others
Attitude toward others	Likes most people, appreciates them for their real worth, friendly, kindly, generous-hearted
Security and independence	Self-assured and at ease in large or small groups. Not unduly dependent upon others for affection, attention, or assistance
Sense of responsibility	Respects his obligations to others in the way of debts, appointments, and the like

Larger Social Relationships

Committees and other group meetings	Appreciates the values of group planning and action. Contributes his best with full awareness of rights of others
Adjustment to coworkers	Does his full share of work, pleasant, appreciative of the efforts of others
Attitude toward neighbors	Friendly, considerate, helpful
Attitude toward community	Interested in his community, accepts community responsibility
Attitude toward world affairs	Interested in the welfare of all peoples. Tries to weigh world problems intelligently and without prejudice. Willing to make sacrifices for the good of a large number.

THE TEACHER CAN FURTHER ADOLESCENT SOCIAL DEVELOPMENT

The teacher can do a great deal in his classes to further the social development of his students. He should, to begin with, represent the socially well-adjusted person himself—not primarily to set a good example although that has some importance, but because what he is, believes, and does influences the mode of social interaction in the classroom. The friendliness, respect for others, and social grace of the members of a class to some extent at least reflect what the leader is, and for many students the effect is long-lasting, particularly if the teacher is the kind students tend to hero-worship.

He should realize that a democratic situation is the best one for good social growth. This means that he must have something better in the classroom than the "teacher decrees—students obey" procedure. The teacher's behavior must show recognition of the fact that these students have intelligence and judgment, along with a considerable understanding of their own and each other's needs, and can make good contributions to the general welfare. There must be recognition also of the fact that there should be a place for group decision and action as well as for individual decision and action.

The teacher should understand the importance of social intercourse to the adolescent and not be critical of sociability of the teen-ager sort. A high school teacher who really understands adolescents and enjoys working with them got on a suburban bus one Saturday afternoon, tired from shopping and glad of the opportunity to relax, when at a bus stop, a crowd of teen-agers got on, boys and girls of about fifteen or sixteen. The bus became a bedlam, with shoving, loud laughter, and noisy conversation. The thought came to the teacher's mind: "How disturbing they are! How noisy! How silly!" And yet at the same time she knew that her attitude was wrong, that she should not judge adolescents by their effect on adults. She knew that she was seeing something normal and wholesome, albeit discomfiting to her at the moment.

A considerable amount of social freedom should be allowed in the classroom. Some college students were observing a high school class with the intention of discovering which students were well adjusted and which socially ill adjusted. They returned from the observation with little in their notes, for, as they said, "What can you find out about a person's social adjustment when he does nothing but sit stiffly in his seat, raising his hand when he knows the answer to a question, reciting when he is called upon?"

Some departure from the traditional rigidity of the classroom situation is certainly necessary if the students are to have full opportunity to learn how to get along cooperatively and well in a nonselected group. This is not a recommendation for license. It is rather saying that adolescents should have opportunity to work together with the easy informality that can be characteristic of a group who respect one another and see purpose and interest in what is being done.

Finally it should be noted that it is entirely possible in the classroom to help students develop the true spirit of brotherhood. Evidence is given in this account:[27]

"Nancy Gaffney taught us mathematics—and respect for one another.

"Protestant, Catholic, Greek Orthodox, and Jewish—we were descended from parents who were Italian, Syrian, Polish, American, Hungarian, Czechoslovakian, German, and Dutch. We were white and Negro.

"And the unfounded prejudices we brought with us from our homes and our neighborhoods were revealed thru our petty snobbishness and antagonisms.

"It was a few months after we had been brought together from all parts of the city as Cleveland's first Major Work Group, in the middle of the second semester of the seventh grade, that she began her campaign for the formation of a homeroom club to include all 22 of us. So subtle was her propaganda that, on the day the formal proposal was made, each of us was convinced that the idea had originated with him.

"We planned skating parties and sledding parties, wiener roasts, and outings. At Tony Caruso's, after an exciting two hours of sledding one evening, we feasted on Italian spaghetti and veal cutlets—and we learned that Tony's people were kind and good, warmhearted and hospitable. We learned the same about Effie Lee Morris' folks who, tho their skin was black, were no different from the Panuskas, the Cechs, the Abookires, or the Mativetskys.

[27] Sanford E. Rosen, "Not Out of Books," *NEA Journal*, 1949, p. 344.

"Before many weeks had passed, we were eagerly discussing our differences of religion, family custom, and origin with complete naturalness. We were growing up with the realization that we were part of America's partially realized dream of human sharing and cooperation and understanding.

"She taught us mathematics—and self-reliance and self-respect.

"Whenever one of our group met with failure in trying to achieve an all-important goal like the basketball team or a position on the newspaper staff or the honor society, Miss Gaffney seemed to know it almost at the moment the blow struck. She would invite the despondent youngster to chat with her after class. If the mere relating of 'the great tragedy' to her was not enough to dispel the feeling of dejection, a reminder of past successes, a tale of herself in a similar situation, or a pat on the shoulder with an 'I-know-you'll-make-it-the-next-time' smile did the job.

"Inadvertently she let us know that failure was as much a part of life as triumph, and that he was wise who profited from disappointment—and used it as a spur to future effort.

"More often, however, it was conceit, not inferiority feelings, that had to be conquered. None of us can recall that she ever put us to shame publicly or that she submerged our overbearing actions with a campaign to show how insignificant we were.

"She merely looked about for the most popular among the older students in the school and informally let us reveal to her and to ourselves their traits of modesty and self-reliance that helped them win their many friends.

"She was eager to help us with our class assignments, but never let us use her as a crutch. She would not tell us the answer. She merely asked a series of questions that invariably led us directly to the core of the problem and suggested related ideas.

"Our mouths would drop in astonishment as the solution came to us suddenly and almost mysteriously. Then she would nod with a smile and say, 'See, you knew how to do it all the time, didn't you?'

"She taught us mathematics—and reverence.

"When Charles Traina died, and the sobriety of permanent separation from one of our number settled like a pall upon us, Miss Gaffney accompanied us to his home. There amid the sobs and tears of family and friends she did what she could to help bereaved parents look to God for solace. She aided us to recall our own good fortune in having known Charles—for he had entertained us for hours with his humorous cartoons and the tales he wove around them.

"She showed us also how to respect the faith of our fathers, and whenever the opportunity presented itself, she encouraged our parents to send us to the Sunday schools of their choice. She never spoke of religion to the two families of 'atheists' among us. Even lack of formal faith is to be respected in a democracy.

"She taught us mathematics—and friendship.

"When the three years had passed by and we moved on to high school, our club remained intact. Later when some of us went to universities and others found employment, we held semi-annual meetings.

"All thru the war we were in constant touch with each other thru Nancy Gaffney. When one of us suffered bereavement or won some special honor, Nancy would be there—calling on us or stopping in to say 'hello' to our folks, if we were not in town.

"Today we are merchants, dentists, housewives, physicians, artists, laborers, ministers, and engineers, and we live in all parts of the United States. Nancy Gaffney still teaches, still inspires, in the same schoolroom.

"Certainly her contributions toward good citizenship and richer, more meaningful lives for us to whom her humble efforts have meant so much extend far beyond the classroom. She is making the most of her sacred responsibility toward the lives she influences as noble teacher and dear friend."

ALL-SCHOOL PROMOTION OF GOOD SOCIAL LIVING

The school is ideal for helping the adolescent in his social development, if for no other reason than that it is the gathering place for large numbers of teen-agers who are amenable to the direction and guidance of the faculty.

The General Spirit of the School

Schools differ greatly in the attitude of administration toward teacher, teacher toward student, and student toward student. In one school the teachers are so much interested in the welfare of their students as people that if one were to call a teacher in his evening leisure hours to discuss some student's problem there would be no resentment of the infringement on his free time. This feeling of kindly interest in the welfare of others seems to be present in all of the social relationships within the school system.

In another school great importance is given to strict routines, considerable formality of behavior, and strong autocratic control on the part of the teachers. Here conformity is of first importance, and there are few opportunities for the easy sociability among the boys and girls that a more relaxed atmosphere permits.

The school that best furthers the adolescent's social development is one where the adults in the school system have a kindly, friendly, cooperative attitude toward one another and toward the students and where they realize that the adolescent should be living a wholesome social life in the school as well as outside.

The Type of Teachers

Miss X is the kind of teacher high schools ought to have. Although she is unreservedly interested in her students and concerned with their welfare, they are not her whole life. She has many adult social interests and concerns outside of the classroom. The students are her friends, but they are not her only friends. She is successful as a teacher, but this is not the only reason for her feelings of worth. Perhaps all of this helps to explain why Miss X can look upon her students as friends and can treat them as friends, for they are not of such moment to her personally that her sense of well-being rises or falls with their treatment of her. Though what is important to them is often not important to her, she feels no need to disparage or disregard their interests. Though what they do could interfere with comfort or ideas of propriety (for adults), she maintains without effort a spirit of live and let live.

. But perhaps this does not sufficiently explain why Miss X is so good for a school that is trying to foster social adjustment. It may be rather that Miss X knows each of her students as a person and gives him that consideration which is the right of another individuality. It may be, also, the fact that Miss X has no desire to dominate, believes in the interchange of opinion, and encourages a friendly, informal atmosphere in her classroom.

Whatever the cause, Miss X does promote the students' social welfare—both purposefully and by the fact that she is the kind of person she is.

Miss Y, in contrast, is the wrong kind of teacher as far as the students' social welfare is concerned. Inevitably she judges her students by what is proper for adults or comfortable for them. As a result she looks with disapproval upon much student social behavior which is actually normal and good. Then, too, Miss Y is a despot. She believe that it is her task to keep the students busy at what she thinks is good for them and to enforce strict discipline. Her classrooms are models of good deportment—if quiet, strict attention to business and rigid following of rules are one's aim. But it would be difficult to find in Miss Y any influence for good if one is looking for the extension of friendliness, consideration for individuality, or growth in social techniques.

Opportunities for Social Interaction

It is probably enough here merely to suggest some of the out-of-class opportunities which do supply the means to social growth.

1. Recreation—parties, dances, picnics, carnivals, mixers.
2. Trips—such as excursions to places of historical interest, industrial centers, big cities, and the like.
3. Participation in government.
4. Clubs and other extracurricular activities.
5. Work experiences in or outside of the school, but under some school supervision.
6. Social service projects.
7. Cafeteria facilities where students may eat together in inviting surroundings.
8. Places to lounge. Adolescents like to gather before school, at noon, or after school and just talk.
9. The home room and its social-development possibilities.
10. Leadership experience for many.

Opportunities for Developing Social Techniques

There are a number of social techniques and social knowledges which are rather easily acquired and which make social intercourse more pleasant. Some adolescents need no help in regard to this, for their parents and their out-of-school activities provide sufficient learning. Others, however, do not have sufficient opportunity and will attain these learnings only at too great effort or only partially. For these the school should provide ways in which students may learn the social conventions, learn to dance, get help in dressing attractively, perhaps get some practice in putting on parties suitable to the home circumstances.

Hutson and Kovar had 2,163 senior high school students give them data on problems in regard to social poise. These are reported in Table 16.

Often these learnings can best be integrated with the work of some course—that is, manners with English and with home economics, dancing with physical education, and so on. But other ways are possible. Thus, at the University High School, University of Minnesota, a unified arts course runs through the seventh, eighth, and ninth grades. Among the most popular activities are telephone conversations between boys and girls, how to ask for, to accept, and to refuse a date, learning games for parties, practicing dance steps, making introductions, illustrating the correct way for boys and girls to walk on streets and enter theaters, and so on.[28]

[28] Louise T. MacKenzie, "Group Action in Personality Development," *School Review*, 56:484–488 (1948).

TABLE 16. PROBLEMS OF ADOLESCENTS IN REGARD TO SOCIAL POISE*

	Boys		Girls	
	Yes	No	Yes	No
Do you feel at ease in introducing people?	57.1	40.8†	69.4	29.3
In general, is it difficult for you to carry on a conversation with the opposite sex?	38.9	57.7	36.7	61.1
Are you afraid lest you make a mistake at a social affair?	50.9	45.3	54.8	42.5
Are there some members of your class whose competency and fearlessness in social affairs make you feel inferior and inadequate?	43.3	50.2	51.4	43.2
To boys: Do you feel at ease in asking a girl to attend some social affair with you?	44.7	47.1		
To boys: Does it bother you much to walk across the floor and ask a girl for the next dance?	34.1	41.4		
To girls: Have you ever wanted to ask a boy to take you to a dance, but didn't do it, because "it isn't being done"?	....	.....	41.7	50.4
To girls: Does it bother you if boys don't "cut in" on you at a dance?	....	.....	16.2	71.4

* Percival W. Hutson and Dan R. Kovar, "Some Problems of Senior-high-school Pupils in Their Social Recreation," *Educational Administration and Supervision*, 28:503–519 (1942).

† "No answer" accounts for lack of 100 per cent.

Help in Particular Social Problems

Anyone who has met with groups of boys and girls will know that inevitably they have problems in regard to their associations with others which they wish to discuss. It is regrettable that the school doesn't make possible more discussion groups under adequate leadership. Classes in family relationships, too are often valuable to the student in verbalizing social-adjustment difficulties and offering solutions, and the library can be of service by making available the many books in this field.

Special Help for the Maladjusted

There are not many adolescents who can be considered near perfection in their social adjustment, but there are a goodly number who are fairly well adjusted and who will continue to make progress if nothing occurs to impede them. In addition to these, unfortunately, there are those who are seriously maladjusted socially. They are:

1. The boy or girl who because of an unpleasing personality is rejected by his fellows.

2. The boy or girl who for other reasons is so rejected.

3. The boy or girl who seemingly chooses to be completely solitary and unsocial.

4. The boy or girl who because of obnoxious traits arouses dissension and mistrust.

5. The boy or girl who because of shyness makes few social contacts or is ill at ease in social situations.

6. The boy or girl who is antisocial.

What should be done for such adolescents? Our first answer is a caution: Be slow to make a direct attack on social inadequacy with the boy or girl personally. An awkward approach, a blunt disparaging statement, or the very fact that the deficiency has been recognized by the teacher may heighten the very insecurity, aloofness, or antagonism which the teacher is trying to lessen.

Unless the teacher is sure of his skill, it is better to depend upon more general means of helping the socially maladjusted.

Make opportunity for the maladjusted boy or girl to enter situations which demand an attempt at social adjustment but which are not such as to result inevitably in failure for him. Small committee groups where he can make a contribution are helpful. Having the student work in a small group where there are some who are better adjusted than he and some who are less well adjusted may be effective.

Sometimes one student can help another. Ruth Cunningham writes:[29]

"Often there are others in the group who can help the left-out child to find his place in the group. 'Big sisters,' seatmates, fellow committee members, partners on a field trip may all be used to this end.

"A word of caution may be in order here. Pairing two rejected children is seldom successful. Usually the only result is that the rejected ones are merely rejected as a pair.

"And pairing the rejected child with the most popular is no more successful. Both are uncomfortable during the enforced companionship.

"It has been our experience in conducting a series of experiments in a number of classrooms that no child is totally rejected by everyone in the group, just as no child is totally accepted by everyone in the group. The discerning teacher may find a child who does not strongly reject Johnny and set the stage for the two to get to know each other."

[29] Ruth Cunningham and associates, "Johnny Doesn't Belong," *NEA Journal*, 55:579, '48.

WHAT CAN THE COMMUNITY DO?

We shall discuss the community's responsibilites in another chapter (Chapter 13). Let us only suggest here that the community which is fully aware of its responsibilities to youth makes available to them many opportunities for wholesome social living. One example will be given.[30] Columbia, South Carolina, has a youth memorial center, a living memorial to those killed in the Second World War.

"A committee, made up of student representatives, was formed to discuss the possibilities of creating just such a place. These were farsighted youngsters, aware of their limitations as well as their abilities.

"From the very start, they knew they wanted a center run by the students with the aid of some adult director who was not a teacher. And they were firm on the point that the enterprise was to be free of any city politics. What they had in mind could never be organized without the co-operation and approval of grownups, so the committee compiled a list of the different kinds of people they wanted for an advisory board. No professional organizer could have been more shrewd and calculating in picking types essential to the needs of the center.

"As the committee saw it, the advisory board should include: a liberal-minded clergyman; a member of some city club such as the Rotary or Kiwanis; a representative of the YMCA and one from the YWCA; one city official; an important member of a local soft-drink bottling company; the mother of a student, preferably wealthy; and a teacher or principal, from the educational system.

"In their mental blueprints, they envisioned a building with an auditorium for plays as well as dances, a game room, a snack bar, craft shop and library.

"With the plans for fund raising, an outline of organization, and a list of advisors and work committees in hand, the students went around the city trying to get someone to sponsor them. There are people in Columbia who are not proud of the record of those few weeks, because boys and girls were turned down all over town. The city recreation office said, No. The YMCA said No. The YWCA said, No. They piled up a stack of refusals which should have been discouraging enough to make them drop the whole thing.

"Instead, they launched a two-day, door-to-door campaign and at the end of the forty-eight hour period had a total of twelve hundred dollars. With this concrete evidence that the project had the support of some adults, they started the circuit again. It was the USO which finally said

[30] Marguerite Kohl and Frederica Young, "Youth Memorial Center," *Woman's Day* pp. 38, 39, 80, January, 1949.

that part of their building could be turned over to the students. The committee raced to spread the news. They hired an executive director, Miss Betty Crews, whose job during the last four years has become everything from business manager, judge of a yo-yo contest, jitterbug expert and wizard of snack-bar finance, to big sister of thousands.

"Now that they had a definite place to go, the students drew up rules for behavior, selected the names to match the types of people they wanted for the advisory board, elected committees from each school and were ready to have their first night at the teen canteen.

"Part of their money went toward buying tables for games, part towards records and a record player. It was at this time they bought their first recording of 'Let's Take the Long Way Home' which has since become a tradition at eleven o'clock closing time.

"The two-year period that the canteen was in the USO building was acknowledged a success by the students and their elders. The undertone of worry on the part of adults soon turned to outspoken praise. Contrary to some expectations, the young people didn't ruin the building, they didn't leave the canteen and run wild on the streets, didn't stop doing their homework or scorn their homes as places to entertain friends. Success didn't go to their heads, though it did cause a few older foreheads to crinkle with wonder.

"But these were determined young people. They had started off wanting a place of their own and, while grateful for the co-operation of the USO, they still aimed at a place of their own. In the spring of 1946, they launched a building campaign which will long be remembered in Columbia. They were out to construct a living memorial, a memorial created by youth, for youth, in honor of those, just slightly older than themselves, who had been killed in the war.

"The impact on the city was shattering. Their story was simple, they told it sincerely. And they told it everywhere. Descending on the town in a mass movement, they hardly missed a person of the 71,000 population. Within two weeks they had amassed thirty-two thousand dollars. This was not the largest amount ever collected, but it represents a greater number of individual donations than any other campaign in the history of Columbia.

"It was a bad time to think of building. Materials were still scarce and costs high, but the people who had laughed at this 'flash-in-the-pan' idea in '44 were not laughing in '46. They were doing everything they could to help.

"Part of a tract of land which had been given to the city for recreation purposes was turned over to the center. The contractor overlooked his normal profit, the county gave $5,000, steel and hardware were secured at cost, the preferably wealthy mother from the advisory board contributed all the concrete block. By the time everyone was through, there was a $90,000 building.

"The Youth Memorial Center was opened in January 1948, but the dedication ceremony was barely over before the murmur of a few remaining skeptics could be heard. 'Now that they have it, will they ever use it?'

"Use it they do: from 3:30 until 6, and 7:30 to 11 P.M. Membership cards are fifty cents a semester or one dollar a year. A constant flow of youthful traffic passes through the center's wide front doors on weekday afternoons, but it is Friday and Saturday nights when about five hundred teen agers come to the canteen with eager anticipation. Spread out between the game room, snack bar and auditorium, even this number doesn't make the building overcrowded, and each group seems to be doing exactly what it wants to do.

"What the center stands for varies with different youngsters and the different things they do there. For some, it is a miniature country club with weekly dances. To others, it is the corner drugstore dressed in new glory, and to still another group, a family rumpus room where you can fit all the people you want and make all the noise you care to.

"There are check rooms for coats, there's a powder room, and there's a dance floor with room enough to try out new steps. And what makes it better than any other place is that there's nothing new or frightening. For all its gaiety and excitement, this is still the center, these are friends dancing near by. Everyone knows just what to expect, what to do. They can all relax and have a good time.

"But Saturday isn't just dance night. In the game room you'll find some intense pool playing going on. The room has atmosphere: low-hanging bright lights, comments from the sidelines as each player makes a shot. This is as much fun as the corner poolroom, and has the added advantage of being a place no parent objects to.

"Ping-pong draws its own crowd of enthusiasts. Those for whom good evening is spelled in terms of a hard, fast game can stand way back and smash away without ever a worry of knocking into furniture, marring the wallpaper or breaking the family's best vase.

"The snack bar is a teen-ager's dream come true. Here they can order ice-cream cones, sodas, milk shakes, sundaes, soft drinks. Everything made with a heavy hand, for the fountain boys are students. Paid fifty cents an hour to work behind the counter, they are taught by a representative of an ice-cream company, and to expert directions they add their own youthful intuition born of teen-age appetites.

"The fountain boys are really learning something constructive. Those who do well are recommended for part-time employment in drugstores throughout the city. They are taught the ways of sanitation, that they have to be polite even when mobbed and that the prize usually goes to the one who can combine good work with speed.

"Though the only ones paid for their labor, excepting the director, the fountain boys are not the only working members of the canteen. Committees are appointed for such jobs as checking membership cards at the door, keeping the record machine going and maintaining order on the dance floor. One of the rules of the center is that everyone must help out in any capacity when needed.

"Not that the duties are very pressing. Sometimes they are very welcome, particularly for those youngsters who haven't yet learned the art of social conversation, even with people their own age. A tongue-tied boy finds an hour spent playing the records gives him a chance to talk to many people and a good start on new friendships. A girl on the door committee forgets her shyness while she's busy checking cards and answering the greetings of all comers.

"Discipline is pretty much group discipline on the part of all. There are hard and fast rules against gambling or drinking and these are enforced, not by the two sets of parents who are invited each evening as hosts and hostesses, but by the young people themselves. There hasn't been a fight in three years because the law, established by the students, says that at the first sign of a fight the center will be closed and everyone will leave. All their rules are like that. A little sterner perhaps than if made by adults, and applied with a hand of iron by the same people who obey them.

"Parents with children who use the canteen are only part of the adults now chanting the center's praises. A juvenile court judge recommends attendance for problem youngsters brought before him. The Junior League has assumed responsibility for staffing the check rooms. Business women, some of whom have worked a full day, take over the cash register at night. The 'phone rings, and a man who has no children of his own asks if there is something he could do to help.

"It started out as something only the young people believed in. Today it is not just a beautiful building, but a project the city has taken to its heart. Columbia believes in the Youth Memorial Center. It believes in the youth who made it possible."

Reminiscences

1. What were the fads of your peer group in your adolescent days?
2. Did you belong to a "crowd"? What was its membership? What advantages did it have for you? What disadvantages?

3. What social experiences did you have in high school? Were they sufficient?

4. What in your home life was outstandingly good in making you social?

5. Did you feel that the lower economic classes in your high school were less well treated and had fewer desirable opportunities than did the upper?

6. Did you have one "best friend" all through high school? How did he or she contribute to your well-being and happiness?

7. Did you have any teacher in high school who seemed unusually successful in promoting social adjustment in his or her class? Describe that teacher's work.

8. Were there any social experiences that you had an insufficiency of? In what way did the lack affect you?

Observation

1. Visit a high school party. Evaluate the experience for those present. Would those who were too shy to come have felt welcomed and happy if they had been there?

2. Visit some adolescent "hangout" such as a drugstore popular with teenagers. What do the adolescents do? Is there any supervision? Is the experience a wholesome one? Does it have any disadvantages?

3. Visit a club meeting. What opportunities do you find there for social development?

4. Visit a place where a great many adolescents congregate, as at a teen center. Look for specific instances of differences in social aggressiveness, in social interests, and in social acceptability.

Participation

1. Get data and prepare a sociogram for some high school class.

2. Prepare a few items for a "guess who" test. Combine with those of the other class members. A committee should edit and organize these and then, if possible, give the test to some high school class. In reporting the results, numbers may be used instead of the students' names.

General Discussion

1. What evidence do we find in this city of the importance of the peer culture to the adolescent?

2. What does this city do, outside of the school, to give the adolescent good social experiences?

3. Can the social stratification of students in the high school be modified?

4. Do you agree with Sister Lucina's conclusions as to how boys differ from girls in attitudes toward best friends?

5. Should a school try to break up cliques?

6. Do you believe that every boy and girl should be a member of a mixed crowd for his best good?

7. Do you agree that adolescents can be cruel to their age mates?

8. Explain how it happens that a boy or girl may move from popularity into a no more than tolerated position among his peers as he goes from the seventh and eighth grades into senior high school.

9. Consider Kuhlen and Lee's list of desirable personality characteristics. Are these characteristics the same as those found most desirable in adults?

10. What different questions might be asked in getting data for a sociogram?

11. How may a sociogram best be used by the teacher to help adolescents?

12. Consider Cook's study. Specifically what would a teacher do to change the social make-up of a class? To what extent is this desirable?

13. Give some very concrete suggestions as to what the teacher might do to promote democracy in classroom and school.

14. Describe any socially maladjusted adolescents you have known.

Movies

Are You Popular? Coronet Films, 10 min., color, 1947.
Brotherhood of Man, Brandon Films, 10 min., color, 1946.
Shy Guy, Coronet Films, 13 min., b. & w. and color, 1947.
You and Your Friends, Association Films, 10 min., b. & w., 1946.

FURTHER READING

ALMACK, J. C., "The Influence of Intelligence on the Selection of Associates," *School and Society,* 16:529–530 (1942).

BELL, REGINALD, "Children's Opinions of Their Classmates," *Progressive Education,* 18:278–283 (1942).

BONNEY, M. E., "Personality Traits of Socially Successful and Socially Unsuccessful Children," *Journal of Educational Psychology,* 34:449–472 (1943).

DYER, DOROTHY TUNELL, "Are Only Children Different?" *Journal of Educational Psychology,* 36:297–302 (1945).

ELLIOTT, M., "Patterns of Friendship in the Classroom," *Progressive Education,* 18:383–390 (1941).

FISHER, DOROTHY CANFIELD, "What Price Popularity?" *Parents' Magazine,* 11:20–22 (1936).

HAND, HAROLD C., "Do School Costs Drive Out the Youth of the Poor?" *Progressive Education,* 28:89–93 (1951).

HANEY, GERMAINE, "Help Your Child Make Friends," *Parents' Magazine,* 21:41 (1946).

HOLLINGSHEAD, A. B., *Elmtown's Youth* (New York: John Wiley and Sons, Inc., 1949).

How to Construct a Sociogram (New York: Bureau of Publications, Teachers College, Columbia University, 1947).

LEVY, J. R., "Social Competence of High School Youth," *School Review,* 51:342–347 (1943).

Low, Camilla M., "The Neglect of the Personal-social Needs of Youth, *Progressive Education,* 28:52–56 (1950).

Meek, L. H., *The Personal-social Development of Boys and Girls with Implications for Secondary Education* (New York: Progressive Education Association, Chairman, Committee on Workshops, 1940).

Northway, M. L., "Outsiders: a Study of the Personality Patterns of Children Least Acceptable to Their Age-mates," *Sociometry,* 7:10–25 (1944).

Smith, M., "Some Factors in Friendship Selections of High School Students," *Sociometry,* 9:303–310 (1946).

Van Dyne, E. V., "Personality Traits and Friendship Formation in Adolescent Girls," *Journal of Social Psychology,* 12:291–303 (1940).

Chapter 6. HETEROSEXUAL ADJUSTMENT

"What do you want from life?"

Let any typical high school senior answer that question and he will probably say: "A good job, a happy marriage . . . ."

Then turn to any person of forty or fifty and ask him what in his opinion makes for a happy life, and he, too, is rather sure to put among the top essentials a happy marriage. Or put the question to a psychiatrist. He will doubtless include in his list a happy marriage as well as a wholesome attitude toward sex.

This would be reason enough for us to be concerned with the adolescent's heterosexual adjustment—that it is an important requisite for a suitable marital choice and a successful marriage. But it is not the only reason. We are equally interested in having the adolescent be happy in his growing up and in having him make the most of years that can be very wonderful. It is therefore important that we have both the good judgment and the ability so to set the stage when necessary and manipulate the environment that his heterosexual relationships may actually be of the kind to make life joyous and good for him. More than that, since we are interested in understanding him in order that our associations with him may be pleasant and helpful, it is imperative then that we understand all phases of his development, heterosexual being among the most important.

What do we mean by good heterosexual development? First of all, we mean that the adolescent will accept his sex role and be reasonably satisfied with the way he fulfills it. The boy will not long to be a girl; the girl will not long to be a boy. Each will accept and find happiness in the mode of life of his own sex. The boy, whatever shortcomings he might find if he compared himself with the most masculine of his sex, accepts himself as he is and feels sufficiently masculine. Similarly, the girl regards herself as adequate. Second, we mean that an adolescent will reach adulthood understanding the biological basis of reproduction, realizing the place of sex stimulation, sex interests, and sex activity in a well-balanced, wholesome life, with attitudes toward sex that make for good mental health, and possessing the ideals and standards which will give sex an importance and a spirituality beyond the purely physical. Third, we mean that the adolescent will come to find the other sex attractive and be attractive to them, that he will pass pleasantly through the period of falling easily in love and out of love and that before leaving his teens or shortly thereafter he will come to the point of being able to love one person deeply, wholeheartedly, and faithfully. Finally, we mean that the adolescent will grow up able to meet the other sex on terms of equality in companionship, in business, and in civic affairs.

We have stressed here what the adolescent should become as an adult. It must be made clear, however, that it is not the end result alone which we are interested in. The process of growing up heterosexually should be good in itself. Good companionship with members of the other sex, such growing awareness and understanding of one's sex feelings as to add to one's sense of aliveness and make one realize how strong are the feelings that bind people together in the world, an enlargement of one's own ability to feel and express tender emotions—these are experiences which contribute greatly to one's pleasure in living and to one's sense that living is worth while.

HETEROSEXUAL INTERESTS

The Importance of Heterosexual Interests to the Adolescent

If we want statistics on the importance of heterosexual interests to the adolescent, we can turn to Jones, who reports that in an investigation of what senior boys and girls talk about 41 per cent of the boys and 61 per cent of the girls said that they talked often or very often about having dates.[1] Or we can look at the answer of the 2,000 boys in Fleege's study[2] when they were questioned about their topics of conversation: the two highest in favor are "sports" and "girls."

But we really don't need statistics. Anyone has but to recall his own adolescence to realize of what major importance seem the early shynesses and excitements of the first adolescent attractions, to realize how pleasant and exhilarating is work when congenial boys and girls are doing it together, how overshadowing to all other events a date can be, how sweet is the youthful love affair, how tormenting its difficulties, how comforting the knowledge that one has an attentive boy friend or an admiring girl friend—and to realize, too, how distressing it may be for the boy or the girl who is not attractive and who does not participate in the gay teen-age life.

The adolescent is drawn into heterosexual interests by the excitements and stimulations initiated by the glandular changes of puberty; but mind body, and emotions soon become absorbed in the feelings and activities

[1] H. E. Jones, *Development in Adolescence* (New York: Appleton-Century-Crofts Inc., 1943), p. 107.

[2] Urban H. Fleege, *Self-revelation of the Adolescent Boy* (Milwaukee: The Bruce Publishing Company, 1945), p. 234.

involved in association with the other sex. Some adolescents move smoothly into the sphere of heterosexuality, and their problems are but the temporary and not too serious ones such as quarrels with the boy friend or girl friend, and the like. Other adolescents enter this stage of their growth slowly and awkwardly, taking a long time to achieve some of the lightsomeness and ease that come so readily to others. Some resist their growing sex interests and cling to their childhood associations and activities. Some mature so early in their psychological acceptance of their sex role that they may settle down into a mature relationship before they are out of their teens.

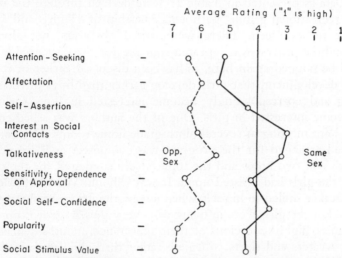

Fig. 27. Social ratings of a twelfth-grade boy, illustrating differentiation of behavior in company of the two sexes. (From F. B. Newman, *The Adolescent in Social Groups,* Applied Psychology Monograph No. 9, Stanford University, 1946, published for American Psychological Association, p. 41.)

For almost any adolescent, however, the adjustment to the other sex involves a certain amount of beginning awkwardness. In some cases there is shyness, self-consciousness, and even blushing, the presence of the other sex being desired yet painful. In other cases behavior while not obviously uncertain is on a trial-and-error basis, the adolescent not being his ordinary self because he is not sure of how what he does will be accepted and not sure of just what he should do to be highly pleasing.

Figure 27 gives the social ratings of a senior boy in the presence of girls as compared with his ratings when with boys, showing that even well along in adolescence there is still a seeming lack of ease and self-confidence in the presence of the other sex as far as some—and probably many—adolescents are concerned.

As one fourteen-year-old lad says:

"I have trouble with the girls. I can't get along with them. I don't know why, but they ignore me. Maybe it's because I am too bashful and don't go near them or ask them to go to parties. It makes me feel very blue."

Social-sex Development

The best picture we have of the adolescent at various stages of his social-sex development comes from Campbell in a study attempting "to define, describe, and measure the social-sex segment of child development." Data as presented in Table 17 were derived through the observations of recreational groups with a membership of 43 girls and 59 boys, aged five to seventeen. There were paired observers, not always together, and the process was repeated annually for three successive years.

It will be noticed again here, as has been discussed earlier in regard to physical development, that girls develop earlier than boys in their sexual maturing and correspondingly become interested in boys earlier than boys become interested in girls. One of the authors was asked to give a talk to a joint meeting of several ninth-grade home rooms. The committee which had arranged for the program was composed, as it happened, of three girls and two boys, and the topic finally suggested for the talk was one that the girls had insisted upon. It was "Should We Go Steady?"

The speaker smiled to himself when he saw the group of about 90 boys and girls. For the girls were in many cases very poised, grown-up-looking young ladies, highly conscious of their appearance, mouths delicately lipsticked, sweaters and skirts collegiate rather than childish, hair shiningly groomed. In contrast, the majority of the boys were very much little boys who looked as if they had some time to go before they could catch up to the girls in sophistication. The girls were ready for at least a theoretical consideration of going steady. The boys looked as if they were innocent of any thoughts on the subject.

This difference makes for particular difficulty in a junior high school for the girls are eager for a kind of social activity with the boys for which the boys are physically and psychologically too young.

Another view of social-sex development comes to us from Meek:[3]

"The interest of boys and girls in the opposite sex takes on new form and new meanings as they go through the pubertal cycle. Behavior and emotions become complicated because children are developing at different rates and because girls usually develop a year or more before boys in their grades. Social life will often become complex because 'little boys

[3] Lois Hayden Meek, "The Immediate Social Relations of Students in Junior and Senior High Schools," *Progressive Education*, 15:610–616 (1938).

will feel the pressure of the more advanced girls and the few more mature boys will be sought by the girls and will feel out of place with the boys.

TABLE 17. SEX DIFFERENCES IN DEVELOPMENT*

Age	Boy	Girl
11	....	Shows self-consciousness at touching boys, except under conventional conditions
12	Shows self-consciousness at touching girls, except under conventional conditions	Begins incessant whispering with friends
13	....	Feels shy in a group of boys
13½	....	Will not admit that any boy could be attractive to her, but from her behavior one knows she is interested
14	Sex modesty appears	Sex modesty appears
14½	Will not admit that any girl could be attractive to him, but from his behavior one knows he is interested. More careful of his appearance and self-conscious about the attention of girls, but he is not interested in dancing until a year later	Beginning the heterosexual phase by primping, being enthusiastic about dancing, admiring the clothes of women, and seeming interest in the attention of boys
15	Loses interest in adult affection	Interested in boys but not in a particular boy. Classifies work on sex lines Definite and open seeking after the other sex
15½	Interested in girls, but not in a particular girl. Shows an enjoyment of the physical contact of dancing. Classifies work on sex lines Definite and open seeking after the other sex	Assumes the external manners of an adult
16	Assumes the external manners of an adult	Shows an enjoyment of the physical contact of dancing

* Adapted from Elise Hatt Campbell, "The Social-sex Development of Children," *Genetic Psychology Monograph*, 21 (No. 4): 527–528 (1939).

Chaffey, in describing the changing relations of boys and girls observed in the Adolescent Study, says:

" 'As for their interest in the opposite sex, the girls were at first not particular whose attention they attracted. Any susceptible boy in the group might be a temporary target. As they grew older they became more and more discriminating and also more disdainful of boys their same chronological age. The boys were thus often inducted into the social life of the girls before they were ready for it and were then dropped suddenly from it as the girls found more mature boy friends. Sometimes they were successful in resisting the attention of the girls, later becoming themselves interested in younger girls. When left to their own devices the boys frequently first became interested in rather boyish girls and girls who were kindly and tolerant of their rather awkward social techniques. The transition to the more demanding and sophisticated "feminine" type sometimes occurred rapidly. There were some girls in the group who were regularly turned to by boys just venturing upon social contact with the opposite sex. At this period, parties and appearance were the chief subjects of conversation among the girls. The boys, although usually older when they showed this interest, showed it just as intensely. They did not go in couples to parties at first, though the effort was always made to have an equal number of boys and girls. Later, a few of the more mature would go in couples, the others going in groups of boys or girls and sometimes mixing to go home after the party. As they grew older, it was not acceptable to go to a party (now a "dance") except in couples. At the "dance" there would be almost no interchange of partners unless couples had gone as a foursome. At that period social security was gained by "going steady" so that it was the thing to do not only to stick to the same companion all evening but for a period ranging from a week to several years.

" 'As members of this group proved themselves acceptable to both sexes and became sure of their social status, absorption in parties, dates, and opportunities for social contact decreased. Individual interests began to emerge. Sometimes these were centered around vocational plans, development of a talent, or pursuit of a hobby.' "

Dating

By dating we mean that the boy and the girl go out alone together (or, of course, may double-date) to engage in some planned activity. On the first date very often the boy and the girl go to a movie, then have refreshments such as a coke, sandwich, or ice cream, and then come home.

According to Punke, who investigated the dating practices of high school youth in 12 high schools in nine states, over half of the freshmen boys and girls have no dates at all, while only about one-fifth of the senior boys and one-eighth of the senior girls report having no dates. About one-tenth of the freshmen boys and girls report having more than 10 dates a month, while one-fifth of the senior boys and one-third of the senior girls have 10 dates or more. These facts are reported in Table 18.

These data lead us to several conclusions. In the first place, it is obviously

what the possibilities for affection, companionship, and congeniality are unless he dates enough to know how people differ. The time for dating is in the teens and beginning twenties. This should be a time for experiencing what many different personalities of the opposite sex are like as companions.

Lowrie has given considerable thought and study to the matter of dating and concludes that it is very important in a young person's life:[4]

"[Dating] serves a long list of functions. Some of these are more or less preparatory for, and lay a foundation for, a wise, more intelligent, more objective choice of a mate. Thus, dating frequently a number of different individuals should normally give, among others, the following interrelated yet distinguishable ends:[5]

"1. Broader experience

"2. Greater poise and balance

"3. Experience in adjusting to others

"4. Reduced emotional excitement on meeting and association with a stranger of the opposite sex. Dating tends to serve certain other functions:

"5. It enriches and develops personality

"6. It gives prestige

"7. It is a means of having a good time and mixing socially

"8. Somewhat more debatable yet apparently real, dating together with the normal interaction and stimulation that accompanies it, seems to give a kind of sexual release, a reduction in sexual tension. As a consequence of all these functions, dating has two other results:

"9. It tends to provide a wider acquaintance from which a mate may be selected

"10. Its continuation over a period of time normally enhances an individual's ability to judge members of the opposite sex sensibly and objectively

"11. Finally it should be repeated that the functions of dating include that of courtship, that of choosing a mate."

Lowrie believes that general association with many of the opposite sex (as in school activities not including dating) will compensate to some extent for lack of dating but will not substitute sufficiently. He thinks that lack of dating or unfavorable experiences in dating may cause personality defects, whereas dating in adolescence may work to correct maladjustments developed earlier in life.

Attending movies is the most prevalent dating activity for all ages from fourteen to nineteen according to Bibb's study and attending dances

[4] Samuel Lowrie, "Dating, A Neglected Field of Study," *Marriage and Family Life*, 10:90–91 (1948).

[5] In the original, the listed items appear in a paragraph rather than as given here.

TABLE 19. MAJOR DATING ACTIVITIES AS RANKED BY ADOLESCENTS ACCORDING TO AGE*

Activity	Age of students						
	14 years	15 years	16 years	17 years	18 years	19 years	20 years
Attending the movies.................	1	1	1	1	1	1	1
Attending dances or parties...........	2	3	2	2	2	2	2
Riding.............................	3	2	3	3	3	3	3
Talking............................	4						
Attending school affairs..............	5	..	5	4	4		
Attending sports.....................	..	4	..	5	5	4	
Participating in sports (bowling, skating, hiking, etc.).......................	..	5	4				

* Frances G. Bibb, "Study of the 1042 Sophomores, Juniors, and Seniors of a Midwest High School" (unpublished master's thesis, Indiana State Teachers College, 1949).

TABLE 20. MOST AND LEAST EXPENSIVE DATES AS REPORTED BY ADOLESCENT BOYS*

Item	Number reporting	Price range	Median price	Per cent of total
Most Expensive				
Formal dance.................	147	$6.00–21.00	$10.00	54.7
Dinner and dance.............	36	3.00– 6.00	4.00	13.3
Carnival.....................	21	6.00–22.00	10.00	7.8
Dinner.......................	21	1.50– 5.00	3.50	7.8
Dance........................	16	2.00– 5.00	3.75	6.0
Dinner and play..............	15	3.00– 7.00	4.00	5.6
Dinner and movie.............	11	3.00–10.00	6.00	4.1
Least Expensive				
Sodas, cokes, etc..............	97	0.10– 0.50	0.30	42.2
Movie........................	54	0.70– 1.40	1.00	23.5
Dance or party...............	38	0.50– 0.70	0.70	16.5
Bus tokens...................	18	0.25	0.25	7.8
Gasoline.....................	17	0.25– 1.00	0.60	7.4
Candy, gum, etc..............	6	0.01– 0.25	0.10	2.6

* Frances G. Bibb, "Study of the 1042 Sophomores, Juniors, and Seniors of a Midwest High School" (unpublished master's thesis, Indiana State Teachers College, 1949).

and parties or riding around in a car come next. These data are presented more fully in Table 19.

Dating, of course, puts a financial burden on the boy, sometimes a heavy one. From a national teen-age survey[6] we learn that New York

[6] *Ladies' Home Journal*, September, 1949, pp. 46–47.

City boys may spend as much as $5 on an ordinary week-end date, though many arrange very inexpensive dates, going to Central Park, the Zoo, museums and the like. In a study of 130 boys in a general vocational school, Horvath[7] found that the expenditures for dates ranged from $0.14 to $19.30 per one six-week period, with the average expenditure $1.75.

Further data on costs are given in Table 20.

Lest this discussion of costs take the mind off more important ideas, we add that the last word on dating must be that it is a social activity which stems from a wholesome, natural, and unsophisticated desire to have a companion of the other sex and which contributes both to the growth and to the present happiness of the adolescent.

Going Steady

The meaning of "going steady" differs from age to age and, of course, from person to person. When the fourteen-year-old girl says that she is going steady, it may mean only that for a period of time (often as short as two weeks) she restricts her dates (which may be few) to one boy, whom she thinks of as her boy friend. When the seventeen-year-old girl says that she is going steady, she may mean that not only has she been going with a particular boy for months but that there is a strong bond of affection between them.

But no generalizations can be made. One senior girl reported that she had gone steady with 10 different boys in her senior year!

The girl is apt to go steady with a boy older than she, and, it follows, many boys go steady with younger girls. In one high school, a third of the senior girls reported going steady with boys then out of high school and either working or going to college.

In Bibb's investigation of 1,040 high school students she found that 13 per cent of the girls and 5 per cent of the boys went steady at fourteen; 20 per cent of the girls and 12 per cent of the boys at fifteen; 22 per cent of the girls and 14 per cent of the boys at sixteen; 25 per cent of the girls and 16 per cent of the boys at seventeen; 26 per cent of the girls and 25 per cent of the boys at eighteen and nineteen. The time during which couples had gone steady varied from two weeks to eighteen months.[8]

Wood gives these advantages and disadvantages of going steady, as they are given by boys and girls:[9]

[7] K. G. Horvath, "Earnings and Expenditures of 130 Boys in a General Vocational School," *NEA Bulletin of Secondary School Principals*, 29:69 (1945).

[8] Bibb, *op. cit.*

[9] M. W. Wood, *Living Together in the Family* (Washington: American Home Economics Association, 1946), p. 201.

Advantages

Gives security (for dates are ensured).
Gives more likelihood of having nice dates.
Don't have to sit at home.
Makes the girl feel more popular.
Gives a chance to know each other well.
May help to determine whether you want to make it a still longer period.
Costs less money.
May make family feel more secure because they know this boy or girl.

Disadvantages

It is easier to get started than to stop.
Boy may have to work; so girl has to stay home.
Makes it hard to make up your mind to a change.
May shut you off from other friends.
May cause unpleasant arguments in the family.
Family may think it too serious.
Family may want you to go with their choice. This produces discord.
One may be more serious than the other and he or she may want to carry on too long.
May not leave you free to make new friends in college or in work.
One person may not satisfy all needs.
Costs more money.
It is hard to get in circulation again after you stop going steady. This is especially true for girls.

As the list of advantages and disadvantages suggests, going steady offers many problems. One attractive senior girl in a small Middle Western city explained: "One difficulty is that boys and girls often go steady for different reasons. I'd like to go steady because then I don't have to worry about having dates—and some of the kids think that you just aren't popular unless you do go steady. But the boys often think that it's assurance that you'll do all the petting they want, and if you just don't want to get too involved, that makes for trouble."

Three high school boys report thus on the matter of going steady:[10]

"Glen isn't going steady now, but he thinks it's a good idea if the right girl comes along. He believes that the boy gets the best deal out of going steady because he doesn't have to call weeks in advance when he wants a date. 'I think it's probably cheaper, too, because you could be real honest when you were broke. I like free lancing, though, because you're not tied down to one person and I like to get around,' Glen says."

[10] *Indianapolis* (Indiana) *Star*, May 1, 1949.

manent love ties so that anyone was free to be attracted by whoever caught his fancy. No deep passions are stirred, no strong and complex feeling develops. The adolescent takes it seriously while it lasts of course, but in almost every case the relationship is on a lighter plane than is the love relationship three or four years later.

We catch some of the spirit of early love in these remarks of twelve- and thirteen-year-olds written in response to the question: "What makes you feel 'blue' (or embarrassed or afraid)?"

"When I come to school and find that my best girl is crazy over another guy, that sure puts me down in the dumps." (*Freshman boy.*)

"My girl friend and I were walking home from a dance one Friday night. We got about half way home when I put my arm around her. She got mad and slapped my face. Boy, did I feel blue afterwards!" (*Freshman boy.*)

"I was walking down the hall with another girl toward our eighth-grade home room when we passed a seventh-grade boy. I said to my girl friend, 'Do you want to see a real cute seventh-grade boy?' Here I turned around and there he was right behind us. I was so embarrassed that I left my girl friend standing there and almost ran into my home room. (I had just started to like him and he knew it.)" (*Freshman girl.*)

"What makes me feel just terribly blue is when my boy friend doesn't talk to me. For about two months now he hasn't talked to me. The girls tell me about what he does with other girls—takes them to the show and to the drug store afterwards. Mother tells me that everything will work out, but if it is true about him what the girls say, I don't know." (*Freshman girl.*)

"I am afraid to say 'Hi' to my boy friend, and he is too bashful to say 'Hi' to me." (*Freshman girl.*)

"When I was in the seventh grade last year, a girl invited me to a Friday night party at her house. Because I hadn't gone to many parties I was eager to go, supposing that it was just a little get-to-gether with dancing and refreshments.

"When I arrived at the party I found some rather unsavory characters there. This didn't bother me too much but a few minutes later one of them hollered out, 'Let's play spin the bottle.' That really scared me because I had never kissed a girl before.

"The first few times around I was lucky because the bottle didn't point to me. Then a girl spun it and the bottle did point right at me. I braced myself against the wall, shut my eyes, and prayed. But the girl only kissed me on the cheek, thank goodness.

"Now it was my turn to spin the bottle. It pointed right toward a girl. I didn't know what to do. Then I got an idea. I kissed her on her hand.

"Well, I got out of that all right, but it was one of the most embarrassing times I have had." (*Freshman boy.*)

We smile tenderly when we read of these fears, embarrassments, and discouragements or when we see the early evidence of love in the budding adolescent. It is to be hoped that we will not make fun of early adolescent love or in any way minimize its importance to those involved.

Love in later adolescence is much the same as romantic love between man and woman at any age. Adolescents fall in love with each other just as adults do, and they manifest their love in ways not too greatly different. They may hold hands when they walk down the corridor or down the street, they look at each other with secret messages in their eyes, they protect each other's interests, they delight in the presence of each other, and they feel real affection for the "boy friend" or the "girl friend."

Nowadays the older adolescents are not apt to be coy or secretive about their love interests when the love is mutual and there is a wholesome recognition of their relationship by themselves and their friends. It would be wise if adults would adopt the same attitude. As Taylor says:[13] "If they feel free to enjoy the beauty of their early loves, without the inhibiting feelings of guilt and shame, they will be more certain to reach the important goal of mature mate love and its transfiguring power."

When a twenty-one-year-old girl, to be married as soon as she is graduated from college in a month, writes to her family, "I am finding it very hard to study. I day dream about Bill and our marriage or write a letter to him when I ought to be working," they read this with sympathetic understanding. It doesn't make them disgusted with her, it doesn't embarrass them, it doesn't excite their curiosity, nor does it impel them to respond facetiously. Adults should respond similarly to the sincere love affairs of adolescents. They are not matters for scorn, derision, curiosity, or a heavy playfulness any more than is sincere affection at any age. We should remember, too, that these are first experiences with being in love and it is to be expected that there will be less decorum, less balance, and more uncontrolled intensity of feeling than there would be in a comparable case involving older people.

WHAT IS THE SCHOOL'S RESPONSIBILITY?

This book is written in the belief that it is the duty of those who work with the adolescent to help him in all areas of his living. Certainly one of the most important kinds of adjustment and growth is the heterosexual.

[13] Katharine Whiteside Taylor, *Do Adolescents Need Parents?* (New York: Appleton-Century-Crofts, Inc., 1938), p. 291.

The school and those connected with the school have the following responsibiities:

1. To give the adolescent adequate sex information if this function is not taken care of by the home.

2. To help the adolescent develop a wholesome attitude toward the sex force in himself and develop standards for using it so as to make his own life happier and so as to contribute to the health of his society.

3. To give much opportunity for wholesome heterosexual association.

4. To help those who are troubled by problems in this area.

5. To help the adolescent prepare for making a marital choice and for being happy in marriage.

We shall consider each of these.

ADEQUATE SEX UNDERSTANDINGS AND ATTITUDES

What Is the Adolescent Like?

We have many sources of information as to where adolescents get their sex information and whether or not they consider it adequate. From all of these sources we may conclude that many adolescents learn about sex in ways which are not apt to give them correct knowledge or desirable attitudes. The data from different groups of boys and girls lack uniformity, however, and the reader will have to judge for himself which most nearly represent the facts for his own community.

TABLE 21. SOURCES OF SEX INFORMATION*

First information			Source	Second information		
Rank	Number of boys	Per cent		Rank	Number of boys	Per cent
1	1,098	54.9	Companions	1	995	49.8
2	692	34.6	The street	5	455	22.8
3	668	33.4	Books	2	777	38.9
4	497	24.9	Magazines	3	646	32.3
5	365	18.2	Priests	4	525	26.3
6	348	17.4	Father	9	346	17.3
7	308	15.4	Mother	10	313	15.7
8	398	14.9	Teachers	6	443	22.2
9	295	14.8	Movies	8	347	17.4
10	289	14.5	Newspapers	7	376	18.8

* Urban H. Fleege, *Self-revelation of the Adolescent Boy* (Milwaukee: The Bruce Publishing Company, 1945), p. 272.

According to Fleege's study (made in 1939), over half of the boys got some of their first sex information from their companions, and over one-third got some of their first information from the street, as Table 21 shows. Of the boys who got their information from unwholesome sources (that is, 1,235 of the 2,000 boys) 53.3 per cent thought the

TABLE 22. EFFECT OF SEX INFORMATION*

Source of information	Number of boys	Effect of information				
		Good	Bad	Both	Neither	Uncertain or no answer
Unwholesome predominant...	1,235	20.5	52.3	11.2	8.3	6.7
Wholesome predominant.....	459	80.0	5.0	8.6	3.7	2.7
Wholesome and unwholesome balanced...............	225	46.2	18.2	24.9	7.1	1.8
Indeterminant.............	81	74.1	18.5	0.0	6.2	1.2

* Urban H. Fleege, *Self-revelation of the Adolescent Boy* (Milwaukee: The Bruce Publishing Company, 1945), p. 279.

TABLE 23. ATTITUDES TOWARD SEX*

	Number of boys	Per cent
Whenever the thought of sex comes to my mind, I find myself regarding it as:		
Something that puzzles me............................	619	31.0
A power of creation we share with God.................	450	22.5
Something sacred.....................................	424	21.2
Something dirty and vulgar...........................	406	20.3
A source of thrills...................................	332	16.6
Something disgusting.................................	251	12.5
An ever-present opportunity for pleasure...............	246	12.3
Something mysterious.................................	240	12.0
Lots of fun..	231	11.5
Something fearful....................................	122	6.1

* Urban H. Fleege, *Self-revelation of the Adolescent Boy* (Milwaukee: The Bruce Publishing Company, 1945), p. 284.

effects on them were bad, whereas of the boys who got their information from wholesome sources (that is, 459 of the 2,000) 80 per cent thought the effects were good.

The present attitudes of those boys toward sex varied greatly, as Tables 22 and 23 will show.

The Washington study, as well as data from Duvall and Motz, who studied 403 girls between fourteen and twenty-four years of age, would lead one to believe that more boys than girls receive their sex information from unwholesome sources. Tables 24 and 25 give the details.

In the *Ladies' Home Journal* survey of teen-age youth, we read:[14]

"Out of this survey two general conclusions can be made: most teen-agers *do not* get information about sex from their parents; they do get information frequently in a distorted and inaccurate form, from books (popular novels, medical texts, lewd pamphlets and comics), and movies (both family type and 'flea-show specials'), and conversation among themselves, usually quoting older friends. . . .

TABLE 24. ACTUAL SOURCE OF INFORMATION ABOUT SEX*

	Boy	Girl	Total
Parents and adults at home...............	38.2	64.6	52.6
Church, Sunday school minister............	3.2	2.5	2.8
Older kids, magazines, movies.............	52.3	26.7	38.3
Class and supervised discussion............	10.5	20.8	16.1
An adult counselor......................	8.7	6.4	7.4
No information.........................	4.3	0.8	2.5

* L. J. Elias, *High School Youth Look at Their Problems* (Pullman, Wash.: State College of Washington, 1949), p. 29.

"In spite of the reticence about sex information in many homes and in most schools, almost all the teen-agers interviewed remembered being curious about sex for the first time at as early as 4 or 5 years. Most of the curiosity remembered was traceable to the very normal incidents and developments that arouse curiosity about sex in any human life:

" 'I saw a pregnant woman on our street and I asked somebody why she was so fat.' . . .

" 'When I started school I realized that boys and girls were kept separate and somehow they were different.' . . .

" 'My mother once told me as a joke that I was left under cabbage leaves. I knew it wasn't true and it just made me wonder more.' . . .

"In later grade-school years, around 10 or 12 years of age, many of the teen-agers—more boys than girls, however—remember owning or having 'one of the fellows show me' one of the innumerable 'dirty comics,' small booklets of pornographic comics which have periodically swept through

[14] "Where Do Teen-agers Get Their Sex Education?", *Ladies' Home Journal*, 54:234–237 (October, 1949). Reprinted by special permission from the *Ladies' Home Journal*. Copyright, 1949. The Curtis Publishing Company.

grade-school or junior-high-school groups in this country for at least the past two decades. . . .

"According to teen-agers, however, it is not until the years between 14 and 16 'sex really gets on your mind.' It is then that many individuals and groups begin 'to trade information about what they know.' As one high school junior explained, 'Among close friends, girls will usually talk. One girl finds out and passes it on to the rest of us.' . . .

TABLE 25. SOURCE AND TYPE OF FIRST SEX INFORMATION OBTAINED BY THREE GROUPS OF GIRLS STUDIED AND ADEQUACY OF THEIR PRESENT SEX KNOWLEDGE FOR MARRIAGE*

	Group 1		Group 2		Group 3	
	Number	Per cent	Number	Per cent	Number	Per cent
First sex information obtained from:						
Family members	58	71.6	66	40.0	71	52.6
Teacher, relative, adult	8	9.9	27	16.4	12	8.9
Other children	8	9.9	52	31.5	36	26.7
Others	7	8.6	20	12.1	16	11.9
Total	81	100.0	165	100.0	135	100.1
Wholesomeness of first sex knowledge:						
Wholesome	64	86.5	101	68.2	94	73.4
Unwholesome	10	13.5	47	31.8	34	26.6
Total	74	100.0	148	100.0	128	100.0
Present sex knowledge is adequate for marriage:						
Yes	23	29.1	84	49.7	82	60.3
No	24	30.4	33	19.5	26	19.1
Doubtful	32	40.5	52	30.8	28	20.6
Total	79	100.0	169	100.0	136	100.0

* Evelyn Millis Duvall and Annabelle Bender Motz, "Age and Education as Factors in Social Experience and Personal-Family Adjustments," *School Review*, 53:413–421 (1945).

"Besides talking with older or experienced friends, much of their sexual information 'especially about techniques' and 'what actually happens,' comes from books and booklets purchased at out-of-the-way newstands or from ads in magazines, according to several teen-agers. . . .

"Several teen-agers interviewed explained that they had bought 'old medicine books' at secondhand bookstores for as little as 25 cents or had read 'an old marriage book we've had around the house for years' in an attempt to get complete and accurate information. In one of these books alone, published in 1872, the following are . . . examples of the endless misinformation which appeared on its pages:

" 'No young man strong in his faith would commit such a deed [masturbation]. It will end only in blindness and insanity, will sap his strength and leave him an accumulation of diseases which terminate only in death.'

" 'During menstruation Nature demands an extra amount of sleep and a girl should be allowed to stay out of school from one to three days as the case may be. . . . At the end of eight days she should again enjoy health.'

"Among teen-agers interviewed, many had read up-to-date and scientifically accurate books to find sex information. . . . Though the information in such books may be accurate and well presented, it often comes to an unprepared teen-ager as a shock."

This information should be balanced against the preceding tables.

It is safe to say that a goodly number of adolescents get their information about sex from sources which either give them inadequate or incorrect ideas or give them attitudes toward sex which are bad—or both. Even if one's sex nature, interests, and functions were much simpler and much less important in life than they are, the existence of such misconception, ignorance, and undesirable feelings would still be a matter for shame on the part of adults who have allowed them to develop.

Everyone should understand himself, whether it be the nature of his physical structure, of his emotions, of his impulses, of the way his mind works, or what not, and, this being true, it is certainly desirable that one understand his sex structure and nature.

The Ideal in Sex Understandings and Attitudes

Ideally, the adolescent would have an accurate knowledge of the facts of sex and would understand the place of sex in life. The gist of a talk given to junior and senior girls in a high school group presents a wholesome viewpoint.

"There are certain activities the body engages in to maintain self-preservation—breathing, consuming and digesting food, taking in water, eliminating waste, engaging in physical activity, resting and sleeping, and avoiding pain and hurt. All of this is of vital essentialness to the individual. Consequently the urges to engage in such activity are very strong and the satisfactions attained are very pleasant.

"There are other activities that the person engages in with a partner of the opposite sex, the purpose of which is conception. Through these activities the race is maintained. Consequently the urge to engage in this activity too is very strong and the satisfactions one attains are also very pleasant.

"All of these urges may be called animal urges in that they belong to the body of the animal, whether that animal be a fox, a cat, a dog, a horse, or a man. All of these creatures, and all of the other animals, are equipped with these urges for the two reasons that we have given: that life may be preserved and that the race may continue.

"One should notice, however, that man has used his intelligence, his imagination, his idealism, to 'civilize' these acts, some more and some less. In some cases this means that he has made the act serve a larger purpose than that for which it was originally intended. By *larger* we mean that it serves in ways that we believe have gone beyond the animal level of existence. Thus eating can be the occasion for a gracious companionship among friendly people, as well as an activity which satisfies hunger and pleases the senses.

"The act of sex has been made more than a highly pleasant act which may result in offspring. It is the foundation of the institution of marriage, which at its best is the noblest and most beautiful of human relationships. Unite two people in liking, in friendship, in admiration, in respect, in love, and you have an association which makes both bountifully happy.

"The sex act can be used for lesser purposes. It may be used merely as a means to physical excitement and pleasure. It may be used merely so that the participants may feel important to someone else and wanted. In using it thus, however, we may destroy our potentiality for using it at times and in ways which are more productive of happiness."

Such understanding, along with accurate knowledge, is important; but it is not enough.

The emotional set in the person toward sex must also be right. We can express the ideal positively by saying that one's conscious and unconscious feelings toward sex should be wholesome. We can be more precise from a negative point of view: one should not view the sex aspects of life with distaste, with horror, with a sly interest, with excessive interest, and one should not have guilt feelings in connection with marital sex relationships.

How Can This Ideal Be Reached?

Sex stimulations and responses are not unknown before adolescence. The child is stimulated sexually and knows sex feelings and sex curiosities. In addition, he lives among older boys and girls and among men and women from whom he learns attitudes and knowledges. As Blos says:[15]

[15] Peter Blos, "Adolescence . . . Its Stimulations and Patterns," *Childhood Education*, 18:79–83 (1941).

" . . . the adolescent approaches the task of heterosexual adjustment dependent on patterns of behavior he has learned in his childhood. His earliest experiences of affection; his early learnings of right and wrong in respect to the body, his own and others, its functions, sensations and pleasures; his earliest feelings about men and women, as well as his observations of adult attitudes toward the body, affectional behavior, and sex appropriateness—all these factors form the groundwork on which he must build the mature love for a suitable mate and the comfortable acceptance of his own role as a man or a woman. Experiences in the family and the kind of relationship he has had to either of the parents will be of importance in determining how fully he can accept the implications of his own sex, and the privileges, limitations, and responsibilities which go with it in the particular culture in which he lives."

Even in the matter of sex knowledge alone, we should realize that much is known before adolescence. In Ramsey's study of the 291 boys,[16] each reported the age at which he first secured information concerning ejaculation, intercourse, and so on.

By the age of ten, 14 per cent of the boys knew about ejaculations, 69 per cent knew about the origin of babies, 11 per cent knew about nocturnal emissions, 10 per cent knew about contraceptives, 5 per cent knew about menstruation, 43 per cent knew about masturbation, 57 per cent knew about intercourse, 23 per cent knew about prostitution, and 3 per cent knew about venereal diseases. By the age of fourteen, 93 per cent knew about ejaculations, 100 per cent knew about the origin of babies, 73 per cent about nocturnal emissions, 86 per cent about contraceptives, 38 per cent about menstruation, 96 per cent about masturbation, 99 per cent about intercourse, 97 per cent about prostitution, and 57 per cent about venereal diseases.

It follows then that those working with the adolescent are not beginning a task. They are continuing one which may have been well begun in some cases or very badly begun in others.

Most adults would agree with the seniors of the Washington study in choosing the home as the ideal source of sex information, though some might reverse the second and third choices:[17]

	Per Cent
Parents and adults at home	61.6
Class and supervised discussion groups	44.8
Adult counselor of their choice	11.6

[16] Glenn V. Ramsey, "The Sex Information of Younger Boys," *American Journal of Orthopsychiatry*, 13:347–352 (1943).

[17] L. J. Elias, High School Youth Look at Their Problems (Pullman, Wash.: State College of Washington, 1949), p. 29.

However in a 100 per cent sampling of the parents in two Oregon communities recently it was found[18] that "about a fifth of the parents are in favor of keeping sex knowledge from children as long as possible. Approximately half feel that nothing should be told about sex until the children raise the question themselves—if they ever do. Nearly a fifth are opposed to the suggestion that children should be allowed to help prepare for the arrival of a new baby and that this event might be used by the parents as an opportunity to teach facts of human reproduction. About two-fifths feel that it is improper for parents to dress or undress in the presence of their children. These results suggest that in many homes sex instruction is restricted and narrow and possibly ill-adapted to the needs of the child."

School living and home living should be a part of the same whole, and consequently anything as important as sex attitudes and understandings should not rightly be left out of either learning situation. And when the home fails, as happens often, it would seem that the school must of necessity supply the lack.

It would be good, and in many communities it is absolutely essential, to have the parents in agreement with the school in all that is done. Meetings of the parents, if this can in any way be arranged, are often advisable. Those in charge of such a meeting should present data to explain the need for sex education in the school, explain the nature of the books which their children might read, show a film which might be used, and so on. This should not be done hastily or sketchily. Parents' wrong attitudes toward what the boys and girls are learning may distort it or even degrade it for their children. Parents' opposition to what is being done may cause much trouble for the school authorities and those who are handling the work.

Sometimes in high school when the support of all of the parents cannot be enlisted, it may be wise to allow only those students whose parents give their approval to partake of special discussion groups, and so on.

Classes in sex education are too often thought of as being the first-ranking need of adolescents in regard to heterosexual adjustment. Actually all that such classes can do is to inform the student about certain facts and viewpoints. In most cases they cannot counteract deep-set—even unconscious—feelings about sex which the adolescent would be better off without; nor can they eradicate long-established habits of thought or behavior. And certainly they cannot give a boy or girl much help, if any, in his social adjustment to the other sex. As Frank says:[19]

[18] Marcille Harris, Berlan Lemon, and Lester F. Beck, "Sex Instruction in the Classroom," *Educational Leadership*, 6:519–524 (1949).

[19] Lawrence K. Frank, "The Adolescent and the Family." Chap. 13 in Nelson B. Henry (ed.), 43d Yearbook, *National Society for the Study of Education* (Chicago:

"It is also ironic to recall that when boys and girls are most eager to make an approach to each other, to discover what a man and a woman mean to each other and how they should act toward each other, we can only offer them 'sex education,' *i.e.*, teaching about procreation which is the last thing they are really concerned about. They want to know, not about babies, but what you do with sex, what you can give and receive from the other, what love means. Instead of giving them our best knowledge and wisest counsel and helping to direct these interests, the cautious parent may instead concentrate upon terrorizing them with the dangers of venereal disease."

As to just what should be done, we would agree with Kirkendall, who does not advocate special "sex courses" but rather suggests that materials should be integrated into the various courses of the curriculum. He would have seven items of emphasis:[20]

1. Biological: An understanding of the reproductive processes, sex as a biological function, and the like.

2. Preparation for marriage, family life, and child care: Points to consider in choosing a mate and thinking of marriage, how to achieve a stable and satisfactory family life, and so on.

3. Sociological: The place of the family as a social institution, divorce, and similar topics.

4. Health: The relationship of sex and sex practices to physical and mental well-being.

5. Personal adjustments and attitudes: Personal problems in regard to heterosexual adjustment.

6. Interpersonal relations: To build a sense of social responsibility.

7. The establishment of values: To develop wholesome values in regard to sex and other areas of living as well.

Environmental Hindrances

No matter how good a job the home and the school do, there are inevitably environmental influences which tend to counteract it.

One is the overemphasis on sex in movies, radio, and advertisements. Sexual attractiveness of the female for the male is beyond a doubt the most publicized theme in this country. All other ideals and ideas take second place to it when judged by the amount of money and effort used to keep it in the public eye and ear—thus to sell movies, radio programs,

University of Chicago, 1944), Part I, *Adolescence*, p. 243. Quoted by permission of the Society.

[20] Lester A. Kirkendall, "Health, Sex, and Human Relations in Education," *NEA Bulletin of Secondary School Principals*, 28:94–100 (1944).

and innumerably varied articles. So presented, sex means physical attraction, nothing more, and one gets the impression that sex is man's sole preoccupation and sex attraction woman's sole function. Thus the youth may experience too much emphasis on a very superficial interpretation which may pervert his viewpoint.

Another undesirable influence comes in the ready availability of pornographic literature. A survey of the magazines on any newsstand, even in the smaller cities, reveals that there are many whose sole purpose is to be sexually provocative and that there are others which are extremely lewd and indecent in the pictures and information they give. These are not for adult eyes alone. They are easily available to the young person and are often meant to catch his eye.

OPPORTUNITY FOR WHOLESOME HETEROSEXUAL ASSOCIATION

Adolescence is the golden time for learning to get along with the other sex, a time when the romantic and also merely companionable association of boys and girls is a fitting and natural expression of the growing sex differentiation and sex feelings.

It is the ideal time for learning to get along heterosexually, for several reasons. The first is that the natural interests and desires make the youth want to be accepted by the other sex and heighten the pleasure he finds in their company. Then because he is in high school where there are such numbers of boys and girls gathered together, he has many opportunities to find among them those special ones who will be congenial—something more difficult a few years later when, unless he is a college student, his associations are more limited. Finally, since he is bound to be awkward, giddy, foolish perhaps, or overintense at times in his attachments and his behavior when he is first experiencing romantic interests and feelings, this is the time to get the "practice period" over—during his teens, when the world feels tolerant and kindly toward adolescent love behavior.

Why Should the School Encourage
Wholesome Heterosexual Association?

Perhaps it is obvious from what has already been said that the school should encourage the wholesome association of boys and girls. Nonetheless, it may be worth while to enumerate the reasons: First, since it is in the nature of things that boys and girls should want to be together a great deal, the school is distorting their lives unwisely if it refuses them this privilege. Second, much of the teen-agers' leisure time will be spent together, but in most towns the opportunities for wholesome recreation are not what they should be. The school can offer such opportunities. In the third place, recreational activity of boys and girls is often on a clique basis with class lines maintained and accentuated. The school can provide recreational and work associations of a more democratic nature. Finally, heterosexual adjustment means that the youth learns to choose suitable companions of the other sex, learns to be at ease in the presence of the other sex, learns to judge members of the other sex without being too much influenced by the emotional halo, dates enough to know what is possible in the way of such companionship, and grows to the point where he can select one to love above all others and can be true to that one. These learnings do not occur without much experience in being with the other sex.

Teacher Attitudes

What teachers believe not only affects what they do but also shows itself more subtly. For example, if a certain teacher thinks that it is shocking for a boy and girl to hold hands as they walk down the street or if she subconsciously envies their being able to do what she cannot do, she may dislike the two or feel spiteful toward them without knowing why. If, on the contrary, a teacher has an approving but highly sentimental attitude toward any signs of heterosexual attraction, she may engender a feeling that such attraction is a matter for congratulation and stir up too much sophisticated self-consciousness about it. A teacher in the ninth grade, for example, who was trying hard to replace her outmoded prudish attitude toward boy-and-girl relationships with a more modern viewpoint developed a coyness and a bright eagerness about such associations which was not good for the subjects of her attention.

If the teacher's attitude can be completely wholesome and understanding, the student will inevitably profit by it. This will be true if the following can be said about him:

1. He is not embarrassed by the idea of sex, horrified by it, shocked by it, fearful of it, sentimental toward it, overintrigued by it—or otherwise maladjusted in his own sex attitudes.

2. He realizes that sex attraction is one of the staples of good living but not the only such staple by any means.

3. He realizes that sex activity properly used is as wholesome and natural as eating good food but infinitely more capable of being the basis for beauty in human relationships and infinitely more capable of being a source of highminded inspiration.

4. He realizes that heterosexual attraction and association among the teen-agers is normal, wholesome, and eminently desirable.

5. He realizes that there are many unobjectionable public demonstrations of affection in adolescent couples toward which he should be completely neutral and which he should consider none of his business—such as when they stand long outside the class door talking, sit rapt in conversation in the classroom before school or at noontime, or hold hands as they walk down the corridor or down the street.

6. He realizes that it is the duty of the school not to prevent or discourage heterosexual association, but rather to provide varied opportunities for it.

The teacher who feels that his own life has not been such as to promote the right attitudes can help himself a great deal by reading Popenoe and other writers who express so well the mature viewpoint.

School Social Activities

School social activities will be discussed in another chapter (Chap. 14), but mention of one will be made here.

Dances are a form of school recreation which offer opportunities for heterosexual association and which, when supervised, are certainly a good part of a school social program. They alone will not suffice, however, for not only are they too limited in the kind of activity they provide, but they are also limited in that they do not attract the whole student body.

Hutson and Kovar asked 2,163 senior high school students to fill out a check list giving reasons for not attending school dances. Those reasons which were checked by 25 per cent or more of the boys are given in Table 26 and those checked by 25 per cent or more of the girls in Table

TABLE 26. REASONS GIVEN BY BOYS FOR NOT ATTENDING SCHOOL DANCES*

	Per Cent
I do not know how to dance	74.1
I did not have the money	25.4
I would only sit or stand around and not have a good time...	36.0
I did not have a special girl that I wished to take	30.4
I lack the nerve to ask a girl	25.2
I could not take a girl because I had no good way of getting her there and back	35.9

* Percival W. Hutson and Don R. Kovar, "Some Problems of Senior-high-school Pupils in Their Social Recreation," *Educational Administration and Supervision*, 28:503–519 (1942).

27. Hutson and Kovar add:[21] "The evening dancing party is too advanced a recreational form for a large number of high-school pupils. It impose

[21] Percival W. Hutson and Dan R. Kovar, "Some Problems of Senior-high-school Pupils in Their Social Recreation," *Educational Administration and Supervision*, 28:503–519 (1942).

barriers in the form of money costs, transportation facilities, expensive clothing, pairing, skill in dancing, and parental jitters. . . . "

TABLE 27. REASONS GIVEN BY GIRLS FOR NOT ATTENDING SCHOOL DANCES*

	Per Cent
I do not know how to dance	38.5
Only those who are paired off with a member of the opposite sex really have a good time	25.7
I would only sit or stand around and not have a good time	30.3
I did not have a special boy friend to escort me	41.6

* Percival W. Hutson and Dan R. Kovar, "Some Problems of Senior-high-school Pupils in Their Social Recreation," *Educational Administration and Supervision*, 28:503–519 (1942).

From the point of view of furthering heterosexual adjustment, then, school recreation should include many different kinds of parties—square dancing, picnics, carnivals, mixers, and so on, as well as sports activities in which both boys and girls can participate.

GIVING HELP TO THOSE WHO HAVE PROBLEMS

The problems met by students in regard to heterosexual adjustment are: (1) those having to do with attracting and holding friends of the other sex; (2) those having to do with such decisions as whether to go steady, when to come in from a date, and the like; (3) those having to do with lack of knowledge or misconceptions in regard to sex; (4) those having to do with crushes (which we shall discuss in Chap. 7 on emotions); (5) those having to do with homosexuality.

Normal Problems in Regard to Attraction and Association

Letters written to Alice Barr Grayson show what the first type of problem in our list is like:[22]

"Could you please advise a lonely girl of 16? I come from a respectable family and live in a nice big house. I dress as nice as any of my girl friends. My hair is cared for nicely. I don't neglect anything in personal cleanliness and wear just the right shade of make-up. But I still don't have dates. I am beginning to get an inferiority complex because I am very tall and a little underweight but nevertheless in a perfect state of health. . . . Once

[22] Alice Barr Grayson, *Do You Know Your Daughter?* (New York: Appleton-Century-Crofts, Inc., 1944), pp. 48, 89, 90. (This book is "a discussion of the difficulties growing up as seen in letters from adolescent girls to the department 'Let's Talk Things Over' in the magazine *Calling All Girls*.")

in a long while I am fortunate enough to go out with a boy. The moment I introduce him to any one of my good-looking girl friends with their 'come-hither' look he has fallen for them and starts asking them for dates. I am very discouraged with life and everything in it for what could be worse than a sixteen year old girl and dateless?"

"I am a girl of fourteen and am at present going in a crowd of boys and girls from 14 to 16 years old. I now find it impossible to continue our friendship. . . . Both my father and I agree that companionship between girls and boys is a healthy condition providing the said companionship does not extend over certain bounds. Because of these bounds my mother has been branded as old-fashioned and I am now considered a prude. However in my heart I know I'm right. Do you think it is normal for boys to come to a party with the expressed purpose of turning out the lights and necking in the living room as well as in other rooms? Each of my girl friends agree with me that necking and such is wrong but at parties they lower their standards for the sake of popularity. Especially in a home where there are sufficient means of entertainment, such as victrolas pianos and so forth?"

"I am a girl of thirteen. I am many years older for my age. We have had many school dances and parties and I have gone. I usually walk home with one or two girls. There have been many boys tried to kiss me and as I do not like it I have asked them not to do it. The boys and girls have called me a snob and a don't-you-dare-touch-me-girl. I don't have many friends because of that. Would you please help me solve my problem?"

It takes a wise person to give the individual counseling on problems of this sort. Grayson, for example, writes this in regard to the girl of thirteen above:[23]

"A 13-year-old, however, *is* young in the number of years she has lived. There is no reason for her to rush into experiences for which she is not ready. She must know that what might be called the 'light' variety of petting may lead—and often more quickly than she may expect—to the 'heavy' type. She might as well accept the fact that many boys find it difficult to control their feelings, once aroused. A fair-minded girl would concede that she has no right to lead a boy on, to tempt, to act provocatively, or, in youth's own language, to 'turn on the current' and then adopt the how-dare-you manner! Girls must learn, too, that what they finally decide about these matters is not a thing apart but involves the total personalities as well as the goals they have set for themselves as girls and women."

There are adolescents who would like help on even simple problems such as this:

[23] *Ibid.*, p. 92.

"Last Saturday night a gang of kids from our church went tobogganing. There were four girls and four boys and one of the boys had a car, which made it easy for us to go. I am new in this town and am just getting acquainted with the kids. We went there and had lots of fun. But on the way back one of the boys asked me if I wouldn't sit with him. I knew one of the girls that was there liked him and I didn't think I should accept. But she was standing there when he asked me and she said, 'Go ahead.' I didn't like the idea, but what could I do. So the next day she wouldn't even speak to me and she told the other girls I did it on purpose. I really didn't because I'm not that kind. I tried to explain to her but she was real cold to me. The funny part is that I don't like the boy as a boy friend. I think he's swell, but I just like him as a friend. What should I do in a case like this?"

Many teachers do not have the necessary wisdom, and of course many boys and girls who need help do not confide in anyone. It is therefore recommended that the school provide not only individual counseling but also such general attacks on personal heterosexual adjustment problems as discussion groups, helps in grooming and in etiquette, classes in ballroom dancing, and informal work and play occasions where those who need help can develop more pleasing personalities or become more skillful in their social relationships.

Ignorance and Misconceptions in Regard to Sex

We have said earlier that sex education should be more than a "course," that it should rather be approached through many avenues and over a long period of time. Nevertheless there must be provision for the high school boy and girl to get direct answers to questions they have on sex—through class or individual counseling, educational movies, library books, or other means.

One of the most harmful pieces of misinformation that boys and girls can harbor is that masturbation may lead to dire physical and mental aftereffects. In a fairly recent investigation of the beliefs of college freshmen as to the effects of masturbation, there were found to be prevalent such ideas as this: "It will drive a person crazy," "It will wreck his morals," "It dulls his intelligence," "It is bad for his health," "It will ruin his eyes," "It lowers his resistance to disease." Table 28 gives further details.

Actually masturbation is not only exceedingly common but is also, to the best of anyone's knowledge, harmless.

In Ramsey's study mentioned earlier[24] he found that by the age of six,

[24] Glenn V. Ramsey, "The Sexual Development of Boys," *American Journal of Psychology*, 56:224 (1945).

5 per cent had had masturbatory experience; by the age of ten, 29 per cent; by the age of twelve, 73 per cent; by the age of fourteen, 95 per cent; and by the age of fifteen, 98 per cent.

Of course, we cannot assume that an act is normal and unobjectionable just because it is widespread, but in the case of masturbation such an assumption is probably justified. Masturbation does none of the things so frequently believed—it does not harm the health or the mind, it does not corrupt the morals, weaken the will power, or cause insanity. One should consider it an unwholesome practice only if it leads to one or the other of these three results: It may bring on worry, guilt, self-doubt, or

TABLE 28. THE BELIEFS OF SEVENTY-FIVE YOUNG MEN CONCERNING THE EFFECTS OF MASTURBATION*

Belief	Number of young men	Percentage of total†
Some type of serious damage.........	62	82.7
Serious physical damage..............	33	44.0
Serious mental damage...............	28	37.3
Serious moral damage................	18	24.0
Serious social damage................	9	12.0
Harmful (not specified)..............	6	8.0
Direct cause of insanity..............	12	16.0
Not seriously harmful................	5	6.7
No response.........................	8	10.7

* E. V. Pullias, "Masturbation as a Mental Hygiene Problem—A Study of the Beliefs of Seventy-five Young Men," *Journal of Abnormal and Social Psychology*, 32:216-222 (1937).

† Overlapping in percentage due to the fact that some of the young men believed masturbation had several types of effect.

the like. It may become such a major source of satisfaction that others are lost sight of. It may be too much relied upon as an escape.

If a boy thinks he is doing something bad when he masturbates, the psychological effects on him may be not only very upsetting but also harmful to his personality development; for anyone who carries around with him the feeling that he is doing something to be ashamed of, who is constantly afraid that he will be "found out," who has lost respect for himself, who thinks that he is ruining his health or going the way to insanity cannot be happy or enter into the affairs of his life with wholehearted enthusiasm.

Nor is it good for a person to find so much satisfaction in the manipulation of his own body that this takes precedence over the many other satisfactions possible to him or that it prevents his enjoying social activities with other boys and girls. And, of course, any pleasure used excessively to escape from the problems, obligations, or disappointments of life weakens one's ability to face life courageously.

In contrast, if a boy masturbates *and* if he is also living a generally satisfying and socially oriented life, masturbation will have but a minor importance in his life and will gradually be used less and less.

Homosexuality

Homosexuality, often referred to as homoerotism, is a more serious matter, for it leads to attractions, interests, desires, and sometimes practices which run counter to those accepted by society as normal and desirable—nor does one, in many cases, "grow out of it."

By homosexuality we mean a personality make-up which inclines one toward a sexual interest in one's own sex rather than in the opposite sex. This may be the result of physical make-up, or it may develop because of environmental pressures.

We know that both male and female hormones are found in every individual, a preponderance of male in the male, and of female in the female. Since the proportions vary, it may well be that the human race is not of two distinct groups, the male and female, but is rather of many different degrees of femaleness and maleness. If this is true, then there are those people who though male or female in structure are actually close to the dividing line between female and male—with body of one sex but sexual interests more similar to those of the other.

Of these people some may never consciously recognize their latent homosexuality as such; they will only know that they have no interest in the opposite sex and are much attracted to certain members of their own sex. Others are aware that their feelings differ from the normal, but the thought of any homosexual practice does not occur to them, and they live the typical life of their own sex, though they are not apt to desire marriage or to make a success of marriage if they do engage in it. Still others become active homosexuals—that is, engage in sexual practices (mutual masturbation) with members of their own sex.

Environmental pressures, too, make people deviate sexually. It is highly probable that such pressures would never affect the strongly masculine or strongly feminine. But we do know that boys have been made very feminine in their behavior and inclinations because their mothers have brought them up as they would girls, and similarly girls have been made masculine. In other cases, a boy or girl's first sex experience has been with someone of the same sex. This is often due to temptation resulting from segregation of the sexes, as in boys' schools, girls' schools, or the armed services. This first experience may place an imprint on the youth's sexual nature to the extent that he comes to desire only that kind of sexual stimulation and gratification thereafter.

It is likely that such a person has some sexual ambivalence to start with, however, for many youths return to normal sex interests as soon as the abnormal pressures are gone.

Ramsey's data[25] show that, roughly, 25 per cent of adolescent boys engage in homosexual play. With many such children and adolescents this is no more than passing experimentation and not a matter for concern. With a few it may induct them early into practices which continue into adulthood.

It is difficult to advise adults on their treatment of the boy or girl with homosexual leanings. We should realize that some cannot help themselves and it is useless for us to make their lives more burdensome by trying to force them into the typical pattern. In one school, for example, a girl had reached her senior year in high school bearing the stamp of masculinity to an unusual degree—dressing in boy's clothing when she could or in very plain suits, wearing her hair short, enjoying woodworking, hunting, and fishing as her hobbies, and, in her later adolescence, assuming an almost courtly attitude toward other girls. When she was a senior, the sponsor of the senior class decided that she would do everything she could to make the girl more feminine in her appearance and behavior. So she advised her on clothes, persuaded her to let her hair grow longer and get a permanent, authoritatively insisted that the girl come to school dances— and all with the sole result of making the girl very uncomfortable and unhappy with her lot, nothing else.

As for the practicing homosexual we should realize that his life has much in it to make him unhappy, because of the very fact that he is adopting a mode of existence which society regards as abnormal and reprehensible. Consequently we are probably safe in assuming that the adolescent with homosexual leanings who comes for counseling should be encouraged to make his life follow the pattern of his own sex as far as he possibly can.

Those working with the adolescent should be warned not to judge anyone's sexuality by his appearance, his voice, or his mannerisms, for all of these may be misleading.

PREPARING FOR MARITAL CHOICE AND MARITAL HAPPINESS

Anyone who studies the adolescent must realize that before very long many of these boys and girls will be making what is perhaps the mos

[25] *Ibid.*, p. 230.

important choice of their lives, the choice of a marital partner, and will be settling down to marriage. No one needs to be reminded of the fact that such choices are often unfortunate and even disastrous—or that marriage even for the happily mated demands qualities of character of a high sort if the marriage is to be the most completely successful.

Whatever can be done to prepare the adolescent for choosing wisely when the time comes and for being a good husband or a good wife will be a real contribution to individual happiness and social welfare.

What Kind of Development Is Ideal?

In this as well as in everything which we try to accomplish we must have our objectives clearly in mind. What should be the course of the adolescent's development if he is to be best prepared to choose wisely and live happily in marriage? There are five requisites. First, he must become as well adjusted as possible. The more secure, the more courageous, adaptable, happy-natured, generous-hearted, and socially skillful a person can be, the better are his chances of being a good marriage partner. Second, he must become heterosexually adjusted—that is, interested in the other sex, able to find companionship among them, and able to center his affections and loyalty on one. Third, he must develop an ideal for marriage —an ideal which would include mutual kindness and consideration, a sharing of duties, responsibilities, and decisions, companionship, unselfishness, appreciation for the other person's good qualities, and forbearance. Fourth, he must recognize the fact that a successful marriage rests on the willingness to put forth effort to make it successful—and he must have a desire to make that effort. Finally, he will have some homemaking skills— among which may be numbered the ability to cook, purchase suitable clothing, spend the household money wisely, skill in budgeting, and so on.

What Can the School Do?

No single class, no single school effort makes an adolescent into a truly marriageable adult. The first two requisites, good general adjustment and good heterosexual adjustment, must be among the major objectives of the whole school program. The second two will be reached only when many teachers and many classes contribute to them—literature can help form the ideal, and so can sociology; but more important than any subject will be the attitudes of the teachers of all subjects. The last, homemaking skills, are more definitely the province of classes in homemaking, industrial arts, and economics.

Doubtless the best results will be accomplished if everyone who works with the adolescent realizes what is needed to make him grow up into a person able to make good in marriage and tries sincerely to help bring about that development.

Reminiscences

1. When did you start dating? For your best good, was the time too early, too late, or just right?

2. Were there many questions in regard to your heterosexual adjustment upon which you received no help in high school though you needed help?

3. Was there as much going steady in high school when you were there as there is now? If not, what do you think has made the change?

4. What did your school do to make opportunities for wholesome heterosexual association?

5. What problems in regard to heterosexual association did you experience? Did you have sufficient help on them?

General Discussion

1. Campbell's data regarding social-sex development were published in 1939. From your observation of adolescents would you agree that it is still a true picture, or have adolescents changed since then?

2. Are adolescents beginning to date earlier today than when you were a freshman in high school? If so, how do you account for the change?

3. When you have an adolescent child of your own, how will you attempt to regulate his dating activities, if at all?

4. Study Punke's table on dating (Table 18). On the basis of this, how would you answer a parent of a teen-ager who asked you: "What is normal dating frequency for a high school freshman girl?"

5. Study the dating activities in Bibb's table (Table 19). Do any of these seem more wholesome than others? Which? Are there any which you think have too much prominence for their worth?

6. Study Lowrie's list of dating functions. Are there any of these functions which will be served equally well by experiences other than dating?

7. Should young teen-agers go steady?

8. If you had an adolescent son or daughter of sixteen, would you want him or her to go steady?

9. Is Popenoe right in his concepts of sex-stimulating and sex-releasing associations?

10. Why do adults so often make fun of or laugh at adolescents in love?

11. What could be done in your major subject to help develop wholesome attitudes toward sex?

12. Do you believe in classes solely for the purpose of sex instruction?

13. Some people say that the average adolescent will get enough heterosexual association outside of school and that therefore the school need not be concerned with this problem. What do you think?

14. In regard to Hutson and Kovar's data, what would you do for these boys and girls?

15. Consider each of the letters to Grayson. How would you answer it?

16. Would you require a course in home and family relationships of all students? In what year? What would it include?

Panel Discussion

1. Adolescents: Boy-girl problems.
2. Parents: Boy-girl problems.

Movies

Are You Ready for Marriage? Coronet Films, 15 min., b. & w. or color, 1950.

Choosing for Happiness, McGraw-Hill Textfilms, 14 min., b. & w., 1950.

Human Reproduction, McGraw-Hill Textfilms, 22 min., b. & w., 1947.

Further Reading

BEACH, RUTH E., "Should Sex Education Be Taught in High Schools?" *Journal of Health and Physical Education,* 14:152–153 (1943).

CARTER, HOMER L. J., and LOUIS FOLEY, "What Are Young People Asking about Marriage?" *Journal of Applied Psychology,* 27:275–282 (1943).

FORCE, ELIZABETH S., "Education for Family Living," *Annals of the American Academy of Political and Social Science,* 272:156–162 (1950).

GRAYSON, ALICE BARR, *Do You Know Your Daughter?* (New York: Appleton-Century-Crofts, Inc., 1944).

KIRKENDALL, LESTER A., and MARK FLEITZER, "The Facts Speak for Sex Education," *Clearing House,* 22:27–31 (1947).

ROCKWOOD, L. D., and M. E. N. FORD, *Youth, Marriage, and Parenthood* (New York: John Wiley & Sons, Inc., 1945).

SCHULTZ, G. D., *Letters to Jane* (Philadelphia: J. D. Lippincott Co., 1948).

STRAIN, FRANCES BRUCE, "Sex Education at Different Ages," *Parents' Magazine,* 20:34–35 (1945).

Chapter 7. EMOTIONAL ADJUSTMENT

Probably not a person who reads this book would have any difficulty in finding in himself (or among relatives and friends) examples of habitual emotional responses which are disagreeable to others, painful to self, inhibiting, or even crippling to the personality. Cases like these are numerous:

Tom is too often irritable and ill-humored. If one of the children in turning on the radio lets it blare forth loudly, he is sure of a sharp reprimand from his father. If dinner is a little late, Tom is as likely as not to eat it in sullen silence. If his stenographer makes a mistake in a letter, Tom mentions it with an ill-humor that makes the offence seem much more serious than it really is.

Helen is married, but she has never been able to do as the Bible suggests: leave her father and her mother, and cleave unto her husband. Instead, her mother comes first in her affections. This inevitably results in quarrels with her husband or hurt feelings on his part. When Helen and her husband were buying a rug for their living room, Helen had to ask her mother's opinion—and took her advice in opposition to her husband's choice. Should Helen's husband want to take a trip on Sunday, it would be impossible because they always have dinner with Helen's mother. When the baby was born, Helen's husband was practically shut out by "Mother thinks . . . ," "Mother wants . . . ," and so on. Helen is emotionally still a child in her relationship with her mother. Adult though she is in years, her love relationships are still immature.

Sarah worries about everything. Whenever any of the family is delayed in getting home at night, Sarah is under tension. If someone has a cold, Sarah is fearful that it may turn into pneumonia. If some purchase proves to be faulty and Sarah must return it the next day, she worries about the unpleasantness of the task until the moment of its occurrence. When Sarah goes shopping, she worries about things at home—whether or not she turned off the electric iron she was using, whether it might rain in through the open windows, or the like. Sarah's life is constantly troubled by needless worries.

Sam is a cold, undemonstrative man who either feels little friendliness for others or else is unable to show what he feels. Acquaintances who come to call on the family or even those who are especially invited to the home never feel sure of their welcome with Sam, for his manner is always distant and constrained.

Amy is a flirt. Her husband often questions her loyalty to him, for any man's affections seem as welcome to her as her husband's.

Irene is unkind to her children, slaps them and spanks them and scolds them—seldom showing them any tenderness.

We could go on almost endlessly with examples of the unhappiness that emotion causes, both to the person who suffers the fears, the depressions, the hatreds, and the ill tempers and to those who flinch at the anger, are hurt by the coldness, are saddened by the depressions, and recoil at the hatred of others.

On the other hand we could with equal ease find illustrations of the happiness that comes from kindness, sympathy, love, response to music and other forms of art, joy in success, and the like.

In the first place, you have but to look at your own life to see how much it is improved by friendship, love, sympathy, and kindness; and you have only to think of the times when you have been exhilarated by success to know what pleasure that feeling can give. We find other examples on all sides.

In one school system in a town of moderate size a few key people (the superintendent, the supervisor of the elementary schools, and the principal of the high school) have so set the tone of the emotional atmosphere of the school by their own kindness and generosity toward others that one feels this pleasantness in human relations throughout the student body. As a result it really seems that everyone in school enjoys his school life more than is usual.

In one small town a man who had retired from business and who was a great lover of gardens and flowers took it upon himself to interest the school children in them. He did this by making his own yard a place colorful with flowers, by keeping the classrooms supplied with flowering plants, by giving away seeds, offering prizes to young gardeners, and visiting and helping those children who started gardens. This happened seven years ago. Today that whole little town is garden and flower conscious as few towns are. Not only are the yards almost invariably beautiful, but also the townspeople and the children rejoice in that beauty. Here is a place where we see every life made happier by an emotional response to beauty.

If some miracle could free people from most of their proneness to fear, anger, hatred, jealousy, shame, and guilt feelings, endowing them at the same time with all of the generous feelings that go with love of others as well as with the uplifting feelings that go with religion and aesthetic appreciations, we should have a world infinitely happier than it is now.

No such miracle is going to occur, of course. We must work out our own salvation in this respect, each one of us. In addition, we have another obligation. Since we are also people who have responsibility for adolescents, we must help them, too, to become emotionally healthy. There is no doubt whatsoever that the right kind of parents and teachers for all children could help them grow into a generation of adults who were emotionally good for themselves and good for others. But such a universally wholesome setting for childhood is as yet no more than a dream. As for the adolescent, his childhood has been lived, and what was done for him for good or bad is beyond our control. Nor can we change his home setting right now if it is bad. But we *can* provide wholesome teachers for youth, and each of us should realize our strong responsibility for making ourselves and our behavior the kind that will promote not only our own emotional welfare but also that of our students.

One's emotions are of course intimately related to one's attempts to satisfy his basic needs, and very obviously when we talk about the adolescent's home life, heterosexual adjustment, social adjustment, and so on, we must consider his emotional adjustment also. Nevertheless it seems wise to abstract emotions from these areas, so to speak, and center our attention on them alone. The teacher must be able to look at the adolescent's development from many points of view, for only then will he know where the youth is lacking and where he is doing well in his development —and only then will he be fully aware of his own successes and failures in helping him.

First of all, the teacher must know what the adolescent should become, ideally, in his emotional development.

EMOTIONAL MATURITY

1. We would like to have the adolescent become an adult who is free of apprehensions, fears, and anxieties in regard to his relationships with people and in regard to what "the world" might do to him. Some people are ill-at-ease in social groups outside the family, minimize themselves in comparison with associates, wonder about their acceptance by others. Some people are likely to be overpessimistic; they have forebodings about evil, and their minds jump to an assumption of the worst when there is the slightest possibility of it.

In contrast to this, we would like to have the adolescent grow up to be an adult with personal security. This would mean that he would welcome new experience without fear, that he would have confidence in his own abilities, that he would be easy in all of his associations with others— forgetful of self and without undue strictures. Someone has said that the person who is thus secure can afford to be kindly and generous toward others and will be so. When we realize that the person who is blessed with security is likely to be both a happier and kindlier person than the one who is insecure, we should place this kind of emotional maturity high on our list of necessities for the adolescent.

2. We would like to have him be good-humored and little dependent upon anger. Irritation and anger are reactions to frustration. That is, when things don't go our way, we may respond by being cross, disgusted, or angry. Usually there are many other and better ways of meeting frustrations than anger—such as having patience with and tolerance for other people's mistakes, ignoring trivial interferences with one's desires, and using one's intelligence instead of one's emotions to manage the situations that defeat and thwart us. The fact that anger is more easily eradicated from the personality than is fear makes it the more imperative that adults feel it a necessity to rid themselves of this unlovely and generally fruitless emotion.

We have been thinking of anger chiefly in terms of irritability, ill-humor, temper, and the like, displays of emotion which are in themselves enough to make life uncomfortable and even highly disagreeable to those in the path of the outburst. But we also see cases of anger which result in cruel, ugly, and even criminal behavior. For example, a man angry with a dog kicks him brutally; a woman angry with a child slaps his face with bruising hard blows; a man angry with another pulls out a gun and shoots him. When we consider all of the ills which come from this emotion, we can see how important it is for the well-being of both the individual and of society to have adults in the world who are seldom angry, unless the anger leads to behavior that is to some truly good effect. This occurs rarely—chiefly when one is angry at injustice and is impelled by his anger to try to improve conditions.

3. We would like to have the adolescent become an adult able to forget himself in his love for others. We look at the adolescent and say: "How good it would be if we could ensure him happy relations with friends and family when he is grown." If we would do this, we must help the adolescent develop into the kind of person who can forget himself in his kindly feelings for others. It is true that everyone likes to be on the receiving end of affection and that we tend to love where we get something back—affection, attention, or service. Actually, however, only those people who can love others without thought of return can know the full pleasure of loving, pleasure which surpasses being loved and surpasses also any love which feeds secretly or unconsciously on the expectation of a return for the loving.

4. We would like to have him too intelligent about his emotions to be

misled by them or to be misled by others through them. We are emotional beings far more than we are intellectual ones, and our emotions are often improperly our guides to action.

Mothers, for example, are overprotective toward their children, impelled by their love and unaware that their love may be leading them astray and doing their children real harm. Fathers may say, "I want my child to have everything I didn't have" without questioning whether the actions their feelings dictate are for good or ill. Any one of us may make remarks which our feelings shape and yet be under the impression that we are speaking on the basis of thought. We may say, "I don't think he would be a good man for the job," "I think it's disgusting that they're raising the bus fare again," "Income taxes ought to be lowered," "That teacher ought to be fired," "She must be a very poor housekeeper," and in every case it is possible that we are giving expression to resentment, fear, hate, or some such emotion or sentiment rather than to thought. We may conclude that a nation is inferior to ours, a race should not be given equal privileges, a certain political figure should not receive a hearing solely because our emotions say so—and yet we may smugly think that we are using our intelligence in making these judgments.

Since emotions do not in any way indicate the rightness or wrongness of a thought, a remark, an action, or a decision, any reliance upon them for guidance without substantiating thought may lead to unwise action. Any emotion may move us to bad behavior or to good. Love can bring about disastrous acts. Anger might be the basis for a reform movement. Fear can lead to despicable cowardice, but it can also save a life. Emotion is not on the side of right or wrong, and it must not be relied upon as a guide. Consequently if our world is going to be marked by intelligent action, it must be marked by emotion that is checked by intelligence.

Emotion can make us the subjects of the will of others. Politicians, advertisers, and others whose welfare depends upon getting a mass of people to behave as *they* want and not upon conviction use this fact all of the time. The emotions of anger, fear, and love are energizing. They prepare one for action. If anyone can arouse enough fear in us and then give us directions as to how to use that fear, we are apt to act upon those directions without thought. Thus the advertiser can make us fearful of ill that may befall us and then say: "Buy this to protect yourself." On the basis of this emotion-plus-direction we buy.

In the civilized world there is *no* slave-making technique half so effective or so frequently used as that of the emotional appeal plus direction for action. As long as human beings will allow themselves to be victimized through emotion, so long will our communities and our countries be run by the few, often the unscrupulous few, who can thus mold public opinion and direct public behavior. As long as human beings will feel-and-act when they should think-and-act, so long will our purchases, our recreations, our reading be governed too much by those who can thus make a profit from us.

We would like to have the adolescent be an adult who knows when he is acting on the basis of emotion and who can then guard himself against unwise choices.

5. We would like to have the adolescent become an adult who can enjoy aesthetic experiences. There is much of this in the world to enjoy —in nature, in poetry, novels, painting, sculpturing, music, plays, and movies—all in such abundance that there are kinds to fit every taste and every ability.

We ask this for the adolescent because it is ennobling. A truly aesthetic experience lifts one from personal preoccupations into a partaking of something bigger than oneself. As Tolstoi says: "Art is a human activity having for its purpose the transmission to others of the highest and best feelings to which men have risen."

6. Finally, we would like the adolescent to become an adult who is capable of gayety and humor. It is very easy to get into the rut of un-relieved seriousness toward life. There are families who never lose themselves in gay conversational frivolity and in happy playfulness toward one another and whose lives are oversomber because of this lack. Any-one who has experienced living for some time with attention only to the serious and who then suddenly enters some light-hearted group where he can forget himself in gayety and fun knows that he has been missing something that his life needs.

In summary, then, we say that we would like to have the adolescent become an adult who has these emotional attributes:

1. He is secure and self-confident, free from the needless fears that beset so many people.
2. He is sweet-natured and little subject to anger and irritation.
3. He is able to forget himself in a wholehearted love of others.
4. He understands his emotions and is not led into foolish action through overreliance upon them.
5. He can enjoy some aesthetic experiences.
6. He is capable of gayety and humor.

If we are to help the adolescent achieve this kind of emotional adult-hood, we must understand what emotion is like as well as what the adoles-cent's particular emotional needs are, and we must also know how we can help him. In addition to the need to help him we must understand him also because we want to be able to work with him without the friction that comes from lack of sympathy.

WHAT IS THE NATURE OF EMOTION?

We can think of the three most prevalent emotions, anger, fear, and love, from three points of view; in doing so we shall have a good way of seeing how they hurt people and how they help them. For whenever a person is emotional, there is a change in his physiological behavior, a change in his mental activity, and—generally—some change in his outward behavior.

The Physiological Changes

The physiological changes that take place in fear and anger are changes that prepare the body for energetic action, that is, for running or for fighting. They are:

1. Release of sugar by the liver — Thus providing the voluntary muscles with the extra sugar they need for strong action

2. Increase in heartbeat — Thus propelling the blood with its extra sugar around the body faster

3. Increase in breathing — Thus providing more oxygen and ridding the body of carbon dioxide more speedily

4. Release of red blood corpuscles by the spleen — Thus providing more carriers of oxygen

5. Dilation of blood vessels to voluntary muscles — Thus sending the blood supply where it is most needed

6. Constriction of blood vessels to involuntary muscles — Thus conserving on blood where it is not needed

7. Slowing down in digestive movements — Thus saving on energy where it is not needed for the duration of the emergency

8. Tension of voluntary muscles — Thus readying them for action

9. Release of adrenin by the adrenal glands — Thus prolonging the actions above

These changes are brought about by the nervous system, but they are not under voluntary control. A section of the brain called the *hypothalamus* sends the impulses down the spinal cord and out the motor neurons which govern the involuntary muscles. This system of motor neurons whose cell bodies lie in the cord acts as a unit. All of the changes mentioned above are brought about in the twinkling of an eye when an anger-, fear-, or excitement-rousing situation presents itself.

It is believed that this emergency system which we have been describing developed in the animal and human body as a protection, for it is certainly true that it does provide extra energy for fighting or running. It seems equally true that the nervous system is so organized that it learns very fast, though often blindly, what situations are "emergency" situations, and gradually the person develops a push-button speed in turning on the emergency reaction. This blind learning we call *conditioning*. For any one of us some words, some people, and some situations will automatically bring on this emergency reaction.

We have been speaking of anger and fear. In the other emotion which we shall discuss, love, we have a somewhat (though not wholly) different body reaction. We do not have as many data from research in regard to love as we have for anger and fear, but we do know that there is a heightening of the energy-supplying activities combined with highly pleasurable sensations. Except for a short period, the increase in heartbeat, breathing, and the like, is a mild one, and the reaction generally provides little wear and tear on the body.

These physiological reactions in anger, fear, and love serve the individual wonderfully well at times, but on some occasions they are detrimental. To evaluate emotion, then, we must first consider the worth or harm of these body reactions.

When we must fight or when we must run, it is extremely advantageous to have the body supplied with the means for prolonged and strenuous effort. But when we are physically inactive, that speeding up of the bodily processes may well be wasteful or even harmful. The sugar, for example, goes into the urine as waste if it is not used. Digestion is interfered with, the heart may suffer strain, the muscular tension may bring on insomnia.

In other words, the physical reaction of emotion is often useless—and, more than that, wasteful and even injurious to the health.

Mental Activity

Second, emotion can be considered from the point of view of the mental activity involved. What there is to be said is so obvious that it need only be touched upon. The mental activity in fear and anger is unpleasant. That involved in love is pleasant. Whenever fear or anger comes into our lives, unpleasantness enters in. Whenever love is experienced, we add something pleasant to our living.

Outer Behavior

Third, we should consider the outer behavior which each of these emotions is likely to stir into action. In general:

Fear brings avoidance reactions. This is good when there is something which will actually endanger us if we stay in its presence. It is bad when it prevents our having experiences which might be of worth to us. If because of fear we run away from work, decisions, social situations, and the like, we lose the strength to handle the difficult and we miss the opportunity to enjoy all that we might in life.

Anger brings aggressive reactions. This is good on the few occasions where attack brings wholesome results. Usually, however, it results in quarrels, harsh words, blows, gossip, temper outbursts, assault, or even killing—and in many cases irreparable damage to relationships or to persons may occur.

Love brings movement toward the loved object, and as we all know, it tends to generate protective and pleasing actions.

A Final Evaluation

In the final analysis, then, this may be said:

Fear is generally unwholesome for the person who harbors it. His body may be harmed if too often there is a speeding up of energy production without use, his mental attitude is unpleasant, and he has an avoidant attitude toward many experiences which would make his life pleasanter and more worth while if he could take part in them.

Anger is unpleasant for the person who harbors it, both mentally and physically. The angry person has disagreeable thoughts monopolizing his mind, and his bodily activity is upset. The person who is the object of the anger suffers.

Love on the whole is good physiologically and mentally, bringing a toning up of the body and pleasant thoughts. The activity that love sponsors makes both the doer and the receiver of the action happier.

WHAT IS THE ADOLESCENT LIKE EMOTIONALLY?

If we are to be on good terms with the adolescent, if we are to adjust ourselves to him, if we are to avoid rousing fears and angers in him, if we are to set the stage of his life so that he can be happy, if we are to help him when he is emotionally upset, if we are to help him get over emotional traits which are bad for him—then we must understand what the adolescent is like emotionally.

We must understand far beyond what we are able to observe. For the emotions of the adolescent often do not show themselves to the casual onlooker or even, many times, to the careful observer. For example, a small group of high school juniors and seniors were invited to visit an adolescent psychology class in order that the college students might receive authentic information concerning adolescent recreational interests, home problems, and the like, through questioning the visiting boys and girls on these matters. The sixteen- and seventeen-year-olds all seemed remarkably poised and at ease. But at the end of the period one college student put this question to them: "How many of you felt distinctly ill-at-ease while sitting here with us and answering questions?" All but two of the teen-agers raised their hands.

Perhaps we cannot depend too much on this response to the question, for some of the boys and girls may have answered in the affirmative just because others did or on the basis of only a slight feeling of uneasiness. But the illustration still gives evidence of the fact that we cannot judge an adolescent's emotional state by what appears on the surface. If we are to know how he is feeling, we must instead have some idea of what to expect and also learn to recognize the small symptoms of hidden emotions.

In addition, we must not be disturbed by emotional states which would be undesirable in the adult but which are characteristic of adolescence. The moody adult, for example, would seem immature to us; the moody adolescent is likely to be nothing more than *adolescent*.

What is the adolescent like emotionally? The answer is: He is unstable, he is moody, he is self-conscious. . . . It must be understood, however, that these descriptions of the emotional nature of the adolescent cannot be applied to every adolescent by any means. Actually all that can be said of these characteristics is that they are found *more often* among adolescents than among adults. This qualification should be kept in mind in reading the pages that follow.

1. The adolescent is unstable. Embarrassment, anger, excitement, and emotional responses to other sex are often touched off very readily in him and are sometimes far more intense than the situation warrants. There are three possible reasons for this. One is that the glandular changes in the body seem to make for greater susceptibility to emotional stimulation. In other words, the body itself is more excitable. Another is that life itself is less stable for him than for either preadolescent or adult. There is now more cause for home conflict, a greater variety of social stimulation, more social competition, and more adult pressure toward conformity when there is less willingness to conform. The third is that the pubertal changes and adolescent social uncertainties engender in many enough insecurity to keep them in a state of slight emotional tension for con-

siderable periods of time. This would make other emotional responses occur more quickly and with greater force than would be true in a secure person.

This instability shows itself in many ways. An adolescent girl, when reproved by her father for coming to the breakfast table in her dressing gown, lashed back at him in a fury of harsh words, to her mild-mannered father's astonishment. An adolescent boy in study hall, shown a cartoon just drawn by a neighboring boy, burst out into a guffaw of laughter that startled the whole room and then was lost in painful embarrassment at the attention he had attracted. An adolescent girl cordially greeted some relative who had come to call but, upon being told in jest that she was getting fat, withdrew into a sulky silence which she maintained for the duration of their visit.

2. The adolescent is moody. We shall use this expression to mean what it so often does imply when the adolescent is being discussed—that he frequently has spells of being downcast, glum, or depressed. One reason for this is that he experiences more fancied failures and, with his ambitious expectations, more cutting disappointments than does the child or the adult. Another is that he is beginning to recognize his own help-lessness in manipulating his world to his satisfaction and he is beginning to sense how impersonal the world may be toward him, his troubles, and his desires. Then, of course, he is interested in himself and leans toward introspection. He is attentive to his own feelings, and since a state of melancholy often gives both some pleasure and some sense of importance, he easily gives way to it unless he is too busily occupied with other in-teresting activities to take the time.

3. The adolescent is self-conscious. He has feelings of uneasiness in re-gard to how he appears to others. The much-used phrase "in an agony of self-consciousness" may seem an exaggeration to the adult who has never experienced acute self-consciousness or who has forgotten how it feels, but for some adolescents it actually expresses the painfulness of the state. Self-consciousness occurs with many an adolescent whenever he is the center of attention—when a direct remark is addressed to him by someone whom he doesn't know very well or of whom he is in awe, when he must walk in front of some assembled group, when he must speak to some audience, when something happens to call attention to him in a social gathering. At such times he may be so intensely aware of himself that his whole body is tight-muscled and unmanageable and his mind overridden with reports of this body awkwardness and tenseness.

Often, of course, the feeling is less strong, as in this adolescent's de-scription of self-consciousness:

"The feeling is very hard to describe. First you have a nervousness.

.Second, you wish you could faint or something to get out of whatever you are going to do. Then when it is over, you feel very relieved. This happens whenever I give a speech on some subject or a talk about myself. I keep wondering if I am saying the right thing. Then I wonder if I am standing correctly. I wonder how my clothes look, if they are mussed or if my hose are straight. I wonder if my posture is all right. Then I see some girls that don't like me very well. Maybe they think I am terrible or that they could do better, and probably they could. What if I should forget my talk? Maybe I'm not talking loud enough.

"I know I feel self-conscious because people are watching me. I think I would feel better if they would turn their backs to me and listen that way to what I am saying."

Two other accounts follow:

"I really don't know how to start this because I've never said anything about this to anyone. I just put on a big act that nothing bothers me and just go on. My trouble is in feeling self-conscious with people I've known for a long time—people that I know well enough to speak to but haven't been real friendly with. Strangers don't bother me. It's the people I know and yet somehow don't know.

"When I'm with them, I often feel almost sick inside and as if I weren't wanted. I feel as if it would be just awful if I said or did anything wrong. I feel as if they're all watching me. I just want to start running, but of course I stay and stick it out.

"I guess feelings like this come with growing up." (*Senior boy*.)

"Feeling self-conscious is one of my traits which shows up often. For that reason I do not like to do things in which I am on a stage or platform. When I walk across the stage I feel as if something terrible will happen. Then I become clumsy and sometimes I do trip and fall or do something equally embarrassing simply because I am afraid that I will. When I stand in front of a crowd my shoulders feel as if they are sagging and my posture feels terrible. I dislike, too, to walk in front of a group of girls because I think they are all staring at me." (*Freshman boy*.)

4. The adolescent is inexperienced in handling a new emotional response, love for someone of the opposite sex. Since this emotion has such strength as to overwhelm adults who are undergoing its full intensity, it shoud be no wonder that it sometimes proves unmanageable to the adolescent, who has far less acquaintance with it. One should not be surprised by the fact that he is at times embarrassed by the attractions he feels, is sometimes impelled to hide his feelings, and sometimes is so carried away by the emotion that thoughts of the loved one preoccupy him completely. The younger adolescent particularly can easily be teased, may look completely uninterested in someone of the opposite sex who is

actually very exciting to him, or may be carried away by his feelings and act giddy and uncontrolled. It is difficult for the adult to realize just how overpowering, disconcerting, or unmanageable this sex excitement may be to someone who is experiencing it for the first time or for the not much more than first time, but he should at least recognize the fact that the adolescent is justified in engaging in extravagant or out-of-the-ordinary behavior when he is under the influence of a powerful attraction to someone of the other sex.

5. The adolescent is "touchy." In the eyes of the adult he is oversensitive to criticism, to reprimands, or to slights. Sometimes a seemingly trivial remark or act will bring forth in him an outburst of tears, anger, or sulking out of all proportion to the cause.

In one school the freshman class customarily entertains the freshman class of a certain neighboring school at a banquet. One day the fourteen-year-old freshman president came to the class sponsor and threw her speech of welcome on his desk. "You'll have to find someone else to give this speech," she said.

"But why?" asked the sponsor.

"It doesn't matter why," she answered. "I'm not going to give it." Then out she stalked. The sponsor inquired of other students what the trouble was and finally received this explanation:

That morning, this girl had chanced to remark to a group of acquaintances that she was worried about not giving her speech right. One of the group had responded rather sarcastically: "Getting mighty important these days, aren't you?"

That was enough to spoil everything. Without another word the girl went to the sponsor's room and delivered her ultimatum. It took much persuading by the sponsor and the girl's friends to get her to change her mind.

Such behavior as this is understandable. The adolescent is often insecure, both in his relationships with adults and in those with his peers. He already has feelings of resentment against the demands of parents and teachers, which some small incident may touch off, and he already has some feelings of unworthiness or lack of success in respect to his comrades, which nothing more than a word may call forth full-flowered.

6. The adolescent is giggly. The author remembers having in a freshman college psychology class during the war eight boys of seventeen on an accelerated plan of work amidst a much older group of students. Some of the discussions, of serious concern to the older students, would set this row of boys giggling, and though they obviously tried to control themselves, they were sometimes unable to do so. Three of the boys came to the teacher's office to explain. They would be listening seriously to

class discussion, they said, when something would remind them of a personal experience in which they had all engaged, and this would set them to giggling. Each effort at control just seemed to make things worse.

One sophomore boy tells about sitting in church during a Sunday service and having his eleven-year-old brother whisper something to him about the minister which seemed extremely funny. He made an effort to control himself but without success. A loud giggle came out, to startle all of the people in his vicinity and to embarrass both the boy and his family greatly.

Adults may have the same sort of predisposing experience, but it is very rare for them to giggle, let alone to have a spell of giggling which they cannot control. Why is the adolescent so susceptible? Partly, because he is still a child and laughs freely as a child will laugh—and as an adult has learned not to laugh on many occasions. Partly, he giggles because, as we said earlier, his body—in the process of change—is more easily excited. Still a third reason may be that since giggling often occurs in situations where it is not fitting, there may have been some tension first, a sudden break in that tension through laughter, and then a reaction with such loosening of control as to bring on giggling.

7. The adolescent is easily carried away by excitement.

A seventeen-year-old girl who had been driving for almost a year and who was a steady, sensible person at the wheel was taking two other girls and three boys to a football game in a nearby town. The highway runs parallel to a railroad line for several miles at one spot, and just as they reached this point a streamliner came along. As chance had it, the car and the engine were exactly even for a few moments. Then the train began to pull ahead. "Race it, Mary," said one of the boys. "Race it!" the others echoed him. "It's gaining on you. Don't let it get away. Step on it, step on it!"

Sensible, dependable Mary put her foot down hard on the accelerator and until the train track and highway diverged tore along recklessly at the fast speed of the train, something that her father would have depended upon her to be too mature to do.

Giving away to excitement in crowd situations is the pattern of behavior which adults expect of the adolescent on many occasions. This may in part account for that type of response. Further, the adolescent *is* more excited by adventure and sports, not having had the time to become blasé about such things.

8. The adolescent is easily embarrassed. Embarrassment is not well understood, but the conjecture that it is often indirectly associated with sex feelings, in many cases unconscious, would explain the fact that the adolescent is much more apt to be embarrassed than the child. Another

factor to explain the proneness of some adolescents to embarrassment is their desire to appear mature and even sophisticated—and their frequent failures. In their own eyes, they fall so short of what is expected of them that they do seem childish and ridiculous.

A freshman boy playing basketball in a preliminary game stooped suddenly and very solemnly and painstakingly tied a shoelace which had come undone. His preoccupation with his task and his innocent unawareness of the fact that he had stopped the game made the audience burst into laughter. When he rose from his stooping position and became aware of the fact that the audience was laughing at him, he was so embarrassed that he began to cry.

9. The adolescent may have worries about his pubescent changes and about sex behavior. This has already been discussed in Chap. 4. Therefore we shall only remind the reader here of the fact that the adolescent may at times, and even for long periods, be in some tension because he is afraid that he will not become, physically, what he would like to be, because he is worried over masturbation or seminal emissions, or because, with the girl, the approach of each menstrual period may bring on premenstrual depression or irritability.

10. He is sometimes hesitant about expressing emotions even though their expression may be perfectly acceptable socially. Some adolescents will keep a blank face, or even frown, when bubbling with elation within; some will act disdainful toward those who awaken the warmest feelings in them; and some will turn away and act unconcerned when their emotional response is really considerable.

A group of five boys were standing at a filling station when the much-liked high school principal of the preceding year, now alumni director of a nearby college, drove by.

"Hi, boys!" he called.

"Hi," they responded and then moved their position or looked away as if completely untouched at meeting their former friend. What warmth of feeling may have been hidden beneath their appearance of unconcern one can only guess at.

WHAT MAKES THE ADOLESCENT EMOTIONAL?

What makes the adolescent emotional? Though we have already considered the cause with some emotions, let us look at what adolescents say:

Embarrassment

"As long as I can remember—as long as anyone can remember probably —my father has been a strong pillar of our church. Nevertheless it has been a weakness of our family to suffer great difficulty in arriving at the little country church in time for Sunday School. We really do try hard. Sunday School starts at ten o'clock, but only too often we slip in at ten-fifteen or so. I am sure that some of the good church people sympathize with my mother who has to get all of us shined up and ready to go, but it is still embarrassing to me to go in late.

"On this particular Sunday morning about which I write, things were different. To the whole family's annoyance, the storm had taken down the telephone line, the radio had blown a tube, and the blamed clock wasn't working. So we guessed at the time by the sun and rushed madly to get to church. I was worried sick for fear church would be completely over, because I was sensitive to being late at all and the sun seemed higher than usual.

"I felt funny when we got there. Not a car was in sight. I was just feeling thankful that we had missed the whole thing and hadn't the embarrassment of meeting people going home, when the minister came out of his house near by and we found out that we were not late, but an hour early!

"When church began, I wasn't paying too much attention until the service began to take on a personal tone. For the minister began his sermon by saying, jokingly, that it might be better if everyone threw away his clock—and then he told the story of our coming early. Everyone in church laughed and stared at us and my face got redder and redder. I had escaped one embarrassment to encounter a worse one just when I was feeling so smug. I couldn't enjoy any of the service after that. I imagined that everyone was thinking about our mistake and I dreaded the time for church to be over when I would have to face people." (*Junior girl.*)

"One time when I was in a neighboring town, I saw ahead of me a boy I thought was a pal of mine. I hurried up to him, slapped him on the back, and said hello. When he turned around, I saw that it was a stranger. I was so embarrassed, I didn't know what to do, but just walked off in a hurry." (*Sophomore boy.*)

"In math class this morning I had very bad posture and our math teacher called me up to her desk and told me I should stand up straight. After I did, she asked the class if I didn't look better. That was the most embarrassing moment I have had in school." (*Freshman boy.*)

"On my first day at school the study hall teacher embarrassed me so much that I felt like two cents. When he gave me my seat assignment, he told me I had to be real quiet. He said it loud enough so that some of the other boys and girls could hear it. I don't believe I was ever embarrassed so much in all my life. I hope I don't have to go through that again." (*Freshman boy.*)

"My most embarrassing moment happened about two weeks ago when some of my boy friends walked into the house just when my mother and dad were having an argument. I was in the living room reading, and don't think I wasn't embarrassed." (*Junior boy.*)

"My most embarrassing moment in the last two weeks was when I went in to class late the other day. Everyone looked up and I couldn't even think to give the teacher my excuse for being absent but went right to my seat. She had to ask me for my excuse and I had to walk up in front with it. When it was all over I was certainly relieved." (*Sophomore girl.*)

"When the sophomores decided to have their skating party, I wanted to ask a boy, but I put it off as long as I could. One morning I saw him walking down the hall and I thought that this would be as good a time to ask him as any. While I was asking him, my face turned red and I felt real embarrassed because everyone seemed to be watching us." (*Freshman girl.*)

"My most embarrassing time in school is when my girl friend comes up to talk to me." (*Freshman boy.*)

"One day just after I went out of sixth period, I was walking up the stairs to study hall and there were several students behind me. One of them stepped on my heel and my shoe came off. I had to wait until all the students behind me got up the stairs and then put my shoes on. Everyone laughed and it about embarrassed me to death." (*Freshman girl.*)

"One day after the last bell had rung, I was going to history class and went by way of the study hall. Just as I walked in the door everyone started laughing. I later found out that everyone was laughing about something the study hall teacher had just said. I thought they were laughing at me for some reason or other and it really got me. I don't know when I've been so embarrassed." (*Sophomore boy.*)

"Last Monday during my noon hour I had just come down from the study hall. While I was walking, I was reading an interesting book. I came down the north stairs and started to the home economics room, but I was very much embarrassed on the way.

"I wasn't paying any attention to where I was going. Opening a door that I thought was the home economics room, I walked into Miss ———'s English class.

"I was so embarrassed that I really don't know how I got out of there. I remember that everyone just looked at me and I at them. No one laughed, for which I was thankful. If there had been a hole in the floor, I would have gladly fallen into it." (*Junior girl.*)

"We were discussing voices and so on in class one day because we are having a unit on public speaking. Suddenly the teacher told me to say something. I couldn't think of anything to say, but I finally got something out. Miss _____ asked the class to comment on my voice. When they were through, she looked at me and said she rather liked my voice. It has a nice tone, she said, he speaks loud enough, and he has a pleasant characteristic drawl. I could just feel my face getting red. I don't know why, but I was certainly embarrassed." (*Junior boy.*)

Anger

"On Thursday of last week I decided to drive the car to school the following day because I supposed it was going to be very cold. I asked one of my neighbor girls if she and her sister wanted to ride. She said they would. I told her to come by at 7:45.

"When the time came, they had not arrived. I waited about ten minutes, and then went on to school. When I got there, she was already there. I asked, 'Say, where were you this morning?' She said, 'We stood out in the road and called to you, but when you didn't come, we went on.'

"Oh, that made me mad. How did she think I could hear them out there? I usually have the radio on, and they know it. I thought they would come to the door. If she thought that I wanted her to ride so bad that I would stand on the porch, in the cold, to see when they went by, I'll be darned if I would. Who does she think she is?" (*Junior girl.*)

"This happened one day in the fifth hour physical education class. We were playing soccer that week. I was defendinig my team's goal—that is, whenever the ball came into the semicircle around our goal, I was either to kick the ball or pick it up and throw it downfield as far as I could. Howard and Kenny, of the other team, came up the field with the ball, kicking it back and forth from one to the other, and got it into the circle. It rolled past me and stopped just outside the goal line. I turned, made a dive for it, and got it, but it didn't do any good. Because the teacher told Howard and Kenny to put me over the goal line; so they grabbed hold of me and dragged me across.

"I was good and mad at the teacher and I told him so. Just last week he had said we weren't to use hands on anyone at any time, and here he actually told Howard and Kenny to drag me through the goal line. He said, 'If you think you can do a better job of teaching than I can, maybe you'd better try it.' I replied, 'You told us last week that we couldn't use our hands. If I told one thing once, I wouldn't turn right around and tell the opposite the next week.'" (*Sophomore boy.*)

"I don't know why, but I never did like Latin. I struggled through one year of it and here I am taking it again, all because my mother insisted. One thing, especially, that I can't stand is the Latin scrapbook. I don't mind scrapbooks if they help you with the subject and give you a clearer picture of it, but the Latin scrapbooks are far from that. The other day one of our assignments for the scrapbook was to take all of the words we had in our vocabulary and get pictures for their meanings. One of the words was *love;* so we get a picture of a girl and boy kissing. Another word was *battle;* so we get a picture of a dog and cat fighting. How in the world are we going to get anything out of Latin by doing this sort of thing? I come home from school and spend the evening looking for pictures that don't help me at all. Another page in our scrapbook is the humor page. We come to class and copy jokes from the board. Example:

"Professor: What does *rex fugit* mean?

"Student: The king flees.

"Professor: Make it present tense.

"Student: The king has flees.

"These jokes are funny, but that is as far as it goes and I would like to know how these things help you to get Latin. All they do is to take up your time. All of this makes me angry." (*Sophomore girl.*)

"I don't get angry very often, but when I do, I want to blow my top. I had an experience in Typing the other day that really made me angry. We had to type business letters and couldn't hand any in with mistakes in them. My machine always skips and I couldn't get any letter perfect no matter how much I tried. Finally I explained this to the typing teacher, showing him the letter I was working on. All he said was, 'Too bad, Jean,' and went on.

"Right then I thought plenty. I believe in treating people fair and in them treating me fair. This was too much. I didn't say anything, but I spent the rest of the time in that class thinking mean things about the teacher." (*Junior girl.*)

"What is more disgusting than for a teacher to make a big assignment when you have other studies to do and a day of other activities? It was the morning of October 27, the day of Homecoming. We went into Shorthand, had our lesson, and then just before the bell rang, she gave us a huge assignment for Monday. Of course that night was the game and the dance. Saturday I have to help my mother. That meant that I had to leave everything for Sunday, and it spoiled my weekend to look ahead to that much work." (*Junior girl.*)

"My girl friend, whom I trusted with some information that I didn't want talked about since it was about a boy, went and called him up and told him that I liked him. This not only made me angry at her but also made him very angry at me. She is not my best friend any more." (*Freshman girl.*)

"I don't mind helping some student with his lesson if I know how to get it and he doesn't. If I can explain it to him so that he understands, I don't mind the time it takes. But when I work all period getting my lesson or maybe take it home and then some student comes along and copies it down in four or five minutes, that gets under my skin. I believe in working for what you earn and getting it honestly. I don't want students to get the wrong impression about me, but after all you don't learn anything from copying." (*Junior girl.*)

"My history teacher makes me very angry. She is so very inconsiderate. I have honestly tried to be kind to her and to do my best work, but I believe it is just a waste of time. The thing that makes me the most angry is that when I ask her a question she just looks at me as if I were dumb. So I'm not smart! Well, teachers are supposed to help the poor dumb kids as well as the brainy ones. A few students are her pets and when they ask her questions she always answers them in the nicest manner. I wish she would treat everyone alike.

"Another thing is my grades in her class. I don't think I should get an A or B, but I do think I should get a C because I work very hard. She gives me a D or a D—, and so I'm supposed to sit and smile about it!

"Some people say she is just nervous, but if she is that nervous, I can't understand why she is hired year after year. She is a headache to some of us students, just as some of us are a headache to her." (*Sophomore girl.*)

"One evening we were all waiting for the bell to ring down in the P.E. room. In about five minutes it rang and we all rushed for the door. As soon as we got out, someone started a snowball fight. I didn't stick around long to see it because one of the fellows who was throwing always likes to pick on me. He only stands about six feet two inches and weighs about 175 pounds, but still he likes to pick on me because I am so much smaller. So I didn't stick around for the fight. Instead I went to sit in the car I always ride home in. What did this fellow do but open the door and hit me with a water-soaked snowball right between the eyes. Boy, was I mad! I climbed out of the car, picked up a snowball to hit him with, but he caught me, took my coat in his grip, and scrubbed me around in the snow and water. I wouldn't feel so bad about it if I had deserved it, but this time I didn't do a single thing to him." (*Sophomore boy.*)

"In my business class the teacher had us file a hundred and seventy cards in two days and these were the two days of the senior class play. I told the teacher that I was in the play and didn't have time to file all those cards. She said I had to get them in. I couldn't help it. I got them in late. After doing all that work, she wouldn't accept them. This is when I blew my top. This didn't flunk me for the six weeks, but it knocked my grade in the head." (*Senior boy.*)

"In this class I am writing about I had always had my lesson prepared and had made A's on tests (without cheating). But on one Monday morning I couldn't remember anything I had read on Friday. We had a class discussion and the teacher asked me a question which I couldn't answer. Then she went on and asked me question after question and I finally got so mad that I don't think I would have answered her if I had known the answers. She made matters worse by giving me a lecture in front of the class about people who could make A's on tests and didn't know anything in class." (*Sophomore girl.*)

"A few days ago a certain person in the office said, Harold, I'd like to see you in the office. I said that as soon as I had reported to class I'd come to the office. When I got there, this person said, Harold, what do you have against me?

"I said, Not a thing.

"Then he said, Why did you throw that snowball at me?

"I said, I'm sorry, but I don't know what you're getting at.

"He said, Don't go beating around the bush.

"Then I got mad and said, I don't know what this is all about. Where did it take place?

"He said, Over on Walnut Street. Yesterday noon.

"I wasn't even over there, I said.

"Well, maybe I got the wrong person, he answered. Do you know who did do it?

"I was so mad I could hardly talk. But all I said was, No. But after this, don't go accusing people of things they didn't do. Then I walked out." (*Junior boy.*)

Feeling "Blue"

"I really feel blue every morning about the third period. That is when I have bookkeeping. In the first place I didn't want to take it, but my folks made me. Every morning I go to that class and work exercises and problems which I don't understand too well. When we discuss the problems I seem to understand them, but when it comes to a test, I don't get them. Each problem has to be done just right or the whole thing is wrong and I am always confused." (*Sophomore boy.*)

"After the third hour I have study hall and then typing. We have been having time tests in typing and that is where I fall down. I can type a letter without making many mistakes but when it comes to speed I just haven't got it. I wish I had a typewriter of my own to practice on. I wish I were out of school because I don't like it. When you're making poor grades and can't seem to bring them up, school makes you very blue." (*Junior boy.*)

"I feel blue about half of the time. When I am feeling blue I am angry with the whole world. I always feel blue when I have to get school work outside of school. I almost always feel blue when I'm at school. I don't like it, that's all there is to it." (*Sophomore boy*.)

"When I feel blue, I feel as if I could cry my eyes out. I don't want anyone to say a word to me. If someone says something I don't like, I start crying. I feel so down-hearted. I don't care if I live or die." (*Freshman girl*.)

"I don't know what makes me feel blue. I guess I just get up on the wrong side of bed. When I am feeling blue, nothing goes right all day long. I don't want anything to do with people, I just want them to leave me alone. I will go out of my way and do extra work just to avoid mixing with people. When I am spoken to, I give a short and complete answer and then escape as soon as possible. In the classroom at such a time my mind wanders and I am not a good listener.

"When I am blue, I find things boring and want to keep busy doing something, but not with other people. The best cure I have found for this blue feeling is to take a long walk by myself or do something else that will exhaust me." (*Senior girl*.)

"I can't seem to describe very well how I feel when I am blue. Once when my girl and I weren't on speaking terms, I felt so blue that I was lower than a toadstool. I wasn't just mad at her, I was mad at everybody. I couldn't have a good time at the basketball games or any place else. I really felt bad. Finally my girl called me up and said she would forgive me if I would do the same. I agreed and everything seemed to clear up so that once again I was sitting on top of the world." (*Senior boy*.)

Fear

"A long, long time ago—really a little over three years ago—I was a freshman. What freshman isn't frightened in high school for about the first six weeks? I remember my freshman year very well. From the moment we graduated from the eighth grade we dreaded the next year when we would enroll in high school. I think I was probably more scared than any of the rest. When I came to school in the morning—which was, by the way, at a very early hour so that not many people would be there —I would go straight to a seat in the assembly and there remain until the bell rang and the assembly was deserted. From there I would trot off to my classes. In the class rooms I was also scared. When I was called upon to recite I would not be certain of anything I would say and that would make matters worse." (*Senior girl*.)

"One night I was baby-sitting at the Johnsons, who had gone to a party out at the Country Club. Their little girl was in bed asleep. It was around ten o'clock and everything was quiet except for the radio. I was reading a book when the back door opened and I heard someone come in. My first thought was to go over to the neighbor's and get help. But then I decided that maybe I had better see who it was. I went to the front stairs and heard him go down the back stairs. I was just shaking all over. I started for the kitchen when I heard who ever it was come down the front stairs. I started for the front stairs when I heard him go back up stairs. I didn't know what to do. I went into the kitchen and there on the stairs I could see half a man. I cleared my throat and asked him if he was looking for the Johnsons. I guess he could tell that I was scared, for he looked me up and down and finally asked me if I was taking care of Ginny. I said that I was and that the Johnsons had gone out for the evening. He told me not to worry, that he just wanted to borrow two quarts of milk. He got the milk and told me to tell the Johnsons that Bob had been there. He then left.

"I found a chair and sat down before I fainted with fright. What if the Johnsons didn't know a Bob? It would be my fault.

"An hour passed before the Johnsons came home. When I told them the story, Mrs. Johnson began to laugh. Bob was her brother-in-law. Just the same, I could hardly sleep that night. I have never been so scared in my life." (*Junior girl.*)

"When the last bell rang in the English room, everyone started quieting down because we knew that we were going to have to give an oral report.

"Our English teacher went to the back of the room and asked if anyone would like to be first, but no one answered. Everyone was so very much afraid that we hardly dared to breathe. When she saw that no one was going to give his report, she started calling on certain ones, picking us by the way we were seated in certain rows.

"This really had me worried because I was the third one in the row that she began in. It wasn't a matter of whether or not I knew what I was going to talk about, because I had been working on it for at least two weeks. It was just that I was afraid to get up in front of those kids. I would have missed school that day but I knew that I'd just have to give the report the next day anyway.

"Finally it was my time, and so when the English teacher called my name, I rose and walked slowly to the front of the room. I felt that everyone was watching me. It made me feel that they were making fun of me right before my very eyes.

"The class had given so much attention to the other reports after the were finished, that I felt now that mine wasn't much good, but I had picked that subject and now there was nothing to do but give it.

"Our teacher had told us to try to look at the class, not at the floor or out the window, but I couldn't do that although I tried awfully hard to. As I went on with the talk, I began to feel easier about it, but I never did get so that I could look at the class.

"Finally it was over. I took my seat and felt wonderful that I was all through with my talk." (*Junior boy*.)

"This is what I am afraid of. It happened one afternoon that I was going around the corner that leads to the study hall when the bell rang to dismiss the students that eat the sixth hour. Out of the study hall the students came like a stampede of wild horses. If I hadn't ducked in behind the corner, they would have trampled me under." (*Freshman girl*.)

"Five years ago this month my grandmother died. It happened just four days before Christmas. She died in her sleep and ever since I have been afraid to go to sleep at night. I know that sounds very childish and silly, but I think that I was just at the age when things like that impress you very much. I think the little prayer I used to say, Now I lay me down to sleep, I pray the Lord my soul to keep, If I should die before I wake, I pray the Lord my soul to take, had something to with it too. I pray that some day I can forget all this nonsense but I don't know if I can or not." (*Junior girl*.)

"When there are dances I'm afraid to go because I don't know how to dance and no one will show me how. People would make fun of me if went because I couldn't dance and they can all dance so well." (*Freshman boy*.)

"The one thing that I have been afraid of in school is going to the general science room and taking a test without having a discussion on the material first. So I'm afraid of getting a D or F on it and having to take t over again next year. I try hard too but I'm never sure that I know nough." (*Freshman boy*.)

"I suppose I have never learned Mrs. _____'s personality and her ctions. Ever since the beginning of this year she has made me afraid when he would bawl the class out. She would never smile while she was doing o but would always look very cross. I have dreaded going to this class nore and more each day. After the first six weeks we started sewing and hings changed some. When she comes around to see our sewing it lways gives me the jitters. It just seems like I can't conquer the fear etween us. It seems to me like a wall is between us. It is a terrible feeling nd I hope some day I can conquer this." (*Freshman girl*.)

"Something that has made me afraid is that I don't know what to do hen I am called to the board. I don't know how to work the stuff and every time I am called on I just shake. The teacher never helps you with anything." (*Freshman boy*.)

"I am afraid to recite in class. When a question is asked I am afraid to answer it. If I don't give the right answer, some of the kids will make fun of me. If I am absolutely sure of the answer I will give it. But if I am not sure, I will say I don't know, or, better, shake my head *no*." (*Freshman boy*.)

"This is what I am afraid of—tests in English. Before we take a test, Mrs. _____, our teacher, says that she will send us to the office if we get an F. Last time we got our papers back she said for all of us who got an F to hold up our hands. My hand was the only one. This was very painful to me." (*Freshman boy*.)

Summarizing the Causes of Emotion

If we were to give one simple answer to the question "What makes the adolescent emotional?" it would be "People." He loves—people. He is embarrassed when he does something stupid, too revealing, childish, or ridiculous in sight of others. He is "blue" when people disappoint him. He is angry when people interfere with his rights, privileges, or conveniences. He is afraid of what people will do to him or of falling short of people's expectations of him. Of course there are exceptions, but in the main the setting for the adolescent's emotions is social.

The immediate causes[1] of each of several emotions may be suggested by the following summary:

Affection for someone of the opposite sex	The answer is obvious
Embarrassment	Being teased about someone of the opposite sex
	Any act which makes him seem funny, ridiculous, or naive to other
	Being made conspicuous through clothing not like that of the group or in other ways
	Any act of his parents, seen or heard about, which makes them objects of pity, humor, or ridicule in a group
	Praise, sometimes
	Family status, family morals, father's occupation, when they are lower in quality or prestige than those of his friends
	Forced association with some student whom other student disparage
	Mistakes made in the presence of others which seem humiliating to him
	Deficiencies in appearance (such as bad complexion) or in physical development

[1] It should be understood that these are not inevitably stimuli to the emotion mentioned.

Depression	Physical sluggishness or lack of buoyancy
	A disappointment
	Social failures or slights; other failures
	Humiliations suffered
	Family difficulties
Anger	Unfair treatment by teachers, parents, or friends
	Unfair treatment of members of family
	Cruel treatment of any child or of pets
	Encroachment on his rights by brothers or sisters
	Being refused some privilege
	Being treated too much as a child by his parents
	Having something go wrong that he is trying to do
Fear	Giving a talk before the class
	Anticipating adult reaction to misbehavior or accidents with adult property
	Teacher's sarcasm or ridicule
	Being sent to the principal
	The prospect of being placed in an embarrassing situation
	Having to do something beyond his capabilities
	Death
Worry*	Tests
	Any public performance
	Illness of members of family
	The prospect of the first date
	Quarrels between parents
	Pubertal development, its normalcy
	Physical development—too tall, too short, too fat, bad complexion, too big a nose, and the like

* Though worry involves fear, it is not like many fears, for it is characterized by a repeated mental rehearsal of the situation feared.

THE POSITIVE APPROACH ON THE PART OF THE TEACHER

Since emotional health and emotional maturity are so important, the teacher must have a program which will embody a positive attempt to further these qualities. That program can be expressed in terms of three types of directives: what the teacher should *be;* how the teacher should treat the adolescent; and what the teacher should attempt to *achieve.* We shall consider each of these.

WHAT THE TEACHER SHOULD BE

What the teacher should be to promote emotional well-being on the part of his students can be expressed in two statements:

I will be a pleasant person in the classroom.
I will be mentally healthy.

I Will Be a Pleasant Person in the Classroom

A class situation represents a group of people working together, supposedly in cooperation and amity; therefore, there is no justification for the relationships within that group being other than friendly and agreeable ones, with people happy in the presence of the others and with the atmosphere conducive to kindly feelings. Unfortunately this is not always the way it is, for the teacher is sometimes ill-humored or at odds with the class, and the students are sometimes cross, rebellious, depressed, displeased with one another, jealous of each other, antagonistic, or the like.

The teacher influences the student's feelings, but of course she cannot control them. Whatever she might wish for in the way of mutual kindness and good will within the class, she can but set the stage for; she cannot guarantee it.

She can, however, guarantee her own emotional behavior. She should realize that there is one person in the group who has no right to be unpleasant. That is the teacher. The teacher has an obligation to be as nearly ideal emotionally in her relations with her students as possible. That means that she should be pleasant—and not irritable, ill-humored, vindictive, sarcastic, or nagging. She should be cheerful—not sad-faced, excessively serious, pessimistic, or depressed. She should be friendly—not just neutral, and certainly not unkind. She should be sympathetic—not unfeeling, harsh in her criticism, or disdainful.

In other words, while in the classroom a teacher should not harbor ill-humor, gloom and depression, unfriendliness, and unkindness. Yet many teachers do. The reason may be any of several:

Some teachers inflict their personal problems on the class. If they rise in the morning feeling irritable, they remain irritable during their teaching. If they look forward to the day with displeasure, they let that displeasure show in their dealings with their students. If they are unhappy for one reason or another, their unhappiness is allowed to mark their spirit in situations which in no way merit it.

Other teachers consider teaching an antagonistic relationship between the teacher and the class and treat the students with spite, vindictiveness, and harshness. Some teachers are grim and cheerless in their attitude toward schoolwork. Others are intolerant or jealous of the younger generation. Still others are of an unkind, irascible nature.

Whatever his provocations to be disagreeable, any teacher should try to be happy, pleasant, friendly, and cheerful with the class. Mere absence of unpleasant emotion is not enough. We sometimes see a teacher who maintains a complete emotional neutrality, but in such a teacher's classes there is not apt to flourish that happy, friendly feeling which one finds in other classes and which is so conducive to a good social atmosphere.

I Will Be Mentally Healthy

Obviously a teacher's own failures in adjustment may interfere with her effectiveness in working with other people. A teacher can best avoid this if she will make an intelligent effort to maintain her own mental health. Naturally a comprehensive prescription for this cannot be given in a page or so, but four suggestions will be made which are preeminently useful.

1. The teacher should guard his physical health, for ill-health can lead to unpleasant emotional states. A headache may make a person irritable. Lack of energy may lead to a lack of enthusiasm for and friendly response to others. Frequent illness may make one worried and so concerned about himself as to be unduly self-centered. Aches and pains may make it impossible for one to act pleasant at all. It is a fact that if one is to be buoyantly cheerful, happy-natured, optimistic, and sweet-tempered, one of his best assets will be excellent health.

2. The teacher should have an ideal of emotional maturity toward which he will strive. Any teacher should have in mind an ideal of emotional maturity as a goal for adolescent development. Such an ideal was presented at the beginning of this chapter. It included personal security, good humor and freedom from easy irritation, crossness, and angers, the ability to love generously and wholeheartedly, freedom from emotional slavery, the ability to enjoy aesthetic experiences, and gayety and humor. Some similar ideal should be a part of the teacher's objectives for himself. Any degree of growth in emotional maturity is worth while, for not only will it make the classroom situation better for the students but it will also make life happier for the teacher.

3. The teacher should maintain an adult circle of friends, and he should refrain from talking shop when he is with them on social occasions. It is doubtless admirable that teachers can become completely wrapped up in their school responsibilities, but when that interest extends to the point where there are no adult friendships maintained, the teacher is weakening himself as a person and losing opportunities for the kind of pleasant and wholesome social life he is entitled to.

4. The teacher should have a creative avocational interest. Every person needs some means to successful endeavor outside of his work. The value to mental health of a hobby or some similar interest is generally recognized by psychiatrists.

Thus far we have talked of what the teacher should *be*. We go on now to the matter of how the teacher should *treat* the adolescent as far as emotions are concerned.

HOW THE TEACHER SHOULD TREAT THE ADOLESCENT

How the teacher should treat the adolescent so as to promote his emotional well-being can be summarized in three statements:

1. I will realize that hidden emotions often dictate behavior and will act accordingly.
2. I will react to the emotional adolescent wholesomely and helpfully.
3. I will not respond to the behavior of adolescents with unsuitable emotion.

I Will Realize That Hidden Emotions Often Dictate Behavior

Examples can readily be found to show how easy it is to misunderstand the emotions back of behavior. Thus Norma is a cold, aloof, unresponsive girl of seventeen, and Miss Wright, her history teacher, has this impression of her: "Norma never smiles at me or talks to me. She always greets me curtly when I meet her. I don't think that she approves of me very much. I wouldn't be surprised if she actually dislikes me." The fact is that Norma is shy, reserved, and inarticulate with adults. Her cold exterior hides a considerable amount of liking for and approval of her teachers.

What should Miss Wright do? She should realize that she cannot judge Norma's feelings by her behavior and should certainly refrain from treating Norma in terms of the way she thinks Norma regards her. Rather she should be to her just as she is to anyone else—pleasant and friendly.

Pete is a flippant wisecracking sixteen-year-old who is frequently, for that reason, a source of trouble to the teacher. He is the kind who mutter in an aside to those around him, "Catch *me* doing something like that," when the teachers ask for a volunteer for a report, who pulls his coat around his face and shivers elaborately when the teacher opens the window a few inches, who ludicrously mimics the teacher when she is writing at the board with her back to the class. Miss Bascomb, Pete's English teacher, thinks of him as being a bad boy and regards him as a real disciplinary problem in her class. Actually Pete is ill at ease in a social situation, and he wisecracks to get a little attention. In talking with a counselor Pete admitted that he is uncomfortable in a group and is hardly ever part of one except at home and in class. For such a person it is easy to get group attention with the unexpected surreptitious remark even though he cannot be easy, poised, and relaxed in normal social give and take. A person who might answer a query addressed to him in a group situation awk wardly, stiffly, and self-consciously can sometimes wisecrack with aplomb when he takes the group by surprise and thus becomes himself the one in ascendance.

How should Miss Bascomb respond? Many times it will be best to ignore Pete's disturbing behavior. Never should she let it irritate her if she can prevent it, for she should be able to view Pete's actions with the same objectivity that a doctor would have in seeing chicken-pox rash on a child's face. It is a fact that Miss Bascomb is seeing in Pete symptoms of internal disorder. She should give thought to what she can do to help him. He needs experiences which would enable him to learn to get proper group satisfactions instead of the kind he does get.

Sam, seventeen, is often insolent and impertinent in class. His teacher of science, Mr. Rollo, is ready to exclude the boy permanently from his class. What should he do? First of all, he should try to understand the motives back of Sam's behavior. Is he covering up insecurity? Sometimes brash, insolent people are compensating (though not always, by any means). Has Sam had reasons to feel at odds with adult authority, and is he "taking it out" on Mr. Rollo? Is Sam just trying to show off? What *is* the reason for his behavior? Perhaps Mr. Rollo cannot know with any surety at all what the explanation for Sam's insolence is, but the effort of looking for causes will at least help him to be clinically objective toward Sam. It should be understood that Mr. Rollo must probably also take a stand on Sam's behavior, and this involves a consideration of what will be good for the class, for Sam, and for the teacher. Prescription cannot be given here, for each case has its own involvements which need consideration before action is taken.

These three illustrations are given to demonstrate the fact that hidden emotions often dictate behavior and that we can not always take the adolescent at his face value. An attempt to understand the fears, the worries, the irritations, and the resentments which underlie some disconcerting acts on the part of adolescents will make the teacher's responses more sympathetic and helpful—if he avoids a brash assurance that his diagnosis is unfailingly right.

I Will React to the Emotional Adolescent Wholesomely and Helpfully

It should be obvious that the adolescent will sometimes be in an emotional state which the teacher does not welcome and of which the teacher may not approve. Often it is best for the teacher to ignore this unwanted emotion, though at the same time it is necessary for her to understand it. At other times the teacher must react to it positively.

The Crush on the Teacher. The crush on the teacher is so common an occurrence that it hardly needs to be defined. An emotional attachment of a student for a teacher, it occurs in all combinations: Boy or girl may have a crush on a teacher of the same sex or a teacher of the opposite sex. Any of these is common enough, the least common being that of the boy on the man teacher. Examples of the others can easily be found.

In a small-town high school the principal remarked: "Most of the boys in the senior class have a crush on Miss Brown. They hang around her when they can like bees around honey. At basketball games, the players are all aware of her presence. After school when Miss Brown is correcting papers, there are sure to be some boys sitting around. A smile from her when they meet her on the street makes them feel good. They are exhilarated by being in her class." Then he added: "No harm in it. She knows how to take it."

This kind of crush, that of boys on an attractive woman teacher, is an entirely normal reaction. Harm can come only if the teacher reacts to it unwisely. The wise reaction is that where the teacher:

1. Is not greatly affected by the feeling directed toward her. She is not eager for such adulation and she is not gratified by it. She develops no crushes on these students. She doesn't try to descend to their level in her actions. She doesn't invite such attention. She hasn't the inclination to be flirtatious and doesn't indulge in such behavior.

2. Is her normal friendly self with them just as she is with all of her other students. She shows no negative emotional reaction. She is not shocked, and her manner toward them is not reproving.

In another high school a young man teacher who is very good-looking is having a similar experience. A number of the girls have a crush on him. They talk to him when they can, they talk about him a great deal, and now and then they write him affectionate little notes. This young man is responding in the wrong way. In the first place the adulation has gone to his head. He feels wonderful because he is so popular, and he is beginning to walk with a little swagger and look with condescension on the other faculty members who are not so much the object of attention. In the second place his manner to the girls is highly personal and somewhat flirtatious. He pays them compliments, and his whole attitude indicates very definitely that he enjoys having them around him.

What is wrong with all of this? Several things: The girls are going to center their attention too much on this young man, who has special prestige in their eyes because he is older and in a position of authority. This may change their relationship with boys of their own age with whom they should be having companionship. What is more, it will charge the classroom situation with excessive emotion which can have no normal outlet—as ordinary adolescent loves do through dating and other informal association.

In all crushes such as these, the recipients should remember that it is highly natural for many adolescent boys and girls to become just a little enamored of the attractive teacher who, because of his age, is more sophisticated than they, who is in a position to demand their attention, who is nice-looking, and who inevitably must give them some attention. The teacher should say to himself, "This is adolescence," and treat it kindly. But he should not become adolescent himself in his response.

Another kind of crush, less frequent in its occurrence, is that of a girl on the woman teacher. This is a different situation from the one we have been describing and is not to be taken so lightly. It usually denotes some lack of affection or object of affection in the girl's life, and the teacher is unconsciously used as a substitute. For that reason, because the need being supplied is a basic one, the feeling focused on the teacher is apt to be very intense. An example will illustrate this:

Jennie was adopted when she was eleven by a plain, austere, well-meaning couple who were chiefly interested in Jennie's presence in their home because she would be company and help for Mrs. Jones, who had periods of ill health. They treated Jennie well, but there was a lack of kindred feeling between her and them which prevented her becoming closely tied to them in affection. When Jennie was thirteen, her home-room teacher, feeling sorry for the rather forlorn-looking little girl, showed her especial kindness, inviting her to her house for lunch on two occasions, talking to her about her interests, and giving her a little gift on her birthday. By Christmastime, Mrs. Howell was to Jennie's eyes a combination of mother, ideal, and good friend. Whenever Jennie could be in Mrs. Howell's room cleaning the blackboard for her, helping with papers, or just talking to her, she was there. She spent the little money she received on presents for Mrs. Howell. She wrote her long letters during vacations and often at other times slipped affectionate notes into her desk.

Mrs. Howell was to Jennie the much-loved, idealized person that a glamorous and not too well-known mother might have been. Mrs. Howell, on the other hand, felt kindly toward Jennie, felt sorry for her, but was troubled by Jennie's attachment for her. Being a wise person, she understood that all of Jennie's pent-up affection for a nonexistent mother was being directed toward her. She realized that Jennie needed someone to love and someone to give her love and that she, Mrs. Howell, must serve in that capacity for a while. Being wholly adult, and happy in her adult life, she was not flattered by Jennie's devotion. Indeed, giving time to Jennie became a real chore.

Still she did continue to do just that—give her time, give her attention, and give her friendship—in exactly the spirit that a somewhat impersonal but generous-hearted mother would, hoping that the girl would outgrow her dependence before long.

Johnson makes these suggestions for the case of a girl's crush on an older woman.[2]

1. Under no circumstances should the individual who has the crush be ridiculed about her attachment.

2. Give the individual with the crush an opportunity to get satisfying attention from her associates.

3. In so far as possible, avoid opportunities for intimate expressions. When other people are present the girl with a crush is not likely to make exaggerated statements of her affection.

The Crush on Someone of the Same Age and Sex. Sometimes we see two girls (or two boys) who have an extraordinarily strong attachment for each other and no interest in other friendships. When such a relationship is marked by an almost loverlike attitude, we speak of it, too, as a "crush." Most associations of this kind will be outgrown in time, and probably the best general rule for adults to follow is to let them alone. However, if such a relationship seems to be seriously detrimental, these suggestions from Johnson will help the adult find ways of remedying the situation:[3]

"Appeal to the girl's altruism. When a girl can be convinced that her excessive affection is detrimental to the future development of the girl she loves, the expressions of the crush, and eventually the excessive emotional tone will gradually disappear.

"Make opportunities for large circles of acquaintances. Extracurricular activities and group project work in school furnish excellent opportunities for girls to get acquainted with larger numbers of young people.

"Provide opportunities for success and genuine approbation. When the girl develops a crush on some girl whom she admires because of her success or appearance, much can be done to assist her by giving her opportunities for attention and approval as a result of her own accomplishments.

"Provide opportunities for activities with the opposite sex. Parties, committees, and dramatizations provide excellent opportunity for normal impersonal contacts with the opposite sex.

[2] Bess E. Johnson, "Adolescent Crushes and the Teacher's Responsibility," *Clearing House*, 13:531–534 (1939).
[3] *Ibid.*

"Forcible separation with change of environment is sometimes effective. To employ this means, without a thorough knowledge of the case and the individuals involved, might do more harm than good."

The Student Who Pouts. One of the seniors in Mrs. Raines's history class is a very opinionated boy, Ed. The other day when Mrs. Raines asked the class a question which required considerable thought on their part, Ed's hand shot up almost as soon as her question was finished. Mrs. Raines said: "Ed, you're always ready with an opinion, but time and time again it's one that isn't worth anything to the class. Now this time sit and think the question over and see if you can't give us something really worth while." Ed glowered at her for a while and then sat back and with elaborate interest stared out the window. For the rest of the period he paid no attention whatsoever to what was going on.

How should the teacher react to the pouting student? First of all, Mrs. Raines must remain herself undisturbed emotionally. It would be easy to let Ed's attitude spoil her friendly feeling toward the class. What she must do is to remove Ed from her emotional consciousness completely, give all of her attention to the rest of the class, and keep her spirit toward them what it was. Ignoring Ed may make him see how childish his behavior is—but it may not. In that case a frank talk with the boy is advisable, in which the teacher explains why she thinks he should modify his behavior. She *must* avoid being emotional herself or being motivated by a desire to placate a recalcitrant student.

The Student Who Dislikes the Teacher and Shows It. Ralph and Miss Brown have never seemed to get along well together. Miss Brown cannot recall any particular reason for Ralph's dislike of her, but Ralph seems to go out of his way to show her that it exists. His manner verges on the insolent but doesn't quite reach that point. He is often patently inattentive in class. When he meets her, he returns her friendly greeting with a curt nod.

How should Miss Brown treat Ralph? She doesn't know. She is doubtful that she would get anywhere through a conference with him. Thus far this has been her policy: She has been ordinarily courteous with him. She has tried to be completely unemotional about his attitude, for it should be of no *personal* importance to her. When Ralph does something well in class, she makes sure that he gets credit for it and that the class knows of her approval but at the same time she tries not to bend over backward and be overgenerous toward him. She is going to ask the principal to call a conference of all of Ralph's teachers in order that they may talk over his work. She will not express herself there about Ralph's attitude, since this is a subjective matter, but will try to get an understanding of the boy which will help her to deal with him better.

The Student Who Is Easily Angered. Rhoda was described by Miss Clarke as a "sassy fifteen-year-old that someone ought to whip manners into." Rhoda and her bad temper make life difficult for Miss Clarke. When anything goes wrong for Rhoda in class, she expresses herself heatedly. For example, in a test the other day, Miss Clarke explained when she handed the papers back that she had given only one-point credit instead of five points to the answer "2" for the problem "$3x + 7 = 6x + 1$; find x," if all of the steps for solving the problem were not shown since, as she had several times explained previously, it was the knowledge of the steps which was important, not the answer.

Rhoda said hotly before anyone else could speak: "That's not fair. You're always thinking up something new to trip us. I hate this class."

While many teachers would become angry themselves at thus having their authority flouted, Miss Clarke only said to the class in her quiet way: "Rhoda is wrong. It *is* fair, as most of you know. Rhoda spoke in anger. I wish that she hadn't said what she did. But I don't think it will help matters by dwelling upon her remarks." And then she went on to something else.

When the Group Dislikes a Student. Suzanne, a senior, was greatly disliked by others in her class and for justifiable reasons, for Suzanne was dictatorial, critical, and selfish. Her behavior in class was not of the kind that either teacher or student could enjoy, for Suzanne listened to discussion, seemingly, only to criticize, was very dogmatic in her statement of her own opinions, and took good care to see that her own interests were always served before those of others.

The teacher saw that Suzanne was an outcast among the students, and though she could not like her, she felt it to be her duty to befriend her. As a result she embarked upon what she afterward decided to be entirely the wrong course of action. She was careful to give the girl not only her full due of praise but also a little extra when she made a good contribution to class discussion. She had the girl help her in the small honorary tasks that teachers ask of students. She was almost fawningly attentive to Suzanne's opinion.

As a result of this well-intentioned but unfortunate behavior on the part of the teacher, Suzanne became unbearably cocky, and the dislike of the class for her was now enhanced by the obvious partiality shown her by the teacher. For that matter, the teacher herself, though she was originally well liked, began to sense that the feeling of the class for Suzanne was extending to her, too.

What should a teacher do when a student is disliked by a class for good reason? Not as this teacher did, certainly. Rather, the teacher must as far as possible restrain the student from inflicting her disagreeable behavior upon the class and then try to help her change.

For one thing, the teacher should have said to Suzanne, when the occasion seemed to merit it, *if she could say it without unkindness and in a purely impersonal way:* "Suzanne, in a class discussion like this, your place is to do more than just criticize: Many of the remarks that are made are well worth thinking about. There is as much value in appreciation for what is good as there is in destructive criticism for the bad, and all of us should try to cultivate that ability to recognize quality."

Second, she might talk to Suzanne privately—*again if she could do it in a kindly, impersonal way*—explaining to her that she was making herself disliked by the class because she was being disagreeable.

A word of caution is necessary here, however. No such prescription for treating the adolescent can be taken at its face value. The teacher must approach the task warily and suit her behavior to the individual case. If she is doubtful about her skill or her success, it would be wise to consult with Suzanne's other teachers first.

The Student Who Is Timid. Earl is an extremely timid boy of sixteen. His every action seems to indicate a desire to be unnoticed. He never volunteers in class; yet tests show that he is an unusually excellent student. Often he has the look of being half asleep or of daydreaming. He is always alone and seems to have no place in the group life of the school.

What should the teacher do for Earl? Certainly she shouldn't single him out for attention, and it is extremely doubtful if she should give any sign of being aware of his timidity. Talking to him about it would, nine chances out of ten, be entirely the wrong thing to do.

Rather she must make it a point to greet Earl when she meets him in the hall or on the street and to call on him in class, just exactly as she would a confident student. She must not react to his shyness with embarrassment or pity.

Earl needs opportunities for small-group activity in class where because of his scholarly ability he will have considerable confidence and where he will have to talk to other students.

It is important that any student with inferiority feelings receive help. This is what may be done:

1. Try to discover what has caused or is causing the feeling (but generally *not* by direct questioning).

2. If it can be done subtly, give the student opportunities to succeed in ways that will win him class approval.

3. Put him in small social situations where he has a chance to take part without fear of failure. A group where there are people who are less capable

than he and people who are more capable than he seems a good training ground.

4. Show by your manner in talking to him and your general attitude that you look upon him just as you do anyone else—neither favor him nor ignore or slight him.

5. There are times when it is a good idea to talk to a student about why he does not volunteer (or whatever it is that he does which indicates inferiority feelings). Do *not* show that you have recognized inferiority feelings in him. Rather, merely open up the way for him to talk about himself if he will. If he should mention inferiorities, reassure him by telling how many are the people who have inferiorities and inferiority feelings. Perhaps you can recommend books for him to read—biographies or popular psychologies—which will give him a sense of kinship with the many others who feel the way he does and thus help him to rise above his feelings.

The Students Who Are "in Love." Most high schools have some boy-and-girl pairs who walk around the hall hand in hand, who stand before the classroom door in long conversations, who give each other meaningful glances in class, or who daydream the class away in thoughts of each other. What should the teacher's reaction be to them? It should *not* be to remark, as one teacher did: "You're the most sickening couple I ever saw." It should *not* be to feel disgust or envy. It should *not* be to beam on them as if they were something special. *Ignore their state.* Consider it their business, not yours.

It is true that if their conduct becomes unseemly, something must be done to get the pair to modify it. The appeal to them then should be on the basis of good taste, not on the basis of what is "right," and it should be unemotional.

The Students Who Are Giggly. Mr. Spence was surprised in class to have a little group of juniors start giggling and laughing about something, he knew not what. He was quite taken aback and quickly searched his memory for what had just gone on in the class. Had he said something funny? Not that he could think of. Was there something wrong with his clothes? Was *that* what they were laughing at?

Mr. Spence could have comforted himself by the knowledge that most spells of such giggling have nothing directly to do with what goes on in class. He should have said to himself: "That's adolescence for you," for adolescents are at times a notably giggly group, and the giggles can start over practically anything. A situation in which they don't feel at home may do it. Or reminders, often very vague or farfetched, may suggest funny situations or emotional stimuli.

The chief thing to do is to keep one's own equanimity: be as easy as possible, smile with them, give them a little time to calm down and assume that they want to. Chances are that they have no ill intent whatsoever and actually can't help themselves. One teacher at such times had the ability to say something humorous and thus get the whole class laughing heartily. That cured the giggle.

The Student Who Is "in a Mood." A high school junior was asked: "Is your behavior ever disturbing to the class or to the teacher?" He answered: "I guess it is when I'm in a bad mood." Then he went on to explain: "Sometimes when I get up on the wrong side of the bed, I just want to start a little trouble. Then I talk quite a lot to those around or do anything I can think of." Of course this is annoying to the teacher, but again he ought to save himself the wear and tear of any unfavorable emotional response, for it does no good. He will be better off himself, and the class will be better off, if he remains emotionally neutral to such a student.

The Student Who Cries. Dorothy cried when reprimanded very mildly by the teacher—who was then aghast at what he had done. Here is another case of needing to understand reasons for the behavior. Dorothy, as it happened, had a test coming up in another class the next period. The teacher of that class had said the day before that he would make it tough for anyone who failed. Dorothy had just settled down to study for the test after dinner that evening when her parents decided to go to a movie and insisted that Dorothy come along. So she didn't get her studying done.

Usually when a student cries in class there is an underlying reason, such as home trouble, loss of a friend, difficulty with the boy or girl friend, failure in another class, illness, anxiety over report cards, and the like.

The teacher's immediate response to a crying student should be the most tactful he can make. Sometimes the best thing to do, if the crying seems but a "summer shower," is to ignore it. If something must be done, it would probably be to have some close friend take the girl to the washroom to wash her face.

Later, when the girl is feeling all right again, the teacher should find out what was wrong in case it is something that needs attention.

I Will Respond to the Behavior of Adolescents with Suitable Emotion

Every teacher on some occasion or other has met with student behavior which might easily anger him, hurt his feelings, or even possibly embarrass him. This is true of insubordination, a student's correcting the teacher, a student's not having prepared his lesson, frequent tardiness, indifference to what is going on, fidgeting, and the like.

Such behavior is not pleasant for the teacher; yet it does seem that the emotionally mature person should see beyond the act to the causes and not let it arouse unpleasant emotion in him.

Symonds says:[4] "A teacher has two attitudes to take toward aggression: one allays it by objective and sympathetic understanding, and the other harnesses it to an attack on the real problems of learning and living." And Redl[5] gives an explanation which will help the teacher to be tolerant of adolescent restlessness: He says that adolescents are often fidgety and eager to handle something or other with their hands because they can thus discharge their overflow of emotional energy.

Finally, Swem gives us three cases which show again that the teacher should respond to the behavior of adolescents not with unsuitable emotion but rather with a sympathetic attempt to get at causes.[6]

Helen

"There was obviously copying on Helen's final examination in beginning shorthand. It was disturbing.

"Should I denounce her for 'cheating'? Tear up her paper in anger, and give her zero? Show her what I thought of dishonesty? Or could it be that a child had revealed a need for some help that I could give?

"Cheat, liar, thief—these are harsh words to be hurled at youth by their elders, to whom they look for instruction and approbation. If those words are ever justified at all, they certainly need handling as careful as that of a surgeon's knife, lest they butcher rather than heal. Let a child once become convinced that you do not believe in him and like him, and your power to mold his character has vanished.

"I summoned Helen and showed her the paper, but with no accusations or slurs on her integrity. Frankly and sincerely she responded: 'That's the only way I can pass. You know, yourself, that when I sat beside Louise, I got good marks. When I was across the aisle, my marks went down. That's what I had to do to pass my bookkeeping. I just can't get it by myself!'

"How glad I was that I had not, by an accusing tone, erected a wall between us and made it impossible for her to be simple and truthful with me! The matter was serious enough, of course. But dishonorable? Not so intended on her part.

"I could easily give a new examination, but here was her admission that she could not pass it if I did. I asked, 'Have you achieved enough short-

---

[4] Percival M. Symonds, *The Psychology of Parent-Child Relationships* (New York Appleton-Century-Crofts, Inc., 1939), p. 179.
[5] Fritz Redl, "Adolescent Changes as a Factor in Delinquency," 1941 Yearbook *Probation and Parole Progress* (New York: The National Probation Association) p. 202.
[6] Boyd R. Swem, "Disturbing or Revealing," *NEA Journal*, 57:194–195 (1950).

hand to go on?' I gave her time to think it over before answering. Next day she returned, and gave her own verdict of failure for the record.

"But more than that; we had plenty of chance to talk over the effect of leaning on a borrowed crutch, of accepting credit even in one's own mind for learning something that was not really learned, and of the use by society of the labels 'dishonest' and 'cheating' where people, knowing what they were doing, got things by false pretenses.

"This absense of matured ethical concepts is important. If we could only recall: just when did I myself finally get this or that standard established? We may think we were born with it, but were we? At what age, and just how, did we achieve it?

Raymond

"Raymond had stolen some things from the highschool shop. They were small items, not of great value. But they led to a suspicion that other things had been taken, too. Rather roughly he was turned over to the police, who searched his room, found some things, and took him to the station. The chief took him aside for a fatherly talk, and he was returned to school.

"Some time after this experience, I tried to discover his reaction toward the school. He explained the friendly attitude of the chief and added, 'I never knew till he explained it to me that if you stole something and didn't get caught at it, the article still was not really yours.'

"Sounds fishy, you say? It didn't to me, as I learned of his sharecropper life in another state. I concluded that the moral code by which he had lived was probably precisely that which he had indicated. Do many of us achieve a higher moral code than that which has been exemplified in our presence?

Ralph

"Ralph, age 15, was truant. Not once, nor twice, but a dozen times and more—maybe all day, maybe just a single period. Parents tried bringing him to school; then they made a special effort to start him off on time. Today it worked; tomorrow it slipped again.

"Promises galore—seemingly sincere at the time. Excuses, even flimsy and wholly discriminating ones, presented freely. A stern lecture by the judge of the children's court had little effect. The incident was disturbing to everyone—to his parents, to us, and to himself.

"We felt that a child of his age who is unable to carry out what he himself intends to do is headed for trouble in later life. From early childhood, he had evidenced less than a normal degree of self-direction.

"Every effort was continued to get compliance, and a careful record was kept, with daily reports to parents at once, if Ralph 'turned up missing.' All adults were encouraged to avoid temper or anger, and to make no threats that would not be literally carried out.

"There was detention after school which was attended or skipped about the same as other appointments. Except in rare cases, Ralph was not personally escorted to his engagements but left to perform for himself, even if he failed. This was believed wise since an attending governess could not be a permanent solution, and might make him all the less self-directing. Punctuality was praised liberally wherever possible.

"Teachers got increasingly restless and irritated at the amount of time and attention given him. Delinquencies still continued.

"Yet one day when a list of chronic absentees was being compiled and Ralph's name was proposed, one teacher spoke out that for two weeks he had been very much improved and should not be listed. Other teachers reported, 'perhaps not good, but certainly better.' At last, something seemed to be taking root, after months of despair.

"If there was any way to force it faster, we were not smart enough to discover it. Perhaps some mental processes, like the knitting of a bone, or recovery after paralysis, require a liberal dose of just plain time. If he succeeds, we have hope for others, and once more have found revelations in disturbances."

WHAT THE TEACHER SHOULD ATTEMPT TO ACHIEVE

There are certain emotions that a teacher should attempt to encourage in adolescents—and there are others she should endeavor *not* to rouse. In other words, the teacher's program should be:

I *will not* cause or encourage unwholesome emotions.
I *will* encourage wholesome emotions and sentiments.
I will set the stage for good emotional living.

I Will Not Cause or Encourage Unwholesome Emotions

Every teacher is the cause of emotional reactions on the part of the students. Sometimes these reactions may be very unwholesome and detrimental to the adolescent.

Fears. There is no justification whatsoever for fear in the classroom. Fear is a useful reaction in a few life situations, but in a great majority it is harmful. The teacher who uses fear as a motivation or causes fear is a bad teacher. Fear in the classroom, as the direct result of the teacher's behavior, may result from any of several causes:

1. The teacher who is over severe and even unkind. One teacher taught algebra better than anyone else in a large school system—if one could judge by the results of standardized tests. But a major element in her success was the fact that she was a stern, fearsome personality. Even a bold student quivered when her unsmiling look was fixed on him. No one ever glanced up from his work in her class; no one ever daydreamed; no one ever failed to do his homework. Examinations were dreaded, and during examination time not a student was free from tension. We cannot say whether this prevailing tension would do any lasting harm. It might. We know for sure, however, that it would be bad for the child while it was going on.

2. The teacher who loses his temper. A young woman of twenty-nine was asked if she had ever had a teacher who lost his temper. "I certainly did!" she responded. "When I was thirteen I had a teacher who actually had temper tantrums when things went wrong. One time she threw a book at a boy and missed his face by about an inch. She was never angry at me because I was both a docile student and a good one, but how I suffered when she got angry! It is painful for me to think of it even now."

All that can be said of this can be summarized in three words: It is inexcusable.

3. The teacher who is inconsistent. The student who never knows when he will be pounced on for behavior that passed uncensured the day before may persistently feel some uneasiness even though he is a moderately well-behaved person, and his enjoyment of school may be unnecessarily marred.

4. The teacher who is sarcastic. Sarcasm can hurt very much, too much for any good it may accomplish. Someone in authority with a gift for pointing up weaknesses or ridiculing can delight himself—and perhaps those not victimized—with his barbs. But the object of his sarcasm may suffer embarrassment or humiliation too great for his offense (if there was one) and not good for his psychological growth; and everyone may be a little bothered about the fact that he may the next time be the butt of the teacher's cruelty.

5. The teacher who gives public scoldings. A college student was talking about the teachers he had had and enumerating those he had liked. His father, who was listening, said with some surprise: "But what about Miss Akers? She was always considered a wonderful teacher, and I know that she was invariably good to you."

The college student replied: "I guess I forget her because I suffered so much in her room."

"Suffered?" said the father. "Ridiculous! She never did anything to you that you could object to."

"No," the young man said. "But she did so much scolding of the students who misbehaved that I just sat there and shivered every time. I think I felt the scolding twice as much as the one it was intended for."

It is doubtful if the teacher should ever scold publicly and with severity those who misbehave in class, for even if the culprit merited the stigma of such a public "whipping," which might be questioned, in the rest of the class are sensitive students who cringe and suffer when they shouldn't have to.

Emotional Dependence on Adults. There are students to whom adult approval means too much. In the classroom they live for the acceptance, praise, and attention of the teacher. It is easy for the teacher to derive so much pleasure himself from this importance in the eyes of such students that he fosters it rather than does as he should—help the students become more independent of adult approval.

Anger. The following illustration speaks for itself.

"I guess I felt good this particular day because I was acting up all morning. Then the fourth period study hall rolled around. There were a lot of people in the study hall that day and I was kind of showing off. The teacher in charge seemed to be half asleep and I guess I thought I could get by with murder under him so I tried it. I tore up three sheets of paper into little tiny bits. Then I hunted for a victim. I picked on Jim because he and I are pretty good friends.

"I put all the little tiny bits of paper in one hand and took a book in the other. Then I walked very quietly to the seat he was sitting in. I opened my book and told him to look at a certain picture. While he was doing this, I spread the tiny bits all over his head and then walked back to my seat and started reading. The next thing I knew there was an awful lot of laughing in the front of the room. The study hall teacher looked around and saw Jim covered with paper. He went over to Jim and asked him who did it, and Jim told him. That is when I started getting embarrassed. The teacher called me up to the front of the room and tried to make me get down on my hands and knees and *lick* up the paper with my tongue. I simply refused to do it and then the war started. I do not remember much that happened after that because I was so embarrassed." (*Senior boy.*)

"A certain study hall teacher made me very angry last week. This is what happened:

"A boy tore some paper into small pieces and then walked up to the front of the study hall and put them on a boy's head. He then turned and walked back to his seat without the teacher's seeing him. When the teacher discovered what this boy had done, he called him up to the scene of his crime, telling him to get down on his knees and lick up the pieces of paper that had fallen to the floor. The boy would not do it and I don't blame him, for the floor was dirty. The teacher then put his hand on the boy's neck and tried to push his head to the floor. When the boy would still not lick up the paper, the teacher picked him up and shook him very hard and then threw him back to the floor. Then he said, "Now pick that paper up." The boy then picked up the paper and threw it in the waste-basket and the teacher went over and took his seat at the desk.

"I admit that the boy was wrong, but was that any way for a teacher to act?" (*Junior girl.*)

Jealousy. Students in the classroom, like people everywhere, can become jealous, and the teacher should try to be so impartial and fair in his dealings that as little feeling of "favoritism" exists as possible.

Irritation. In all probability, no teacher lives who isn't at times irritating to some of the people in his class. Irritation should be avoided when possible. It can be avoided to a large extent if the teacher will review his own classroom behavior from time to time to see if there are mannerisms or habits which he should rid himself of—such as standing at the window so that the class must look at the light all of the time when paying attention to him, such as playing with chalk, saying "-a-a-a-" when talking, rubbing his face, and so on.

Feelings of Inferiority. It is a serious charge to make of any teacher that he has fostered feelings of inferiority in a student. Yet many teachers are guilty of this. A college student was discussing with the college psychologist the fact that she had a severe inferiority complex. The psychologist was trying to find events in her youth which would account for it. The girl said: "One thing that helped me feel this way, I know, was an English class I had as a freshman in high school. I don't know how you would explain that teacher. She never failed to use me as a bad example for the class. I remember so well all the difficulties I had in grammar. Well, that teacher would get me in front of the class to diagram a sentence at the board. I'd do it wrong and there I'd stand while she tried to make me see *what* was wrong. Sometimes I'd be up there for half the period. This didn't happen only once. It was at least a weekly occurrence, sometimes oftener, and I was ashamed and miserable every time. But I took it, and I suppose I am suffering from it today."

No teacher should ever use a student as a bad example. No teacher who appreciates the importance of helping adolescents develop wholesomely should ever have the poor judgment to diminish a student in the eyes of others.

There are other ways in which teachers and schools can engender an inferiority complex.

When the course of study becomes more important than the student, some students are going to have to suffer needless frustrations again and again, with resultant feelings of inferiority. Robert was such a student. When Robert was a senior, he was one of the best-liked students in the school, friendly, sweet-natured, gentle-spirited, honorable, unselfish, decent, cooperative. Any sensible teacher might have predicted that Robert would be a fine husband, a fine father, and a fine citizen some day. But Robert was not good in academic work. The curriculum of the school was a cut-and-dried affair suited only to preparing for college work, if indeed that. It was entirely unsuited to Robert's interests, his abilities, and his future plans. Nevertheless, Robert had to traverse that particular course in order to graduate from high school. So he did his best, failed once in a while, never got more than a D in any but two classes, though now and then he did get a C in a test or a project, at which he beamed.

Most of Robert's school life was a life in which he was doomed to feel inferior and in which his inferiority was deliberately impressed upon him day after day. It is doubtful if one could find any benefit to Robert in all of his academic experiences, which were so uniformly disheartening. And when one thinks of the waste of having a fine boy endure four years of near failure, it seems pitiful and shocking indeed.

I Will Encourage
Wholesome Emotions and Sentiments

There are certain feelings, emotions, and sentiments which deserve all of the encouragement which the teacher can give them. Students will be affected in this respect by what the teacher is himself, by what the teacher says, by the general atmosphere of the classroom, and by the types of activity engaged in.

The wholesome emotions that the teacher should encourage wherever she can are the generous emotions toward people, love for work, and the aesthetic emotions. Some suggestions can be made for doing this; much must be left to the teacher's ingenuity.

Friendliness, Unselfishness, Sympathy for Others. The teacher can promote these feelings in three important ways: (1) By his own friendliness, ability to find something to like in *everyone*, refusal to take personally any unlikable behavior, and recognition that the class is a social situation. (2) By being alert to opportunities he may find ways of letting those who are selfish practice being good to someone else. Tommy, in the eighth grade, was a rough, tough boy, seemingly without a spark of kindly feeling toward anyone. But when Mary Sue fainted in class, it was Tommy that the teacher asked to open the window, Tommy who was later re quested to get Mary Sue's wraps for her when she felt well enough to go home—and Tommy who seemed to show a little difference in his attitude toward his classmates the next day. (3) By having the class activity on such a basis that the social interaction demands politeness and kindness.

Love for Work. Many people—and unfortunately many teachers—have values such that to them work is unpleasant and to be avoided. They never realize that there is work for everyone which can exhilarate, exalt, and bring pleasure to life. The adolescent has a right to grow up with the ability to take pleasure in working as well as in playing; and since so much of the work that he does is schoolwork, it is especially important that teachers foster the ability to enjoy that. They should not *preach* enjoyment of work, of course, but they can make the work that the students do as inviting as possible and of the kind that gives joy in doing. And they can see that *they themselves* find joy in the work they are doing, for this attitude will be contagious.

The Aesthetic Emotions. The teacher would do well if he could help his students see beauty in the affairs of their everyday living—beauty in the outside, beauty in the variations of the weather, beauty in a neat classroom. Many teachers, of course, work in areas where it is their primary objective to foster aesthetic appreciations. They should take care to see that what they do is enlivening and not deadening.

I Will Set the Stage
for Good Emotional Living

The Teacher's Manner. The teacher who is sweet-tempered, even-tempered, happy in his work, considerate, and courteous will help make the classroom atmosphere such as will encourage the pleasant rather than the unpleasant emotions.

Discipline. Discipline that is fair, effective without being harsh, quiet and unobtrusive, and conducive to self-discipline will not engender needless fears, angers, or resentments.

Motivation. Motivation which leads the students to work with zeal and interest will make endeavor pleasurable rather than a source of discomfort, irritation, or rebellion.

A Socialized Classroom Situation. If the students have opportunities to carry on their schoolwork through committees, through excursions, through group discussions led by their own members, as well as through more formal methods, they will probably be happier and be more likely to feel the good social emotions than they would in a completely formal situation.

Discussion of Emotions. In some classes there may be opportunity to discuss the harms and values of emotions, to get an exchange of viewpoints on anger, fear, affection, depressions, and excitement which will lead to admirable standards and ideals of emotional conduct.

Books. There are so many popular books nowadays on principles of mental hygiene that the school or the teacher should take definite steps to make these available to the adolescent.

Reminiscences

1. Try to describe how you have changed in your emotional reactions since adolescence.

2. Were there any teachers in your experience who frequently made you fearful or angry? Describe what they did to cause these emotions.

3. Were there any teachers in your experience who promoted a warm friendliness in the class? How did they do it?

4. Did you have a crush on a teacher in high school? Was it good for you or bad? How did you get over it?

5. What were you like emotionally as an adolescent?

6. What did specific adults do for you in your adolescence to help you develop emotional maturity?

General Discussion

1. Look at the list of attributes of the emotionally mature person. How many of these imply good social adjustment?

2. The emergency system, useful in the days of frequent physical emergency, is often a handicap in civilized existence. Give as many examples of this as you can.

3. Consider the 10 emotional attributes of the typical adolescent. For each, tell how the parent or teacher of such an adolescent should react.

4. Consider the summary which gives the causes of each of the several emotions. For each cause listed, tell what the general policy of adults should be in their treatment of the adolescent.

5. Is it ever appropriate in the classroom for the teacher to be angry, irritated, hostile, or depressed? If, so, why? If so, when?

6. Give more specific suggestions than does the text for the maintenance of good mental health in the teacher.

7. Give any examples of adolescents or adults that you can to illustrate the point that hidden emotions often dictate behavior.

8. Give any example that you can of adolescents who were disturbingly emotional in the classroom, and then tell how the teacher handled the situation.

9. Can you recall and describe any teachers who handled crush situations with excellent judgment?

10. Describe any concrete situations you know of where the classroom is often pervaded with fear.

11. Why is emotional dependence upon adults as found in an adolescent sometimes pleasing to the teacher?

12. Give any instances you can of teachers who succeeded in inspiring students with sympathy for others, love of work, and aesthetic feelings.

13. Describe the teacher in your experience who best set the stage in the classroom for good emotional living.

Movies

Act Your Age, Coronet Films, 13 min., b. & w. and color, 1949.

Emotional Health, McGraw-Hill Textfilms, 20 min., b. & w., 1947.

Understand Your Emotions, Coronet Films, 14 min., b . & w. and color, 1950.

Further Reading

BETTELHEIM, BRUNO, "The Social Studies Teacher and the Emotional Needs of Adolescents," School Review, 56:585–592 (1948).

CONRAD, HERBERT S., and MARY C. JONES, "Some Results from an 'Annoyance Inventory' in a Cumulative Study of Adolescents," Psychological Bulletin, 39:475–476 (1942).

FRIEDLANDER, K., "Significance of the Home in Emotional Growth," New Era, 29: 41–43 (1948).

HAMALAINEN, ARTHUR E., "Developing Maturity in Youth," Educational Leadership, 8:412–416 (1951).

LAYCOCK, SAMUEL R., "Problems in the Adolescence of Exceptional Children, Part I. Growing Up Emotionally," Journal of the Exceptional Child, 8:171–176 (1942).

THOMPSON, G. G., and S. L. WITRYOL, "Adult Recall of Unpleasant Experiences during Three Periods of Childhood," Journal of Genetic Psychology, 72:111–123 (1948).

ZACHRY, CAROLINE B., and MARGARET LIGHTY, Emotions and Conduct in Adolescence (New York: Appleton-Century-Crofts, Inc., 1940).

Chapter 8. ADJUSTMENT TO LIFE VALUES

Hidden away in the personality and in some cases never known even to intimate friends are ideas and feelings in regard to behavior and accomplishment which are of tremendous importance to the individual who harbors them and also to those who feel the effects of that person's behavior. These are one's standards, ideals, morals, and religion. Often unverbalized, often not even subject to much thought, they still contribute greatly to making the individual what he is.

All these directives of behavior are not only closely interrelated but are also at times and in some respects indistinguishable. A selected dictionary definition for each will illustrate the truth of this:

Standard: an accepted or established rule or model.
Ideal: a standard of perfection.
Morals: principles concerned with the practice of right conduct.
Religion: the profession or practice of religious beliefs.

We see that morals may involve standards, that religion may be based upon ideals of behavior, and that the person who practices his religion would be expected to be moral. Other interrelationships may be found as well. At the same time we realize that each of the four types of behavior directives may occur independently of the others. One may make a moral choice without having religion enter into it. One may have standards without ideals, and so on.

If you will look up any of these terms in the dictionary, you will find that there are so many definitions for each one that it is easily possible to become confused as to how each should be interpreted. Therefore, in order that we may have a uniform basis of understanding for the purpose of this discussion, we shall define these four terms very specifically. If the definition does not fit the reader's concept, he is urged to accept it while he reads the chapter, for not the terms but the underlying ideas are the important matter.

DEFINITIONS

Standards

When there are degrees in the quality of behavior or goals, we may choose (or adopt without conscious choice) a certain quality as being a necessity for us in some situations. This "necessary quality" is a standard. Any number of examples might be given. We shall mention only a few for illustration:

In regard to	Situation	Standard may be
Fingernail cleanliness	At school	They must be absolutely clean
Typewriting	A letter of application	There must be no mistakes
Eating	At the dinner table	One should not butter the whole slice of bread at once
Relationship with others	Buying something at the store	One should not be rude

Most of us have standards in regard to our personal cleanliness and grooming, the quality of the clothes we buy, the care of possessions, courtesy toward others, and the like. We do not necessarily have a standard, however, just because it is possible to have one. For example, if I own a home I may let my yard go and never mow it at all; or I may let it go until the contrast with the neighbor's well-mowed lawn becomes uncomfortable to me. In neither case am I governed by any standard. But if I believe that unless I cut it every two weeks, it gets "too high," then I have set a certain condition of the grass as being essential to me. I have a standard.

Some standards are so agreed upon by the great middle class of society that the school makes a strong effort to compel all of the students to conform to them. Examples of these are standards in regard to English usage, letter writing, clothing (as in the case of girls not wearing slacks to school), and behavior in the classroom.

Ideals

When we possess a picture or an actual representation of a "best state" desired but at present beyond our reach, we have an ideal. We can thus have ideals wherever attainment is possible. We may have an ideal of the kind of person we would like to be, the kind of friends we would like to have, the kind of house we would like to live in, the kind of job we would like to hold, and the kind of neighborhood, community, and world we would like to be a part of.

As we say, an ideal is possible wherever attainment is possible. One does not necessarily have an ideal in such cases, however. If we go back to the illustration of the lawn, we see that I might harbor an ideal which pictures a lawn always velvety smooth and free from weeds or bare patches. On the other hand, I might have no such idea of a best state at all.

Morals

In many cases we have a choice of two kinds of behavior, one of which is "right" and the other of which is "wrong." When we do what is right, we are being moral.

What is considered moral may vary from person to person, from family to family, and from community to community. However there is a considerable amount of agreement, at least verbally, as to the "wrongness" of some actions. The Ten Commandments are an example:

"Thou shalt have no other gods before me.
"Thou shalt not make unto thee any graven images.
"Thou shalt not take the name of the Lord thy God in vain.
"Remember the sabbath day, to keep it holy.
"Honor thy father and thy mother.
"Thou shalt not kill.
"Thou shalt not commit adultery.
"Thou shalt not steal.
"Thou shalt not bear false witness against thy neighbor.
"Thou shalt not covet thy neighbor's house, thou shalt not covet thy neighbor's wife, nor his manservant, nor his maidservant, nor his ox, nor his ass, nor any thing that *is* thy neighbor's."

In any situation standards, ideals, and morals may or may not be interrelated. Thus in the first case below, they are; in the second, they are not.

Interrelated	*Not Interrelated*
Standard: I vote at elections	Standard: I brush my teeth twice a day
Morals: I think this is right	Morals: None
Ideal: What good citizenship means	Ideal: None

Religion

By religion we may mean an organized church to which allegiance is expressed, we may mean a belief in a supernatural Being and in His laws, or we may mean a spiritual concept of the significance of life, a concept which is accompanied by certain principles of living. Since this last interpretation embraces all creeds and is broader than denominational interpretations, it is the one we shall use in this chapter. Black has expressed the idea more fully:[1]

"The religions of man can and should be a unifying force, for all the great religions reveal a basic unity in ethics. Whether it be Judaism,

[1] Algeron D. Black, *Ethical Faith* (New York: The American Ethical Union), p. 5.

Catholicism, Protestantism, Buddhism or Confucianism, all come out to a sense of the sacredness of the individual. This moral sensitivity to the sacredness of life—the will not to kill, not to hurt, not to put a stumbling block in the path of the blind, not to neglect the widow or the fatherless, not to exploit the servant or the worker—all this is to be found in the Bibles of man, in what they call their sacred books. They all teach in substance: 'Do unto others as you would that others should do unto you.' . . . most of the great religions agree on mercy, justice, love—here on earth. And they agree that the great task is to move men from apathy, from an acceptance of the evils in life, to face the possibilities of the world, to make life sweet for one another instead of bitter."

THE IMPORTANCE OF STANDARDS, IDEALS, MORALS, AND RELIGION

As we have said, a person's standards, ideals, morals, and religion direct his behavior in innumerable ways. What is more, not only is his own happiness affected by what these directives are, but even more so is the happiness of those who are in any way associated with him affected. The neighbor whose standards in regard to care of garbage, attention to his lawn, and so on, are low, is not a pleasant neighbor and can make for some discomfort in our own living. The school teacher with no ideals for his students' development, can waste their time or even do them harm. The government worker to whom expediency is more important than right can cheat and swindle those whom he serves. The friend who does not believe that he should do unto others as he would be done by is not a good friend.

Standards, ideals, morals, and religion are revealed in a person's behavior if we look for them, but since this requires a very searching examination which must be continued for some time if we are to get the whole picture, we tend to forget both their presence and their importance in the adolescents we teach. This is not good, for actually we cannot do our best in helping boys and girls to become socially desirable people if we fail to give thought to these directives of their behavior. We shall therefore examine each one of them in detail.

STANDARDS

Why Be Concerned with the Adolescent's Standards?

There are many reasons why the adult should be concerned with the adolescent's standards.

1. In the first place, the possession of certain standards contributes to the individual's well-being. Consequently, when we ask ourselves, "Is this adolescent getting along all right?" we must look to see if he has the standards in regard to personal grooming, the standards in regard to healthful living, the standards in regard to work, and the standards in regard to his social relationships which he needs to be happy.

2. In the second place, it will help us to understand each boy and girl if we know something about the standards he or she holds and follows. To make this idea concrete, think of how much better you would understand each of your acquaintances in the classroom if you knew that one has no feeling about the necessity for paying back money that he borrows, that he believes it sufficient to change his underwear once a week, that his standards of scholarship are nonexistent—and so on, in great detail for each.

One should remember, however, that the lack of some particular standard or the presence of a certain undesirable standard can distort your understanding of the person under consideration. If you see one of your students standing at your desk and reading a letter which lies open upon it, you may condemn her as "no good" because this act offends you so much. Similarly, someone with high standards of politeness may seem a splendid person to you just because of the halo effect of her courtesy. In either case it is important that you be aware of the fact that you have not really reached an understanding of the person. You are only making a snap judgment on the basis of one characteristic, about which you have strong feeling.

Another difficulty that may arise in the line of understanding is that we may condemn someone for violating a standard which is important to us when that other person may be completely unaware that such a standard exists. The student who stands reading the papers on your desk has probably never been taught any standards in regard to observing another person's right to privacy. She does not deserve disapproval, dislike, or reprimand. She deserves to be understood and helped.

3. Finally, an adolescent will be almost certain to carry into his adulthood some of the standards he adopts in his teen years. Consequently, it is important that he be helped to see the value of those standards generally considered good and be encouraged to adopt them.

Where Does the Adolescent Get His Standards?

The adolescent gets his standards from many sources.

1. From the home. The adolescent reflects his home standards more than any others, naturally. In regard to all of the following, and more

standards have been imposed on the adolescent by his parents or have been developed from home experiences without any specific teaching:

How often should the house be cleaned? How thoroughly should it be cleaned? How neat should the rooms be kept from day to day? How should the table be set? Should napkins be used?

What special preparations should be made when a guest is in the home? Should the guest be treated like one of the family or should certain formalities be observed?

How much sleep should one get at night? How much fresh air should one have in the bedroom? Is it all right to drink coffee instead of milk as far as health is concerned? Need one have some fresh fruit every day?

How often should one brush his teeth? How often must one bathe? Is it necessary to wash one's hands before eating? How often should one put on clean underclothes?

How polite should one be to his own family? How polite to people on whom one wants to make a good impression?

Home standards are of all kinds—some bad, some good. In many cases the adolescent is but carrying along into another generation, with little change, standards which are shoddy and inadequate at best.

Parents have a great responsibility in determining their children's standards. Yet, as Rautman says,[2] because of our society's emphasis upon youthfulness, parents often will model their behavior after that of the adolescents, making themselves ridiculous in the eyes of young people and giving them no mature standards to aspire to.

2. From the school. The school makes itself the official purveyor of certain standards—those in regard to the English language, proper politeness to teachers, classroom etiquette, and behavior on the playground and at parties. Many of the standards which the school enforces the best are those having to do with school docility—standards which are of no particular use for the future and serve only for adults' present convenience.

3. From their age groups. Conformity to group standards seems imperative to the adolescent. Consequently, we find that in any school certain standards of dress, hair style, mode of greeting, and so on, have marked uniformity. Most of these standards are but a passing fad and have no lasting effect on the adolescent's life.

4. From other adults, from the movies, from the world of commerce. Here is an example, which shows how adults may influence the standards of young people in regard to driving:[3]

[2] Arthur L. Rautman, "Youth in Search of a Standard," *Mental Hygiene*, 30:597–605 (1946).

[3] *Indianapolis Star*, Sept. 26, 1949.

Put Young Drivers on Honor

"A traffic safety campaign which really gets at the heart of the matter has been launched by the Indianapolis Automobile Trade Association. It deserves the enthusiastic co-operation of every parent of teen-age drivers in the city. A widespread response to the idea is certain to result in a significant drop in the accident rate.

"The main feature of the campaign will be the signing of printed 'good driver agreements' between fathers and their teen-age sons and daughters who are licensed to operate autos. Among other things, the pledges put the youngsters on their honor not to allow their cars to be driven by anybody who has been drinking, not to 'show off,' not to drive more than 50 miles an hour, not to take right-of-way for granted and not to break any traffic regulations.

"To promote the distribution of the 'man-to-man' and 'dad-to-daughter' agreements an open meeting will be held at 7:30 p.m. Tuesday at Caleb Mills Hall under the auspices of the Auto Trade Association, the Shortridge High School Parent-Teacher Association and the city and state police departments. The meeting is not limited to Shortridge parents, but open to all. Persons who cannot attend may obtain agreement blanks and wallet cards from member firms of the I.A.T.A.

"Parents have good reason to be concerned about their youngsters who drive the family car. The teen-ager accident rate is 89 per cent higher than that of any other age group and accounts for 33 per cent of all traffic deaths. The driver agreements give fathers a unique opportunity to exercise an influence for good. Youth may be naturally inclined toward carelessness—but the average boy or girl is not going to break a written honor pledge. All dads who possibly can should attend Tuesday night's meeting with their teen-age sons and daughters."

Movies may provide youth with some of their standards in regard to relations with others. The world of commerce will try to get them to adopt standards which will impel them to buy deodorants, tooth paste, electric-light bulbs, insurance, and so on.

The many sources of standards bring conflicts. As Zachry says:[4] "In the larger community now accessible to him he finds himself confronted with an elaboration of standards of conduct and a diversity of ideals of personal worth. . . . In the widening circle of peers, among teachers and other adults, through newspapers, motion pictures, and radio, he meets with mounting evidence of disparity of standards, with evidence of conflict among authorities."

[4] Caroline Zachry, *Emotion and Conduct in Adolescence* (New York: Appleton-Century-Crofts, Inc., 1940), p. 171.

Improving the Adolescent's Standards

Anyone who works with the adolescent should have a clear idea of what standards he should and can do something about. These will differ from school to school. The level of courtesy that one school must strive for, as an example, will be low compared with that attained in another. The areas where something should be done can be listed, however.

1. In regard to personal appearance and grooming.
2. In regard to health practices.
3. In regard to the care of one's own living quarters.
4. In regard to the treatment of people.
5. In regard to public places and public property.
6. In regard to public duties.

Some methods for establishing standards which are often tried the teacher should be dissuaded from using: "preaching," nagging about lack of standards, enforcing the use of certain standards through threats, and the like. The reason is perhaps obvious. These techniques for molding people's behavior are unpleasant and make the social atmosphere disagreeable. This is inexcusable if it is not a necessity—and that it is not, for other pleasanter methods are available which are also more effective.

Then what should the teacher do?

1. He can himself exemplify the kind of standards he wishes to foster. A young man went to a small town for his first year of teaching and found the students there, particularly the boys, very careless in their grooming and manners. The young teacher said nothing and did nothing about it. He just continued to be the same kind of person he always was—very neat and clean, extremely courteous in all of his dealings with faculty and students. Because he was a likable person, he became a favorite of the boys, and many of his standards were adopted by them. They began to keep their hair combed, their fingernails cleaned, began to see that they had clean handkerchiefs each day, and came to adopt some of the courtesies their teacher employed.

2. The teacher can encourage standards of behavior in the classroom which will be equally serviceable outside of school. "Your written work represents you. Don't let it be something that will give people the wrong impression" or "Someone else will be reading your writing. Please be considerate" represents the spirit of this better than does "I'll take five points off your grade if your papers aren't neat." It is regrettable that teachers spend so much time promulgating standards which will serve

no further purpose when school is over, standards for classroom and other school behavior, for form of papers, and for studying. The learning would be more meaningful and worth while if it were the kind to be of use in out-of-school living and also serviceable in adulthood. Consideration for others, for example, is the right reason for being courteous, but often all the adolescent is led to understand is "That's the way the teacher wants it" as a reason for the conduct demanded.

3. The teacher can help students understand the need for standards through group discussion. Standards most often become a part of a person through deliberate or, sometimes, unintentional indoctrination (particularly that of the parents) or through imitation. For this reason it is good for anyone to take stock of his standards, examining them for their real utility. While we cannot say where such opportunity can be made in the school, the teacher should keep in mind that such a deliberate weighing of standards would be of value to adolescents and seek occasions where it may be furthered.

4. He can work with leaders. Suppose that a teacher is troubled because the students are very careless of any obligations to chaperones at parties and dances. If he knows Jack rather well—one of the real leaders of the school and therefore, one would have reason to expect, a boy of good will and common sense—he might ask him what could be done to get students to make an effort to greet the chaperones, converse with them a little, and see that they have a pleasant time. If he and Jack do come to an understanding as to what would be desirable and Jack agrees to do what he can to influence his classmates, much may be accomplished.

IDEALS

"He's an idealist!" We often hear these words said scornfully and in an attempt to discredit the person described.

How does it happen that the word *idealist* is frequently used in derision in referring to an adult and yet is said tenderly and with a note of praise when it is an adolescent that we are describing? The answer is that the ideal is not only the unreal but may also be the imaginative and forward-looking. In the adult, realism and practicality are important qualities, and one is apt to be scornful of the person who appears to be disregarding them. In the adolescent, who is supported by adult realism and practicality, these qualities are not so important, and we feel that idealism can be afforded; we admire the youth who sees fine possibilities for himself, for friendships, for world relationships, and the like, even should they seem very farfetched to us.

What Are the Facts about Ideals?

Except for this critical or admiring attitude, we really give little thought to the ideals others hold—or to ideals in general. What *are* the facts about ideals?

Ideals differ not only in kind but also in respect to their wholesomeness and their attainability. As we have said, ideals may be for one's own development, for friendships, for jobs, for homes, and so on. Ideals may be good, or they may be bad. One adolescent may hold an ideal for himself that involves being honorable, wise, beyond pettiness, and always courteous. Another adolescent may have as his ideal an older boy in the neighborhood who is a tough, rowdy bully.

Ideals may be well founded on reality or may be very unrealistic. Many a young woman or young man marries with an ideal of perfection in marriage which is utterly impossible, considering the imperfections of human beings and considering also the unwisdom of one person's adjusting himself completely to the wishes of another. On the other hand, some young people do have a sensible ideal of what marriage can be if both husband and wife work to create a successful union, know what is involved in the attainment, and know that at its best marriage will hold some conflict and some unhappiness.

People differ greatly in the extent to which they are motivated by ideals and in the kind of ideals which operate in them. The adult idealist—the adult who is motivated in many areas of his living by clear concepts of what more nearly perfect living could be—is probably a rare person. One reason for this, and perhaps the major one, is the great emphasis in this country on shrewdness and on being sophisticated even to the point of cynicism.

The adolescent is characteristically idealistic. The reasons for this are simple enough. The adolescent is just beginning to comprehend what the adult world with its adult relationships and adult achievements is like. Both his own wishful thinking and the ideas of teachers, textbook writers, and others, prompt him to picture adulthood in terms of the desirable and the happy situation.

The adolescent is also characteristically unrealistic. He fails to recognize the long distance between what exists and what he dreams of. He hasn't been enough tempered by experience to know that one need not have perfection to have something good. As a result he expects the impossible and is unreasonably disappointed when he finds that it cannot be attained.

Ideals are seldom consciously or systematically developed. They grow haphazardly. Their extent, kind, and detail are largely a matter of accidental attainment. Sometimes they are the piecemeal result of many experiences. Sometimes, in contrast, a fully worked out ideal is presented by someone with the ability to influence, and the ideal may be accepted in a matter of minutes. This is particularly true with the adolescent, who may be inspired to a complete change in viewpoint upon, say, hearing an impressive minister speak, reading an inspiring book, or meeting some admirable person.

Ideals may be within the bounds of attainment, and they may be a wholesome, inspiring asset to the possessor as well as to society. We need more adults who are idealistic and more adolescents who are possessed of ideals that are in harmony with reality. We need more people who can envisage better states for themselves and for all of us. For illustration, think how much different it would make the world if everyone had for his ideal the attainment of a personality marked by a genuine love of fellow man, by prevailing kindness, and by the absence of easy irritation or severe anger. Blos quotes Edward Sapir as saying:[5] "Man's conception of himself and of the kind of person he would be is of more importance individually and socially than almost any other phase of his life."

How Do Ideals Serve Us?

Ideals serve us in many ways:

1. They help us maintain our standards. Fifteen-year-old Albert says that his ideal is his history teacher, Mr. Rensmith. He would like to be just like this teacher. Mr. Rensmith is, of course, most appealing because he is a lively, interesting young man with a good sense of humor. But he is also very clean and very well mannered, and it is these qualities in his ideal that help Albert maintain his own often wavering standards of cleanliness and courtesy.

2. Ideals inspire us. Sixteen-year-old Helen says that her ideal is Mrs. Owens, a young married woman who lives near her. She admires Mrs. Owens's ability to keep her two little children, her house, and herself always neat and attractive and still have time to take part in the Little Theater and the Woman's Club. She would like to be another Mrs. Owens when she is grown up, and as a result she is for the first time taking an interest in the cooking and the housework at home.

3. Ideals give us a faith to tie to. Superintendent Blackwell often gets discouraged about the progress he is making in trying to get all of the children in school more conscious of their "civic" duty in keeping the school grounds clean. But when he is the most discouraged, he thinks of

[5] Peter Blos, *The Adolescent Personality* (New York: Appleton-Century-Crofts Inc., 1941), p. 318.

how fine it would be if all of the young people in the schools of his town *were* considerate enough to make an effort to keep school property in good condition. This renews his hope.

4. Ideals determine the direction of social and individual progress. They set the pattern for our strivings. The high school students to be mentioned later who accepted the ideal of the golden rule had much of their behavior at home and elsewhere determined for them by this ideal. Because in our country we have an ideal of democracy, ill formed and ill expressed though it be in the minds of most, we move awkwardly and slowly forward in the direction of greater brotherhood.

5. An ideal can be a unifying point around which to rally. In one school a girl of seventeen who was known to all of the students as being unusually generous-hearted and democratic and was loved by everyone who knew her was tragically killed in an automobile accident. Some days later, one of her friends remarked, "There's one thing we can do for Barbara— get rid of all the snobbery and cliquishness in this school. That's what she wanted. We can do it."

The ideal of a truly democratic student body took hold of all of the students and in itself became a means of unification, as of course did the specific efforts made in that direction.

Where Do We Get Our Ideals?

Those for Ourselves. Havighurst and Taba write:[6]

"Boys and girls form an image of an 'ideal self' which acts like a magnet, attracting and directing their behavior. The 'ideal self' contains something of the father and the mother, various teachers and youth-group leaders, important people in the local community, heroes read about, and ordinary successful young adults.

"The 'ideal self' is especially important in directing behavior and shaping character during the years of adolescence when major life decisions must be made and when parental example and precept are no longer accepted with blind faith.

"It may be assumed that the 'ideal self' develops out of experience with people and reflection upon that experience. Such experience may be direct person-to-person contacts, or it may be limited to observation from afar, to seeing pictures, or to reading about persons of the present or past. These experiences, direct and indirect, are the raw materials out of which the 'ideal self' develops."

[6] Reprinted by permission from *Adolescent Character and Personality* by R. J. Havighurst and H. Taba, published by John Wiley & Sons, Inc., 1949, p. 70.

Table 29 gives us information as to where adolescents may get their ideals for the kind of people they would like to be.

Movies are sometimes the source of ideals. Thus one sixteen-year-old writes:[7]

"First of all I'll say my ideal, Robert Taylor. I don't know what I'd do first if I could become his twin brother right now. The main things I like about my ideal are his looks, occupation and his beautiful female surroundings. When I go to a picture played by Robert, I sit and envy him most of the time and don't get much meaning from the picture. The age, I am not sure of how old Robert Taylor is, but I'm sure he is over twenty-three, the age I would like to be this instant. In that case that

TABLE 29. THE PERSON I WOULD LIKE TO BE LIKE: TYPES OF PERSONS SELECTED*

Type of Person	Percentage of Mentions
Family member	14
Glamorous adult	5
Hero read about	0
Age mate	3
Attractive, visible adult	15
Composite, imaginary character	57
Not classified	6

* Reprinted by permission from *Adolescent Character and Personality* by R. J. Havighurst and H. Taba, published by John Wiley & Sons, Inc., 1949, p. 72.

would have to be Mr. Taylor's age also if we were to be twin brothers. When I am old enough I am going to try every means possible to improve my looks. I am going to wear a Taylor mustache, train my hair to be nice as to my liking. I have light hair, brown eyes. According to this it would be quite easy to make my hair darker."

Ideals for Friends. Our ideals for the kind of people we would like to have as friends similarly come from many sources. We hear remarks at home about what makes this person likable and what makes that one displeasing, and we incorporate some of these ideas into our own thinking. In addition we read of people who have many delightful qualities which we feel we could admire and enjoy. Then, too, we experience many kinds of pleasures with people, and we also experience dissatisfactions. From all of this we make up our ideal of a friend.

For Human Relationships. Ideals for human relationships other than those in one's personal sphere are in most people nonexistent, though they are well formulated and emphasized by the Bible and the church. It is this

[7] Reprinted by permission from *Adolescent Character and Personality* by R. J. Havighurst and H. Taba, published by John Wiley & Sons, Inc., 1949, p. 99.

fact that has led many educators to feel that there should be definite propagandizing of the ideal of democracy. If many people in our country instead of a few had a clear picture of just what is involved in the democratic ideal of human relationships, we would move toward it more quickly and more decisively. As it is, it is largely when someone suffers from slights, unkindnesses, snobbery, intolerance, deceit, dishonesty, and so on, that he responds with an "I wish," which actually is a partial concept of what the spirit of good will to men might be.

For Marriage. Most young people have a concept of marriage which is in some respects sensible and down to earth. This answer of an eighteen-year-old girl is typical of what a great many seniors in a large Middle Western high school said: "What would I like to be doing ten years from now? I would like to be married to a man I love, have two children, have our own home—a six-room house in a good neighborhood with a lawn and a garden. We'd have a car—new, but one of the inexpensive ones would suit me fine. And we'd have a dog. If I had all that, I'd be content."

No one could complain about the lack of reality here. But along with such a picture there almost surely exists another ideal of mate and marriage which is very unrealistic. For young people are so constantly fed the material for this romantic ideal by popular magazine stories, advertising, and movies that almost inevitably they combine ideas thus derived with their own ability to dream up perfection and end with a thoroughly unattainable picture of what their marital future can be as far as husband-and-wife relationships are concerned.

What Ideals Should the Adolescent Hold?

Beyond question, there are ideals which can be bad for one or, while not bad, without any influence for good. The boy who in response to the question, "What person would you wish to be like?" answers, "Like Robert Taylor because of his looks, occupation and his beautiful female surroundings," has an ideal which is probably not going to help him at all in growing to be someone worth while as a person.

There is a skill to attaining and maintaining good ideals. Fine ideals often require thought and imagination for their formation—and then to maintain them and work toward them in the face of inevitable discouragements at times requires vision, courage, perseverance, and faith.

Knowing this, we cannot feel that the ideals of the adolescents we work with are their business alone and none of ours. They *are* our concern, for the adolescent often needs help in seeing the importance of ideals, in being introduced to ideals he might never conceive of, in formulating his ideals, in relating them to reality, and in clinging to them in adversity.

Therefore it is important that the teacher know what the direction of adolescent ideals should be in regard to each of the following:

For himself: The body and grooming, appetites, emotions, personal integrity, personal adjustment, growth, relationships with people.
For friends.
For human relationships and a way of life.
For marriage.
For government.

Furthering Desirable Ideals

The authors have asked college students in many classes to give a written account of their ideals. Inevitably the task proves to be a very difficult one. Yet it is hardly possible for a teacher to further the ideals of the young most helpfully if he hasn't verbalized his own. For that reason, if a faculty will individually go through the process of putting their own ideals into writing, they will have the best single process for understanding the nature of ideals and for making their goals with the adolescent concrete.

It is the task of the teacher (1) to build and implement good ideals and (2) to see that the adolescent understands how the ideal and the real differ. The first requires verbalizing the ideal and then making it so attractive to the adolescent that he desires to accept it. The second requires that the adolescent know the odds against him in his reaching toward the ideal. He must see the world as it really is, but he must also see its possibilities for improvement. He must know how great idealists have moved mankind further along the way to good living, but he must also understand the difficulties they have encountered and overcome. He must realize that he should carry on his living on two levels: He should live in the present and the real and make the necessary adjustments to its deficiencies. He should at the same time maintain an awareness of how life might be better; and he must see and want to take the steps that bridge the real and the ideal.

Too many adolescents are eventually disillusioned and go in one step from idealism to skepticism. This is wasteful. It results from the fact that their ideals have been so farfetched in comparison with what the real situation is that when they become fully aware of the greed, the dishonesty, the unkindness, and the misery in the world, they conclude that their ideals are impossible and cast them aside.

This is something that we must not countenance. It is so easy to say, "The adolescent is inevitably disillusioned," and thereby relieve ourselves of any responsibility for the process. But we are failing in a most important task if we do so. The adolescent must be helped to find good but not too fanciful ideals. He must understand the value of ideals, and he must learn to be tolerant of the un-ideal while he continues to strive.

The school can foster ideals in many ways:

1. By example. In the Prairie City study, the sixteen-year-olds mentioned teachers 21 per cent of the time in naming adults with admirable qualities. There can be no doubt that admired qualities in teachers do help to make the picture of the ideal self for the adolescent.

2. By experience. There is no reason why the adolescent should not experience ideal situations in minuscule, at least as far as personal relationships are concerned. A school can be so democratic in its relationships and give such practical experience in living in a true democracy that the students actually do *experience the ideal*. Similarly, the attractiveness of the school grounds and the cleanliness of the school buildings may give experience with ideal working conditions.

3. By direct inspiration. Some adults can inspire adolescents with their ideals through the things they say about them and the enthusiasm they express. Other adults only succeed in sounding "preachy" and should avoid this method.

4. By discussion. As an adult, have you ever listened to adolescents seriously discuss principles of living? If you have, you know that their common sense and vision are quite as good as that of adults in a similar situation. Discussion of ideals clarifies them and makes them more real. With a little guidance, adolescents being as idealistic as they are, such discussion almost inevitably leads to conclusions and formulations which are genuinely uplifting. Rivlin's account of a discussion of college students would apply as well to the high school years:[8]

"At one of these informal meetings at which a group of students and an instructor met in the late afternoon and merely chatted about anything that came to mind, one of the girls remarked that she had just received a bid to join one of the most popular sororities on the campus. The others immediately congratulated her on being admitted to so select a group. Then the girl went on to say that she did not know whether she would accept the bid because she had always considered sororities snobbish and undemocratic. Within a few minutes the group was in a spirited discussion on the place of sororities and fraternities in a democratic college. A number of related and significant problems entered the discussion naturally. On the whole, the quality of the reasoning was high, and when it was not, the other members of the group quickly pointed out flaws in

[8] Harry N. Rivlin, "Meeting the Problem of Moral Conflict through Realistic Teaching," *Mental Hygiene*, 26:58–70 (1942).

the arguments advanced. Much can be said for the kind of relationship that makes it possible for a group of college students to discuss a problem that they feel to be important with an instructor whom they respect. Is not this an effective way of helping students to resolve moral conflicts?"

5. By propaganda. It is sometimes held that the school should maintain such neutrality that it doesn't even propagandize for democracy. This seems a foolish viewpoint, for there are ideals—and this is one—which are so generally accepted as good (accepted in thought though often not in action) that the school must feel obligated to throw its weight on their side and thus help fortify them. The techniques of propaganda are many—movies, posters, the pointing up of examples of the ideal wherever they occur, an attitude toward the ideal of "Of course, we all want it like this," the advocation of the ideal by people with prestige, publicizing it through the school paper, and so on. They should all be utilized. Too often it is the supporters of selfish aims who make the great efforts to propagate them. Those on the side of generous and noble objectives must be equally energetic.

6. By books and movies. A movie of some years ago, *Mrs. Miniver*, depicted a very wholesome and happy husband-wife relationship in such a way as to give it great appeal. Such a picture can do even the older person a distinct service in delineating graphically and attractively an ideal which is worth striving for. Similarly books—novels and biographies particularly, but others as well—can picture an ideal in such a way as to inspire one to try to reach it. Surely many of the readers of this text have memories of books or articles they have read which have led them to accept an ideal not previously held.

MORALS

Chave defines morality in this way:[9] "Morality is the self-regulation of conduct with due consideration for both one's own welfare and the welfare of others." He goes on later to say: "One cannot be moral until one recognizes the social consequences of one's acts, and one is moral to the degree that one controls one's conduct with concern for these consequences." Putting it in another way, he says: "Speaking generally, one may say that an act is right to the degree that it furthers the rights and welfare of all those involved in the act and that it is wrong to the degree that it hinders the welfare and growth of anyone."

Too often we think of morality as having to do with sex behavior, in which society has stamped certain kinds of behavior as "right" and other kinds as "wrong." As Chave's definition indicates, morality is something

[9] Ernest J. Chave, *Personality Development in Children* (Chicago: University of Chicago Press, 1937), pp. 202–203.

infinitely bigger and more important than such a limited view would show.

If one is moral, he is good—good in the sense that his behavior does no one ill and in the sense that if everyone were moral, life would be good for all of us.

We have occasion to make many different kinds of moral choices. We make such a choice when we are tempted to be dishonest in a test, when we are divided in action upon being given too much change after making a purchase, in deciding whether or not to drink; we make such a choice when we drive too fast on the highway, when we loaf on our job, when we lie. But we are moral or immoral in each of these cases not because our conscience judges us to be one or the other or because society labels us moral or immoral but only because the results of our action have been good for us and others or bad.

Sometimes we make our moral choices on the basis of a code that has been given to us, sometimes on the basis of a personal code which we have worked out, and sometimes on the basis of no code at all but rather through an examination of the situation upon which the choice depends.

No one should ever put his whole trust in society's dictates as to what is right and what is wrong, for a social code can never be so flexible or so minutely detailed as to take care of every situation. What is more, the social code may be wrong. Everyone should be able to make moral choices upon the basis of his own judgment.

If everyone were truly moral as Chave defines morality, we would have a wonderful world to live in, for it would be a world of brotherhood and a world where no outward compulsions would be needed to make people good. In such a world one would not have to be on guard against meanness, dishonesty, or cruelty.

But this is only an ideal and a long way from reality. Nevertheless in working with the adolescent we can help to move mankind a little way closer to that ideal. There are two necessities. One is that the adolescent accept a wholesome social code. The other is that he learn to make moral choices where that code does not function or where it needs to be superseded. As Chave says:[10] "While most of a person's conduct may be guided by conventional mores, progress depends upon revision of conventional practices and requires keen judgment."

What Is the Adolescent Like?

We get some understanding of what the adolescent's code of morals is like when we look at reports from the Chicago study on adolescent

[10] *Ibid.*, p. 221.

character and personality, with respect specifically to the qualities of *honesty, loyalty, moral courage, and responsibility:*[11]

"The concept of honesty is dominated by ideas about the use of property and telling the truth. Such acts as borrowing things without permission and using small sums of the family's money without permission are highly disapproved. Telling the truth to employers, teachers, and parents is uniformly and rigorously accepted. Compromises occur only when telling the truth involves betraying another student, thus suggesting tattling. Usually, also, some compromise is attempted when protecting friends conflicts with being honest and truthful towards school authorities. Rigorous and even extreme standards are used in judging other people's honesty. . . .

"Beliefs in [the] area [of loyalty] seem to be confused and uncertain. . . .

"Loyalty to personal friends is often subordinated to other values. Apparently for Prairie City subjects there is a code of not betraying friends outright, but not a similarly strong code of pleasing or cherishing friends.

"Loyalty to school seems to be limited to obeying school rules—attending school parties and school activities is not taken very seriously. A somewhat more positive attitude is expressed in connection with the problem situations. These suggest willingness to contribute to school welfare, willingness to carry on certain activities in spite of the razzing of immediate friends, and willingness to stand up for worth-while causes against the criticism of peers. This suggests that loyalty to school is seen in terms of obvious, concrete actions but that a generalized concept of loyalty to school as an institution is lacking.

"Loyalty to leaders is qualified by an unwillingness to support them if one disagrees with them.

"The least-developed aspect is loyalty to ideas, principles, and values. A high degree of uncertainty characterizes reactions to all issues involving conflict of several loyalties with other values, such as defending the family against criticism or dropping a friendship if one's reputation is endangered. . . .

"The strongest aspect of moral courage is that of defending and protecting one's own rights and those of others. There is practically a unanimous feeling that one must defend anyone against gossip. Yet doubt and fear are expressed about any opinion or action, no matter how right, which is likely to arouse the displeasure of any person in authority or

[11] Reprinted by permission from *Adolescent Character and Personality* by R. J. Havighurst and H. Taba, published by John Wiley & Sons, Inc., 1949, pp. 84–86.

jeopardize one's popularity with peers. There is hesitance in raising questions of rightness and wrongness in criticizing peers, for fear of being regarded as a prig. Subjects also show unwillingness to undertake action which may be needed for the benefit of a group or project, if that action suggests direct or implied criticism of other students. They seem inclined to leave other's business alone, even though other values may be sacrificed. Following the group, even into wrongdoing, is rather highly approved.

"On the whole, rebels show more moral courage than do students who are generally amenable to accepted standards. This suggests that rebels and negatively disposed individuals have greater opportunity to develop moral courage because their personal makeup predisposes them to act in ways which are conducive to moral courage. Individuals with positive moral values, but more submissive dispositions, have fewer opportunities for defending their positive and desirable values. . . .

"Standards of responsibility are highly developed, and they are applied under a variety of circumstances. Duties toward school, home, and employment are taken seriously. Punctuality in attending meetings, completing accepted jobs, and aiding the family financially stand high on the list of approved items. Especially rigorous standards are set up for other people, and lenience toward athletes or talented or forgetful people is highly disapproved.

"There is a great assurance that the first duty of a student is toward his own success, whether in earning grades or in preparing for life work. Very few of our subjects consider it wise to sacrifice this value to any demands that might be made by the general school welfare. On the whole responsibility toward work outside school is taken more seriously than responsibility toward school work or school activities.

"Uncertainties occur most frequently in the case of conflicts between family loyalty, school responsibilities, and friends."

Beller[12] gives us information about honesty in boys from nine to fifteen. Items used describe how a boy would act in a certain situation and also how he would feel about that act. One item from the scale is:

"A boy took a bus. The crowd pushed him so that he could not drop a nickel in the box. He thought it was not his fault that he did not pay the fare and got off at his stop without paying the fare.

"If that happened to you would you do what he did?

"Would it be right for you to do what he did?"

Beller concludes: "We are confronted with the finding that older boys are less honest than younger boys in their behavioral disposition. In in-

[12] Emanuel K. Beller, "Two Attitude Components in Younger Boys," *Journal of Social Psychology*, 29:137–151 (1949).

terpreting this change in honesty we shall proceed from the assumption that underlying the modification in social behavior in most cases is a conflict of motives. It will be remembered that most of the items in the honesty scale were constructed around conflicts. At the age of puberty boys have to give up many well established habits of their childhood and adjust to a new habit system. During this period, frustrations and conflicts mount and therefore deceitful behavior is more likely to occur as a means of mastering new and difficult tasks. Resentment of adult morality and rebellion against it are often found among 12- and 15-year-olds."

While he found that there was a drop in honesty as far as behavior went, he found too that there was an increase in honesty as far as attitudes were concerned. This dichotomy between expressed attitude and behavior is too remindful of adult hypocrisy to be anything but disturbing.

The Adolescent's Moral Conflicts

The adolescent's life is certainly not free from moral conflict and may be unusually troubled at times by the need for moral decisions regarding which he feels inadequate. At the same time, he makes choices where moral issues are involved without realizing what the alternatives and their values are.

Most adolescents have to make moral decisions in these three areas:

1. Relationships with the other sex.
2. Smoking and drinking.
3. Honesty, and obeying the law.

Moral conflicts in regard to relationships with the other sex are generally of the "How far should I [or we] go?" variety, although other choices of a moral nature are also made, usually without being recognized as such. Of this latter group are questions of this sort: How far should a girl allow herself to go in arousing a boy emotionally when she wants little if any physical expression of his feelings? How much should a boy urge a girl to intimacies such as kissing and mutual caresses when no real affection is involved but only a desire for pleasurable sensations? How much responsibility should each feel for the choices the other makes? These should be recognized by adolescents as moral issues and the alternatives and outcomes fully understood.

As for the first question, "How far should I go?" we have here a really difficult problem faced by many a boy and girl, complicated by the fact that three different viewpoints in regard to it exist among adults and adolescents. Some adults—the majority, perhaps—and a few adolescents, believe that any kind of "touch" behavior is wrong for the teen-ager; other adults believe that it may be good for the boy and girl who love each other to engage in intimacies short of intercourse; many adolescents think that "it's all right" to do anything except have intercourse, and some think that that, too, is permissible. This third viewpoint differs from the second in that it is based not on the matter of wholesomeness but on the matter of "rightness" as opposed to "wrongness."

We see that the youth has no certainties here to which he may cling. With his emotion pressing him toward physical expression of his feelings, his mind may say, "It's wrong," at the same time that it says, "But the others do it."

Adults could help him in this quandary if they themselves would recognize this as a moral choice where right or wrong does not exist by ordinance but must be discovered by weighing the effects of the action on the participants and on society as a whole. Then they could at least clarify the issues for the adolescent and help him to make his decisions with wisdom and understanding.

Conflicts in regard to smoking and drinking[13] are not of the same nature as conflicts in regard to sex behavior, for here the issues are more clean-cut and there is no question of a strong natural urge demanding expression.

When "Should I smoke?" becomes a matter for decision with the teen-ager, he knows, in most cases, that his parents would rather that he didn't smoke but that a lot of the "fellows" (or girls) do—and he is not convinced that there is any harm in it. With drinking he knows that his parents think it harmful, but here he realizes that they are right, although he is apt to feel that he himself will be able to handle the drinking better than do those who get into trouble with it. The pressure to drink comes from the fact that others in the crowd do it, from the desire to try something which has the halo of adult sophistication about it, from the pleasure in the effect—or from all of these.

Here the adolescent needs facts upon which to make his choice. He should realize that he is not deciding between what is mysteriously 'right" or "wrong" but is rather choosing in terms of what is good for him (and others) or bad. With both smoking and drinking, the advantages and disadvantages are rather easily discerned. However, the desire to be like the others, the tantalizing temptation of forbidden fruit, the feelings of importance the act may give, and the physical pleasures that result all cloud the issue and make choice difficult. The fact that both smoking and moderate drinking are considered acceptable behavior for adults puts still further weight on the side of the adolescent's so indulging himself.

[13] Of course it is realized that the problems of the adolescent's smoking is not to be compared in seriousness with that of the adolescent's drinking.

The adolescent makes many moral choices in regard to honesty and in regard to obeying laws or regulations although he seldom understands the moral issues involved. Most unfortunately, there is the feeling with many an adolescent that the adult is his natural antagonist and that if he can circumvent adult-made rules, it is all to his credit. This attitude often prevails in the case of cheating in a test, smoking on the school grounds, faking excuses for absences, getting out of study hall, letting some other student do one's classwork, or (outside of the school) getting into a movie for the children's admission price and driving a car before one is old enough.

We can say about all of this, "It's adolescence," and let that be the end of the matter, justified by the fact that this type of adolescent dishonesty is not necessarily the forerunner of any large-scale adult dishonesty of character. Yet then we are acting on the assumption that adults as they are are good enough, are moral enough—an assumption which is not valid if our goal is a world where adults are truly as good to themselves and others as possible. If it is our hope that *adolescent development* means the development into better adults as a whole than we now have, then we cannot say, "They seem to turn out all right," and be content with adolescent behavior as it now is.

In trying to help the adolescent be—and continue in adulthood to be—a highly moral individual, we are greatly handicapped by the fact that adults provide an example of seeming to get along well in the world without having high standards of behavior. The grasping competitiveness in business, the willingness to let others suffer if one thereby may get ahead are only a part of this. Outside of business, too, in relationships with neighbors, with coworkers, and with government, and of course in government itself, all kinds of shoddy behavior for personal gain are countenanced, if not by actual expression of approval, at least by absence of criticism.

Perhaps then we should be much more concerned than we are about the adolescent's dishonesty—not in the sense that we express shocked disapproval, but rather that we examine our responsibilities as adults and do something about them.

If this is the case, then we should be careful to have adolescents cooperate in setting up all of the regulations by which we expect them to live, in order that they may be governed by rules that make sense, have purpose, and of which they approve. Then they would not be forced into dishonesties by unreasonable rules or adult dictatorship, and their choices could be based on a full realization not only of consequence but also of obligations.

Some adolescent moral conflicts arise because obligations to parents or teachers are in opposition to immediate desires. The boy would like to do what his parents wish, but he's lazy, he has other uses for his time and energy, or he has other wishes, and he must then make a choice. "Save your money," says his mother. But his desire is to spend it. "Clean the garage," says his father. But when the time comes, he wants to be out with the other boys. Sometimes he believes that what his parents want is the right thing to do. Sometimes he thinks they are wrong, but he still feels a sense of duty toward them. In either case his choice involves allegiances as well as issues, and it is for that reason one which may leave him dissatisfied regardless of the choice he makes.

Finally, some of the adolescent's moral difficulties come from the fact that his own age group pull him away from what he thinks is right and from what he actually would prefer to do.

"Come on, let's see if we can get in this tavern and have a drink."
"But we shouldn't."
"Aw, be a good sport."

"Let's see if you can get the car up to ninety."
"No, that's dangerous."
"Go ahead, don't be a sissy."

"Let's play the slot machines."
"No, I don't believe in those things."
"What's the matter? 'Fraid you'll lose a nickel?"

In such cases moral courage is greatly needed, for to take opposition against a group of people you like or by whom you want to be liked requires a considerable strength of character, particularly in adolescence when the opinion of others means so much. Even here, too, the choice may not be unequivocal. For there are times when being a good sport or being willing to follow the group may be worth more than the safety which the other choice might entail.

Probably the school could give no better service in these conflicts involving allegiances than to provide opportunities to the adolescent to discuss such problems in heterogeneous groups. For in such groups there are sure to be others who champion the viewpoint of the adolescent who feels that he stands alone in doing the right thing, and knowing others who feel as he does will give him strength. Then, too, it is important that the youth have an opportunity to objectify his conflicts, see them as an outsider would, and thus remove them from the realm of his feelings. This, too, comes about when such problems are discussed by many of his own age group.

What Is the Source of Moral Values?

According to Havighurst and Taba, there are six motivational sources of moral values:

1. Ambition and social mobility. In this case the person tries to be what will make him acceptable to the social group he wants to enter or whose support he wants. His moral choices will not depend upon a personal code or upon judgment as to what is good and wholesome. Rather they will depend upon his estimation of what other people require or have respect for. If the social group he is trying to conform to have good morals, then his choices will tend to be good; if not, the reverse will be true. However, even if the results are good as far as his behavior is concerned, this way of reaching them is not conducive to inner security or even self-respect, for he must always dance as someone else calls the tune.

2. Affectional responsiveness. Similar to the one above is the person who tries to be what others want because he wants them to like him. He is "good" because this particular kind of "goodness" will bring him the approval and even the affection that he craves.

3. Submission to authority. Some people get their directions as to what they should do or what they shouldn't from whatever authority is concerned with them. First it will be the parents, then the school and the parents, and then whatever groups or individuals have an authoritative position toward them. Such people are likely to be timid and to find it difficult to make a choice when their personal desires conflict with authority.

4. Impulse and emotionality. There are people who let their feelings and desires of the moment decide many of their choices. All of us can doubtless think of some situations, particularly in our youth, when we have acted upon impulse. Some people are characteristically impulsive.

5. Negativism. Some people who don't get along well react by adopting a negative policy toward the customary and the expected. They, then, to quote Havighurst and Taba, "tend to develop a morality which represents the reverse of the one expected of them."

6. Rationality and reflection. Some people arrive at their moral code and moral choices through a thoughtful consideration of possibilities and principles. Their values are of their own choice; they approve of them and they have made them a part of themselves. When choice is not on the basis of this personal code, it is put on a basis of deliberation and careful judgment. This is the desirable situation, for it implies self-regulation of conduct. It is not sufficient, of course, unless that self-regulation of conduct is regardful both of personal good and of the welfare of others.

Developing Morality

As Havighurst and Taba say:[14] "The ability to apply moral beliefs to an increasing range of conflicting life situations is quite undeveloped at the age of sixteen. These subjects see the more obvious lines of action but seem at a loss whenever a subtle weighing of values is called for. They find conflicts hard to face; they tend to solve conflicts by using slogans rather than by using concepts of the relative significance of values."

To the extent that the high school students referred to by Havighurst and Taba are typical of all, we may conclude that the school has not done much to develop the ability to make moral choices except in stereotyped situations where a rule of thumb will work. We cannot conclude, of course, that such adolescents will invariably become adults who similarly cannot make intelligently-thought-through moral choices, but we can be sure that many will grow up thus limited if something is not done to make them different in high school.

This is the essence of character education, and its importance cannot be stressed too much. Every teacher should be concerned about it; the teacher who is not concerned cannot be called a good teacher.

Just what can be done?

1. The teacher should realize how wide is the variety of situations where moral choice functions.

In the student-union building of a small college, the top floor has seven "hotel" rooms which are rented to teachers and to transient guests of the college. One night two of the rooms were rented to four high school seniors, intelligent, well-mannered boys who were at the college as part of a high school choir on tour.

In the small attractive lobby on this floor were two delicate figurines standing on the radio. When the maid came to clean the rooms on the morning following the day of these boys' arrival, she found the figurines missing. Rightly or wrongly, she decided to glance in the traveling bags standing in the two rooms used by the boys. In the second one she opened, she found one of the figurines; in the third, she found the other. The boys were taking them home.

This is what we popularly call a "boyish prank." But it was stealing. It was an immoral choice, for it was a choice which profited the boys at the expense of someone else.

On that same campus, there is one building in which smoking is not allowed because of fire hazards. The men congregate between classes out-

---

[14] Reprinted by permission from *Adolescent Character and Personality* by R. J. Havighurst and H. Taba, published by John Wiley & Sons, Inc., 1949, p. 95.

side the doors to smoke. At these places there are containers for refuse, and it would be very simple to toss the cigarette butts in them. But few bother. They throw them wherever they happen to be standing, and by noon the sidewalk immediately in front of each entrance is cluttered with them.

Here too we have a moral choice made, a choice which makes someone else the victim of these people's carelessness and selfishness.

Both of these cases are trivial, and we cannot assume that people who are thus careless of the rights of others in minor issues will be similarly careless in more important ones, for this is often not true at all. We mention them for two reasons: (1) to show how commonplace are occasions where a moral choice must be made; (2) to suggest that even "trivial" moral choices when added together make for a great deal of pleasantness or unpleasantness in the living of those who are affected by them.

Morality is involved wherever honesty is concerned, in responsibilities set by the law, in discrimination, in keeping one's word, in doing one's work conscientiously, in sex behavior, in drinking, in the whole question of expediency, and the like. The teacher should have enough understanding of the variety of moral choices to recognize a moral choice as such wherever it occurs.

2. The teacher must realize that the truly moral person depends upon reasoning and judgment in addition to a moral code he has accepted. He should see that it is better to think "It is right because . . . " than "It is right." He should examine his own code and his precepts for youth to see that they are justifiable in the light of common sense and good will. It is not enough for the teacher to say, "Don't do this." Youth demand a reason, and we should be glad that they do. It is imperative that we be able to give them reasons that are honest and convincing.

3. The teacher should stress consideration for others, which is a necessary background for good moral choices. As we have said, true morality involves knowing the effect of behavior on ourselves and also on others and wanting to follow the path that will be good for ourselves and/or for others and that will hurt no one. It involves respecting the rights of others and not encroaching on their rights in order to make ourselves happier.

Just how this consideration can be fostered is a most difficult problem. That the teacher should exemplify it himself goes without question. Nonetheless, many do not. In a history class, for instance, every student was required to give a brief current events report before the class once every two weeks. One boy of sixteen stuttered and found it very difficult to appear before the class. He went to the history teacher, explained this and asked if she would allow him to stand by his seat rather than go to the front of the class for his report. The teacher said, "Why, you won't have to give a report at all." The boy protested, saying that he wanted to do his part but wished only the concession of not having to stand facing the class. The teacher repeated that he wouldn't have to give any reports, and the boy left, thanking her for her kindness. Since he was a good student and all of his test results were high, he was amazed to find a D in History on his first report card for the year. Confident that a mistake in recording had been made, he went to the teacher to ask her about it. She replied, "I couldn't give you anything more since you have failed to give your current event reports." And in spite of the boy's protests, this is the grade that remained on his card.

The teacher's lack of respect for the rights of others may not influence the class other than to hurt those who suffer by it. But his efforts to get others to feel that respect cannot amount to much if he himself cares so little about them as did this teacher.

How else can consideration for others be fostered? One way is to allow students to set up their own regulations for class and school, for such a process necessitates thought for the welfare of all. Another way is for the teacher to make sure that no one encroaches on the rights of others, using his authority if necessary. Other techniques must be left to the teacher's ingenuity and good judgment.

4. The teacher should further an understanding of what moral choice involves. Two girls, good friends, are both taking third-year Latin. Though each is a good student, one is so busy with extracurricular activities and dates that she has little time for study. Consequently she relies on her friend to get her Latin assignments for her and has even persuaded her to give her help in tests. Both girls have made choices which we would term *moral choices*. Would they recognize them as such? It is doubtful. And yet they should.

Adolescents should realize that there are many occasions when they must choose between their own pleasure and the welfare of others or between a trivial satisfaction, but an immediate one, and a far more important satisfaction, but a remote one. They should recognize the fact that in the first type of choice they are morally obligated to consider the good of others as well as their own good; in the second type of choice they are morally obligated to consider their own best welfare.

Such realization cannot be achieved by lecturing. The learning must come more naturally and must be in line with adolescent interests. Classes which involve the study of people lend themselves to discussions of moral issues—literature, history, government, social studies. Extracurricular groups frequently must meet problems which involve moral issues and therefore are a means to growth of moral understanding.

5. The teacher should try to make morality and moral courage attractive. His own appreciation of students who are "doing the right thing" is the beginning of this, but he must avoid the danger of seeming most appreciative of those uninteresting students whose only personality virtue appears to be their model deportment. The students should realize that personality strength, attractiveness, and morality can and often do go together, and any illustrations which can be brought to their attention without patent moralizing should be helpful. There are people in public life today, as any day, in politics, in the movies, and on the stage, who do combine glamour and goodness, just as there are adolescents who are popular and socially successful as well as being possessed of a fine sense of moral responsibility. These combinations should be high-lighted when such people are being discussed.

6. The teacher should provide opportunities for students to get experiences in making good moral choices. A method suggested by Evenden seems applicable here.[15] He proposes that we give students a "budget of power" just as we might give them a budget of money, to use in any way they see fit. They might be given complete power, for example, to spend the proceeds from the freshman fair in whatever way they chose. No adults would try to influence their choice or hedge it about with restrictions. There would be no criticisms or "I told you so's" if what the students did was not in harmony with what adults thought they should do. Just as with money, at times there would be an auditing of how the budgets of power had been used, but this would be undertaken without any attitude of or assumption of superiority on the part of adults. A teacher giving over budgets of power would want to make the amount of power small at first and then to increase the budget as students learned to use power wisely.

Another suggestion pertinent to this and other points comes from Ciernick, who describes a volunteer student congress organized to study the problem of cheating. The 18 members of the congress were selected by the 36 social science classes of the high school.

The congress, working quietly and without publicity, studied the question with care and finally came to the following recommendations:[16]

"1. More emphasis should be placed upon honor, and the dishonesty of cheating should be stressed.

"2. Whenever a test is being given, teachers should watch carefully to prevent cheating. This should be done, not just to catch cheaters but to protect the student who really doesn't want to cheat but who may be put on the spot by his classmates.

[15] Dr. Edward S. Evenden, in an address given in Terre Haute, Ind., April 20, 195
[16] Sylvia Ciernick, "What Can We Do about Cheating?" *NEA Journal*, 39:57 (1950)

"3. More theme-type tests should be given, even if they are short.

"4. Plenty of warning should be given before a test so that students who are willing to study for it will have time to do so. Students get frantic when hard surprise tests are given.

"5. The philosophy should be accepted that cheating is definitely wrong and undesirable. Cheating cannot be stopped if most of the kids and some of the teachers think it is smart.

"6. Teachers should try to make school work interesting and help the kids see how what they learn will be of help to them later.

"7. Students should be allowed to help decide the value which will be given to different kinds of marks, such as: recitations, oral quizzes, maps, notes, and notebooks.

"8. Teachers should try to have several marks in their books for each student before deciding on the mark for the period.

"9. More oral quizzes should be given and more oral work required.

"10. Teachers should try to get together and arrive at some uniformity as to the amount of work to be assigned and ways of marking."

7. The teacher should emphasize a positive morality. Murray, in an article, "Time for a Positive Morality,"[17] stresses the fact that our social philosophy has had a negative orientation and that it is time for us to stress a positive ideal of moral development. We have been able to agree on what we *don't* want, he says, but we have not been able to agree on what we *do* want. He suggests that instead of setting up a lofty image of perfection as a spur to our efforts, we should work out clearly the steps to attaining it; instead of preaching moral absolutes, we should define the conditions under which they should operate; instead of imposing ideals from above, we should devise a democratic way of modifying and improving ourselves.

8. The teacher should have in mind a goal of mature morality toward which he helps the students grow. Titus lists eight marks of a mature morality:[18]

"*a*. A mature morality judges an act right or wrong on the basis of its effect upon persons or upon human welfare.

"*b*. A mature morality is one in which concern for persons expresses itself in a spirit of love or selflessness, and even when necessary in self-sacrifice. This spirit of love at its highest embraces the entire human family.

"*c*. A mature morality is one which places a premium upon knowledge and intelligence.

[17] Henry A. Murray, "Time for a Positive Morality," *Survey Graphic*, 36:195–196, 214–216 (1947).

[18] Reprinted by permission from Harold H. Titus, *What Is a Mature Morality?* (New York: The Macmillan Company, 1943), pp. 68–102.

"*d*. We are morally mature only when we rely on inner rather than upon outer controls.

"*e*. A mature morality judges the entire act, which includes a motive or motives, means, and consequences.

"*f*. A mature morality recognizes that for a better society we need both transformed individuals and social reconstruction.

"*g*. We are morally mature only when we are willing to grow along with the growing, changing world.

"*h*. A mature morality interprets our human duties as duties to God and thus it gives cosmic significance to the moral life."

RELIGION AND ETHICS

Though there are many adults who do not profess any particular religious faith and though there are many who are not members of a church and do not attend church, there are probably few who would not agree that what one gets from religion at its best is a necessity to every individual:

An emphasis on the spiritual in living.
An emphasis upon a way of life that is altruistic and good for all.
An opportunity for fellowship in good works.

As Black says:[19] "Man's moral life, the effort to work out a meaningful existence, is the struggle to fulfill the most precious of human possibilities in one's personal life; to achieve relationships which are mutually liberating and creative and a society which gives security and support to the upward movement for a better world."

In the homes of some adolescents there is considerable emphasis on the spiritual and the altruistic. The same adolescents in many cases also receive inspiration from church attendance. As to this, the Washington data given in Table 30 are fairly typical.

Our knowledge of the variations that exist in homes and the data in Table 30 tell us that there are many adolescents whose lives are not being influenced in a religious way by the home, the church, or any other institution. For these students particularly, but for the others, too, the school has its responsibility. This responsibility is not to introduce religion into the schools as it is denominationally practiced. It is rather to find opportunities to stress spiritual values.

Weaver writes that youth have three needs for religion:[20]

[19] Black, *op. cit.*, p. 3.
[20] Paul Weaver, "Youth and Religion," *Annals of American Academy of Political and Social Science*, 236:152–160 (1944).

"First, there is a need for a clear outlook on life. The lives of young persons, no less than of adults, must have adequate meaning. The fragmentary elements of experience must be held together. It is precisely in adolescence that the tendency to generalize begins. There is a search for continuity in experience and for a philosophy that gives life purpose.

"It is not easy for youth to find manageable meaning in the kind of world they inherit today. Not only the war and political unrest, but also the contradictions in our culture between a realistic, scientific outlook and a traditional religious outlook (that for the greater part has not effectively come to terms with scientific mood and assumptions) block the path to an integrated, assured universe of meaning. . . .

TABLE 30. ATTENDANCE AT CHURCH, SUNDAY SCHOOL, OR OTHER YOUNG PEOPLE'S RELIGIOUS ORGANIZATIONS*

	Boy	Girl	Total
Every week..............	23.1	33.4	28.7
Usually.................	14.3	22.5	18.8
As often as not...........	10.1	10.0	10.1
Seldom attend............	36.4	24.4	29.8
Never attend.............	10.6	4.3	7.1
No information...........	5.5	5.4	5.5

* L. J. Elias, *High School Youth Look at Their Problems* (Pullman, Wash.: College Bookstore, State College of Washington, 1949), p. 32.

"Second, youth is in almost desperate need of ethical clarity and ethical conviction. The mores of our culture have been changing rapidly. An older reserve about sex, based on fear of consequences and rigid moral convictions, is gone. Science has circumvented the fears, and the temper of the times has weakened moral conviction. Drinking has moved from the saloon into the drawing room. Statutes and smart legal practice have replaced stern moral principles in judging acceptable procedures for making money. Hollywood has pushed the divan from the shadows into the center of the spotlight. Smoking is no longer just fashionable, but the taken-for-granted habit of healthy adults. The speed of all these changes has increased in wartime conditions as it has sharpened youth's need.

"Most parents have not made mental adjustments in their expectations for youth behavior; nor have they evolved realistic and acceptable reasons as a base for reserve in young people. The dichotomy and the confusion create a severe problem. . . . In my own course in beginning philosophy for college students, the most intense questions I find raised have to do with ethics. 'What is the difference between right and wrong? What

makes a right thing right?' These questions are raised in deepest seriousness, and in some instances in a kind of panic. They want to know—and
they want to know what is true—not just what is believed by older persons, including ministers, parents, and teachers. . . .

"Third, youth needs emotional sensitivity. Morals that have grown
threadbare decreasingly claim allegiance. Recreation, increasingly becoming commercialized amusement, dulls the edge of emotional creativity.
Strivings of youth for maturity become imitations of the collegiate set
glamourized by pictures. Boom conditions in many cities take youth out
of the home. Careless workmanship and *naïveté* of religious education
workers frequently keep religious programs for youth aesthetically poor
and emotionally trivial. Much of our 'character building' work with youth
has been done with little regard for the basic importance of emotions."

Emphasizing the Spiritual in Life

First of all, those working with youth must understand just what a
religious but nondenominational emphasis means. It means an emphasis
upon respect for the individual and upon kindness and generosity toward
others. It means a belief in the possibilities for improving personal and
group integrity and goodness and a willingness to work for that improvement. It means attention to the noble and uplifting aspects of life rather
than to the materialistic alone.

Second, they must themselves be guided by spiritual values in their
own lives and in their school practices. They must try to be honorable
in all of their relationships, to evaluate people for their true worth, to
appreciate goodness, honesty, responsibility, careful workmanship, and
all other such virtues not measurable by dollars, immeasurable in their
worth to society.

Third, they must seek every opportunity to promote the kind of living
which, to use Black's words previously quoted, faces the possibilities of
the world and makes life sweet for one another instead of bitter.

One junior high school has short devotionals each morning at nine
o'clock. The program is broadcast over the public-address system. First
a hymn is played. Then the 300- to 400-word devotional is read by some
capable boy or girl. In this school, life is concretely related to principles
of spiritual living.[21]

In a senior problems class in a Los Angeles high school, the students
agreed to practice the golden rule in relation to the members of their

[21] Maude McElvaney, "Devotionals in Highland Park," *Phi Delta Kappan*, 30:190-
192 (1949).

families, without telling anyone. Here is what some of them said about the experiment:[22]

"During these ten days I have become closer to my parents than ever before. By meeting them halfway I am able to discuss my problems with them, whereas previously the discussions had been arguments."

"I really feel good about being helpful and kind to my family, and I'm sure from what I've done in the past ten days my family appreciate me more than ever before. I've also found that happiness can be yours, if you just go about it in the right way."

"The way my family noticed things was incredible. The first two days my mother thought I wasn't feeling well, and wanted to borrow the car. My sisters practically fainted, they couldn't believe that I could be so generous and thoughtful. As a whole my family wondered if I could continue. I told them I would try to be that way forever."

"During these ten days I didn't have any fights with either my sister or my brother which was very unusual and I could tell that they were trying to get me mad at times because they didn't know what was going on. My family all appreciated the fact that I was helping my mom more than what I already did and my dad wasn't as crabby with me as he usually was. Both my brother and sister when they saw how I was helping my mom decided they were going to do the same and they did. I found after this that we were all getting along better than ever before."

Reminiscences

1. Can you think of any standards you now hold which were definitely acquired in your adolescence? What made you adopt them?

2. Were you more idealistic in your adolescence than you are now? In what respects?

3. Try to explain how and when your present religious beliefs developed?

General Discussion

1. What standards and ideals are adolescents likely to pick up from movies and the radio? Speak in terms of specific movies and specific radio programs.

2. How does Chave's idea of morality differ from the popular idea of what morality consists of?

3. Consider Havighurst's remarks on honesty, loyalty, moral courage, and responsibility. Then tell as concretely as possible what adolescents you have known are like in these respects. What should they be like, ideally?

[22] "Progress Reports from Junior and Senior High Schools, Moral and Spiritual Values in Education," Publication No. SL343, May, 1947, Curriculum Division of Los Angeles City School Districts, as reported in *Phi Delta Kappan*, 30:107–108 (1948).

4. Consider the six motivational sources of moral values. Describe in an illustrative way people you have known who have exemplified each of these.

5. Consider the suggestions for what the school can do to further character education. Try to find illustration of these from your own experiences in high school.

6. Consider Titus's eight marks of a mature morality. Do you agree with all on his list? Are there some that you would rate higher than others?

7. Consider Weaver's account of youth's three religious needs. How can the school and the teacher help supply each of these?

Panel Discussion

1. What standards would you like to have an adolescent son or daughter have?

2. Should adolescents smoke?

3. Why should one encourage adolescent honesty? How can it be done?

4. How can an interest in the subjective aspects of life as contrasted with an interest in the objective aspects be furthered in adolescents?

5. What can be done in the high school to promote universal brotherhood?

6. Should high school teachers try to exemplify in every respect the standards, ideals, morals, and religion they would like adolescents to adopt?

7. What moral choices are common in adulthood? Are they different from the moral choices of adolescence?

8. Does organized religion give us answers to all moral questions?

Further Reading

BECKER, I., "Emotions in the Religious Development of Young People," *Religious Education*, 42:281–284 (1947).

FROST, B. JOHN, "Some Thoughts on Censorship and Youth," *Library Journal*, 70:792–793 (1945).

GRUENBERG, SIDONIE, "The Comics as a Social Force," *Journal of Educational Sociology*, 18:204–213 (1944).

HAVIGHURST, ROBERT J., MYRA Z. ROBINSON, and MILDRED DORR, "The Development of the Ideal Self in Childhood and Adolescence," *Journal of Educational Research*, 40:241–257 (1946).

HAVIGHURST, R. J., and H. TABA, *Adolescent Character and Personality* (New York: John Wiley & Sons, Inc. 1949).

HORNE, E. P., and W. H. STENDER, "Student Attitudes toward Religious Practices," *Journal of Social Psychology*, 22:215–217 (1945).

McCONNELL, T. R., "College Students and the Problem of Values," *School and Society*, 53:713–719 (1941).

MORGAN, EDWARD D., and J. B. VASCHE, "The American Way: Oakdale's Freshman Laboratory Course in Social Living and Democratic Ideals," *Clearing House*, 16:259–263 (1941).

NELSON, E., "Student Attitudes toward Religion," *Genetic Psychology Monograph*, 22:323–423 (1940).

NELSON, RAYMOND, "Citizenship Laboratory," *School Review*, 56:156–162 (1948).

NICHOLS, MARION, "A One-year Curriculum in Social Living for High School Freshmen," *School and Society*, 53:541–543 (1941).

ORAM, GERTRUDE, "Meeting the Grown-up World," *Parents' Magazine*, 14:24–25 (1939).

RAUTMAN, ARTHUR L., "Youth in Search of a Standard," *Mental Hygiene*, 30:597–605 (1946).

REMMERS, H. H., and N. WELTMAN, "Attitude Inter-relationships of Youth, Their Parents, and Their Teachers," *Journal of Social Psychology*, 26:61–67 (1947).

TARKOFF, IRMA, "History Classes Visit Churches of 3 Faiths," *Clearing House*, 20:39–41 (1945).

THURSTON, MARY E., "510 Assistants," *Clearing House*, 18:288–289 (1943).

WILLIAMS, LILLIAN, "Teaching Them to Feel," *International Journal of Religious Education*, 19:10–11 (1943).

WORTH, HOWARD A., "A Decade of Youth Works in the Church," *Religious Education*, 46:111–114 (1951).

ZORBAUGH, HARVEY, "The Comics—There They Stand," *Journal of Educational Sociology*, 8:196–203 (1944).

Chapter 9. PERSONAL ADJUSTMENT

If we could guarantee to each high school student that he would be a truly well-adjusted person by the time he left high school, we would be doing him a service greater than all others that we might do put together. We would be assuring him the best possible basis for happiness. We would be saving him from all of the misery that can come to a person from his own personality difficulties.

What would he be like? Let us look at a hypothetical well-adjusted high school senior, Tom, to see what good adjustment actually means.

THE WELL-ADJUSTED ADOLESCENT

Tom has inner security. He has strong confidence in himself. There are few situations in which he experiences inferiority feelings, fear, o worry. He can say in all honesty that there is no person who gives him a sense of inferiority, although, of course, there are many people whose abilities or accomplishments he recognizes as being superior to his own He is never overawed by any person's rank, assumption of importance or aggressiveness.

Tom's self-assurance and self-satisfaction spring from a true estimation of his own worth and not from conceit. These feelings of confidence and pride in self are not aggressive and are not meant to impress others. The are the state of his inner being and are in no way offensive or obnoxiou As a result of this inner security, Tom's attitude toward other people one of liking and well-wishing. Criticisms of others, on the rare occasion when they do occur, are deserved ones and do not spring from any de sire to undermine reputations in order that he may thereby enhance h own.

Tom is also courageous and zestful toward life. His days are not un mitigatedly pleasant, of course, but he finds them good on the whole an worth living. He is indeed exhilarated by the very lack of predictabilit in life, by the need for struggle, and by the calls upon his strengths an abilities.

Tom likes people, and they like him. Tom has a friendly, kindly at titude toward others, and he conducts himself in such a way as to mal them feel good in his presence—not from policy, not because he expec any return, but just because his impulses toward people are genero ones. There is nothing mean, selfish, or grasping about him. Instead, I is considerate of others, pleasant in his dealings with them, and quick to put their needs before his own.

People like Tom because of other admirable qualities. He enjoys life. He is independent enough so that he can go his own way without leaning on others. He is objective and can laugh at himself in a ludicrous situation just as heartily and sincerely as can the next person.

Tom feels that what he does from day to day is worth while. Tom is the kind of boy who uses his abilities in worth-while ways. Since he is still in school, this includes accepting the challenge of some of his subjects and working at them with good will. But it also includes finding commendable uses for himself in other school and out-of-school activities. He did some work on the Annual this year, work of minor importance but enthusiastically performed. He has belonged to the Hi-Y Club for all of his high school years, was the treasurer as a sophomore, and is vice-president this year. At home he regularly takes care of the furnace and the lawn, and being a born mechanic, he keeps his father's car in good repair. In addition, he has an afternoon paper route.

As one might expect, Tom has a feeling of accomplishment from his days. He isn't bored, and he has no reason to feel worthless or useless.

Tom welcomes new experience and has a variety of interests. He enjoys tennis, he is a chess enthusiast, he plays the clarinet—not well, but not too badly. One summer he worked on a highway construction crew. Another summer he and two friends took a canoe trip to New Orleans.

Tom has a wholesome attitude toward his body needs. Moreover his body needs are wholesome ones. He follows sensible health practices, eating what is good for him, getting enough sleep, refraining from over-indulgence.

Tom faces reality. There are two kinds of painful reality that people sometimes try to run away from. One is the unpleasant reality of problems to be faced, discomforts and disappointments to be endured, failures, embarrassments, and deprivations to be suffered. This is the reality of the outside world in its disagreeable aspects. People also sometimes try to run away from the second kind of painful reality, disagreeable truths about themselves.

Tom is not an escapist. He recognizes the problems and the difficulties that confront him and does his best to meet them strongly, constructively, and honorably. He philosophically accepts the pain, the sorrow, and the failures that are unavoidable. He is neither a quitter nor a dealer in excuses but makes a firm stand and a good fight when wisdom dictates that he should.

Tom is also realistic about himself. He recognizes his own failures and doesn't blame others for them. He doesn't try to gloss over his own weaknesses through such devices as boasting, rationalization, lying, and the like. He is honest with himself and feels no need to present a false picture to the eyes of others.

Tom is psychologically tough. Since he has faced whatever problems have arisen in his life realistically and mastered them to the best of his ability, Tom has attained real character strength. Little can worry or daunt him. He doesn't give up easily; he doesn't whine. His personality stays sound and sweet in spite of any frustrations and adversities encountered. He is psychologically tough.

Tom is adaptable. He fits himself easily into the plans of his family and of his friends, having no allegiance to his own desires, plans, or schedules just because they are his own. He is broad-minded, glad to hear ideas that may be opposed to his own; nor is he critical of others just because they differ from him. At the same time, he has high principles, high personal standards, sturdy, well-defined values, clear and decisive opinions. In other words, he is a boy of strong standards, clear-cut opinions, and decisive choices, but also one who can adjust himself wisely and easily when his own good or the good of others demands it.

Tom's emotions, in general, further rather than hinder his well-being. He hates no one, has seldom in his life been jealous; he is fearful only on the rare occasions when danger actually threatens those he loves or himself. He gets angry on occasion, of course, and expresses himself without fear when he thinks the expression merited, but he is not easily roused to anger, and he always has himself under control. He is affectionate and friendly, gets along well with girls, and has been going steady for the past two months.

Tom is not afflicted with those useless mental habits which make trouble for the personality. He doesn't "whip himself" when he makes mistakes. He remembers the bad experience as a valuable lesson—not as something to brood about. He isn't suspicious of others. He doesn't give undue attention to trivial occurrences. He doesn't worry. He doesn't anticipate the worst when the outcome of something is problematical.

All in all, Tom is an extremely well-adjusted boy, and we may be sure that he will continue to have these fine attributes when he is an adult.

THE MEANING OF ADJUSTMENT

Adjustment refers to the way we get along (the way we adjust ourselves) in satisfying our needs in an environment which is sometimes helpful, sometimes unyielding, and sometimes hurtful toward us. The process of adjusting ourselves occurs only because we have needs, because we can use various ways of seeking and satisfying these needs, and because the environment in which we must find our satisfactions is in a sense neutral or even antagonistic toward us as far as our wants are concerned.

WHY IS THE MATTER OF ADJUSTMENT SO IMPORTANT?

Sellery writes:[1]

"According to statistics from national headquarters of Selective Service for the period January 1944 to August 1945, of 5,767,000 registrants, 2,535,800 were rejected for general military service. The *leading cause* for all rejections during 1944 was mental disease, accounting for 26.8% of all rejections.

"The greatly increased incidence of mental disease, the breakdown of family life as shown by our rapidly rising divorce rate, the mounting wave of crime and venereal disease among our youth—all point to the fact that in the field of mental health we are failing dismally."

The well-adjusted person is a happy and effective person. He is getting the satisfactions he needs. He is only rarely troubled by unpleasant emotions. Change is not a source of great discomfort to him. His frustrations do not leave him embittered, disagreeable, or without the satisfactions he needs. He is not bothered by suspicion, self-mistrust, worry, or prolonged regret and self-condemnation over the minor mistakes he makes.

The well-adjusted person also makes others happy. He is friendly and possessed of friends. He is happy-natured. He is not jealous of others, and he does not try to undermine them. He is not unduly aggressive or unkind. He is not unpleasantly critical of others. He does not lose his temper or easily get depressed.

In other words, if we are to help people be happy and socially effective, we must help them to be well-adjusted.

Personality maladjustment in the adolescent is largely the result of childhood experiences, and personality maladjustment in adulthood is largely the result of childhood and adolescent experiences. This suggests one reason why the period of adolescence is so important as far as personal adjustment is concerned. The maladjustments of childhood will not then be so well set as they will be when adulthood is reached, and therefore they will be easier to overcome. The earlier that counteractive measures can be undertaken, the better, naturally. What is more, attention to personality maladjustments in adolescence will not only help with those already formed but will also prevent further ones from forming.

[1] C. Morley Sellery, Director Health Services, Los Angeles City Schools, *NEA Journal*, 37:586 (1948).

A second reason why attention to adjustment is so important in adolescence is that it is a time unusually suited to helping the individual make changes in himself. The adolescent tends to be critical of himself and eager to improve. He is doing more conscious experimenting with living than in childhood. He is making new adjustments and is therefore likely to be flexible and amenable to change. His social experiences—a good laboratory for learning to adjust—can be made broad and varied.

We have an example of the adolescent's sensitivity to his own personality needs in Blos's account:[2]

"The adolescent is usually aware of the necessity of 'learning' self-control. . . . In this connection, the following excerpt from an interview with a sixteen-year-old girl may be illustrative: May said there was a great fight in social science class this morning, in which she opposed the child-labor amendment, and Mr. Thurman, the teacher, came out flatly against her stand. She then spoke of an assistant teacher who was in Mr. Thurman's room when she went to speak to him during a free period. She said: 'He makes me so mad. I can't stand these know-it-alls. And I think people who argue about the superiority of men over women are crazy. It's something you just can't measure.'

"Worker asked what it had all been about.

"May explained that the assistant had said that women are not as good losers as men.

"May said again: 'It's not measurable!' She laughed and said, 'But you should see the self-control I'm developing. I don't blow up any more. I just didn't say anything. And even when I'm typing or playing ping-pong I don't swear; I just snap my fingers and say "Nerts." '

" . . . Worker had the feeling that May's new self-control is the result not so much of a forcible restraint imposed by May upon herself, but rather, a genuine integration."

A third reason why the period of adolescence demands attention to adjustment is this: The maladjusted adolescent is an unhappy adolescent who needs help. The school and the teachers who give no thought to the many maladjusted students are ignoring one of the greatest responsibilities they have toward people they are presuming to help.

SOURCES OF ADOLESCENT ADJUSTMENT DIFFICULTIES

Let us look at six boys and girls who are having difficulty with their adjustment.

Ronald is fifteen, small in stature, above average in intelligence, and

Inc., 1941), pp. 306–307.

[2] Peter Blos, *The Adolescent Personality* (New York: Appleton-Century-Crofts,

from a good family. He is extremely conscious of his appearance because of his shortness and also because his face is badly broken out with pimples. When he is called upon to recite in class, he blushes and stammers to such an extent that he can barely answer. One notices, however, that when he is with a group of boys he seems fairly at ease.

Alice is a sophomore in high school. She has the feeling that she can't do anything right although her intelligence would rate above average. In geometry, she may begin to demonstrate the proof of a theorem for the class, but before she has gone very far, she is almost sure to say, "I can't do it," and take her seat. In sewing class, she always chooses an extremely simple pattern, and her feeling about anything more complicated is "I wouldn't dare to try it. I couldn't do it." When her English teacher asked her to be in an auditorium skit, her answer was "Oh, I couldn't. Why, I'd make a complete flop of it."

Margaret is a nice-looking girl of normal intelligence who comes from a respectable family in the low-income bracket. In grade school she did average or better work. In high school she is on the verge of failing. She seems to dislike school very much, will not recite in class, doesn't associate with the other girls, and looks very unhappy. She confessed to her counselor that she longed for the time when she could quit school. When asked why, she said, "I guess it's just that I'm so ashamed of my clothes. We don't have money for anything at home. Even what I earn working after school and Saturdays has to go for food. I don't belong here in high school. I look so shabby and I feel so out of things."

Bill is a fifteen-year-old boy, a sophomore in high school. He is a little above the average in intelligence, has a good scholastic record, and is well liked by his classmates. He has taken part in various extracurricular activities. In his physical education class, however, he does not get along so well. Although he is a little bigger than many of the other boys of his age, he has been late in developing physically. As a result he has taken a locker off in the corner, is very modest about undressing before the other boys, avoids taking the required shower after each session, rarely talks to the other boys in the dressing room, and has been absent from class a great deal.

Virginia is a girl of sixteen. Although she has a brother and a sister, she has a status in the family almost equivalent to that of an only child, for she is eight years younger than the next oldest. As a result she has been pampered to such an extent that she still has tantrums and crying spells in order to gain her own way, and in the last year she has used the excuse of sickness very often to gain her objective.

Ralph is a well-built fifteen-year-old freshman, 5 feet 11 inches in height. The coach said of him:

"He seemed so interested in sports that it never occurred to me to ask him to report for practice but when he was absent the first night, I did ask him if he was interested and if he would come to practice. He said that he would come out and was at practice every afternoon after school for about two weeks. Suddenly he stopped coming. I asked him the reason but he seemed reluctant to tell me.

"It was that afternoon that I overheard two of the boys talking in the dressing room and overheard the words 'Ralph and religion.' I asked Ralph the next morning if it was because of religion that he was 'quitting' basketball. He said it was and with tears in his eyes, turned and walked away.

"After practice that evening I drove out into the country to see Ralph's father. Mr. C. said he wouldn't 'have a boy of his in front of a mixed audience, naked.' He was very sincere. He also wanted me to know that the boy had been punished for 'sneaking behind his back' and practicing basketball for two weeks. He said he had forbidden it and Ralph had gone ahead and practiced and then lied to him about it.

"After that Ralph grew more and more unsocial. I tried to give him important duties in our intramural program, thinking this would help him. He wasn't interested; in fact being around sports must have made him all the more bitter. The only thing he dreamed of was playing on the team."

Ronald, Alice, Margaret, Bill, Virginia, and Ralph are not getting along so well as they should. What is the source of their difficulties?

Margaret and Ralph: The environment is upsetting their lives in ways beyond their control.

Ronald and Bill: It's adolescence. Ronald's extreme self-consciousness and easy embarrassment in a mixed group and Bill's worry about his development both occur because these boys are in their adolescent period.

Alice and Virginia: These girls have personality faults which interfere with their well-being.

As these six cases illustrate, we can locate the cause of an adolescent's adjustment difficulties in one or more of three sources:

1. The environment.
2. Adolescence itself.
3. The personality.

In the discussion which follows, we shall make frequent reference to the individual's psychological needs, which we believe to be:

1. The need for security.
2. The need to love and be loved.
3. The need for companionship.

4. The need for ego satisfaction, that is, for a sense of worth through accomplishment and through the regard of others.

5. The need for variety.

Much of an individual's striving occurs because he is seeking satisfactions for these needs. Much of his unhappiness is due to the fact that he doesn't receive such satisfactions in sufficient amounts.

THE ENVIRONMENT

No matter how much a person wants sufficient companionship, love, ego satisfaction, security, and variety, and no matter how much he tries to find these satisfactions, his success is partly dependent upon what his environment has to offer him. A child whose parents dislike each other and quarrel frequently will almost inevitably feel some insecurity. A boy or girl from a low-income home whose schoolmates are for the most part both more wealthy and snobbish about their wealth may find it difficult to secure the companionship, affection, and acceptance wanted in school. A teen-ager whose community offers little of recreational interest to youth except, say, movies, will be hard pressed to find in desirable ways the exciting variety he longs for.

It would be impossible to discuss here all the ways in which the environment may fail the adolescent in his efforts to find the satisfactions that he needs and merits. But we can suggest how many are the difficulties the young person meets by listing some of them:

1. In his need for physical well-being:
   Home circumstances that provide poor food, inadequate space, poor sanitation.
   Limited recreational facilities.
   Parents who set poor examples in health procedures.
2. In his need for security:
   Home:
   Parents quarrel excessively.
   Parents are apprehensive, fearful, timid people.
   Parents belittle child.
   Parents show preference for some other child.
   Parents never did want this child.
   Parental discipline is inconsistent.
   Parents are dead, one or both.
   Parents are separated or divorced.
   Child is illegitimate.
   Parents expect too much of the child.
   Home is in financial difficulties.
   Father loses his job.

School:

    Scholastic requirements beyond his ability.

    Discipline too strict.

    Discipline inconsistent.

    Teachers sarcastic.

    Rejection by other students because of his lack of social position.

Community:

    War.

    Unemployment.

    High crime rates.

3. In his need for love and companionship:

Home:

    Parents are emotionally unresponsive.

    Parents refuse to allow friends in the home.

    Parents try to select his friends.

    Home is too far removed from school or other students' homes.

    Parents are migratory workers.

    Parents keep him too busy to allow him much time to be with friends.

    Parents refuse him the normal freedom that other adolescents have.

School:

    Teachers unfriendly.

    Classroom situations very formal.

    Few social activities.

    Exclusive social activities.

    Cliquishness in the school.

Community:

    No youth centers.

    Strong social stratification.

4. In his need for ego satisfaction:

Home:

    Poor family reputation.

    Home is in bad neighborhood.

    Home is ugly or ill kept.

    Parents have inferiority feelings.

    Parents have low social status.

    Parents are ignorant.

    Parents have little respect for child.

    Parents are overcritical of child.

    Parents unwilling to let child conform to youth standards of dress.

    Parents compare child unfavorably with siblings.

    Parents expect too much of child.

School:

    Discrimination.

    Leadership positions given to the few.

    The grading system forbids success to some.

Work too difficult.

Favoritism.

5. In his need for variety:

Home:

Too many home obligations.

Too strict parents.

Home isolated geographically.

Parents' interests very limited.

Home finances demand that the child work.

Parents overprotective toward child.

School:

Unimaginative teachers.

Few extracurricular activities.

Little use of visual aids, excursions, and the like.

Schoolwork limited to abstract and verbal.

Classwork always sedentary.

Community:

Too few interests for youth.

Unwholesome adult interests stimulate indulgence in wrong kind of variety.

A few examples follow showing how the environment can be directly and immediately responsible for an adolescent's not being able to get along well in satisfying his needs:

Jasper lives in a small town in Ohio. His family have recently migrated from another state and are living a hand-to-mouth existence. Their home is a shack on the outskirts of town. Jasper's wardrobe consists of one tattered shirt, worn overalls, and a broken-down pair of shoes that are too big for him.

Jasper is ridiculed by the "town kids" and the "country kids" alike. A good way to tease a girl is to say that Jasper is her boy friend. The boys whose families are well to do will have nothing to do with him.

It is unnecessary to remark that Jasper through no fault of his own is being made very unhappy.

In a rather small community there was recently an outbreak of vandalism in the form of minor destruction of property, which caused the citizens much concern. The vandals were apprehended in nearly every case and were found to be high school boys. These boys were questioned as to their motives, but there was no satisfactory explanation forthcoming. It seemed that in most cases both parents of each boy worked in factories in a nearby city, and the boys formed the habit of loitering on corners downtown. A survey of the community was made, and it was discovered that there were no clubs, no amusement activities, no organizations of any kind with which the boys could associate themselves. It may be assumed that they turned to the excitement of misbehavior for want of anything else interesting to do.

Marilyn's parents belong to a very strict religious group of which there are few members in the community. Marilyn is limited to the academic program in school, all extracurricular and social activities being forbidden to her because they don't conform to the parents' idea of what is proper. She is not allowed to have intimate friends outside of her faith, and her social activities are limited to church affairs, where she goes always with her parents. There is little Marilyn can do to widen her social contacts and activities.

Patricia's father committed suicide two months ago. Patricia, who seemed well adjusted socially up to that time, has withdrawn from class participation and social activities. She refuses to recite in class, avoids talking to the other students in school, and goes home as soon as her last class is over.

Virgil's family was a very happy one until his mother died three years ago. Following her death, Virgil's father made a great effort to be a good companion to his twelve-year-old son, and the boy basked in his father's attention. Last year Virgil's father married again—to a pleasant woman who would like to be a good mother to Virgil. But to Virgil she was only the woman who took his father away from him. Now there is a new baby boy in the family, and Virgil feels himself less important to the home group than ever.

When we look at these boys and girls, we see that they are unduly handicapped by their environment. We are not suggesting that the adolescent should be spared frustration, for that would be both impossible and bad for him. But he should have the kind of home, community, and school which would allow him to find sufficient affection, companionship, ego satisfaction, security, and variety to give him reasonable happiness. Frustrating circumstances which are too big to be handled by the boy or girl, which defeat him, and which warp his growth are not good for him. They interfere too much with his present well-being, and they interfere, too, with the best development of his personality.

We cannot predict just what effect extreme environmental deprivations will have on an adolescent, but we can be sure that if the stumbling blocks are insurmountable, the effect will not be good.

IT'S ADOLESCENCE

Adolescence itself can be a breeder of unhappiness and disjointedness with the world. In the first place, the youth's pubertal development may temporarily affect his attainment of satisfactions. Both insecurity and questionings about his own worth may be engendered by such things as:

Puzzlement about the normality of his genital development.
Worries over masturbation.
Being different from his fellows because of early maturing or late.
Awkwardness.
Skin eruptions.
Emotional instability.
Sex curiosities.

In the second place, the very time of adolescence, with its need to become heterosexually adjusted and to become independent of the home, offers its problems which interfere with the attainment of needs, problems such as:

Clashes in the home over authority.
Problems of necking and petting.
Insecurity over acceptance by the other sex.
Troubles over unhappy love affairs.

Howard, on the basis of psychiatric work done with 117 students at Smith College, summarizes the problems brought on by the emotional difficulties of adolescence in this way:[3]

1. Conflict over unsolved family ties.
2. Anxiety, guilt, or depression in connection with the heterosexual and aggressive drives.
3. Rebellion against social restrictions.
4. Adolescent asceticism and intellectualism as a recoil from heterosexual and aggressive drives.
5. Masculine identification (in girls) as a means of avoiding heterosexual conflicts.
6. Reversion to the "security" of earlier family ties as an escape from problems.

An illustration of how adolescence can precipitate problems is shown in the case of Shorty, as described by Stolz.[4]

Shorty came to the Child Study Institute at eleven and along with other boys his development was studied for the next seven years. At eleven and in the sixth grade, Shorty seemed to get along well with the other students. But in the last two years at junior high school, we read,

---

[3] Edgerton McC. Howard, "An Analysis of Adolescent Adjustment Problems," *Mental Hygiene*, 25:363–391 (1941).
[4] Herbert R. Stolz, "Shorty Comes to Terms with Himself," *Progressive Education*, 17:405–411 (1940).

" . . . the attention-getting techniques which had given him status in the elementary school were less acceptable in junior high school. His clowning and wise-cracking attracted some following among the less mature boys but did not give him the satisfying status with the 'big shots,' nor, indeed, with the rank and file of his classmates. The restless activity which seemed to flow naturally from Shorty at an earlier stage became sporadic and more obviously compulsive. . . .

"It was during his second junior high school year that Shorty began to talk about his lack of height. No doubt he had worried some about it before that, but now he seemed to fasten on it as the chief cause of his failure to achieve his goals in social recognition. Each time he was measured he stretched up as far as he could and even lifted his heels from the floor if he was not carefully admonished. Before the measurement could be read he would inquire eagerly: 'How much have I grown?' and he was always disappointed by the answer.

"The growth situation *was* hard to accept. The lad was not only distinctly short but his puberal acceleration was retarded a year in relation to the average among his fellows. This meant that while the other boys in his class were shooting up by inches every six months, Shorty was growing only by fractions of an inch. . . .

"With Shorty as with other boys there was a close timing relation between puberal development in height and development of appropriate male characteristics. He did not talk directly about this aspect of his retardation but from his 'wise cracks' and his comments about the changes in other boys it seems very probable that it disturbed him."

Shorty had never been one to play with girls, and when the other boys of his age became interested in heterosexual activities, Shorty found it difficult to adapt himself to mixed groups. As a result he found himself on the sidelines.

"This threw him with a group of younger and less mature boys who, while keeping an eye on the girl-dominated activities, expressed their frustration by exaggerated little-boy tactics.

"This retrogression in status made it harder than ever for Shorty to accept himself. Coupled with his misgivings about his size and developmental retardation and with his waning prestige in athletic performance (and doubtless with other factors) the failure to achieve satisfying social relations with girls brought out in him the first obvious signs of serious disturbance. The quality of his school work became worse. Periods of compulsive hyperactivity alternated with periods of apathy and moodiness. . . . His mother reported that he showed a new tendency to pick quarrels with his sister. There appeared an edge of malice in his wise cracks and a flavor of sullenness in his responses to adults. . .

"In high school, the staff agreed, he was not happy, although he did show considerable enthusiasm in shop where he worked at reconditioning a junk-yard car for his own use. One day, toward the end of his first year in senior high school, he was arrested for stealing auto parts from the junk yard. For two weeks he was kept in the Detention Home, where he was first like a wild animal trying to get out and then later broodingly silent.

"Shorty had never been able to define his feelings verbally and so one can only guess at the causes and nature of the crisis which were precipitated by the Detention Home episode. From his behavior and from piecing together things he said to his mother and to the school counselor it seems reasonable to suppose that during those terrible days he was cornered and completely overwhelmed by the accumulated insecurities which had developed through the years. Without consciously defining the situation he probably sensed for the first time the futility of the evasive techniques he had used in trying to achieve social significance and self-respect.

"Fortunately the drive for significance was still there, and gradually with sympathetic support of his mother and an unusually wise counselor Shorty built a new and much more realistic pattern of self-expression. He gave up trying to become a football hero and, with the connivance of the dean of boys, undertook the responsibilities of assistant manager for the team. For this he had real qualifications which quickly established his prestige. . . . "

He obtained after-school and Saturday work, improved his school work, established a new bond of understanding with his mother, all of which contributed to his sense of well-being. After graduating from high school, he seemed to be adjusting well, coming to terms with himself and his world.

Another case in which "adolescence" brought on the trouble is found in this account by a high school teacher: "Last year in our school we were blessed with four boys who had remarkable talent as singers. They were enthusiastic and eager to win their acclaim as a quartet, and it wasn't long until they were very much in demand. Their ages were 18 years, 18 years, 17 years, and 14 years. Jim was 14 and had a very fine tenor voice. Not only was he a good singer, but he was also an excellent student and played on the first squad in basketball. Things went smoothly until suddenly Jim's voice began to develop a squeak and he had to stop singing with the others. The quartet found another member and poor Jim was left 'out in the cold.' His grades began to drop; he was not his old alert self on the basketball floor; and to talk to him—'his life was an utter wreck.' This was a case of an adolescent going from the sublime to a status of despair —all because his voice was changing. Fortunately this stage passed rapidly and Jim is his old self again."

A college student writes: "It seems that during my first year in high school I sprang up over night and as a result I was the tallest boy in the class. Accompanying this was an outstanding pair of feet that seemed to me at that time to protrude several blocks long. As a result I was continually kidded about my big feet and was given the nickname 'land paddles.' This was very disturbing to me and as a result I shied away from participation in class plays and any activity that would mean a performance before the class, and on more than one instance, I simply played sick and would not go to school."

A certain boy of fourteen is exceptionally well developed physically —muscular, larger, stronger, and more athletically inclined than the other boys of his group. He looks like a man in his ninth year of school, and he does the work of a man on his father's farm. As a result, adults expect mature behavior from him. He looks like a man; they expect him to act like a man. But he is only a boy, and his "kiddishness" is always getting him into trouble with his teachers and the coach—and he is always hearing reproofs beginning: "For a boy as big as you. . . . "

Adolescence is the cause of his troubles, too, and we may assume that time will bring a cure.

Mabel is five feet seven inches at fourteen. She is large-boned, well developed, and weighs 165 pounds. Her posture is poor because of her efforts to conceal her size; she diets strenuously at times, producing an unevenness of disposition. She is frequently downhearted in the thought that boys like only dainty little girls. The acuteness of her distaste for herself is typical for her years.

Kenny at sixteen is in love with a girl who is very capricious in her demands and fluctuating in her affection. Kenny is very hard to get along with these days at home, but his parents have the good sense to be tolerant and undemanding, for they know that in this case "It's adolescence."

Often the only thing that we can say about some youth's difficulties is "It's adolescence." That does not mean that the difficulties may not be hard to bear at times or that they may not be bad for the boy or girl in some cases. But it does tell us that the cause lies in a period of physical growth and of social adjustment over which we have little if any control and that in general the best response on the part of the adult is great patience and understanding.

THE PERSONALITY

The word *personality* refers to all that a person is—his intelligence, his attitudes, his skills, his hopes, his fears, his aspirations, his habits, his interests, his understandings, and the like. The personality is the means by which we win the psychological necessities of life for ourselves; it is our tool, our instrument.

When we use the terms *well adjusted* or *maladjusted*, we are customarily referring to the personality structure, although actually the terms would be fittingly applied to the satisfaction of needs. That is, we might properly say that the person whose wants are being satisfied is well adjusted and the person whose wants are not being satisfied is maladjusted or unadjusted. But since the terms are so often limited to the personality alone, we shall use them in that way. When we speak of a person as being well adjusted or maladjusted, we shall mean that his personality is "well put together" or "ill put together," that it is a good instrument for securing the psychological necessities from life or that it is a poor instrument.

If the teacher wishes to understand how the adolescent's personality is helping or hindering the boy or girl in his adjustment, he must look at it from this point of view, that it is an instrument for achieving satisfactions in life. What is more, he must look at it in some orderly way so that he really can make careful assessment of what the personality is like. We are *not* suggesting that the teacher act as a psychiatrist. But we are saying that *a teacher is obligated to understand his students* and that such understanding should not be the vague "He's maladjusted" or the often poorly understood "He's insecure" but rather should be as clear and definite as possible.

Consequently, we recommend that the teacher look at the student's personality from five points of view:

> *How effective is it in its role of supplying security, love, companionship, ego satisfaction, and variety?*
> *How effective is it in meeting frustrations?*
> *How adaptable is it?*
> *How free from emotional difficulties is it?*
> *How free from troublemaking mental habits is it?*

All of these actually center around the one problem of winning satisfactions, but the make-up and effectiveness of the personality become clearer if we consider each of them separately.

Is the Personality Able to Win the Needed Satisfactions?

The Personality and the Need for Security. Fred was born with a birthmark on his left cheek. It isn't an unpleasant mark, but it is very noticeable, especially to strangers, who are not used to it. As Fred grew up, he became more and more sensitive about this mark, and now in high school he is a shy, retiring, self-depreciating boy who acts as if anyone who said "Boo" would frighten him away.

Barbara is the youngest of a family of four children. The older three are bright-spirited, aggressive, highly social young people, very much like their father, who is an extremely likable person, very popular with everyone including his own family. Barbara is quiet and reserved, has never received much attention from her father, whom she adores, and cannot compete socially with her lively brothers and sister. Now a junior in high school, Barbara has developed the appearance of considerable poise and self-assurance, but actually she feels as her family has unintentionally made her feel—inferior and not desirable.

Helen is an only child. Her parents, themselves insecure people, have brought her up to be overcautious and apprehensive. She has heard too often as she grew up, "What will people think?" "That won't *look* right," "I'm afraid," "Be careful," "Watch out." Helen is always viewing herself through the eyes of other people to her own disadvantage, and Helen is also always afraid of what may happen to her—if someone who sits near her gets the "flu," Helen is sure that she will be next. If the family goes on a motor trip, Helen is sure that they will have an accident.

Fred, Barbara, and Helen have personalities so afflicted with feelings of inferiority, fears, and apprehensions that they suffer greatly from insecurity.

The insecure adolescent is subject to many discomforts, anxieties, frustrations, discontents, fears, and compensatory actions. Insecurity is thus one of the most disabling maldevelopments in a personality.

Just what do we mean by insecurity?

Along with satisfactions and pleasures and good feelings in life, there are pains, discomforts, losses, deprivations, and sorrows. This kind of unhappiness may be inflicted upon us by people, by failure in our own efforts to reach some goal, or it may be visited upon us by "the world." Examples of unpleasantness from people might be some sharp criticism, or some refusal of a much-desired privilege; an example of failure in achievement is seen when the baby tries to walk and falls repeatedly; an example of what the world may do to us is seen when someone is struck down by a car, when a bank fails and savings go with it, when war comes.

Now the experiences of children in growing up may be of such a nature as to foster in them fears in regard to any or all of these sources, or it may be the opposite. In other words, there may be bred into the child through such experiences a pervading discomfort or apprehension about how people regard and accept him, lack of confidence in his own ability, and fearfulness (conscious or unconscious) about accidents of fate or about the future in general. If this is true, he has, we say, an insecure personality. If the reverse is true, if he is free from such apprehensions, if he is easy and confident in his associations with people, if he has respect for his own ability, and if he has a general serenity of spirit as far as what might befall him is concerned, he has, we say, a secure personality.

The insecure personality develops through such experiences as these:

1. Lack of love on the part of the parents can cause lasting insecurity. The parents are the protectors, the bringers of comfort, the strong. If they are definitely on the side of the child, the child feels safe and this feeling, like so many strong feelings of childhood, is likely to persist long beyond the time when the child is greatly dependent on his parents. If they are not loving and reasonably protective, the child may develop an ever-present expectancy of hurt or deprivation (conscious or unconscious) which may stay with him for a long time or even all of his life.

2. Fearful, apprehensive parents can cause insecurity in the child. If people as important as his mother or father express fear of something, either in words or unspoken attitude, the child is apt to be fearful too. The child whose parents frequently warn him about dangers, who talk about their own inadequacies, who threaten him, who express feelings of inferiority will learn to be insecure and will retain that learning for a long time, in some cases for life.

3. A balance of failure over success in the child's many and various attempts at achievement will be likely to make him doubtful of his own ability and of the outcomes of his endeavors.

4. Some difference or inadequacy which sets a child off from other children or which doesn't allow him to compete successfully with them in games or schoolwork may develop inferiority feelings in the child.

5. A child may actually be taught to feel inadequate if parents, brothers and sisters, or teachers think of him or speak of him as stupid, belittle him, criticize him, and act as if they expect him to make failures and mistakes.

6. A sheltered, overprotective atmosphere in the home may leave the child feeling insecure when he gets into a less protected situation.

Insecurity in some people shows itself very clearly in their behavior. In other people its signs are less easy to detect. Some of the outward manifestations of an insecure personality are:

Retreat or withdrawal from those experiences where the person might not be sure of his success, his acceptance, or his safety.

Jealousy of others.

Excessive criticism of others.

Attempts to undermine others.
Self-consciousness.
Bullying.
Touchiness.
Excessive eagerness for flattery and praise.
Attention getting.

The Personality and the Need for Love and Companionship. One of the most obvious personality failings that an individual can have is the inability to be pleasing to others so as to merit their affection and secure their companionship. Any teacher and any student can point out a number of associates who are not so likable or so companionable as they should be to get along well in the world. For this reason, we shall not present any illustrations here of adolescents with this type of personality failing.

Less obvious a flaw but equally serious is the lack of ability to feel affection for others. This is an ability whose existence we take for granted in people; yet actually many have too little of tenderness, kindness, and sympathy in them, and some are almost devoid of such feelings.

People like this will make others unhappy. We should remember, too, that they will also make themselves unhappy.

The Personality and the Need for Ego Satisfaction. Janice's parents are both college graduates. Her father was a football star at a great Middle Western university, and her mother made Mortar Board on that same campus. Their only child is far from being the shining success that her parents were, though she tries very hard; for her parents—as they often tell her—want her to be at the top, to be the best. Poor Janice's ambitions are set so much higher than she is capable of achieving that she can never feel that she is successful.

Tom, whose IQ is 98, is taking English, algebra, Spanish, and woodwork. In none of them is he doing well. Without the abstract mental ability necessary for doing academic work successfully, Tom is also unfortunate in that he has no gift for doing precision work with his hands. What he saws comes out crooked, the glue goes on messily, the paint is applied unevenly. Tom works after school helping in the kitchen of a restaurant, the money he earns being used almost entirely for such necessities as clothing and school supplies. In the evening he may listen to the radio, do a little homework, or hang around downtown with a bunch of boys among whom he is a tolerated member without influence or prestige.

Tom has no hobbies, no skill at any sports, no abilities to make him successful at school—no interests of any kind which would lead him into activities at which he could be successful. Everyone needs some successes as a person, and the boy or the girl like Tom who is without any abilities, hobbies, or interests which will win ego satisfaction for him is unfortunate. We can easily find examples of people who use unwholesome ways of getting ego satisfaction. Jack is a grind who overworks himself, not because he enjoys his endeavors, but because he must be better than the others. Betty is a braggart who gets her feeling of worth by boasting about herself, her possessions, and her family. Sarah is not happy unless she is the center of attention. She may come into class with her jacket on backward, happy in the laughter she arouses. She often raises her hand to make a recitation, only to go into a long story of some personal experience which has little bearing on what the class is discussing. In a small group she is absent-minded when others are talking about their affairs, but quick to get a remark in when there is opportunity to talk about herself.

There are many adolescents whose personalities are so constituted as to prevent their winning the successes and respect that all of us crave. Some go without these satisfactions. Others like Jack, Betty, and Sarah seek them in ways that are not good for them or are disagreeable to others.

The Personality and the Need for Variety. There are some people who have enough interests, enough play skills, and enough zest for new experiences so that they are never bored. There are others whose personalities in these respects are so limited that their lives are lived on a much less interesting and fruitful level than might otherwise be.

Alice is an example. Seventeen years old and not an unattractive girl, she has one recreational interest, reading. While other girls of her age get pleasure from tennis, swimming, roller skating, extracurricular activities, and parties, Alice is so limited by her sparsity of interests that she is tasting very little of the pleasures that life might have for her. Of course her personality is at fault in other ways, but it would be improved considerably if it could be changed in one respect—if she could have more interests and recreational skills.

Is the Personality Effective in Meeting Frustrations?

By frustration we mean any thwarting or blocking of need, desire, expectation, or plan. Frustrations range from the most insignificant such as being bitten by a mosquito to the very serious such as a death in the family, from the momentary such as having to wait for the stop light to change to the long-lasting such as an unhappy marriage between two people who do not believe in divorce, from those we accept as inescapable such as taxes to those that we rebel against strongly such as a cut in salary.

How we handle our frustrations makes a great difference in our lives.

If we avoid the difficulty we ought to face, we not only fail to win what we want but we gain no strength for future struggles. If we meet our troubles with temper, jealousy, or depression, we make life needlessly unpleasant, not only for ourselves, but also for those who associate with us.

Burton is an example. Burton resents tests. Almost invariably after a few minutes of writing he will stop and sit with eyes blazing in a perfect rage of temper. Toward the end of the period he usually calms down enough to write a little more, but not enough to give him the grade that would be commensurate with his high intelligence. He often displays a similar technique at class parties, going off to one side and refusing to participate for a while if something occurs to disturb him.

Patty is a high school senior. Since childhood she has pretended to be ill whenever she cannot have her own way. She has convinced her parents that she has "heart trouble." Once a doctor had said that she had "a very slight murmur." This was all she needed to prove her illness.

One day she became very ill ("a pain in her heart") during school. Her father was notified and when he arrived, he and four large boys were needed to carry her to the car.

Later it was discovered that she had quarreled with her boy friend and that the senior class had turned down all of her suggestions for class colors, class motto, and class flower.

Joyce, a high school freshman, quite literally runs away from trouble. Her mother made an unscheduled visit to her class and happened to arrive just at a time when Joyce was being reprimanded for failure to get a certain assignment. Instead of going home on the bus that night as she was expected to do, Joyce went to the home of a girl who lived near the school.

On another occasion, Joyce was seated in the hall to work because she was whispering too much in class. When the teacher went to get her, Joyce was not to be found. Thorough searching failed to reveal her whereabouts. Before the school day was over many people were looking for her.

Joyce didn't appear until suppertime, when she came walking home from the woods where she had been hiding for almost five hours.

The person who lets his frustrations get the better of him has much to regret. He is weak, and he grows weaker with each occasion when he gives in to his troubles. He sometimes causes much trouble to others, and he often feels ashamed of himself or guilty about his behavior.

In general there are five bad modes of meeting frustration: (1) running away; (2) easing one's frustration by finding something to compensate which is not wholesome; (3) antisocial behavior; (4) responding to frustration with anger, jealousy, or depression; (5) being indecisive when one is troubled by conflicting choices or demands.

1. Running away. Examples are:

Staying away from parties because the person feels that he won't get along as well as the others there.

Being negativistic toward any suggestions for new experiences or experiences that might be unpleasant, like the girl who is asked to be in an auditorium skit but says *no* automatically and without thought because that is her customary response to any suggestions that might involve discomfort.

Quitting too soon, like the boy who gets a job on the school paper, finds that it entails considerable drudgery instead of glamour, and quits.

Daydreaming, like the girl who finds the classwork too taxing and withdraws into fantasy.

Procrastinating, like the boy who puts off his book report until the last possible minute.

Malingering, that is, playing sick to get out of something unpleasant, like the girl who is supposed to give a report, is afraid, and stays home "with a headache" on the appointed day.

2. Compensating in unwholesome ways.

In daydreaming one makes up for actual failures by fancied successes.

Undermining the prestige or reputation of others makes the insecure person feel good because it brings envied ones down from their eminence. Tattling is an example of this in many cases.

Eating is sometimes indulged in purely to make one feel good when some frustration is causing unhappiness.

Compensation, as with the boy who is truly a grind because he feels himself unsuccessful socially.

Identification, as with the girl, without popularity herself, who becomes a hanger-on of some group of popular girls because she thereby gets a vicarious satisfaction.

3. Antisocial behavior. This result of frustration will be discussed in the chapter on delinquency, and for that reason nothing further will be said of it here.

4. Anger, jealousy, and depression. These three states *are* responses to frustration, nothing more. A certain amount is normal in the adolescent, but with some it will be seen that the dependence upon anger and other unpleasant emotional states is becoming a permanent part of the personality. This is to be deplored; for the adult who is easily irritated or made angry, who often gets "blue," or who is jealous is not good for himself and certainly not pleasant to be with.

5. Indecision. It is bad for anyone to let conflicts drag on without solution, for not only is one thereby prevented from acting but he is also kept in a state of mental, and sometimes emotional, upset.

An adolescent, like all of the rest of us, experiences many different kinds and degrees of frustration. Common ones are:

> Getting back a test with a low grade.
> Having to be in school when he wants to be elsewhere.
> Having to study.
> Giving a talk in English when he feels self-conscious before the class.
> Being nagged at by his mother or father.
> Being teased.
> Being unsure of himself with the other sex.
> Not being liked by someone he admires.
> Being less popular than he longs to be.
> Having a quarrel with the boy friend or girl friend.
> Not being "understood."
> Doing something awkward.
> Being displeased with his appearance.
> Not getting on the team.
> Having parents quarrel.
> Being "too young."
> Being refused the family car.

Some adolescents, of course, are frustrated in far more serious ways. The parents get a divorce. The father or mother dies. The adolescent himself suffers from some chronic physical malady. His classmates reject him. He is successful at nothing in school. He lives in extreme poverty.

But whether the frustration is serious or but a minor one, the way it is met will determine how successfully it is overcome and will also help form the pattern of adult strength and adult ways of meeting difficulty.

Is the Personality Adaptable?

One must be able to adjust himself to circumstances or he may be disagreeable to others and himself uncomfortable. There are three kinds of unadaptable personalities.

1. The rigid personality. Glen is a boy of sixteen who is extremely set and precise in his ways. In his geometry class, which has been in progress now for three weeks, the teacher requires that neatly written out proofs of problems be handed in. Glen's work is the neatest and most attractive in appearance of all handed in. The teacher hesitates to put corrections on the paper when she finds mistakes, for she hates to see the beautiful

layout disfigured. But of course she must. She does not know, though his mother does, that Glen is greatly disturbed when this happens, not because he has made a mistake, but because he cannot bear to see the perfection of his paper marred. In other ways, also, Glen is too easily disturbed. He doesn't believe anyone should smoke, and he cannot endure being around those students who do; when he sees a teacher smoke, he can think nothing good of him from then on. Glen's room is always meticulously neat. In a way his mother is pleased, but it disturbs her that Glen is so bothered by having anything there moved even a little from its accustomed place.

2. The person who feels himself to be the center of a world which must revolve around him. Gloria might be termed extremely selfish. She is that, but she is more than that, for she is so self-centered that she is completely unaware of the needs and wants of others. One day, for example, she drove her mother over to her aunt's and parked her car in the driveway. Her mother protested because the uncle would soon be coming home and would be inconvenienced. "Oh, don't let it worry you," Gloria replied. "Uncle Tim's a dear; he won't scold." And that was the end of the mattter as far as her thinking was concerned. When class rings were being discussed, Gloria wanted an expensive hand-engraved one chosen. When a friend protested to her that many of the students couldn't afford such a ring, Gloria shrugged her shoulders and continued her efforts. Gloria sits in the school library and talks to her friends, to the disturbance of others who are there to work. Gloria isn't even aware that she is interfering with what they are trying to do.

3. The person who is always "right." Paul is a very bright boy who almost invariably insists on having everything done his way because he is sure of his own rightness. In history class Paul explained his viewpoint on United States policy abroad and then sat back with an air of having given a final answer. Others in the class very ably pointed out many flaws in his argument. When the teacher then turned to Paul and asked, "What do you think now?" Paul quickly summarized his original point of view and added, "I just can't see it the way the others say." He was speaking the truth: he *couldn't* see it.

When the family took a trip East in the car this summer, Paul wanted to stop at the hotel a classmate had told him about, but his father decided to stop at another. For the duration of the four days' stay, Paul was convinced that his father had made the wrong choice and on many occasions explained to the family why this was so.

These three people have personalities that are maladjusted because they are unadaptable. Glen makes life difficult for himself as a result, and Gloria and Paul are hard to live with because of their lack of adaptability.

Is the Personality Free from Emotional Difficulties?

Brad, a high school sophomore, is a well-built, well-coordinated youth, good in athletics but often a drawback to the team. For he simply can't take getting hit or roughed up in a game by smaller boys or having officials call a foul on him; whenever anything like this happens, he loses his temper and is so angry for a while that his value to the team is greatly diminished.

We can forgive many emotional outbursts in the adolescent if we understand that his time of life sometimes makes for greater sensitivity and irritability. But we should nonetheless recognize the fact that the adolescent who loses his temper often or who has many hates or fears is not so well off as the adolescent who is more on an adult level of emotional maturity.

Is the Personality Free from Bad Mental Habits?

Alex is a thirteen-year-old boy of above-average intelligence who is highly suspicious and always expecting the worst. He is often afraid to go home after school for, in his own words, he knows "the boys are laying for him." His home-room teacher has on several occasions walked home with him, for the boy's fear is genuine, but never has the teacher seen anyone "laying for" Alex. Alex is also very pessimistic about the world. His father was out of work for awhile and Alex told his home-room teacher with obvious concern: "I know he won't get a job. What will we do then? What will we eat? We won't have any rent money. I suppose we'll be put out, and then where will we go?"

Suspiciousness, worry, self-disparagement, and the needless reviewing of past mishaps are bad mental habits which often stem from deep-seated insecurity; nevertheless many boys and girls who fall into these bad habits without being otherwise seriously distorted in their personality could rid themselves of them just as they would overcome any other undesirable habit—by seeing its harmfulness, being convinced of the need for change, and rigidly abstaining from practicing the habit from then on.

This topic, "What Are the Sources of Adolescent Adjustment Difficulties?" is complex, and for that reason we insert a summary of it here:

What Are the Sources of Adolescent Adjustment Difficulties?

I. The environment is at fault.
II. It's adolescence.
III. The personality is maladjusted:

1. In its role of supplying security, love, companionship, ego satisfaction, and variety.
2. In its role of meeting frustrations:
   a. Running away.
   b. Easing the frustration by finding something to compensate which is not wholesome.
   c. Antisocial behavior.
   d. Responding to frustration with anger, jealousy, or depression.
   e. Prolonged indecision in the case of a conflict.
3. In its adaptability:
   a. The rigid personality.
   b. The person who is highly egocentric.
   c. The person who is always "right."
4. In its emotional maturity.
5. In its mental habits.

CONDUCT PROBLEMS AND PERSONALITY PROBLEMS

Ackerson, who has studied the recorded case material for a consecutive series of 5,000 children examined at the Illinois Institute for Juvenile Research, Chicago, distinguishes between conduct problems and personality problems. This is a worth-while distinction for the teacher to remember. Many teachers punish for personality problems, not recognizing the fact that punishment in such a case will not help the situation and may do harm.

Ackerson lists these personality problems as showing a definite rise in incidence with chronological age:[5]

Depressed spells.
Daydreaming.
Self-indulgent attitudes.
Unhappy appearance or manners.
Sensitiveness over particular fact or episode.
Inferiority complex.
Preference for younger children as playmates.
Worry over some specific fact or episode.
Abused or injured feeling or manner.
Seclusiveness, unresponsiveness.
Oversuggestibility.
Lack of initiative or ambition.
Listlessness.

[5] Luton Ackerson, *Children's Behavior Problems* (Chicago: University of Chicago Press, 1931), p. 185.

DO YOU RECOGNIZE PERSONALITY PROBLEMS?

Ives[6] gives some interesting information on teachers' understanding of students' adjustments. During the Second World War from October, 1943, to January, 1946, a Teacher Appraisal Blank was filled out for every seventeen-year-old boy attending a secondary school in the United States. This blank asked for the teacher's impression of the student in regard to schoolwork, truancy, his ability to make up his mind, participation in physical activities, responses from classmates, attitude toward teachers, dependability, and these "characteristics:"

1. Seclusive
2. Moody
3. Suspicious
4. Effeminate
5. Deceptive
6. Markedly nervous

7. Temper tantrums
8. Strikingly immature
9. A "show-off"
10. A "daydreamer"
11. Peculiar

Certain physical difficulties were also listed for checking.

Ives compared the Teacher Appraisal Blanks for 284 men who were rejected for service for neuropsychiatric reasons with those of 284 men accepted for service and matched in socioeconomic status. She concluded that the questionnaire was of negligible value as an aid to neuropsychiatric diagnosis, a primary reason being "the consistency of ignorance displayed by the teachers," both in actual omissions and in a confounding of factors. The reasons for this, she suggests, may be lack of time for the individual student on the part of the teacher, the teacher's proneness to evaluate behavior in terms of the smooth functioning of the classroom rather than of the happy adjustment of the individual, lack of background in adolescent psychology, carelessness, or fear of prejudicing the student's career.

As she says: "Teachers should not become overly analytical, yet it is certainly of value to them to have clear-headed knowledge of possible difficulties experienced by their students."

How good are you at judging the seriousness of personality and conduct problems? Here are 55 such problems.[7] On a separate sheet of paper list them in order of their seriousness, putting the most serious first, the least serious last.

[6] Olive Lord Ives, "A Critique of Teachers' Ratings of High School Boys," *Teachers College Contributions to Education*, No. 950 (New York: Bureau of Publication, Teachers College, Columbia University, 1949).

[7] Rearranged from E. K. Wickman, "A Study of Teachers' and of Mental Hygienists' Ratings of Certain Behavior Problems of Children," *Journal of Educational Research*, 36:292–307 (1942).

1. Active, full of life
2. Attracting attention, demanding attention
3. Carelessness, carelessness in work
4. Cheating
5. Cowardliness, physical cowardliness
6. Cribbing
7. Cruelty, bullying (pinching, hitting, etc.)
8. Curiosity
9. Defiance, impertinence
10. Destructiveness, destroying school materials
11. Disobedience
12. Disorderliness
13. Domineering (self-assertive)
14. Dreaminess, daydreaming
15. Easily discouraged, giving up easily
16. Enuresis, bed-wetting
17. Fearfulness, showing fears of persons, of situations, etc.
18. Heterosexual activity (sex experience, immorality)
19. Imaginative lying
20. Impudence, rudeness
21. Inattention
22. Inquisitiveness
23. Interested in the progress of others
24. Interrupting adults' conversations, talkativeness
25. Lack of interest in work, uninterested, bored
26. Laziness, laziness about the home
27. Masturbation
28. Nervousness
29. Obscene notes, obscene talk
30. Overcritical of others, fault finding
31. Poor concentration
32. Profanity
33. Quarrelsomeness
34. Resentfulness
35. Restlessness
36. Selfishness
37. Sensitiveness
38. Shyness
39. Slovenliness in appearance
40. Smoking
41. Stealing, repeatedly taking things
42. Stubbornness
43. Suggestibility, easily influenced
44. Sullenness
45. Suspiciousness
46. Tardiness
47. Tattling
48. Temper tantrums, fits of temper
49. Thoughtlessness
50. Truancy
51. Unhappiness, feeling depressed
52. Unreliableness
53. Unsocialness, not social, withdrawing
54. Untruthfulness, lying
55. Whispering

These traits have been rated by a large number of mental hygienists. Turn now to page 321, and compare your rating with theirs (Table 31).

WHAT SHOULD BE DONE ABOUT THE MALADJUSTED?

Recognize the Maladjusted Adolescent

In many cases (but by no means in all) there are outward signs of maladjustment, and the wise teacher is at least alerted by them. The most common are:

Truancy. This generally[8] indicates that the student is not happy in school, and we can assume therefore that the school is not meeting his needs—that is, is not giving him sufficient ego satisfaction, companionship, affection, sense of worth, and variety. In many cases truancy is a definite sign of the fact that the truant is not able to achieve sufficient success in school or that he finds it monotonous and dull.

Solitariness. There are some students who keep very much to themselves and obviously are not getting companionship and affection, at least as far as the school is concerned. One must be careful in making a judgment here too, however, for people differ in the amount of solitude and of companionship that they need. Some are unhappy when they are alone. Others, though they like to be with people at times, have admirable solitary pleasures also. It is not these whom we should worry about. Rather it is the ones who are always alone and who give evidence of being lonely, of being excluded, of being wistfully on the edge of things.

Frequent or Prolonged Daydreaming. The teacher cannot know how much the student daydreams, and there are many boys and girls who might daydream excessively without the teacher's being aware of it. But if she does know of a student who seems to spend much time in daydreaming and if there is substantiating evidence in his not participating in the typical activities of the boys and girls of his age, she may suspect that his life is not meeting his needs sufficiently. The reader, if he is a well-adjusted adult with a busy satisfying life, will himself probably give evidence of this fact, for since he is getting his satisfactions in real life, he is not likely to spend much time in daydreaming.

We should keep in mind, however, that adolescents almost invariably do *some* daydreaming. The world is all before them to daydream about. Then, too, by contrast to what is happening today, daydreams offer exciting and glamorous successes, and experience has not dulled hope. But some adolescents do much daydreaming and little participating in activity around them. These are the ones for whom daydreams are too often a substitute for real satisfactions.

Shyness. Shyness is a symptom of feelings of inferiority or of the inferiority complex. We may be sure that the shy adolescent does not have the sense of security that a person must have to be happy, and we may be sure that he is not getting the social pleasures which are his due if we are trying to see that he is happy.

Attention Getting. Merrill gives us this example:

[8] A great many young people have "played hooky" now and then in a spirit of caprice, and though this is disturbing to the teacher, it is certainly not a cause for any alarm about the culprit.

"Harry . . . has already been labeled a 'problem child' at school and referred to the school clinic because of his troublesome behavior in class. This school behavior has always been of the attention-getting variety. He is noisy, talks continually, and is fond of dramatic recital. In the classroom he is a nonconformist—if the class is to write a composition, Harry wants to read; if they are to go out to the playground, Harry wants to stay inside—no matter what the situation, Harry must contribute to his prestige by drawing attention to himself. . . .

"As we see Harry at the age of twelve, he presents an almost classical picture of the attempt to adjust to inferiority feelings by resorting to defense mechanisms. His scholarship is poor, but he is outstanding by reason of his negative and nonconforming behavior. Not a very adequate adjustment, but a pseudo-achievement, often like this of aggressive character, serves as an outlet when real achievement is thwarted."[9]

Delinquency. The delinquent child, as we shall show in a subsequent chapter (Chap. 11), is often a frustrated child. When an adolescent is known to be engaging in delinquent acts, it is in many cases (though not all) a sign that he is not getting sufficient affection, companionship, variety, or ego satisfaction.

Bullying. The bully, it may be assumed, is not getting enough ego satisfaction in normal ways and must resort to mistreating those younger or smaller or weaker than he to get the sense of importance he craves.

Bragging. Similarly, the braggart, too, lacks a sense of worth, and his bragging is an attempt to win the regard of others by verbalizing his claims to importance.

Proneness to Criticize Peers Excessively. This is an almost sure sign of insecurity and inferiority feelings. The adolescent who has nothing good to say of others is using the technique of belittling his classmates to lower their reputations and by contrast raise his own.

Crushes. As we have said in another chapter, many crushes are normal and occur in the most wholesomely adjusted adolescents. Intense crush of girl on girl and of girl on older woman, especially when a slavish worship and attendance are involved, indicates a lack of sufficient affection or heterosexual success.

A Look of Unhappiness. We sometimes see adolescents who unmistakably *look* unhappy. As we have said, we cannot judge by outward appearance but the teacher who is impressed by an adolescent's woebegone look at least has some cause for giving thought to that boy's or girl's adjustment.

[9] Maud A. Merrill, *Problems of Child Delinquency* (Boston: Houghton Mifflin Company, 1947), pp. 199–200.

Be Cautious in Your Interpretation

In the first place, remember these rules:

1. View the whole child. We all have some maladjustments, both because of environmental interference and because of personality flaws. With some, each of us might look at ourself and say: "Yes, this isn't so good, but taking my life or my personality all in all, it really isn't serious." But with another we might, for example, come to a conclusion like this: "I am entirely too intolerant of other people's opinions. This is interfering with my friendships enough so that I must choose between staying as I am and not being very likable and making a change in my personality."

In other words, a maladjustment must be viewed in its relationship to the rest of a person's life. From that point of view, something that at first looms rather large may on a more careful evaluation be rather insignificant. And something that seems trivial may at times be a cue to a difficulty needing attention.

Anyone working with the adolescent should be warned not to stereotype him in terms of a maladjustment, something that is very easy to do. One can think of a boy, for example, as being "John who is so shy" and give little further thought to the complexities of his personality. Stereotyping of anyone automatically prevents the achieving of a full understanding of that person's personality, and any teacher who finds himself thinking of a boy or girl as representing a certain type and does nothing further to comprehend the complexities of that individual should realize that he *doesn't really understand him.*

2. View the whole child in his environmental setting. It is similarly important to see the child in relation to his home, community, and school setting. Two sisters living in lowly circumstances, for example, were sent across town to the high school which served the wealthier section, sent there because that was where the mother had gone as a girl. These girls, with their somewhat shabby clothing, lack of spending money, and inability to talk about the out-of-school affairs the other girls participated in, felt out of place; and being gentle-natured their reaction was to withdraw and keep to themselves. Such behavior was actually not characteristic of them usually, and it took on significance *only* in terms of the immediate environment.

Another example of the importance of this principle is given in the case of Gwendolyn, described by Dimchevsky.[10]

"Gwendolyn is reported for cheating in English. She had handed in as her own composition a story copied out of an old magazine. Judging her

[10] Esther M. Dimchevsky, "Counseling in Emotional Problems," *Mental Hygiene,* 32:549–559 (1948).

behavior solely on the basis of breaking classroom rules and regulations would call for discipline which in her case would only create a greater problem. The counselor needs to understand Gwendolyn as a girl with average mental ability, but with parents who expect her to do A and B work because her sister did. The counselor needs to see her as a somewhat ungainly, retiring adolescent, whose family is constantly comparing her with that attractive outgoing sister. The counselor needs to appreciate the lack of satisfactions in this student's life and her intense drive for acceptance into a sorority, which depends on her grade in English. Understanding gives an entirely different slant on the situation in which Gwendolyn is trying to meet very basic emotional needs for belonging and acceptance, recognition and approval by her own age group, as well as that of the adults of importance to her. It is not through judging, but through complete and sympathetic understanding that the counselor can help Gwendolyn strike a healthy satisfaction-giving balance between her emotional needs and her manner of meeting them."

Behavior must be placed in its relationship to the environmental forces which are affecting it if it is to be truly understood, and the teacher who neglects to see *the child in his environment* will make many misjudgments.

3. View the whole child in his developmental setting. What an adolescent was in his adjustment and what he is moving toward are important considerations. Of course, we cannot see this whole line of development, and we can only conjecture what the future will bring. But such "foresight" is important, as the following case will demonstrate:

In describing a very well adjusted woman, Roberts and Fleming write:[11] "She matured slowly and was not interested in boys until after many of her friends were already dating steadily. At times she felt backward and unpopular because of her lack of boy friends and wondered if she would have an opportunity later to have dates. She used to say to herself that she wondered what it would be like to kiss a boy, and she knew when she had a chance she would try it. Her mother urged her to accept all invitations and if no other provision was made for an escort her brother took her, an arrangement which both children hated. However, toward the end of high school she began dating. With many adolescents this feeling of lack of attraction for boys and the lack of social skill with them which was related to her slow physical maturation would have become major problems. But for Marjorie there was some steadying influence within herself and in those around her that saw her through to a successful adjustment."

[11] Katherine Elliot Roberts and Virginia Van Dyne Fleming, "Persistence and Change in Personality Patterns," *Monographs of the Society for Research in Child Development*, 8 (No. 3):8 (1943).

Here we see someone who was getting along all right, viewed in her whole developmental setting, although the immediate picture in her adolescence was one of failure to progress normally.

In addition to these three general principles, remember in the second place that with many boys and girls the problems of adolescence bring reactions which one might label personality maladjustments but which really are but temporary adjustment techniques which the adolescent employs to ease a difficulty and which in many cases will disappear as the youth approaches or achieves maturity.

For example a 21-year-old girl came home at Christmastime having been away since September on her first teaching job. One day when her 15½-year-old sister, Marian, was gone for the afternoon, she decided to clean out Marian's bureau drawers and start her out right for the new year. About an hour and a half later she came downstairs to the living room where her mother was sitting reading, swinging three rather worn looking brassières by their straps.

"Mother," she began, "look at these . . . ."

Just then Marian came home, and the sister turned to her with "Marian, you shouldn't be wearing brassières like this. They're ready to be scrapped. Why—"

Marian looked at her in rage. "Where did you get those?"

"Why, I was cleaning out your drawers. . . . "

"My drawers? How dared you!"

Then for the next ten minutes Marian stormed at her sister as well as at her mother, finally going upstairs in tears.

Such behavior in an adult might seem excessive. In Marian at 15½ it betokened nothing more than the natural response of a high-spirited girl to an invasion of her privacy.

Excerpts from Blos will emphasize this point that behavior which in adulthood would be a sign of personality maladjustment, in adolescence may be only a temporarily helpful device to tide the boy or girl through some difficult period:[12]

"At about fourteen or fifteen, sometimes sooner or later, the pattern seems to shift. The child is still an unstable, moody, and rather unpredictable person—battling with adult authority and with himself—overanxious, self-conscious, and over-confident by turns, apparently sophisticated but frequently only on the verbal level, desperately wanting help and guidance but often quite unable to ask for it or to accept it from those he likes best. . . .

"In any phase of growth in which the individual is experimenting with new powers and capacities, his behavior is apt to be extremely unstable

[12] Blos, *op. cit.*, pp. 272, 277, 284, 285, 289, 293.

It shifts from violent intensity to weak indifference, from overdoing to underdoing. . . .

"The swaggering bravado so typical of the adolescent age is a thin disguise for self-doubt, inadequacy, or fear. . . .

"It is easy, also, to misinterpret the withdrawal and secrecy of the adolescent as implying that he has attained a comfortable self-sufficiency and feels no further need of adult help. Some adolescent secrecy is, of course, simply self-protection from adult interference, for boys and girls make their first ventures into independence and try out new standards and activities which they feel will not be approved or permitted. This sort of secrecy is merely the cloak for disobedience and rebellion when open defiance would prove too uncomfortable. . . .

"But sometimes secrecy is more significant, revealing a deep sense of guilt or inferiority and a profound need for help that the child is afraid to express. . . .

"But within reasonable limits and as temporary relief, fantasy is a healthy safety-device, and the day-dreaming of adolescents serves an important function in easing strains that would bring him in open conflict with reality. Adults are ordinarily too readily alarmed at the unhealthy possibilities of this typical adolescent behavior, failing to credit its positive values or to capitalize upon its educational possibilities. . . .

"Another device, that of temporary compulsive habit formation, is frequently used to avoid anxiety: it is manifested in over-meticulousness, orderliness, keeping belongings strictly in assigned places, doing things at certain times, and keeping an unwritten schedule about free time. . . .

"Though rationalization is anything but rare among adults, its transitory and protective character gives it a unique function during adolescence."

Redl says:[13] "If the adult over-reacts to *all forms* of adolescent behavior as though they were the signal for character decay, he only pushes the youngster in question into deeper insecurity and thus introduces the disturbances which he is out to fight."

Be Cautious in Your Treatment of the Maladjusted Adolescent

Bearing in mind that one should be cautious in interpreting behavior, be very cautious, too, about attempting any specific therapeutic procedures. The human personality is complex, and it is difficult even for someone who is trained in psychology or psychiatry to be sure that he

[13] Fritz Redl, "Adolescent Changes as a Factor in Delinquency," in Marjorie Bell (ed.), *Probation and Parole Progress*, 1941 Yearbook (New York: National Probation Association, 1941), p. 199.

is diagnosing correctly and offering the right help. The most well-meaning teacher in attempting to help an adolescent overcome some particular maladjustment may bungle the procedure and do more harm than good. One cannot depend upon his good intentions. This is an area of teacher activity where even the most delicate skill may not be delicate or skillful enough. The fact that some of the best-known techniques for helping the maladjusted are very lengthy gives us evidence from the experts that in many cases one should not hope to bring about a cure by advice, dictation, and the like. Psychoanalysis, for example, depends upon month after month of daily conference with someone who has been trained not only medically but also in the process of psychoanalysis. The nondirective techniques of counseling, which have achieved so much prominence in recent years, demand many hours of listening and reacting on the part of a counselor whose resources include an extensive knowledge of the human personality and also extensive knowledge of a special technique for helping the person who is troubled.

Therefore, instead of attempting specific treatment in many cases of individual maladjustment, the teacher of the adolescent is advised to depend instead upon the techniques that follow:

Study your students. If you cannot do this for all of them, at least get to know those that you feel to be maladjusted. One of the simplest and best ways of finding out what your students are like is to spend some time talking to them individually. There are few adolescents who do not welcome the chance to talk to a sympathetic teacher about their interests, how they spend their time, the difficulties they have in and out of school, what vocation they hope to follow, and so on. If the teacher does not have time to do this out of school, he should try to arrange each class now and then so that the students are working by themselves in order that he may then be free to talk to three or four students, one at a time, during the period. This should be as a conversation between friends. Under no circumstances should the teacher use the occasion to criticize the student unfavorably or express negative attitudes toward his interests and activities.

There are many written devices, too, for finding out about the individuals in the class, and these are more economical of time though less personal in feeling. A questionnaire on this order might be used:

Name	Age
How many sisters?	Their ages?
How many brothers	Their ages?
What does your family do together for recreation?	
What do you do by yourself for recreation?	

What do you do with your friends for recreation?

Do you read any magazines?   Which ones?

Do you read books?   What have you read recently?

Whom do you like best to be with?   Your friends?

                               Your family?

                               Alone?

Where do you like to be the best?   At home?

                               At school?

                               Or where?

Do you earn any money by working?

If so, what kind of work do you do?

How many hours a week do you give to this?

If you had an unexpected holiday today, how would you spend your time?

Another often-used and helpful technique is that of asking the student to write his biography. Then, too, there are adjustment inventories and tests made especially for high school students which are effective in getting information about the student's personality.

Ask for teacher conferences on students who seem to need help. This should be a procedure used in every high school, and time should be made available for this without burdening the teacher excessively. If Bill Brown seems disturbed, unhappy, or unable to get along with the other students, a conference of all Bill's teachers to pool information and ideas will lead to more understanding of Bill's case, better ideas of how he can be helped, and a greater unity of effort in his behalf.

Beware of situations that hamper good adjustment. There are many classroom situations which are bad for the student. They are often situations which just "happen" and continue to exist in the normal course of events without the teacher's being aware that something detrimental is present. At least three such general situations might be mentioned:

1. Dooming some students to failure hampers good adjustment. Usually in a high school class a few students receive A's for their work, a somewhat larger number receive B's, more receive C's; and then we have a fewer number receiving D's and a smaller group again getting failures. This distribution approximates the normal curve, and naturally, therefore, approximates the normal distribution of intelligence. The reason for this paralleling of grade distribution with intelligence distribution (if the teacher does not actually make the grade distribution fit the normal curve) is that success in most schoolwork depends upon academic, verbal, abstract intelligence.

The result of this is that the students with high abstract intelligence experience school successes again and again; the students with the low verbal intelligence experience failure or near failure equally as often. It is unnecessary to stress the point that this is an unwholesome situation for the ones at the bottom of the intelligence range. And if the argument is advanced that life is like that, one should give that argument short shrift whether or not it be true, because the way "life" is is not at all necessarily what is good for adolescents' development. The reader needs only to consider how he would feel if for the goodly part of his working day he was doomed to do work that could not be commended by those whose place it was to appraise it, to do work that would almost inevitably be disparaged, to do work that would surely be inferior to that of his associates.

One cannot say just what effect such experiences have on the high school student, for the effect is often not discernible but only adds to conscious and unconscious memories and emotional sets. But we might assume with justice that any or all of the following habits and attitudes might result:

> Careless habits of work.
> Dislike for work.
> Feelings of inferiority.
> Antagonism toward school.

Most teachers feel that grades are an evil; but most teachers find that grades are a necessary evil in the sense that their school system requires them. What should the teacher who is concerned about the personal adjustment of her students do then to minimize the ill effect of grades? First of all, if grading must be done on work of a purely abstract verbal nature, the teacher can compensate for the inevitability of some students' receiving D's and perhaps F's by seeing that everyone in the classroom can contribute successfully to class activities and also grow and be aware of his growth. For example, a teacher of English uses a tape recorder in oral composition, and with this motivating device there is no student in her class who isn't strongly interested in his own progress in clarity of enunciation, accuracy of English and sentence structure, and so on. Every student without exception has that opportunity, among others, to feel proud of himself, to receive the commendation of the teacher, and to win the respect of his classmates. This is as it should be and it compensates for the fact that these particular students are graded comparatively—that is, each person's grade represents his relative achievement; and consequently many never get above or can hope to get above a C.

It would be better, of course, if the boys and girls in school could all receive equal recognition for work well done even though the results are not comparable. The traditional grading system frustrates the teacher who wants to work on this basis, but it might be within reason to let the class consider the matter of grading and the possibility of letting grades reflect contribution to the class and growth. They might draw up a list of activities, achievements, and the like, which would merit an A, those which would deserve a B, and so on. Such use of the grading scale would be less frustrating to the student and more productive of real effort than the traditional application of it.

2. Ignoring the life needs of students hampers good adjustment. As we have stressed again and again, adolescents have the same vital needs that we adults have:

To be liked.
To have companions.
To know some success, to receive some praise, to be admired, to feel pleased with oneself.
To be free from worry, anxiety, fear.
To have interesting variety.

They also have the very specific desires:

To make heterosexual adjustments.
To have help on personal problems.
To have help on home problems.
To have help in choosing a vocation.

A classroom situation that persistently ignores these needs, many or all, is allowing the student but a sterile environment for developing wholesomely.

3. Ignoring the individuality of students hampers good adjustment. It is very easy to stereotype a student in terms of a few characteristics or only one, thinking of him as no more than "a poor student," "that little mouselike thing," "the straight-A student," "that conceited Mary Brown," and the like. The results are bad, as we have indicated earlier, for they prevent one's knowing the student as well as one should and tend to minimize him.

Make your classroom situation one that promotes good adjustment. Have the attitude that the student should enjoy his life in the classroom. Don't look upon yourself as a taskmaster. Everyone should learn the pleasure of work; he can't learn it if he must continually work without purpose and without feeling a need for what he is doing. Nor can he learn it if the teacher is grim and joyless in his participation in classroom activities. Then keep always in mind that you should try to make the classroom a place where the student can feel secure, where he can feel worth while, where he can experience the liking and companionship of others, and where the routine is not unvaried.

To show that personality adjustment can be changed and changed by fitting the environment to the adolescent, we present the case of Calvin:[14]

"Calvin came to us at the age of fifteen and a half. He had become extremely rebellious in his foster homes. Once when he ran away he got as far as Texas. Calvin was an illegitimate boy who knew nothing about his parentage. He had been reared in an orphanage, county homes, and foster homes. He was aloof, restless, and resentful. He was untruthful, he bullied other children, he was nervous and short-tempered. He had all the coldness commonly found in children of his deprived emotional background. He was suspicious and mistrustful of adults, and only tolerated his contemporaries if they did not make demands upon him. A psychologist reported his inability to deal with reality as strongly suggesting the neurotic. By virtue of his personality setup and his success at running away, he was considered a poor candidate for our school; however, the following is the outcome of his two years' residence there.

"He now is in first class standing in citizenship. He is stable, reliable, and sufficiently qualified in his trade as cook to substitute for the chef when he is absent. There is an elasticity and softness to the boy that was not there when he arrived. He is friendly and jovial but he still does not permit himself to become attached to adults. He ran away several times during the early part of his stay but he always came back of his own volition.

"There seem to be two crucial group experiences in the rehabilitation of this boy, his athletics group and his trade group. Though small and slight of stature, he proved to be a natural athlete. His interest in athletics became apparent at the time of his enrollment when he asked to change his first name to correspond to that of a big league baseball player. All vicissitudes of his early adjustment at the school were tolerable in anticipation of his hours on the athletic field. He has won varsity letters in every sport since he enrolled. He frequently said that the only thing that kept him at the school was athletics. His skill and sportsmanship have given him prestige and recognition from the boys and the faculty.

"He first selected printing as a trade but was unqualified for this and the restlessness and defiance previously reported became much in evidence. When he was transferred to cooking and baking, his whole attitude changed. He was competent in his work, he was accepted by the group, and his growth throughout the program has been continuous. There is limited, if any, identification with the coach and chef whom he greatly respects.

[14] Kenneth I. Wollan, Director, Connecticut Junior Republic, "The Value of Group Living in Institution Treatment," *Bulwarks against Crime*, 1948 Yearbook (New York: National Probation and Parole Association, 1948), pp. 132–134.

"What has happened here can be stated only briefly. This cold, resentful, rebellious boy was accepted with the hope that the deprivation in meaningful human relationships which had characterized his life could be compensated for best by the enrichment of social contacts experienced in group living. This boy has achieved a remarkable degree of basic socialization due primarily to his experience in athletic groups and a vocational group where no threatening emotional demands were made upon him by the adult leaders. He found acceptance and prestige in these groups and developed the ability to relate himself meaningfully to his contemporaries though only in a limited degree to adults. He has built up self-esteem on proven achievement. He no longer looks upon the world as a hostile, rejecting place, but accepts his environment as essentially friendly and approving, though still holding some reservation about the complete trustworthiness of adults. Personality change has been achieved within the limits of his impoverished emotional background."

We see from this account that even in a relatively short time good living conditions in home and school can help an adolescent grow nearer to the good adjustment that is so necessary to his happiness, present and future.

Reminiscences

1. What problems of adjustment in your teen-age years could you profitably have had help on from adults?

2. What adjustment problems did you outgrow well enough without help?

3. Can you think of any examples of high school companions who were seriously hampered in adolescence by environmental conditions? Describe them.

4. Can you think of any boys or girls who were unhappy in their adjustment because of "adolescence"? Describe them.

5. Did the high school you attended contribute to maladjustments in any way? If so, how?

6. Did you experience any major frustrations in high school? How did you meet them?

7. Can you remember any seeming maladjustments in adolescence which loomed large at the time but which in retrospect seem very trivial?

General Discussion

1. If you were to put the basic needs mentioned on page 286 in a hierarchy from the most important to the least, which would you put first? Next? Next?

2. What personality maladjustments would you feel to be the most easily overcome in high school?

3. What would be the most difficult to overcome?

4. What personality maladjustments are likely to be hidden from the teacher?

5. Which ones are fairly obvious?

6. Give all the specific cases you can of environmental factors which interfere with adjustment.

7. Consider each adjustment difficulty which might be classified under "It's Adolescence," and discuss whether the adult's response in general should be to ignore it, adjust to it, or give help on it.

8. Consider Howard's summary of adolescent problems. Give examples of each category.

9. What would you have done for Shorty had you been his teacher and had you understood as much about his case as is given in the account of it?

10. We might diagram the personality and its adjustment in this way:

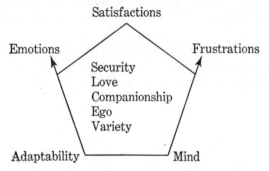

What is the question about personality which each of these five words suggests?

11. Give as many specific examples as you can of people you know who have personality failings in regard to one or more of these five aspects of personality. How are they therefore hampered?

12. Consider the experts' ratings of behavior (Table 31). Discuss why those at the top of the list in seriousness were so placed. Do the same for those low on the list.

13. Consider each of the outer signs of maladjustment listed on pages 308 to 309. What should the teacher do for the class as a whole to help overcome individual maladjustments which these suggest?

Panel Discussion

1. What the high school can do to promote good mental health in its students.

2. What the home can do.

3. What the teacher can do to promote good mental health in himself.

Movies

Attitudes and Health, Coronet Films, 10 min., b. & w., 1949.

Feeling of Rejection, National Film Board of Canada, 23 min., b. & w., 1947.

TABLE 31. A STUDY OF MENTAL HYGIENISTS' RATINGS OF CERTAIN BEHAVIOR PROBLEMS OF CHILDREN*

	Behavior problem	Ranking†
Serious	Unsocialness, not social, withdrawing...............	1
	Unhappiness, feeling depressed.....................	2
	Cruelty, bullying (pinching, hitting, etc.)............	3
	Fearfulness, showing fears of persons, of situations, etc.	4
	Stealing, repeatedly taking things...................	5
	Nervousness.....................................	6
	Suspiciousness...................................	7
	Enuresis, bed-wetting.............................	8
	Cowardliness, physical cowardliness.................	9
	Easily discouraged, giving up easily.................	10
	Overcritical of others, fault finding.................	11
Undesirable	Resentfulness....................................	12
	Unreliableness...................................	13
	Dreaminess, day dreaming.........................	14
	Untruthfulness, lying.............................	15
	Cheating..	16
	Sullenness.......................................	17
	Temper tantrums, fits of temper....................	18
	Poor concentration...............................	19
	Quarrelsomeness.................................	20
	Heterosexual activity (sex experience, immorality).....	21
	Suggestibleness, easily influenced...................	22
	Destructiveness, destroying school materials...........	23
	Lack of interest in work, uninterested, bored..........	24
	Truancy...	25
	Cribbing..	26
	Obscene notes, obscene talk........................	27
	Shyness...	28
	Sensitiveness....................................	29
	Selfishness......................................	30
	Imaginative lying................................	31
	Tattling...	32
	Restlessness.....................................	33
	Laziness, laziness about the home...................	34
	Defiance, impertinence............................	35
	Carelessness, carelessness in work..................	36
	Attracting attention, demanding attention.............	37
	Masturbation....................................	38
	Stubbornness....................................	39
	Tardiness..	40
	Profanity (swearing).............................	41

Table 31. A Study of Mental Hygienists' Ratings of Certain Behavior Problems
of Children.*—(Continued)

	Behavior problem	Ranking†
Slightly undesirable	Domineering (self-assertive).....................	42
	Impudence, rudeness............................	43
	Disobedience...................................	44
	Slovenliness in appearance.......................	45
	Thoughtlessness................................	46
	Smoking.......................................	47
	Inattention....................................	48
	Disorderliness.................................	49
	Interrupting adults' conversations, talkativeness........	50
	Whispering....................................	51
Desirable	Inquisitiveness..................................	52
	Interested in the progress of others.................	53
	Curiosity......................................	54
	Active, full of life. . :...........................	55

* E. K. Wickman, "A Study of Teachers' and of Mental Hygienists' Ratings of Certain Behavior Problems of Children," *Journal of Educational Research*, 36:292–307 (1942).
† By 96 mental hygienists, psychiatrists, and psychologists.

Feelings of Depression, McGraw-Hill Book Company, Inc., 30 min., b. & w., 1950.

Learning to Understand Children, Parts I and II, McGraw-Hill Book Company, Inc., 21 min. and 20 min., b. & w., 1947.

Overdependency, National Film Board of Canada, 32 min., b. & w., 1949.

Further Reading

Bernard, Harold W., *Toward Better Personal Adjustment* (New York: McGraw-Hill Book Company, Inc., 1951).

Bettelheim, Bruno, *Love Is Not Enough* (Glencoe, Ill.: Free Press, 1950).

Blos, Peter, *The Adolescent Personality* (New York: Appleton-Century-Crofts, Inc., 1941).

Brogan, Peggy D., "Building Self-respect in Children," *Childhood Education*, 19:5–8 (1942).

Cole, Doris M., "Bad Boys and Their Books," *Wilson Library Bulletin*, 16:532–538 (1942).

Elsbree, Willard S., "School Practices That Help and Hurt Personality," *Childhood Education*, 18:197–204 (1942).

Evans, Diana R., "The High School Stage—a Laboratory for Personal Development," *NEA Bulletin of the National Association of Secondary School Principals*, 32:74–80 (1948).

Gardner, George E., "The Mental Health of Normal Adolescents," *Mental Hygiene*, 31:529–540 (1947).

GRAHAM, ALVA WHITCOMB, "Personal and Social Adjustment of High-school Students," *School Review*, 55:468–473 (1947).

HANKINS, DOROTHY, "Mental Hygiene Problems of the Adolescent Period," *Annals of the American Academy of Political and Social Science*, 236:128–135 (1944).

HENDERSON, KENNETH B., "Diagnose Before You Treat," *Educational Leadership*, 8:101–104 (1950).

KATZ, BARNEY, "What Teachers Should Know about Personality Disorders," *Education*, 61:598–601 (1941).

LEWIS, VIRGINIA, "I Spent the Summer in a Mental Hospital," *NEA Journal*, 39:25 (1950).

LOUTTIT, C. M., "The School as a Mental Hygiene Factor," *Mental Hygiene*, 31:50–65 (1947).

MANGUS, A. R., "Personality Adjustment of Rural and Urban Children," *American Sociological Review*, 13:566–575 (1948).

McKINNEY, FRED, "Developing Personalities in High School and College," *Education*, 63:591–595 (1943).

MURRAY, JOHN M., "Conscience during Adolescence," *Mental Hygiene*, 22:400–408 (1938).

PRESTON, M. I., "Children's Reactions to Movie Horror and Radio Crime," *Journal of Pediatrics*, 19:147–168 (1941).

REDL, FRITZ, and WILLIAM W. WATTENBERG, *Mental Hygiene in Teaching* (New York: Harcourt, Brace and Company, Inc., 1951).

RESNICK, JOSEPH, "A Study of Some Relationships between High School Grades and Certain Aspects of Adjustment," *Journal of Educational Research*, 44:321–333 (1951).

ROSE, A. A., "Insecurity Feelings in Adolescent Girls," *Nervous Child*, 4:46–59 (1944).

SAUL, LEON JOSEPH, *Emotional Maturity* (Philadelphia: Lippincott, Company, 1947).

SMITHIES, ELSIE MAY, *Case Studies of Normal Adolescent Girls* (New York: Appleton-Century-Crofts, Inc., 1933).

STEVENSON, GEORGE S., "Mental-Hygiene Problems of Youth Today," *Mental Hygiene*, 25:539–551 (1941).

THORPE, LOUIS P., "Danger Signals of Needed Pupil Adjustments," *School and Society*, 46:799–801 (1937).

TURNEY, AUSTIN H., and FLOYD I. COLLINS, "An Experiment in Improving the Personality of High School Seniors," *Journal of Educational Psychology*, 31:550–553 (1940).

Chapter 10. VOCATIONAL ADJUSTMENT

It is the day before graduation. Mr. Hollis, the mathematics teacher, walking to school overtakes a student of three years earlier, Joe, now a senior.

"Won't be long now, will it, Joe?" he greets him.

"Nope! One day more."

"What are you going to do then, Joe?"

"Don't know. Get a job, I guess."

"What do you have in mind?"

"Well—nothing, really."

"But you've got to find something?"

"Oh yes, I've got to work. I figure I'll start looking Monday."

With that they separate, leaving Mr. Hollis to ponder on the case of Joe—average boy of average ability, leaving the routinized existence of high school, all on his own to try to find his rightful place in the work world, with little knowledge of what he is good for, of what jobs are possible for someone like him, or of how he should go about looking.

And he thinks of how many others throughout the country will be looking for work too, like Joe ill prepared for the searching and the choosing they must do.

Since only 17.6 per cent of all high school graduates continue their education and the majority of dropouts and graduates go directly to work upon leaving school—57 per cent of the graduates and 65 per cent of those who drop out earlier—the matter of choosing a vocation and of finding work is obviously one of immediate concern.[1] Figure 28 shows how many *must* make their vocational plans while in high school.

As it is now, the first job is often not one chosen for its especial suitability but is rather one arrived at through the play of mere chance factors. One boy's uncle can get him a job in the railroad yards; another boy's family has always worked at the steel mills, and he, too, will try for a place there; a third boy thinks he'll apply for work in a shoe store—looks like a fairly easy way to earn a living, he says. One girl has worked in a department store at Christmas, and she believes that she'll ask for a permanent position there; another girl has had typing and shorthand in high school—she wants a stenographic job though she doesn't know just

[1] Data from Warren W. Coxe, "The Opportunities of High School," *School Review*, 58:220–224 (1950).

how she'll go about getting it; a third girl has heard that one can always get something to do at the penicillin plant.

Peters asked 700 central Missouri high school seniors to check the factors which influenced them most in selecting the vocation they desired

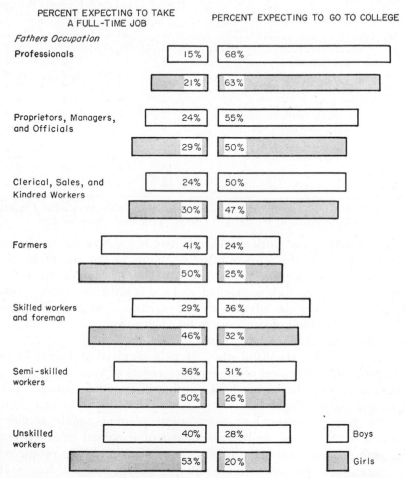

FIG. 28. Future plans of high-school students and occupation of fathers. Social Research Service, Michigan State College. [From *Youth and the World of Work* (East Lansing, Michigan: Michigan State College, 1949), p. 19.]

to enter. The results of the survey, as shown in Table 32, indicate that the influence of relatives and acquaintances is a far more important factor in vocational choice than is knowledge of one's capabilities.

In other words, with many adolescents the beginning job is whatever happens to offer itself or else the result of choice on a very superficial

TABLE 32. FACTORS WHICH CONTRIBUTE TO YOUTH'S VOCATIONAL CHOICES*

Factor	Most influential		Second most influential	
	Rating	Per cent	Rating	Per cent
Parents...............................	1	20.5	1	13.6
Friends...............................	2	11.0	6	8.1
Professional acquaintances...............	3	10.5	7	7.5
Relatives other than parent..............	4	10.0	3	11.0
Teacher..............................	5	9.5	5	9.3
Opportunity for study...................	6	8.4	5	9.3
Opportunity for quick employment........	7	7.4	4	9.8
Result of vocational-guidance tests........	8	5.8	11	2.9
Social recognition of the vocation.........	9	5.3	10	3.4
Opportunity for advancement.............	10	5.3	2	12.7
Result of hobbies......................	11	4.7	8	6.8
Advertisements........................	12	1.6	9	5.2

* Edwin F. Peters, "Factors Which Contribute to Youth's Vocational Choice," *Journal of Applied Psychology*, 25:428, 430 (1941). Table made from his data.

basis. For a start in the work world, this may not matter too much. Unfortunately, though, the worker often continues in the line of his first employment even though it is not very satisfying or suitable; for it is in this work that he now feels acquainted, and it is in it that he is able to offer to his next employer the advantage of experience. And even if he does change to another kind of occupation, his choice may again rest on what is available rather than on what is suitable.

The results of the Maryland study of 1936, as given in Tables 33 and 34, are probably still typical of the job preferences of youth.

About a fifth of the high school youth will go on to college. They will choose their colleges for various reasons—proximity to their home being the most common, low costs, social prestige, family tradition, reputation of the school, and an assessment of its actual value in terms of learning opportunities being others. Some of these young people will have chosen their professions upon entering college and will have well-planned courses ahead of them. Many of the others will not know what they want to do and will enter college in the trust that time, experience, and the college will settle their problem for them.

These prospective college students need help, of course, just as the other boys and girls do. They need to understand their own temperament and ability as they pertain to work choices, they need to recognize their personal vocational limitations and assets, and they need to know, too, what work opportunities are available in the world. Many of them would

TABLE 33. THE JOBS YOUTH WANT AND THE JOBS THEY GET*

Male youth		Female youth†	
Ten occupations most frequently preferred	Ten occupations most frequently followed	Ten occupations most frequently preferred	Ten occupations most frequently followed
Engineer	Farm laborer	Nurse	*Housewife*
Mechanic	Industrial laborer	*Teacher*	*Family domestic*
Farm owner	Inside salesperson	*Stenographer*	*Inside salesperson*
Aviator	Unpaid family worker	*Housewife*	Textile operative
Physician	Textile operative	Secretary	*Stenographer*
Lawyer	Clerk	Beautician	*Teacher*
Electrician	Truck driver	*Family domestic*	Waitress
Teacher	WPA	Artist	*Secretary*
Musician	Helper	Musician	Clerk
Machinist	CCC	*Inside salesperson*	Clothing operative

* Howard M. Bell, *Youth Tell Their Story* (Washington: American Council on Education, 1938), p. 134.

† The italicized jobs in the *female* group show that six of the jobs they most preferred are found in the list of those they followed. Bell says: "These comparisons suggest, among other things, that there is either less vaulting ambition among the young women, or else there is a good deal more realism in their understanding of themselves and the kind of world they are living in."

TABLE 34. PERCENTAGE OF YOUTH WHO PREFERRED THE OCCUPATIONAL FIELD IN WHICH THEY WERE EMPLOYED*

Occupational Field in Which Youth Were Found to Be Employed	Percentage of Youth Who Preferred This Field
Semiskilled	10.7
Unskilled	13.6
Office-sales	35.5
Domestic-personal	36.6
Skilled	40.8
Managerial–farm owner	44.5
Professional–technical	91.2

* Howard M. Bell, *Youth Tell Their Story* (Washington: American Council on Education, 1938), p. 134.

like to have help in high school both in choosing a college and in choosing a profession.

They are not, however, in such urgent need as are the boys and girls who must go directly to work or to a short-term work course (as in business school or trade school), for they have, in many cases, four more years of schooling to give them both time and the possibility of professional help in choosing a vocation.

The Importance of the Right Choice

It is generally recognized that one's lifework is of the greatest importance to one's happiness. The job's forty hours a week skim from the five or six work days their most vigorous and productive hours and take from the person his most energetic efforts. Such hours wasted in work that is drudgery, in work that is distasteful, boring, or without challenge, or in work that is harmful to the personality mean that a goodly part of an adult lifetime is given over to the production of unhappiness.

In contrast, the right job can be a means to fulfillment and enjoyment for the person who has found what is the best for him vocationally. Such a person has a sense of doing something worthy of his ability. He enjoys the hour-by-hour activity of his job. He generally awakens to the thought of work with pleasure and seldom wishes his working hours away.

The adolescent may not realize all that a wrong choice may mean to him, but he certainly is seriously concerned with the whole problem of selecting and finding a job. In Bonar's fairly recent study of sophomores, juniors, and seniors of Manitowoc, Wisconsin, 186 of the 364 seniors said that getting a job or preparing for a vocation was their most important problem. These problems also were picked as the most important[2] by 198 of the 422 juniors and 185 of the 443 sophomores.

WHAT IS THE ADOLESCENT LIKE IN RESPECT TO HIS VOCATIONAL ADJUSTMENT?

What Is the Nature of His Choices?

There is some statistical evidence to indicate that the adolescent is down to earth in his vocational choices. His choice may not be a wise one, it may be made without sufficient thought or sufficient data, but at least it is not ridiculously lofty nor is it highly impractical as far as work opportunities in general are concerned.

Boynton and Woolwine[3] questioned 2,361 girls in the eighth to twelfth grades about their occupational preferences and expectations and then compared the choices of girls of low, higher, higher, and highest economic status. Table 35 gives the percentages for the first seven occupations[4] chosen. I represents the lowest economic status; IV represents the highest.

[2] Hugh S. Bonar, "High-school Pupils List Their Anxieties," *School Review*, 50:512–515 (1942).

[3] Paul L. Boynton and Ruth Dowell Woolwine, "The Relationship between the Economic Status of High School Girls and Their Vocational Wishes and Expectations," *Journal of Applied Psychology*, 26:399–415 (1942).

[4] These seven occupations cover 73 per cent of the first choices.

As the authors say, it is interesting to compare the preferences and expectations. Many of the girls of the higher economic status do not want to be stenographers, but they expect that they will have to be. Many of the girls of the lower economic status would like to be nurses but do not think that their hopes will eventuate. The teaching situation is somewhat similar to that for stenography. Girls of higher status do not want to teach in as great numbers as they expect to.

It is a little sad to contemplate the differences between preferences and expectations. On the surface at least, these girls do not seem to be aiming

TABLE 35. THE RELATIONSHIP BETWEEN THE ECONOMIC STATUS OF HIGH SCHOOL GIRLS AND THEIR VOCATIONAL WISHES AND EXPECTATIONS*

Expectations	Percentages							
	I		II		III		IV	
	P†	E†	P	E	P	E	P	E
Stenography.................	26	21	27	32	21	28	14	25
Nursing.....................	25	17	21	16	13	10	7	7
Teaching....................	15	16	12	14	10	12	9	16
Marriage....................	5	4	9	6	11	7	13	6
Beauty-parlor work...........	7	10	8	9	5	4	2	3
Clerical work................	5	10	3	6	4	5	6	5
Music......................	2	2	5	1	4	2	6	4

* Paul L. Boynton and Ruth Dowell Woolwine, "The Relationship between the Economic Status of High School Girls and Their Vocational Wishes and Expectations," *Journal of Applied Psychology*, 26:399–415 (1942).

† P refers to Preferences. E refers to Expectations.

too high; yet a considerable number do not expect to see their modest ambitions fulfilled. Figure 29 gives us somewhat similar information for boys.

Drier and Kreitlow[5] studied 2,622 seventh- to twelfth-grade students in four Minnesota counties. The first five vocational choices for both the farm girls and the rural nonfarm girls were, in the order named, to be a secretary, a nurse, a teacher, a beauty operator, and a housewife, with the first three receiving 55 per cent of the choices. The first choice of the farm boys was to be a farmer (about 40 per cent). The first choice of the rural nonfarm boys was to be an engineer (10 per cent), with

[5] William H. Drier and Burton W. Kreitlow, "The Educational Plans of Minnesota Rural Youth," *Journal of Educational Sociology*, 23:37–38 (1949).

farmer (8 per cent), mechanic (6 per cent), and aviator (5 per cent) coming next.

Moser[6] asked 550 students in the Pittsburg (California) Senior High School to select three occupations of interest to them as possible future

Fig. 29. Twelfth-grade boys' occupational aspirations and expectations, compared with gan State College. [From *Youth and the World of Work* (East Lansing, Michigan:

careers. Then he compared the average IQ of the students choosing each occupation with the Army General Classification Test ranking. He concluded that the students in general chose in relation to their ability.

[6] W. E. Moser, "Vocational Preference as Related to Mental Ability," *Occupations*, 27:460–461 (1949).

Carp[7] studied the total male population of a union high school in southern California (165 boys), asking them to give their desired occupation, their probable occupation, their father's occupation, and their grandfathers' occupation. She found that the mode for the students' choices

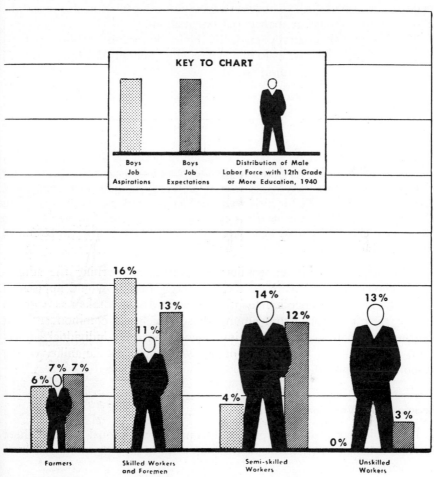

the occupational distribution of the male labor force. Social Research Service, Michi-Michigan State College, 1949), pp. 4–5.]

was neither higher nor lower than that for the fathers and grandfathers and concluded from this that high school boys are realistic about occupations.

[7] Frances Meichant Carp, "High School Boys Are Realistic about Occupations," *Occupations*, 28:97–99 (1949).

In contrast to evidence which would seem to show that adolescents *do* choose their vocations with considerable realism, we have other data which point to a tendency in many youth to be overoptimistic in regard to their vocational possibilities.

Fleege[8] studied 535 students and found that a large percentage chose occupations beyond their mental capacities, 50 per cent, for example, choosing professional or managerial occupations.

Myers writes of a survey made by Helen D. Staples of 444 students of the graduating class of 1940 of Eastern High School, Washington, D.C. His conclusions may be summarized:[9]

Making a definite vocational choice: 66 per cent of the girls and 52 per cent of the boys.

Choosing above their level of intelligence: 46.4 per cent of the boys and 28 per cent of the girls.

Choosing unrealistically as far as community needs are concerned: 54 per cent of the calls for boys coming to the District Employment Center were for clerical workers, but only 10.3 per cent of the boys chose this occupation; 63.3 per cent of the calls for girls were for clerical workers, and 71.3 per cent chose this work; 25.7 per cent of the calls for girls were for stenographers, and 58 per cent chose this work. Few chose retail selling, but many will be forced to enter this occupation.

All of this seemingly contradictory evidence concerning the adolescent's choices may actually harmonize better than it would appear on the surface. All together it may mean that adolescents taken as a group choose their vocations from among those which are common and not demanding of unusual talent or intelligence, but that individual adolescents often choose vocations out of line with their specific ability or the community's opportunities.

Readiness for Vocational Choice

The adolescent is often ill prepared to make a vocational choice. There is much evidence of the truth of this statement in investigations that have been carried on.

Roeber[10] studied 2,000 ninth-, tenth-, eleventh-, and twelfth-grade boys and girls in 22 high schools of Illinois and Wisconsin. Students from small

[8] Urban H. Fleege, "Motivation in Occupational Choice among Junior-Senior High School Students," *Journal of Educational Psychology*, 37:77–86 (1946).

[9] William Myers, "High School Graduates Choose Vocations Unrealistically," *Occupations*, 25:332–333 (1947).

[10] Edward O. Roeber, "High School Students Need Vocational Information," *Occupations*, 23:97–101 (1944).

schools and large ones, from agricultural, residental, and industrial communities, and from all economic levels were represented. The objective was to get answers to two questions:

1. How accurate is the knowledge of high school students concerning the world of work?

He found that most of the students were well informed as to the necessary abilities, necessary types of leadership, hours per week, salaries for beginners, salaries for experienced workers, and trends in employment. They did not know how much demand there was for women workers and for young workers in common occupations, and they did not know what educational training was necessary or how school subjects related to occupations.

2. How much knowledge is possessed concerning occupations in which they profess an interest?

He found that students were victims of little information rather than of misinformation. Most knowledge was shown about the salaries for beginners, abilities needed, advantages and disadvantages for their chosen occupations. Even here, however, information was inadequate, as is partially shown by the following:

Advantages of Occupations

Lots of people dying. (Undertaker)
You make lots of money. (Farmer)
You are sure people will always be sick. (Doctor)
No worry about rent, light, or gas. (Aviator)
You don't have a big-shot telling you what to do. (Farmer)
The satisfaction of one's soul. (Artist)
Good hours. (Farmer)
Vacation every year. (Teacher)

Disadvantages of Occupations

Too long a vacation. (Teacher)
I wear rose-colored glasses. (Stenographer)
Too much of a chance to become an old maid. (Teacher)
None—work will never hurt anyone. (Farmer)
Hard work. (Farmer)
Uncertain and low income. (Farmer)

He concluded that adolescents "have only a few notions of what lies ahead; they are eager for facts, and know not where to turn for such information . . . ."

Spaulding,[11] in writing about the youth of New York State, says that

[11] Francis T. Spaulding, *High School and Life* (New York: McGraw-Hill Book Company, Inc., 1938), p. 55.

he found a large number of boys and girls on the point of leaving school either to have no vocational plans or to have plans quite out of line with their own demonstrated abilities and with opportunities for employment. Many of the leaving pupils had uncertainty about their immediate jobs, while 17 to 40 per cent of the various groups of pupils questioned had no long-range vocational objectives.

TABLE 36. PROPORTIONS OF YOUTH IN SPECIFIED GRADE LEVELS WHO HAD RECEIVED VOCATIONAL GUIDANCE*

Grade completed	Received vocational guidance
Seventh grade......................	1 out of 10
Ninth grade.........................	2 out of 10
Twelfth-grade graduate...............	3 out of 10
4 or more years beyond high school.....	4 out of 10

* Howard M. Bell, *Youth Tell Their Story* (Washington: American Council on Education, 1938), p. 74.

Few adolescents receive vocational guidance—that is, have an opportunity to learn about their own vocational fitness and to learn about jobs. In the American Youth Commission's study of the young people in Maryland between the ages of 16 and 24, in which 13,528 individuals were studied by personal interview, we learn that only 22.7 per cent of all

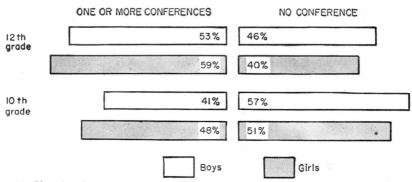

FIG. 30. Showing help in the form of conference about life work given students. Social Research Service, Michigan State College. [From *Youth and the World of Work* (East Lansing, Michigan: Michigan State College, 1949), p. 22.]

youth received vocational guidance. More specifically, we have the facts in Table 36.

When the Washington students[12] were asked if the school had given them the information necessary to help them choose the proper vocation, only 51 per cent said that they had received "all desired information" or

[12] L. J. Elias, *High School Youth Look at Their Problems* (Pullman, Wash.: State College of Washington, 1949) pp. 23, 28.

"a great deal of information." When they were asked what the school could do to make them better prepared for their life beyond high school, 43.8 per cent answered "Give more vocational courses." Figure 30 shows how much help in the form of conferences about their lifework was given 6,789 Michigan students interviewed.

THE EMPLOYMENT SITUATION FOR YOUTH

Any statement about the employment situation in the country should be suited to the particular year and even the particular month in which the statement is made and will be the better if it is suited to the month and the year in which the statement is read. Despite this, there is some value in quoting from the Maryland study even though it does go back to 1936, since that study was so comprehensive and so carefully carried out. We read:[13]

"In spite of the fact that most of the 13,528 young people considered in this study were interviewed at a period when the influence of industrial recovery and the impetus of agricultural activity were being generally felt, . . . of every ten youth in the labor market approximately four (38.8 per cent) were not employed on full-time jobs, and three of these four had no employment whatever. When only the youth 16 to 20 years of age are considered, we find that of every ten youth in the labor market approximately five were employed on full-time jobs, one had some kind of part-time work, and the remaining four had neither the constructive activities of the schools nor the absorption of jobs to fill their empty days."

Even when boys and girls do find work, their adjustment to it may not be easy.

According to Moyer,[14] the business novitiate finds it necessary to make adjustments in regard to at least four types of problems:

1. Human relations: As may not have been necessary before, he must be able to get along with all sorts of people.
2. Physical environment and working conditions. Adjustment must be made to:
   a. Lost freedom—regular hours.
   b. Long hours of confinement.
   c. Learning to work all day, sometimes standing for the whole period.
   d. Living in a new place among strange people, in the case of some.

[13] Howard M. Bell, *Youth Tell Their Story* (Washington: American Council on Education, 1938), p. 105.
[14] D. H. Moyer, "Business Novitiate," *Occupations*, 18:169–173 (1939).

3. Business philosophy, ideology, and attitudes. He must often adjust to:
   a. Demand for blind submission to authority.
   b. New scale of values—tempo of work increases, advancement slows up.
   c. Evaluation of people in terms of service to company rather than in terms of individual progress.
4. Work performance:
   a. He must give 100 per cent accuracy in place of the 60 per cent or so accepted in school.
   b. He must learn to think and to stand on his own feet in place of reading, memorizing, and repeating back.

WHAT IS THE IDEAL FOR VOCATIONAL ADJUSTMENT?

Considering how many types of work there are in the world and how many divisions there are within each type—considering the fact that there is work to suit all tastes and work to suit all degrees of intelligence and skill, it is a great tragedy and seemingly a needless one that so many adults are doing work for which they are ill fitted. So prevalent is such maladjustment, particularly in the less highly paid jobs, that we can probably all think of examples of it among the people we know. We also have evidence of job dissatisfaction from other sources.

Thus Super studied 273 men from twenty to sixty-eight years of age in respect to avocations. Some of his questions, however, pertained to job satisfaction, and the results from this part of the study, given in Table 37, indicate much vocational maladjustment.

TABLE 37. OCCUPATIONAL LEVEL AND JOB SATISFACTION*

	Satisfied		Dissatisfied		Total
Professional.........	77	85.56%	13	14.44%	90
Managerial..........	28	74.22	10	25.78	38
Commercial.........	36	41.86	50	58.14	86
Skilled..............	19	55.88	15	44.12	34
Semiskilled.........	10	47.62	11	52.38	21
Total	170	63.33%	99	36.67%	269†

* Donald E. Super, "Occupational Level and Job Satisfaction," *Journal of Applied Psychology*, 23:550 (1939).
† "Unskilled" not included.

Sometimes the vocational disappointment is very serious. Thus Gordon F. had his own insurance agency and was making an excellent living for his family when he had a nervous breakdown and had to give up his business entirely for two years. One day when he had sufficiently recovered to be about again, he met a friend of his, a highly outgoing, socially easy person. When this friend said, "Tell me, Gordon, just what *did* happen to you?" Gordon answered:

"The whole trouble was that I didn't have your kind of personality. You don't know how I've envied you all these years."

"What do you mean?" the friend asked.

"It's easily explained. I've been in work all of my life that's gone against the grain. There are times when I've hated it, and I guess I never did much more than tolerate it at best.

"You know that I started working with my uncle. I was a quiet sort of person. I had always found it difficult to be aggressive towards people. But I had this good chance with Uncle Dan—and I was ambitious and determined to succeed. So I set about being the kind of person I wasn't meant to be—and on the surface at least I made myself over.

"I made a lot of money selling insurance—but it was always an effort to be the kind of person the work demanded. Finally"—he shrugged— "well I guess it was just too much for me."

Not all vocational maladjustment is as serious in its consequences as this, to be sure, but there is nonetheless needless unhappiness in the lives of many people because they are in jobs that they dislike.

Ideally the adult would be doing work that he could fully enjoy. It would be suited to his personality, as that of Gordon, in the illustration above, was not. It would also be so suited to his intellectual ability that it would allow him to utilize his intellectual best but not demand more than he was capable of; it wouldn't become monotonous for him; and it wouldn't allow him to stagnate. It would utilize other abilities, also, so that he really could feel that he was expressing himself in his work. It would give him returns in the way of achievement and self-respect, and it would allow him and those dependent upon him to live in comfort and have security for the future. This is our goal for the adolescent's vocational adjustment as an adult.

What should be going on in the adolescent's development right now, ideally?

1. He should be learning to appreciate the values inherent in work. He should turn to work as well as to recreation in seeking pleasure and fulfillment.

2. He should be developing the qualities that make for good workmanship— pride in careful work, a sense of personal responsibilty for what he does, willingness to put forth effort, and the ability to recognize his own degrees of accomplishment, whether poor, mediocre, or good.

3. He should be developing the qualities that make for a good worker—the ability to get along with others in work relationships, the desire to give honest measure, punctuality, and dependability.

4. He should come to understand his own qualifications for work—his in-

telligence level, his special abilities, his personality characteristics, and his interests.

5. He should learn what vocational possibilities are open to him.

6. He should learn what the chances are for entering such vocations.

7. He should learn what the opportunities for success in these vocations are, what rewards will come to him, and so on.

8. He should understand the process of preparing for these vocations and entering them.

HELPING THE ADOLESCENT BECOME A GOOD WORKMAN

Since the school is the place of work for the adolescent and since teachers are universally and constantly concerned with "getting the students to work," one might almost assume that making the boy or girl into a good workman would be one accomplishment that the school could be rather sure of. Actually, however, as any college teacher who deals with beginning freshmen and as any businessman who hires graduating high school seniors will be only too willing to verify, the average high school student is not a good workman. He lacks diligence and self-discipline, his standards of work are not high, and he regards work without enthusiasm. He does do a considerable amount of work in high school, of course, but too often he works in ways which develop incompetency rather than the qualities that are desirable.

Look at a boy of fifteen who is making a bookcase for his mother for her birthday and who is working with care because he has a deep personal interest in having the undertaking turn out as well as possible. He knows the reason for each of the steps he is taking, he knows their continuity, and he comprehends the whole pattern of his undertaking. No one outside of himself needs to prod him into action or to keep him going. He is self-governing and self-disciplining because he has a goal of his own choosing, because he has a personal desire to succeed, and because he knows the importance each step has to the finished product.

In this job he is experiencing what it means to be self-motivating, painstaking, and persevering in his work. If these qualities are frequently characteristic of what he does, they are likely to become a part of him. In the main, it is probably true that only when the high school student is doing work with appreciation of its purpose, with acceptance of that purpose as his own, with a real desire to do it well, and with understanding of the progression of the steps of his work—only then can we say that he is learning to be a good workman. When he does work at someone else's behest, with little understanding of its purpose and also with as little expenditure of effort as he thinks he can get by with, he is developing or perpetuating shoddy standards and slipshod methods.

ACQUAINTING YOUTH WITH VOCATIONAL POSSIBILITIES

Everyone should have a comprehension of what variety of work there is in the world and of what some of this work entails in the way of ability, effort, and rewards. He should have this whether or not he has immediate need of such information and understanding in order to make a vocational choice. Man's work is too important a part of life, too important a part of our country's economy, and too important a part of happiness to be ignored in our general effort to understand and adjust to the world we live in. It would therefore seem sensible for all high school students at some time in their high school life to have a course which would acquaint them with the kinds of work done in this country as well as with the importance of that work in the lives of individuals and in the welfare of society.

Such a survey should be a general one but might also involve a more detailed study of a few occupations. Some classification should be used to give a manageable comprehension of the whole field of work. The following is offered merely as an example of what might be done:

I. Work with people:
   A. Indoors:
      1. Service.
      2. Selling.
      3. Managerial.
   B. Outdoors: managerial.
   C. Traveling:
      1. Selling.
      2. Service.
II. Work with machines:
   A. Indoors:
      1. Building machines.
      2. Repairing machines.
      3. Operating machines.
   B. Outdoors: operating.
   C. Traveling: conveyance.
III. Work with other objects of the man-made environment:
   A. Office jobs.
   B. Housework.
   C. Construction.
   D. Factory work.
IV. Work with the land:
   A. Farming and gardening.
   B. Forestry.
   C. Hunting and trapping.

V. Work on water:
    A. Fishing.
    B. Conveyance.
VI. Work depending mainly on physical strength and endurance:
    A. Outside.
    B. Inside.
VII. Work involving a special talent:
    A. Writing.
    B. Music.
    C. Dramatics.
    D. Painting and sculpturing.
    E. Modeling.

Some grouping of occupations of the above nature would probably be more interesting to adolescents than the one which follows:[15]

Professional and managerial occupations:
    Professional occupations.
    Semiprofessional occupations.
    Managerial and official occupations.
Clerical and sales occupations:
    Clerical and kindred occupations.
    Sales and kindred occupations.
Service occupations:
    Domestic-service occupations.
    Personal-service occupations.
    Protective-service occupations.
    Building-service occupations.
    Building-service workers and porters.
Agriculture, fishery, forestry, and kindred occupations:
    Agricultural, horticultural, and kindred occupations.
    Fishery occupation.
    Forestry (except logging) and hunting and trapping occupations.
Skilled occupations.
Semiskilled occupations.
Unskilled occupations.

It seems to the authors that the ideal situation would be to provide every adolescent with a thoroughgoing survey of the work world such as we have suggested, involving the use of books and movies, speakers from industry and professions brought to the classroom, individual interviewing, excursions to places of business, and work experiences.

Many schools are as yet approaching this problem in more limited

[15] *Dictionary of Occupational Titles* (Washington: Government Printing Office, 1939), Part II, p. ix.

ways—though in ways helpful to the student. In one large city,[16] for instance, a series of senior job conferences were held on a city-wide basis. First, the students were polled as to their first and second job choices. Second, plans were made with various business- and professional men to hold conferences with the students. Third, an orientation meeting was held with the students, conferences were scheduled, and the students met in groups according to their interests. Altogether 70 conferences were organized, conducted by 52 different conference leaders from the city. Meetings were frequently held in the places of work and often were carried on through informal discussion.

In another school[17] a course in occupations has been worked out which includes choosing a vocation, studying that occupation, spending a day or two actually doing the work, visiting an employment office, and so on.

In still another school[18] a course, Diversified Occupations, is given for students who are not academically-minded and who are ready for job training. The class meets four days a week, the fifth day's period being used for personal interviews with individual students by the teacher. Each pupil also spends part of his school day on a job which he finds for himself or which is found for him by the teacher.

The class sessions center around four big units: (1) Know yourself. (2) Know your job. (3) How to play—enjoy this day! (4) How to grow up. As these titles indicate, the teacher endeavors to help the student in his general development as well as in his vocational adjustment. Materials for this course are found wherever available—reference books are used, as are various personality and interest tests, magazine articles, speakers, and the like.

WORK EXPERIENCES FOR YOUTH

Real work experiences are good for students in many ways and for many reasons. They give adolescents an opportunity to have the adult status they crave, demand endeavor that has real meaning and seriousness, and promote a chance to get acquainted with actual work situations, thus giving boys and girls a means of learning their own abilities, tastes, and interests through trying them out. They offer the youth a gradual induction into the work world. They give him actual experience which

[16] Margaret E. Andrews, "Five Steps to Minneapolis' Senior Job Conferences," *Clearing House*, 22:334–338 (1948).

[17] C. A. Heuss *et al.*, "High School Seniors Study Occupations," *Occupations*, 26:290–293 (1948).

[18] Katharine Dresden (describing a course taught by Mrs. Daugherty), "Current Materials in a Work-experience Program," *School Review*, 57:165–167 (1949).

will be to his advantage in applying for a full-time job when that time comes.

There are various ways in which such experience can be given. Here, in her own words, is what one ingenious teacher did:[19]

" 'The Vocational Guidance Period should be a most pleasant one,' say vocational guidance authorities.

"Our guidance period, forty minutes each week for each eighth grade, was pleasant, but it didn't go beyond that point. Information was passively received. Something was wrong. Assuming that lack of interest lay in the fact that the need was not immediate, I suggested we look for jobs. Then began a survey of our neighborhood, lasting two weeks.

"A few in each class had after-school jobs—they suggested possibilities. Several girls found jobs staying with youngsters a few hours during the evening. (Two had to leave these jobs because the parents disregarded the time agreed upon and remained away until long after midnight.) The neighborhood bakery could use a girl on Saturdays. The corner barbershop needed a boy to clean up between five and six each night. One neighbor wanted a dependable girl whom she could trust to go into her house at noon and after school to care for a pet dog, because she worked from eight until five.

"Several boys removed ashes for neighbors on ash collection day, and added the job of carrying oil to those living on the second floor. A few, who couldn't find jobs, assumed added duties at home for which their parents rewarded them financially.

"At the end of the two-week survey period, each pupil reported on his new job. We checked our 'Personality List' and 'How to Find a Job' list in reference to their aid in finding jobs. We formed a club, restricting membership to job holders. Dues were decided upon. Some of the money is used for new materials in vocational guidance; the remainder will be spent on a club trip to New York in June.

"After our club had been operating for two months, I asked each member to state frankly whether or not his particular job had helped him. These are some of the replies:

" 'I've learned how to understand people better.'

" 'The blind woman I take to the bus is the most uncomplaining person I have ever met.'

" 'I've learned to work quickly but well.'

" 'I must be neat and clean to hold my job.'

" 'I must be more careful of my English.'

" 'I've learned that sometimes it takes money to make money.'

" 'I've acquired a sense of responsibility.'

[19] Helen M. Carroll, "Eighth Graders Find Jobs," *Occupations*, 24:506 (1945).

" 'I know the value of being prepared.'

" 'My job at the grocery store has helped me to understand how to sell things, make change, and wrap articles neatly.'

" 'My job in the Central Plumbing Supply helped me in Mathematics.'

" 'I've learned to clean a house well.'

" 'I've learned not to shout at little children.'

" 'I've learned to get to work on time.' "

A technical high school has the following program:[20]

"All the members of last year's graduating classes at the Technical High School [St. Louis] participated in the school-work program which has been in effect for the past two years. Under this plan, the student in his last term in school attends school one-half day and works in the field of his major specialization for the other half-day. The student receives credit for this work experience; the work on the job is considered practical laboratory experience in which he applies the techniques and skills learned. The counselor-coordinator visits the place of employment, checking on the actual work experience, the work habits, attitudes, and personal adjustments of the student. The students participating in this program meet the counselor for one school period each day in a conference to discuss common problems. Although wide latitude is permitted in the questions discussed, they are woven into the over-all pattern to give the student a well-balanced view of himself, and the relationship between training and job activities, as well as proper work attitudes and habits. The major areas include: analysis of the individual's abilities, training, and job requirements; discussion of personality, leadership, and health, and how each affects job efficiency; the importance of good telephone technique —including demonstration voice testing; job attitudes and ethics; job-finding techniques including practice interviews; employer-employee relationships; budget and income and grooming. This program has proved advantageous to the student, the employer, and the school. It assists the student in bridging the gap between the school and the job; the employer has the student broken into the job routines and has some idea of potential skills by the time the beginner is ready to begin full-time work on the job, and a closer relationship and better understanding are developed between the school and industry. This program is being continued during the current year."

Sometimes boys and girls can be given work experiences by setting up situations within the school which approximate out-of-school job situations. Some schools, for example, have a school bank, chartered by the state and organized and run by the students.

[20] Marguerite Stuehrk, "How One School Helps 'Tween Age Youth," *Occupations*, 4:87–88 (1945).

Ivins and Wey[21] tell of one high school which had a planned program of informal work experiences for all students. One such project was the selling of magazines to raise money for themselves and the school. Before and during the sales campaign commercial and mathematics classes studied salesmanship, social studies classes discussed how to meet and get along with the public, the magazines to be sold were discussed and evaluated in the English classes, and so on. Another such project was the improvement of the school's physical plant through cooperative pupil effort. Thus the students had wholesome work experiences and all of the teachers did what they could to make these experiences educational.

Many students, especially juniors and seniors, will find part-time work of their own if they can, as Table 38 suggests.

TABLE 38. RESULTS OF A WORK CENSUS FOR A CITY'S 12,548 SENIOR HIGH SCHOOL STUDENTS*

	Number	Per cent
Employed...	5,468	43.6%
Want jobs...	4,837	38.5
Not interested in jobs...	2,243	17.9
Total...	12,548	100.0%

* May Carmody and O. I. Schmaelzle, "The Value of a High School Work Census," *Occupations*, 22:348–351 (1944).

Concerning another group of seniors, we read:[22]

" . . . in the college-preparatory high school of a large industrial city in Ohio during April, 1948, seventy Senior boys were interviewed regarding their jobs. Forty were employed at that time; seventeen had held jobs but, for various reasons, were not working at the moment; twelve had worked only during school vacations; and only one had had no work experience besides his paper route. In the same school, of fifty Senior girls reporting, twenty-one were employed, nine formerly had held jobs, eleven had worked only during vacations, and nine had never worked outside their homes."

Self-found work opportunities may not be so educational as one might wish and in some cases may be actually harmful. Nevertheless many schools accept them as either necessary or educational or both and make special provision for their working students.

[21] Wilson H. Ivins and Herbert Wey, "Capitalizing on Educational Values of Informal Work Experiences," *School Review*, 57:485–489 (1949).

[22] Mabel M. Riedinger, "The High-school Teacher's Service to the Employed Pupil," *School Review*, 57:83–88 (1949).

Gilbert[23] writes that information was requested from the 100 largest cities in Missouri concerning the school adjustments they were making to allow for paid work experiences for pupils. Sixty-six replies were received. According to them, the following arrangements were being made to provide for some better combination of school and work experience for high-school youth:

Earlier opening hour of school.

Establishment of Saturday classes.

Opening of evening high-school classes.

Scheduling of required subjects both morning and afternoon to accommodate students who work the first or second half of the day.

Setting up classes outside the regular school buildings.

Relaxation of graduation requirements in individual cases.

Allowing credit toward graduation for paid work experience.

Riedinger[24] suggests that the teacher can make the work experience more profitable to the student (and the school experience more profitable as well) if he will find ways of relating work to school. She finds that group discussions of the work experiences the students are having will not only give the teacher more information about the students' activities but will also give the students an opportunity to organize and to clarify their own thinking about what they are learning at work. She believes that written compositions in regard to work experiences are also helpful for the same reasons.

To be the most helpful to a student, a work experience should have the following characteristics, according to Walker:[25]

"1. An acceptable work station will present no undue social or physical hazards to the worker.

"2. It will be considered by both the school and management to be primarily a training situation—a cooperative educational project fully and freely subscribed to by the school, the trainee, and management.

"3. It will pay the student worker the prevailing entrance wage for the kind and quality of service he renders. Unproductive workers will not be recommended by the school for parttime employment.

"4. The nature of job activities will be in line with the basic school training program, or training in related phases of the total occupational field. Sales trainees, for instance, may profit from experience in nonselling departments, such as the filing department, the personnel department, or the adjustment de-

---

[23] A. W. Gilbert, "Work Experience for Secondary-school Pupils," *NEA Bulletin of Secondary School Principals*, 28:36–40 (1944).

[24] Riedinger, *loc. cit.*

[25] A. L. Walker, "Job-centered Business Education," *NEA Journal*, 38:348–349 (1949).

partment. Similarly, stenographers may be assigned to these or other departments as a means of gaining a broad understanding of the total business establishment.

"5. The work-experience program will be no longer than is required for
the trainee to gain the desired degree of occupational orientation, and the perfection of special skills it has to offer. The usual 15 hours a week for 36 weeks
may well be, in some cases, twice as much time as is necessary in order to provide adequate orientation to fulltime working conditions.

"6. The parttime work agreement should be in writing and should be subscribed to by the school, the trainee, the employer, and the parent.

"7. A good work-experience program will provide for periodic (30- to 60-
day intervals) employer evaluation reports that reveal occupational and personal deficiencies as well as the progress achieved by the trainee.

TABLE 39. THE EFFECT OF WORK EXPERIENCE ON HIGH SCHOOL EXTRACURRICULAR
ACTIVITIES*

Schools	Mean number of activities	
	Workers	Nonworkers
Bloom Township High School............	1.26	1.16
Hobart High School....................	1.95	2.44
Waukegan Township High School........	1.40	1.99
All schools...........................	1.56	1.86

* Richard M. Bateman, "The Effect of Work Experience on High-school Extra-
curriculum Activities," *Educational Administration and Supervision*, 36:265–274
(1950).

"8. While eventual fulltime employment may well be a resultant of the
cooperative parttime agreement, there will be no obligation on the part of
either principal to project the work arrangement beyond the internship period.

"9. There will be an inschool related training program of studies designed
to complement the work-experience phase in business.

"10. The cooperative parttime program will be under the administration
of a competent teacher-coordinator who has sufficient nonteaching time
scheduled for making and maintaining contacts with employers, prospective
employers, and fulltime and parttime employees."

A work experience may have several disadvantages:

Bateman[26] paired working students with nonworkers as to school,
grade, sex, intelligence, father's occupation. Then he worked out a

[26] Richard M. Bateman, "The Effect of Work Experience on High School Students'
Scholastic Achievement," *Occupations*, 28:353–356 (1950).

scholarship rank for each, calling A 4, B 3, C 2, D 1, and E 0. The average for the workers was 2.16, for the nonworkers 2.34. It would seem, he concludes, that working does lower the scholarship.

He also compared these students as to the number of extracurricular activities in which they participated. His data are given in Table 39.

Bell writes:[27]

"It would be much too naïve, however, to assume that a plan which involves part-time schooling and part-time work is an unmixed blessing. It has very real dangers and limitations which should not be ignored. For example, such an arrangment may offer unscrupulous employers opportunities for exploiting their students, or 'learners,' and evading their responsibilities under the Fair Labor Standards Act. The possibility of such exploitation should be taken into account by the sponsors of a cooperative program.

"There is, moreover, the question of how such a plan affects the interests of the youth who are out of school and unemployed. Let us assume that 2,000,000 of the more than 7,000,000 pupils in our secondary school could be brought under a half-work-half-school program. This would mean that 2,000,000 half-time jobs, or 1,000,000 full-time jobs, are filled by students. It is true that students so affected would enjoy the benefits of a vitalized educational program. But what of the 4,000,000 youth who are totally unemployed?"

Although not necessarily connected with the school, another type of work experience may be mentioned here—the work camp. Work camps originated in Europe and were introduced here by the American Friends Service Committee in the summer of 1924. As one example of what youth might do, Henderson[28] mentions a Kentucky camp group which cultivated, harvested, and canned 6½ tons of vegetables, crated them, and packed them on a freight car to start them on their way to Austria.

Henderson quotes Kenneth Holland and George L. Bickel as they visualize thousands of separate camps scattered all around the country, housing small groups of high school boys and girls:[29]

"For eight weeks the campers spent from five to seven hours a day in voluntary work on projects of community benefit. Old barns, vacant and dilapidated buildings, deserted shacks, were transformed into useful, at-

[27] Howard M. Bell, *Matching Youth and Jobs* (Washington: American Council on Education, 1940), p. 62.

[28] Richard L. Henderson, "Work Experiences through Work Camps," *School Review*, 47:391–396 (1949).

[29] Kenneth Holland and George L. Bickel, *Work Camps for High School Youth*, (Washington: American Council on Education, 1941).

tractive community centers. Roads and paths and fences were built, mile upon mile. Community services received free aid. Thousands of underprivileged children were given care, furnished with food, afforded brief vacations in the country. . . . Young campers spent some 300 million boy- and girl-hours of hard, earnest labor. . . .

"But labor was not the whole life of the camps. A million and a half boys and girls looked at the United States in a new way. Into factories, mines, homes, and farms they swarmed on special trips, and there they saw with their own eyes how Americans work and live. . . . In the evenings they sat around campfires and discussed what they had done and seen during the day. Large and small issues were pondered, songs were sung, a new kind of comradeship was formed. . . .

"Back to their homes they went at last—a million and a half boys and girls who were healthier, who knew more about living and working conditions, who had more realistic experience in work and in ways of gaining a livelihood, and who had grasped an understanding of how to get on with one another more firmly than any large group of high school pupils in the history of the United States."

THE QUESTION OF ACTUAL VOCATIONAL TRAINING

Just how much actual vocational training should be given in high school is a debatable question. Some argue that except for the commercial subjects, vocational training can be given most effectively on the job. However, there are students who know what they want to prepare for, and the training given them in high school then not only gives them a good start in the work world but also makes them happier about all of their high school work. An interesting plan is used in St. Louis:[30]

"Through a high school cooperative program the technical high school offers specialized training to the students in the upper grades of the 8 metropolitan high schools. Students attend their 'home' school for one half-day, and attend the Technical High School for the other half-day. The student is thus given the opportunity to supplement the general foundation secured in the 'home' high school, and is equipped with skills to offer an employment manager when he applies for work. At the same time the student can take part in the social and other school activities of his graduating class. This term, 98 school 'co-ops' or nearly 9 per cent of all senior students are enrolled in almost all departments of the Technical High School. Enrollment is on the recommendation of the principal and the counselor of the 'home' school."

[30] Stuehrk, *op. cit.*, pp. 88–89.

THE ADOLESCENT MUST UNDERSTAND HIS OWN POSSIBILITIES

Tests

Since occupations can be rated as to the level of intelligence each demands for success, an intelligence-test score has value in helping the student find his vocation. It is questionable whether it is good for all students to be told their IQ's, and it is not suggested here that that be done, but such information can be used in conjunction with other facts about the student to give him a general picture of his capabilities and probabilities for success in particular vocational fields.

There are a number of vocational-aptitude tests which are helpful to students. Thus for mechanical aptitude there are the Minnesota Paper Form Board, Stenquist Mechanical Aptitude Test, the Minnesota Mechanical Assembly Test, Purdue Pegboard, and others. For clerical aptitude there are the Detroit General Aptitudes Examination, Minnesota Vocational Test for Clerical Workers, Science Research Associates Clerical Aptitudes Test, and others. There are a Medical Aptitude Test and a Law Aptitude Examination.

A valuable kind of test for vocational information is the vocational-interest inventory. There are several of these, the best known being the Strong Vocational Interest Blank for Men, the Strong Vocational Interest Blank for Women, and the Kuder Preference Record (Vocational). These are devised for adults but are used with considerable success with the older high school student.

The Strong Vocational Interest Blank begins by explaining to the reader that the test is not one of intelligence or school work, but rather measures the extent to which one's interests agree or disagree with those of successful men in a given occupation. There follow 400 items on which the person taking the test rates himself. Thus a list of 100 occupations is given, each to be rated L (if you like that kind of work), I (if you are indifferent), or D (if you dislike it). Following this is a list of 49 amusements for a similar rating, then a list of activities, and so on.

When the test is scored, a rating is given on 35 occupations such as artist, psychologist, architect, physician, dentist, mathematician, engineer, and the like. The scoring for the Strong test is a complex matter and must be done by someone who is professionally competent. The expense of having the scoring done might make the use of the test impossible in many high schools. The Kuder Preference Record is simple to score. It gives the person a rating on nine areas, mechanical, computational, scientific, persuasive, artistic, literary, musical, social service, and clerical.

The test consists of 168 groups of three activities each. The subject selects the activity he likes most and the one he likes least in each group.

Vocational Counseling

Every student should have direct personal help from someone who is competent to assist him in evaluating his own capabilities. Such a person, generally known as the *vocational counselor*, has other responsibilities as well. According to Bell, these are the duties that the vocational counselor should assume: [31]

A. Helping the applicant to evaluate his vocational assets and liabilities:
  1. To review his occupational experience thoughtfully.
  2. To examine his education and training critically.
  3. To consider his aptitudes and abilities intelligently.
  4. To discover certain fields of work to which he is particularly adapted.
  5. To discover some of the reasons that have prevented him from gaining greater success in any vocational field in which he has accumulated experience.
B. Interpretation of the facilities offered by the community to the unemployed individual:
  1. To understand some of the significant changes occurring in various occupations and industries.
  2. To learn of professions or occupations in which the successful workers have tastes, interests, and abilities similar to his own.
  3. To put him in touch with facilities through which he might prepare himself for an appropriate occupation.
  4. To find opportunities to add new skills necessary in his work.
  5. To plan avocational activities that would employ and develop special abilities and interests for which his occupation gives little opportunity.
C. Broader aspects of adjustment:
  1. To work out a life program that would contribute to greater happiness and success.
  2. To make contacts that would be helpful in putting his plans into successful operation.
  3. To gain a better command over his own life and over the conditions under which he is living.
  4. To avoid certain fields in which he is weak.

Strang[32] makes the point that vocational guidance should have as one objective helping the student see the social importance of prospective vocations and, as well, the worth of the job as a means to self-fulfillment.

[31] Bell, *Matching Youth and Jobs*, pp. 25–26.
[32] Ruth Strang, "Social Aspects of Vocational Guidance," *School Review*, 48:326–334 (1950).

RECORDS AND INFORMATION FOR EMPLOYERS

Spaulding writes:[33] "Analysis of the reports showed that high schools in general know little about many of their pupils beyond the facts implied in records of school marks." Later he says: "A study of the reports for various groups of pupils suggested that high schools know most about boys and girls from well-to-do homes, who graduate from the college-preparatory curriculum; they know least about young people from economically poor homes, who leave school without graduating."

When a boy or girl has been in a school throughout his junior and senior high school years, one would expect that the school would know something about his intelligence, his social adjustment, his strengths and weaknesses as a person, his workmanship, and the range of his interests and abilities. This information could be both garnered and recorded if the administration would provide the incentive and plan techniques for getting the information on permanent records.

One example of a helpful technique is described by Heuss,[34] who tells of the introduction of personality rating charts into the junior-senior high school of Dobbs Ferry, New York. Each teacher has a small chart for each pupil on which she records ratings for accuracy, cooperation, effort, attitude, reliability, initiative, leadership, self-control, voice and enunciation, personal appearance, and courtesy. The students know that they are being rated and seem to like the idea, on the whole, and be stimulated to improve because of it.

YOUTH SHOULD KNOW EFFECTIVE PROCEDURES FOR FINDING JOBS

According to the findings of the Remmers-Shimberg Youth Inventory,

35 per cent ask "How do I go about finding a job?"
24 per cent want to know where they can go for help in finding a job.
27 per cent don't know for what kind of job to apply.
19 per cent are concerned about how to act during an interview.
18 per cent wish they could write good letters of application.

Assuming that the school has prepared the youth for his vocational choice by giving him an understanding of what the world offers in the way of work possibilities, by helping him to know himself, and by making meaningful work experiences available to him, one thing remains to be done and that is to see that the boy or girl knows how to go about getting a job.

[33] Spaulding, *op. cit.*, p. 159.
[34] Charlotte A. Heuss, "We Introduced Rating Charts," *Occupations*, 25:216–219 (1947).

It is a fairly simple matter to provide this knowledge. The ability to write a proper letter of application and some experience in being interviewed can be achieved in a few learning periods. Information about the use of want ads and of employment agencies, along with some actual practice in using them, is also rather easily acquired.

It is particularly important that the high school job seeker know of the help he can get from the United States Employment Service and its state affiliates. He should know not only that this Service will help him find a job but also that it will give him a general aptitude test, which will help him find the *right* job. This test, requiring 2½ hours to take, consists of 15 parts and measures aptitude in 10 major fields, thus covering over 2,000 occupations. Such testing service is available to the public and is also available to high schools in that trained administrators will come into the school and give the test to any group that desires it, as, for example, an entire senior class.

Reminiscences

1. How much help did you have in high school in selecting your lifework?

2. What led you to choose the work you are now preparing for? **Try to** mention all of the major factors involved.

3. Did anything in high school help better your understanding of the great complexity of kinds of work in the world, as well as add to your understanding of what the work life of individuals in widely different kinds of work is like?

4. Can you think of any particular classes or any particular teachers who did much for you to make you a better worker? How was it done?

Observation

1. Arrange to have some high school seniors visit the class. Find out how many have made vocational choices and upon what basis they have made them. What are their vocational aspirations for the future of 10 or 20 years hence? What do they feel are their responsibilities as workers?

2. Visit the United States Employment Service. Find out what services are offered to prospective workers. If possible, take some of their tests.

Participation

1. Arrange to take high school students to visit some place of business. Be sure there is opportunity for the students to ask questions.

2. Take the Kuder Preference Test or the Strong Interest Inventory yourself so that you know what such a test is like.

3. Find five books on vocations which you would recommend to a high school student.

General Discussion

1. Look at Peters's list of factors in vocational choice (Table 32). How would you rate them as to what *should* be first in importance, second, and so on?

2. Study the preferences and expectations of the girls in Boynton and Woolwine's data. Do they have any significance for the educator? What is it?

3. Look at Dreier and Kreitlow's list of choices of rural boys and girls. Do they seem realistic?

4. Consider Moyer's problems for the business novitiate. How troubling to youth is each of these likely to be?

5. What would you do in the classes you will be teaching, to make youth into good workmen?

6. Consider the characteristics of a desirable work situation. Do you know any students who work? How desirable is their activity?

7. What could be done in your own state as to work camps for youth?

8. Consider Bell's listing of the duties of a vocational counselor. In the light of these, what kind of training would you say a vocational counselor should have? What experience?

Panel Discussion

1. An ideal vocational-adjustment program in high schools.
2. A part-time work program for youth.

Movie

You and Your Work, Coronet Films, 10 min., b. & w., 1948.

Further Reading

ANDREE, ROBERT G., "Training Youth for Intelligent Membership in Labor Unions," *Clearing House*, 17:3–5 (1942).

BAKER, R. W., V. M. JACKSON, and P. R. STEVICK, "Fewer Square Pegs in Round Holes," *Junior College Journal*, 13:387–389 (1943).

BARBER, LEROY E., "Why Some Able High-school Graduates Do Not Go to College," *School Review*, 59:93–96 (1951).

BATEMAN, RICHARD M., "The Effect of Work Experience on the Attitude of High School Students toward School and School Subjects," *Educational Administration and Supervision*, 35:157–164 (1949).

BELL, HOWARD M., *Matching Youth and Jobs* (Washington: American Council on Education, 1940).

BELL, HOWARD M., *Youth Tell Their Story* (Washington: American Council on Education, 1938).

BURNS, NORMAN, "Work-adjustment Plans for Youth," *School Review*, 59:10–12 (1951).

DIMICHAEL, S. G., "Using Interests as the Basis of Vocational Choice," *Occupations*, 20:270–275 (1942).

EDMISTON, R. W., and C. S. STARR, "Youth's Attitude toward Occupations," *Occupations*, 26:213–220 (1948).

FORNWALT, RUSSELL J., "Vocational Guidance for the Delinquent Boy," *Occupations*, 25:149–151 (1946).

FORNWALT, RUSSELL J., "Vocational Guidance for the Socially Maladjusted Boy," *Mental Hygiene*, 31:599–604 (1947).

FORRESTER, GERTRUDE, *Methods of Vocational Guidance* (Boston: D. C. Heath and Company, 1951).

JACKSON, J., "A Note on the Crystallization of Vocational Interests," *Journal of Social Psychology*, 26:125–130 (1947).

KLEIN, LOUIS M., "Our Junior Vocational Course," *Clearing House*, 20:537–539 (1946).

KOPP, T., and L. TUSSING, "The Vocational Choices of High School Students as Related to Scores on Vocational Interest Inventories," *Occupations*, 25:333–339 (1947).

LIPSITZ, HERBERT J., "The Exploratory Program as a Factor in Student Choice," *Occupations*, 24:92–94 (1945).

McDANIEL, H. B., "Guiding Youth to Service Today," *Occupations*, 21:363–368 (1943).

MOYER, DONALD H., "Advice from the Apprentices," *Occupations*, 18:411–416 (1940).

PATERSON, DONALD G., "Vocational Interest Inventories in Selection," *Occupations*, 25:152–153 (1946).

PEPPER, JAMES N., "Effective Living: Richmond's Course for Seniors," *Clearing House*, 21:31–33 (1946).

RECHTENWALD, L. N., "Attitudes toward Occupations before and after Vocational Information," *Occupations*, 24:220–223 (1946).

SCHLOERB, LESTER J., "Guidance Program and Problems at the Secondary School Level," *School Review*, 54:202–207 (1946).

SCHNEIDMAN, EDWIN S., "Information Form Useful in Vocational Counseling," *Occupations*, 25:108–109 (1946).

SELDER, JUNE, "A Work Experience Program," *Childhood Education*, 26:415–417 (1950).

SLATER, HENRY L., "A Cooperative Training Program in a Small School," *School Review*, 49:761–765 (1941).

STONE, C. H., "Are Vocational Orientation Courses Worth Their Salt?" *Educational and Psychological Measurement*, 8:161–182 (1948).

TRAXLER, ARTHUR, "Guidance toward College Preparation," *School and Society*, 73:113–116 (1951).

Chapter 11. JUVENILE DELINQUENCY

Whoever the reader of these pages may be, he must inevitably have heard something about juvenile delinquency. If he has not come across one of the almost innumerable books on the subject or read one of the frequent magazine articles, he has at least seen newspaper reference to some youth who has transgressed the law and thus become technically a "juvenile delinquent."

WHO IS A JUVENILE DELINQUENT?

Juvenile delinquency is behavior defined by law both in regard to the age of the offender and in regard to the nature of the act. As far as age is concerned, in most states the juvenile delinquent is a young person over seven and under eighteen, but in some states the upper age limits differ from this.

What a child does to be termed a juvenile delinquent also differs from state to state. For example, in the statutes of the state of Indiana, we read:[1]

"Sc. 4. Delinquent child defined.

"That the words *delinquent child* shall include any boy under the full age of eighteen years and any girl under the full age of eighteen years who:

"1. Violates a law or municipal ordinance or regulation of the State or any subdivision thereof; except in proceedings concerning any child over sixteen years who has violated any of the traffic laws of the state or any traffic ordinance of a subdivision of the state;

"2. Commits an act, which, if committed by an adult, would be a crime not punishable by death or life imprisonment;

"3. Is incorrigible, ungovernable or habitually disobedient and beyond the control of his parent, guardian or other custodian;

"4. Is habitually truant;

"5. Without just cause and without the consent of his parents, guardian, or other custodian, repeatedly deserts his home or place of abode;

"6. Engages in an occupation which is in violation of law;

"7. Associates with immoral or vicious persons;

"8. Frequents a place the existence of which is in violation of the law;

"9. Is found begging, receiving or gathering alms, whether actually begging or under the pretext of selling or offering anything for sale;

"10. Unaccompanied by parent, patronizes or visits any room wherein there is a bar where intoxicating liquors are sold;

[1] Acts of Indiana General Assembly, 1945, 84th session, Vol. II.

"11. Wanders about the streets of any city between the hours of ten o'clock P.M. and five o'clock A.M. without being on any lawful business or occupation;

"12. Is found in or about railroad yards or tracks; or who jumps on or off trains; or who enters a car or engine without lawful authority;

"13. Uses vile, obscene, vulgar or indecent language;

"14. Uses intoxicating liquor as a beverage, or who uses opium, cocaine, morphine or other similar drugs without the directions of a competent physician;

"15. Knowingly associates with thieves or other maliciously vicious persons;

"16. Is guilty of immoral or indecent conduct;

"17. Deports himself so as to wilfully injure or endanger the morals or health of himself or others;

"18. Deports himself so as to wilfully injure or endanger the person or property of himself or others."

Here, as in several states, the child who commits a capital crime (an offense punishable by death) is not tried in the juvenile court but is rather tried as a criminal and in the criminal court.

REFERRAL TO THE COURT

The great majority of cases are brought to the court following arrest of the child or youth by the police. There are, of course, other sources of

TABLE 40. JUVENILE-DELINQUENCY CASES, 1945: SOURCES OF REFERENCE TO COURT, IN BOYS' AND IN GIRLS' CASES DISPOSED OF BY 374 COURTS*

Source of reference to court	Number			Per cent		
	Total	Boys	Girls	Total	Boys	Girls
Total cases.....................	122,851	101,240	21,611			
Source of reference reported........	96,262	79,534	16,728	100	100	100
Police........................	68,682	60,049	8,633	71	75	52
School department..............	6,976	5,027	1,949	7	6	12
Probation officer...............	2,974	2,224	750	3	3	4
Other court....................	1,590	1,343	247	2	2	1
Social agency..................	1,592	752	840	2	1	5
Parents or relatives.............	5,751	2,951	2,800	6	4	17
Other individual...............	7,477	6,304	1,173	8	8	7
Other source..................	1,220	884	336	1	1	2
Source of reference not reported....	26,589	21,706	4,883			

* "Juvenile-court Statistics, 1944 and 1945," *Social Statistics*, Supplement to Vol. II of *The Child* (November, 1946, Supplement) Federal Security Agency, Social Security Administration, U.S. Children's Bureau, p. 5.

Table 41. Juvenile-delinquency Cases, 1945: Reasons for Reference to Court, in Boys' and in Girls' Cases Disposed of by 374 Courts*

Reason for reference to court	Number			Per cent		
	Total	Boys	Girls	Total	Boys	Girls
Total cases.....................	122,851	101,240	21,611			
Reason for reference reported......	111,939	92,671	19,268	100	100	100
Stealing......................	40,879	38,610	2,269	37	42	12
Act of carelessness or mischief...	19,241	17,779	1,462	17	19	8
Traffic violation...............	9,852	9,659	193	9	10	1
Truancy......................	8,681	6,164	2,517	8	7	13
Running away.................	9,307	5,652	3,655	8	6	19
Being ungovernable.............	9,840	5,542	4,298	9	6	22
Sex offense...................	5,990	2,579	3,411	5	3	18
Injury to person...............	3,224	2,828	396	3	3	2
Other reason..................	4,925	3,858	1,067	4	4	5
Reason for reference not reported...	10,912	8,569	2,343			

* "Juvenile-court Statistics, 1944 and 1945," *Social Statistics*, Supplement to Vol. II of *The Child* (November, 1946, Supplement) Federal Security Agency, Social Security Administration, U.S. Children's Bureau, p. 5.

Table 42. Juvenile-delinquency Cases, 1945: Ages of Boys and of Girls When Referred to Court, in Cases Disposed of by 374 Courts*

Age of child when referred to court	Number			Per cent		
	Total	Boys	Girls	Total	Boys	Girls
Total cases......................	122,851	101,240	21,611			
Age reported.....................	110,415	91,435	18,980	100	100	100
Under 10 years.................	4,172	3,763	409	4	4	2
10 years, under 12..............	8,032	7,311	721	7	8	4
12 years, under 14.............	18,362	15,558	2,804	17	17	15
14 years, under 16.............	40,872	32,645	8,227	37	36	43
16 years and over.............	38,977	32,158	6,819	35	35	36
Age not reported.................	12,436	9,805	2,631			

* "Juvenile-court Statistics, 1944 and 1945," *Social Statistics*, Supplement to Vol. II of *The Child* (November, 1946, Supplement) Federal Security Agency, Social Security Administration, U.S. Children's Bureau, p. 5.

referral, as Table 40 shows. Table 41 gives the reasons for referral, the most common for boys being stealing, acts of carelessness or mischief, and traffic violations. For girls the most common are being ungovernable, running away, and sex offenses. As for age, more children between fourteen and sixteen years of age are referred to the court than are children of any other age, as Table 42 shows.

WHERE ARE THE CHILDREN DETAINED PENDING HEARING?

It is a shocking fact that children who are arrested or otherwise referred to the court are often detained in the jail along with adult prisoners pending their hearing. How bad it is to have a youth in jail if even for but a short time can be seen from this comment by Roy Casey, Inspector, Federal Bureau of Prisons:[2]

"During recent months assignments have taken me on two occasions into the county jail in the capital city of one of our northern states . . . the county jail, an institution which, measured by any standard of sanitation and decency, would disgrace the most backward community in Christendom, . . . has no quarters for the segregation of juveniles yet the state law permits their being confined there, nor is there any intelligent classification or segregation of adults. At the time of my last inspection the jail held four children somewhere within the dark and filthy cells of its vermin-infested cell blocks, along with criminals, vags, sex perverts, and the insane. The officials spoke of how they were handicapped by not having segregation quarters for juveniles, but it did not appear that they were greatly concerned over the matter and had considered it only a minor thing to have to put fifteen, sixteen and seventeen year old boys with hardened criminals and perverts."

One need not add that children should never be held in jail. Yet as will be seen from Table 43, of the cases reported in 1945 8,735 were so held in the jail or police station.

Twenty-two thousand six hundred fifty-nine were held in detention homes. Ideally the child should be paroled to his home or in the care of someone with whom he can feel security and ease. The use of the detention home is a second-best procedure but necessary in those cases where the home is unsuitable, where the parents have referred the boy or girl for being ungovernable, or where no satisfactory friend can be found to care for the child. The detention home should, of course, have the aspects of a good home—the surroundings pleasant and the atmosphere friendly.

[2] Roy Casey, "Children in Jail," in Marjorie Bell (ed.), *Delinquency and the Community in Wartime*, 1943 Yearbook (New York: National Probation Association, 1943), pp. 174–182.

TABLE 43. JUVENILE-DELINQUENCY CASES, 1945: PLACES OF DETENTION CARE OF BOYS AND OF GIRLS, IN CASES DISPOSED OF BY 374 COURTS*

Place of detention care	Number			Per cent		
	Total	Boys	Girls	Total	Boys	Girls
Total cases.....................	122,851	101,240	21,611			
Detention care reported...........	76,002	62,353	13,649	100	100	100
No detention care over-night.....	43,100	36,824	6,276	57	59	46
Detention care over-night or longer	32,902	25,529	7,373	43	41	54
Boarding home...............	331	292	39	†	1	†
Detention home‡.............	22,659	16,948	5,711	30	27	42
Other institution.............	760	503	257	1	1	2
Jail or police station§........	8,735	7,507	1,228	12	12	9
Other place of care‖..........	156	75	81	(†)	(†)	1
Place of care not reported.....	261	204	57	†	†	†
Detention care not reported........	46,849	38,887	7,962			

* "Juvenile-court Statistics, 1944 and 1945," in *Social Statistics*, Supplement to Vol. II of *The Child* (November, 1946, Supplement), Federal Security Agency, Social Security Administration, U.S. Children's Bureau, p. 5.

† Less than 0.5 per cent.

‡ Includes cases of children cared for part of the time in detention homes and part of the time elsewhere but excludes cases of children also cared for in jails or police stations.

§ Includes cases of children cared for part of the time in jails or police stations and part of the time elsewhere.

‖ Includes cases of children cared for in more than one place but in places other than detention homes, jails, or police stations.

Unfortunately, a goodly proportion of detention homes are little better than jails in spirit and sometimes but little superior even in appearance.

HOW MANY JUVENILE DELINQUENTS ARE THERE?

As given for 1945, the total number of cases was 122,851—101,240 for boys and 21,611 for girls. But this is not the complete picture. In the first place, the best information we have comes from the juvenile-court statistics as collected by the U.S. Children's Bureau, and these statistics have certain limitations:[3] "Some courts report only cases that they have disposed of officially. . . . Other courts report, in addition, those cases disposed of unofficially—without formal action—by judges, probation officers,

[3] "Juvenile-court Statistics, 1944 and 1945," in *Social Statistics*, Supplement to Vol. II of *The Child* (November, 1946, Supplement), Federal Security Agency, Social Security Administration, U.S. Children's Bureau, p. 5.

or referees. Some courts may handle certain types of cases as dependency or neglect cases whereas the same cases in other courts might be handled as delinquency cases."

In the second place there are many children who commit offenses without ever being apprehended. There are also many children who are detected but never brought to court, their cases being handled by a social agency.

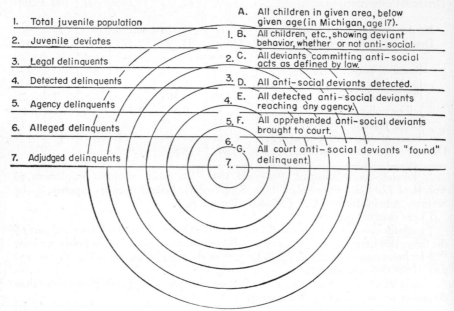

1. Total juvenile population
2. Juvenile deviates
3. Legal delinquents
4. Detected delinquents
5. Agency delinquents
6. Alleged delinquents
7. Adjudged delinquents

A. All children in given area, below given age (in Michigan, age 17).
I. B. All children, etc., showing deviant behavior, whether or not anti-social.
2. C. All deviants committing anti-social acts as defined by law.
3. D. All anti-social deviants detected.
4. E. All detected anti-social deviants reaching any agency.
5. F. All apprehended anti-social deviants brought to court.
6. G. All court anti-social deviants "found" delinquent.

Fig. 31. Showing how the number of delinquents varies depending on which ones are being counted. [From L. J. Carr, *Delinquency Control*, rev. ed. (New York: Harper and Brothers, 1950), p. 90.]

Carr's diagram (Fig. 31) shows how the numbers may vary depending on which delinquents are being counted.

WHAT IS THE DELINQUENT LIKE?

For our answer to the question of what the delinquent is like we shall rely in the main on an authoritative research into the causes of juvenile delinquency, under the direction of Sheldon Glueck and Eleanor Glueck.[4] In this study extending over a 10-year period, 500 boys, really serious offenders, were paired with 500 boys free from delinquent behavior.

[4] Sheldon Glueck and Eleanor Glueck, *Unraveling Juvenile Delinquency* (New York: Commonwealth Fund, Division of Publication, 1950).

TABLE 44. WHAT THE JUVENILE DELINQUENT IS LIKE

Age	The modal age is between fourteen and sixteen*
Sex	There are about five times as many delinquent boys as girls*
Intelligence	In one study the average IQ was found to be 88.74. In another, 64% of the cases were of average or above intelligence. In a third, 41.6% were average or above.* Glueck and Glueck (1950) found that delinquents have less verbal intelligence, less capacity to approach problems methodically, and tend to express themselves intellectually in a direct, immediate, and concrete manner
Residence	The delinquent most often comes from an underprivileged neighborhood*
Physical makeup	Less healthy than nondelinquents, more solid, closely knit, and muscular, less disharmony in physique. Growth spurt occurred late
Personality	More extroversive, more vivacious, more impulsive, more destructive and sadistic, more aggressive and adventurous, less self-controlled. More hostile, resentful, defiant, and suspicious. Less fearful of failure or defeat. Less concerned about meeting conventional expectations, less submissive to authority. More socially assertive. More likely to have feelings of not being recognized or appreciated
Misbehavior tendencies	More in habit of stealing rides, hopping trucks, committing acts of destructive mischief, running away from home, keeping late hours, gambling, begging, smoking, and drinking
Leisure	Less leisure time spent at home, more spent in distant neighborhoods and hanging around street corners, vacant lots, water fronts, railroad yards, and poolrooms. Greater preference for adventurous activities and more seeking of vicarious adventure through movies
Companions	More membership in gangs, more chumming with delinquents, more companionship with older boys

* Data on age and sex from "Juvenile-court Statistics, 1944 and 1945," *Social Statistics*, Supplement to Vol. II of *The Child*, Federal Security Agency, Social Security Administration, U.S. Children's Bureau. Data on intelligence from William C. Kvaraceus, *Juvenile Delinquency and the School* (Yonkers, N.Y.: World Book Company, 1945); William Healy and Augusta F. Bronner, *New Light on Delinquency and Its Treatment* (New Haven: Yale University Press, 1936); Sheldon Glueck and Eleanor T. Glueck, *One Thousand Juvenile Delinquents* (Cambridge: Harvard University Press, 1934). Data on residence from Clifford R. Shaw and Henry D. McKay, *Social Factors in Juvenile Delinquency*, Report on the Causes of Crime, Vol. II, National Commission on Law Observances and Enforcement (Washington: Government Printing Office, 1931).

TABLE 44. WHAT THE JUVENILE DELINQUENT IS LIKE.—(*Continued*)

Parents	More emotional disturbances, mental retardation, alcoholism, and criminalism among families of mothers. More emotional disturbance and criminalism among families of fathers More physical ailments, mental retardation, emotional disturbances, alcoholism, and previous history of delinquency in parents. Less ambition, less self-respect, less planning for the future, less ability to support family
Siblings	More physical ailments, mental retardation, emotional disturbances, excessive drinking, and delinquency among brothers and sisters
Affectional relationships	Family indifferent or frankly hostile to delinquents
Discipline	Extremes of laxity and harshness
School attainment	On an average, 1 year behind grade
School adjustment	More dislike of school, less interest in academic tasks, less attentive in class, more often tardy, less reliable, more careless in work, lazier, more restless, less truthful, more effort to attract attention. More truancy, disobedience, disorderliness, stubbornness, sullenness, impertinence, defiance, and impudence

These boys were matched in four respects: (1) age, (2) general intelligence, (3) national (ethnicoracial) origin, and (4) residence in underprivileged neighborhoods. Then for each boy the family and personal background was studied, the body build classified, a medical examination administered, an intelligence test, achievement test, and Rorschach test given, and a psychiatric interview held. The resulting data were then classified and studied to discover the fundamental differences between the delinquents as a group and the nondelinquents, thus isolating probable causal factors.

Table 44, which presents a picture of the delinquent, utilizes the conclusions of this research unless otherwise stated.

WHAT ARE THE CAUSES OF DELINQUENCY?

The causes of delinquency in any particular child are seldom simple, and the teacher who accounts for some piece of delinquent behavior with a glib explanation is demonstrating ignorance of the complex nature of the motivation of much of human behavior.

In general, however, as Carr says, children become delinquent for one or both of two reasons:[5] "(1) Because of some inadequacy in themselves or in their relation to their environment they become frustrated, thwarted,

[5] Lowell Juilliard Carr, *Delinquency Control* (New York: Harper & Brothers, 1940–1941), p. 69.

emotionally disturbed, and *fall into deviant behavior as a way out*. And/or (2) because *the immediate environment presents predominantly deviant behavior patterns*, as in a slum or an area of delinquency traditions, they adopt such patterns and become social misfits outside of their own circle."

Intelligence and Delinquency

One can find many reasons for expecting the child of below-normal intelligence to be delinquent. He is subjected to more frustrations in school both scholastically and in extracurricular activities. He does not comprehend the full significance of his acts. He is more easily persuaded or seduced.

Nonetheless, much of the evidence on delinquency would indicate that the distribution of IQ's is not greatly skewed to the lower levels. As Louttit says,[6] if delinquents are compared with other children of their *own socioeconomic* level, they are found to be similar in intelligence.

Adolescence and Delinquency

Thirty-eight per cent of juvenile-delinquency cases are in the fourteen- to sixteen-year-old range. Another 34 per cent are between sixteen and eighteen (assuming eighteen to be the top age limit). Quite evidently, delinquency is much more typical of adolescence than of childhood. One reason for this is doubtless the fact that the adolescent's "world" is less confined to the home sphere. Plant suggests three other factors:[7]

"(1) The adolescent is a more 'vulnerable' creature than his older or younger brother; he is more easily affected by problems and stimuli. (2) In adolescence the child often strikes back for the first time, just because he is now strong enough or well enough integrated against a problem that has actually been quite as pressing for a number of years. (3) The adolescent is freshly aware of a whole new set of problems and adjustments— those involved in the awakening of the sexual drive."

The Psychopathic Personality

Seemingly there are some children who cannot be socialized. They give evidence of being unable to develop any feelings about what is right

---

[6] C. M. Louttit, *Clinical Psychology* (New York: Harper & Brothers, 1936), p. 374.
[7] James S. Plant, "Who Is the Delinquent?" Chap. I, in Nelson B. Henry (ed.), *Juvenile Delinquency and the School*, 47th Yearbook, National Society for the Study of Education (Chicago: University of Chicago Press, 1948), Part I, p. 27. Quoted by permission of the Society.

and what is wrong. They are devoid of compassion. They may indulge in senseless perversions or cruelties. Such people are often referred to as *psychopathic personalities*.

Whether heredity has made them what they are or whether they are the result of unwholesome environmental forces, no one as yet knows.

The Home and Delinquency

When Basic Needs Are Frustrated. In an earlier chapter we explained that everyone needs and seeks (1) physiological satisfactions, (2) companionship, (3) love and affection, (4) success, (5) security, and (6) variety. Since these satisfactions bring a feeling of well-being, the child, the adolescent, and the adult will long for them and strive for them. If they are not as fully attained as one needs, his personality and his mode of living may be skewed away from what is wholesome.

In childhood and even in adolescence, the most important source of security and of affection (the second helping to supply the first) is the home, particularly the parents. In childhood, the home is also a major source of feelings of success and worth. The child who is deprived of these satisfactions is not only unhappy but may also develop personality flaws which will prevent his getting the satisfactions he needs all of his life.

The child in a home where he is not loved, where his parents are not harmonious, where the parents favor another child, is almost surely a frustrated, unhappy child. The ways in which he reacts to his unhappiness will vary. Many of them will not be of a nature which we would label delinquency. But in some cases the child *will* seek his satisfactions in antisocial ways because that is the only way he can get them or will feel bitter and resentful and take out his hurt on society; in other cases because of an unsatisfied craving for more excitement and variety than he is getting he may engage in delinquent acts for the thrill they give him, and in still other cases the friction between him and his parents may result in an unmanageable child.

A convincing indication of the importance of having the basic needs satisfied in the home is seen in Healy and Bronner's statement that among the 145 cases treated, 92 per cent had major emotional disturbances:[8]

Feeling of being rejected, unloved, or insecure in affectional relationships—53 cases.

Deep feelings of being thwarted in self-expression and other self-satisfaction—45 cases.

[8] William Healy and Augusta F. Bronner, *New Light on Delinquency and Its Treatment* (New Haven: Yale University Press, 1936), p. 49.

Marked feelings of inadequacy or inferiority in some situations or activities —62 cases.

Emotional disturbance about family disharmonies, discipline, etc.—43 cases.

An example of a child who was delinquent at least in part because of the frustration of his basic needs is found in the case of Tommy:[9]

"Tommy became a specialist in maintaining his self-esteem by stealing. He was never very important to anyone until he began to steal. John, his older brother, was always a comfort to his mother and a source of reliance in the fatherless household; and Cyril, the illegitimate younger brother, with his lively ways and sunny disposition, was sought by the other boys in the neighborhood and a general favorite. Tommy was, to quote Anna Freud's young charge, 'Nobody's nothing.'

"The family was very poor and there was never any money for the things children want—indeed, not even enough for the essentials. The mother was worried and harassed over finances and the desertion of Cyril's father whom she had expected to marry. Ill health further complicated her problems. Never a good manager, she had little time or inclination for household tasks. Her county and state aid she supplemented by her irregular employment as a charwoman—there was no state aid for Cyril because he was illegitimate. The supervision of her three boys was desultory and lax.

"In this home atmosphere the three boys developed quite different personality patterns. John was grave, and rather prosy, and always carried more than a child's share of the burden of household cares and of responsibility for his younger brothers. Cyril was carefree, rather sure of himself, confident of being liked, and, while he engaged in one or two episodes of childhood stealing in the process of acquiring his adjustments to an expanding social environment, delinquency never became for him a pattern of response to frustrating conditions.

"With Tommy the situation was different. Unlike Cyril, secure in his feeling of being loved and wanted, and John, mature beyond his years and socially secure in his consciousness of being an important person in the household, Tommy had no way of being sure he was loved or socially important either at home or at school. He was never a good student; Cyril was always a better student, and important in both academic and social ways in the school world; and John was a plodder and teacher's standby. Tommy was shy and sensitive and continued, long beyond the period where his brothers had left off, to engage in the imaginary exploits of their childish play. He was much by himself, engaging very little in organized play on the school grounds or in other group activities.

[9] Maud A. Merrill, *Problems of Child Delinquency* (Boston: Houghton Mifflin Company, 1947), p. 134.

"His first contact with the probation officer was at the age of ten when he stole gum and cigarettes from a barber shop. For this offense he was admonished, but was not brought into court. His first court appearance was when he was twelve years old, at which time he was charged with attempted extortion."

When Specific Desires Are Unfulfilled. Many children are denied the things that other children receive as a matter of course—a bicycle, spending money, the use of a car in the case of the older adolescent, attractive clothing, and so on. Some children feeling these wants endure their frustration or try to overcome it in legitimate ways; other children will steal.

When Other Members of the Family Engage in Undesirable Conduct. The child's first teachers of what is right and what is wrong are his parents. He learns both from their conscious instruction and also from their example. If his parents are criminal, immoral, or no more than slovenly and dishonest in their standards of behavior, the child may well be the same.

When Discipline in the Home Is Bad

"Don and Carl Elno live with their parents and five brothers and sisters in four rooms of a Chicago tenement, which neighbors call the 'Beehive.' Its back yard runs up to the Illinois Central Railroad tracks.

"The Elno's are poor; in good times they spend everything they earn on food, rent, and clothes. In bad times, they have to go on relief. At all times, Jim, the father, spends too much on liquor. . . .

"Don, the oldest child, has been babied by his mother all his life. She has unconsciously favored him over Carl and the other children. When first married, she wanted a baby, and loved Don intensely. (She did not want Carl.) Furthermore, Don spent most of his first three years in the home of his grandmother; both she and two doting aunts competed with his mother to coddle him. Restraint and punishment were at a minimum in his early life. To Don, his mother was a permissive, loving person, with very little punishment or warning in her voice.

"Don's father, likewise, punished him very little when he was a baby. Later, when Don was in school, however, his father did whip him severely a number of times. . . . But the father's discipline was erratic and inconsistent. . . .

"All in all, Don has grown up in an atmosphere of inconsistent discipline. As he said when he was eleven, '*I don't really know what's bad, till I do it.*'

"Punishment does not stop Don from his bad behavior, because this behavior brings him reward, whereas no reward is offered him for good behavior. This probably explains why the practice of whipping children, which is common in lower class families, often fails to improve their behavior. The case of Don is typical. In his inconsistent way, Don's father has whipped and punished him for stealing. Why does Don not stop? The reason is clear; he gets the powerful rewards of (1) the stolen goods, and (2) the approval of his gang-mates. These certain rewards easily outweigh the occasional punishments he gets for stealing."[10]

When the Child Fails to Accept and Adjust to the Regulations and Restrictions of Home and Society. When a small child can't get what he wants or do what he would like, he hits or kicks or screams. As children grow older, most of them learn to accept many frustrations without rebellion, learn to accept the ways of home and society as necessary and adjust themselves to them. But a few are never taught the necessity for some of these adjustments or refuse to make them. One boy

" . . . has apparently been coddled and pampered during his boyhood with the result that he has never developed any sense of responsibility. He admits that he received speeding tickets on approximately twelve occasions during the past year but dismisses the matter as being of little consequence. He has no realization of his social obligations so far as the operation of a car is concerned. He is unconcerned over the present situation except as his own selfish interests may be affected.

"This impulsive, immature boy has no respect for the rights and privileges of other individuals. This attitude is perhaps directly traceable to faulty training. . . . "[11]

The Neighborhood and Delinquency

Some of the most thoroughgoing studies of neighborhood sources of delinquency have been made by Clifford Shaw and Henry McKay.[12] They found that in Chicago the areas of marked concentration of delinquents were around the stockyards, steel-mill districts, industrial districts, central business district, along the north and south branches of the Chicago River, and on the near West Side. These areas were characterized by physical deterioration, decreasing population, high rates of dependency, high percentage of foreign-born and Negro population, high rates of adult offenders, and disintegration of the traditional institutions and neighborhood organization.

[10] W. Allison Davis and Robert J. Havighurst, *Father of the Man* (Boston: Houghton Mifflin Company, 1947), p. 184.

[11] Marjorie Bell (ed.), *Social Defenses against Crime*, 1942 Yearbook (New York: National Probation Association, 1942), p. 217.

[12] Clifford R. Shaw and Henry D. McKay, *Social Factors in Juvenile Delinquency*, Report on the Causes of Crime, Vol. II, National Commission on Law Observances and Enforcement. (Washington: Government Printing Office, 1931), pp. 28, 108.

One instance of how the neighborhood can influence youth is shown in the account of Larry:[13]

"Larry, living in a tough neighborhood, became a member of a 'cellar' club. Here he found a certain importance and affection which the adult world denied him. He developed a new conscience based on the morals and mores of the gang. Crimes against your brother members were strictly forbidden. Crimes against your own neighborhood were bad taste. Crimes against outsiders were permissible—in fact commendable. Imprisonment for property crimes was a sign of daring and courage and thus a mark of distinction. Sex crimes in contrast were regarded with contempt. But there was no restraint on sex as long as the relationship was voluntary. Half a dozen girls attached themselves to the gang and held free relationships with all members of the gang. But they were bound to keep themselves 'pure' from outsiders."

Recreation and Delinquency

Anything that helps make life better for children and youth will contribute something to the prevention of delinquency. This is true of the provision of good recreational facilities for young people. One is sometimes given the impression, however, that if the recreational facilities are good enough and made available to all children, then delinquency will before long be largely eliminated.

The effectiveness of wholesome recreational opportunities in combating delinquency can easily be overrated, for it will not singlehandedly rid a community of delinquency.

Writing on this topic, Tappan makes these points:[14] A boy who is a good athlete is not necessarily immune to delinquency; recreational activities may still leave time and energy for antisocial acts or even in some cases stimulate delinquent acts "for fun"; the recreational program may not reach the children who need it the most; if poor adjustment, the delinquency tradition of the neighborhood, poor home training predispose toward delinquency, then games and sports are not enough to prevent it; delinquent acts often provide thrills which make recreation seem tame by contrast.

Tappan is not implying, of course, that wholesome recreation is not the right of every child; he is rather emphasizing the fact that recreation is not a cure-all for delinquency.

[13] James S. Wallerstein, "Roots of Delinquency," *Nervous Child*, 6:399–412 (1947).
[14] Paul W. Tappan, *Juvenile Delinquency* (New York: McGraw-Hill Book Company, Inc., 1949), pp. 150–151.

Solomon[15] writes that if recreation is to reduce delinquency, it must be preventive recreation of a special sort. The leader must seek out the stayaways, get them to come, and then hold their interest. He must be highly skilled in understanding young people and causes of delinquency and must be able to organize a program so as to improve character, thought processes, and choices. This, rather than team successes and the like, must be the aim of the real leader of children.

Street Trades, Domestic Service, and Delinquency

Glueck and Glueck, in their study of 1,000 delinquents, found that 58.1 per cent were engaged in street trades as newsboys, bootblacks, errand boys, or messengers. Boys in such work are on the street when many other boys are engaging in sports, working with hobbies, reading or listening to the radio at home, or enjoying the comradeship of their friends. And while on the street at these particular jobs, they meet all kinds of people—some decent but some corrupt—and they see meretricious standards of behavior which may attract them unduly.

Harris,[16] writing on delinquency in adolescent girls, says that young girls in jobs of waitresses, domestic workers, maids in hotels have opportunities for casual sex contacts which, because of the girls' ignorance and bewilderment, becomes a real moral hazard.

The School and Delinquency

The adolescent must spend five or six or more of his most active hours in the school. Surrounding him are the boys and girls with whom he must work and play and, because they are his daily associates, whom he will want to impress and by whom he wants to be accepted and liked. Depending on how they view him, he can achieve social success, mediocrity, or rejection; he can feel secure or insecure.

In charge of him is a teacher, an adult with complete authority over him, an adult who tells him what to do, praises him or punishes him, likes, puts up with, or dislikes him, an adult who has prestige in his eyes, in the eyes of his classmates, and often in the eyes of his parents. How this teacher treats him will likewise be a determining factor in his feelings of security and in his sense of importance.

Schoolwork is often work of an academic nature. For many young people this work is uninteresting drudgery, and for some it is work at

[15] Ben Solomon, "Preventive Recreation," *Recreation*, 44:562–566 (1951).
[16] Dale B. Harris, "Delinquency in Adolescent Girls," *Mental Hygiene*, 28:596–601 (1944).

which they cannot be successful no matter how hard they may try to follow directions and to win the 100's or the A's that are given for good achievement.

It need hardly be said, so obvious is it, that the school for some youth is a source of an unbearable amount of frustration. A teacher who is unsympathetic, school requirements that are dull or beyond his ability, handicaps which prevent his getting along well with the other students —any or all of these may intensify a student's feelings of insecurity, feelings of worthlessness, and feelings of boredom to the extent that he may seek his satisfactions elsewhere legitimately or not—or to the extent that he may become punishingly aggressive toward the society which has failed him.

WHAT CAN THE SCHOOL DO TO PREVENT JUVENILE DELINQUENCY?

Minimize Needless and Harmful Frustrations

Too many teachers and principals are not sensitive to the fact that the adolescent deserves to live happily while he is in school or to the fact that the soundest and the most far-reaching learning occurs when the adolescent is enjoying what he is doing, seeing its use to him, and taking a vital part in the planning and the learning process.

One of the biggest questions for the teacher and the school is this: How can we see that no student is subjected to the major frustrations that are so often the lot of some and see, too, that life is recognizably worth while for all? The answer lies in making a strong effort to meet the basic needs of all of the students. These needs are as follows:

1. The need for security. A sense of security in school will be present if the students believe that all will be treated justly, if discipline is not harsh, if the student feels that the teachers are his friends, if the work is not beyond his capabilities, if order and consistency characterize school regulations and patterns of activity.

2. The need for companionship and affection. The adolescent, like all of us, needs to be a part of a group where he can make a contribution, where he will be liked, and where he can receive some approbation. He also needs intimate friends with whom he can talk over personal matters, with whom he can walk to class, go to basketball games, and so on, and who will give him support in his ventures. Neither the school as an organization nor the teacher can supply these directly to those who seem unable to find them for themselves. But they can do two things: They can provide friendly adults who will give to each student kindly at-

tention, interest, and concern for his welfare. They can call upon all their ingenuity to provide social groupings and social occasions in which the less-liked adolescents may perhaps find a place.

3. The need for a feeling of worth. We have no right to force a youth to spend three years in junior high school and three years in senior high school if we are going to make life there devoid of success, devoid of accomplishment, and devoid of a feeling of satisfaction with the way he is spending his time. We have no right to do this to another person's life. But we do it, and we surely thereby hasten some young people into truancy and delinquency.

The customary high school pattern is academic and favors those of higher IQ's. High school teachers, having been brought up in such a system throughout their schooling, naturally fall back into it when they teach. As a result there are students who inevitably get the F's and D's, those who get the D's and C's, those who get the C's and B's, and those who get the B's and A's.

As far as the average students are concerned, in all probability many of them are not depressed or discouraged by their mediocre grades. One may suppose that they adjust and go their way without bitterness or great discouragement. But it is a waste that these students have so few opportunities to do what they can be proud of, to achieve what they feel a need for, to experience the joys of real creativeness and the pleasure of seeing real growth take place.

We do not doom students to mediocrity of intelligence or to mediocrity of talent. Their inheritance may be entirely responsible for that. But we do doom them to mediocrity of experience. Since we do this so often with little thought to the real needs and the real interests of these students, we are without excuse.

As for those students whose lot it is to get F's and D's, we are not only depriving them of happy experiences and feelings of worth through accomplishment, but we are also labeling them as worthless or nearly so in the hierarchy of our opinion. Under these circumstances we inevitably contribute to the rebellious feelings of some youth and to feelings of distaste for school.

4. The need for variety. The high school boy and girl have an abundance of energy, and at the same time they do not have deeply channelized interests. As a result, they are not able to endure unchanging routine, dullness, and the commonplace as well as the adult. School could be exciting and interesting; often it is dull and without appeal. Boredom in school might not be the only factor which leads a child to find excitement in harmful ways, but it helps.

Locate and Help Predelinquent Children

Kvaraceus suggests that the following conditions or signs are suggestive or indicative of a boy or girl who is particularly vulnerable to delinquency:[17]

"1. Feels dissatisfaction with school
  "*a*. Is unsuccessful in his academic work, and often in other school situations as well
  "*b*. Shows little academic aptitude
  "*c*. Has repeated several grades
  "*d*. Transfers frequently from school to school
  "*e*. Dislikes school intensely
  "*f*. Intends to leave school as soon as the law will allow
"2. Plays truant
"3. Belongs to no recognized or supervised recreational or character-building agency
"4. Has unsatisfactory home conditions
  "*a*. Comes from an atypical or broken home
  "*b*. Has a mother who is employed
  "*c*. Lives in a family in which conflicts abound
"5. Lives in a high-delinquency area
  "*a*. Lives in a poverty-stricken or marginal home
  "*b*. Lives in overcrowded conditions (more than 1.5 persons per room)
  "*c*. Has changed residence frequently (four or more times)
"6. Feels rejected in home, school, or neighborhood

"Not every child who shows one or more of these signs will become a delinquent. However, from the evidence at hand, it is safe to say that a major portion of those unfortunate children who will appear in the juvenile courts of tomorrow will be drawn from the reservoir of children who show several of these characteristics."

Obviously this means that the teacher must *know each student he teaches*. He should know what kind of home he comes from, what his reactions to his home are, how he spends his time outside of school, what satisfactions he is finding in school, and how well adjusted he seems to be.

What to do about those who need help is another matter—unfortunately often in no wise simple. Every teacher may, over a period of time, have

---

[17] William C. Kvaraceus, "The Role of the Administrator in Relation to Juvenile Delinquency," Chap. VI in Nelson B. Henry (ed.), *Juvenile Delinquency and the Schools*, 47th Yearbook, National Society for the Study of Education (Chicago: University of Chicago Press, 1948), Part I, pp. 136–137. Quoted by permission of the Society.

one or two or more students who are incorrigible, beyond his help and beyond assimilation into the class situation. It is highly probable that there is nothing that he can do for them. They need the counsel of someone who is trained to give it to them.

Even with less difficult cases the teacher must be careful, of course, for giving help in adjustment and attitudes can be a very delicate matter which even the most skillful person may possibly bungle. Generally speaking, the teacher will do the best for any student if he will try to do well by everyone in his classes. He may:

1. Talk to him privately about the nonintimate affairs of his life—recreation, reading interests, clubs, likes and dislikes, family organization, health habits. Questions can be kept free from any attitude of prying if the teacher asks them in the spirit of genuine interest in the young person's welfare.

2. Provide variety in the class's activities, with group work, individual work, movies, excursions, and the like.

3. Put the class on such a basis that every student has a chance to make friends through work associations.

4. Put the class on such a basis that every student has an opportunity to make real contributions and win the respect of others for some of his achievements.

The faculty can use its ingenuity in other ways to counteract delinquent tendencies. Thus in Central High School of Chattanooga, Tennessee, there is in operation Club X, membership in which was extended to 20 boys, actually the 20 boys most often referred to the principal for punishment, though this fact was kept a secret. The club's purpose is to give these boys a sense of responsibility, a consciousness of their own importance, and an opportunity for service. The result is that the boys in the club so enjoy their wholesome activities there that their conduct has improved greatly in other respects as well.[18]

WHAT CAN THE COMMUNITY DO?

Clifford Shaw, mentioned earlier, initiated the Chicago Area Projects. Under his plan a neighborhood or larger unit is organized to develop through its own resources a program which will promote the welfare of its children. The committee which plans and oversees the program is made up of people of the area; the leaders of the various activities are secured from the community as far as possible; all the facilities of the community—churches, schools, industries, recreation centers, clubs, and

[18] J. Pope Dyer, "An Experiment with 'Problem' Boys," *Clearing House*, 20:360–361 (1945).

so on—are coordinated and utilized. In other words, the betterment of the community comes from within it.

One such area project is that of the Russell Square community. Some indication of what has been accomplished there is given by the fact that the number of boys arrested in 1940 was only one-third of the average per year for the five-year period before the program was initiated in 1932.[19]

Another plan of community work is that of coordination through community councils whose purpose is to work for the prevention of delinquency. Such councils are found in cities, towns, and villages throughout the country and generally meet once a month, with committee meetings in between. Members are usually representatives from the schools, police, welfare department, library, churches, service clubs, parent-teacher organizations, and the like. Most of these councils feel that the most serious problem they have to meet is the lack of recreational facilities for youth.

Such coordinating councils have had many good results to report. They succeed in increasing the recreational facilities of the community; they educate their own members as to the importance of youth needs; they stimulate the better use of existing facilities in the community; they sometimes make special provision for adult education; they create new services for children. Thus:[20]

" . . . as a result of the work of the Berkeley coordinating council a public school behavior clinic was established which includes on its staff a psychiatrist, a pediatrician, a psychologist, and four visiting counselors. Richmond, Virginia, secured a juvenile crime prevention officer from the department of public safety to act as a liaison officer between the individual child and the court, the police department, the social agencies, and society at large. A number of councils have been instrumental in persuading police departments to appoint special officers to handle juvenile cases."

A comprehensive answer to the question "What can the community do?" can be found in a Children's Bureau publication for 1943. Four goals are given for community action. The first three are:

"I. *Strengthening of resources needed by all children.*

"II. *Protection of groups of children especially vulnerable to delinquency.*

"III. *Control of harmful influences in the community.*"

[19] Edward Haydon, "Community Organization and Crime Prevention," in Marjorie Bell (ed.), *Social Defenses against Crime*, 1942 Yearbook (New York: National Probation Association, 1942), p. 34.

[20] Kenneth S. Beam, "Delinquency Prevention through Coordination," *Journal of Educational Sociology*, 10:9–34 (1936).

Space forbids giving the details of any except the last goal:[21]

"IV. *Services for the delinquent child and the child with behavior problems.*

"A. Social Services.

"1. Social services adapted to the needs of any child who presents behavior problems in the home, school, or elsewhere, and made available to parents, teachers, police, court officials, and others who deal with the child.

"2. Full utilization of these social services by law-enforcement officials and by courts in order that children and young persons coming to their attention may be dealt with understandingly and sympathetically, and that their needs for special services may be met with a view to preparing them for healthy, wholesome, and productive lives rather than merely to meet an immediate emergency.

"3. Utilization by social agencies of all available services that are pertinent to the treatment of delinquency and behavior problems.

"B. The Police and the Juvenile Court.

"1. Law enforcement with provision for special handling of children's cases through a special unit in the police department (in larger communities), a staff of policewomen, or a selected officer.

"2. Court procedure for children's cases—based on the idea that children should be helped and protected rather than punished for specific acts—through either a juvenile court or specialized court procedure.

"C. Adequate Detention Care.

"1. Quarters entirely apart from those used for the detention of adults.

"2. Standards of care that assure understanding and protection of children while in detention.

"3. Limitation of detention to children for whom it is absolutely necessary.

"4. Authority for discharge of children from detention vested only in the juvenile court or the agency designed to provide social services for the juvenile court.

"D. Provision for Institutional and Foster-family Care.

"1. Assumption by the local public-welfare agency of responsibility for providing foster-home services in communities where no facilities exist or where existing facilities cannot meet the entire need.

"2. Payment of adequate boarding rates, essential to obtaining the kind of foster parents who can deal wisely with such children.

[21] "Controlling Juvenile Delinquency," U.S. Department of Labor, *Children's Bureau Publication*, 1943, p. 301.

"3. Pooling the efforts of child-placing agencies to stimulate applications from desirable foster parents.

"4. Consideration of the place and contribution of child-caring institutions in the total child-welfare program of the community, in the light of wartime needs.

"5. Standards of care of foster homes and institutions which are in conformity with the standards established by the State public-welfare agency.

"*E.* Child-guidance Services.

"1. Establishment in large communities of child-guidance services under public auspices to serve parents, the social agencies, the schools, and the juvenile court in handling of children showing personality difficulties.

"2. Provision for funds to obtain service on a fee basis from psychiatrists engaged in private practice or from private child-guidance clinics, with social services available for all children referred.

"3. Utilization of traveling clinics or special consultant services that may be provided by State agencies."

Passaic, New Jersey, has established the Passaic Children's Bureau to help children who need special treatment. Organized in 1937, the Bureau is now a part of the school system in charge of an assistant superintendent of schools. Any complaint about a child is referred to the Bureau, whether it be by a teacher in regard to troublesome behavior in the classroom or truancy, by some recreation agency, or by parents or police. The staff consists of the director, a psychologist, a psychiatric social worker, two attendance officers, and a unit of four police officers (including one policewoman) who are assigned by the chief of police to serve the Bureau.

When a case is reported to the Bureau, a thorough study is made of the boy or girl, conferences are held with those concerned, and finally, a program is set up whereby the parents, the school, and any other agencies involved cooperate to help the child become better adjusted.

The case of Michael will show how the Bureau operates:[22]

"Already well known to the police, and a persistent disturber of the classroom, Michael was brought to the attention of the Bureau almost as soon as the agency opened. Michael was referred after attempting to poison his father. With the background of vicious conduct which had preceded this episode, there is small doubt that, had it not been for the Bureau, he would have been almost summarily committed to a juvenile institution. The staff of the newly created Bureau, however, decided that perhaps the clumsy and ineffectual effort to poison his father presented

[22] William C. Kvaraceus, *Juvenile Delinquency and the School* (Yonkers, N. Y.: World Book Company, 1945), pp. 46–47.

a clue to the protracted maladjustment of the boy. It is worth noting that the first person to make this suggestion was the police lieutenant in conference with the representative of the psychiatric clinic whose help was invoked in this case.

"Bit by bit, the home life of Michael's family was unfolded. A father, born in eastern Europe, himself diagnosed as psychopathic after a series of arrests for wife-beating; a none too bright mother, whose sole aim in life was to placate her husband. In this situation, the care of the child fluctuated from excesses of barbaric severity to indifference which even allowed absences of several days to go unnoticed. The 'poisoning' episode followed a particularly brutal phase of family discord.

"Enlisting the help of a private child-placement agency, the Bureau arranged for Michael to live on a farm outside the city. Freed from the harassment of school and from the fear of his father, his disposition improved and with his disposition, his conduct. Through a long adjustment period, close contact was maintained with Michael and the interview reports indicate how far-reaching were the questions which were troubling him and how helpful the Bureau worker was in resolving them. Throughout this case, the Bureau kept Michael in close touch with the psychiatric clinic and acted on its advice. Several years after the Bureau closed its files on Michael, his father was committed to a mental hospital with an alcoholic psychosis. Michael himself has been well adjusted and represents a definite Bureau success."

Some evidence of the Bureau's worth is shown by the fact that the crime rate (number of offenses known to the police per 100,000 population) went down from 1,445.9 in 1937 to 1,080.3 in 1941 in Passaic, whereas in the state of New Jersey it went up from 1,053.8 in 1937 to 1,098.7 in 1941, and in the United States as a whole it went up from 1,438.1 in 1937 to 1,572.3 in 1941.[23]

Recently the state of New Jersey has established the New Jersey State Diagnostic Center in Menlo Park. Young people are sent here for diagnosis and may remain for as long as ninety days. Eventually it will be open for diagnosis to all ages.

In attendance are 4 psychiatrists, 5 psychologists, 3 psychiatric social workers, 4 nurses, 1 X-ray technician, and 25 aides.[24]

It should not be forgotten that sincere individual efforts are also worth while. Every town probably has one or many examples of this to report. Here is one example:[25]

[23] *Ibid.*, p. 41.
[24] Marion Robinson, "Mental Health for Child and Delinquent," *Survey*, 86:293–297 (1950).
[25] Terre Haute (Ind.) *Tribune-Star*, June 25, 1949.

"Frat Men Make Bad Boys Good

"EASTON, PA. (U.P.). It took only three months for 12 members of Lafayette College's Zeta Psi fraternity to transform a dozen street urchins with police records into model citizens.

"Acting with the co-operation of probation officers, each of the fraternity men adopted one of the youngsters, all of whom had been charged with offenses ranging from thefts of autos to shoplifting. The big brothers took the boys on hikes, boxed and played games with them, and heaped encouragement on their young charges for their successes.

"In almost no time, the personal touch technique paid off and the once bad boys were attending school regularly and keeping out of juvenile court.

"Now, however, the eight- to 14-year-old lads are going to lose their college friends temporarily. The fraternity men . . . are leaving for three-months summer vacations.

"Probation officers are seeking other big brothers to carry on the good work during the summer."

WHAT CAN A STATE DO?

The Michigan Child Guidance Institute[26] was a good example of how the state can help in the prevention of delinquency. This Institute was under the Board of Regents of the University and was managed by an executive committee and the director with a staff consisting of a full-time psychiatrist, a psychiatric case worker, a field unit consisting of one psychologist and two psychiatric case workers, a field sociologist to assist in community coordination, a full-time research worker, and a clerical staff.

Any responsible person in the state could refer a maladjusted child under twenty-one to the Institute. To this person would be sent an application blank, a physician's examination blank, a social-history blank, and a blank for the legally required consent of the parent or guardian to permit the child's examination. When these blanks were returned, properly filled out, a date would be fixed for the child to be sent to Ann Arbor, his stay there to be for from three to thirty days, depending on the needs of the case. There he would be given medical, social, psychological, and psychiatric examinations, whereupon the staff would discuss the case and draft recommendations, which would be sent back to the referring individual or agency.

Any county which agreed to match the state's expenditure in the

[26] Carr, *op. cit.*, pp. 382–403.

county and which would organize to cooperate might have a field unit come there to study the cases of children selected as needing help.

Innovation in the child-welfare field often meets resistance. The Institute went out of existence June 30, 1943.

THE JUVENILE COURT

There is no uniform system through the country for court hearings in the case of the juvenile delinquent. Some juvenile courts are a part of the criminal court, with the same judge and similar procedures, but separate hearings. Some are linked with the family courts. Some are set up specifically as children's courts.

Tappan[27] believes that wherever it can be avoided the child should not be subjected to court procedures, but that if he is brought to court, it should be a court specially set up for children and young people with specially trained and well-trained personnel, and with the power and procedures of the court limited and clearly defined.

INSTITUTIONS FOR THE DELINQUENT

As Tappan says, the juvenile court has three questions to consider after adjudicating a child:[28]

"1. Should he be left in his own home with suspended sentence but no treatment, or under the guidance of probation, and/or under some program of assistance from some community agency?

"2. Should he be placed in a foster home under the guidance of a probation officer or some other agency?

"3. Should he be committed to an institution?"

Table 45 shows the disposition generally made.

It is generally considered that if a child is able to make his readjustment in a home situation, he is better off there than he would be in an institution. But with many children, either because their own home or a foster home cannot give them the proper care or because outside of an institution they actually endanger society, it is necessary to institutionalize them. For this, there are many training schools or reformatories throughout the country. Some are so conducted that the only end they serve is to keep the child incarcerated. Others have programs which really help the child become better adjusted and more social.

[27] Tappan, *op. cit.*, Chap. 9.
[28] *Ibid.*, p. 416.

TABLE 45. JUVENILE-DELINQUENCY CASES, 1945: DISPOSITIONS OF BOYS' AND GIRLS'
CASES, DISPOSED OF BY 374 COURTS

Disposition of case	Number			Per cent		
	Total	Boys	Girls	Total	Boys	Girls
Total cases.....................	122,851	101,240	21,611			
Disposition reported..............	114,887	95,027	19,860	100	100	100
Case dismissed, adjusted, or held open without further action....	49,040	42,184	6,856	43	45	35
Child supervised by probation officer.....................	34,981	28,829	6,152	30	30	31
Child committed or referred to an institution..................	10,101	7,748	2,353	9	8	12
State institution for delinquent children................	5,789	4,640	1,149	5	5	6
Other institution for delinquent children...........	3,157	2,346	811	3	2	4
Penal institution	222	206	16	*	*	*
Other institution	933	556	377	1	1	2
Child committed or referred to an agency or individual..........	5,400	3,546	1,854	5	4	9
Public department..........	1,751	1,183	568	2	1	3
Other agency or individual...	3,649	2,363	1,286	3	3	6
Other disposition of case	15,365	12,720	2,645	13	13	13
Disposition not reported	7,964	6,213	1,751			

* Less than 0.5 per cent.

The unfavorable side of the picture is presented in this description:[29]

"As has been shown, there are two kinds of training in a penal reformatory, namely, that intended by the institution's officials and that gained from inmates in the yard and cell block. Even though education takes hold, to some extent, so that the mind is improved and the hands given skill, it is nevertheless imparted in an atmosphere heavily charged with resentment and unhappiness and accompanied by deteriorating effects on character. The work-habits established at a reformatory are, in the mind of the youth, habits associated with a temporary, abnormal and despised existence. Life, work and play, he hopes, will be vastly different when he is released; he will certainly wish to make his life of freedom differ as much as possible from his life of punishment. Since it is extremely

[29] Leonard V. Harrison and Pryor McNeill Grant, *Youth in the Toils* (New York: The Macmillan Company, 1938), pp. 118–121.

difficult for the state to succeed in education which is viewed as one of the forms of punishment, it is easy for the released prisoner to turn his back upon the whole training experience.

"In addition to institutional work-habits there are institutional companionships. These are not of a normal variety in that they are entirely limited to persons goaded into abnormal attitudes. The effects of the associations, unlike the work-habits, are virtually inescapable and they are lasting. The worst boys in the reformatory are the leaven in the whole loaf, not the welfare and educational activities.

"The dual aim of punishment and rehabilitation through education and training in a reformatory is bound to yield meager returns in the improvement of human beings who are selected on the basis of their marked deficiencies and poor beginnings in life.

"Is there any ground for a belief that wholesale reformation of convicted offenders can be effected with large groups? We think that there is not. The belief that feelings of penitence will arise under punishment dies hard but it must be uprooted if we are to deal realistically with the problem of stimulating aspirations of right living among young offenders. The reformatory is a high type of prison well adapted to the purposes of incapacitating the most incorrigible offenders who cannot be handled safely in any other way. But to regard it as a training school suited to the improvement of congregate masses of five hundred to two thousand young persons, or old, is to deceive ourselves with wishful thinking. Just as a prison for adults is in the nature of a university of crime, so is a large correctional training school all too often a preparatory school leading to the university."

If an institution is really to serve in helping a child develop a better personal and social adjustment, it must have facilities for understanding what the child is like in intelligence, attitudes, and adjustment; it must have a staff which is devoted to the task of rehabilitating the youth in its care, which is sympathetic and kindly, and which understands the psychology of childhood and youth and of the delinquent; it must provide suitable living conditions, suitable employment, education, and recreation; it must encourage self-discipline and democratic procedures of group government; and it must have some arrangement to give continuing help to the child after he is released.

For illustration, let us describe two private schools, not "reformatories" but showing what can be done with youth who have problems in their adjustment to society. They are the Children's Village at Dobbs Ferry, New York, and the George "Junior Republic," at Freeville, New York.

The Children's Village is an accredited, nonsectarian school incorporated under the laws of the State of New York and in operation twelve months a year. The school is for boys only and serves 400 students whose ages range from ten to sixteen years.

As to the type of boy accepted:[30]

"He may be one who has lost his parents and does not respond to life in a foster family, but who requires training in a group environment.

"He may be a lad who was prevented from receiving proper early training because of the illness of his parents or because of a broken home.

"He may be a boy who is unhappy or rebellious because he cannot adjust to the ordinary school program or because he does not get along well with his brother, sister, or playmates.

"Other boys come from families who feel that their youngster is beyond control or in danger of becoming delinquent.

"Then there are those who have already offended the community and have been brought before the Children's Court for special planning."

The Village is set up as a real community. The boys live in 20 cottage homes, each in charge of a married couple who act as the cottage parents. Each boy shares in the home duties, participates in the government of the community, earns money for the time he puts in on his regular program in school, shop, and service assignments, and has a bank account through which his expenses are paid. The Village has a psychiatrist, psychologist, physician, dental hygienist, registered nurse, and nine social workers who serve as the liaison between the school, the child and his parents, and the judge or referring agency. In the nearly one hundred years of its existence the Children's Village has helped over 50,000 troubled young people find themselves and prepare for happy and useful adult lives.

The George Junior Republic, founded by William R. George, is, as the name suggests, a self-governing community whose citizens are 125 boys and girls between the ages of thirteen and nineteen on admission. It is situated in rural New York State upon 550 acres of land. In literature sent out by the school we read:[31]

"The Republic program adequately meets the needs of the normal child, and at the same time is particularly successful with children showing behavior difficulties, but not presenting problems serious enough to warrant custodial care. We do not have a resident psychiatrist and for that reason do not accept children in need of intensive psychiatric treatment.

"The Republic does accept boys and girls referred from juvenile courts, providing it is felt that their problems are not too deep-seated and that

[30] Quoted from pamphlet sent out by the Children's Village, p. 2.
[31] 1952 Catalogue of the George Junior Republic, Freeville, N.Y.

they have the desire and capacity to make a good adjustment. A number of youngsters come to the Republic on the referral of social agencies. Most children, however, are referred directly by families who feel that the Republic offers them better opportunities for development . . .

"Individual responsibility for community life is learned by junior citizens through the operation of their own government. Each young person learns that the only way of securing a better community is to exercise his rights and responsibilities as a citizen. Being dealt with by a government which he himself has helped to elect, has a sobering effect on the irresponsible boy or girl who hitherto has been dealt with by adults not of his own choosing, according to a system which he has had no part in creating. Acceleration in growth and maturity and the development of social understanding are shown by young people when given the right of self-determination in a school setting. It goes without saying that they will be more intelligent and responsible citizens of the community into which they graduate than those who, never having handled the problems nor experienced the failures and achievements of an active civic life, suddenly acquire voting privileges with a no more significant reason than the arrival of their 21st birthday. . . .

"At the George Junior Republic the concept of 'social illness' is one around which an important part of the program is developed. The physically ill person is seen by a medical doctor to whose care he entrusts himself. He temporarily forfeits his right to decide what he shall do and allows the doctor to prescribe the best treatment for him. Similarly, the socially ill citizen of the Republic is seen by his 'Social Doctor,' a trained social caseworker who is alert to symptoms of social illness and devotes his skills to its cure. Having been diagnosed socially ill, the citizen renounces his right to choose what course he shall pursue with relation to society, and undergoes his Social Doctor's prescribed treatment, which may vary greatly from one patient to another. For instance, the patient whose illness shows up in excessive shyness may be required to attend certain recreational functions, while another may need to spend a period of time in the special cottage known as Treatment Center.

"Residents of this cottage are isolated from the rest of the community; they eat, sleep, work, study and play separately from the other citizens, and are closely supervised and restricted. Placement in Treatment Center is not considered as punishment, but as the provision of conditions under which the patient may achieve the most rapid and permanent recovery. Not confronted continually with the necessity of making decisions for himself which he is not yet prepared to make wisely, the citizen finds a certain relief and security in the knowledge that the right decisions will be made for him. In this protected environment he can cultivate good habits and develop strengths which give him a status and a sense of achievement within the small group. This in turn equips him with a degree of confidence and good judgment which renders him more able to handle his responsibilities in the larger community."

In other words, youth at the Junior Republic grow because they have a real community, genuine self-government, and the guidance of sympathetic and specially trained adults.

PENALTIES FOR PARENTS

Many people, realizing how frequently delinquency stems from home conditions, advocate punishing the parents, for they say that since the parents are often to blame for the child's maladjustment, they should bear the penalty for it.

In answer to this, Whitman writes:[32]

"The most serious fallacy found in the thinking of the zealous critics [of parents] lies in the assumption that parents are aware of their own shortcomings and deliberately plan to misguide and mistreat children. Common sense tells us that this is a false assumption. From the cases seen in child-guidance clinics, it has been observed that the type of parental guidance contributing to a child's poor adjustment is largely unintentional and unwitting."

Judge Paul W. Alexander of Toledo's juvenile court has been punishing parents of juvenile delinquents for the last ten years. He concludes:[33]

"In fine, we might say our study seems to show that to punish parents who contribute to the delinquency or neglect of their children accomplishes very few, if any, of the things claimed for it except revenge; that in some cases where the parent is refractory and resists the casework approach, a certain amount of actual punishment may bring about cooperation; that in selected cases, where other methods have failed, prosecution and the threat of punishment, without actual punishment, are rather effective. . . . But punishing parents is no panacea."

Reminiscences

Look at the many subdivisions in the definition of the words "delinquent child." Did you ever engage in any such behavior? When? Why? For how long?

[32] Samuel Whitman, "Stop Sniping at Parents," *Child*, May, 1947 (reprint).
[33] Judge Paul W. Alexander, "What's This about Punishing Parents?" *Federal Probation*, March, 1948 (reprint).

Outside Speakers

In any community there will be, doubtless, social workers who can tell the class of particular cases of adolescents they have worked with.

General Discussion

1. Consider the subdivisions in the definition of the words "delinquent child." Rate these as to seriousness for society and seriousness for the child, from the most serious to the least.

2. Why do the most common offenses for girls differ so much from the most common for boys?

3. Consider how many children were detained in jail pending hearing. To bring out the wrong that is done through this, name some of the mild offenses for which a child might be thus held in jail.

4. Consider the description of the juvenile delinquent. To the extent that time allows, show how each characteristic mentioned might help lead to delinquent behavior.

5. Describe a delinquency neighborhood in your own home town.

6. Describe preventive recreation in more detail than the text gives.

7. How would you organize your own community to prevent delinquency?

8. What state services would you offer to prevent delinquency?

9. Consider the listing of services for the delinquent child and the child with behavior problems. Which of these does your community have?

10. If you had the opportunity to set up a correctional school for juvenile delinquents, what would you have it like? Give full details.

Movies

Children in Trouble, New York State Department of Commerce, 10 min., b. & w., 1947.

Children of the City, British Information Service, 30 min., b. & w., 1945.

Children's Village, RKO, 19 min., b. & w., 1948.

Who's Delinquent? RKO, 16 min., b. & w., 1949.

Youth in Crisis, March of Time, 17 min., b. & w., 1943.

Further Reading

BANAY, RALPH S., *Youth in Despair* (New York: Coward-McCann, Inc., 1948).

BARRON, MILTON L., "Juvenile Delinquency and American Values," *American Sociological Review*, 16:214–216 (1951).

BELL, MARJORIE (ed.), *Current Approaches to Delinquency*, 1949 Yearbook (New York: National Probation and Parole Association, 1950).

BLADES, LESLIE B., "Why Institutions Fail," *Survey*, 77:291–292 (1941).

CARR, LOWELL JUILLIARD, *Delinquency Control* (New York: Harper & Brothers, 1950).

DEUTSCH, ALBERT, *Our Rejected Children* (Boston: Little, Brown & Company, 1950).

ECKENRODE, C. J., "Their Achievement Is Delinquency," *Journal of Educational Research*, 43:554–560 (1950).

ELLINGSTON, JOHN R., *Protecting Our Children from Criminal Careers* (New York: Prentice-Hall, Inc., 1948).

FREEMAN, DOROTHY, "The California Youth Authority," *Social Service Review*, 22:211–233 (1948).

GLEASON, GEORGE A., "It's Up to the Family," *International Journal of Religious Education*, 20:18–19 (1944).

GLUECK, SHELDON, and ELEANOR GLUECK, *Unraveling Juvenile Delinquency* (New York: Commonwealth Fund, Division of Publication, 1950).

HEALY, WILLIAM, and B. S. ALPER, *Criminal Youth and the Borstal System* (New York: Commonwealth Fund, Division of Publication, 1941).

HENRY, NELSON B. (ed.), 47th Yearbook, National Society for the Study of Education (Chicago: University of Chicago Press, 1948), Part I, *Juvenile Delinquency and the Schools.*

HOOVER, J. EDGAR, "Today's Irresponsible Parents," *Nation's Schools*, 37:42 (1946).

KVARACEUS, WILLIAM C., *Juvenile Delinquency and the School* (Yonkers, N.Y.: World Book Company, 1945).

LEONARD, CHARLES W., "Relationship of the Correctional Institution to Community Agencies from the Viewpoint of the Institution," *Journal of Correctional Education*, 2:121–127 (1950).

MACKAY, JAMES L., "Juvenile Welfare in Relation to Home and School," *Journal of Educational Sociology*, 19:111–119 (1945).

MERRILL, MAUD A., *Problems of Child Delinquency* (Boston: Houghton Mifflin Company, 1947).

MOORE, A. E., "Instruction in Family Living Will Help Prevent Juvenile Delinquency," *Nation's Schools*, 38:41–42 (1946).

PITKANEN, A. M., "Salvaging the Juvenile Delinquent," *Nation's Schools*, 35:47–48 (1945).

REDMONT, ROBERT S., "The Functions of a Juvenile Detention Home," *Social Casework*, 31:205–208 (1950).

REISS, ALBERT J., "Delinquency as the Failure of Personal and Social Controls," *American Sociological Review*, 16:214–216 (1951).

ROBINSON, REGINALD, "Beneath the Surface," *Survey*, 83:41–52 (1947).

TAPPAN, PAUL W., *Delinquent Girls in Court* (New York: Columbia University Press, 1947).

TAPPAN, PAUL W., *Juvenile Delinquency* (New York: McGraw-Hill Book Company, Inc., 1949).

VALENTINE, P. F., "They Blame the Home for Delinquency," *Educational Forum*, 11:285–287 (1947).

WATTENBERG, WILLIAM W., "Family Recreation and Delinquency," *Focus*, 29:6–9 (1950).

Part III

MAJOR INFLUENCES ON THE ADOLESCENT

Chapter 12. THE ADOLESCENT
AND HIS HOME

The adolescent is so much a product of his home that the teacher cannot be said to understand boys and girls unless he has a general understanding of how the home influences development and behavior; and he cannot understand a particular youth unless he knows something of the home from which that young person comes. What is more, if the teacher is concerned with helping the adolescent, he must also then give thought to the possibility of assisting the youth in solving his home difficulties.

There are three questions, therefore, that we must consider:

How has the home contributed to what the boy or girl is today?
How is he getting along at home right now?
How can the school assist the youth who is having difficulties in regard to his home?

HOW DOES THE HOME AFFECT DEVELOPMENT?

Relationships with Parents

The strongest factor in molding a child's personality is his relationship with his parents. If his parents love him with a generous, even-flowing, nonpossessive affection and if they treat him as a person who, like themselves, has both rights and responsibilities in the family group, then his chances of developing normally and well are good. But if they diverge from this desired pattern, the child's development may be distorted.

Parent-Child Relationships in General. How the parental relationship affects the child is shown in the results of Roberts and Fleming's intensive study of 100 college women, who were divided into two classifications, those who came from happy childhood homes and those who came from unhappy childhood homes—the happiness or unhappiness being explained largely in terms of good or bad relationships with parents. They found the following differences:[1]

[1] Katherine Elliott Roberts and Virginia VanDyne Fleming, "Persistence and Change in Personality Patterns," *Monographs of the Society for Research in Child Development,* 8 (No. 3):45–51 (1943).

The happy childhood group: Better adjusted socially, more understanding attitude toward parents, fewer religious conflicts, more church participation, more insight in regard to others, happier, less feeling of inferiority, better coordinated physically.

The unhappy childhood group: Accept criticism and teasing better, feel the need for more money regardless of the actual size of the income.

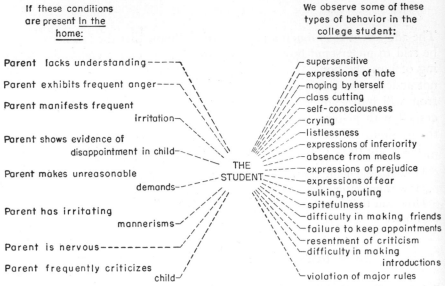

If these conditions are present in the home:

We observe some of these types of behavior in the college student:

Parent lacks understanding
Parent exhibits frequent anger
Parent manifests frequent irritation
Parent shows evidence of disappointment in child
Parent makes unreasonable demands
Parent has irritating mannerisms
Parent is nervous
Parent frequently criticizes child

THE STUDENT

supersensitive
expressions of hate
moping by herself
class cutting
self-consciousness
crying
listlessness
expressions of inferiority
absence from meals
expressions of prejudice
expressions of fear
sulking, pouting
spitefulness
difficulty in making friends
failure to keep appointments
resentment of criticism
difficulty in making introductions
violation of major rules

FIG. 32. Some relationships between home adjustment and the behavior of junior college students. (From M. D. Woolf, "A Study of Some Relationships between Home Adjustment and the Behavior of Junior College Students," *Journal of Social Psychology*, 17:285 (1943).

In another investigation we see again that unfavorable relationships with the parents seem to cause maladjustments in the child. Figure 32 gives the result of Woolf's study in which he compared 106 girls with excellent home adjustment with 105 girls with unsatisfactory home adjustment.

Specific examples can easily be found of adolescents whose development has been bad because of unhealthy family relationships.

The Overlyprotective Home. Ralph was the only child in the family. His father and mother both worked, the mother having a position just five blocks from school and one which was purposely arranged to allow her time to be with her son at noon and also allow her to be ready to go home with him when school was over. Consequently she had lunch with him alone in one of the classrooms every day and took him for a walk afterward, if the weather was favorable. When the school day ended, she called for him and they went home together.

Since Ralph had an exceptionally good mind, he learned to read at an early age and he spent his time after school hours preparing his school-work and reading books, many of which were far above the level of books chosen by his classmates. In recitations, while he was timid and retiring, he would at the same time astound both teacher and classmates with the insight he showed in regard to his assignments and also with the breadth and depth of information he had gained from reading.

Ralph had no close friends among his classmates. The pupils who associated with him through elementary and high school regarded him as a "brain" and held no strong feeling either for or against him. In fact they didn't know him.

Ralph was kept in an extremely sheltered atmosphere not only for the eight years he was in the elementary school but also until he was ready for his junior year in high school. Then his mother was transferred to another position, which permitted Ralph to be free from her domination at least during the school day.

In many respects Ralph's life was better than most boys and girls have the privilege of experiencing, for his home was comfortable, his parents harmonious in their own relationship and affectionate toward him. But some influences, as has been suggested, were very bad; for during those years of childhood while Ralph was growing physically and mentally his parents made his decisions for him, and as time went on he became more dependent upon them rather than less, as would be desirable. Then, too, he had no opportunity to develop friendships with boys and girls of his own age, for he was not encouraged by the parents to become a part of the play groups in his neighborhood or to join in those activities in school which are of a socializing nature.

Long before Ralph reached his senior year in high school, he had begun to realize that he was different from the rest of the students, but it was in his senior year that he himself felt that difference the most keenly. In spite of his efforts to be friendly and a good sport, he could not succeed in gaining acceptance in the groups he envied, for he had never learned how to be easy with those of his own age or interesting to them. At home his parents' solicitude galled him, and yet at the same time it gave him the attention and companionship that he failed to get at school.

This case history need not be continued further. Ralph has made some progress since leaving home for college, but he is still stiff and constrained in social groups and without any close circle of friends. Unfortunately, too, he is unsure of himself in his choices and decisions and too often relies on following the path that he feels his parents would approve of.

What help could Ralph have received from his teachers in elementary school and in high school? They certainly noted what was wrong. In fact they often talked about how much they pitied Ralph because his mother was unwilling to allow him to make his own decisions. They saw how his opportunities for socialization were limited. Could some teachers along the way have called Mrs. D.'s attention to what her well-meant interest in her son was doing to him? Doubtless something could have been done, though nothing was, probably because Ralph's mother was so sure of herself and so resentful of even the mildest suggestion that she might be pursuing the wrong course. Could Ralph's teachers in high school have found ways of drawing him into some of the extracurricular activities? With his deep interest in science, could he not have been led to take some responsibilities of leadership in the science club? Since Ralph excelled in all types of scholastic work and never "caused any trouble," could it be that his teachers overlooked the great need for development of the social side of his nature? Whatever the explanation, the school did fail to do what it might have done in directing Ralph's social development and giving him more independence.

The Divided Home. Herbert came from a home in which the ordinary comforts needed by a child were present, for he had a good, well-furnished house in which to live and a sufficient amount of wholesome food to eat. But in another respect the home was not good for him. He was the youngest in a family of three children, Mary, the first-born, being eight years his elder and Peggy, the second sister, six years his elder. Attention was showered upon Herbert from infancy by his mother and sisters. Overprotection, however, was only one cause of the difficulties Herbert encountered in growing up.

Herbert's father had real affection for his son, but since he didn't agree with the mother's and daughters' methods of directing his development, there were often quarrels about the boy with Herbert "listening in." In addition, Herbert witnessed unpleasant battles that came about because of parental differences in political and religious views. For the mother had left the church with which she had been affiliated since childhood and become a convert to another faith, the elder daughter following her mother's action and likewise joining this church. The father and younger daughter remained as followers of the church to which the family originally belonged. This alignment of two members of the family against the other two was the source of much conflict when Herbert was about six years old, and he was affected emotionally by the clashes between the older members of his family.

The bickerings and arguments he found himself in the midst of did not provide the atmosphere of mutual love, altruism, and self-sacrifice necessary to develop in Herbert a sense of emotional security. By the time he entered the first grade of elementary school, the teachers saw a boy who was very nervous and restless, unable to keep his attention on any job which required many minutes of sustained interest although his entrance tests showed him to have an intelligence quotient of 135.

What is more, Herbert didn't know how to make friends among his equals. He was inclined to pinch, push, or otherwise inflict minor torture on children if they came within his reach both in the classroom and on the playground outside the school.

The child did not achieve a satisfactory degree of success at school. Even this was a cause for conflict. The mother, and the daughter holding her views, blamed the school for not being able to direct Herbert's development in a satisfactory manner. The father and other daughter insisted that the mother and older sister had protected Herbert too much and that his failure to succeed in school was all their fault.

The principal and the teachers understood very clearly what the home life was like, and conference after conference was held with both the mother and the father on numerous occasions during the years Herbert was in the elementary school. The parents admitted that what was taking place in the home might not be conducive to the development of emotional stability, but they never fully acknowledged their responsibility for being the source of Herbert's trouble. The teachers were sympathetic with Herbert; they tried to help him and actually did much with him to counteract some of the influence in the home.

Age twelve found Herbert ready for the seventh grade, but with only a poor record of past achievement. Instead of having high marks he had barely passed in most of the six grades he had gone through. The mother then decided to send him to a private school which had a good reputation for dealing with such cases. At the close of one year the private school refused Herbert's continuance, and back he came to the school he had previously attended.

Herbert's record in junior and senior high school was much the same as it had been for the elementary grades, except that he occasionally failed a subject and had to repeat it. Home conditions remained about the same, and Herbert continued to be a restless, unstable, and friendless boy at school.

After graduation from high school Herbert entered college. He was dropped at the end of his first year because of low scholarship. After a period of one year he has been readmitted to college. Many of the habits of childhood remain with him, but now he is taking hold of himself and trying to improve.

At the present time, he appears to be on his way to becoming a productive citizen. Fortunately he faces the situation he is in very realistically and understands the causes for the trouble he had while growing up. He finds it very difficult to apply himself to study, for the years in elementary and high school were not what they should have been. But Herbert gives his teachers much credit for holding on to him through those trying times. If it had not been for their thorough understanding of his home situation and their patient and sympathetic attitude Herbert might have been another among those who dropped out of school at sixteen and into an unwholesome existence.

Parental Repression. Jenkins, describing types of children encountered in psychiatry, gives us the following three pictures:[2]

"The overinhibited personality structure is extremely familiar to mental hygienists. Typically it develops in an atmosphere of parental repression. The parents are likely to be cold and unsocial, the mother compensating for some rejection by overproduction and over-restriction, the father perfectionistic and intolerant. Both parents are inconsistent in methods of discipline. Both parents are restrained, socially disciplined persons. They are typically of a social stratum and a level of education above the clinic average. The mother is likely to be ill frequently from one affliction or another. The child himself is likely to have experienced an unusual amount of illness which contributes to his insecurity and dependence. He is likely to be jealous of his siblings in their relation to the parents, feeling his own relation less secure.

"In order to understand such a personality structure we need only to consider the dynamics of personality development. The child obtains his sense of security from his parents. A young child has no other source of security. He is utterly dependent upon the parents, and there is no frequent childhood fear which produces such chronic anxiety as the fear of loss of the parents, or the fear of loss of the parents' love. Just as the parent is the fundamental source of security to the young child, the fear of loss of the parent is the fundamental source of insecurity and of anxiety. This fact is so simple and obvious it is often overlooked.

"Here we are dealing with the unsociable, cold, distant parent, lacking

[2] Richard L. Jenkins, "A Psychiatric View of Personality Structure in Children," in *Delinquency and the Community in Wartime* (National Probation Association, Yearbook, 1943), pp. 202–208.

in warmth, perhaps the rejecting but overprotecting mother, and perhaps the perfectionistic, hyper-critical father. The child lacks the assurance of acceptance and affection which comes through close emotional contact with the parents. These are parents whose approval (and presumably whose love) can be won only by very good, very conforming, very inhibited behavior. Any violation of parental taboo is met by disapproval which this insecure child feels or fears means rejection. There is deeply implanted as the result of this experience the pervading fear that if he is not a good child his parents will not love him. As a result any aggressive act by the child throws him into a panic of anxiety. He can feel secure only by being excessively good, by being excessively inhibited. To protect himself he screws down the safety valve on his central core of primitive impulses, and the pressure there mounts to produce an acute situation of internal conflict which may be relieved by neurotic disorders.

Unloving, Ill-natured Parents. "This child's problem centers around his uninhibited hostile treatments of others. He is cruel, defiant, prone deliberately to destroy the property of others as well as violently to attack their persons. He shows little feeling of guilt or remorse. He is seldom able to get along with other children, but is always quarreling, fighting or engaging in mischievous tricks to annoy them. He is inclined to bully and boss them and is boastful, selfish and jealous. He is rude or defiant toward persons in authority, openly antagonistic toward his teachers, and has outbursts of temper when crossed. He will deceive others and refuses to accept the blame for his own misbehavior. Because of his personality makeup he has few close friends if any, and his classmates have little to do with him.

"Even if others attempt to become friendly with him, this boy does not respond with friendship for he is suspicious of other people and reacts negatively to questions. He is non-committal and evasive when questioned and usually appears sullen. He seeks vengeance against those he dislikes. In our small series we find even arson and murder. His frequent petty thieving at home or at school sometimes results from the same vengeful attitude. His language is profane and obscene. He displays an unusually overt interest in sex, and is known to indulge in masturbation."

This is a child, he goes on to say, whose parents' relationship is apt to be fraught with bitterness and disharmony, whose parents are probably violent-tempered and abusive toward each other, whose parents are indifferent toward the child or even openly hostile and rejecting.

"The product of this background is a child of bottomless hostilities and endless bitterness who feels cheated in life, who views himself as a victim although he is constantly the aggressor, who is grossly defective in his social inhibitions, and who is grossly lacking in guilt sense over his misconduct. . . . " The reasons are that the child receives no love from his parents, he has no affectional tie to an adult through which he could incorporate standards of behavior, and he actually sees before him in his home examples of selfish and inconsiderate behavior.

Inadequate Supervision and Surroundings. "This is the pseudosocial boy —the loyal gang member, the good comrade of a delinquent sub-culture. Within his own group he is commonly a socialized and adjusted individual. It is only in relation to the larger group that we can consider him maladjusted and antisocial.

"While his behavior bears certain resemblances to that of the unsocialized, aggressive boy, there are important differences. These differences are related to the fact that he is socialized in his own group and loyal to his comrades. This boy also is deceptive and defiant toward authority. When possible he avoids self-incrimination by not accepting the blame for his own acts and he feels little guilt over his delinquent depredations. On the other hand, should he violate the code of his group, as by informing on his companions when caught, he would feel deeply guilty. Even more than the unsocialized, aggressive boy, he engages in petty stealing at home or school, but this behavior would appear to be motivated more by acquisitiveness than by a desire for revenge. He is also extremely antagonistic toward school attendance, but expresses this antagonism chiefly in truancy. This antagonism toward school is not due to a lack of friends there, for compared with the average child seen at the clinic, this boy is popular.

" . . . Typically he comes from an impoverished overcrowded home in a downtown deteriorated delinquency area. But this child was not rejected from birth. His mother, although inadequate to control him as he grew older, never lacked maternal feeling. As a result he achieved a basic socialization. But his father was more inadequate than his mother and there was a failure particularly of paternal function—the guidance, training and control of the older child. Hence he drifted into contact with the delinquent associates of his neighborhood and achieved his adolescent socialization within a delinquent group. As a result of his behavior and parental inadequacies, an acute conflict with the parents finally developed."

Indulgent Parents. Fitz-Simons describes the behavior that indicates overacceptance on the part of a parent as being:[3]

[3] M. J. Fitz-Simons, "Some Parent-Child Relationships as Shown in Clinical Case Studies," quoted by Percival M. Symonds in *The Psychology of Parent-Child Relationships* (New York: Appleton-Century-Crofts, Inc., 1939), p. 25.

Parent indulges child—cannot refuse requests.
Parent cares for child's physical needs to an unusual degree.
Parent sleeps in same bed with child.
Parent spends all possible time with child.
Parent pushes child.
Parent gives money, toys, special privileges.
Parent does not want child to leave for recreation.
Parent spends time with child—playing with or amusing child.
Parent gives in to child.
Parent excuses child—defends him.
Parent is proud of child—praises him.
Parent sleeps in same room.
Parent sees few if any faults.
Parent protects child from unhappiness.
Parent protects child from what he considers harmful.
Parent makes an effort to improve child's condition—by carrying out recommendations, etc.

Symonds says that if either or both parents overprotect a child, that child is likely to be characterized as:[4]

Overdependent.
Infantile.
Possessing feelings of inferiority.
Withdrawing.
Having poor social adjustment.
Having poor work habits.

Rejectant Parents. Rejection of a child by one or both parents is one of the most harmful home experiences the child can know. According to Fitz-Simons, the parental behavior that indicates rejection is:[5]

Parent sees mostly shortcomings.
Parent uses severe punishments.
Parent deserts child.
Parent evicts child.
Parent turns child over to an authority.
Parent puts child in institution, reform school, boarding school, convent (for discipline or to avoid trouble).
Parent does not provide financial support.
Parent criticizes child.
Parent threatens to evict child.
Parent deliberately frightens child.

[4] Symonds, *op. cit.*, p. 46.
[5] M. J. Fitz-Simons, *op. cit.*, p. 26.

Parent locks child away—in closet, basement, outside house.
Parent threatens to report child to authority.
Parent pays no attention to child—gives no money, toys, treats.
Parent spanks child, whips child.
Parent does not provide advantages, special education.
Parent does not spend time with child.
Parent neglects child—movements unsupervised.
Parent compares child unfavorably.
Parent is hard on child—holds to standard unsuited.

Symonds says that if either or both parents reject a child that child is likely to be characterized as:[6]

Aggressive.
Rebellious.
Hostile.
Jealous.
Attention-getting.
Hyperactive.
Annoying in school.

We read further about the rejected child in Bonney, who writes:[7]

"The patterns run about as follows: They have experienced some form of rejection by one or both parents or they have had excessive emotional ties with one of the parents—usually the mother, while at the same time lacking even normal relationships with the other parent. This rejection and this abnormal pulling of the child toward one side of the parental axis results in various forms of personality distortions such as a sense of inferiority, a deep-seated desire for revenge, an immature and confused love life, and an expectation of greater pleasure without effort or responsibility than the world affords."

Other Home Influences

We have discussed at length how relationships with parents affect the child's development. All of the aspects of the home must be considered, however, if we really wish to understand why the adolescent is what he is.

These are summarized by Bossard thus:[8]

[6] Symonds, op. cit., p. 47.
[7] Merle E. Bonney, "Parents as the Makers of Social Deviates," Social Forces, 20:77–87 (1941).
[8] James H. S. Bossard and Eleanor S. Boll, Family Situations (Philadelphia: University of Pennsylvania Press, 1943), pp. 111–112.

A Classification of Family Situations

Intrafamily Relationships

I. Affectional relationships

    A. Excess of affection

        1. The possessive home
        2. The oversolicitous home
        3. The overindulgent home

    B. Normal affection

        1. The companionable home

    C. Discrimination in affection

        1. The divided home
        2. The favored-child home
        3. The "impartial" home

    D. Inconsistency of affection

        1. The bickering home
        2. The unreliable home

    E. Displacement of affection

        1. The home with a new member

    F. Lack of affection

        1. The nagging home
        2. The frigid home
        3. The neglected home

    G. Frank rejection

        1. The home of the unwanted child

II. Subjectual relationships

    A. Repression

        1. The mother-controlled home
        2. The father-dominated home
        3. The overdemanding home

    B. Anarchy

        1. The child-dictated home

    C. Confusion

        1. The home with too many bosses

    D. Approaching Balance

        1. The democratic home

Family Patterns

    A. Size

        1. The large family
        2. The one-child family

    B. Organization

        1. The cooperative family
        2. The independent family
        3. The incomplete family

    C. Activity

        1. The nomadic family
        2. The "joiner" family
        3. The family of the intelligentsia
        4. The "cliff-dweller" family
        5. The community-benefactor family

D. Values and goals

1. The social-climber family
2. The materialistic family
3. The overlyreligious family
4. The scientific family
5. The superstitious family
6. The conventional family

External Factors

A. Socioeconomic status

1. The inadequately financed home
2. The suddenly wealthy home
3. The large-inheritance home
4. The mother-supported family
5. The family marked by peculiar occupational characteristics
6. The home of culture conflict
7. The disgraced home
8. The family in the public eye

B. Neighborhood

1. The farm family
2. The small-town family
3. The city family
4. The summer-resort family
5. The misfit-in-the-neighborhood family
6. The family in a sub-standard neighborhood

C. Health

1. The home of the invalid
2. The home of the defective

HOW IS THE ADOLESCENT GETTING ALONG AT HOME?

Like all of the rest of us, the adolescent has his problems and frustrations. With some boys and girls, many of these troubles stem from the home, and sometimes it is the home problems that are the most unmanageable.

These problems may be divided into two groups:

1. Those having to do with the home setting.
2. Those connected with personal relationships within the home.

Problems Having to Do with the Home Setting

Home of Another Culture. In our country it is not uncommon to find boys and girls in school coming from a home where the father and mother were reared in a different culture. The difficulties of adjustment which these young people face call for a type of guidance and understanding teachers often fail to give. The case of Sammy is illustrative: Sammy's father and mother were emigrants from Russia who had come to America at the age of twenty. They settled in a Middle Western city of 70,000, locating in the old part of the city which had in an early day been the most important business district but which as the city grew became a slum section. Factories grew up in this portion of the city, the rental rates for homes were low, and it soon became populated with the under-privileged. Saloons, gambling places, and houses of prostitution flourished in this section where Sammy was born.

The father opened a secondhand store in the very center of this old section of the city and housed the family in two rooms attached to the rear of the store. The parents, who were unable to speak the English language when they came to America, were honest and God-fearing citizens, anxious to rear Sammy and his brother, Tommy, to be the same. Though they were eager to see their children take full advantage of the opportunities furnished for getting an education, their failure to under-stand the contrasts the children faced between home and school caused much conflict in the lives of the two boys.

By the time Sammy entered junior high school, he was well aware of the fact that he was different from the other students. For one instance, his parents could not see why it was necessary for Sammy to take part in certain school activities after school hours since they kept him from getting home early and helping in the store. For another, Sammy had no home to which he would dare take any of his classmates. When he was invited to their homes, he had a feeling of guilt because he was unable to show them the same courtesy by asking them to his home. Then, too, while his mother and father wished to show their cooperation with the school and would often come to programs to which parents were in-vited, they were different in dress and manners from other parents and Sammy was conscious of this and embarrassed by it.

Sammy's teachers and his counselor understood his difficulties. Con-ferences were held with his parents to give them a better understanding of what the school was trying to do. But not enough was accomplished to change their way of thinking about their boys.

After completing the eighth grade Sammy had a heart-to-heart talk with his counselor. He said: "Mr. J., I guess I am through school now. Dad says he can get me a work permit; so I think it best that I quit." The counselor understood the struggles Sammy had been experiencing. He told him that before such action was taken it would be good for the two of them to consider at length what Sammy proposed to do. In the conversation Sammy unburdened his soul. He said: "There's no use in me trying to go ahead. I can never hope to amount to much with father and mother like they are. I know it's wrong for me to be ashamed of them, but I can't help it. They are so different from the parents of the other boys. They try to make me behave so different from my friends. I can't get clothes like my friends wear. My parents complain about me all of the time because I want more than they want to give me. So I think I had better quit."

The counselor told Sammy that he was a good boy and that, although unhappy at times, he had made satisfactory progress generally. He showed Sammy that those who knew him and his family did not look down upon him just because his parents were "different." In fact, he said, he admired Sammy very much for the way he had been brave enough to stick to it as he fought an uphill battle. The counselor promised Sammy all the help possible if he would remain in school. Whenever he felt discouraged, it was suggested, he should come in for a talk.

Sammy did graduate from high school. Today he holds a position which he was able to secure because of his school training in commercial subjects. He seems to be reasonably well adjusted and is a useful citizen, pursuing work which gives promise of enabling him to make a decent living. We don't know what might have happened to Sammy if his school and counselors hadn't understood him and his problems.

The Immoral Home. The problems to be faced by the adolescent growing up in a home where one or both parents have no decent standards of conduct are very different from the problems arising in homes like Herbert's and Sammy's.

Ronald's father spent most of his time away from home, and the care of Ronald, their only child, was left to the mother. The mother's reputation in the community was bad, for she engaged in keeping a "rooming house" for girls.

The problem of adjustment for Ronald became serious for him when he was about twelve years old. For some time previous to adolescence he had been conscious of what went on in his home, but it was in adolescence that the conditions surrounding him gave rise to serious emotional disturbance. He was ashamed of the low moral standard held by his mother. Perhaps his father's standards were no higher, but since the father was away from home most of the time, Ronald knew little about him.

Ronald's classmates, while they had heard of his family's reputation, were friendly and accepted him as their equal in most school situations, for he was a bright boy and especially attractive physically. But by the time Ronald was fifteen he noticed that he was not invited to their homes. Though the girls treated Ronald in a courteous manner, they knew enough about his home background to be afraid to invite him to dances and parties. The boys did not ask him to home affairs because they knew of the girls' objections.

Ronald's counselor talked with the mother. It was evident that she gave very little thought to the boy's welfare. She admitted it was a difficult situation for him but could see, or desired to see, no other way to live. She conceded that there was much noise and confusion in the house at night and that Ronald's sleep was disturbed but said that she had to make money to clothe and feed him. She described Ronald's father as being a shiftless and irresponsible man.

Ronald lost interest in school. His attendance had been good until he reached his sophomore year, during all of which time he had made normal progress. But one day in his sophomore year he disappeared. Upon inquiry at his home it was learned that he had left with a few of his belongings the previous night. The mother found a note in the room which read: "I want to be somebody, but I can't do that here. So I am going away where people don't know me. I hope you won't try to find me."

At the time this is written, Ronald's whereabouts are unknown to his family and his teachers. He may have had the necessary moral courage to live up to the ideals he caught a glimpse of in school. What he learned at home would certainly not have helped him to be an honorable and upright citizen.

Did the school fail to do what it could and should have done for Ronald? Were the citizens of the community responsible for this boy in any way? Did social and law-enforcement agencies fail by permitting a home where children were growing up to become such a place that the adolescent boy could no longer remain in it? The answer to all of these questions seems clear. The responsibility for Ronald was a joint one. All of the agencies of the community—law-enforcement, child-welfare, service clubs, churches, and school—might have made conditions more favorable to his development had there been intelligent cooperation in meeting his needs.

Broken Homes. Curtis and Nemzek[9] investigated the effect of certain unsettled home conditions on the academic success of high school pupils. Fifty students from broken homes were paired with pupils from normal

[9] Erta Agnes Curtis and Claude L. Nemzek, "The Relation of Certain Unsettled Home Conditions to the Academic Success of High School Pupils," *Journal of Social Psychology,* 9:419–435 (1938).

homes on the basis of intelligence, chronological age, grade in school, sex, and nationality. They found that the achievement of pupils from broken homes is inferior to that of pupils from normal homes. No other casual factors were found to account for this difference.

Broken homes, of course, may affect the adolescent in many ways. Thus two boys of fourteen and sixteen, whose mother had died, had to keep house for their father—with the result that they were always unkempt and unwashed and looking for every excuse to be somewhere other than at home during most of their waking hours.

The woman's influence in the home or the man's is too important to prevent some lack of balance when the mother or father is gone from the home. Not just in housekeeping or in breadwinning but also in many more subtle ways are needed influences lost.

Lack of Privacy in the Home. One girl writes: "My mother, father, and I live with my grandparents. The house is really not big enough. Although we do have 5 rooms, I do not have a room of my own. I think every boy and girl should have their own room. You don't like to have someone else always knowing everything you do."

Another girl says: "My home is quite satisfactory and I have hardly any complaint, except that my room is fairly open and I have very little privacy which I believe all girls need. Now I have no trouble with my parents—they never gather in my room, but still I can't close the door and feel alone. My bedroom is off the front room and the rooms are joined by an arch door. So you see I can't very well close my room off and be alone."

It is easy to understand why it is disturbing to the adolescent not to have a place in his home which is his own and which is private. With the attention of adults so often upon him, he needs at times to be safe from prying eyes and free from distractions. In addition he needs a place for his belongings arranged just as he wants them—and left that way—a place where he can express himself and his ideas of good living without interference.

Lack of Money in the Home. Probably no one who reads this is so affluent that he cannot appreciate the troubles that poverty can bring to the adolescent. Lack of proper food, lack of conveniences, lack of health services, and other deprivations not only interfere with his physical well-being but also sometimes cause feelings of inferiority, shame, and jealousy. Often, too, the adolescent has to spend his leisure time working, both to help his family and to get necessities for himself, and he is thus deprived of opportunities for the kind of association and recreation others engage in.

Problems in Personal Relationships

Parent-Child Relationships. Home life for the majority of adolescents is comforting and comfortable; but for every one of them, some more and some less, it has its unpleasant moments arising from trouble with father or mother, brother or sister.

Almost invariably there are sources of friction and displeasure in adolescent-parent relationships. This is true in child-parent relationships as well, of course, but difficulties often become more severe in adolescence

TABLE 46. ADOLESCENTS' DISLIKES REGARDING PARENTAL BEHAVIOR

	Farm		Town		City		
	Boys	Girls	Boys	Girls	Boys	Girls	
I. Discipline and control	31.8	23.1	18	28.9	21.3	21.5	Father's
and other personal relationships between parent and child	33.3	33.1	26.9	35.9	15.7	26.7	Mother's
II. Temperamental traits	9.1	15.6	15	19.5	11.7	27.8	Father's
and behavior affecting members of the family and others	8.5	13.8	11.8	25	13.5	14.4	Mother's
III. Personal habits and behavior	20	30.6	34	19.5	34	22.8	Father's
	6	2.3	8.6	5.1	23.6	16.7	Mother's
IV. Emotional adjustment	12.7	15.6	7	6.7	11.7	6.3	Father's
and control	12.8	16.9	9.7	9.6	16.9	13.3	Mother's
V. Ideas, attitudes, beliefs	0	0.7	3	2.7	0	0	Father's
	3.4	2.3	4.3	3.2	0	0	Mother's
VI. Work, self-sacrifice	0	0.7	3	2.7	0	0	Father's
	12	8.5	12.9	8.3	12.4	7.8	Mother's
VII. Social matters	1.8	1.4	0	2.7	0	3.8	Father's
	3.4	1.5	5.4	1.3	5.6	2.2	Mother's

when the boy or girl is consciously pulling away from his parents' dominance and when he is becoming more aware of his parents as people.

Stott[10] gathered data from 1,878 young people (694 living on farms, 639 living in small towns, and 545 living in a city) in regard to the question of what they disliked about their parents' behavior. He asked them, "What does your mother do that you *don't like?*" and "What does your father do that you *do not like?*"

[10] Leland H. Stott, "Adolescents' Dislikes Regarding Parental Behavior and Their Significance," *Pedagogical Seminary and Journal of Genetic Psychology*, 57:393–414 (1940).

He classified their replies into six groups (plus a group of miscellaneous items of trivial importance). From his extensive data we present Table 46, giving only the per cent of total criticism.

According to this report, and it is as we would expect it to be, the most frequent parent-child difficulty in normal homes lies in direct clashes between parent and child. We have further evidence of this in written opinions of high school boys and girls: [11]

Parents won't listen:

"I can't discuss anything with my father. He won't listen to my side of anything. He is head-strong and what he says goes. He says I'm not old enough to know anything."

"My friends influence me most. It seems I just can't get mother to sit down and talk real sense about my problems."

"Mother just never has time to talk things over with me."

"My mother won't answer any of the problems I bring home and ask her—especially sex problems. She just says that I'll find out sooner or later."

Parents don't trust you:

"Why do parents always expect you to account for everything you do while out of their sight? It makes you have a feeling that they don't trust you."

"If I have a date, I must be home at an early time. If I am just five minutes late, I have some tall explaining to do. Why parents can't trust their children is beyond me."

"My parents are always suspicious of everything that I do. I'm getting to the place that I'm not caring much any more if they keep doubting me. There is no reason for them to act like this toward me, and there never has been any. It just makes me keep my thoughts to myself and then there's _____ to pay because 'You don't say anything—you don't tell me anything.'"

Parents treat you as a child:

"My mother will not let me go out at night with my girl friends. She will not let me have a date with a boy who has a car. She says anything could happen. She doesn't seem to know that I'm old enough to take care of myself and that my friends are nice."

[11] All unpublished data from James F. Conover, Principal, Garfield High School, Terre Haute, Ind.

"When I was fifteen my parents said I could have dates when I was sixteen. It's gone on this way for two years. Now, I'm seventeen and they say for me to wait until I'm eighteen. I suppose it will continue this way the rest of my life."

"My mother and father don't think that I have enough sense to drive a car—even though I've passed the test. They want me to wait another year, and I'm a senior now."

"They always introduce me to people as their *baby*."

Parents interfere with your friendships:

"My parents are entirely suitable to me. I have only one gripe and that is that my Dad worries too much about me. Dad can't be at ease when I'm gone for the evening. He is so worried that sometimes he is sick for a few days. He acts as if he doesn't trust me, but when I ask him he re-assures me, 'I could trust you to the end of the world.' *His very words.* My problem is how can I make him trust my *friends* whom I trust and like? This especially means the boys that I date."

"Mother doesn't like for me to go out on school nights, and then when someone comes she doesn't like it because we make noise. You can't keep kids quiet, and if you can't go anywhere, what are you to do?"

"My parents seem to think that I can entertain my friends when they are in the same room. For some reason you can't be natural when you feel that your mother or father is listening to everything said."

"I don't think my mother has a right to pass judgment on all of my friends when she doesn't really know them."

"My mother is jealous of my friends. If I mention going some place with some one, she complains that I don't think much of her or I would spend all of my time with her. Thus, I find myself without close friends, just because I dread bringing them home."

Parents try to decide what you should be:

"My parents expect me to be a future genius and anyone can tell that I am not."

"Parents try to decide your future instead of trying to work it out with you."

"My parents continually compare me with other boys in what they have done and I have not. It could be possible that I do not have the same interests or ambitions, or as far as they know, could be handicapped in some way, thus preventing my participation in the activities in which those other boys are so successful."

Parents want you in too early:

"They expect you to be in from a party when the party is just starting."

"It happens that I get to go out rarely. I can't have a good time because I'm worrying about being home on time. I have to be home before anybody else, 9:30 P.M., and it makes me feel plumb silly, like an old wet blanket. I want to go out just once and have a good time—no worries or cares about being home at a reasonable time. I don't see why my mother out of a million other mothers has been so strict with me."

"My mother demands that I come straight home from school every day. I wish that she would let me stay at least for half an hour once in a while, so that I could mix in with the crowd."

"Dad insists that I get in at nine o'clock when I'm out with anyone but when I'm out with him, time makes no difference."

Parents invade your privacy:

"Sometimes a friend phones me. My mother always wants to know who it was and what the person wanted. I don't think this is fair. I should be able to have a little privacy."

"Parents always think that you have something up your sleeve when you go out at night with a bunch of boys and always give you a general quiz. I think it is all right to ask me where I've been—but without the *quiz*."

Parents complain too much:

"I'm talked about in front of my grandparents and other relatives. My parents call me lazy because I play basketball until it gets dark and then I'm tired and want to go to bed early."

"It would be better if my parents would go out and have a good time themselves once in a while instead of just sitting around and grumbling."

"Father is always trying to find things wrong with the way I do things. He has never complimented me on anything—just gripes."

Parents quarrel:

"I believe that when parents have troubles between themselves, they should keep it to themselves and not be constantly raving to their children about them. It is embarrassing for the children. They can't even express their views. It only makes them unhappy."

Actual quarrels with parents are more typical of adolescence than of childhood. Punke has investigated the matter of family quarrels as far as high school youth are concerned; the causes of such quarrels are given in Table 47. As we see from this, the daughter engages in more quarreling in regard to social life and friends, clothes, and other members of the family. The opposite is true when it comes to economic factors, education, and vocation. The differences are perhaps not large enough to be the basis for generalization, but it can at least be said that we would expect

TABLE 47. CAUSES OF PARENT-ADOLESCENT QUARRELS*

	Per Cent
Social life and friends:	
Father and son	40.2
Father and daughter	50.6
Mother and son	36.1
Mother and daughter	41.7
Economic factors relating to work and spending money:	
Father and son	34.7
Father and daughter	25.1
Mother and son	30.5
Mother and daughter	32.2
Clothes:	
Father and son	1.0
Father and daughter	4.8
Mother and son	5.8
Mother and daughter	17.5
Education and vocation:	
Father and son	6.6
Father and daughter	4.7
Mother and son	7.9
Mother and daughter	2.9
Other members of the family:	
Father and son	2.3
Father and daughter	3.7
Mother and son	4.8
Mother and daughter	5.4
Other causes:	
Father and son	15.2
Father and daughter	11.1
Mother and son	14.9
Mother and daughter	9.3

* Data arranged from Harold H. Punke, "High-school Youth and Family Quarrels," *School and Society*, 58:507–511 (1943).

them to fall as they do. In the first place, parents are more protective toward their daughters and therefore feel more necessity for keeping a watchful eye on their friendships and social engagements. Second, the very fact that the girls' clothes are more varied than the boys' and that the girls probably want to indulge themselves oftener in small additions to their wardrobes may account for greater quarreling in this area. Third, it may be that girls tend to bicker more in regard to the privileges of other members of the family; it would be difficult to say.

Boys are more likely to engage in work outside the home, spend more money for dates, and have more at stake, most parents would believe, as far as their vocations are concerned. This may account for the fact that quarreling in these respects seems to be more frequent with the boys.

Punishment of children, whether or not they be of adolescent age, is not a pleasant affair for either the punisher or the punished. To the adolescent, however, it may seem worse because at his age he may feel more humiliation at the idea of being punished.

Stott[12] asked 1,878 high school students these questions:

Were you scolded or punished at home last week?
If so, how were you punished?
By whom were you punished?
For what were you punished?

Six hundred fifty of the students reported that they had been punished. The causes of the punishment are given in Table 48.

TABLE 48. REASONS WHY PARENTS PUNISH ADOLESCENTS*

	Per Cent
Getting home late from a date..............	12.9
Disobedience.............................	
Being impudent or "sassy".................	
Neglecting work.........................	22.3
Getting home late from school.............	
Other reasons (70 are given in all)..........	46.2

* Leland H. Stott, "Home Punishment of Adolescents," *Pedagogical Seminary and Journal of Genetic Psychology*, 57:415–428 (1940).

The three common methods of punishing were:

Scolding.
Made to stay at home.
Slapped.

The mothers administered the punishment in 64.3 per cent of the cases as compared with the 31.1 per cent administered by the fathers.

Quarrels between the parents are always a source of disturbance to the child, and the adolescent, with his greater understanding, is perhaps more bothered by these now than when he was younger. Punke, securing his data from 7,021 pupils in high schools of nine different states, gives us information about parents' quarrels in Table 49.

[12] Leland H. Stott, "Home Punishment of Adolescents," *Pedagogical Seminary and Journal of Genetic Psychology*, 57: 415–428 (1940).

Sibling Relationships. Another cause for difficulty in the home is quarreling between brothers and sisters. This is doubtless inevitable with young people living in the intimate situation of the home, and if not carried to excess it is probably not damaging—although it is disturbing, and life would be happier without it. Actually it may be that we should consider friction between siblings a necessary "training school" for learning mature adjustments to other people, remembering that if the parents are wise in the treatment of the children they will as time goes on grow in

TABLE 49. QUARRELS BETWEEN PARENTS*

Frequency of quarrels between parents:

	Per Cent
No quarreling	67.9
Quarreling from one to five times a month	26.3
Six or more times a month	5.8
Causes of quarrels:	
Economic factors	43.9
Social life of children	21.0
Personal habits of spouse	16.0
Education of children	1.5
Jealousy of spouse	4.2
Other weakness of spouse	1.8
Relatives and kinfolks	2.3
Neighbors	0.4
Other	8.9

* Harold H. Punke, "High-school Youth and Family Quarrels," *School and Society*, 58:507–511 (1943).

the ability to respect each other's rights and individuality and in the habit of settling differences amicably.

In this connection a fourteen-year-old girl writes:

"The thing that I hate is being the middle child. Like, the other day I came into the living room to watch television. My sister was watching a silly program and I wanted to watch something different. I turned the channel. She screamed and told my mother. I was sent to my bedroom for the rest of the day. Then again, when I was watching a program another day, my big brother came in. He changed the channel and there it stayed. I had nothing to say about it. The only time I see what I like is when someone else wants it too. When my sister and I are watching a program my brother doesn't like, he doesn't say anything because it's my little sister's program and she's always babied.

"The same thing happens with clothes and toys. My sister is always playing dress-up in my clothes or getting into my things. I tell my mother, but she only says, 'Let her have some fun.' But if I wear my brother's clothes or play with his basketball, he gets angry and then my mother tells me to leave his things alone.

"I sure wish I had a voice in the arguments."

Relatives. The presence of relatives of the family—a grandmother, an uncle, and so on—can also make trouble for the adolescent. If the added adult is a person who thinks that he has jurisdiction over the adolescent and who therefore proceeds to criticize him, order him around, and the like, life may be made almost unbearable for the boy or girl who has to put up with this. For example, an older unmarried brother of the father of a fifteen-year-old girl came to live with the family, and after he had been there for six months, the mother and father agreed that for the sake of the girl he would have to leave. For his two prevailing ideas in regard to her were that she was there to wait on him and that she should be made to profit by all that he had learned in his sixty years. Consequently, it was "Run and get me a drink of water" and "See if the paper has come yet" and "Sit up straight" and "You shouldn't use lipstick at your age" until the girl became too irritable to let her parents be easy about her.

Disapproval of Parent's Behavior. We must always remember that a certain amount of disagreement between the adolescent and the members of his household is so commonplace as to be considered normal behavior. Similarly, when the adolescent disapproves of his mother or father at times, we can only say: "That is to be expected." As Gildea writes:[13]

"A boy gets up from the dining-room table, tips over his chair, and in reaching for it knocks his plate to the floor. A girl lunges into the dining room late for breakfast, and as she falls hastily into her chair, shakes the table so that each cup spills coffee into its saucer. An agony of embarrassment and self-consciousness follows, for the child's orientation is changing now. He begins to wonder, 'What will people think of me?' Until now his only concern has been what he thought of them.

"The next step, of course, is, 'What do people think of my parents, or my relatives, or my friends?' I shall never forget the amazement I felt when I first heard the adolescent daughter of a friend urge her mother please not to say 'damn' when friends were in the house, and another girl exclaimed with disgust, 'Oh, Mother, you're *never* going to wear *that* bathing suit on the *beach!*' And what father has not taken thought when his hitherto unobserving son notices that his parent's trouser creases need renewing? All families go through a trying period when the food served appears to be not up to the standard of the family next door, or when the automobile is observed to look pretty shabby.

"Fortunately, this grim evaluation of his home—and of himself—by

[13] Margaret C.-L. Gildea, "The Modern American Parent," *Mental Hygiene*, 27:43–54 (1943).

what the child conceives to be the standards of society, is enormously alleviated by the new development and burgeoning of adolescent humor, which, because it is a social phenomenon, is an integral part of the developing social consciousness. This is the age when children stand around school halls for hours just kidding one another."

THE SCHOOL AND THE ADOLESCENT'S HOME DIFFICULTIES

Understanding the Adolescent's Home Background

Understanding is the beginning of any teacher's help to the adolescent, and knowing what the home is like is an essential part of this understanding. The teacher should know something about the economic background of the boy or girl and realize that if the youth is poor he may possibly have inferiority feelings connected with his home, be handicapped in his extracurricular opportunities in the school, be bothered by the fact that he cannot compete with other students in dress, spending money, and the like, and may possibly be unduly retiring or unduly aggressive. If these handicaps are understood, the teacher may be able to help the student succeed in school in spite of his home limitations and should certainly be impelled to be tolerant of behavior which is actually a compensation for deprivations. He must realize, too, that if the boy or girl comes from a home where money flows freely, there may similarly be handicaps and undesirable reactions—egocentrism, snobbishness, attitudes of superiority, inability to accept frustrations, an extreme need to compete and be successful, home pressures to excel in school, and the like.

The teacher should realize that home conditions may be such that the boy or girl doesn't get proper food, has little opportunity to study, or is overworked, and he must make allowances to prevent being too demanding or too censorious of him.

The teacher must recognize the fact that one child's parents may differ strikingly from those of another in educational and cultural background and must realize that his own background is such that he will have certain expectations in the way of "proper" behavior which may differ greatly from what some of his students' homes have instilled in them. It is not enough, therefore, to understand the effects of his students' home training; he must also take account of the effects of his own.

The teacher must be aware of the fact that the social status of his students may lead him to discriminate in favor of some and against others, even though he is not conscious of doing so. Knowing the ease with which such discrimination occurs, he must be on his guard against it.

Working Directly with Parents

Teachers in the elementary school have learned how valuable is the experience of visiting the home and of talking to the parents, for not only does the teacher come to know the child and his home setting better but also the parents get acquainted with the teacher and can get firsthand information as to what the school is trying to do and as to what are the successes and difficulties of their child. With adolescents, however, home visits are often of questionable value, for the teen-ager feels that he is being treated like a child when teacher and parent must thus confer, and the parents of the adolescent may feel that he is too grown-up to require this kind of parent-teacher conference. Consequently it is often more advisable to get the parent to the school.

If an adolescent is in trouble at school, conferences may be held at which the counselor and one or both the parents are present or at which the counselor, the parent, and the adolescent are all present. Aside from such problem cases, however, it is good if parents and teachers can meet in a friendly way from time to time. Techniques such as open-house nights for parents, panel discussions for parents, and anything else the ingenious principal can do to get parents to school to further mutual understanding will help.

The parent-teacher movement was conceived by its early leaders as an organization which could bring parents and teachers together for the purpose of making the efforts of both pay bigger dividends in developing better adjusted children and youth. In many communities such organizations have realized their potentialities and have conducted programs which were really beneficial to all concerned. Parents have come to understand that education is a continuous process a good part of which takes place in the home. As someone has said, they no longer think, "I send my child to school to get an education," but rather "I send my child to school to supplement the education which I give him at home."

The teacher and administrator are the ones who must take the leadership in such organizations usually, for it is they who have the necessary understanding of the child in all areas of his living and the broader educational viewpoint.

Promoting Adolescent-Parent Understanding

Punke, after studying high school youth and family quarrels, arrived at the following conclusions as to how the school might improve home life for the adolescent:[14] The school might help students learn to live

[14] Harold H. Punke, "High School Youth and Family Quarrels," *School and Society*, 58:507–511 (1943).

happily within the family's budget; it might help parents understand youth's recreational needs and help youth understand the reasons for their parents' conservatism; school buildings might be used more for recreational purposes, thus to ease parents' worries as to their children's whereabouts; the school might help parents and children learn how habits might be modified when they are disagreeable to others.

Most adolescents cannot view their home with complete objectivity and cannot see their parents as people with problems which they are making a good effort to solve to the advantage of all in the home. They may not realize that they have an obligation to understand their parents, to be helpful and tactful with them. At the same time they may not be aware of the fact that the home problems they experience are similar to those of other adolescents. If the school has psychology classes, family-relations classes, or discussion groups for youth problems, it is highly probable that it may give the adolescent the knowledge and the understanding which will help him to do his part in bettering his home situation.

THE GOOD HOME FOR THE ADOLESCENT

A real understanding of the adolescent and his home requires that we have a picture of what the home is like if it is to be ideal for the adolescent. To begin with, let us see what some adolescents themselves say:

What the Adolescent Says

"My parents have very good sense. They believe in doing what they think is right for me. Like everybody else's parents, they want me to finish school, for various reasons. I feel secure because Mom and Dad can talk to me and I can talk to them. Not every kid my age can do that. You see Mom had twelve children. Being two from the youngest, I can do almost anything—that is, I go with my girl friends anywhere I want to! Do anything I feel like doing. Mom and Dad would do anything for me." (*Freshman girl.*)

"My parents are understanding—they let me explain things before they say 'No.' They want me to have fun, go places, see things and have dates. They aren't old-fashioned, nor are they too lenient. They feel they have given me nearly 18 years of training and by now I am a fairly responsible and trustworthy girl. I hope to maintain this standard." (*Senior girl.*)

"Being 17 is a difficult time and age. One is expected to act as an adult, have the responsibilities of an adult, but doesn't have the credit or receive the rewards of an adult. Probably this misunderstanding of my 'stage' is the most unsatisfactory thing about my parents. Another point is actual lack of interest in me and things in which I am interested. I am expected to be interested in the occupations, vocations, and hobbies of my parents, but it seems a one-sided affair. Their lack of confidence in me and my judgment are often alarming and discouraging to me. I realize that the thought, 'I am not appreciated' is supposed to be characteristic of my age; however, I have that feeling." (*Senior boy.*)

"My parents treat me as their equal in all family discussions and problems. We discuss financial problems, problems of our relationships with each other, and the problems concerning my future. They make me feel that I am old enough to make decisions and that I must abide by my decision even though it may be unpleasant. I appreciate my parents' efforts to teach me to take disappointments and I am free to go to them and more or less pour out my heart. I'm not wise enough yet to smile and forget troubles, but when I talk to them, I can reason about why or what is important. Lastly my parents are free and happy together around me and I wouldn't ever do anything knowingly to take away their happiness. I guess I've never thought about good or bad except that I just want to please my family." (*Senior girl.*)

"My only objection to my relations with my parents is on the topic of sex instruction. They have always been open and frank with me and made it plain that I should consult them about questions instead of cheap sex manuals. This has been good and I have appreciated it, but during the last year of my high school they have taken the 'better be careful' attitude. I guess I feel they should know my behavior will always be up to my teaching and I will always abide by their creeds for us children. Mom tells me that every girl or boy thinks they will have right conduct and never mean to be wrong. I think I will tell my daughter that I know from experience with parents that if a girl or boy has ambition for a successful life that good common sense will carry them through the 'tender years' we're going through." (*Senior girl.*)

"I think I am one of the luckiest young men in the world to have had the parents and the upbringing which I have received from them. As far as their intelligence is concerned (and this I think is an important factor in dealing with this question) theirs is much above average. They have taught my sister and myself all the necessary things which well-behaved, intelligent young men and women should know. I only hope we do them justice! I used to think when I was little that my parents were too strict, because I saw that those of my friends were lenient. But now I realize that they were trying to teach me things which I should know, and since I am so hard-headed, they had to use many methods of discipline. They have always treated me fairly and squarely and with much understanding." (*Senior boy.*)

"They are too set in their ways. If a debate comes up and I voice my opinion, I'm always wrong and they can't understand why I don't think the same way they do." (*Junior boy.*)

"There is one way they are not satisfactory toward me and it is that they sometimes do not seem interested in what I am trying to tell them. Some things I do don't seem important to them although they do to me." (*Sophomore girl.*)

"My parents are not so satisfactory in the following ways: sex instruction, understanding of motives in doing certain things, understanding me as a high school student who naturally acts non-adult." (*Senior boy.*)

"They give me about everything that most guys my age have. I get to pick out my own clothes and I can have money whenever I want it if it's for a sensible cause. They're fairly broad minded and I can talk freely to them in anything. They do not seem shocked or surprised that 'the baby of the family' should know such things." (*Junior boy.*)

"My main kick is that they won't let me have the car and they won't even teach me how to drive, even though I'm 17. I think everyone should know how. My brother, who is older, gets it without asking; he just tells them. I can't smoke, yet everyone in the house does but mother and me. If they can, why can't I? Everyone teases me and compares me with my brother. Then when I get mad they kid me into laughing and that makes me madder than ever. They will not let me have any parties at my house. I can go to them, but never have them. This is without reason!" (*Junior girl.*)

"When I ask my parents for money, maybe more than I should, they always start telling me they didn't have those sort of things in their days; after all, I believe times have changed." (*Sophomore girl.*)

"We do not have a front porch. Our home has a sun-porch, with windows around the front of the house. I like a big porch. In the summertime when my friends come and it is too hot to be inside, I have no place to take them, except the back porch, and who wants to sit and look at the alley? In my future home, I am going to have a front porch." (*Sophomore girl.*)

"My parents take my word as something of value. If Mother or Father ask me something regarding my activities, my answer is accepted without any hesitation. My opinion concerning matters of interest, family or otherwise, is frequently requested. This makes me feel a part of my family." (*Sophomore boy.*)

"The thing that makes me angry is when my parents treat me as though I were still three years old.

"I suppose that when you're a parent you hate to see that little boy or girl grow up, start dating, get married and leave you, but sometimes it just gets on my nerves terribly.

"When you reach the teens you start thinking of going to shows at night and going to the sweet-shop after Friday night dances. Last year when practically every girl I knew went to the show at night and to the sweet-shop after the dance, Daddy still picked me up and took me home. Going to the show at night was out of the question. I was too young for that sort of thing!

"If I act like a younger person though, Mom and Pop tell me that I'm old enough and should act my age. If I do, I'm told I'm too young.

"You just can't win." (*Freshman girl.*)

Characteristics of the Good Home

In most respects, the home that is good for the adolescent is the home that is good for the child at any age. Such a home will have the following characteristics:

1. Affection. What Taylor[15] says of the adolescent can be said of children of all ages: "Only as the adolescent feels that he is loved, enjoyed, and respected as a separate individual, and that his parents really believe in him, will he feel free to become himself." Affection is one of the marks of a good home. The members of the family like one another and feel tender and loving toward one another. In contrast to some homes where affection ebbs and flows, where it flourishes only when the one who is loved is particularly pleasing, or where it is given or withdrawn to reward or punish a child, in the good home this affection is an even, mutual feeling that shows at all times.

2. Democracy. Since democracy implies that the rights of every individual are respected and the growth of each is given consideration, it follows that democracy is the best medium for the development of each person. In a democratic home there is seldom a condition of subservience to the will of someone else and no feeling that one counts for little in the home organization. There the child learns self-respect because he is respected. He develops self-confidence because he is aware of the fact that he does count as someone who contributes to the group's happiness. There he learns social responsibility because he is a part of a group organization and must recognize the needs of others as well as his own and help supply them.

3. Lack of conflict. In any home there will be differences of opinion, but in the good home, particularly as the children get older, there will seldom, if ever, be strong, unpleasant emotion arising over conflicting viewpoints or desires. An atmosphere of quarreling, bitterness, and vindic-

---

[15] Katherine Whiteside Taylor, *Do Adolescents Need Parents?* (New York: Appleton-Century-Crofts, Inc., 1938), p. 124.

tiveness not only makes the home unpleasant and breeds further unpleasant emotional states but also teaches the child the wrong way of interacting with others.

4. Comradeship. A spirit of comradeship in the home puts the home activity on a friendly, pleasant, agreeable basis. The parents come to know their children better; the children take joy in doing things with their parents and learn from the ways of adulthood.

5. Good personal adjustment on the part of the parents. When parents are maladjusted, it is almost inevitable that the children, who learn so much from the parents, will develop some maladjustments too. It is almost inevitable, too, that the home where parents are maladjusted will not be the best home for children to grow up in for other reasons as well. For the maladjusted person is usually hard on those he lives with. It may be that he is more quick to take offense, he may often be gloomy and depressed, he may be jealous of others, vindictive, overdependent, or in any number of other ways disagreeable or unreasonable.

6. Development of the parents. In the good home the parents grow with their children. This being true, the parents' idea of what is good for the adolescent and of what is proper is the idea of the 1950 decade and not that of the 1930 one, thus preventing unnecessary conflict between the parent and the teen-ager or surreptitious teen-age behavior with resultant guilt feelings. One cannot expect confidence and comradeship between parents and children if the parents are living according to ideas of what is proper, right, or wrong which the children cannot in their best judgment accept.

7. Interest in the children. Children feel more secure and more satisfied with their experiences when they know that their parents are interested in them—not in any smothering, coddling way, but as one good friend is interested in the ideas and activities of another.

8. Firm, consistent, fair, and objective discipline. In a good home the reaction to an error will not be "How bad you are" or "You have disgraced the family" or "I am disgusted with you" or "I don't like you" but rather "You've made a mistake. We don't believe in what you have done. What should we do about it?" The child will come to understand that there are standards of right action and that there are boundaries for what is good and right. He will know why he should behave in certain ways, and he will realize that punishment is not a matter of the whim of the parent but a way of teaching him to do what is right.

9. A wholesome attitude toward sex and adequate sex instruction. Ideally, the parents are well adjusted sexually and have no unpleasant feelings about sex. They have made opportunities to give the child sex knowledge gradually and in connection with natural events, such as the

birth of a brother or sister. They have answered his questions simply and honestly, without embarrassment and without undue elaboration.

10. Gradual release of responsibilities to the child. In the good home, responsibilities are gradually released to the child as he becomes able to assume them. He is given the home duties he is capable of performing and allowed to be on his own wherever this is possible. One mother of a five-year-old decided that she should let Johnny go alone on his tricycle to kindergarten although the way lay across the main street of the small city and involved a distance of nine blocks. "I'm afraid," she explained to a friend, "but I know Johnny can do it and will do it and so I let him go." The good home allows the child to make more and more choices for himself, nor do the parents influence that choice through their authority unless a mistake would do the child too great harm. For example, a freshman boy, having his heart set on owning a horse, set about earning money to buy it. When he had accumulated $40, he decided that he would spend that money on a fine saddle for his yet to be acquired horse. His parents remonstrated, but the boy insisted, and after the parents had seen that he understood their viewpoint as to the unwisdom of the purchase, they let him make his own decision. He bought the saddle. He never did get enough for a horse, and the saddle still hangs unused in the garage. He has often regretted spending his hard-earned money for something which proved the most useless luxury. His parents have regretted it too, but they felt that the boy would have to grow by making decisions for himself even if they proved to be unwise ones.

In addition to having these qualities the home good for the adolescent will have one other.

11. *It will allow him to take on adulthood as fast as he can handle it.* This is often a difficult thing for parents to do. They are used to offering advice which is almost automatically accepted; they are used to protecting the child and to having his full confidence. As a result, it is hard for them to make a sudden change from being parent to the child to being parent to a near-adult. There are other reasons, too, for the parent to cling to the parent-*child* relationship. As Dollard writes:[16]

"Many restrictions . . . serve the function of giving ego gratification to the parents: they want their child to be dependent upon them as long as possible; they want to make him conform to the approved ways of the group because they are afraid that in the eyes of their contemporaries he will not be socially acceptable; and many of them hope that through discipline and training he will be able to rise beyond their own social and

[16] John Dollard, *Frustration and Aggression* (New Haven: Yale University Press, 1939), p. 98.

economic level so that they may eventually identify themselves with his success."

Thus both because of well-set habit and the satisfactions derived from their position of ascendancy, the parents of the adolescent tend to cling to their authority. Yet if they are to make the home a good one for the boy or girl, they will discipline themselves into different attitudes and behavior, letting their son (or daughter) go his own way, keep his own confidences, choose his own friends, and make his own decisions—except when the results would be calamitous.

At the same time they must continue to provide the haven of affection that the young person still needs in spite of his feelings of independence. Every parent should learn early in the life of his children that warm love does not need to carry with it—and, indeed, should not—possessiveness, overindulgence, complete protectiveness, or authority. The parent of the adolescent *must* realize that he can love without giving advice, without prying, without being solicitous, and without dominating; and he must remember that such generous love is essential to the adolescent's security.

TEEN-AGE RIGHTS

Doyle proposes this bill of rights for teen-agers:[17]

1. The right to free choice in respect to
   a. Friends.
   b. The sports he wants to engage in.
   c. His clothes.
   d. The advantages he would like to have (music lessons, and the like).
   e. Expressing his own ideas.
2. The right to make mistakes at times.
3. The right to a new deal in discipline—to greater freedom along with greater responsibility.
4. The right to his parents' confidence—an insight into family affairs.
5. The right to his parents' esteem and approval.
   a. Consideration for his suggestions and preferences.
   b. Respect for his opinions.
6. The right to clear, dispassionate answers to his questions on sex.
7. The right to some definite time of his own without its being subject to questioning—to read and dream, to work at hobbies, to play, to idle away time, and to date.
8. The right to privacy.
   a. A room of his own if possible; if not, a room shared with someone

[17] Kathleen Doyle, "A Bill of Rights for Teen-agers," *Parents' Magazine*, 23:20, 82–86 (1948).

congenial and then a closet or desk or chest of drawers completely his own.

b. His mail not subject to prying or curiosity.

c. Telephone conversations not subject to prying or curiosity.

9. The right to be free of the petty tyrannies we are apt to impose on children.

   a. Criticism by comparison with another child.

   b. Physical "pushing around" by parents.

   c. Depreciating by such statements as "You'll never learn, will you?"

Reminiscences

1. In what ways was your home a good place for adolescent development?
2. In what ways was it poor?
3. What were the causes of any conflicts that occurred between you and your parents?
4. How fast were you allowed to "grow up"? Be specific, telling what responsibilities and privileges were given you at thirteen, fourteen, and so on.
5. What major home influences were especially important in making you the kind of person you are today?

General Discussion

1. Using Woolf's conclusions, explain how the parent's behavior might bring about some of the child's traits as they are given there.
2. Consider Fitz-Simon's listing of behavior traits of the overacceptant parent. For each item tell what the ideal parent would be like, describing his behavior in some detail.
3. Do the same for the list of traits for the rejectant parent.
4. Following Bossard's classification of family situations, give as many concrete examples of each type as possible.
5. Consider Stott's data on what adolescents dislike in parents. Give concrete examples to illustrate his groupings. What would be the parents' proper procedure, in your opinion?
6. Consider the adolescents' opinions as to what's wrong with parents. For each case try to describe the personality of the parent that has led to this kind of behavior. What was wrong with that personality?
7. Consider Punke's data on family quarrels, Table 47. How would you explain differences in amount of quarreling between father and son and between father and daughter? Mother and son, mother and daughter?
8. Consider Stott's data on home punishments of adolescents. If you were a parent, what would you do about the kinds of misbehavior mentioned?
9. Consider the 11 characteristics of a good home for the adolescent. For each, try to give a concrete example from among the homes you are acquainted with.

Panel Discussion

1. Problems in rearing adolescents. (A panel of parents.)
2. What's wrong with parents? (A panel of adolescents.)

Movies

1. *Feeling of Hostility*, National Film Board of Canada, 27 min., b. & w., 1948.
2. *You and Your Family*, Association Films, 10 min., b. & w., 1946.
3. *Your Family*, Coronet Films, 10 min., b. & w. or color, 1948.

Further Reading

BAYTON, JAMES A., "Personality and Prejudice," *Journal of Psychology*, 22:59–65 (1946).

BLOCK, VIRGINIA LEE, "Conflicts of Adolescents with Their Mothers," *Journal of Abnormal and Social Psychology*, 32:193–206 (1937).

BOSSARD, JAMES H., "Family Situations and Child Behavior," *Journal of Educational Sociology*, 18:323–327 (1949).

BOSSARD, JAMES H., and E. S. BOLL, "The Role of the Guest," *American Sociological Review*, 12:192–201 (1947).

BRODY, DAVID S., "The Utilization of an Interest Inventory in a PTA Project for the Purpose of Fostering Parent-Child Understanding," *School and Society*, 72: 311–312 (1950).

CROW, LESTER D., "Living with Teen Age Boys and Girls," *Educational Forum*, 9:467–470 (1945).

DAVIS, KINGSLEY, "The Sociology of Parent-Youth Conflict," *American Sociological Review*, 5:523–535 (1940).

DAVIS, W. ALLISON, and ROBERT J. HAVIGHURST, *Father of the Man* (Boston: Houghton Mifflin Company, 1947).

FREUND, R. H., "We Don't Keep Our Children in the Dark," *Parents' Magazine*, 20:72 (1945).

GARDNER, L. P., "An Analysis of Children's Attitudes toward Fathers," *Pedagogical Seminary and Journal of Genetic Psychology*, 70:3–28 (1947).

GARDNER, L. P., "A Survey of the Attitudes and Activities of Fathers," *Pedagogical Seminary and Journal of Genetic Psychology*, 63:15–53 (1943).

GRAYSON, ALICE BARR, *Do You Know Your Daughter?* (New York Appleton-Century-Crofts, Inc., 1938).

HARTRICH, PAULETTE, "Parent-Teacher Cooperation in Relation to the Developmental Tasks of Youth," *School Review*, 59:38–44 (1951).

HIRSHBERG, BERNARD, "Extrovert Mother and Introvert Child," *Hygeia*, 24:426 (1946).

JUROVSKY, A., "The Relations of Older Children to Their Parents," *Pedagogical Seminary and Journal of Genetic Psychology*, 72:85–100 (1948).

KIRKWOOD, FRANCES L., "Can They Count on You?" *Parents' Magazine*, 21:31, 104–106 (1946).

LEE, RUTH W., "Make It Fun to Stay at Home," *Parents' Magazine*, 19:62 (1944).

McNAUGHTON, E. B., and M. T. NELSON, "Our Responsibility to Boys and Girls," *Journal of Home Economics*, 39:271–272 (1947).

MEAD, M., "Back of Adolescence Lies Early Childhood," *Childhood Eucation*, 18: 58–61 (1941).

MELLON, EVELYN E., "Living and Letting Live with Adolescents," *Parents' Magazine*, 21:34–35 (1946).

MEYERS, C. E., "Emancipation of Adolescents from Parental Control," *Nervous Child*, 5:251–262 (1946).

MITCHELL, MORRIS R., "Yes, It Can Be Done," *Progressive Education*, 24:88–91 (1947).

REMMERS, H. H., and W. A. KERR, "Home Environment in American Cities" (abstract), *American Journal of Sociology*, 51:233–237 (1945).

RICH, G. J., "The Tradition of Force and Punishment," *Nervous Child*, 5:222–225 (1946).

SHERMAN, ARTHUR WESLEY, JR., "Emancipation Status of College Students," *Pedagogical Seminary and Journal of Genetic Psychology*, 68:171–179 (1946).

SMITH, WILLIAM C., "The Stepchild," *American Sociological Review*, 10:237–242 (1945).

TAYLOR, KATHERINE WHITESIDE, *Do Adolescents Need Parents?* (New York: Appleton-Century-Crofts, Inc., 1938).

TORRANCE, PAUL, "The Influence of the Broken Home on Adolescent Adjustment," *Journal of Educational Sociology*, 18:359–364 (1945).

WILLOUGHBY, RAYMOND R., "A Study of Some Poorly Adjusted Families," *American Sociological Review*, 7:47–58 (1942).

WOLBERG, L. R., "The Character Structure of the Rejected Child," *Nervous Child*, 3:74–88 (1944).

Chapter 13. THE ADOLESCENT AND THE COMMUNITY

If you were the parent of a very young child, what would you want from the community for the sake of that child? He will not be old enough for school for several years; so schools are not a matter of immediate concern to you. He won't be going to the movies, listening to the radio, frequenting the library; he won't be studying the display of magazines on the newsstands; so these elements of the community will not matter for his sake one way or the other unless thereby you get helpful information on child rearing. Actually, of especial concern to you may be only whether or not the air is free from smoke and dust, whether or not you can find suitable housing at the price you can afford, whether or not the water and milk are pure, and whether or not the pediatrician is easily available.

But it is an entirely different matter if you are the parent of an adolescent. For your teen-aged boy or girl will be directly affected by the community in many ways, both within the home and in out-of-the-home activities. First of all, he will go to school, and at least five to seven of his most active hours will be spent in the buildings the community provides and under the direction of teachers the community hires. At other times, he will listen to the radio or look at television, go to movies, study parts of the daily paper, and skim through or read some magazines. All of these means of communication will affect his taste in entertainment, his emotional reactions, and his understandings—in ways you would approve of in some cases, but not in others.

Your teen-aged boy or girl will be greatly dependent upon the community for other recreation and other uses of his leisure time. Where will he spend his leisure with companions? The drugstore? The skating rink? Joe's Place? The Teen-Center? Which of these will have a good influence on him? Which will have a bad? Where can he go on a date? To a movie and then to a drugstore? Are there any other dating facilities?

What sports can he enjoy in the summer? Will the playgrounds be inviting? Will they be well supervised? Will there be some place where he can swim without cost? Play tennis? Play golf? Baseball? Will there be someone to teach him, if he doesn't know how and wants to learn?

How about winter sports? Does the community offer anything that will get him out into the open air in the winter?

How inviting will the church be to your teen-ager? Will it recognize the fact that he is not yet an adult, that he has special needs and special interests? Will it be able to work out a program of activities so pleasing that one adolescent will tell another that here is something that he shouldn't miss?

Will there be opportunities for young people to work together in the community, and will the opportunities be varied enough so that there will be appeal to all tastes, all interests, all abilities, and all of the adolescent age levels? Will the Boy Scout troops, the Boys' Club, the 4H clubs, and the like, be well organized and well directed?

What cultural opportunities will there be for your boy or girl? Will he be able to hear good music, see good painting and sculpture, take part in creative activities such as dancing, acting, and the like? Will the library win his patronage?

And how about the unfavorable side of the picture? Will there be temptations put in his path in the way of salacious literature, taverns, gambling, houses of prostitution, peddling of drugs, and burlesque shows?

If you were the parent of an adolescent, all of these matters would be of serious importance to you as you studied your community with your mind on your son's or daughter's welfare. But you would not be finished with your assessment even then. The whole picture would be something like this:

EVALUATING THE COMMUNITY'S SUITABILITY FOR YOUTH[1]

I. Does the community supply the resources needed by all children?
  A. Does it do everything possible to make the homes proper places for rearing children through:
    1. Adequate housing, street lighting, neighborhood beautification, and sanitation?
    2. Adult education for parents?
    3. Parent-teacher meetings?
    4. Promoting unified action by small groups of parents in setting standards and establishing policies governing the social activities of their children?
  B. Does the community provide adequate schooling?
    1. Are there good and well-equipped school buildings?
    2. Are there enough teachers, well prepared and adequately compensated?
    3. Are the school-attendance laws enforced?

[1] Adapted from "Controlling Juvenile Delinquency," U.S. Department of Labor, *Children's Bureau Publication* 311, 1943. Part IV is quoted in the chapter on Juvenile Delinquency.

4. Is there social service available to help the school with those students who are social and emotional problems?

5. Are the school buildings used to good purpose throughout the day and throughout the year?

C. Are the churches such as to provide real spiritual guidance and wholesome fellowship activities?

D. Does the community have good recreational facilities to take care of the needs of all areas, groups, and individuals?

II. Does the community protect the groups of children especially vulnerable to delinquency?

A. Children of employed mothers:

1. Does it provide the parents with counseling and information service?

2. Does it provide for their care in the absence of the mother through:

a. Foster-family day care?

b. Day-care centers?

c. Nursery schools?

d. Before- and after-school programs?

e. All-day vacation program?

B. Boys and girls in employment:

1. Does the community publicize good employment standards for young people?

2. Does it have an adequate staff for issuing employment and age certificates?

3. Does it see that boys and girls get good counseling and placement service?

4. Does it inspect workplaces?

5. Does it see that youth have adequate adult supervision on the job?

C. Mentally and physically handicapped children:

1. Does the community provide services whereby the handicapped may be discovered and diagnosed early?

2. Are the community services such that all handicapped may have adequate treatment, education, and social service?

D. Children in families in economic need: Are such families given financial assistance in line with the requirements and resources of the family?

III. Does the community have effective and suitable control of the harmful influences within it?

A. Does it have the legal authority for controlling places offering public refreshment or entertainment?

B. Does it have the legal authority for dealing with individuals contributing to the delinquency of minors?

C. Does it have the legal authority to eliminate the sale of obscene literature, liquor, and marijuana and similar drugs to minors; to close houses of prostitution and control conditions that lead to prostitution?

D. Does it have effective enforcement of these legal measures?

E. Does it have provision for observing and protecting youth in such public places as those providing public refreshment and streets, parks, and bus, train, and ferry terminals?

F. Has it secured the voluntary cooperation of commercial establishments in guarding the welfare of youth?

Obviously, the community in all of its aspects as they touch on youth is too large a topic to discuss in a chapter. We shall therefore give attention only to the social stratification of the community and its effect on the adolescent and to those phases of community life particularly of concern to youth and not discussed elsewhere—the church, the library, youth organizations, recreational opportunities in general, teen centers, youth participation in government, movies, television, and the radio, and influences in the community harmful to youth.

THE EFFECT OF SOCIAL STRATIFICATION

The social structure of a community affects the adolescent in many ways, depending on where his family falls in the social hierarchy. We shall illustrate this point by details and conclusions from Hollingshead's study[2] of the impact of social classes on adolescents in "Elmtown," a Middle Western community with a population of 6,000.

Five social classes are found in Elmtown:

Class I. The "society class," marked by wealth and inherited position.

Class II. Less exclusive than Class I, but having prestige because of economic success and civic leadership.

Class III. The middle class.

Class IV. Poor but honest and hard-working.

Class V. "Resigned to a life of frustration and defeat in a community that despises them for their disregard of morals, lack of 'success' goals, and dire poverty."

This social stratification affects the youth in several ways—in the courses he takes in high school, in the grades and honors he receives, in discipline (see Chap. 14), in his extracurricular participation, in the cliques of which he can become a member, in the people he can date, in the places he can go for recreation, and in his reasons for leaving school if he leaves before graduating.

There are three courses offered, the college preparatory, the general, and the commercial. Classes I and II concentrate on the college preparatory; Class III on the general; Classes IV and V on the general and com-

[2] August B. Hollingshead, *Elmtown's Youth* (New York: John Wiley & Sons, Inc., 1949).

mercial. The two upper classes, too, take it for granted that the good grades, honors, and student offices will fall to them, and teachers tend to fall in line with this idea and "act judiciously in their relations with the children of the powerful."

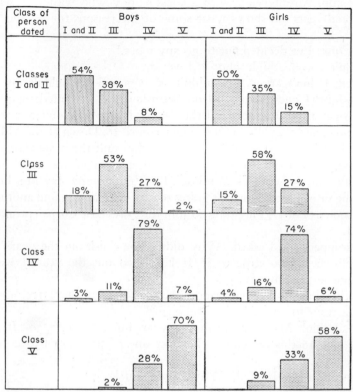

Fig. 33. Intraclass and interclass dating patterns of boys and girls, April, 1942. All dates reported by the Student Group are included. (Reprinted by permission from *Elmtown's Youth* by A. B. Hollingshead, published by John Wiley & Sons, Inc., 1949, p. 231.)

Every Class I and II student participates in extracurricular activities, but only 75 per cent of Class III, 57 per cent of Class IV, and 27 per cent of Class V participate.

Clique relationships are within the same class in 63 per cent of the cases and cross one class line in 33 per cent. In only 4 per cent of the cases were two class lines crossed. The situation is similar with dating, as Figure 33 shows.

There are three movie theaters. At the lower level is the Bright Star, patronized by Class V, with some Class IV's. At the upper level is the

Elmtown, patronized by Classes I, II, and III. Similarly with dances, the lower classes patronize one place, Morrow's Hall; the upper classes attend Country Club parties.

All of the Class I's and II's finish high school; only 11 per cent of the Class V's do. An interview with a Class V boy who withdrew when he was sixteen years old shows what some of the reasons for leaving school are:[3]

" 'I've quit. I've decided not to go any more.'

" 'Didn't you like high school?' I asked.

" 'Well, I don't know. I wouldn't say yes and I wouldn't say no. It was all right, I guess. I was 16 on Saturday, and I wanted to quit. I'm going to get a job. I understand they're paying twenty dollars a week at the Factory, and they'll take you when you're 16. Down at the Mill, they won't take you until you're 18. Frank Burton quit the other day, and he was down there a few days; when they found out he was only 16, they made him quit, so he's back in school. But Frank won't stay in school the rest of the year. He told me he's going to stay until he can find another job. Just as soon as I'm 17, I'm going to join the Navy Air Corps [pronounced Korpse].'

"He stopped, and I asked, 'Why didn't you finish out the year?'

" 'Well, there's no sense to it. If I finished out the year, I wouldn't finish high school anyway.'

"Another long pause. 'How does May [younger sister] feel about it? Does she want to go on?'

" 'No, I think May will finish this year, but she won't go after she's 16. She'll be 16 this December. Neither one of us wanted to come this year.'

"To prompt him I asked, 'Why didn't you?'

" 'Well, money and other things.'

"Another pause. 'What do you mean, money and other things?'

" 'You see, Dad's on pension [father, age 67, on old age assistance]; he's too old to work. My sister Josie, she's the one that works at the Mill, bought my books this year, and an aunt in the country bought May's books. Otherwise, we couldn't have come [this year].'

"A pause. 'Have you had a job?'

" 'I've set pins at the bowling alley all winter. I was just an extra down there. I worked after school sometimes to about midnight. The regular boys go to work at one o'clock in the afternoon and work until midnight or one o'clock. Us extra fellows didn't have to work after supper unless we wanted to, but I used to work most of the time. They pay you 5 cents

[3] Reprinted by permission from *Elmtown's Youth* by August B. Hollingshead, published by John Wiley & Sons, Inc., 1949, pp. 341–342.

a line, and what you earn depends on how many there are. The most I ever made was $9.85, but I worked every afternoon after school until one o'clock that week and all day Saturday and Saturday night. I usually made about $3.75 to $4.00. Of course, some weeks I only made $1.50 or $2.00. It just depends on how many lines you set up.'

"A long pause. I then asked, 'Did you have a good time in school?'

" 'I can't say I did. I was going out for football last fall and then I didn't. The folks didn't want me to. They were afraid I'd get hurt. I didn't go to any games all last year, and I didn't see any basketball games this year. I went to one dance, the Freshman Mixer. I didn't have a date. When I get a job, I'll have money, and I can have dates.'

" 'Whom are you going to date?'

" 'There's a girl that lives down on Eastern Avenue close to the canal. I want to date her. I don't know her name. I just know her and I like her.'

"After a long pause, I asked, 'If you could start over again and have things the way you wanted them, what would you do?'

" 'I'd like to live uptown, I'd like to have money, and I'd like to have clothes and dates. I'd like to go out for basketball and football, and I'd like to be in things. There are fellows like that in school.'

"Another pause followed by, 'How did you get along with them?'

" 'They treated me all right. They'd speak to me when they saw me, but I was different from them and they were different from me.' "

Hollingshead agrees that the operation of the class system in the schools brings inequalities of opportunity and treatment to youth not in harmony with the democratic ideal but that the whole problem of the class system in society is very complex and difficult to grasp, let alone try to solve.

In contrast to the conclusions of this lengthy report on Elmtown, we have a brief study of "Midwest," a town of 700 in the corn belt, by Barker, Wright, Nall, and Schoggen.[4] They conclude that there is no class bias in Midwest's high school.

The reader cannot judge the school in which he teaches by either report, of course. But knowing about Elmtown, he will be better able to evaluate conditions in his own locality.

THE IMPORTANCE OF UNDERSTANDING THE COMMUNITY'S SOCIAL STRUCTURE

The teacher is likely to be from a middle-class home himself, and he may too readily judge his students by his own background and interests. This will mislead him in many cases and work a hardship on those he mis-

[4] Roger G. Barker, Herbert F. Wright, Jack Nall, and Phil Schoggen, "There Is No Class Bias in Our School," *Progressive Education*, 27:106–110 (1950).

understands and misjudges. Havighurst believes that if all teachers understand the community's social structure (1) they will understand the motivations of their pupils better—why some take to books, others don't; why some value education, others don't; (2) they will understand better the abilities of children from social classes other than the teacher's; (3) they will understand the peer culture better; and (4) they will understand better what the school means to the different social classes.[5]

As an example, we may cite the class differences in Elmtown as far as attitudes of parents toward school are concerned:[6]

Class I and II: High educational goals for them set by parents. Parents expect them to be leaders.

Class III: Parents place great emphasis upon grades and extracurricular activities.

Class IV: Have little appreciation of the work the school is doing or of what the child will get out of it, but "some of these parents have a blind, almost pathetic, faith that education will enable their children to gain something from life that was denied to them."

Class V: "A high school education is outside the experience of class V parents, and beyond the expectancy of most of their children. The principal ambition of the class V child is to grow up and escape from the authority symbolized by his parents and teachers."

THE CHURCH

The church is the institution whose avowed purpose is to offer spiritual guidance to a people. It also provides wholesome fellowship opportunities. No one would deny that the adolescent would profit by such guidance and such fellowship if the church could reach him, nor, probably, does any church fail to realize the necessity for working with the adolescent. Sermons are sometimes given especially for him, Sunday school classes are maintained for him, and youth groups are organized under church sponsorship—youth groups such as American Unitarian Youth, Girls Friendly Society, International Society of Christian Endeavor, International Walther League, Luther League of America, Methodist Youth Fellowship, Youth Fellowship of the Reformed Church of America, B'nai B'rith Youth Organization, and others.

In spite of this fact, probably 50 per cent of the adolescent population does not participate in church activities, as witness the data in Table 50.

We may assume that the strongest reason for the presence or absence of adolescents in church, Sunday school, or other church activities is

[5] Robert J. Havighurst, "Knowledge of Class Status Can Make a Difference," *Progressive Education*, 27:97–105 (1950).

[6] Hollingshead, *op. cit.*, p. 178.

family attitude and custom. In this respect homes may be classified into four groups:

Group I. In this type of home the parents attend church conscientiously each Sunday and see that the children are regular in their attendance at Sunday school, and perhaps at church as well. There is a strong feeling that such participation is necessary and right for all.

Group II. In this type of home the parents' attitude toward the church is favorable although their attendance is intermittent. The children go to Sunday

TABLE 50. YOUTH PARTICIPATION IN CHURCH ACTIVITIES*

Location of study	Year	Number	Findings
Maryland......................	1938	13,528	71% are members of some church 44.5% go to church once a week 43.7% participated in recreational activities
Washington....................	1949	5,500	53.3% are members of some church 28.7% attend church or other religious group once a week
A Middle Western town of 6,000...	1946	81	71% attended church regularly
Missouri......................	1947	840	50.2% engage in religious activity each week

* Howard M. Bell, *Youth Tell Their Story* (Washington: American Council on Education, 1938), pp. 196, 197, 203; L. J. Elias, *High School Youth Look at Their Problems* (Pullman, Wash.: State College of Washington, 1949), pp. 3, 32; Emma Beekman, "What High School Seniors Think of Religion," *Religious Education*, 42:333–337 (1947); Edward B. Olds, "How Do Young People Use Their Leisure Time?" *Recreation*, 42:458–463 (1949).

school, but the parents relax their insistence on some church participation when adolescence comes.

Group III. In this type of home the parents do not attend church, and it does not make much difference to them whether or not the children have any church experience.

Group IV. In this type of home the parents are antagonistic toward the church.

The church is fairly well assured of support from adolescents of the first type of home. It must win and hold those from the three other types. What does it have to offer them?

A spiritual experience through prayer, ritual, music, and the very atmosphere of the church.

Inspiration for living more worthily.

Directives as to how to live.

Guidance and counseling on personal problems.

A sense of fellowship with others in the church.

A sense of security.

A sense of worth.

Actual companionship.

Recreation through church-group programs, social get-togethers, and parties.

All of this is good, but that does not necessarily make it appealing to many adolescents. In their revolt against adult authority, they revolt too against church demands for spirituality and goodness. In their desire for companionship and recreation, many of them will not seek the church—both because it has associations with sanctimony which they dislike and because there are competing activities which promise more entertainment, more excitement, or more freedom.

Nevertheless, if the church *is* to appeal to the adolescent who is not church-minded, it must win him through the avenues of companionship and recreation offered and then it must hold him by meeting his needs for spiritual direction, guidance, and counseling in terms and in ways that have meaning for him and are adjusted to his problems in the present-day world.

THE LIBRARY

Almost every community has a public library which provides many services to the adolescent. Popular teen-age magazines (*Open Road for Boys, Model Airplanes, Stamps, Seventeen, American Girl*), many shelves of boys' books and girls' books, a quiet place to study with all of the standard reference books available, librarians who are sincerely interested in being helpful—all are there for the adolescent who will use them. Some do; many don't.

At first thought the fact that many teen-agers do not use the library, is a matter for regret. The library has much pleasure in store for those who will partake of it—books of adventure, travel, biography, science, and fiction. Those who "read the library through" in their youth know what delight it gave them and wish the same for all of today's boys and girls. But many of these young people are spending their time in more lively pursuits than in reading. For the period of adolescence these may be worthy alternatives.

In other words, while we are pleased when a well-adjusted adolescent includes the library resources in his leisure-time activities, still we must not bewail the fact that many do not *if* their lives are otherwise well filled with happy and wholesome school, social, and sports activities.

YOUTH ORGANIZATIONS

There are a great number of organizations for youth which offer opportunities for recreation, for learning new skills, for group work activities, and the like. Some of these are church auxiliaries, some are associated with other adult organizations, and some are independent of any adult affiliation and exist solely for youth. A number of these will be described, for certainly anyone who is working with the adolescent should know what organizational opportunities the community offers him.

American Junior Red Cross. Membership in 1946: 19,326,747. This organization is affiliated with the American National Red Cross, and it exists in the elementary and high schools only, not outside the school. It engages in service activities, and its purpose is "to contribute to the educational objectives of schools, to the social education of young people, and to provide participation in the achievement of the general objectives and responsibilities of the American Red Cross."[7]

Boy Scouts of America. Youth membership: 1,457,402. Its purpose is "to promote, through organization and through cooperation with other agencies, the ability of boys to do things for themselves and others; to train them in Scoutcraft; and to teach them patriotism, courage, self-reliance, and kindred virtues, by placing emphasis upon character development, citizenship training, and physical fitness."

There are three groupings of members:

Cub Packs (nine through eleven), with activities centered around the home.
Scout Troops (twelve and up), with activities based on outdoor life.
Senior Scouts (fifteen and up), with activities based on three programs—air scouting, explorer scouting, and sea scouting.

"Each Scout unit is supported by a church, school, service club, or a group of citizens. The permanency of each unit is guaranteed for at least a year by the institution; a meeting room and facilities are provided (except in the case of Cub Packs), and every boy has an opportunity for ten days and nights of outdoor experience under the guidance of three male adults."[8]

Boys' Clubs of America, Inc. Membership, boys between eight and

[7] M. M. Chambers, *Youth-serving Organizations* (Washington: American Council on Education, 1948), pp. 10–116. All of the data on youth organizations have been obtained from this source unless otherwise indicated.
[8] *Ibid.*, p. 12.

twenty: 275,000. This is an organization for the underprivileged boy. Each club usually has its own building and offers such opportunities as "recreation, social activities, physical training, athletics, swimming and life saving, libraries and reading rooms, vocational classes, group clubs, Boy Scouts, medical examinations and correction, vocational, behavior, and attitude guidance."[9]

Camp Fire Girls, Inc. Membership: 360,000. There are three groups within this organization: Blue Birds (seven to nine), Camp Fire Girls (ten to fifteen), and Horizon Clubs (fifteen to eighteen). They offer wholesome leisure-time activities with considerable emphasis on woodcraft and camping. As Wrenn says: "A distinctive characteristic of the Camp Fire Girls is an elaborate ritual incorporating elements from Indian legend. This is intended to stimulate imagination and invest the ordinary relationships of life with beauty and a new significance."[10]

Girl Scouts, Inc. Membership (girls and women): 1,213,913. Though not affiliated with the Boy Scouts, this is similar to that organization. It too has three groupings: Brownie Scouts (seven to nine), Intermediate Scouts (ten to fourteen), and Senior Scouts (fifteen to eighteen). There is a volunteer leader and assistant for each troop, and the activities engaged in offer practical information about homemaking, nature, outdoor living, sports and games, music and dancing, literature and dramatics, health and safety, arts and crafts, community life, and international friendship. As with the Boy Scouts, merit badges are earned through proficiencies developed.

Grand Council of the Order of DeMolay. Membership, boys fourteen to twenty: 85,467. Though DeMolay is not a Masonic organization, each chapter is sponsored by some Masonic group. Any youth of suitable age and good character is eligible. "For the development of all-round character and good citizenship, the organization promotes good scholarship, student leadership, vocational selection, athletics, amateur music and dramatics, self-control, and thrift, in addition to numerous other activities pointing toward the ideals it upholds."[11]

Order of the Rainbow for Girls. Membership, girls thirteen to twenty: 125,000. As in the above, membership in this organization is not restricted, although each chapter is sponsored by Masons or Eastern Stars.

Young Men's Christian Association. Many communities in the United States have a YMCA association with a building offering gymnasium, clubrooms, hotel facilities, a swimming pool, and so on.

[9] *Ibid.*, p. 13.
[10] C. Gilbert Wrenn, *Time on Their Hands* (Washington: American Council on Education, 1941), p. 115.
[11] Chambers, *op. cit.*, p. 16.

" . . . the typical 'Y' program contains an assortment of young people's clubs, either of specialized interest or intended to promote general, all-round development. There are said to be over 15,000 of these groups for young men.

"Hi-Y clubs enroll 200,000 members in 6,500 local units. They encourage voluntary activity among boys for the improvement of school and community life. State, regional, and national camps are popular parts of their program. Some attention is given to social affairs, sports, and hobbies."[12]

Young Women's Christian Association. This is similar to the YMCA though the building facilities are not so elaborate. The YWCA sponsors the Y-Teen clubs for girls of high school age, many of which are located in schools although sometimes the meeting place is the library, the YWCA building, or elsewhere. These clubs supply wholesome companionship in recreation and work projects of various kinds as well as help on the problems of adolescence through discussion, talks, panels, and so on.

4-H Clubs. Membership, between ten and twenty-one: 700,000 boys and 800,000 girls. These clubs, conducted by the Extension Service of the U.S. Department of Agriculture, give instruction in farming and homemaking. Each club has "regular meetings, demonstrations, tours, exhibits, judging events, and social and recreational activities."[13] The girls for the most part work on clothing, management of the home, preparing of meals, and so on. The boys for the most part have garden projects, poultry, sow-and-litter, and dairy-calf projects, and the like.

Future Farmers of America. Membership: 206,039. The boys that belong to this organization are those studying vocational agriculture in public high schools under the provisions of the National Vocational Education Act.

Future Homemakers of America, Inc. Membership: 168,259. Membership is voluntary but is limited to those in homemaking or home-economics classes in high school or those still in school who have been so enrolled.

American Youth Hostels, Inc. Hostels where young people on bicycling or hiking tours may stay overnight at a cost of 25 cents per person are found in chains and networks in 28 states of the United States. They are under the supervision of a resident house parent and his wife. Their purpose is "to help all persons, especially young people, to a greater knowledge, understanding, and love of the world; to enable them through hosteling to enjoy the cultural benefits of travel and live happier and healthier lives."[14]

[12] Wrenn, op. cit., pp. 116–117.
[13] Chambers, op. cit., p. 65.
[14] Ibid., p. 116.

Many other organizations of the nature of these might be mentioned. The reader is urged to find out which ones are serving his own community and the nature of the services they are rendering.

How many youth participate in the activities of community organizations? Table 51 indicates what three studies have found.

From a Missouri study of 840 high school students, we have the record of participation given in Table 52.

TABLE 51. YOUTH PARTICIPATION IN CLUBS*

Location	Date	Participation	Per cent
Maryland...............	1938	Belong to no club	74.5%
Missouri................	1947	Engaged in club activity	46.0%
		Average hours per week	2.75
New York...............	1940	Engage in club activity often	12.9%

* H. M. Bell, *Youth Tell Their Story* (Washington: American Council on Education, 1938), p. 168; Edward B. Olds, "How Do Young People Use Their Leisure Time?" *Recreation*, 42:458–463 (1949). Nettie Pauline McGill and Ellen Nathalie Matthews, *The Youth of New York City* (New York: The Macmillan Company, 1940), p. 222.

TABLE 52. TYPE OF ORGANIZATIONAL AFFILIATIONS OF UNIVERSITY CITY HIGH SCHOOL STUDENTS*

Type of organization	Total	Boys	Girls
Libraries...	126	47	79
School clubs and councils...........................	65	21	44
Jewish national program groups......................	22	2	20
YMCA and YWCA.................................	93	45	48
YMHA and YWHA...............................	33	20	13
Boy and Girl Scouts...............................	73	62	11
Other Community Chest agencies.....................	8	4	4
Music organizations................................	5	3	2
Religious bodies (choirs, Sunday schools, youth associations, churches, and so forth)......................	360	158	202
Masonic junior organizations........................	35	19	16
Hobby clubs......................................	19	18	1
Game clubs.......................................	20	11	9
Skating and riding clubs............................	6	2	4
Sports groups.....................................	8	3	5
Country clubs and Missouri Athletic Club..............	4	4	0
Social groups other than sororities and fraternities........	279	114	165
Miscellaneous.....................................	14	5	0

* Edward B. Olds, "How Do Young People Use Their Leisure Time?" *Recreation*, 42:458–463 (1949).

These figures do not add up to the total of young people included in this survey because some youths reported several organizational affiliations.

The value of each of the numerous organizations for adolescents depends upon the objectives of the organization, the kinds of activities engaged in, the facilities for making the work inviting and effective, and the leadership secured. On the surface all of the youth organizations have the best of intentions to do well by their members. In practice a particular organization's worth may be high in one community, low in another. Just the information that a boy or girl belongs to a certain youth group is no assurance that he is benefiting by that membership.

RECREATION

Everyone needs recreation. No life can be called well balanced if a place is not made in it for a variety of healthful and enjoyable recreational activities. William C. Menninger, writing on recreation and mental health, tells of a survey made some years ago at the Menninger Clinic. A group of well-adjusted individuals were compared with a group of people, now psychiatric patients, in regard to the matter of the type, number, and duration of their hobbies. It was found that the well-adjusted had many more hobbies and pursued them with much greater intensity than did those who were now patients. The conclusion was that people are well adjusted partly because they have strong recreational interests.

Menninger discusses three ways in which recreation contributes to mental health. First, he says, people are often prevented from expressing their need to be aggressive by the restrictions of school or their jobs. Such persons can satisfy their aggressive desires in games of all kinds, though particularly in games in which there is bodily activity. Second, we all have a drive to be constructive or creative, he says, and this drive can be satisfied through creative hobbies. Third, we need relaxation, and this is something that listening to music, seeing a ball game or a movie, reading a mystery book, or studying art masterpieces can give us.[15]

Health, whether it be physical or mental, is not the only reason for engaging in recreation. Recreation also provides opportunity to satisfy one's social needs more fully. This is important at any age, but it is especially so during adolescence, when the youth is making his heterosexual adjustments and developing his adult viewpoints, standards, and habits of living. There is, of course, social opportunity at school and at home, but the greatest variation in social participation can only occur in recreation where the boy or girl may engage in physical activity or in quieter games with others, in dancing, in working at something pleasurable together, or in just talking. If knowing many people in many different situations

[15] William C. Menninger, "Recreation and Mental Health," Recreation, 42:340–346 (1948).

and in many different activities gives one some of the rewards of living, then recreation is a necessity.

Everyone takes pleasure in creative activity of one sort or another—in making a hat, in painting a picture, in doing carpentry, in raising vegetables, in decorating a room, in writing a poem, in tinkering with a car, and so on. Here is another need that recreation serves, as Menninger has

TABLE 53. COMPARATIVE PREFERENCES FOR ENGAGING MORE IN EACH ACTIVITY*

| Activity | Engage in activity more if there were more | | | |
| | Time | | Facilities | |
	Boys	Girls	Boys	Girls
Supervised sports	66	45	40	31
Unsupervised sports	60	17	47	33
Concerts, plays, and lectures	24	50	32	51
Watching sports	39	21	31	30
Hobbies	33	37	24	15
Reading	28	65	3	6
Chaperoned parties	15	26	25	25
Musical activities	19	43	7	8
Unchaperoned parties	26	31	8	12
Movies	19	31	8	12
Games	17	15	26	15
Classes	6	27	8	31
Loafing with friends	20	23	8	9
School activities	17	18	8	10
Jobs or housework	18	7	17	11
Club activities	12	16	11	13
Radio listening	15	12	5	5
Religious activities	7	10	4	9
Scout activities	11	3	3	5
Studying	6	9	2	2
Loafing alone	1	2	1	1

* Edward B. Olds, "How Do Young People Use Their Leisure Time?" *Recreation*, 42:458–463 (1949).

mentioned from a different point of view. It provides enjoyable ways of accomplishing something into which one has put his wholehearted interest. Hobbies are of countless variation, and every adolescent should be introduced to some, both for his present well-being and for the sake of his having such habits and interest in adulthood.

In Olds's study (Table 53) we see that some of the 840 Missouri high school students said that they would engage in more sports, concerts, plays, and lectures, hobbies, chaperoned parties, musical activities, games, and club activities if there were more facilities. When we consider that among the boys there were 212 such expressions of desire for better facilities and among the girls 191, this takes on significance.

It is generally recognized that many communities, if not most, do not have adequate recreational facilities. We get an idea of how communities vary when we look at the survey for community recreation in 1946 presented in Table 54. Notice that although 1,268 cities reported having softball, only about half as many offered social dancing, less than a half as many offered skating, and only about one-fourth offered other winter sports. Other comparisons will be interesting.

According to an article in *Recreation*, the outstanding lacks in present services are (1) not enough recreational space and facilities, (2) not enough adequately trained personnel, (3) poor coordination of recreation services, (4) lack of balance and quality in community programs, (5) girls and women, minority, low-income, rural, and aged groups underserved, (6) inadequate financial provision, and (7) hospitals and institutions inadequately served.[16]

An account of the recreation of a city of 10,000 (Presque Isle, Maine) pictures the opportunities in one community:[17]

"Briefly, the present setup of the recreational program is this. Headquarters for all recreational activities is the ornate building erected as a USO center during World War II and purchased by the city last September at a cost of $25,000.

"The building, located on South Main Street within easy walking distance from the business section, boasts a large auditorium, a lounge and snack bar, a stage for the presentation of amateur theatricals, two music rooms at one end of the hall, three offices at the other end, ample checkrooms for public functions and a hobby room downstairs currently in use as a darkroom for amateur photographers.

"When the auditorium is in use, it is just that. The hall has been used for banquets, dances and meetings of a public nature. The last adult visitor will hardly be out of the hall before a transformation occurs.

"Out from their places beside the walls come ping-pong tables, pool tables, a miniature bowling alley, juke boxes, domino, checker and chess sets—almost every kind of equipment one needs for amusement. The lounge serves, ordinarily, as a spot where the more serious may read papers, magazines and other literature made available to youth . . . .

"An outstanding feature of the recreation program is Club 21. This organization is composed of teen-agers, has already admitted 100 to membership and is in the process of admitting many more. It has its own officers, a bank balance—and more constructive ideas than one could

[16] "Recreation—A Basic Human Need," *Recreation*, 41:578–579 (1948).

[17] Elmer Ingalls, "Recreation Center Pays Dividends," *Recreation*, 41:335–336 (1947).

TABLE 54. COMMUNITY RECREATION IN 1,268 CITIES*

	Cities Reporting		Cities Reporting
Arts and crafts:		**Music:**	
Art activities	642	Community singing	485
Handcrafts	968	Opera groups	32
Athletics and games:		Choral groups	335
Archery	448	Symphony orchestras	86
Athletic tests	598	Other instrumental groups	314
Badminton	800	**Outing activities:**	
Baseball	1,212	Camping	245
Basketball	1,099	Gardening	139
Bowling—indoor	196	Hiking	567
Bowling on the green	110	Nature activities	407
Boxing	539	Picnicking	792
Croquet	657	**Water sports:**	
Field hockey	101	Boating	141
Football—regulation	345	Model boating	74
Football—six-man	179	Swimming	981
Football—touch	721	Swimming tests (NRA)	369
Golf	331	**Winter sports:**	
Handball	294	Coasting	284
Horseshoes	1,072	Ice hockey	246
Paddle tennis	685	Skating	594
Roque	69	Skiing	284
Shooting	116	Tobogganing	143
Shuffleboard	584	**Miscellaneous:**	
Soccer	406	Activities for old people	264
Softball	1,268	Card clubs	231
Table tennis	946	Circus	155
Tennis	1,003	Community celebrations	580
Track and field	667	First-aid classes	357
Volleyball	1,049	Forums, discussion groups	207
Dancing:		Game-room activities	580
Folk dancing	515	Hobby clubs or groups	414
Social dancing	659	Holiday observances	477
Square dancing	472	Model aircraft	316
Tap dancing	235	Motion pictures	491
Drama:		Photography	295
Drama clubs	302	Playground newspaper	183
Festivals	283	Safety activities	384
Little-theater groups	172	Social recreation	654
Pageants	252	Supervised bicycling	197
Plays	399	Supervised roller skating	238
Puppets and marionettes	192		
Storytelling	807		

* *Recreation*, 41:109–118 (1947).

enumerate in a ream of paper. Latest proposal is a mimeographed newspaper and don't be too surprised if it makes its appearance shortly. These
youths have a way of getting things done.

"When the weather gets a little warmer, the youngsters will be flocking
outdoors—to the community swimming pool and playground named for
the Rev. Milton Grant, an ardent exponent of recreation for children.

"At the swimming pool, there are life guards in attendance constantly,
playground directors in charge of the swings, slides and extensive equipment available to the children. It is at this spot that the Abnaki has been
staging its annual Children's Day observances, which draw thousands of
youngsters.

"Located also at the playground is a softball diamond, used during the
day by the youngsters, after supper by a multitude of adult softball teams
playing a rigorous schedule.

"During the winter months, Presque Isle's youths may participate in
the activities at the Recreation Center—or may avail themselves of
facilities at Aroostook State Park, Echo Lake, or, if the brisk outdoor air
appeals, the Veterans of Foreign Wars run a supervised skating rink on
Presque Isle stream. The Community Association helps in the support of
this project, the city itself contributes and, most of all, the veterans themselves pour plenty of time and money and effort into keeping it going.

"Most of this story has dealt with the youth and their program. What
of the adult? The recreational program takes in the projects sponsored
by the Presque Isle Community Association—and they are almost too
numerous to mention. Briefly, a Little Theater group starts a series of
offerings this month. There is a photography club. A city bowling league
has just completed its schedule. There is adult competition in softball.

"In short, the city of Presque Isle offers its youths and adults almost
any kind of recreation desired—so long as it's clean and wholesome."

A community should provide good public recreational resources for
the adolescent (as well as for the other age groups, of course). This is not
enough, however, to ensure all adolescents partaking of them as much as
would seem advisable. Lack of time on the part of those who work will
prevent their participation. Inertia will prevail against it for others. And,
as Edgren says,[18] many do not respond to recreational opportunities because in them fear conflicts with desire and fear wins out.

In addition the community provides commercial recreation or loafing
spots which draw patronage from youth. This is of all varieties—some
wholesome, some not, some supervised for the good of the teen-agers,

[18] Harry D. Edgren, "Recreation—Its Meaning for Youth," *Recreation*, 43:439–440
(1949).

most supervised only to the extent that property is protected from damage. Examples, described by college students observing them, are:

A bowling alley: "On Saturday mornings the high school youth have their bowling league. They meet promptly at ten and utilize all twenty-four-lanes from ten through the afternoon. Approximately 120 boys and girls participate. The manager has several adult supervisors and parents attend the league once in a while."

A drug store: "After school the high school students, average age 16, sit in booths, smoke, joke, laugh, show off, drink cokes, eat sundaes, and make dates. There are usually about twenty there in the late afternoon. These students also meet at the drug store at night just to loaf and kill time. Fellows bring dates in for a coke and to talk after a show. The place teems with activity after athletic events. The proprietor is very strict. No loud talking, no singing, no scuffling, no feet on furniture, no loud cursing, no drinking, and not too much loafing are allowed."

A pool room: "Between 3:30 and 5, and between 7 and 11 there are usually twelve to fifteen high school boys of ages from 14 to 20 here playing pool, snooker, and the pin ball machines, and as well kibitzing, cussing, wagering, arguing, drinking soft drinks, and loafing. There is almost no supervision except that scuffling or fighting is stopped and the property of the pool room is protected. The behavior and talk are sometimes very rough and crude."

The roller-skating rink: "A great many adolescents are here every evening where they roller skate, clown on skates, play games on skates, smoke, gossip, and make new acquaintances. There is not much supervision. Some drinking occurs immediately outside the rink."

Ideally, all community meeting and recreational places for youth would have standards ensuring decent conduct. But both this problem and that of getting all young people to use the recreational facilities provided by the community (assuming that the community *is* making adequate provision) are not ones that can be solved overnight. The best ready-at-hand instrument for furthering good recreational interests is the school. If the school can see that each adolescent develops the skills needed in a variety of games and sports, gets an enjoyable taste of a wide range of ways of spending his leisure time, and becomes habituated to engaging in several kinds of worth-while activities, then the youth can be better trusted to use good judgment in where he goes and what he does during his leisure.

YOUTH CENTERS

Probably everyone understands what the youth center (otherwise known as the *teen canteen, youth canteen,* or *teen town*) is—a room, a number of rooms, or a building where young people can get together and enjoy the kind of recreation they choose, whether it be dancing to a juke box, playing ping-pong, just talking, eating, playing cards, or engaging in some project. Youth centers are generally youth-managed though customarily there is also adult supervision.

The youth center grew up during the war, and it has been estimated that by the spring of 1945 at least 3,000 were in existence.[19] At present there are doubtless many more, for in any state one is apt to hear periodically of a new one being built.

There are many problems that arise in connection with youth centers:

Financing: First of all, a place must be provided, a place that is large enough to supply plenty of space for many adolescents and for many different kinds of activities. Naturally the attractiveness of the building, of the rooms, and of the equipment will contribute to the appeal the youth center has for the community's young people. Second, there is the matter of upkeep, not only in the way of electricity, cleaning, fuel, and so on, but also in the matter of employing trained adults to guide the center. Sometimes this is taken care of through taxation; more often it is handled through private contributions. It is probably unnecessary to point out that many difficulties arise in connection with getting adequate funds and that often there is such insufficiency that not only is the place unattractive but also the adult supervision dangerously limited both in quantity and quality.

Membership: Bridges writes:[20]

"Experience has caused thoughtful questions about membership to arise. For example, can youngsters of junior and senior high school ages be mixed? Apparently it cannot be done satisfactorily, for many canteens are assigning special periods for junior high members only. Can youth who go to school and youth who work be mixed? Some say yes, believing in the advantages of shared experience. Others say that interests are different and that provision should be made for separate programs. The advantages and disadvantages of large memberships are questioned. The downtown urban center for those who like to go in search of activity versus the convenient neighborhood center is a debated point. Can rural youth and youth in small communities use the same center? Although one center reports that on Saturday nights when rural youth come in, local youth stay away, these two groups are using some centers."

[19] George B. Corwin, "The Teen-age Canteen and Social Group Work," *Proceedings of the National Conference of Social Work* (New York: Columbia University Press, 1947), p. 244.

[20] Bernice Bridges, "Teen-age Centers," *Proceedings of the National Conference of Social Work* (New York: Columbia University Press, 1945), pp. 265–266.

In a youth center in one town the boys and girls who are the socially elite have largely taken it over, and while some young people of lower income brackets do go there, a number stay away because they are not comfortable competing with those socially and economically better off. Another center has won the reputation of being for the underprivileged, and when a boy of wealthy parentage was asked whether or not he ever went to the teen canteen, he answered scornfully, "Why, of course not."

Ideally, one would think, young people of all social and economic levels might mingle and enjoy life together, and this leveling of class barriers could well be one of the objectives of the adult leaders. It cannot, of course, be achieved by preaching it or by authority. When youth centers are obviously "managed" for the "good" of the boys and girls, their usefulness declines, for adolescents feel that they have too much "managing" as it is, and they are not likely to spend their free time where they will get more of it.

Leadership: Boys and girls should have much of the management of the center put in their hands. They want this, they are able to handle their own affairs, and they need the chance to learn to make plans, to handle money, to set up standards, to provide group discipline, and the like. With this they need skillful adult help from leaders who have the ability to get along well with young people, who know what boys and girls want in the way of relaxation and recreation, who have vision as to the kind of wholesome pleasure they might enjoy, who have confidence in the ability of youth to manage their own affairs, and who feel no personality need to dominate. Bridges[21] notes that "in one youth-serving agency, six young case workers in addition to two experienced group workers, mingle regularly with the boys and girls. They are liked by the youngsters and find ample opportunity to help." She also says that professional workers have two major responsibilities, to help youth work out a satisfying and desirable program and to assist volunteer leaders in understanding how they can be the most helpful.[22]

Standards for behavior: Again we quote from Bridges:[23]

"One of the questions which must be dealt with, both by active youth councils and by adult leaders, and for which there is no simple answer, is: 'How much behavior which does not conform to accepted middle-class patterns can we afford to allow?'

"Quite generally, youth councils have voted to confine smoking to certain rooms, and to rule out drinking, gambling, necking, rowdyism, and property destruction. Where the majority of the members consider

[21] *Ibid.*, p. 267.
[22] *Ibid.*, p. 269.
[23] *Ibid.*, pp. 270–271.

such behavior as unfitting and antisocial, it is comparatively simple for the teen-agers themselves to enforce rules which serve as controls to the few who might break over. If, however, a majority of the members is accustomed to such behavior, too rigid enforcement of rules at the beginning may leave us without a group. If we want these youngsters to come in, we may have to relax a few of the usual standards somewhat. This does not mean giving approval to such behavior; rather it means that this antisocial behavior is usual for some youngsters. If we hope to see them move toward socially acceptable behavior and attitudes, we must begin where they are, not where we think they should be. Judgment about what is too fast or too slow progress requires the most skilled leadership."

In summary, Barbour suggests these four "musts" for teen-age centers:[24]

1. The club should serve only one community or neighborhood and a limited age range. The boys and girls who frequent the club center should know each other, for then all will feel a greater responsibility for the common good. The anonymity of a large organization can be dangerous.

2. The club center should be governed by a small elected body, with one of the members some well-liked and capable adult.

3. Loose financial management will wreck a club. The receiving and spending of money should be controlled by a joint committee of young people and adults.

4. Club activities should always be chaperoned by responsible adults.

YOUTH PARTICIPATION IN COMMUNITY COUNCILS

Communities are run by adults. The mayor or the city manager, the city council or board of commissioners, the policemen, the judges and juries, the teachers, the voters—all are adults, of course, and properly so. But within their community is a large body of near-adults—people who read adult newspapers, partake of adult recreation, are led into adult crime, suffer from adult mismanagements. Many people have questioned whether true democracy and true regard for the rights and the needs of youth would not insist that youth have some share in community government.

Some communities which have tried to meet this problem have invited representatives from the community youth to participate as full-fledged members of the community coordinating council.

When adolescents are members of a community council, as Stein says:[25]

[24] Richmond Barbour, "Whoa! 4 Musts for Teen-age Centers," *Clearing House,* 20:220–221 (1945).

[25] Abe B. Stein, "Adolescent Participation in Community Co-ordinating Councils," *Journal of Educational Sociology,* 21:177–183 (1947).

"[They] should not be exploited and asked to perform chores that are as hateful to them as they are to adults unless both groups share equally in the performance of these chores. The adolescents' duties as members of the council are not to be belittled and disdained by asking them to clean up the parks, to be kind to animals, to do one good deed a day, etc. These may be admirable services, but adolescents may consider such requests as being childish and overworked, and they can easily point to adults who violate these same 'boy scout' details. The council must maintain complete respect for its young constituents by allowing them equal representation and respect together with all groups. Boys and girls should not be asked to do the work without having participated in the planning, and without an understanding of the values of the outcome. If a group of students accepts a phase of a community problem to work on, helps plan the method of attack, carries it through to conclusion and evaluates the outcome in terms of its purposes and plans, the service has been an excellent learning experience for all concerned."

In some communities the youth participate actively in organizing and supplying the recreational opportunities for young people. An example is the Manhasset Youth Council.[26] This is a body of more than 400 boys and girls between the ages of thirteen and eighteen, governed by an Executive Board made up of elected officers and members of the executive committee, presidents and chairmen of all clubs and activities within the Council, and the boys and girls who have been designated the official representatives for each youth group in the city, such as Boy Scouts, Girl Scouts, Junior Red Cross, Police Boys' Club, and the like.

The Youth Council has a committee designed to lessen vandalism, another to strengthen controls on the sale of liquor to minors, and committees to provide a varied and attractive program of club and other activities, such as a chess club, a drama group, rifle club, radio club, square dancers, and the like.

The Youth Council is in charge of the Youth Center (the "Juke Box").

Any young person of any sect or race may join the Youth Council. There are no dues, but each member purchases the sterling-silver recognition pin (at a cost of 78 cents) which is required for entrance to the Juke Box, for voting, and for participation in other Youth Council activities.

MOVIES, TELEVISION, AND RADIO

Every person is molded by the life he lives from infancy on. He learns by what he sees, hears, tastes, touches, and feels. He is a mosaic of the

[26] Jay Jostyn, "The Manhasset Youth Council," *Journal of Educational Sociology*, 18:417–425 (1945).

thousands upon thousands of experiences he has had. We should realize, then, that since radio, television, and movies contribute to the experience of almost every child and youth in our culture, they are inevitably some of his teachers. They help make him what he is.

What then do they do for the adolescent? Is their influence good or bad?

In most cases they probably do nothing spectacularly bad. In one study of what psychiatrists believe regarding the effect of these media on children,[27] there seemed to be a consensus to this effect: Radio and the movies do not originate personality disorders in children. Rather they only re-awaken or intensify them if they are already existent in the child.

In a similar way we may make the following statement about the adolescent: No radio, television, or movie programs originate anxieties, unwholesome attitudes, bad habits, or delinquent behavior in the boy or girl, but if the seed for these things already exists, some radio, television, and movie programs he hears and sees may stir them into action or give them emphases which are not wholesome. A girl who has the idea that sex appeal is all that counts in a woman's search for happiness will have substantiation for her belief in some of the movies she sees. A boy whose understanding of the responsibilities and obligations of marriage is so slight as to allow him to believe that one can fall in love one week and properly propose the next—and then be happily married and live that way "forever"—can discover in some movies that (moviewise!) it *does* happen that way. The boy who is already moving in the direction of delinquency can see the bad man idealized in a movie and can learn techniques of crime.

One question we must ask about movies, radio, and television, then, is: What are they doing to the young person who is already growing in undesirable directions? In writing about the movies, Forman concludes:[28]

"A number of adolescent and youthful criminals give circumstantial accounts of their path to, and arrival at, criminality, and, rightly or wrongly, but very positively, they blame the movies for their downfall. In cases cited by both Blumer and Thrasher, they tell of learning their criminal techniques from certain of the movies; Blumer's list alone included thirty-one different techniques culled from autobiographic accounts of delinquents—all movie-acquired. . . .

"Similarly, large percentages of girl inmates in an institution for sex delinquents rightly or wrongly attribute to the movies a leading place in stimulating cravings for an easy life, for luxury, for cabarets, road-houses

---

[27] "Chills and Thrills in Radio, Movies and Comics," some psychiatric opinion reported by Josette Frank, *Child Study*, Spring, 1948, pp. 42–46, 48.

[28] Henry James Forman, *Our Movie Made Children* (New York: The Macmillan Company, 1935), pp. 280–281.

and wild parties, for having men make love to them and, ultimately, for their particular delinquency. Male delinquents, likewise, testify to using certain types of movies as excitants for arousing and stimulating the passions of girls . . . .

"Motion pictures, however, at times can and do, according to the evidence, have an effect of deterring young people from crime, misconduct or delinquency . . . ."

We have been talking about those adolescents who are, so to speak, ready to be seduced by what they see and hear. They are, of course, in the minority. What about all of the others?

First of all, we can say with certainty that radio, television, and movies have the adolescent's ear and eye.

In Elias's study of the Washington seniors 10.3 per cent saw one movie a month, 17.9 per cent saw two, 15 per cent saw three, 22 per cent saw four, and 27.2 per cent saw between five and nine a month. In Olds's study of 840 Missouri adolescents 92.5 per cent reported listening to the radio each week, the average number of hours so engaged a week being 7.6, and 69.5 per cent reported going to movies each week, the average number of hours spent being 4.15. In McGill and Matthews's study of New York youth 62.5 per cent said that they went to movies and the theater often, and 76.9 per cent said that they listened to the radio often.[29] Doubtless we would find the same heavy reliance on movies and radio for recreation in whatever part of the country we surveyed. As soon as television sets are as common as radio, the data will probably be similar for television.

It is generally believed that movies have a more vivid effect on the personality of the individual than does the radio, not only because they appeal to sight as well as to hearing, but also because they demand longer sustained attention and give meaningful representation of life (not just witticisms, tests of knowledge, panel discussions, commentaries, music, and the like, as is so often true of the radio). Forman[30] gives us evidence from Holaday and Stoddard to the effect that movies are long-remembered. They found that in tests given six weeks after a movie was viewed and given without warning, the high school children remembered 88 per cent of the movie facts they knew the day after the movie was seen.

Attitudes: Movies can be powerful instruments for determining atti-

[29] L. J. Elias, *High School Youth Look at Their Problems* (Pullman, Wash.: State College of Washington, 1949), p. 10; Edward B. Olds, "How Do Young People Use Their Leisure Time?" *Recreation*, 42:458–463 (1949); Nettie Pauline McGill and Ellen Nathalie Matthews, *The Youth of New York City* (New York: The Macmillan Company, 1940).

[30] Forman, *op. cit.*, pp. 61–63.

tudes. One effective movie such as *Lost Boundaries* or *No Way Out* will definitely change racial attitudes. Conversely, of course, a movie may equally well instill undesirable attitudes. One reason for this is the fact that they customarily deal in stereotypes and in stereotyped attitudes. Pictured as types and not as individuals are teachers, farmers, certain minority races, the big businessman, the newspaper reporter, the taxi driver, the clubwoman, the politician, and others. The attitudes that go with these stereotypes are often undesirable. Another effect is to deaden the sensitivity of people to other people as *individuals*. Only a few movies have enough artistic truth to heighten that sensitivity.

Ideals: One has but to look at the tremendous sale of Hopalong Cassidy attire to see how movies affect the ideals of children. The effect on the adolescent is probably similar, but he cannot so easily become like Farley Granger or Betty Hutton as can the eight-year-old whose mother buys him a Hopalong Cassidy suit complete with spurs and holsters. The adolescent must be content with longing to be like his idol or with taking on some of his mannerisms for a while. Actually, as far as ideals are concerned, movies for the adolescent probably do no more than this, supply some never-to-be-satisfied longings. With one exception—and that is in regard to the American romantic ideal, which is the stock in trade of the movies and is therefore inevitably impressed on the adolescent. This is the ideal of the perfectly matched man and woman, the man all stalwart chivalry and masculinity, the woman all charm, tenderness, and femininity, with a great passion binding the two. This ideal overemphasizes the importance of romantic love in the relationship between a man and woman and underplays the importance of congeniality, adaptability, forbearance, and the like. It is likely to make the adolescent believe too much in a "fated," storybook type of love and expect of marriage continuing happiness with little effort.

Knowledge of the world: When over 1,000 high school seniors in 15 schools across the United States were asked what experience or experiences during their lives, in or out of school, were most important to them in "developing an understanding of other countries or in arousing interest in world affairs," movies came third in importance, the films most often cited being *Gentleman's Agreement, Dragon Seed, Open City, Shoe Shine, Wilson,* and *The Iron Curtain.*[31]

There are many movies which do picture life truly and with insight, and through them adult and adolescent alike have their comprehension of the world broadened and deepened. But a far greater number give a superficial or even completely misleading representation of what people,

[31] Leonard S. Kenworthy, "High School Seniors and World-mindedness," *Progressive Education,* 27:205–207 (1950).

localities, professions, and so on, are like. We have but to consider how unwilling we would be to have people of a foreign country take our movies as telling the truth about us to realize how misinforming they can be.

Emotions: Inevitably movies, radio, and television affect the emotions of child, adolescent, and adult. Sometimes this is uplifting, as when the experience is artistic. Sometimes it is healthfully relaxing, as when we laugh heartily. Sometimes it has no noteworthy effect on us at all; and sometimes it is harmful. For the ennobling experiences they may offer and for the relaxation they often provide, movies, radio, and television are undoubtedly emotionally beneficial to the adolescent. On a few occasions they may do him some harm emotionally as when they portray scenes of horror or suffering too great for him to keep in perspective. Otherwise their effect is probably unimportant.

Effect on the mind and on recreation habits: Fred Allen has said that television threatens to change Americans into creatures with eyeballs as big as cantaloupes and no brains at all. We must agree when we consider that most of what the adolescent (or adult) experiences in movies, television, and radio is a type of recreation which requires little if any thought. Through it all the boy or girl sits with inactive body and, on the whole, inactive brain. Recreation can be the means to developing a vigorous, well-rounded personality, but too great reliance on a passive kind of recreation with entertainment value only prevents the utilization of the many varieties of recreation possible and makes for a deadening rather than an enlivening of the mind and creative spirit. One needs self-expression through doing. Extensive movie or television attendance develops the observer, not the doer.

On the other hand, it would seem that television is going to restore to the home whole-family participation in recreation; and the fact that mother, father, and children gather around the television screen to enjoy programs together certainly seems beneficial to family life.

In summary, then, we may say that movies, television, and radio provide a major source of recreation for the adolescent but while their effect could be to stimulate the mind, uplift the spirit, broaden the understanding, and refine the taste, as well as to provide relaxation, too often they dull appreciations and limit mental activity.

PITFALLS IN THE COMMUNITY

Every day in the average American community some adolescents are confronted with unnecessary choices between good and evil just because the community provides easy opportunity to action which is in minor ways unwholesome or in major ways disastrous. As a result, there are boys and girls who become habituated to behavior which may stultify their personality resources, lead to deterioration of character, or result in some catastrophic occurrence the effect of which can never be wiped out.

In most communities taverns and liquor stores are more frequent than restaurants and grocery stores. While young people are excluded from taverns until they are twenty-one; they see them on almost every street corner and cannot help realizing that many adults find much pleasure in drinking. As for procuring liquor, adolescents have little difficulty in buying it if they want it, for they either can have it delivered to their homes when that is expedient or can find some unscrupulous older person who will go into a liquor store and purchase it for them.

Though many adolescents drink, probably only a few develop a long-lasting habit of drinking. Liquor is dangerous to many an adolescent because under its influence he is apt to do something which he will spend a lifetime regretting. All of us have read of automobile accidents which have had tragic results, the reason for the accident being that the young driver of the car had been drinking. We know, too, that many boys and girls indulge in sex activity beyond that of which they would normally approve—again, because too much to drink has aroused them sexually at the same time that it has weakened their control over their behavior.

The adolescent cannot be kept isolated from any possibility of mischance. Inevitably he will make mistakes; and the adult must understand that this is a necessary part of growing up. But there are missteps from which he cannot recover or as a result of which he will always bear too deep a scar. Unfortunately, the adult allows such experiences to take place when he makes it easy for the adolescent to drink—and, most particularly, to drink and drive or to drink when in an unchaperoned heterosexual group.

Other community sources of harm to the adolescent are the many unsavory places of amusement and loafing which are open to him. These range from poolrooms where the talk is vulgar and where gambling is going on in the back room to night clubs where the entertainment is suggestive to "vice dens" where liquor flows freely, drugs are sold, and sexual excesses are encouraged. Every community of any size will supply all of these, and almost surely some boys and girls of fourteen, fifteen, and up, will be found frequenting them.

Less serious, no doubt, is a third type of community evil—the sale of magazines, pictures, and comic books of a lewd nature. These are sold near high schools in all small or large cities, and there will always be some high school students who will buy them and a great many more will read them.

Finally, we should mention as the worst danger of any community people with evil intent toward youth. Every town or city has some—men and women who for money, for personal pleasure, or because of sadistic natures willfully set out to seduce or pervert the young. Nothing definite can be done to rid a community completely of such evil people. But there should be such control of places of recreation and such opportunity for wholesome recreation that those who are bad have little chance to make their influence count.

Reminiscences

1. Movies: How often did you attend the movies during your adolescence? Did any movie, as you remember, have a particularly good or a particularly bad effect on you?

2. Radio: What programs did you listen to? Do you still listen to the same type of program? Are you satisfied with your radio listening in retrospect as far as its effect on you and its worth to you are concerned?

3. The library: How much time did you spend in the library? Do you wish now you'd spent more? Less? Would you say that such library experiences are indispensable to a young person's life? Why, or why not?

4. Youth organizations: What organizations did you belong to? Did you have any leadership opportunities? Do you feel that the leadership of adults was wise enough for your good?

5. Playgrounds: How much did you use city playgrounds as an adolescent? Were they easily available to you? Were they made sufficiently attractive to you? Was your physical activity varied enough? Were you encouraged to engage in creative activities?

6. The church: Did you spend at least an hour a week on religious activities? Why, or why not? Did the church meet your religious needs as an adolescent? Explain.

7. Other recreational facilities: Did your community have a youth center? If so, evaluate it. If not, do you think your community should have had one? Why?

8. As an adolescent, were you aware of your community's social stratification? Did you feel its effects favorably, unfavorably, or not at all?

9. All in all, was your community a good place for you to grow up in? Why, or why not?

Observation

1. Visit one or many of the following:
A playground.
A meeting of some nonschool youth organization.
Some commercial entertainment or recreation provided especially for youth.
A teen center.

A church activity primarily for young people.

Observe for the following:

Is the situation a wholesome one for youth?

Is there an adult who oversees the activities? Does he seem well suited to his responsibilities?

Is there a particular type of youth that seems to be drawn to this activity?

Are there some changes which could be made to broaden and improve the appeal, if this seems desirable?

2. Attend church some Sunday with the purpose of deciding how the services would appeal to and serve the adolescent.

3. Read some of the typical magazines for teen-agers as well as some of the sections for adolescents in women's magazines. Evaluate them in terms of their worth to youth.

4. Visit the "slums" in your city. What do you think of them—to the extent that you can decide upon such superficial observation—as a place for a young person to grow up?

General Discussion

1. Consider each of the youth organizations mentioned, in turn. What have been your experiences with each?

2. Consider the questions given in the text by which a community's suitability to youth may be evaluated. Answer each question for your own community and with concrete details.

3. Consider the report from Elmtown. How does your own community compare?

4. What might the church do to draw more youth to it?

5. Consider each of the leisure-time activities listed by Olds. How does your community meet youth needs in regard to each?

6. Consider the 1946 survey of community recreation. Tell whether or not your community has each recreation and, if not, whether or not it should.

Panel Discussion

1. Ideal recreational facilities in our city.

2. A perfect community for youth.

3. Unwholesome temptations to youth in our city.

4. What communities throughout the country are doing for their adolescents.

Movies

Leaders for Leisure, Association Films, 21 min., color, 1949.

Lessons in Living, National Film Board of Canada, 22 min., b. & w., 1945.

Make Way for Youth, Association Films, 22 min., b. & w., 1948.

$1,000 for Recreation, Association Films, 12 min., color, 1946.

Playtown, U.S.A., Association Films, 23 min., color, 1946.

Further Reading

"About Boys," *Recreation*, 42:455 (1949).

BRIGHT, MILDRED, "Harlan County (Ky.) Organizes for Youth Welfare," *School and Society*, 55:588–590 (1942).

CHAMBERS, M. M., *Youth-serving Organizations* (Washington: American Council on Education, 1948).

DUCAS, DOROTHY, "Learning to Live," *Parents' Magazine*, 22:28–29 (1947).

FEINGOLD, G. A., "Newspaper Tastes of High School Pupils," *School and Society*, 59:316–319 (1944).

"4-H in a Changing World," *Practical Home Economics*, 24:83–84 (1946).

GAUDET, H., "High School Students Judge Radio Progress," *Education*, 60:639–646 (1940).

HAINFELD, HAROLD, "Our Summer Program in Movies," *Recreation*, 42:5 (1948).

HOLLINGSHEAD, AUGUST B., *Elmtown's Youth* (New York: John Wiley & Sons, Inc., 1949).

KAPLAN, EVELYN E., "Civic Center in the North," *Recreation*, 42:58 (1948).

KINNEMAN, F. C., "Comics and Their Appeal to the Youth of Today," *English Journal*, 32:331–335 (1943).

LE-BOUTILLIER, P., "Out of Doors with Irvington Youth," *Recreation*, 38:258 (1944).

LOVELESS, JAMES C., "Community Meets Youth's Problems," *Recreation*, 35:245–248 (1941).

MUSSLEMAN, VIRGINIA, "Teen Trouble," *Recreation*, 37:6–10 (1943).

"Neighborhood Play Centers," *Recreation*, 42:87 (1948).

PINCKNEY, JEANIE M., "Becoming Superior to Community Discouragements," *School Activities*, 15:299–300 (1944).

WITTY, PAUL A., "High School Students and the Radio," *Journal of Educational Psychology*, 32:176–185 (1941).

WRENN, C. GILBERT, *Time on Their Hands* (Washington: American Council on Education, 1941).

Chapter 14. THE SCHOOL FOR THE ADOLESCENT

Any institution which governs the activity of a young person for six or more of the most energetic hours in his day will have considerable significance in his life. Such significance we must grant the school just on the basis of the time element alone. Actually many reasons combine to make the school of paramount importance in the life of the adolescent.

1. The school is where his planned learnings go on—where he acquires the knowledge, habits, skills, and attitudes involved in history, English, home economics, industrial arts, mathematics, science, languages, and so on.

2. The school provides the only professional help that many a boy or girl will get in his endeavor to live well today and in adulthood.

3. The school is the adolescent's society. Gathered together there are the many people of his own age and interests among whom he finds his place and his companionship.

4. The school is the center for many of the adolescent's experiences in group processes. Group discussion, other than that of the family, group decisions, committee work, group projects—these experiences for many a boy and girl are limited to school life.

5. The school is the social world which provides the transition from the life within the home, intimate and protective, to the life within the community, often impersonal and competitive.

6. Many of the adolescent's most seriously felt responsibilities and most serious problems are those concerned with schoolwork and school living.

The junior high school and the senior high school are in existence not only to serve the adolescent but also to serve society. But since we believe that a social nature and an altruistic outlook are a necessity for happiness in the individual, we assume that what is truly the best for each boy and girl is also the best for society. Therefore we can say that it is the primary purpose of the junior and senior high schools to promote good living for the adolescent.

It follows then that it is the function of the high schools to meet whatever needs of the adolescent are not expressly or incidentally being met elsewhere in sufficience. His needs[1] are:

---

[1] This list has been kept to minimum essentials.

1. The needs that he has in common with all people of his culture:
   To feel secure.
   To have a sense of worth.
   To have companionship and affection.
   To have variety.
   To maintain physical well-being.
2. The special adjustment needs of adolescence:
   Adjusting to his physical changes.
   Adjusting heterosexually.
   Emancipation from childhood dependence and restrictions.
3. The need for adult help on personal problems of adjustment.
4. The needs set by coming adulthood:
   Learning the ways of democracy.
   Developing adult directives of behavior.
   Developing the ability to work, and making a vocational choice.
   Preparation for marital choice and marriage.
   Acquiring the other knowledges, abilities, and attitudes which are of genuine necessity in adulthood.

In brief, whoever is connected with the school must ask two questions: How is the adolescent getting along as an individual? How is the adolescent getting along in accomplishing the specific adjustments and learnings he needs to move him into a happy adulthood?

If the boy (or girl) is making good adjustments in school and is finding school profitable—that is, if the school is really meeting his needs as it should—he will stay in school as long as he can. If the school is *not* rewarding to him, he will be tempted to drop out upon reaching the legal age for doing so.

The fact that so many *do* drop out is evidence that high schools are not so properly "schools for the adolescent" as they should be.

Four brief accounts will illustrate this:

"A Stranger and Afraid[2]

"[Mike's] troubles began before he was born. He has problem parents and an oversensitive Syrian temperament he inherited from them. He has two sisters, both high-school graduates, and a younger brother. Although above average in ability, he was failing in school and he didn't have any friends, so he just quit. He loathed English courses. 'I don't like poetry! I can't understand it,' he exclaims in pure anguish. He hates Julius Caesar personally.

"'It's not what you know in this world—it's *who* you know that counts,'

[2] *Ladies' Home Journal*, January, 1951, p. 51. Reprinted by special permission from the *Ladies' Home Journal*. Copyright, 1951. The Curtis Publishing Company.

Mike keeps saying. He got a job, after much hunting, as a bus boy in a hotel grill. After two months he quit to take a better job in a small factory where he now earns ninety-two cents an hour. Eighteen years old, Mike lives alone in a rented room and takes his meals at restaurants. He takes a glum view of life, but thinks things may be looking up, now that he has a good job. 'If the Army don't get me,' he sighs.' "

"Undershooter[3]

"The principal looks at [Bobby's] school record and says, 'I don't know why boys like that get away from us.' Bob doesn't know either—he would have been a sixteen-year-old senior this year, but he failed three out of five subjects his junior year and it didn't seem worth the effort to him to make them up: 'I just don't like school—I don't like anything about it' is his explanation. Yet his I.Q. is above average; he is a healthy, amiable young man. He wants to drive a truck, but he will have to wait until he is twenty-one to drive for big trucking concerns. 'At a couple of places they said they wasn't hiring nobody but high-school graduates. I don't know.' He really doesn't know what he wants to do or what he can do. But of one thing he is certain: he will never go through that Silas Marner again if he starves to death. He wants his stepmother's permission to join the Navy when he is seventeen. In the meantime he has no steady job. He plays baseball, loafs on street corners."

"Apathetic Average[4]

"In all respects except vitality, Harold . . . is as near to the statistical average as boys come. His is an average-size family—one brother and one sister, both high-school graduates. His I.Q. is average; his scores on reading tests are in the middle bracket; even his grades were average, usually between 75 and 80. His only failure in high school was a course called American Democracy.

"But his teachers gave him the impression that he is much *below* average and they seem to believe it themselves. 'He is just one of those slow, dull boys,' a woman teacher said. (Many people believe 'average' is a great deal higher than it really is.) Harold's health has been below par—he's had a bout or two with rheumatic fever and a twenty-day session with tonsillitis complications that took the last wind out of his sails. He 'just didn't feel like going back' to complete his sophomore year, although his family wanted him to. 'We even tried bribing,' his sister said."

[3] *Ladies' Home Journal,* January, 1951, p. 51. Reprinted by special permission from the *Ladies' Home Journal.* Copyright, 1951. The Curtis Publishing Company.

[2] *Ladies' Home Journal,* January, 1951, p. 51. Reprinted by special permission from the *Ladies' Home Journal.* Copyright, 1951. The Curtis Publishing Company.

"Brilliant Nonconformist[5]

" 'School is a dull routine,' Tom . . . says. He has quit twice. Tennis and dramatics interested him, but not enough to hold him. In his opinion, most teachers are dictators and all of them think they are smarter than he —a demonstrably false assumption. Tom's I.Q. is far above average and his reading ability is superior.

"He earns about $45 a week working as 'houseman' in a bowling and billiard hall. Last summer, during the slack season, he collected state unemployment compensation, carefully avoided other work. One of five children, he has a twin brother not at all like him. An older brother is an outstanding student at Annapolis. Tom, 18, is a member of the Air Force Reserve and expects to continue formal education, if ever, in military service. A thoughtful and sophisticated reader, he would make a superior college student if he had a high-school diploma. One sympathetic teacher said, 'It's not that Tom is a smart aleck. He's just too old for his age.' "

Again we say, it is the function of the school *to meet the needs of the adolescent.* We shall discuss the school's specific responsibilities in regard to each person shortly, but first we must consider the demands made by the fact that in a school we have a considerable number of people working together and often dealt with as a group. These demands are:

1. Promoting good working relationships.
2. Understanding how the individuals in the group differ one from another.

PROMOTING GOOD WORKING RELATIONSHIPS

We can expect that the majority of students will be generally law-abiding and considerate of others. A few may be antisocial, and for their own good and the good of the group they must be restrained and prevented from continuing their unsuitable behavior.

If a class group or the school as a whole differs adversely from this "normal" ratio, then the school leader or the teacher must assume that he is setting up a situation that is too contrary to the needs and natures of the students to allow them to adjust to it easily. An example will illustrate what is meant.

Miss X is an English teacher in a school where each teacher works at one specialty and nothing else. All day Miss X teaches grammar, punctuation, correct usage, and composition to eighth-graders. She is a con-

[5] *Ladies' Home Journal*, January, 1951, p. 50. Reprinted by special permission from the *Ladies' Home Journal*. Copyright, 1951. The Curtis Publishing Company.

scientious, painstaking teacher who works very hard at the job of seeing that her eighth-graders learn what they are supposed to. But she is extremely tired after each day's labors—too tired to contemplate the next day with anything but forboding. The reason for this is that she must work so hard keeping her students quiet and busy. They too readily get noisy and break into horseplay.

Miss X should realize that when so many students are almost always on the verge of being unruly there is something wrong with the way the classroom situation is set up for them. There may be something wrong with the teacher's behavior or attitude, or there may be something wrong with the activities the students are engaged in.

In Miss X's case, the latter is the source of the difficulty. Let us examine the situation in one class. In it are 34 boys and girls between the ages of twelve and fifteen. Their IQ's range from 92 to 137. Some of them have the kind of minds that delight in grammar; more of them dislike it; a number find it almost if not entirely impossible to comprehend. Similarly with the weekly themes they write, some of the students enjoy them; more of them find the task distasteful or very difficult. What is worse, they see no purpose in it.

Actually many of these students are doing work which has little meaning for them, does not interest them, and offers them no enjoyment. Is it any wonder that they find their own ways of making the class period more exciting and more interesting and that some of them rebel against the teacher's dictates?

Miss X, an attractive, likable person, but one who was forcing her students to be discipline problems, realized one day what she was doing, and after much thought she came to the following conclusions:

I must vary the work from group to group within this class so that each student is getting what he needs and can see a need for.

I must give more opportunity for the whole group, and smaller groups within the whole, to plan their own work so that they can see more fully the purpose in what they do and their success in reaching their purpose, so that they have the opportunity of enjoying each other's companionship in work, and so that they learn better how to work together.

I must put as much variety into the week's activities as possible. For example, the tape recorder might be used in oral composition. Then, too, we can, as a class, seek out interesting experiences to write about.

I must change my ideal of discipline from the idea that it means perfect quiet and complete concentration on the work at hand to the idea of its meaning that the boy or girl is engaged in purposeful endeavor, that he is aware of how his behavior affects others, and that he governs himself with growing consideration for them.

As you would probably expect, her discipline problems grew fewer and fewer as she put this program into action.

There are certain principles of discipline which apply to any situation, whether it be with young children or adolescents, whether it be in home or in school. They are as follows:

Promote Self-discipline

Self-discipline can be furthered in the adolescent by developing an understanding in him of what is good for oneself and others, the desire for these "goods," and the ability to choose wisely and abide by that choice. We are self-disciplined when we brush our teeth regularly because we think it good for us, want this well-being, and can make ourselves do what is necessary to attain it. Every one of us is self-disciplined in many respects by the time we reach early childhood. We choose the good of our own accord, and we live up to our choice through our own efforts.

What we want for the adolescent is not that he become to some extent self-disciplined, because he already is that, but that he become more and more completely self-disciplined. In all areas of his living we would like him to come to

Know of more good choices to make.
Want to make them.
Be habituated to governing himself in respect to these choices.

We must not fall into the error of thinking of self-discipline as meaning that the adolescent behaves himself as the adult wishes and without too much adult coercion. That would be comfortable for adults but is not necessarily a mark of the best self-discipline. Rather true self-discipline means such things as these:

In regard to health: Believes in the desirability of outdoor exercise, sufficient sleep, wholesome food with few sweets, undereating rather than overeating, little if any indulgence in alcohol. Without too much effort, lives according to this belief.

In regard to work: Believes in good workmanship and can make himself put forth the necessary effort to do well what he undertakes. Is able to concentrate. Wants to use his time wholesomely and to good effect.

In regard to spending money: Makes choices that consider future good as well as present pleasure. Regards money not as an end or value in itself but as a means to good.

In regard to the rights of others: Believes in doing unto others as he would be done by. Is aware of the rights and needs of others in any situation where others are directly or indirectly participants. Wants their well-being as well as his own.

In regard to appearance: Takes pleasure in personal cleanliness and neatness as well as in attractiveness and suitability of clothing.

In regard to the care of belongings: Believes in orderliness, neatness, and carefulness, and abides by his belief.

Self-discipline is often thought of as involving effort. Someone who is dieting, for example, may endure much painful struggle in his effort to withstand pastries and candies. Here indeed is self-discipline achieved only with difficulty. But we can find countless examples of our disciplining ourselves painlessly and as a matter of course. If *discipline* means *control*, then self-discipline or self-control of a gentle yet wholly effective sort can certainly be achieved within oneself just as one person can gently discipline another (as a mother her child).

The highest form of self-discipline is the effortless kind. An adolescent boy, Oliver, for example, is painstaking in his work, is orderly and careful in regard to his belongings, follows healthful practices in his living, and is considerate of others. He is "just naturally" what he should be, we say. He doesn't have to struggle with himself to be good. He likes to be good, not because he wants to be *good*, primarily, but because that is the kind of behavior which gives him pleasure.

How can we further such self-discipline in all adolescents? The answer is to make desirable behavior pleasurable. This is not as difficult as it might sound, for behavior that is good for the individual and others does bring real rewards. In other words, adolescents who experience "being good" of their own free will usually find it adding to their happiness. But such behavior must as a rule be self-chosen or at least assented to in spirit; for if it is forced on a person, his rebellion will counteract the pleasure it brings.

Promote Group Discipline

Groups, too, must learn to discipline themselves. When a group can organize itself (selecting a capable leader from among its members), and when it then can decide what it wants to do, work out plans for the doing, and carry out those plans effectively—when it can do this with the full cooperation of its members and without direction or coercion from the outside, then we say that the group is self-disciplining.

The teacher should always remember that these are skills that must be learned. It is true that adolescents are accustomed to being members of groups which engage in joint activity. But their techniques of group work are casual ones which occasionally are very effective in getting the best from the group but are not dependably so. More and more is being done today to discover what the best methods are for group organization and united effort. The teacher should bring himself up to date on these methods and then help groups that he works with to get practice in using them.

Pflieger and Weston write:[6]

"John and Harry were the kind of teenagers to whom every event seemed funny. They held up class procedures with their silly antics. Precious time was wasted waiting for their cooperation. They were at the stage of growth and development where they needed to defy authority in order to show their independence of adults.

"Traditional means of discipline, such as sending them to their counselor or to the principal, keeping them after class, scolding them in front of the group, had no effect. John and Harry were not afraid of school authority.

"The case of John and Harry is only one example of classroom situations in which some kind of discipline seems necessary. The nature of the discipline usually depends upon the relationship which exists between teacher and pupils.

"These boys were members of a class where democratic living was the objective. The pupils as well as the teacher were involved in planning the work for the semester, and so it was natural that the class accepted the responsibility for the behavior of both the group and the individuals in it. Taking responsibility meant making judgments in terms of some criteria. These judgments were made on the basis of criteria for democratic living.

"John and Harry's behavior was freely discussed in their presence by the class. The decision was that in any democratic group all members have the responsibility to assist in perfecting a smoothly-operating organization and, therefore, that John and Harry had the duty to contribute to such an organization.

"On the other hand, the group had the responsibility to see that John and Harry did not continue present behavior and to impose sanctions, if necessary, to keep the group from disintegrating.

"This procedure was effective because students themselves measured their behavior against statements of democratic living which they were developing. Further, the behavior of John and Harry changed because the need to defy authority was supplanted by a more potent need—to be well-thought-of by peers.

"The action on the part of the group achieved results which the teacher, acting as an individual, had never been able to achieve with John and

[6] "Democracy," *NEA Journal*, 56:256 (1949).

Harry. The type of classroom organization which provided a democratic atmosphere had made it possible for students to assume obligations toward classroom problems and to attack them as a group.

"As more and more students and groups are given actual practice in working on such problems, we can hope that gradually we may have an adult society which can make a more intelligent attack on the social behaviors of the day."

Understand the Motivation behind Misbehavior

Both to ensure tolerance of the individual (though not of his act, necessarily) and to ensure the proper treatment of the behavior, it is necessary to know the reason for the adolescent's acts when they are out of line with what is desirable. Such understanding is not always easily arrived at—not only because motivation is complex and hidden below the surface, but also because an act may result from any of a number of different causes. This is illustrated in Cohler's discussion of the reasons for insolence.[7] Often, he says, what appears to be insolence is not that at all. It may be only that the student is behaving as he normally does with adults outside of the school and the worst that the teacher should say of him is: "He doesn't have the manners I expect." It may be that the teacher is unfamiliar with modern "high-schoolese" and therefore takes affront at what is customary present-day behavior among high school students. The primary cause of true insolence is the need for release of tensions— tensions which may arise from physical ill-being, from home difficulties, from school frustrations, and from other sources. In many such cases the teacher is bearing the brunt of something for which he is in no way responsible. The teacher must give help through individual conference and adjustment—a method diametrically opposed to that of indignation and punishment.

To understand the motivation behind misbehavior, it is necessary to understand common human motivations (that is, the desire for attention, for importance in the eyes of others, for emotional response from others, and so on), to understand typical adolescent behavior, and to understand as much as possible about the particular person involved.

Understand Reasons for This Form of Misbehavior

We have suggested above that one should know why the adolescent is moved to behave as he does. It is also important that we know if possible why the particular form of behavior engaged in is chosen.

[7] Milton J. Cohler, "A New Look at the Old Problem of Discipline," *School Review*, 56:468–475 (1948).

To illustrate what we mean, let us look at the matter of stealing. First, when a young person steals we must understand why he is stealing—what are going to be his primary gains? Hightower[8] suggests that the motivations for stealing are three: to have what others have, to gain attention, and to have an emotional outlet for one's conflicts.

But many adolescents at times want what others have, at times want more attention than they are getting, and have conflicts that trouble them; yet they do not steal. What impels those who do to engage in this particular form of behavior?

In some cases it will be that neighborhood practices are such that stealing is not considered a serious offense—or it may even be considered desirable. In other cases it will be that the boy or girl is not used to disciplining himself; what he wants he takes, what he wants to do he does. In still other cases the youth may resent the fact that others possess what he lacks and may persuade himself that he has as much right to these things as they.

Whatever the reason, the teacher should try to discover it; for both the reason for the act and the reason for the form of the act should be understood if he is to treat the offender in a way which will really help him.

Respond Intelligently to Misbehavior

On many occasions the best response of the teacher to misbehavior is to ignore what the boy or girl does. This is particularly true when the class is unaware of the act and when the behavior itself is the result of high spirits, temporary mischievousness, or something else which will pass and leave no lasting effect. At other times, of course, some definite reaction on the part of the teacher is necessary. In that case, the teacher should think before he speaks and consider what the real good of both individual and group demands. The following suggestions are helpful:

1. Don't have a sense of emergency when someone disrupts the class. In 99 per cent of all disturbing situations the teacher will be able to resolve them effectively. Most high school students are fundamentally people of good will—not the ogres that a few teachers take them to be. Given understanding and fair treatment, with work that has meaning and worth to them, adolescents will be pleasant to deal with. Many teachers, unfortunately, *do* have a sense of emergency whenever someone misbehaves, and this feeling frequently makes them react unthinkingly and emotionally, to the detriment of both teacher and class.

[8] Howard K. Hightower, "School Problems of Pupils Who Steal," *Educational Administration and Supervision*, 33:229–234 (1947).

2. Don't make mountains out of molehills. A teacher can give so much attention to minor disturbances that the class seems like nothing more than a series of disciplinary actions with a little learning activity sandwiched in between reproofs, scoldings, pleas for good behavior, and the like. The teacher should follow the rule of parsimony in censure and punishment—use the mildest, briefest, and least generally noticeable action which will be effective. Often a negative shake of the head, walking over to stand by the offender, or something equally unobtrusive will be enough. Let the rest of the class be as little involved as possible. Generally it is not their concern, and they do not deserve to be bothered or upset.

3. Don't talk too much. There is hardly ever a troubled occasion when the teacher is not wise to cease action and think. There is hardly ever a time when it is good to rant at a student and let angry, nagging, sarcastic, or tearful words fall in a torrent from your lips. Thought, well-considered decision, and then action mean strength. A flurry of unconsidered or ill-considered words shows weakness.

4. Act from conviction, and act in accordance with your convictions. Don't respond to a student with behavior which someone else has suggested or with what you think "ought" to be done if you actually don't approve of it. Listen to advice, read what experts say, then try to reach your own well-thought-through conclusions. When you act on the basis of belief, your action is much more effective and is likely to have sounder justification.

5. Keep cool. Do not yourself become emotionally involved. Anger, hate, fear (or tears!) weaken any personality that is attempting to be intelligent, sensible, and adult.

6. Don't make an emotional or a personal appeal for good behavior. An adolescent's behavior should be based on an understanding of his own needs, a recognition of the needs of the group, and an acceptance of social regulations. No teacher should try to make an adolescent so sorry for what he has done that he makes extravagant promises of good behavior. Nor should a teacher attempt to make an adolescent behave by using a strong personal appeal—the "do it for my sake" approach. In either case the appeal is emotional and the resulting promises not easily lived up to when the emotion dies down—with the result that the adolescent is apt to fall from grace again and then feel enmity toward the teacher who has brought on the guilty feeling that results. What is more, as we said in another chapter, the adolescent should make *moral* choices whenever possible. When the teacher descends to securing good behavior through an emotional appeal, she is failing to give the adolescent the practice in moral choice that he needs.

7. Don't threaten. This is almost always a weak response. The students

know that it is an in-between measure of a teacher who can't be the kind of leader who inspires a group to work amicably together and yet who can't act decisively, a teacher who wants to postpone action, a teacher who depends on fear to get good behavior.

8. Do something to take care of the immediate situation. Have devices of your own in mind; if possible, don't ask for help from some higher authority. It is true that a boy or girl may disturb a class greatly by talking, insolence, humming, showing off before a class, and so on. The teacher must have some plan for seeing that the class is not disturbed long. One source of strength is to know ahead of time what can be done if certain difficulties arise. This readiness for trouble will not be an invitation to trouble. It will merely prevent the teacher's seeming worried and indecisive, or acting without wisdom when the necessity for some immediate action occurs. It is difficult to give prescriptions here as to what might be done, for what will be effective with one teacher and one class may not be with another. Some of the measures often used are:

To stand by the student's desk, without otherwise giving him any close attention.

If the teacher and the class are in good rapport, to explain to the student before the class how he is disturbing the group and why he should change his behavior.

To change the student's seat, thus removing him from temptation.

9. In most cases have a conference with the student. At that conference:

a. Try to understand the student. Talk to him enough so that you get his explanation for his behavior and something about his life, interests, likes, and dislikes as well. Be friendly, not sternly disapproving.

b. Avoid stirring up emotion in yourself or him. Explanations and decisions need a clear mind on the part of both teacher and student.

c. Think before you speak. A word may be said which will spoil the tone of the conference, where the relationship is a delicate one at best.

d. Be honest. Some teachers will make threats they don't expect to live up to, make misleading remarks about how others regard the boy or girl, exaggerate the seriousness of his misbehavior, promise an unpleasant future —none of which is the truth. A teacher will always promote better relationships in such a conference if he is not deceitful. He should be honest —but of course not blurt out everything he knows. A student recognizes and respects sincerity in a teacher, and a teacher will therefore do well to refrain from dealing in platitudes, exaggerations, or actual lies.

e. Consider results. Compromise if it will help the boy or girl. Try to plan a mutually happier situation.

f. Clarify the future without threats. Say calmly and clearly what you expect of the boy or girl and what he or she can expect of you.

10. Punish the offender if he needs it; never punish the whole group. A young high school teacher tells of sitting in study hall and hearing something bounce, bounce, bounce on the floor. She did nothing, but remained at her desk trying to figure out just who was causing the disturbance. It took a long time before she spotted the troublemaker. Walking over to him very quietly and with no evidence of anger or of being upset, she took the object he had been bouncing, a dried-up apple. This quiet control of the situation was all that was needed. There was no more disturbance.

Many teachers might not have found the culprit and then, baffled, might have punished the whole group in some way. This is bad. It is completely unfair and inevitably arouses resentment against the teacher—and justifiable resentment. No one can feel that a teacher is a person of good will if he thus punishes indiscriminately.

11. Do not discipline the student by humiliating him. To deprive a boy or girl of his feelings of self-respect, his pride, to make him feel unimportant, is not only cruel but also is bad for the personality. No punishment should hurt the child's welfare, and humiliation does just that.

12. Do not punish the student by depriving him of experiences he needs. The mother of a thirteen-year-old girl came to talk to one of the authors about some problems she was meeting in connection with her daughter. Her daughter was shy, she said, and didn't seem to get along well with other boys and girls. It bothered her, too, that her daughter was not obedient. She had told the child that she could go to the basketball games on Friday nights if she would come right home after the game. A few days after the second game, some evidence came to the mother that her daughter had not come home directly after the affair was over. When she talked to the little girl about this, her daughter admitted that she had gone with four other girls to the drugstore and hung around "with the crowd" for half an hour. There was nothing at all harmful in what she was doing, but the mother didn't like the fact that she had been disobeyed.

"What did you do?" the mother was asked.

"I haven't let her go to any basketball game since," she replied.

Here is a case of punishing a girl by depriving her of the very experiences she needed, those of mixing more with boys and girls of her own age.

13. Don't punish for revenge or to bolster your own ego. But remember that there is a place for punishment at times. Jenkins says that since punishment has been so much misused, many people have concluded that there is no place for it at all in human control. However, it is his contention

"that children cannot be socialized without a discerning use of punishment, and that a society cannot exist without sanctions of punishment."[9]

Punishment can be thought of as serving three purposes: It may prevent the recurrence of the socially or individually harmful act. It may, as Jenkins says, "relieve tension in the individual or the group that disapproves the punished act, by exacting payment for it through punishment." It may also relieve tension in the punished. "The offender may be in a destructive state of self-accusation which may be relieved by punishment, and he may thereby be freed for a more constructive social adjustment, if the self-condemnation has been excessive."

Many factors, Jenkins says, enter into the determination of which reaction or what combination of reactions may follow punishment. Some of the factors are the following:[10]

1. The sense of acceptance or emotional security left to the punished person. He is most likely to react adaptively to punishment if, in spite of the punishment, he still feels sure of the interest, respect, and affection of others.

2. The clarity of the prohibition to the punished.

3. The reasonableness of the prohibition to the punished.

4. The severity of the punishment. Too mild punishment may be ignored; too severe punishment may result in disorganization.

5. The reasonableness of the type of punishment to the punished.

6. The consistency with which the punishment is applied. This means not only the consistency with which it is applied to all who deserve it but also the consistency with which it is applied to one individual for a repetition of the same offense.

7. The sense of the punished regarding the penetrability of the limitation or the conquerability of the force behind the punishment. If counteraggression will be successful, the punished will be apt to try it.

8. The effect of group attitudes. If the group supports the offender, there will be almost surely a conflict situation.

The punishment is unsuccessful when it leads to counterhostility, disorganization, or acceptance of the punishment without acceptance of the limitation.

We have finished this discussion of keeping good order in the school with a consideration of punishment. Let us come back again to the fact, however, that in a good school students will be working happily together, self-discipline and group discipline will prevail, and punishment will seldom be needed.

We pass now to the second general necessity in any school for the adolescent—the understanding of individual differences.

---

[9] R. L. Jenkins, "The Constructive Use of Punishment," *Mental Hygiene*, 29:561-574 (1945).

[10] Jenkins, *loc. cit.*

UNDERSTANDING INDIVIDUAL DIFFERENCES

We cannot make the best adjustment to an individual unless we know what he is like. Every person is unique, and we can understand him only by studying him.

Unfortunately the teacher often does not have enough time to know each student as well as would be desirable. Then he is helped if he has some general ideas as to how adolescents differ.

They differ, as we know, in intelligence. Some are bright, some are average, some are dull. They differ in their special aptitudes. Some have musical ability, some mechanical ability, some a talent for writing or painting—and many have no pronounced gift at all. They differ in their physical fitness. Some are in splendid physical condition and of fine structure. Others are weak, without energy, and often ill—or may be handicapped by poor vision, deafness, or other defects.

The student of adolescence should know something about all of these differences and is urged to investigate them in further reading. Here in this chapter there is space only for a limited discussion of intellectual differences. We shall discuss the gifted and the dull.

The Intellectually Gifted

Who Are the Intellectually Gifted? The Educational Policies Commission of the National Educational Association suggests that, roughly, individuals with an IQ above 137 be classified as "highly gifted" and that individuals with an IQ between 120 and 137 be classified as "moderately gifted."[11]

What Are the Intellectually Gifted Like? Terman has for many years been carrying on a longitudinal study of highly gifted individuals. The majority of the subjects were located as children in 1921–1922, and more were added later. Altogether, 1,444 cases have been studied up to the present time.

Terman gives us this picture of the average highly gifted child.[12]

Parentage: Generally superior in cultural and educational background and also in heredity.

Educational achievement: Accelerated about 14 per cent of his age. In mastery of subject matter he is accelerated about 44 per cent of his age.

[11] *Education of the Gifted*, Educational Policies Commission, National Education Association of the United States and the American Association of School Administrators (Washington, June, 1950), p. 43.

[12] Lewis M. Terman and Melita H. Oden, "The Gifted Child Grows Up," Vol. III in *Genetic Studies of Genius* (Stanford University, Calif.: Stanford University Press, 1947), pp. 55–57.

Interests: Many-sided and spontaneous. Learns to read easily, reads more and better books than the average child, and largely educates himself. Makes numerous collections, engages in all kinds of childhood activities, acquires far more knowledge of plays and games than the average child of his years.

Character: Less inclined to boast or overstate his knowledge, more trustworthy when under temptation to cheat, reading preferences, character preferences, and social attitudes are more wholesome than average. Scores higher in emotional stability.

He cautions us to remember, however, that this composite portrait will not give us the inevitable pattern for the individual gifted child, for gifted children, naturally, fall into an infinite variety of patterns.

A better idea of what the highly gifted adolescent is like will come from this description:[13]

Donald, a case of brilliant achievement and social balance: "Fourteen years old and in the third year of high school, Donald presents a picture of a happily functioning boy. Not only is he superior mentally and scholastically but he is also in excellent physical condition and well adjusted socially.

"He comes from fairly well-educated people of superior stock on both sides. His paternal grandfather had a year of college and his maternal grandparents were both normal-school graduates. His father, a most successful business man, is a college graduate, and his mother attended college for one year. The prevailing occupations of his forbears have been farming and business on the paternal side, and law and teaching on the maternal side. The family live in a delightful home in an excellent residential section where Donald, who is an only child, is surrounded by every cultural advantage.

"Donald showed a marked interest in drawing at three and a half years, learned to read with little help at four and a half, and at five years composed his first story. He entered school at eight years of age, beginning in the fourth grade. It was less than a year after he entered school that he was located by us in the 1921–22 survey. His IQ was 157, and he was making an excellent school record. His scores on the achievement tests given then showed him capable of doing work about three grades in advance of the one he was in. He stood out particularly in history and civics, literary knowledge, and all-round information. On the basis of the Plays and Games questionnaire, his play interests were rated as more than ordinarily social and as rather masculine. The teacher reported that his companionship was especially sought by other children.

[13] Reprinted from "The Promise of Youth," Vol. III in *Genetic Studies of Genius* by Lewis M. Terman and others with the permission of the authors and of the publishers, Stanford University Press.

"At the time of the follow-up study he was fourteen years old and was making practically a 'straight A' record in the third year of high school. His early interest in cartooning does not appear to have persisted to any extent, but his fondness for reading and his literary interests have grown rapidly. He has a real love for books, has read extensively, and is collecting a library of his own. One of his favorite occupations is writing stories, of which he has a great many to his credit. He recently won the first prize in a short-story contest sponsored by a well-known bookshop. In this contest he also took third prize for an essay and received honorable mention for general reading. He is an enthusiastic collector and during the past few years has accumulated in addition to his library about 3,000 stamps, 1,000 lead soldiers, 50 rare coins, 25 toy dogs, 800 baseball pictures, and 600 bottle tops. His lead soldiers have been a persistent hobby, and he spends many hours arranging them in battle array and maneuvering them. Donald is physically active, and fond of playing football, baseball, and tennis. He is a great 'fan' of all the sports, always following in season scores of teams, standing of the colleges, names of players, and technicalities of the game. At high school he is a member of the R.O.T.C., a sergeant in rank, and soon to be a lieutenant. (A later report informs us that he was advanced to captaincy by his senior year.) A short time ago he won a medal for the best work in sergeant's individual drill in an annual, city-wide, R.O.T.C. competition.

"On our 1927–1928 Interest Blank Donald lists as his favorite pastimes reading, playing with other children, and playing with his soldiers. His taste in companionship is illustrated by his own description of his best chum, a fifteen-year-old boy who is athletic, fond of reading good books, an Eagle Scout, sociable, and good-natured.

"Donald's most notable achievement was his selection, at the age of eleven, as Boy Mayor of one of the largest cities of California. The judges made their choice by examining the candidates on city government, current events, and affairs in general. Two outstanding boys from each school were chosen by the principals to compete, there being 150 boys in all. During his week as Boy Mayor, Donald was of course featured in all the papers; he was feted, called on for many speeches, and otherwise made much of, but he came through it unspoiled.

"At the age of fourteen Donald was 6 feet 1 inch in height and weighed 155 pounds; otherwise he was the same healthy, wholesome, freckle-faced, red-haired lad that he had been six years before. His manner was poised and unassuming, and he spoke of his achievements as interesting experiences, with no taint of bragging. He mixes well with his schoolmates and is much interested in school affairs. He is out for debating and baseball, and also holds a position as assistant in his school bank. (A later report has been received to the effect that he was made head of the school bank in his senior year.)

"Though his family is in most comfortable circumstances, Donald likes to work and earn money. When he was only thirteen and a half he spent his Christmas vacation as clerk in a bookshop. The following Christmas vacation he again worked as a clerk, this time in the book section of one of the large department stores. His vocational ambition is to enter law.

"On the tests which he was given in the follow-up study he made excellent scores. At age 14-8 his Terman Group Test point score was 203, or 12 points higher than the median for our fourteen-year-old gifted boys. His scores on the educational tests were correspondingly high.

"We have in Donald a rather extreme case of acceleration which has had none of the unfavorable results so commonly believed to be inevitable. Size and mature appearance, as well as natural social gifts, have probably contributed to this happy outcome. No better illustration could be given of the necessity of considering each case as an individual problem when the question of extra promotion arises."

Cynthia is an example of a moderately gifted adolescent. Her IQ is 124. One thinks of her as being bright, quick, understanding, and a good student but not as being far and amazingly beyond the rest of her class in brilliance or accomplishment. Unlike the highly gifted adolescent who, if such a one be found in a school, far surpasses most high school teachers in intellectual interests and abilities, Cynthia is similar to her teachers in her mentality.

Cynthia likes school and no wonder, for her mind delights in the many academic subjects on the "required" list as well as in the subjects she elects to take. She has the reward, too, of high grades, receiving all A's and B's, with more A's than B's. She takes a lively interest in class discussions and her contributions are always well thought through and sensible.

Cynthia takes part in many extracurricular activities and is the able treasurer of the senior class. She is a well-rounded girl in her interests, and although she loves to read, she also has time for outdoor sports and for just "hanging around" with the gang.

Since the highly gifted are rare, it is adolescents like Cynthia who are most typical of the brightest students of any class. One should be fully aware of how important it is that such young people get an education suited to their abilities. For it is these people who, as adults, will hold positions of leadership and who will work at jobs where knowledge, breadth of understanding, good adjustment, high ideals, and integrity will affect the welfare of many people. These are the future teachers, ministers, doctors, writers, engineers, architects, lawyers, senators, representatives, mayors, and governors. If we fail to help them become the best that they can be, we fail society. What is more, for each gifted boy or girl who spends his life in school to less than full advantage, we have failed a deserving person in his quest to fulfill himself.

The Education of the Gifted. The Educational Policies Commission suggests that there are four methods of adjusting to the needs of the gifted:[14]

1. Acceleration, which has many advantages but which may, in some cases, cause or aggravate social and emotional maladjustment.

2. Grouping, which has many advantages, but which also has disadvantages in that it seems to be undemocratic, stigmatizes those excluded from the "better" groups, provides an unrealistic social environment, fosters feelings of superiority, and is sometimes difficult or impossible to arrange where schools are too small and where teachers dislike too much being assigned to classes of the less bright.

3. Enrichment, through creative expression, much firsthand experience in the community, reading and the study of literature, opportunity to delve more deeply into fields of special interest, and opportunity to explore a wide variety of both intellectual and nonintellectual activities.

4. Elective courses, advantageous if they are selected with care and with proper guidance.

Many teachers will be left to their own devices in the matter of making the education they are providing more suitable to the bright than it ordinarily is. They must not content themselves with giving longer assignments or "busy-work" reports to these superior students. Rather they should find time for a personal conference with each of them so that teacher and student together may decide what is needed, keeping in mind the following:

1. The gifted generally like to read. They read well, their vocabulary is large, and their ability to comprehend is high. They should be given the time and the encouragement to read widely in the fields of biography, travel, history, science, psychology, and literature.

2. The gifted generally enjoy learning for the sake of learning. They should have an opportunity to try out many different kinds of study—science, music, painting, creative writing, languages, and so on.

3. The gifted are capable of meticulous, high-grade workmanship in intellectual matters and should be helped to reach this standard.

4. The gifted often have an abundance of activities to fill their out-of-school hours. For that reason, the teacher should be more concerned with making

[14] *Education of the Gifted,* Educational Policies Commission, National Education Association of the United States and the American Association of School Administrators (Washington: June, 1950), pp. 49–65, 75–79.

every minute of their in-school time count than with adding to outside assign-ments.

5. The gifted are capable of planning and directing their own work with a little guidance and should be encouraged to do so.

6. The gifted are capable of fine insight into their own personality and that of others and should have opportunities to develop this understanding.

Contrary to popular ideas, young people in the upper IQ levels will be well adjusted if impediments are not put in their path. The school should beware of fostering the following mental-health difficulties:

1. Thwarting of the drive for obtaining the satisfactions of intellectual learn-ing. Parents and teachers sometimes try to restrain this drive in order that the boy or girl may spend more time on social activity and recreation. This is unwise. Rather they should balance intellectual interests by giving special encouragement and opportunity for recreation, social activities, and manual work.

2. Social rejection or feelings of social inferiority. It is good to encourage the development of nonintellectual interests as well as intellectual interests so that the gifted adolescent may have some interest bonds with the less gifted.

3. Concentration on intellectual achievement as compensation for social re-jection. Prevention and cure of such compensation can be achieved by the provision of many wholesome socializing experiences. One should beware, however, of thinking that all concentration on intellectual achievement is com-pensation.

4. Egotism, from favoritism, excessive praise, or being shown off.

5. Infantilism, from oversolicitude.

The Dull

By the "dull" we mean those who are not intelligent enough to be called average but who are also not low enough in intelligence to be classified as feeble-minded or even as borderline cases. Specifically, they are those with IQ's between 80 and 90.

When we read accounts of the highly gifted, we realize that here are people who are strikingly different from the average. Such is not the case with the moderately gifted, who are very much like the average boy and girl in interests and viewpoints, though more able mentally. It is to these moderately gifted that the dull correspond. The adolescents with IQ's between 80 and 90 are not startlingly different from the average. Rather they are much like them in interests and attitudes, though with *duller* minds.

The words *bright* and *dull* actually are dependable descriptions of the group directly above and the group directly below the average. With the bright adolescent, the mind is sharper, the thinking faster, more complex, and more clean-cut. With the dull, the machinery of the mind seems to be blunted and to move at a slower and more awkward pace.

Martin is an example of a dull-normal adolescent. His IQ is 85. He is nineteen years old and a senior in high school. He is a well-built boy, healthy and active, with a pleasing, sweet-natured face. In talking to him one might not be aware of the fact that his intelligence is below the average. He expresses himself well, and his answers to one's questions come readily. He works after school and on Saturdays, as he has for several years, helping his father, who is a carpenter in the small town where they live. When he tells how he spends his money, we realize that he seems to use good judgment in what he buys. He is saving some of his earnings; he wants to get married before very long, though he is afraid that he will be drafted and will have to postpone marriage. He has been going steady for two years. What does he like about his girl? The fact that she's pretty and very clean. She doesn't smoke or drink, and this pleases him. What do they have in common? They like movies; they like the same programs on the radio; they both belong to the same church and attend all of the young people's meetings there.

"What do you think of installment buying?" is one question we ask among many. "I don't know what that means," he replies. We explain, and he says, "I don't think that's a good idea." We ask him about drinking, and he answers that he doesn't approve of it because "you can do some pretty bad things when you're drunk and besides it's a waste of money."

"If you were given too much change in buying something, would you return it?" we ask. He says he would. In fact, as we continue with questions having to do with right and wrong behavior, we find that he gives all of the approved answers.

"What do you read?" we ask. "No books," he replies. But he does read *Life*, and the headlines, sports, and comics of the daily paper. His favorite subjects in school, he tells us, are woodworking and physical education. There are few others that he likes.

It is not until we ask him questions demanding, not a *typical, habitual* response, but actual thought that we begin to realize that his mind does not work quickly or well.

From the Stanford-Binet[15] we ask: "Bill Jones's feet are so big that he has to pull his trousers on over his head. What is foolish about that?"

"You always put your trousers on over your feet," Martin replies.

"The fireman hurried to the burning house, got his fire hose ready, and after smoking a cigar, put out the fire. What is foolish about that?"[16]

[15] Lewis M. Terman and Maud A. Merrill, *Measuring Intelligence* (Boston: Houghton Mifflin Company, 1937), p. 103.
[16] *Loc. cit.*

"He might set something else on fire," Martin answers.

We turn to the Stanford-Binet vocabulary list, and for some of the words we receive the following replies:

Scorch: When you iron, you scorch something.
Mars: I don't know.
Juggler: You throw it up in the air (and he demonstrates with his hands).
Priceless: Not worth anything.
Disproportionate: I don't know.

Martin, as with all of us, reflects the experiences he has had. His life has been such as to make him kindly, well-meaning, and well behaved, and in these respects he is like many people of normal or higher intelligence. As with all of us, Martin has by this time acquired a number of habits, attitudes, ideas, and emotional conditionings typical of many of the populace. In many cases these habits, attitudes, ideas, and emotional conditionings provide ready-made responses which require little if any thought. It is for these reasons that Martin—and all of the dull—appears in so many ways to be little differentiated from the average or the bright; his ordinary reactions to the affairs of daily life are the typical habitual reactions of a great many of the population.

In other respects, however, Martin is *unlike* those of the higher levels of intelligence. In the first place, his vocabulary is less extensive than is that of the average or above. In the second place, he doesn't enjoy learning through words; he likes to deal, rather, with the concrete and the manipulable. In the third place, he is not good at abstract thinking. His mind works slowly and easily gets lost if the problem or the idea is complex.

Those who are dull-normal will hold simple, uncomplicated jobs. The girls who work for a living will be maids, waitresses, elevator girls, laundresses, and so on. The boys will be janitors, taxi drivers, countermen in restaurants, railroad section workers, miners, and the like. It is important then that the school give them the particular kind of education which will be meaningful and helpful to them both during adolescence and in adulthood. Let us see just what this would involve.

Most of them will marry	Sex education
	Information in regard to choosing a mate
	Knowledge and skills for homemaking and care of children
Many of them will work for a living	Habits of good workmanship
	Information for choosing a vocation
	Vocational skills, in some cases

Most of them will handle money	Knowledge, habits, and skills regarding: Budgeting Saving money Spending money wisely Paying taxes
All will need to keep in good mental and physical health	Healthful habits of living Principles of mental hygiene A well-adjusted personality
All will need and engage in some recreation	A number of varied and desirable play skills Familiarity with a number of different kinds of recreation
All will converse with others, read, write a little, and use arithmetic	Pleasant, distinct speech Enough reading skill and discrimination to read the daily paper Enough ability to write legibly and express oneself clearly, as, for example, in a simple business letter Simple arithmetic
All will have dealings with others	Simple rules of etiquette Ability to get along with people in the ordinary relationships Simple rules of good citizenship An altruistic outlook
All will use their community and participate in government	Firsthand knowledge of community Firsthand knowledge of government Understanding of duties of citizenship

This is what the dull need. The directive to the school for the adolescent is: Give it to them. At the same time, don't force upon them the many kinds of "book learning" which would be suitable for those better equipped mentally but which are completely unsuited to the dull—unnecessarily difficult, without meaning for them, and serving no justifiable purpose.

The teacher should remember that the dull learn best and most happily when they deal with the concrete and when they can learn by firsthand seeing, hearing, tasting, feeling, and smelling. Like all of us, they learn by experiencing, but their experiences are the best for them when they allow the boy or girl to be personally and actively concerned in them.

The teacher should also remember that the dull are no different from any other adolescents in their need for security, a sense of worth, companionship and affection, and variety, or in their need to make the adolescent adjustments to physical self, to the other sex, and to adult independence.

Having discussed two general necessities, (1) promoting good order and (2) understanding individual differences, we pass on to the function of the secondary schools—to meet the needs of the adolescent.

What should the school for the adolescent be like? First of all, it should meet the adolescent's basic human needs. We shall discuss each need separately, bearing in mind that all are interrelated and that satisfying one may serve other needs as well.

I. THE BASIC NEEDS

The School Should Give Each Boy and Girl a Sense of Security

The school has at least three major ways of contributing to the adolescent's sense of security: accepting him, assuring him of freedom from mistreatment, and enlarging his experiences. These are the adolescent's due, and no school can be called a proper school for the adolescent if it fails him in these.

Acceptance. We all know what is meant when it is said that a young person is rejected by his parents or by his group—they don't like him; they don't want him around. Such rejection may be expressed very plainly in action, or it may be felt but outwardly concealed. In either case the rejected person is likely to be aware of his status; for even when those who reject him endeavor to hide their feelings, there are usually many subtle indications of the true attitude.

We believe that no adolescent should be personally rejected by the adults who work with him in school and that ideally he will be accepted by all of them. Just what is meant by this acceptance is often not understood. It does not imply that one must like or accept the acts of a boy (or girl) or his ideas; it does not even imply that one must like him—let alone, as some assume, be effusively pleasant to him. When we accept the adolescent, it means only that we look upon him with no personal feelings of animosity, jealousy, or irritation, that we have something akin to divine sympathy for the fact that he has his hopes, fears, sorrows, and pains, as we have, that he is striving to win a place in the world, response from people, and success, as we all are, and that he is not necessarily what he would choose to be but is to a considerable extent a reflection of the kind of life he has led and the kind of environment he now knows.

Many teachers have this desirable openhearted attitude toward all adolescents they meet. Such teachers are incapable of entering the emotional arena with the insolent adolescent, or the lazy, the mischievous, the antagonistic, the argumentative, or the dishonest, to respond personally with feelings which match in childishness those of that boy or girl. Other teachers who are by nature less magnanimous will find that there is a golden path leading to the ability to accept all adolescents—again remembering that this does not mean that they necessarily approve of *what he does*. That path is understanding. It is said that to understand all is to forgive all. Certainly it is true that the teacher who really understands a boy or girl is not likely to be personally affronted, disgusted, dismayed, embittered, or angered by that young person's behavior.

Fair Treatment. Just as the adolescent has a right to acceptance by the adults who work with him, so he also has a right to fair treatment from them. He doesn't always get it. When one group of people have absolute jurisdiction over another group, there is always possible the misuse of authority and in school this takes the form of "picking on" a student, sarcasm, harsh punishment, and discrimination of various kinds. An account of discipline in Elmtown high school will illustrate this.[17] At a teacher's meeting after an hour of discussion, the teachers voted to send all tardy students to detention (which meant an hour after school); no excuses were to be accepted.

"The second week of the new regime, the daughter of a prominent class II family did not go to detention. Instead, she kept an appointment with a beauty parlor to have a permanent wave. The next morning the Superintendent walked into the principal's office, diffidently fingered the mail in the teacher's boxes, sauntered over to the windows with his hands in his pockets, looked at the autumn leaves moving across the yard, and in a disinterested way asked, 'How is the detention room working?' The principal answered:

" 'All right, except we are running into the old stall of some students who think they can do as they please!'

"[Superintendent] 'Yes, I know. The idea is all right, but I do not think it will work in every case. Last evening Mrs. Newton called Evelyn [the Superintendent's wife] about the church supper next week. She mentioned that Kathy [her daughter and the girl in question] was at the hairdresser's last night!'

"[Principal] 'That is just what I had in mind. Last evening I called Mrs. Newton and told her Kathy was not in detention and I wanted to know where she was. Mrs. Newton told me she had to have her hair fixed for the dance at the Country Club tonight. When I get Kathy in here, I am going to tell her a thing or two.'

"[Superintendent] 'Now, be careful, Alfred. I do not think there is a thing we can do in this case.'

[17] Reprinted by permission from *Elmtown's Youth*, by A. B. Hollingshead, published by John Wiley & Sons, Inc., 1949.

"The principal sat silently at his desk and shuffled excuses. The Superintendent walked out of the office.

"When Kathy came in for her lecture, she was dressed neatly in a brushed wool sweater and tweed skirt. She walked coyly to the principal's desk and asked in a naive voice, 'Did you want to see me last night?'

"The principal looked up and quietly asked, 'Did you forget about detention?'

" . . . A pause. 'No, I had an appointment at Craig's to have my hair set.'

" . . . 'Did you have to go last night?'

" . . . 'Yes, tonight I have to go to Mrs. Nettle's to get my dress for the dance.'

" . . . 'All right. Go on to class, but don't let this happen again.'

"After Kathy left the office, the principal threw a pack of excuses on the desk and muttered, 'There it goes again! The next time one of these prominent families puts pressure on me, I am going to raise hell!'

"The following Wednesday morning, Frank Stone, Jr. (class I) parked his father's Cadillac in front of the high school at a quarter after eight, climbed out leisurely, picked up his notebook, and walked into the office and casually remarked, 'I guess I'm late again.'

"The principal looked hard at him and spoke firmly, 'What's the story this time?'

" . . . 'I didn't wake up, I guess.'

" 'This time you are going to detention like everyone else.' He wrote young Frank an excuse, placed his name on the detention list, and, as he handed him the excuse said, 'This means one hour in detention. I want to see you there at three-fifteen tonight.'

"When the principal checked detention at three-thirty, he noted that young Frank was absent. He walked down the hall to the Superintendent's office where the one telephone in the building was located and called Frank Stone, Sr., at his office. He told Mr. Stone that young Frank had been late that morning and he had not come to detention. He ended with, 'I want him down here right away.'

"The Superintendent heard the telephone conversation from his partially enclosed office. As the principal hung up the receiver, he walked into the outer office and asked, with a studied effort to be calm, 'What did Mr. Stone say?' The principal replied, 'He is going to get young Frank down here right away. I have to leave now to practice my solo for this Sunday with Mrs. Henderson, but I will tell Mr. White to check young Frank in when he comes.' (The principal sang in the Methodist choir 'for policy's sake.') The principal returned to detention, spoke to

Mr. White, then came back to his office, locked his desk, put on his coat, and left.

"About a half hour later, Mr. Stone drove to the high school with young Frank. The Superintendent waited in his office with an eye on the street. As Frank came into the building, the Superintendent slowly walked down the hall toward the principal's office. The two met at the head of the stairs, and the Superintendent asked in a pleasant voice, 'Haven't you gone home yet?' Young Frank, burning with rage, retorted, ['Mr. Principal] made me come back for detention. Dad is really sore.'

" 'Frank, come into my office, and let us talk this over.' The two walked into the Superintendent's office and discussed the matter. After ten or fifteen minutes, the Superintendent told Frank to sit in the outer office for a while and not go to detention. Some days after this, he said to us:

" 'I did not want to put young Frank in the detention room with the rest of the kids; so I sat him there in the outer office, and I deliberately worked around in my office until about five-thirty. Then I came out and said, "Frank, I guess you have been here long enough. You go on home and let's not have any hard feelings." I talked to his father later about the whole thing and I think we have come to an understanding.'

"The principal was enraged when he learned what had happened, but he could do nothing. This practically ended uniform enforcement of the new detention rule. Thereafter, class I and class II students and many class III's flouted it on the least pretext; the office gang returned to its old ways. However, it was enforced more rigidly for many others.

"Three weeks after the Frank Stone, Jr., incident, 'Boney' Johnson, a 15-year-old class IV boy came late one morning, and the English teacher refused to admit him to class without an excuse. As 'Boney' walked into the office, the principal was sitting at his desk. Before 'Boney' could say a word, he barked, in a sarcastic tone:

" 'So my pretty boy is late again! I suppose it took you half an hour to put on that clean shirt and green tie!' The principal arose from his desk, walked around, and looked at Boney's trousers and shoes and went on. 'Ha, you have your pants pressed today! I suppose you took a bath last night, too. New shoes, and they're shined.'

" 'Boney' said nothing, but his face flushed and he bit his lips. The principal walked back to his desk, sat down, and wrote out an admission slip. He put 'Boney's' name on the detention list and handed over the excuse with the remark, 'I want to see you in detention tonight. Now go on to class and show the girls what a pretty boy you are.'

" 'Boney' turned, and as he walked toward the door, said in a low voice, 'I'm not going to your damned detention room tonight or any time.'

"The principal apparently did not hear him as he went on with his work. In a few minutes, he walked across the room and said:

" 'Now there's a hot one. He's one of our wise guys. He thinks he's a hotshot. His old man is a laborer out at the fertilizer plant, and the kid thinks he's someone, umph! He'll be on the W.P.A. if they have one twenty years from now. There's one guy I'm going to see put in detention.'

"When school was out that afternoon, the Superintendent stood in the hall near the side exit, Mr. White, a teacher, watched the front door, while the principal patrolled the building. Mr. Gardner, another teacher, was in the detention room. After the building was cleared of students and most of the teachers had gone home, the Superintendent walked back to his office, but the principal stood outside the front door. Suddenly the door was thrown open from the outside, and angry voices were heard. The Superintendent rushed out of his office and stood at the head of the stairs. The principal pushed and shoved 'Boney' up the stairs as he repeated, 'You can't get away with that stuff.' As they neared the top, 'Boney' broke from his grasp and started down the hall toward the side door. The Superintendent blocked his path, and 'Boney' ran upstairs. The principal leaped and grabbed him by the coat collar with his left hand. 'Boney' turned and started to fight. The principal spun him around, seized the visor of his cap with his right hand and yanked it down over his eyes. While 'Boney' was fighting to get the cap off his face, the principal hit him three times with the heel of his hand on the back of the neck near the base of the skull. 'Boney' cursed, struggled, and hit in all directions. Soon he broke free and ran toward the Superintendent, who shook and slapped him three or four times. Both men then grabbed him by the arms and shook him vigorously. The Superintendent angrily screeched, 'You're going out of this building. You're never coming back until you bring your father and we talk this over.' By this time, the three had reached the front door. 'Boney' was shoved outside. He stood there, cursing and threatening both men with violence. In a few minutes he composed himself, straightened his clothes, and walked away, muttering to himself.

"The principal and the Superintendent came upstairs and walked into the Superintendent's office. The Superintendent dropped into his swivel chair and said, when he had caught his breath, 'I can stand a lot of things from kids, but one thing I can't stand is a sassy kid. No kid's going to sass me.' He puffed a few minutes more. The principal said nothing, and the Superintendent resumed, 'That boy is a trouble maker. I've had my eyes on him all year. Look at the gang he's running with.'

" 'Yes, I know. They're trouble makers around here. I had trouble with them all last year, and they're starting out again this year. If he wasn't that type, he wouldn't be running with that bunch.'

"After a pause, the Superintendent composed himself and remarked, 'That boy will have to bring his father back here, or he'll not get in this school.' The principal agreed, 'Yes, I'll stand with you on that. We have got to stop this thing some way.'

"After the principal had walked out of the office, the Superintendent slumped wearily in his chair and said:

" 'I ought to know better than that. I would have really liked to smack that boy, but that's one thing I've learned. You can't pop these kids even though they deserve it. The hardest thing I have to fight all the time is to keep from popping these smart kids. I shouldn't have lost my temper but, damn it, sometimes it gets too much for me. When a kid sasses me, I see red and that's all there is to it. I don't think anything will come of this, his background being what it is.'

"The Superintendent was right; nothing came of it, except—'Boney' quit school."

Perhaps the best thing for any teacher to remember in this respect is the golden rule: "And as ye would that men should do to you, do ye also to them likewise."

Rich Experiencing. The country boy of long ago knew what the elements of his life were. He knew the people he would associate with outside the family; indeed he had known them all of his life. He knew how he would spend each day, for the pattern of daily living changed little from year to year. He knew what his recreation would be like. He knew the little town well where he went to school, and nothing that happened there could surprise him greatly.

In contrast the modern boy, and particularly the city boy, lives among unknowns. Family life has changed in the short time of his existence, if in no other way than through the radio bombardment of world events and the appearance of television. School is big, and many in it are strangers to him. In his passage through the city on his way to school or to recreation he meets many that he does not know, and he moves among many who do not know him. The city abounds in evils—crime and cruelty well described in the daily papers.

We can see that present-day living for the adolescent lacks the quiet serenity that we find when life has a simple aspect and unchanging pattern in a well-understood environmental setting. We can see, too, that for this very reason present-day living lacks the security that older ways of life offered.

The unknown often appears frightening and hazardous even though it actually may have no harm in it whatever. It is for this reason that we say that it contributes to the adolescents' sense of security to become as widely acquainted as possible with the many friendly and pleasant aspects of living which are available to him. The school too often depends almost entirely on giving the adolescent "book-learning" experiences and little else. Yet it could acquaint him also with the life around him through many firsthand experiences. Just meeting and getting to know more people would be most salutary—getting to know more students through socialized classes, extracurricular activities, and school projects; getting to know more townspeople through participation in community affairs and excursions into the community to study it directly. Another way of enlarging the experiences of adolescents would be to let them study at firsthand community government, community recreation, community industries, and so on.

The adolescent should have many experiences in the large and multitudinously varied world of recreation, also. We know that play and other kinds of recreation are good for a person and are not to be dismissed as frivolity. The adolescent's knowledge of the world should include a firsthand awareness of its many recreational pleasures.

The School Should Give the Adolescent a Sense of Worth

If the secondary schools are really schools for the adolescent, they will be places where he can feel successful, where he can win respect, and where he can feel that he is putting his time to good use.

First of all, the school must let the adolescent grow up. Someone in writing about her father's treatment of her during her adolescence said: "He was a very wise man. He knew when to treat me as a child and when to treat me as an adult."

The school often forgets how many times there are when the adolescent can be treated as an adult. Instead they tend to treat him with protectiveness and circumvent him with restrictions as they would a child, and he reacts to the frustration of his desire for importance with rebellious behavior.

As we have said elsewhere, adolescents can be people of good sense and dependable good judgment in many situations if they are allowed to exercise these abilities. Everyone who reads this book has probably experienced the discomfiture of being considered less able or less intelligent than he is. The adolescent feels similarly mistreated when he is reduced to a state of childhood which he has actually grown beyond.

Second, the school is a place where the adolescent works. Does he have a chance to do the kind of work which he feels is worth doing? Does he have a chance to do the kind of work at which he can be successful? In other words, is the curriculum a suitable one? This is not the place to discuss the matter in detail since so many books have been written on that subject alone. But it can be said that the essential characteristics of a good curriculum are that it:

Meet *real present* as well as *real future* needs.
Be suited to the abilities of the students.
Be recognizably worth while to the students.
Allow for actual participation in the whole process of learning.
Allow for genuine experiences in success.

It is easiest for the teacher to teach traditional subject matter in the traditional manner, letting the students adjust as best they can to the method and material used, rather than making a careful adjustment to the needs and abilities of the students. Yet adjustment to those needs and abilities is a moral obligation of the teacher.

The task is not so difficult as one might think. One workable plan is suggested here:

Teach by whatever method is comfortable at first. Get a routine established which brings about good relations with the class and good working order. Continue this way for a while.

In the meantime, study your students. Observe them, and have them write about themselves (biography, questionnaire, or the like). Then for a few minutes each day when you are alone, get out your seating charts or your class lists, taking as much time as you can spare to think about each student and consider his needs.

Thereafter watch for an opportunity to adjust your class procedure if only a little in the direction of meeting the real needs of all of the students—or even of only one. When that change has been tried out and, if found good, retained, watch for another opportunity to make a further improvement. Little by little you will move into a kind of teaching which, because it has come gradually, is not difficult and disrupting for you and which, as it moves away from too traditional schoolwork, may be far better suited to the requirements of adolescents.

Third, the teacher should value many things about the adolescent besides academic success. If the teacher can see and be pleased by curiosity, imagination, courtesy, kindness, integrity, social ability, leadership, zest for living, cleanliness, humor, and every other desirable human quality, his students will be the happier for it and their personalities will be the better. Look at Joe, for example. His IQ is recorded as 91, and his success in his traditionally oriented classes is low. But Joe is a sociable boy, always generous and helpful to others, and the teachers in most of his classes respect him and like him for this. They don't necessarily say so, but Joe is aware of the fact that he has stature in their eyes, and it makes him feel good about school and worth something there even though his grades are always discouraging.

Fourth, it is important that the student help set his goals and help evaluate his own accomplishments, for then he sees himself grow and earns his own self-respect. Ideally the student and teacher would sit down together, talk over what the student wants to get out of life and how he thinks the school can help him. Together they would plan what he would do and how he would do it, and together they would decide, later on, how well he had succeeded in doing what he had hoped.

As schools are now organized and financed, few students—perhaps no student—can have such an opportunity. But anything the teacher can do to give the student a real stake in his planning, learning, and evaluating will not only give him a better motivation for working but will also give him a more genuine sense of accomplishment.

The School Should Help the Youth Secure Companionship and Affection

We cannot stress too much the importance to the adolescent of happy social relationships, both with adults and with his own age group. Teachers should be friendly and interested in every one of their students, and opportunities should be made for boys and girls to be together in many different kinds of informal situation.

A class can be socialized through whole-class discussion, small-group discussions, committee work, and group or whole-class projects or through the class's having lunch together, dinner together, a picnic, or something similar. One class which met from eleven to eleven-fifty did have lunch together once each week in the classroom, with a resultant growth in acquaintance that was good for the students and the teacher both. One new high school is being built with a large lounge, where students may meet to talk or read at noon or before or after school. A teacher may schedule the use of the lounge, too, for a class any day during school hours if she wishes the class to be on a less formal basis than the classroom allows.

Noontime is usually an occasion for informal social activity, which is good in itself, though some schools feel it wise to provide organized games and dancing at this time for those who have their lunch at school. The cafeteria, too, should be made attractive, for it is another place where students can enjoy each other's companionship, particularly if they may eat at leisure in pleasant surroundings.

Excursions by foot, car, bus, or train about the community or farther afield are generally good opportunities for boys and girls to get to know one another better and to learn better how to get along with one another.

Parties, mixers, and the like, also have their place.

In addition to all this, an effort should be made to *know* how each boy or girl is getting along. That we act the watchdog and smother adolescents with care is not the intention. But we should have enough interest in this very important part of an adolescent's life to take pains to find out whether he is getting the companionship he craves and needs, and if he is not, to manipulate situations so that they are made more favorable for him.

The School Should Provide Variety

"School is boring," say many adolescents.

Perhaps some boredom is inescapable, but very much is inexcusable. There are so many worth-while interesting activities for the adolescent to engage in and so many methods of learning—trips, group work, movies, panel discussions, demonstrations, wire recordings, actual participation in community affairs, dramatizations, individual projects—that every boy and girl should look forward to the day at school as something interesting and even exciting.

The School Must Promote Physical Well-being

The school is not primarily the source of the adolescent's physical well-being, nor can it do a great deal about such things as food and rest. But where it can, it should help the adolescent maintain good health as well as learn how to continue in good health in the future. Yearly health examinations, a health counselor, medical and dental care without cost and *without publicity* to those who need it but cannot afford it, physical education that is helpful and appealing enough to establish lasting interests and habits, a cafeteria that makes healthful foods very attractive—all of this and more might be considered in helping the adolescent be and stay healthy and vigorous.

II. THE SPECIAL ADJUSTMENT NEEDS OF ADOLESCENCE

As we suggested in the second chapter of this book, Why Study the Adolescent?, the period of adolescence is a time when certain adjustments are not only desirable but are actually forced upon the boy or girl. These imperative adjustments are those to his body changes, those to the other sex, and those bringing about emancipation from childhood dependence and restrictions.

The School Should Help the Adolescent
Adjust to His Body Changes

Information. At the time of this writing the authors are teaching a class of adolescent psychology composed of college seniors and graduate students. Also attending the class regularly, as an experiment, are 10 high school seniors, 5 boys and 5 girls. The class has just finished studying the physical and physiological changes of adolescence—the facts about the growth spurt, early and late maturing, the primary sex changes, the secondary sex changes, and so on. Four of these adolescents have thus far taken occasion to say privately to the teachers something on this order: "If I had only known about this when I was twelve [for example], it certainly would have saved me a lot of worry."

The adolescent should know all of the facts about his own development that are presented to you in Chap. 4. In most cases he will not learn these at home, and consequently it behooves the school to give him this information. This can be done in a high school psychology class, in classes in health or biology, through making pertinent books easily available in the library, or if need be through special lectures.

Sympathetic Understanding on the Part of the Teachers. The teacher should also know all of the facts of physical change and in addition should be well aware of the psychological effects of these changes so that he may react to the growing boy and girl with understanding, tact, and helpfulness.

Just for example, the big girl of twelve whose adult size overshadows that of all of her companions in the seventh grade feels awkward and out of place enough without being embarrassed by having a teacher say: "My, you're growing fast, Barbara." And the teacher should know that she is still child enough in spite of her size to feel bewildered by the teacher who chummily talks to her as she would to another adult about the "children" who make up the rest of the class. The boy of fourteen with gangling arms and legs who knocks over an inkwell in his fourteen-year-old awkwardness is disconcerted enough by his lack of coordination without having the teacher scold him. The teacher should know that the girl of fifteen who has grown tall without having "filled out" may resent being called "Skinny" by her companions and should never do anything or say anything to add to this self-consciousness.

If the teacher knows all the delicate nuances of feeling that attend changes in body structure, he may be able to create just the right at-mosphere and say just the right word to make an adolescent more com-fortable in his presence, rather than less, and better able to manage his changing body and changing feelings than he would be otherwise.

The School Must Help the Youth in His Heterosexual Adjustment

Proper Attitude on the Part of the Teachers. The principal and teachers should realize the importance of heterosexual association in the eyes of the adolescents, its complete normality and desirability, and its necessity as far as good mental health is concerned. They should be sure that they don't harbor ideas that the desire of boys and girls to be together is fool-ish or disgusting or something to be eradicated from their nature.

Sex Information. It should be kept in mind that the giving of sex informa-tion occurs most suitably in the home, but if the home does not meet this need, the school must do so. Properly, the facts, understandings, and attitudes about sex would be a part of the learning from the primary grades on and there would never be any blunt proclaiming of "sex facts" in a class or in lectures when the boy and girl reached senior high school.

Opportunities for Heterosexual Association. Boys and girls will inevitably associate together, and while there are work and play situations when boys want to be by themselves and girls by themselves, often both students and teachers will be better off if boys and girls can work together in groups or enjoy recreation together. The school must be careful not to overdo the matter and surround heterosexual association with an air of unnatural solicitude. Principal and teachers need to be wholesomely matter-of-fact about it.

The School Must Help the Youth Free Himself from Childhood Dependence and Restrictions

We condemn the home when it refuses to let the son or daughter grow up. The school must see that it does not fall into the same error, an easy possibility since it is generally comfortable to adults to keep the adolescent in the restraints of childhood.

Adolescents should not have great freedom given them without prepara-tion, for if they are used to following the plans and procedures of adults, freedom may be unmanageable. But they should be given as much as they can handle and then unremittingly groomed for more.

III. THE NEED FOR ADULT HELP ON PERSONAL PROBLEMS OF ADJUSTMENT

If a school does its share in supplying the basic human needs of the adolescent and in helping him make the typical adjustments of the teen age, he will, in many instances, be happy and be able to get along well in life. But there will still be some in the group who need special help on their problems.

These problems can be classified under two headings. There are those which the adolescent recognizes rather clearly and which impel him to seek aid if it is available. There are others not so clearly recognized by the adolescent himself but identified by the adults who work with him.

Problems Impelling the Adolescent to Seek Help

Many teen-agers have problems on which they would like help. We have data on this from Hoppock,[18] who asked the students in seven senior and eleven junior high schools this question: Do you want any of your teachers to help you on any of the problems listed below? The total number of students is not mentioned, but 709 senior high school students said they wanted help on choosing a vocation. Next in importance came educational guidance, then moral guidance, social guidance, and recreational guidance. Of the junior high school students 1,068 said they needed vocational guidance, with educational, recreational, social, and moral guidance following.

Norton writes of the problems submitted during one school month to 235 teachers by 1,586 pupils in 57 public high schools located in 54 Michigan communities. Table 55 presents the data on the non-school-related problems.

We see from Hoppock's study that there are many students who say that they want to take problems to teachers for help. From Norton's study we see that some students actually seek out that help.

Whether the number of adolescents who need help on personal problems be large or small, no one would deny that any young person who wants assistance should have it. What is more, the school must take the responsibility for this if other suitable agencies do not.

What the boy or girl needs is a friend on the faculty who has his real interests at heart and who has more than ordinary wisdom and understanding of the adolescent. Every school faculty has such people, and it would

[18] Robert Hoppock, "What Kinds of Guidance Do Students Want?" *Occupations*, 23:472 (1945).

TABLE 55. CLASSIFICATION OF 1,822 NON-SCHOOL-RELATED PROBLEMS OF 1,586 HIGH SCHOOL PUPILS*

Type of problem	Number	Per cent
Home situation:		
Broken homes........................	119	6.5
Financial condition of family............	114	6.3
Parent-child relationships...............	90	4.9
General home conditions...............	30	1.6
Illness in family or family history........	20	1.1
Sibling relationships..................	13	0.7
All home problems................	386	21.2
Personal characteristics:		
Sense of inferiority, lack of self-confidence, timidity, shyness..........	136	7.5
Resentment, insolence, defiance..........	56	3.1
Emotional instability, borderline psychiatric cases.........	46	2.5
Immaturity, unreliability...............	43	2.4
Appearance, grooming...............	34	1.9
Superiority complex..................	17	0.9
Attitudes, mental states...............	13	0.7
All personality problems............	345	18.9
Social relationships....................	383	21.0
Health and physical conditions...........	357	19.6
Personal (general, not specified).........	227	12.5
Boy-girl relationships..................	81	4.4
Racial discrimination..................	25	1.4
Religious conflict....................	18	1.0
Total.........................	1,822	100.0

*Stanley K. Norton, "Student Problems Met by the Teacher," *School Review*, 56:494–499 (1948).

seem a suitable procedure to lighten their teaching load enough so that they could be generous with their time for individual conferences when needed.

Other Adjustment Problems

There are boys and girls who have personality problems or problems of adjustment about which they do nothing. In cases of this kind some adult must recognize the difficulty, and effort must be made to help the student overcome it. Problems of this nature were discussed in the chapter on Personal Adjustment as well as in that on Juvenile Delinquency and will not be reviewed here. It is perhaps sufficient to say that if the school feels a strong responsibility for the adolescent's welfare, it will make a worthy effort to help all students become well adjusted, for few things that the school can do for boys and girls will contribute so much to their future welfare and the welfare of all who will associate with them.

IV. THE NEEDS SET BY COMING ADULTHOOD

One big task of the school is to help the adolescent make the most of each day. It is unfortunate when the assumption is that he lives only for the future and that the days of his adolescence do not count except as they prepare for adulthood. Every person has but a limited number of days to live, and each should be made to contribute its best to a person's life.

In a sense, living well for the present will help take care of the future; for a happy, well-rounded life from day to day in childhood and adolescence will produce a well-adjusted adult. Nevertheless, we do not feel that actual preparation for adulthood should be neglected, and along with the needs of each day must be considered the needs of the future.

The Need for Learning the Ways
of Democracy

We believe in democracy. If democracy is to prevail in the future, and in a more nearly ideal state than now, adolescents must reach adulthood habituated to living as the spirit of true brotherhood would dictate, skilled in the group processes, and—in the case of some—able to act as leaders.

The Spirit of Brotherhood. If a school is to further democracy, it must further a kindly, generous spirit among all of its members. To a large extent, the faculty can set the stage for this by treating each other and the students as one would actually treat brothers whom he loved and respected. More than this, they can work to break down class bars and prejudices. We know that the class system prevails in high school to the disadvantage of the economically underprivileged, and we also know that there is likely to be racial discrimination. No right-thinking adult can approve of either kind of discrimination, but he has reason to wonder what can be done about it; for it can certainly not be done away with to any great extent by regulation.

It would seem that the best counteractive to discrimination is this:

Scrupulous fairness on the part of the staff toward every student.
Acceptance of all students (as we have discussed this earlier in the chapter).
Providing as much opportunity as possible for students to come to know each other well.

If the faculty set the tone of the school through their friendliness and respect for the rights of all and if the students come to know each other well enough to be forced to go beyond superficial marks of worth in their evaluation of associates, these things alone will markedly improve the status of the underprivileged.

It is believed by many people that a high school must refuse to harbor fraternities and sororities if it would be democratic. Green gives these arguments against secret societies:[19]

1. They are undemocratic.
2. They divide a student's loyalty, putting loyalty to the society first.
3. They often try to dominate the social life of the school and frequently succeed.
4. They provide undesirable pressure groups in school elections.
5. Their secret meetings cannot be supervised as they should.
6. They generally have no responsible adult leadership.
7. Their initiation is sometimes cruel and harmful.

He suggests that the school administration and school board abolish these organizations, but he emphasizes the fact that this will not be successful unless an adequate social program for the entire school be substituted and an educational campaign be carried on to make clear to students and parents why such secret societies are undesirable.

Group Process: Solving Problems through Democratic Action. Since we live in a country where much is done through group discussion, group decision, group planning, group action, and group evaluation, it is important that all adolescents have many experiences in learning the ways of group action and how that action may most effectively be carried on.

Some of this learning must come in classes where the teachers make a distinct effort to help a group develop the ability to carry on profitable discussions, plan group action, and so on. Some of it should come through other situations often more realistic than those the classroom affords.

One such situation is the student council, an organization of students elected by students. Other extracurricular activities also provide such experience. Dramatics, chorus, band, orchestra, the school paper, the annual, debating groups, honor societies, and clubs of all sorts offer the student opportunity for practice in working as a part of a group. They have many other advantages as well, of course—opportunities for creative expression, for practice in getting along with others, for widening one's friendships, developing particular skills, getting leadership experience, and having the security which comes from being an accepted part of a valued group.

[19] Raymond A. Green, "Secret Societies," *NEA Journal*, 338–339 (May, 1950).

In any school there are several problems that need to be considered in connection with extracurricular activities:

1. Is there sufficient variety so that there will be some that will appeal to every taste and every interest?

2. Are they properly supervised by teachers who are interested and not already so overburdened with work that they begrudge the time they must spend on their supervisory duties?

3. Is the sponsor enthusiastic and ready to give help, but *not* domineering?

4. Does the sponsor see and further the educational possibilities of the activity (development in social skills, leadership, and the like)?

5. Is each student helped to maintain balance in his extracurricular choices?

6. Is *every* student helped to find extracurricular activities which will prove enjoyable to him and which will further the enrichment of his personality?

Developing Leadership. Leadership is important in any society, but in ours we are concerned with the kind which assures good returns to the group being led instead of returns primarily beneficial to the leader. We don't want leaders who exploit the group, nor do we want leaders who, though well intentioned, lack wisdom and skill.

In any group of people some will emerge as leaders. This is as true in school as it is in outside-of-school life. In high school these leaders are usually from the upper income bracket and they excel nonleaders, generally speaking, in scholarship, intelligence, and personality traits.[20]

In answering the question "What makes leadership?" Cunningham answers:[21]

1. The leader is sometimes one who is able to achieve in an area which has prestige for the group. For example, she says, the big boy, able in sports, easily becomes the hero-leader.

2. The leader is sometimes one who is feared. For example, the girl who can confer or withhold "belonging," as a social arbiter, may well be feared by many in the group.

3. The leader is sometimes one who is able to help the group achieve what it wants through group action. She continues: "Subtly but significantly different from the leader who rules through fear, is the one who has ability, recognized by the group as uniquely required, to help the group move toward its goals."

A consideration of leadership brings two conclusions:

Leadership has great importance to the welfare of the group being led

[20] Floyd Johnson Reynolds, "Factors of Leadership among Seniors of Central High School, Tulsa, Oklahoma," *Journal of Educational Research*, 37:356–361 (1944).

[21] Ruth Cunningham and associates, "Leadership and the Group," *NEA Journal*, 502–503 (1948).

as well as to other groups affected by that one. The fact that a person is a leader does not mean that his leadership will be good. For that reason, it is important that leaders be trained to be *good* leaders.

Leadership is a rich experience, and if the leadership is wholesome, then it is probably desirable that as many adolescents as possible have the experience in at least a minor way.

There are various ways of developing *good* leadership. Any classes which deal with people (history, social studies, literature) may involve a consideration of leaders, and much can be learned from such study. Any group of people in a student body who are choosing a leader, as a class president, for instance, may be encouraged to give serious and lengthy thought to what qualities they want in him. The elected leaders in a high school may meet for a weekly conference and under good adult leadership can learn a great deal about how they may develop and what they should aim for in their growth. Community leadership may be observed and studied.

Brophy describes a leadership-training class in his high school:[22] Students admitted for training must be juniors, must be recommended by their teachers, must have an average of 85 per cent in English, a satisfactory scholastic average in other classes, and no adverse character ratings. The group discusses the need for high ideals and fine character in leaders and gets its practice in leadership through leading discussions, first in the class itself and later in other classes, in assemblies, and even in the community.

Broadening the opportunities for leadership means primarily that there must be more small groups within a school to lead. Every well-supervised extracurricular group added to the school adds such opportunities; as does every committee within such groups. Every class where students work in small numbers under their own leadership makes its contribution.

Thus, we repeat, through the development of leaders, through practice in the group processes, and through a prevalent spirit of brotherhood, a school will do much to help its adolescents learn well the ways of democracy.

The Need for Developing Adult Directives of Behavior

As we have set forth in an earlier chapter, an adult is to a large extent what his standards, ideals, morals, and religious principles make him. The school must recognize the fact that these directives of behavior are largely formulated in adolescence. The importance of this development can

[22] John M. Brophy, "Our Leadership-training Class," *NEA Journal*, 39:52 (1950).

hardly be exaggerated. Yet often a school will almost completely ignore its responsibility in this line.

If the school is to fulfill its duty to the adolescent, it *must* know what is desirable in the way of standards, ideals, moral choices, and ethical principles and then set machinery into motion to give the adolescent actual experience in becoming mature in these respects.

The Need for Learning to Work and Making a Vocational Choice

We make the adolescent work, it is true, but because *we* choose the type of work he will do, set the goal, and decide the mode of working, the student's interest is often halfhearted and he learns little more than to make some show of satisfying the teacher's demands. If we are to develop capable workers who insist on a high standard of achievement, who take pleasure in what they are doing, and who do not need to be whipped to their task, we must let the students engage in activity which they themselves think good for them and where they themselves see the goals and find them desirable.

This is part of the task of preparing the student for a happy and fruitful work life. It is also necessary for the school to help that student find the work for which he is in ability and temperament the best suited. To do this, it must give every boy and girl an opportunity to become acquainted with vocational possibilities and an opportunity to assess his own capabilities and desires.

Preparing for Marital Choice and Marriage

More and more colleges are including a course in marriage and family living in their curricula. This is fine for the students who go to college, but most adolescents are done with their schooling when they finish high school, and they, too, need all of the help that can be given them on choosing a marriage partner wisely, making a success of their marriage, and rearing their children well.

It is ridiculous, when one thinks of it, that in all of the high school's vaunted "preparation for the future," it has done nothing to help the adolescent in the most delicate and important choice he can make, in the most vital and difficult human relationship he can maintain, and in his greatest responsibility, that of rearing his children.

One would be tempted to put this task of the school first in the list of needs set by coming adulthood. If that seems too strong a contention, certainly everyone would agree that it merits equal ranking with the three we have already discussed.

Acquiring Any Other Knowledges, Abilities, and Attitudes Which Are of Genuine Necessity in Adulthood

Finally we come to those needs of the adolescent which are probably given the most attention by the average high school—the need for certain subject matters (English, history, mathematics, and so on), the need for certain abilities (effective communication, clear thinking, ennobling appreciations, and others), and the need for certain attitudes (toward one's duties as a citizen, toward work, toward one's fellow men, and the like). These must not be minimized. They *are* important. But they are no more important than all of the other needs we have discussed in this chapter.

Certain subject matters and skills—and presumably certain habits, attitudes, and understandings resulting from their study—have made up our curriculum for many years. The very fact that all of this has been taught for a long time gives it prestige in our eyes, and we think it necessary for the adolescent whether or not it actually be of worth to him at all. It is important that we examine afresh all that we customarily teach in the secondary school. If its worth to the adolescent is not convincing, if it does not merit the time spent on it, from the point of view of the welfare of the adolescent or of society, then it should be taken out of the learning experience of the adolescent. There is too much to learn of real worth to waste time on the inessential or the futile.

IN CONCLUSION

We conclude with a statement, the spirit of which underlies the material of this whole book: The adolescent has many needs which must be met if he is to make the most of his life as an adolescent and develop into the best kind of adult. *It is the duty of the school to help him meet these needs.* We repeat them for a last consideration:

1. The needs that he has in common with all people of his culture:
    To feel secure.
    To have a sense of worth.
    To have companionship and affection.
    To have variety.
    To maintain physical well-being.
2. The special adjustment needs of adolescence:
    Adjusting to his physical changes.
    Adjusting heterosexually.
    Achieving emancipation from childhood dependence and restrictions.
3. The need for adult help on personal problems of adjustment.
4. The needs set by coming adulthood:
    Learning the ways of democracy.

Developing adult directives of behavior.

Developing the ability to work, and making a vocational choice.

Preparing for marital choice and marriage.

Acquiring the other knowledges, abilities, and attitudes which are of genuine necessity in adulthood.

Reminiscences

1. Look at the final summary of the school's obligations to the adolescent. Point by point, evaluate the high school you attended. Substantiate your statements by illustrations.

2. What adjustments to individual differences were made in your high school during your day there?

3. What seemed to be the principles of discipline followed in your high school when you were there?

4. Using the ideas about good discipline developed in this chapter, select the teacher in your experience who was the best disciplinarian, and explain why. Then select the teacher who was the worst, and explain why.

General Discussion

1. What practices on the part of high school teachers are likely to stir up misbehavior in the classroom?

2. Presumably if teachers would adjust to the adolescents' interests and needs, there would be few so-called "discipline problems." Just what would such adjustment entail?

3. Can you originate some techniques for providing experiences for adolescents which will encourage the development of self-discipline?

4. What techniques must groups learn if they are to work the most effectively as groups?

5. Do you believe that there are times when a teen-ager must be punished? If so, when? If so, how?

6. What would you do for a boy or girl in your class who was truly among the intellectually gifted?

7. What would you do for a boy or girl who was among the dull-normal?

8. What qualities must we develop within ourselves if we are to accept all of the boys or girls we teach even though we may not accept their ideas or acts?

9. If you were to broaden the wholesome high school experiences of an adolescent, what experiences would you add to the present curriculum?

10. For your own major subject, what would you do to give the class activities variety?

Panel Discussion

1. The most modern of today's high schools throughout the country.

2. The high school of fifty years hence, concretely described.

Further Reading

ALBERTY, HAROLD, *Reorganizing the High-school Curriculum* (New York: The Macmillan Company, 1947).

Association for Supervision and Curriculum Development, *Fostering Mental Health in Our Schools*, 1950 Yearbook (Washington: National Education Association, 1950).

Association for Supervision and Curriculum Development, *Toward Better Teaching*, 1949 Yearbook (Washington: National Education Association, 1949).

BAGLEY, W. C., "New York Public Schools Base 'Promotion' on 'Social Maturity,'" *School and Society*, 60:67–68 (1944).

BERRY, MARY, "Social Conduct," *Clearing House*, 19:222–224 (1945).

BLOTT, EVELYN M., "Community Schools for Adolescents," *New Era*, 23:128–129 (1942).

BOYD, GRACE, "Development of Non-academic Courses in Evanston Township High School," *Education*, 60:17–24 (1939).

DIEDERICH, PAUL B., "Simplifying a Crowded Schedule," *School Review*, 53:162–169 (1945).

Educational Policies Commission, *Education for All American Youth* (Washington: National Education Association, 1944).

Educational Policies Commission, *Learning the Ways of Democracy* (Washington: National Education Association, 1940).

HANNA, PAUL R., *Youth Serves the Community* (New York: Appleton-Century-Crofts, Inc., 1936).

HENDRICKSON, GORDON, "Mental Development during the Preadolescent and Adolescent Periods," *Review of Educational Research*, 20:351–357 (1950).

HERRON, JOHN S., "The Community School vs. Community Recreation," *Recreation*, 38:339–342 (1944).

LEWIS, W. D., "A Comparative Study of the Personalities, Interests, and Home Backgrounds of Gifted Children of Superior and Inferior Educational Achievement," *Journal of Genetic Psychology*, 59:207–218 (1941).

LEWIS, W. D., "The Relative Intellectual Achievement of Mentally Gifted and Retarded Children," *Journal of Experimental Education*, 13:98–109 (1944).

Ohio State University High School, Class of 1938, *Were We Guinea Pigs?* (New York: Henry Holt and Company, Inc., 1938).

OLSEN, EDWARD G. (ed.), *School and Community Programs* (New York: Prentice-Hall, Inc. 1949).

OTTOSEN, A. H., and J. W. M. ROTHNEY, "A Practical Reorganization of a Junior High School to Meet Student Needs," *Education*, 63:29–39 (1942).

Progressive Education Association, *Thirty Schools Tell Their Story* (New York: Harper & Brothers, 1943).

THOM, DOUGLAS A., and NANCY NEWELL, "Hazards of the High I.Q." *Mental Hygiene*, 29:61–77 (1945).

THORNDIKE, R. L., "Growth of Intelligence during Adolescence," *Journal of Genetic Psychology*, 72:11–15 (1948).

TYLER, R. W., "Cooperation and Conflict in Mental Development of the Child," *Mental Hygiene*, 32:253–260 (1948).

YOUNG, THEODORE, "An English Class Explores the Community," *Education*, 63:639–644 (1944).

NAME INDEX

A

Ackerson, Luton, 305
Alexander, Paul W., 384
Anastasi, Anne, 135
Andrews, Margaret E., 341
Arnold, Martha, 63
Atkinson, William B., 91

B

Baldwin, B. T., 84
Barbour, Richmond, 447
Barker, Roger G., 102, 431
Bateman, Richard M., 346
Bayley, Nancy, 78, 81, 82, 99–101
Beam, Kenneth S., 374
Beck, Lester F., 182
Beekman, Emma, 63, 433
Bell, Howard M., 34, 327, 334, 335, 347, 350, 433, 438
Bell, Marjorie, 367
Beller, Emanuel K., 263
Best, Charles Herbert, 88
Bibb, Frances G., 51, 128, 167–169
Bickel, George L., 347
Black, Agernon D., 246, 274, 276
Blos, Peter, 34, 180, 254, 284, 312
Blumer, H., 449
Boll, Eleanor S., 398
Bonar, Hugh S., 56, 328
Bonney, Merle E., 398
Bossard, James H. S., 398
Boynton, Paul L., 328, 329
Bridges, Bernice, 445, 446
Brink, W. G., 50
Bronner, Augusta F., 361, 364
Brophy, John M., 497

C

Cameron, W. Jaffray, 42
Campbell, Elise Hatt, 162, 163

Carmody, May, 344
Carp, Frances Meichant, 331
Carr, Lowell Juilliard, 360, 362, 378
Carroll, Helen M., 342
Casey, Roy, 358
Chambers, M. M., 435–437
Chave, Ernest J., 260, 261
Chenoweth, L. B., 93
Ciernick, Sylvia, 272
Clark, W. R., 50
Cohler, Milton J., 465
Conover, James F., 406
Cook, Lloyd Allen, 140
Corwin, George B., 445
Coxe, Warren W., 324
Coyle, G. L., 131
Cunningham, Ruth, 151, 496
Curtis, Erta Agnes, 403

D

Davis, Allison, 46, 367
Diehl, Harold, 87, 88
Dimchevsky, Esther M., 310
DiMichael, Salvatore G., 57
Dimock, Hedley S., 32, 35, 50, 122, 124, 133, 137, 141, 142
Dollard, John, 21, 420
Doyle, Kathleen, 421
Dresden, Katharine, 341
Drier, William H., 329
Dupertuis, C. W., 91, 94
Duvall, Evelyn Millis, 177, 178
Dyer, J. Pope, 373

E

Edgren, Harry D., 443
Elftman, Herbert, 91
Elias, L. J., 34, 50, 57, 63, 177, 181, 275, 334, 433, 450
Evans, Bergen, 23
Evenden, Edward S., 272

503

SUBJECT INDEX

A

Acceptability to peers, 109–113, 133–136
Acceptance by teachers, 480–481
Achievements, adolescent, nature of, 62–63
Adaptability of personality, 302–303
Adjustment, to body changes, 490–491
emotional, 196–243
heterosexual (*see* Heterosexual adjustment)
importance of, 283–284
to life values, 244–279
meaning of, 280–283
personal, 280–323
social, 115–158
vocational, 324–354
Adjustment difficulties, sources of, 284–305
Adolescence, definition of, 3
and delinquency, 363
length of period of, 3
love in, 172–174
metabolism in, 96
as source of adjustment difficulties, 290–294
Adolescent, aspirations of, 60–62
and community, 425–456
definition of, 1–9
description of, older, 44–46
younger, 41–44
emotional, 225–233
and library, 434–435
problems of, 52–56
reasons for study of, 10–39
securities of, 65–66
sex differences in younger, 43
world of, 40–69
social, 59–60
Adolescent cruelty, 131–133
Adolescent period, and adult responsibilities, 12–15
and psychological changes, 16–27

B

Basic needs, 480–489
Behavior directives of adulthood, 18, 497–498
Behavior problems, rating of, 321–322
"Blues," 216–217
Body changes, adjustment to, 490–491
Boy Scouts of America, 435
Boys' Clubs of America, Inc., 435
Bragging, 309
Breast knots, 90–91
Breast development, 94–95
Broken home, 403–404
Brush Foundation Study, 34
Bullying, 309

C

California Adolescent Growth Study, 32
Calvin, case of, 318–319
Camp Fire Girls, Inc., 436
Character, 33
Chicago Area Projects, 373–374
Children's Village, 381–382
Church and adolescent, 432–434
Citizenship, 14–15
Civilization, hazards of, 20–26

Adolescent problem, 11
Adolescent secrecy, 117
Adolescents, number of, 4
Adults, responsibility of, toward adolescent, 27–31
Aesthetic experiences, 201
American Junior Red Cross, 435
American Youth Commission, 33–34
American Youth Hostels, 437
Anger, 199, 213–216
Arm growth, 104–105
Aspirations of adolescent, 60–62
Attention getting, 308